The EDGAR
CAYCE
Collection

The EDGAR CAYCE
Collection

FOUR VOLUMES IN ONE

General Editor
HUGH LYNN CAYCE

BONANZA BOOKS
New York

Edgar Cayce on Dreams copyright © 1968 by the Association For Research and Enlightenment, Inc.
Edgar Cayce on Healing copyright © 1969 by the Association For Research and Enlightenment, Inc.
Edgar Cayce on Diet and Health copyright © 1969 by the Association For Research and Development, Inc.
Edgar Cayce on ESP copyright © 1969 by the Association For Research and Development, Inc.

This 1986 edition is published by Bonanza Books, distributed by Crown Publishers, Inc., 225 Park Avenue South, New York, New York 10003, by arrangement with Warner Books.

Printed and Bound in the United States of America

LIBRARY OF CONGRESS CATALOGING-IN-PUBLICATION DATA

Cayce, Edgar, 1877-1945.
    Edgar Cayce collection, 4 volumes in 1.

    1. Psychical research—Collected works. 2. Occult
sciences—Collected works. I. Title.
BF1023.C372 1986   133.8   86-8209
ISBN 0-517-60668-2

h   g   f   e

Book design by Cynthia Dunne

CONTENTS

INTRODUCTION

THE BOOKS THAT have been written about Edgar Cayce have totaled well over a million in sales. Many other books have devoted sections to his life and talents. He has been featured in dozens of magazines and hundreds of newspaper articles dating from 1900 to the present. What was so unique about him?

It depends on through whose eyes you look at him. A goodly number of his contemporaries knew the "waking" Edgar Cayce as a gifted professional photographer. Another group (predominantly children) admired him as a warm and friendly Sunday School teacher. His own family knew him as a wonderful husband and father.

The "sleeping" Edgar Cayce was an entirely different figure—a psychic known to thousands of people, in all walks of life, who had cause to be grateful for his help. Indeed, many of them believed that he alone had either "saved" or "changed" their lives when all seemed lost. The "sleeping" Edgar Cayce was a medical diagnostician, a prophet, and a devoted proponent of Bible lore.

In June, 1954, the University of Chicago held him in sufficient respect to accept a Ph.D. thesis based on a study of his life and work. In this thesis the writer referred to him as a "religious seer." In that same year, the children's comic book *House of Mystery* bestowed on him the impressive title of "America's Most Mysterious Man!"

Even as a child, on a farm near Hopkinsville, Kentucky, where he was born on March 18, 1877, Edgar Cayce displayed powers of perception which seemed to extend beyond the normal range of the five senses. At the age of six or seven he told his parents that he was able to see and talk to "visions," sometimes of relatives who had recently died. His parents attributed this to the overactive imagination of a lonely child who had been influenced by the dramatic language of the revival meetings which were popular in that section of the country. Later, by sleeping with his head on his schoolbooks, he developed some form of photographic memory which helped him advance rapidly in the country school. This gift faded, however, and Edgar was only able to complete his seventh grade before he had to seek his own place in the world.

By the age of twenty-one he had become the salesman for a wholesale stationery company. At this time he developed a gradual paralysis of the throat muscles which threatened the loss of his voice. When doctors were unable to find a physical cause for this condition, hypnosis was tried, but failed to have any permanent effect. As a last resort, Edgar asked a friend to help him re-enter the same kind of hypnotic sleep that had enabled him to memorize his schoolbooks as a child. His friend gave him the necessary suggestion, and once he was in a self-induced trance, Edgar came to grips with his own problem. He recommended medication and manipulative therapy which successfully restored his voice and repaired his system.

A group of physicians from Hopkinsville and Bowling Green, Kentucky, took advantage of his unique talent to diagnose their own patients. They soon discovered that Cayce only needed to be given the name and address of a patient, wherever he was, to be able to tune in telepathically on that individual's mind and body as easily as if they were both in the same room. He needed, and was given, no other information regarding any patient.

One of the young M.D.s, Dr. Wesley Ketchum, submitted a report on this unorthodox procedure to a clinical research society in Boston. On the ninth of October, 1910, the *New York Times* carried two pages of headlines and pictures. From that day on, troubled people from all over the country sought the "wonder man's" help.

When Edgar Cayce died on January 3, 1945, in Virginia Beach, Virginia, he left well over 14,000 documented stenographic records of the telepathic-clairvoyant statements he had given for more than six thousand different people over a period of forty-three years. These documents are referred to as "readings."

The readings constitute one of the largest and most impressive records of psychic perception ever to emanate from a single individual. Together with their relevant records, correspondence and reports, they have been cross-indexed under thousands of subject headings and placed at the disposal of psychologists, students, writers and investigators who still come, in increasing numbers, to examine them.

A foundation known as the A.R.E. (Association for Research and Enlightenment, Inc., P.O. Box 595, Virginia Beach, Virginia 23451) was founded in 1932 to preserve these Readings. As an open-membership research society, it continues to index and catalog the information, initiate investigation and experiments, and promote conferences, seminars and lectures.

EDGAR CAYCE

ON DREAMS

by Harmon H. Bro, Ph.D.

CONTENTS

PART III

ESP in Dreams

PART IV

Self-Development Through Dreams

INTRODUCTION

THIS VOLUME PRESENTS the data from more than six hundred Edgar Cayce Readings on dreams.

Harmon H. Bro, Ph.D., worked with Edgar Cayce for the better part of a year—from 1943–1944. He observed the regular schedule of daily readings. Coming to Virginia Beach as a skeptic he asked probing questions, interviewed persons who came for readings and read correspondence. Careful detailed notes became the basis for a doctoral thesis a few years later at the University of Chicago.

Recognizing as many students of the Readings have that Edgar Cayce placed unusual emphasis on the value of an individual's study of his own dreams, Dr. Bro has examined and thoroughly indexed the hundreds of dream readings.

Here is his first popular study of these readings. It is designed not only to present the challenging new concepts on dreams which are contained in this psychic's unusual approach to the subject, but also to enable the reader to apply these ideas in working with his own daily dream material.

In my opinion this is one of the best and most important studies ever made of the Edgar Cayce Readings.

—Hugh Lynn Cayce

PART I

The Dreams of a Young Woman

CHAPTER 1

THE DREAMER

SHE WAS YOUNG, just twenty-one. She was attractive, proud of her figure. She was ambitious, from a leading Mississippi family. She was bright, a graduate of a select women's college.

And now she was married. She had picked a Pennsylvania banker, eight years older, whom she had met at a family resort. She knew that his associates called his future promising, and she could imagine him on Wall Street someday.

She could hardly guess that within four years he would be not only a Wall Street banker, but a millionaire, a financial marvel even in the prosperous Roaring Twenties.

Right now, freshly married, she had a problem on her hands. How was she to justify to her relatives her husband's consuming interest in a middle-aged Ohio psychic named Edgar Cayce? She had told them about Cayce: her parents, her sister, and most of her uncles, aunts, and cousins. But they had stayed skeptical. She could see why.

Cayce was uneducated. He had no respectable profession at present, although he had been a successful Alabama photographer until a couple of years ago, in 1923, when he had moved to Ohio. He had no money, although not far back he had held a million dollars in oil properties located by his psychic gift for his Cayce Petroleum Company—and had lost it all in drilling gambles and business calamities. He didn't even have a home of his own, for her husband was helping to finance the costs of moving his family to Virginia Beach, Virginia, where Cayce's psychic source had long insisted he would be most productive.

7

There were only a few things she could say to her relatives in Cayce's favor.

He was a southerner, from good Kentucky stock that could trace its ancestry back to France, as could some of her own relatives in the Deep South. He was a family man, with a petite but regal southern wife, and one son in third grade and another in high school. He taught Sunday School in the Christian Church, a Baptist-like church which was popular in the South. And he was helping her husband, Aaron, become a rich man.

She had heard story upon story from Aaron, telling how Cayce was coaching him and some Ohio businessmen to use their natural psychic talents to become wealthy. Cayce offered them no miracles, for he gave business counsel only to those who were already active and effective in their fields: manufacturers, real estate brokers, corporation executives, product inventors, distributors, stockbrokers, insurance salesmen and bankers like her husband. Even to these his counsel was limited, she knew. For while he could evidently see an astonishing array of facts with his psychic vision, he called on his talent only to train others to use their own talents: their hunches, their impressions, their promptings, and their dreams. But he had convinced her husband that was all the aid he needed, for he was rapidly becoming wealthy, as were a number of his associates—especially two brothers who were stockbrokers.

Cayce was certain, Aaron had explained to her, that psychic ability was a normal potential in every healthy, creative person. He saw it as an outreach of the personality that could be trained as one might train musical or philosophic or executive abilities.

Frances was especially fascinated with what Cayce could do with dreams. She knew that for months her young husband had been presenting his dreams to Cayce for interpretation—especially on business matters but also on sex, aggression, health, personality patterns, fears, religion, attitudes towards associates, hobbies, death, and even on what sorts of brides his girl friends might become. Now he was encouraging her to present her dreams to Cayce.

So Frances, a bride of one week, wrote down some recent dreams and mailed them to Edgar Cayce in his new home at Virginia Beach, to be interpreted in the trance "readings" which he took twice daily.

She began one of the most colorful chapters in the history of twentieth-century dream interpretation—a century that had started with Freud's monumental volume, *The Interpretation of Dreams*, but which left dream study in the hands of analysts until its midpoint, when the first "sleep laboratories" began to appear on university campuses.

Frances' dreams, interpreted by Edgar Cayce, may one day prove to be only a novelty in the century which rediscovered dreams. Or they may prove fresh leads to the workings of dreams, to the makeup of dreamers, and to things worth dreaming about.

Over a four-year period she submitted to Cayce, largely by mail, 154 dreams, with which he dealt at varying length in fifty-five of his readings—almost all of them given in the first three years. Only three other persons, one of whom was Cayce himself, submitted such extensive collections of dreams for his psychic analysis. During the two decades after 1924 during which he interpreted dreams, others also sought dream guidance—a total of sixty-nine people before Cayce's death in 1945. All together, Cayce was given some 1650 dreams for his interpretation in about seven hundred readings—approximately one reading in twenty of the thousands that were recorded and saved in the forty years of his psychic efforts.

What sort of dreamer was Frances? What sort of waking life lay behind her dreams?

During the time that Cayce served as her dream analyst, and as her coach in learning to interpret her own dreams, Frances went through both calm times and rough. Her dreams mirrored both.

She lived well in an expensive home in New York City, with servants to do her wishes. She traveled to Europe, and often to her girlhood home in Mississippi, as well as to Virginia Beach, Palm Springs, Florida, and Chicago. She bought lovely clothes. She read a great deal, but she also worked energetically at entertaining. She found time to indulge in lazy memories of her childhood, and in fantasies of old love affairs.

She went through ecstasy when Cayce assured her she would bear a child who could be an intellectual and spiritual leader in her times. Then she had a miscarriage, of which both Cayce and her dreams warned her—and she left the hospital just in time to attend her mother's funeral. She bore her son at last, over a year later, but before she left the hospital with him, her father died suddenly in Mississippi. Frances knew pain as well as she knew joy, during the time she worked on her dreams with Cayce.

The dream records show that she quarreled with her mother-in-law, but not too bitterly, and always made up. She had her rows with Aaron, too. She was apparently jealous of his intellectual and psychic abilities, while he was inclined to be condescending toward her. But they seemed genuinely fond of each other, and their marriage went along quite well sexually and socially, until it was hit by a series of earthquake-like shocks, all of which were foreshadowed in her dreams.

Eight years after she married Aaron, she divorced him.

Frances does not seem to have been neurotic, although her dreams showed that she could be temperamental, sharp-tongued, stubborn, and even selfish. In most of her dreams she appeared as a fairly normal young woman, going through the adjustments and awakenings of early marriage and motherhood. But she also went through several shocks, which laid bare her personality structure in her dreams.

First, she went through the problem of transference, so familiar to psychoanalysis. She came to see Cayce not only as a father-figure but almost as a prophet, despite his repeated insistence that she turn to the divine, rather than to him, for her devotions. Identifying with Cayce, she showed the familiar love-hate ambivalence: she hoped one day to give readings as he did; she sulked when he did not magically prevent her from her miscarriage. Her resolution of the transference came hard, as it sometimes does in analysis, for she went through a disappointed and nearly permanent rupture with Cayce when her husband (caught in a transference problem of his own) quarreled with Cayce over financing of the Cayce hospital, during Depression days, and withdrew all his support and contact.

Second, Frances experienced the collapse of her security, toward the end of her dream series, when her marriage began to break up.

Third, she underwent a slow but drastic change of religious orientation. She was Jewish, as was her husband, a fairly liberal though family-oriented tradition which called a house of worship a "temple" instead of a synagogue or "schul." She was familiar with Yiddish phrases and mannerisms, and they helped her defend her dignity as part of a vulnerable minority in American society. She and her relatives went to Jewish resorts, and enjoyed them, as her dreams show.

But it wrenched her that she found Edgar Cayce in his trance state, however tolerant in waking life, adamant that Jesus had in truth been the most complete pattern for men to follow, whatever their religious affiliation. She knew that Cayce did not push her to become a churchgoer, and in fact encouraged her in hopes of rearing her son to be a religious leader in Israel. But the force of the respect which he gave to the figure of Christ put her under inward stress, as well as under outward tension with relatives.

Fourth, Frances developed what seemed to be a measure of psychic ability of her own. She did not turn towards business affairs, as did her husband, although she developed her ability, as he did, in her dreams. She turned to the woman's world of family and relationships, securing impressions of the health, attitudes, welfare, and potentials of her son, her husband, and her relatives. However great her husband's interest in psychic matters—and he was even more interested in these than in making money, at which he worked hard—she found she could not live in his atmosphere alone. She had to deal with friends and relatives, bustling in and out of her life, and often ridiculing her psychic interests and stories. Her otherwise normal ego was thus put under an unusual strain, and her dreams showed her floundering over how to think of herself and her psychic interests, in front of her peers, despite her wealth and social position.

Frances took four full-strength jolts, besides the death of both parents, in eight years of marriage. It is not surprising that her dreams showed not only the usual stresses, but one major thrust which must have greatly compensated for the blows in her waking life. She began to have vivid dream experiences of her dead mother, whom she came to feel, with Cayce's assurance, was alive beyond the grave. She found in these experiences a source of awe and wonder, as well as practical guidance, which meant a great deal to her—as we shall see.

She never remarried. Later in life she underwent an emotional breakdown, as her dreams with Cayce previewed. She pulled out of it by devotedly serving her son, and by a hard-won career in nursing. The sturdiness which showed in her early dreams seemed to ripen in later years into a strength and compassion which could well have made her a woman to know and to cherish.

CHAPTER 2

LEVELS OF DREAMING

As EDGAR CAYCE interpreted dreams in hundreds of trance sessions, and as he talked about the function of sleep and dreaming in a few essay-type readings, he set forth his view of how dreams work.

They work, he said, to accomplish two things. They work to solve the problems of the dreamer's conscious, waking life. And they work to quicken in the dreamer new potentials which are his to claim.

Why Dreams?

In describing dreams as problem-solving, first of all, Cayce anticipated many of the findings of sleep laboratories which would not be established for another quarter of a century after he counseled Frances.

Although he noted that some of her dreams expressed body-tensions, he did not see her dreams as giving her vicarious satisfaction of subterranean wishes for sex and aggression. Sex and aggression were in her dreams aplenty, and with plots that gratified them. But such dreams, he said, contained more as well; they contained suggestions for how to evaluate and direct these basic drives. Her dreams, he pointed out, would deal with primitive drives only when these became a problem to her; then they would be taken up in dreams as would any other problem, with possible solutions—both realistic and unrealistic—dramatized and evaluated in the dreams.

Although Cayce did not use the term employed by modern dream researchers in their laboratory work with normal human subjects, he described the process now called the "perseverative effect." It is the process that appears whenever a person becomes involved in a problem or task; he tends to persevere in it until it is worked through. Modern dream research shows that normal people tend to persevere into the night in the questions that absorbed them in the day—not only in the questions of their role and status with others, but in very practical questions of money, of studies, of trips, of food, of skills, and even questions of how to get enough sleep.

In describing a large part of dreaming as problem-solving, Cayce also underscored that kind of dreaming which has long interested artists and inventors: the "incubation" dream. This is the dream which either presents a surprising solution to a problem or design on which the dreamer has been working, or awakens him in a state of mind where the solution he needs springs easily to his thoughts. Here, again, Cayce paralleled the work of modern sleep and dream laboratories, some of which today are not only exploring the mind's capacity for creative incubation in dreams, but even its use of ESP in sleep, as part of its problem-solving work.

But when, on the other hand, Cayce described the rest of meaningful dreaming as quickening the dreamer to his own human potentials, he came nearer to the viewpoint of psychoanalysis, in its various schools.

Over and over he pointed out how dreams signal to the dreamer that it is time for him to carry new responsibilities, or to develop more mature values, or to stretch his thinking. Such dreams, he said, are not simply solving practical problems. They are helping the dreamer grow.

He described whole cycles of dreams as devoted to developing a new quality in a dreamer: patience, balance, manliness, altrium, humor, reflectivenss, piety. Some of these self-remaking dreams he saw as coming from the efforts of the dreamer's personality to right itself in breakdown—as psychoanalysts see every day in the dreams of those on their couches. Other such dreams Cayce saw as spontaneous, healthy presentations, occurring when it was time for a new episode of growth in the dreamer's life.

Frances accumulated vivid evidence, in four years of Cayce's help, that her dreams functioned both to solve her outward problems and to quicken her to inner potentials.

There were plenty of practical problems reflected in her dreams. Many were about arguments with relatives or husband. Some were about travel plans. One was about a cold her husband had caught. Two dealt with a maid who had stolen some clothing from her. Numbers of them dealt with her diet and exercise as she prepared for motherhood. Not a few of them displayed her mannerisms and life style exactly as others would see them. There were even dreams that urged her not to rely too heavily on Cayce, as he pointed out in interpreting them.

But mixed in with these problem-solving dreams, and sometimes part of the same dreams, were dream materials that served a different purpose: arousing Frances to a richer and more mature self. Her dreams appeared to invite her to use her good mind more systematically in study. Others prompted her to give herself more freely to her baby, rather than leave him so much to his nurse. A few dreams confronted her with memorable religious experiences. As Cayce saw her dreams, nearly half of them contained some reference or challenge to her life-orientation, to her ultimate values and commitments, as these showed up in prosaic daily living.

He would not let her use her dreams as a handy divining kit.

What might seem a message of a forthcoming illness, he said, could instead mirror a sick attitude in the dreamer's present behavior. What might seem guidance to an advantageous stock sale could be the dreamer's "stock-taking" on himself or a friend. An awesome bearded man in a dream could well be the dreamer's stern conscience, rather than the heavenly messenger she might rather believe. He made it clear that dreams cannot be approached simply as messages from a higher realm. It is important, he explained, "to differentiate between the spiritual inception and the conscious conception" which appear in dreams.

Yet Cayce did insist to Frances that dreams often incorporate realms of consciousness that are wider than waking, if not higher. They can, he said, draw easily on whatever ESP the dreamer possesses as a natural talent or a developed art, to show him problem-solving items from the future, the distant, the past, or the private.

And there are those dreams, he added, which can bring into play more easily than much of waking consciousness certain structures of great importance to the dreamer. Frances might in dreams contact her own best or higher self; or she might even reach to something beyond herself which Cayce called "the Creative Forces or God." Cayce treated these dream contents, not congenial to either modern laboratory or couch, with great respect. Though he picked out a small minority of dreams as embodying explicit, direct contact with the higher self, or with the divine, he did not hesitate to identify some dreams in this way—and thus his dream interpretations come under some question in the century which has rediscovered dreams in the laboratory and the clinic, but not in the church.

Often he summarized the function of dreams in words such as those which he used for a businessman, whom he urged to consult his dreams for "self-edification, and for the building up of the mental and spiritual, as well as the financial, self."

As Cayce counseled Frances and others about their dreams, it became clear that he saw their dreams as coming from different levels within them. In this view the dreamer is somewhat analogous to a ship.

The Level of the Body

The ship is a big machine. It has a hull, engines, propeller, decks, steering devices, anchors. Some of its equipment must be operated by the crew. Some of its equipment, such as life jackets, can be used by passengers. Some of its equipment operates to serve other equipment—as do governors, emergency circuits, oiling devices, and automatic pilots.

In dreams, as Cayce saw them, the dreamer's body presents its operating problems just as the machinery of a ship occupies those who sail it. The body's need for exercise, sleep, a balanced diet, play, hard work, healthy eliminations, medical care, sexual orgasms, quiet meditation—all of these and more seemed to him to crowd the stage of dreams, as expressions of what Cayce called "the physical." To be sure, Cayce said, some dreams originating in the body are merely hallucinogenic, and not worth interpreting, produced by the same body chemistry that prompts the visions of an alcoholic, the mirages on the desert, or the fantasies of a man in deep fatigue.

Still other body-originated dreams, in Cayce's view, are products of the body working on itself, as some of a ship's machinery call other machinery into play.

When Frances asked him to recall for her one dream she had forgotten, as he often did, he said that this one was merely the body giving itself a workout, and did not require study or interpretation.

Still other dreams, Cayce explained, show the body calling for aid which its own mechanisms alone can't supply. Frances dreamed:

> Saw the boat *Leviathan* and cousin Ted and his wife very sick; and it seemed something was the matter with Ted, and he was dead, for his wife was in a mourning veil.

Cayce pointed out that she had been thinking of taking an ocean trip, and speculating what seasickness might do to her—or might do even more drastically to her cousin Ted, who was ill at the time. This imagining set the body astir (somewhat as hypnotic suggestion can easily do) with fear of seasickness, fear that caused the dream. (Happily, Cayce not only interpreted the dream, but prescribed for Frances a sensible compound medication which he had given to others to prevent seasickness, with surprisingly good results—considering that it came from an unconscious, uneducated psychic.) Frances' body-machinery got the help for which it seemed to have signaled.

The Level of the Subconscious

A ship is operated by a crew. They are trained to make it run day after day, which they often do automatically. Sometimes their orders conflict, and they must iron out their differences in duties and routines. Sometimes they receive cargo or passengers which they are not trained to handle, and they must question the load. Sometimes they are baffled by machinery or storms, and must appeal to higher authority for help. Sometimes they are given new shipmates with skills or equipment they did not know existed.

Cayce referred to the "subconscious" or the "subconscious forces" in dreams much as one might refer to the crew of a ship. These "forces" he saw as very common in dreams, whether presenting problems of their own functioning, or presenting special information which they have retrieved by their own ESP radar. The language of these forces he saw as characteristically "emblematic"—somewhat like the salty dialects and figures of speech of seamen. The dreamer's subconscious—his hidden structures, habits, controls, mechanisms, complexes, formulas—uses the dreamer's own peculiar memory-images and figures of speech to get things done.

Sometimes the crew of the subconscious may, in the Cayce view, give the body-machinery a dry run in dreams, to prepare it for a forthcoming workout.

Frances had been through a miscarriage, and had some earlier fears of childbirth, when her dreams came up with the following vivid experience. The time was a little more than nine months before her baby was actually born. Cayce's dream interpretation included a challenge that she choose now to become pregnant, and a promise of a happy outcome. Her dream, he said, was caused by her subconscious, which he saw as having charge of all vital functions, giving to her "body-conscious that experience of the condition through which the entity passes to attain" childbirth.

Her crew was warming up the machinery of sexual and maternal instinct. Frances reported:

> I had some inner trouble that prevented my having a baby. The doctors told me that to have it corrected would necessitate a slight operation. I objected on the grounds that I couldn't take ether. "Oh yes you can," they replied, and I found myself on the operating table being given the anesthetic. Slowly I felt myself losing consciousness under this influence. I felt their fingers grow lighter in touch and their voices seem further and further away. I was unconscious of myself losing consciousness, and of the latter's consummation. Then I came to—regained consciousness, the operation having been done. I mentioned to the nurse that I supposed now I could not have a baby. She replied that I could—very soon. I wanted to get up and go out.

In interpreting this dream, which he saw as wholly positive and encouraging, Cayce not only touched on the theme of motherhood, but picked up, as any analyst would, the word "consummation" which Frances had used to describe her "operation." He suggested to her that the word referred not simply to childbirth as the consummation of her preparation for motherhood, but to sexual release, which she could choose as pleasantly and safely as the dream showed in the touch of fingers and the drifting off to unconsciousness.

Her crew had set the machinery humming.

Frances' dreams showed her continuous concern with the people she held close. They showed her struggling not only with her personal relationships with them, but with their own problems. What bothered them bothered her, because she carried them in her psyche—as a ship carries passengers.

She knew, for example, that her husband longed for a direct psychic experience of his dead father. In her concern for his longing, she had a unique psychic experience of her own, a cryptic but lovely little dream that probed prophetically accurate: *"Saw five chrysanthemums on the grave of my husband's father."*

Cayce responded that in five weeks her husband would have an experience of being taught in dreams by his dead father, which would bring him some of the greatest joy of his life. Five weeks later, right on schedule, the dreams came to Aaron.

Frances had spoken aloud about the flowers, in her sleep, and Cayce commented on this performance, as well. The same subconscious, he said, which had looked ahead to the contents of her husband's dreams had also prompted her to speak aloud about them, and to interpret the dream. But the sound of her own voice had wakened her as she spoke. She could, he continued, train herself to let the subconscious have more initiative, so that such experiences could become spontaneous little "readings" for those she cared about. Her speaking out loud in sleep would be not unlike his own trances, and quite natural expressions, once in a while, of what went on in her dreams. Frances tried, somewhat gingerly, to encourage her subconscious crew to take over in this way.

The next time she talked out loud in her sleep, it was to advise her husband not to change toothpastes! Modest counsel, but sound, according to Cayce. Later her ventures took her much deeper, though the experiences were infrequent. One of the most important found her talking out loud about her own preoccupation with "looks," with her face and figure—a theme which Cayce said was a central motif in her personality, because of its overtones of power over men.

Not every passenger in Frances' ship was easy to handle, as Cayce pointed out in response to another dream she sent him:

> All of us, my mother-in-law, her friends, my husband and I were back home in Mississippi, way back in the old days when we lived downtown. We were preparing to go to Sandy Beach for the summer. My mother's friend said she wouldn't go, but was going home to White Plains, New York. Mrs. B., another friend, said she would go back to the beach with us. We all got into automobiles and started. Then my mother-in-law got very angry and irritable with me, as she was this past summer. Was very unpleasant.

Cayce contended that Frances' subconscious (or what might be called her crew) had picked up on its ESP the response that would be forthcoming from relatives and friends in the near future, to some things Frances was going to say or do. He urged her to be prepared for this unpleasantness, and not to let it upset her unduly.

The Level of Consciousness

In most dreams Cayce saw calls to conscious decision and action. The process was like the crew of a ship appealing to the captain for his orders.

As he started to discuss the motherhood dream already mentioned, Cayce commented that anyone who could dream and remember it was capable of learning from dreams, capable of adding conscious insight and behavior to the unconscious impact of the dream experience: "For as we find," he said, "each and every individual who is possessed of the faculty of visioning the various conditions of experiences which pass through the various consciousness of an individual"—he meant the various levels active in dreams—"is capable also of gaining those lessons or truths from same which are . . . the truth as shown to the individual through the various phases of its consciousness."

Nobody dreams who is unable to interpret and learn from his own dreams.

Every man's crew has a captain who must act like one, when the crew approaches him in dreams.

Sometimes the crew might appeal to the captain against the captain!

In the first few weeks of marriage, when Frances was fairly intoxicated with Cayce's interpreting of her dreams, and with his entire outlook on life, she plunged into psychic and occult studies. Like her impatient husband, she wanted to understand the whole business at once, so that she could begin practicing her own small psychic feats. Then she dreamed:

> Saw myself going down a large chute into water. It widened as I neared the bottom, and branched out in two directions. Someone said, "It is fourteen feet there where you land. What will you do then?"

Cayce observed that Frances was being warned from within herself that the "mental forces"—her own captain or consciousness—were pushing her beyond her depth, at a time when she was just beginning to understand "elemental conditions" of psychological development. If she would take the time to move "step by step," he said, her mind would broaden in a healthy way, showing her new avenues for using its energies, as the dream depicted with the broadened chute. But if she forced her development by "will," she would bring "destructive forces" onto herself.

The captain had to chart a wise course.

In Cayce's view the captain of consciousness also has definitive powers in determining the cargo for the crew to handle. He saw the subconscious as highly active, constantly molding and shaping whatever was put in its care. Over and over he insisted that "thoughts are things," that "thoughts are deeds," because of their impact on the subconscious.

Frances moved in social circles where bridge and small talk could occupy many hours of a day, building an undercover pettiness that could not always be seen, until one day a part of the bridge player had become a glowering shrew. This dream showed her as much:

> Regarding the playing of bridge, I beheld standing in front of me right in the room, as real and living, the Queen of Clubs. I became frightened and jumped for my husband.

Cayce explained that whatever consciousness dwells on is stored in the subconscious, or "stamped upon the subconscious forces," until it takes on body and form and an independent life of its own.

A new figure had joined Frances' crew in this dream, a Frankenstein's monster created at the bridge table where the captain played and gossiped.

The Level of the Superconscious

A crew needs information from beyond the ship, to operate it effectively. Some of this it can secure by its own devices. In times past, sailors took bearings from the stars, time from the sun, news from passing ships.

Cayce spoke repeatedly of the capacity of the subconscious to get its bearings on practical matters by the use of its own natural ESP. He told Frances that it was her own natural psychic talent that brought her unknowns in many of her dreams, from toothpaste to the future behavior of relatives.

But in Cayce's view another source of help is also available. He called it the superconscious, which he described as a higher realm of the subconscious.

Modern sailors might be turning to something like this if they radioed to home port for guidance from a computerized maritime institute, one which could tell them instantly the latest information on ocean currents, on tides, on weather, on other shipping, on their passengers, and even on the markets in ports ahead of them.

Cayce insisted that there are what he called "Universal Forces" that the individual can contact, according to his need and his training to use them. These forces can provide him with boundless information, and with relevant patterns of guidance. They are in effect the creative currents of the divine itself, moving through human affairs like some great unseen Gulf Stream.

In dreams one may reach far beyond his own faculties to tune in on these Universal Forces, through his own superconscious.

Early in her dream study with Cayce, while still uncertain what to make of Cayce's religious outlook, Frances recorded the following:

> Dreamed I had an earache and was waiting for my mother in front of a drugstore in my old home town. My mother came and my ear hurt so, I wanted her to take me to a doctor. "You don't need one," she said. "You can overcome that yourself." I did and it so surprised me that I went driving with my friend C., and told her all about it. "What you need," she said, "is Christian Science. You ought to try it, for that is Christian Science. Become a Christian Scientist." "No," I replied, "I have my own science. Jewish Science. I cured myself, just naturally."

In interpreting the dream, Cayce evinced no surprise at her ear trouble, for Frances had already brought him a warning dream of an old mastoid condition. Nor did he comment at length on the manner of healing in the dream. Such aid from the superconscious was as real to him as aid from the medication which he had already prescribed for her ear. He took up, instead, the question of whether such aid from the superconscious is the private property of any one faith. Her dream, he said, was showing her that such forces and energies are objective realities which may be found and used by anyone who will meet their conditions, including "faith in the God-force manifest in an individual, see?" He urged her to study the laws of such aid in healing, no matter who claimed to have a corner on them, nor how offensive they might seem to her friends and relatives. Man may divide up his theories into traditions, Cayce observed, but man is talking about laws that could not be parceled out, for "they remain a oneness, whether Jewish, Gentile, Greek or heathen."

The crew has a resource of energy and guidance beyond anything on shipboard, if they know how to contact home port for it, and really need it.

The Level of the Soul

A ship is operated by its crew, working under orders from the captain. But the captain in turn is subject to orders which he violates at his peril. He is answerable to the owner of the ship.

In the Cayce view, unlike that of some modern psychology, the picture of the total person is not complete without including the owner, the best self, or the soul. This part of the person, well-removed from consciousness, carries his real ideals and commitments, whether verbally formulated or not. It gives character and flavor to this conscience (a function of the subconscious according to Cayce), but the soul is not limited to the conscience. It is also a structure more enduring than consciousness, that captain of daily life, for the soul survives death, and consciousness does not.

The soul determines how long and well the captain and crew endure in their task. It sets their large course for them, while leaving them the daily operation of the vessel. It may, as owner of the ship, make its own representations to the captain through dreams. But its desires may be frustrated by the captain, for decision and action—and therefore growth—are his on the voyage of a lifetime.

After Frances' baby was born, and she was past the critical strains of birthing, she grew careless about diet, laxatives, physiotherapy, her temper, and other matters which she had concluded in her dream study with Cayce were important to her own health and peace of mind, as well as to the baby's. Then she dreamed the following:

> It seemed I was to marry cousin William, but when it came to it I hesitated because he was my cousin and he had had so much trouble. Thus I hemmed and hawed and hesitated, undecided what to do.

Cayce warned her that her now "real inner self," her "self's own best self," was protesting her failure to follow through on promises made to herself (a "relative" whom she liked). He described her failure as being as serious as failing to honor an engagement for marriage. And he nailed down the challenge by picking out a warning to her from a dream had by Aaron, weeks before, in which he had seen that his wife should take Pluto water for her eliminations. She had concurred then, but now was careless, and her nursing baby suffered while she procrastinated.

The owner had rebuked the captain, in this dream, for sailing an unsteady course.

Long before, while pregnant before her miscarriage, Frances had also dreamed a contact with her best self, or soul, in this vivid anxiety dream:

> Dreamed that I could never have a child—that none would ever come to me—that I would never give birth.

Cayce assured her flatly that she would one day have a child (as in fact she did, but not the one she was carrying). He told her to forget any literal interpretation of the dream. Instead, he urged her to note the careful preparations she was making for motherhood: diet, physiotherapy, attitudes, exercise. These were her "highest service to the Maker, and to the one held dear," her husband. By reflecting she might see why the dream took up these current preparations for birth as an emblem for the cleansings and disciplines she also needed, to prepare not for the baby, but for her own highest self, which needed to assume a larger place in her life. This was the birth that was in jeopardy, not her baby's. This was the child, the highest self, which would one day be her own greatest gift to her growing offspring.

A shipowner may trade in his ship for a new one.

It was part of the Cayce outlook that the soul reincarnates, taking successive voyages in lives on earth, of long or short duration. Each voyage is meant to enrich and enlarge the soul's total creativity in some specific way.

No single claim of Cayce's alienated so many people in his lifetime.

For years he had used his gift only for medical counsel. Then he had added not only counsel on oil wells, but even counsel on the affairs of nations. Through all of this psychic counseling, until he was forty-five years old, he had remained a psychological oddity—a marvel for some, an instance of self-delusion for others. But shortly before Frances and her husband had appeared in his life, he had commented, in trance, that people live on earth many times. From then on he was not only an oddity, but often someone to be shunned, by those who might otherwise have been drawn to him by his obvious gifts. Yet his psychic sources, at whatever cost to his personal popularity and self-esteem (for the idea of reincarnation was foreign to him as a Southern Protestant) insisted that such rebirth was a fact, to be observed as dispassionately as the broken legs which he described in medical counsel, or the stock trends that he described in business counsel, or the buried oil fields that he had located so brilliantly a few times in the past.

In the first reading that he gave to Frances, he told her, at her request, that in one of her past lives she had been a maid, an attendant, to Henrietta, the wife of Charles I of England. It had not been a particularly helpful life, for she had absorbed much of the spirit of court intrigue, especially from her mistress, and a style of "get even with you yet," when rejected or crossed. Cayce told her firmly that she would need above all in the present lifetime to learn not to act in spite or grudge—a warning he repeated many times. He saw it as the course of her soul to learn forgiveness and patience with others, while serving as Aaron's wife.

Her test eventually came, as it does to many, in marital conflict. Frances stayed with her husband eight years, but finally left him, not without some hints of the spirit of the English court. Her dreams showed her toying with the idea of a romance with an old boyfriend, to get even. But mostly her dreams urged her to patience and steadiness with her husband, when stresses came.

Frances' first dream drawing on past lives came as early as on her honeymoon, according to Cayce. Then, almost exactly a year later, came another, forewarning the blowup in her marriage several years afterwards:

> My husband and I were on a boat, and there seemed much thundering or shooting and fighting. It ended with the boat being struck by lightning and the boiler exploding. It sank. We were blown up—killed.

Cayce told her there would one day be conditions in her life (as in time there were), which would remind her of this dream, which he called a "vision" instead of a dream, because of its accuracy and depth. He told her that her subconscious was using the boat voyage as a symbol or emblem of the voyage of life. And he warned that there would indeed come a crisis in her passage through the affairs of her life, with turmoils and troubles. He spoke sternly to both husband and wife, saying that the warning of the vision had come to both, so "that the paths of each might be made more in accord one with the other." Yet he was not fatalistic, in speaking to Frances of this coming test of her ability to avoid spite or grudge. The "blowup" (Cayce insisted that dreams often dramatized figures of speech) could be followed by a "settling down" to a more perfect understanding by each marital partner, rather than by destruction.

The owner of the ship had called for preparations to meet a serious challenge.

In later years Frances had to meet once more such a challenge. Her son, like his father, was drawn into a marital tangle, and he suffered a nervous breakdown. This time she drew on deep resources of patience and fidelity, seeing him through in ways that won the admiration of friends, and could well have won from Cayce his cryptic remark of highest praise: "the entity gained, in that lifetime."

Three Levels in Dreaming

While Cayce described all of the above structures to Frances as operating in her dreams, he told her, as he did many others, that there are in effect only three levels in dreaming: the levels of body, mind, and spirit.

The body can initiate meaningful dreams, calling for physiological help through the assistance of the subconscious. Or it can produce meaningless dreams by sheer body chemistry acting on the nervous system, often from foods eaten, though sometimes from abnormal involvement of the endocrine glands, or through impaired circulation to the nervous system. He urged Frances to note that "there may be taken into the body physical . . . elements that produce hallucinations; or the activity . . . induced in the system," trying to handle troublesome foods or poisons "produces hallucinations, nightmares, or abortions to the mental forces of an individual."

Such dreams, or non-dreams, need to be distinguished from the more common dreams, he noted, which are initiated by mental or psychological activity.

Dreams of a primarily mental character are sometimes only conscious worries and concerns rehashed in the night.

But sheer worry dreams, Cayce said, are rare for those who work with their dreams. Usually, when conscious thought and effort are restaged in the night, they are shown in order to get a reaction from the subconscious, which proceeds to interpret conscious experience in new light, or to add its own ESP information from subconscious channels. As Cayce told Frances, some dreams are stimulated "from the mental mind of an entity, by deep study or thought" on a problem or an interest or a relationship. In such dreams, the outward "experiences of the individual entity are correlated" with inward structures and perspectives "through the subconscious forces of the entity—the latent forces of the entity—the hidden forces of the entity," which present the correlations "in a vision or a dream. Often these are as symbolic conditions, each representing a various phase to the mental development of the entity."

In yet other mental dreams, as Cayce saw them, the initiative lies more with the subconscious, warning or alerting the dreamer about something that has not yet entered his conscious experience, but is showing up on his internal radar because of the source on which he is headed.

To illustrate this latter kind of warning by the subconscious, Cayce singled out a dream of Frances that a close friend had committed suicide. The dream, said Cayce, accurately depicted a tendency in the friend which had passed. Such a dream developed by the "correlation between mentalities or subconscious entities" of the two dreamers, bringing "from one subconscious to another . . . ac-tual existent conditions, either direct or indirect, to be acted upon" by loving care.

Finally, there are dreams from the dreamer's higher self, often given expression by a nameless voice in the dream, dreams from the superconscious, touching the Universal Forces. Cayce called such dreams "spiritual."

On her honeymoon, early in her recording of dreams, Frances heard just such a voice in a dream:

> I dreamed I saw a woman, stretched on a bedspring, and the spring seemed to sway backward. I dreamed that something inside of me said, "Frances, you will awaken to something different," and I suddenly felt a smile on my face.

In interpreting the dream, Cayce spoke explicitly of the "good pleasure" of "consummation" in the marriage, dramatized in the sexual imagery of the bed, postures, and swaying. He also spoke of the fullness of womanhood and person-hood awakening in Frances as she gave herself in the sex act, and he described the voice that she had heard as "the superconscious," answering happily to the sexual experience and bringing a smile to her face in the dream. He gave her the impression that she was awakening at many levels at once—as many a bride has felt. Here, as in many other dreams, he noted that the typical function of the soul or of the superconscious in a dream was that of quickening or awakening to the dreamer to new inward potentials.

CHAPTER 3

Solving Problems Through Dreams

Edgar Cayce encouraged Frances to interpret her own dreams.

Sometimes in his readings he quoted the saying, "Every tub must sit on its own bottom." It was this sort of self-reliance in Frances which he saw hinted in the following dream:

> I was at the table with my husband and he was talking of my green water glasses. "Now just you keep quiet," I told him; "don't you criticize my glasses."

Although Cayce often told Frances that her dreams of others criticizing her were representations of her own sharp tongue, he took a different approach in commenting on this dream. The green, he said, was an emblem of healthy development—like the green in nature. She should therefore stick to what made sense to her "concept of creative forces." The glasses were vessels for what would be put into her body and life, whatever she chose to absorb and trust. He advised her, "Then do not care what others may say," just so what she saw and did squared with her inner version of the "Creative Force" or God.

When Frances wanted to rely too heavily on dream messages from her dead mother, he again encouraged her to rely on herself. She reported to him the following: "Dreamed that my mother-in-law would tire of California and return home in six weeks." He told her that her perception was fairly accurate (as it proved to be), but when she asked if this perception had been guided from the next plane, he stressed that she had arrived at the dream conclusion from conscious reasoning in a dream state, rather than from any psychic experience. However, he encouraged her to develop within herself, by entering into periods of silence, the ability to achieve telepathic contact with those close to her, rather than seeking "spiritualistic conditions."

When she dreamed, more than a year before the 1929 stock crash, of the exact date on which she and her husband should sell their stocks, because of the "great changes" beginning then, he encouraged her to note how she could gain through such experiences whatever leads she needed for her daily activities.

Cayce invited Frances to do more than study dreams and dreaming. He pressed her to do more than study a psychic at work on her dreams. He coached her to interpret and use her own dreams on the problems of everyday life.

Problems with Relatives

There was, at the start of her dream-series, the problem she had with her relatives in her close-knit family of Southern Jews. They had shown not only the usual doubts about a northerner taking the flower of Southern womanhood, and some private family doubts over whether her husband's checkbook was as good as it looked. They had openly criticized his psychic interests. How was Frances to handle these relatives?

Even on her honeymoon trip, she dreamed of her family, as she reported to Cayce on successive days, in beginning her dream series.

I dreamed I saw my uncle stirring black coffee.

I dreamed I was on a train riding back towards home in Mississippi.

I dreamed I was on horseback and fell off. The same morning I dreamed of my father at home in Mississippi and awakened thinking of Cayce.

Cayce told her that the first dream was of her uncle's actual views of her marriage—as mixed up as stirring black coffee which had no need to be stirred. The second dream, he told her, was a continuation of what she had been thinking before she dropped off into a nap (note that Cayce supplied this verifiable fact from hundreds of miles away, and several days later), which was that her actual train trip on a honeymoon was very different from a train trip she might be taking back home to her folks. The problem she was solving here, he said, was one of getting into perspective all that she was, as a bride, leaving behind. It was Frances' version of every bride's problem.

The third dream Cayce promptly corrected, as he often did, by telling the dreamer that she had left out a good deal of it. He then supplied the missing details for her to verify and study!

There had been not only the horse and rider, he said, but a vision of a roadway with various obstructions, and then an event to cause the horse to shy and the rider to fall.

This dream he treated as engaging the young bride at a much deeper level than the others—as an analyst might have guessed from the dynamic imagery of the horse, the presence of the father, and the hint of the awesome Cayce. But Cayce stressed no Oedipus problem in the dream, although it was likely that Frances' ties with her father were being brought to light by her having taken a man in marriage. Instead he saw the dream as continuing to handle the problem of the relatives' acceptance of her marriage, and of her husband's interests in psychic things.

He saw the horse as bringing a "messenger," a call that comes to everyone from his own best self. And he described her wonder at the things the rider had said, as well as her efforts to match the message with the views of people she held dear—such as her father. He saw the obstructions in the road as graphic dream images of the obstacles ahead in her new life path, and he warned her that the riders falling off meant possible rejection of the message (which in fact occurred, as her dreams continued to warn, some five years later). Cayce spoke to Frances with unusual seriousness in interpreting this dream. He described her confronting of issues in sleep as "very, very good." Then he left her with the impression that in this dream she had gone beyond strategic problems of family harmony, to tackle the deep problem of what she was going to trust with her very life—what outlook, what faith, what principles. As always, he urged her to trust her own best judgment.

Emotional Problems

Frances' problems were not all so abstract. Still on her honeymoon, she sent to Cayce a sex dream that brought a different kind of response from him. She wrote:

> I saw clearly a beautiful house on fire. The same night I dreamed a girl friend of mine was at a dinner table with many guests, including myself. It was back in Mississippi. She was making violent and demonstrative love to her old sweetheart of single days, who was seated next to her. The guests all criticized her for this.

In interpreting this dream, Cayce departed from his usual method. Typically, he had the dream read aloud to him by his wife, while he was in his trance state, after which he would interpret it. But in this case he jumped into the interpretation after the first sentence, interrupting his wife, who was "conducting" the reading as hypnotists do. Ignoring the text of the dream, he proceeded to talk about it as though by ESP he had it all in mind—which in fact he did, as his comments showed.

Why the interruption? It seemed to occur, once in a while, when Cayce felt a special urgency about the subject of the reading he was about to give. Here the urgency showed in what he said to Frances.

He told her that the beautiful house on fire was but one of a series of dreams she had experienced, presenting something beautiful destroyed. In each case, he said, the destruction was represented by some symbol standing for misunderstanding with those of her household. Here it was fire, standing for *ire* in her dreams—a not uncommon dream symbol, he noted.

He was saying to a new bride just this: your dream is showing that your beautiful new relationship may well end in misunderstanding and bitter anger. Was Cayce justified in his warning? Eight years later the marriage ended in just this way.

Yet Cayce was no fatalist. "This should never begin," he said, as he urged the couple to begin working at once on understanding themselves and each other. And if the fire of rage should one day come between them, he added, they could come out of it better people, made more perfect or sound by passing through trial of fire, if they chose.

He stressed the importance of will power in each partner, and he traced its action in a tendency which the dream showed, for Frances to withhold a portion of herself in the marriage. She had repressed a part of the dream already, he pointed out, for he reminded her that only part of the front of the house was destroyed in the dream, while she had also seen blackened ruins in the rear.

What did the blackened ruins stand for? The answer lay in the violent love-making scene from earlier days, which followed in the dream, and brought criticism on the friend who was a stand-in for the dreamer.

Cayce spoke carefully of this portion of the dream, warning Frances that sexual improprieties could be expected to "shadow the life" ahead of her. In interpreting this dream (unlike another which Frances had much later, where her husband appeared in a doubtful light and left her to drown), Cayce spoke to Frances, herself. The trend of his comments was that she was keeping back part of her fantasies for her old sweetheart, and dwelling on these even during her honeymoon—and then finding herself accused by conscience pangs. He warned her, as he often warned others, that thoughts are deeds, with very real consequences. Apparently he was pointing to a chain of events familiar to psychiatrists: one partner in a marriage reserves a portion of himself from the marriage, but becomes so vulnerable to guilts as to be unable to forgive the other when the spouse in turn strays down similar paths. Was Cayce seeing something in Frances that might block reconciliation in later marital quarrels, and urging her to find the block for herself? Certainly he was not speaking of her activities, for she was freshly and happily married; nothing like an affair was in the picture.

Five months later he again interrupted a dream of Frances' being read to him:

> My mother-in-law, my husband and I were living together in a house in Pennsylvania, and I heard much shooting and excitement. All of the windows of our house were open, and as it was raining and storming out, we rushed to close and lock them. Some terrible wild man seemed to be running through the town, shooting and causing great trouble, and the police were chasing him.

Here the unconscious Cayce interrupted the reading of the dream to tell the dreamer, as though she were in the room with him at Virginia Beach, instead of hundreds of miles away in New York, that "the large man, the bugaboo" was herself and her temper. Then he waited while the rest of the dream was read:

> Conditions were chaotic and troublesome. We stopped the police to ask if they had caught this terrible person, and they answered, "Not yet."

Cayce responded at once that Frances should control herself, if this seemingly "terrible person" were to be "caught and conquered." To him the picture of her dream at work trying to solve the problem of her temper seemed completely clear—as it might to anyone living with Frances while she stormed about the house, making things chaotic and troublesome.

Not all of the problems which her dreams worked to solve were so serious. Some were as prosaic as her diet.

Problems of Health

She wanted to keep her girlish figure. It was important in her social circles, and of course carried sexual overtones to which both she and her husband were responsive. She dreamed of trying on clothes, and later, in pregnancy, she dreamed of her discouragement at being too large to go out for a formal evening. She frequently dieted, even though she was still in her early twenties, and not over-weight. She cut out starches and sweets, as her strong will allowed her to do, and she created, according to Cayce, a problem for the economy of her body. Dreams were forthcoming to try to solve the problem.

> Dreamed I said to my husband, "Now my cramps are all gone." He said, "That is fine." Then I awakened and all the pain was gone.

Cayce took a good deal of time with this little dream, showing her that the cramps she had actually been having in waking life, as well as in the dream, were caused by her reducing diet. He traced the effects of that diet, on digestion, eliminations, cell rebuilding, glandular operation, and circulation of the blood. Then he urged her to correct the diet as her own better judgment was already telling her. He also showed her how her figure-consciousness looked in her dreams when she told him a dream from the next night. *"Dreamed I saw J.B. and his sister. Something regarding looks."* He reminded her that she viewed the man and his sister as people overconcerned with their looks. She had dreamed of them because to her own inner mind her superdieting for looks seemed just as unreasonable as they were.

A week later Frances dreamed further about her diet:

> I was sitting at a table eating, but more than eating—I was packing it in. There was chocolate cake and all kinds of sweets and goodies—and I just had a great time eating it all up.

Patiently Cayce explained that this, too, was a problem-solving dream for her body, and that she should eat more sweets, rather than damaging her body by her reducing diet. But he added that she should not take the dream literally, eating sweets only in moderation.

A year later she was still experimenting with diets to protect her figure, and she dreamed this:

> It was raining starch, and I dreamed that I should go out in the rain of starch and put it on my side to ease the pain.

Here again, said Cayce, the body was problem-solving through a dream. He explained at some length that the lack of starch in her diet was causing fermentation in organs on the right side of her body, producing pain, and that the lack of starch was not good for the foetus she was carrying, either.

Problems with Associates

The same night Frances had dreamed of a quite different kind of problem, which Cayce said showed her ESP warning her of coming distress:

> I fainted on Fifth Avenue, falling to the street and knocking out several teeth. Leo seemed to have something to do with this.

Somehow picking up the unknown Leo with his own clairvoyance, Cayce responded that this little dream came to warn her of coming distress from unkind things Leo was going to say about her. Then he added, as he often did in interpreting precognitive dreams, "Being forewarned, be prepared." He urged her to overlook and forgive the remarks when she heard them, not letting them "take root in the mind" as unkind jibes often do, leading to sharp words as hard to replace as teeth.

Quite another kind of associate was central in a dream drama which he said also called on Frances' ESP. She had lost a lovely jeweled pin that her mother had given her and she suspected that a servant had taken it. She dreamed:

> Bob pointed out my lost pin to me as attached to my string of pearls. Upon investigating, I found it was another pin than that which my mother gave me, and not the one I wanted at all.

To unravel this dream, Cayce had to read Frances' mind, focusing on her memory of how she had handled a suspected theft of clothing by one of her servants, some time back. Rather than accusing the servant and setting up her defenses, Frances had taken more positive steps to show the maid her own feelings and commitments about honesty, and the clothes were returned.

This time, however, Frances was impatient. The dream commented on her impatience. It showed her, Cayce said, that if she forced the issue with the present employee, a substitution would be made by the accused servant, to cover up the theft. Or else the servant would leave, and Frances would never regain the pin. Cayce urged her to do as she had done with the incident of the clothes, and as her own best judgment, he said, was already prompting her: to wait, to watch, to pray.

Then, typically, he pointed to an opportunity that lay before Frances—an opportunity to be to her maid a quiet kind of witness. He said the girl was ready to learn, if not too frightened. And he urged Frances to handle the incident so that she herself would not steal something from the thief more important than silver and gold: her self-respect, her chance to grow, her soul. He asked Frances to "put it into the heart, the mind" of employees and relatives about her "that the fear of the Lord—not law—is the beginning of wisdom."

By stressing the strength of the total orientation of a person, as greater than conscience and fear of punishment, and by trusting the relationship between Frances and her servant to bear good fruit, Cayce showed his own ultimate values. Such values inevitably affected all of his serious dream interpretation. In Cayce's view, nobody's problems were simply his own, and one function of dreams was to bring to light all the factors in a situation, as well as the most creative total solution.

Problems of Money

Frances held some stocks in her name, but it was her husband who did the investing—and the dreaming about investing. Still, she could not avoid being concerned with his concerns, and early in their marriage she had the following two dreams about stocks:

> My husband and I were down South and saw thousands of little children learning to swim in a big lake. They were on some kind of rope contraption that went down at the sound of a whistle and thereby allowed them to swim in water up to their waists. I wondered how the rope thing worked, and what it was. Many older girls were also swimming.

Cayce characterized the dream as one about the staple product of the South (where Frances had been reared): cotton. The big device was showing her the rise and fall of prices in the cotton market, in response to the whistle—call or demand—for cotton. The thousands of children represented new industries in the South, needing cotton, while the larger girls were the larger users and brokers, who affected the price-setting device the most. The water was there to show that the market affected real-life support and sustenance for many people.

He told Frances to take her cotton hunches to certain brokers outside the family (not to her husband, who was himself an experienced investor!); these would help her to use her dream tips to good advantage. Later, she came up with stock leads for her husband, as well:

> My husband and I went to the L and N Railroad Station. He had missed his train. The first train had gone. I said to him, "You should never have missed that L and N train. You should watch the time better. You are too slow." He called a taxi to go to another railroad, but the taxi he called was a slow horse hack. Then I saw a fruit stand, and turning to my husband, said, "Buy me a piece of fruit."

On this dream Cayce got right down to market details. Encouraging Frances to use such dreams for financial guidance as he had encouraged her husband, Cayce pointed out that the dream was correct in showing that her husband had in fact missed a chance for a rise in L and N stock, on which he was short. He also pointed out that while Aaron could get out of his situation with L and N stock, as shown through the taxi, he couldn't make much money on the deal, as the slow hack indicated. The part about the fruit he called precognitive, insisting that the railroad and a fruit stock were soon to join in a combine that would affect their holdings. He urged Frances and her husband to be ready to buy when this occurred.

So Frances had her initiation into the world of market dreams, which were making so much money for her husband and his associates in the stock market.

When the great stock crash of 1929 began to come over the horizon, Frances and her husband both had clear and ample warnings, months in advance. The result was that her husband went through the crash and the early years of the Depression relatively unharmed, financially. He even went off to Europe at the trough to the Depression. It was his psychic guidance which he credited with saving his wealth, as it had earlier made him rich.

With the marriage break, Frances was left alone to support her son. In a few short years she had gone from modest means to exceptional wealth, and then to stringent need, with both of her parents dead. She needed every resource in her being.

One resource was her astonishing—and to her, at least, convincing—experience of reaching through death to her mother.

CHAPTER 4

ADVENTURING THROUGH DREAMS

IT WAS TYPICAL for those who turned to Edgar Cayce for coaching on their dreams that they began to adventure through their nightly productions.

Many of their dreams focused on solving problems at all levels of their lives, as Frances saw.

But some of their dreams could only be called adventures. These were apparently bent on quickening hidden potentials in the dreamer—the second great function which Edgar Cayce saw in dreams.

Some of the systematic dreamers pursued mechanical inventions in dreams, such as a container for oil which made a great deal of money for one man. Some dreamed their way back into history. Some heard music, some investigated physiology in dreams. Three college students dreamed accurately of buried treasure. A housewife dreamed the answers to a contest on vitamins in Wonder Bread.

Most of the adventuring, however, went deeper. It led the dreamer into avenues which would broaden and transform his entire selfhood.

Transformation marked the adventuring that unfolded for Frances, in the four years that she sought dream counsel from Cayce. She explored, first through her dreams, and then in a few semi-waking experiences, the country of death.

Psychic Experiences in Dreams

Not all of Frances' psychic experiences in dreams had to do with the departed, with "discarnates," as psychic investigators call them. Some of her ESP went in quite other directions.

What appeared to be ESP took her back in time, into what Cayce called past lives. An early hint of this came in a dream six weeks after marriage. *"Dreamed my husband wasn't coming home any more, and I cried bitterly."* Cayce told her this dream imagery reached into her very soul. "The greater awakening of love, in self, for him, awakens those possibilities of the separate conditions." The deep stirrings which she was feeling as a young bride were also calling forth what Cayce called her karma: all the testings and questionings about men and love that lay locked in her inmost being.

The picture of real love bringing with it the possibility of real alienation was one which psychiatrists and poets alike would recognize, without the Cayce framework of reincarnation.

Despite such daunting episodes in her dreams, Frances was determined to develop her ESP, and her psyche seemed ready for some such awakening, if Cayce's interpretation of this early dream was correct: *"Dreamed I died."*

Here she was seeing, he said, the death of attachment to "physical forces," preoccupation with physical pleasures and diversions, so that her capacity for serious thought and creativity could be born. It was a dream of an ending to prepare for a beginning.

The same night she dreamed further of the awakening that was stirring in her, in response to the interests she saw in her husband and in Cayce:

> Saw someone wearing a dress which I copied and wore. As I tried on the left sleeve it was very tight. They told me that is the way it should be. "Make me two, just like this," I said.

Cayce described her "putting on of apparel" as evidence of the awakening of her subconscious to put on its new potentials, especially for psychic experiences such as she might wish to copy from her husband and others. But he warned that when the dream showed her ordering two dresses, it showed a bit of her pride that had to be tamed.

His basic counsel was Biblical: "Seek and ye shall find. Knock and it shall be opened to you." Yet he noted that the dress would be tight, for she would have to yield a desire to show off to a "desire to show self acceptable to Him, the Giver of all good and perfect gifts, making manifest in word, action, and deed those lessons gathered." The psychic outreach she sought could not be ordered up like dresses, but "little by little, line upon line," as she learned to share her discoveries fruitfully with others. He continued in the same vein when she reported a further dream from the same night: *Saw myself in various costumes."*

By reviewing this dream, he said, she could see herself gradually developing, gradually putting on exactly what she needed, at all levels, for her new awakening—spiritually, physically, mentally. And in his typical language for serious readings, he paraphrased two passages of the New Testament: "Put on the whole armor . . . those conditions that give of the spiritual kingdom. With this awakening"—awakening to the right kingdom first, he told her—"all physical, material will be added unto you" in gifts as helpful as her husband's and Cayce's gifts which she so admired.

It was not long before Frances began to show, in her dreams, an awakening of ESP talents that took two directions which stayed with her throughout her four years with Cayce. One direction was counsel on health matters, for herself and those close to her. The other was telepathy. These two gifts, together with her later capacity to reach through death to her discarnate mother, made up her special psychic profile—different from the profiles of others who sought dream counsel from Cayce.

The health tips in her dreams were simple. But they were helpful. One of the first was a short dream: "Dreamed my husband's cold was worse." Cayce reminded her that she already had prescriptions to give him, and should do something about them.

Something more like ESP seemed evident in a portion of a later dream:

> My husband and I went into a store and bought some candy, at which I said, "There you are bothering around buying candy. You know it is not good for you and that you should not eat it."

It was time, Cayce told her, for her to guide and guard her husband in his appetite for sweets.

Aaron might well have listened to her, for a month before she had come up with a vivid dream for him that proved medically sound:

> My ear seemed to trouble me and I said, "I know—it is a return of my old ear trouble." My ear pained me dreadfully. Yet it seemed to be my husband's ear—not mine."

The last part of the dream, Cayce said, showed her the correct direction to look. For the dream was in fact a warning about an infection in her husband's Eustachian tube, leading to his ear. The dream had simply used her ear trouble to dramatize his need. Helpful as her dream was, Frances still had to ask Cayce which of her husband's ears was involved, and was told "the left"—as a doctor verified.

The same night Frances dreamed yet more strikingly of her brother-in-law's health:

> Saw him get so terribly sick that I interfered, telling them that they should not permit a duplication of what happened in my mother's case.

Cayce responded that she had correctly seen in the dream the gravity of letting her brother-in-law postpone medical aid, as her mother had fatally postponed it. But the interference, he said, was a depicting of helpful steps she had already taken in the family circle, which were beginning to bear fruit.

In six months she had an unforgettable experience of ESP at work in protecting the health of her loved ones. It seemed to her in her dream that her parents (who were by then both dead) appeared to her in a dream and were glad to see her. However, they expressed great concern:

> They told me about my sister, that she had committed suicide, or killed herself.

Cayce insisted that the dream was showing her the actual workings of her sister's mind, and that the sister was in fact carrying the thought of suicide, night and day.

Frances and her husband, alarmed, got on the phone at once to her sister, who broke down and admitted she was contemplating killing herself, as her father had done before her. Only the timeliness of the dream and the call, followed by long hours of counsel, saved the sister from death.

The ability to know, through dreams, the thoughts of others close to her, was not always so disturbing for Frances. She sent Cayce a brief note, along with other dreams, about a scene involving a favorite cousin: *"Dreamed my cousin William was married."* Here she was having a correct premonition of his intentions, Cayce told her, and within the next three months she would receive a message that the marriage had happened. He suggested that she make a record of the dream, as he often suggested to others, first studying the outreach of the subconscious and its ESP. "Follow this," he said, "and it will be seen."

Cayce did not make clear whether Frances was sender or receiver in the delightful instance of dream telepathy which occurred when she was in early pregnancy. On the night of December 2, 1925, Frances' sister-in-law *"Dreamed Frances, my sister-in-law, had a new diamond flexible bracelet."* She sent the dream to Cayce, as some of Frances' relatives were now doing. He told her that it represented Frances making preparations for motherhood, "for the greater bonds that bind self to the commendation of self, to the magnifying of spirit forces in earth plane." Cayce held a high view of motherhood, which could draw a helpful and talented soul into the earth plane for a new incarnation. To him pregnancy was fittingly symbolized by precious jewelry, and especially by jewelry which adorned the arms that would hold a baby.

On precisely the same night, Frances herself dreamed the following:

> Dreamed I had bands on my fingers, which opened up into diamond flexible bracelets to my elbow. I was at home at the time, going to college, and was so excited I decided to stay home and not go to school. I was dressed in my red sweater and skirt. My mother urged me to remain home and celebrate the good fortune, and anyway I lost my schedule of my studies or hours, so could not go to college that day. I stayed home in excitement to enjoy the wonderful jewelry.

To Frances, Cayce was even more detailed about the bracelets. They had first appeared as bands, he said, because of the bands on fingers that signify marital union. They had opened into arm bracelets because her marriage was opening "now, into that wonderful development, of that to occupy the entity in the arm full of jewels, as it were, from that union."

But now Cayce went beyond what he had told Frances' sister-in-law. To Frances he added that the full term of the baby would bring its birth in the middle of June, and that it would be a boy.

However, he warned her sternly that the birth might not take place, if she did not observe the necessary preparations and precautions, both mental and physical. (As a matter of fact, this pregnancy terminated in a miscarriage, two months later.) The dream about staying home from school and losing her schedule, he said, was showing her that she could be "lost in the maze of conditions or speculation" on motherhood. He urged her to take care of matters of diet and physiotherapy, as well as rest and freedom from worry, which he had outlined for her previously in a medical reading.

Frances was learning about ESP in dreams, though she had much to learn of motherhood.

Previewing Death

Like her husband, Frances was fascinated by the question of whether human personality survived bodily death. In the early twenties there was still no systematic laboratory research on ESP. Indeed, Dr. J.B. Rhine, who was to invent the term, had not yet appeared on the scene of psychical research, as he was to do at Clark University, some years later, for a symposium with the famous psychologist MacDougall, and in the company of a young man destined to become dean of American psychologists, Gardner Murphy.

For Frances and her friends, psychic phenomena were almost synonymous with the question of life after death. Their interests followed the pattern of interests in the British-born Society for Psychical Research, which was then placing its sharpest attention on the investigation of mediums and spirit phenomena. The attention was not a morbid desire to retain contact with dead loved ones, but rather a desire to show that "mind" was an independent principle in man, something that survived his death and therefore deserved more attention during his lifetime than did "matter" and materialism. The search was basically for a philosophy of life, from which enthusiasts for psychic phenomena thought they could derive a new and compelling scheme of values for their world, still marked by the scars of the First World War.

Frances' interest in life beyond the grave was evident in a dream she had recalled early in her marriage, where the vehicle was of a type not uncommon for those who submitted their dreams to Cayce: a discussion dream, on a topic important to the dreamer.

> I was in a discussion with Ted. I remember only a portion of this. Recall and interpret and explain to me so that my mind may grasp the significance and I may better understand the lesson intended. That I recall is as follows: Talking to Ted, I said, "Now, Ted, you see, death is not the grave as many people think. It is another phenomenized form of life."

As he often did, Cayce began by telling the dreamer what part of her mind was at work, and how, in a particular dream. Here it was Frances' subconscious giving to her conscious mind, he said, lessons about the psychology of mental forces.

Then he went on to recall the dream for her, as she had asked:

> This as the conversation, as we gain here. The discussion regarding that seen by the life in an individual, and the taking of same by any sudden action, see? And the discussion went into the particular condition regarding individuals' lives that were taken in heat of passion, or in war. And as the mental developed in discussion, we find the entity sees then in same something of that suggestion as was placed in waking life by one Ballentine, in the discussion of life after death. And the entity then sees, through subconscious forces, that death is as but the beginning of another form of phenomenized force, in the perspective of the earth's plane.

The term "phenomenized" was one much used by Frances' husband at the time, to suggest that one life force was at work behind the phenomena in which a person expressed his being, whether in a "third-dimensional" earthly body or a different "fourth-dimensional" form beyond the grave.

Cayce continued his report by emphasizing, as he often did, that post-death existence could not be grasped rationally and logically, but had to be experienced by psychic attunement which could put an earthly person *en rapport* with that other state.

> And may not be understood by the third dimension mind from third dimension analysis, but must be seen from that fourth dimension force as may be experienced by an entity gaining the access to same by development (psychically and spiritually) in the physical plane, through the mental processes of an entity.

He added that Francis was gaining the ability for just such an attunement. Then he went on to explain further, as she had asked.

> We see in the physical world the condition (of death) in every form of life. As is taken here: we find in a grain of corn or wheat that germ that, set in motion through its natural process with Mother Earth and the elements about same, brings forth corn after its kind, see? The kind and the germ being of a spiritual nature. The husk or corn, and the natural or physical condition of it, being physical forces, see? Then, as the corn dies, the process is as the growth is seen (in the dream) in that as expressed to the entity. And the entity expressing same, see? That death is not as commonly viewed, is not that of the passing away, or becoming a non-entity.

Cayce was agreeing with the comments Frances had made in her dream, where she identified life beyond death as "another phenomenized form" of the life force. The body would be left behind like the husk of a seed, and something new would come forth from its germ. Cayce was, however, stressing something he never failed to underscore in discussions of life beyond death, the matter of the *kind* or quality of post-death existence that a person was building in his earthly life. This was the essential *spiritual* question, he suggested to Frances, the question of the spirit or trend or quality of a person's being—not just his enduring or surviving. To be sure, the husk would be discarded. But what would be the pattern of the emergent germ?

Frances had no idea that her dreams of life beyond death were serving a purpose other than developing her intellectual interests. But within a month and a half her mother, now well, would be dead of cancer. And within a year and a half her father would be dead by his own hand, an instance of the process about which Frances was dreaming: "lives that were taken in the heat of passion." Slowly her dreams seemed to be preparing her. A dream which came two weeks later was one which Cayce said specifically was *not* a foreboding.

> Dreamed my father died. It must have been in the near future, because my mother was still limping from a recent accident in which her foot was hurt.

The dreaming of the father's death, he said, was simply an echo of her conscious concern over his diabetic condition. To help her, he spelled out for her father a correct diet, physiotherapy manipulations, and a detailed prescription for a four-part tonic to be taken three to four times daily. Regarding the mother in the dream, Cayce came up with a contrasting interpretation. Frances' letters to her mother were hurting her feelings, "crippling" her, so to speak, and Frances should use "more care in the manner and way in which the communications were addressed to the mother."

But the dream which came two weeks later was of a different order. By then Frances' mother was in the hospital for surgery on her eye, which revealed a malignant growth.

> Dreamed that my sister and myself were on my bed with our mother. Mother was unconscious. Both my sister and myself were crying and saying, "Don't leave us!" Suddenly our mother awakened and started to talk out loud, very loud, but it didn't seem like our mother talking at all.

Worried, Francis asked whether the dream meant that her mother would recover or would not recover. Cayce replied that it did not mean either, but was instead a lesson from the subconscious, giving "possibilities of actual conditions that might be existent in the physical forces" of her mother. Frances' subconscious was showing her the truth of "the soul liveth," as he put it, and Frances was to study the dream, in order to "gain the strength to bear with the weaknesses of the heir of fleshly conditions," or to bear death.

Reassuring her, Cayce turned to what her husband had dreamed, but not reported to him, the same night—Aaron had seen Frances weeping. The important point was not death-loss, Cayce said, but was the lowly spirit of the weeping, in which Frances could be seen emptying herself of physical understanding, in order to receive a grasp of spiritual conditions as they really stood with her mother.

Meantime, Frances' mother was having her own dreams in the hospital, one of which she asked Frances to send to Cayce for interpretation.

> I saw all my children, husband, and even my cook and maids—all with whom I am associated—I saw them as Dead.

Cayce told the sick mother that in this dream her subconscious was viewing from a superconscious perspective, how far each person in the dream fully comprehended the relations between earthly and post-death life. (Such a survey dream, wherein the dreamer explored the attitudes of each participant, was a not uncommon type of dream, in the Cayce view.) She saw the individuals as dead, he reported, because they would each have to go through a kind of "death" to false attitudes and convictions, if they were correctly to understand what she was going through in her own extremity.

Her opportunity, then, lay in what she could show them in the manner of her own dying (he called it what "the physical is passing through"). She could be an example of real strength of spirit, which might help each of her loved ones to grow towards "the full awakening to each," by the dying to live again which must take place in each—not just bodily but totally, existentially. By such dying or death needed for each, he added, "the whole force of life is meant, see?"

The dreams that came to Frances seemed to continue to prepare her for the loss she dreaded.

> I saw handwriting on the wall, with "Well." I didn't understand and went back to sleep and saw myself in a blue and white dress. I was kneeling down on my knees before the doctor and he patted me on the head, and I said, "Through you and God Almighty has our mother been spared to us"; and then he said, "Let us pray again. . . ."

At about this time Frances' mother did make a temporary recovery, even leaving the hospital for a while. Later, Cayce said that the respite had been brought almost entirely by prayer. But he must have had little doubt of the eventual outcome, for he interpreted the dream, again, as one preparing Frances to accept death. Under the existing conditions, he said, the dream was showing Frances herself that "there is only then for the entity to put self into the hands of the Giver of all good and perfect gifts. For in choosing the physician"—or "The Physician"—this would be "the best, then, for self, and for the good of the mother." The blue and the white of the dress he interpreted as he did the same colors elsewhere under similar dream conditions, as truth and purity—this time in her prayer and supplication. The handwriting she had seen, he said, was like that of Biblical times, and it meant "All is well"—not necessarily medically, but in the more perfect understanding of death that would come to Frances if she put her trust where it belonged. It was the answer to her prayer, but in God's terms, not hers.

Cayce was showing Frances, as he did many others, that dreams were a natural and appropriate vehicle in which the answers to prayer might be given.

Later the same night France had her first dream of the sort that Cayce often called a vision, because of its strong effect on the dreamer and its classic symbolic language.

> I saw a man with a gray beard, dressed in pure white like a sheep. It so impressed me that I said, "I can't believe it." I saw him pull my mother by the arm out into the light.

Such dreams or visions always had a direct effect on Cayce as he spoke of them, calling forth from him the Biblical imagery in which his own faith was held. Though Frances' mother was Jewish, Cayce explained the vision in Christian terms:

> This, as we see, is presenting to the dreamer that as is none other but

the Lamb, the Redeemer. For as is given (in scripture), through Him is there gained access to that throne of mercy, grace and pardon. And in complying with those ways that He taught, as is set through His words, may we all be led into the light, see? That the wool, though red like crimson, shall be white, in His obedience, His ways, His precepts. And these, as we see, bring all to that great white Light, see?

There was no question to Cayce but that Frances' mother had lived the kind of life which would give real quality to that part of her that survived bodily death, and would place her in living touch with the highest spirituality Cayce knew.

Then, a little over a month before her mother died, Frances had her final warning dream.

> My mother was well and to be married and all were celebrating. I was sad because I could not join in the merry-making, because I knew she had to be operated on again, and would die. Also, I was disappointed because I was not invited to her wedding.

As it turned out, her mother did require another and unexpected operation, after this dream, and died from it.

In interpreting the dream, Cayce acknowledged the sadness, born of what Frances correctly knew was happening to her mother. Yet he insisted, "The mother is well—will be well." Here he echoed the imagery of the dream, with its note of joy and of a very special turning point coming to the mother. But he added that the mother's welfare lay "not through an operation, but through the applications of spiritual forces that may be awakened in the individual." Frances' mother was awakening to the next plane of her existence, and it was an occasion for merrymaking, despite Frances' inevitable sadness that she would not be invited along. Patiently, Cayce urged Frances to review the seemingly impossible drama of the dream, in order to catch the spiritual lesson through her own awakening, not judging from physical reasoning alone.

Clearly, if survival of death were a fact, then dreams which anticipated death for someone who had lived long and well could not be limited to imagery of grief, real as the sorrow of survivors might be. Nothing less than a wedding could set forth the event!

Dreaming through the Barrier of Death

On the night after her mother died, Frances had a peculiarly vivid dream of an old friend of her mother's, who had died three weeks previously in another part of the country, but who had quite slipped her thoughts in her anxieties over her mother.

> I heard a voice that I recognized as our old friend from Mississippi, who loved me dearly as a child, yet whom I have not seen in two or three years. The impression of her talking to me was very pronounced, and for a while I did not see her figure, yet I felt that she was with Mother

at the hospital, as Mother changed from this earthly consciousness to the other. She was there as the transition was made, and was now with Mother as she said to me, "Your mother is as happy as ever." More she told me about Mother which I can't remember. Recall and explain to me, please.

Cayce assured Frances that she was being shown in her dream "what is meant by the life other than the physical." Recalling the Biblical phrase, "As the tree falls, so shall it lie," he pointed out how natural it was for someone who had loved her mother in life to continue that same love in the next plane, by helping her mother through the events of death.

Frances should take strength, he said, from the knowledge that the dream had explicitly given her, of the companionship her mother was finding. Emphatically he told her, "She is *well, happy* and *free,* from the care as is given in earth's plane." Frances could attune herself to psychically grasp the facts, if only she would not condemn herself for whatever she felt she had failed to do for her mother—a condemning which Cayce said brought needless sorrow to Frances.

Her dream was showing Frances in the clearest terms how friendship and love rule death as well as life. Through the dream experience, which was not symbolic but literal, Frances could know for sure, *"not alone* does the mother go out; not alone in that unseen world; yet with that same care, that same love (which she knew on earth), raised to a better *understanding* of the forces as are manifested" in life and in death.

When Frances asked whether someone such as her mother's friend would actually guide a dying person, Cayce answered that it was exactly this way, and only lack of understanding prevented the living from knowing it. He reminded Frances of two Biblical sayings as he tried to quicken her to a realization of what seemed to his vision to be unshakeably true: "Lo, I am with thee" and "Though I walk through the valley of the shadow of death, my spirit shall guide thee."

Frances had experienced something else on the night her mother died. It was just a voice speaking to her quietly in her sleep, which said, *"Your mother is alive and happy."* But by then she knew that Cayce interpreted this kind of voice as her own higher self, her own soul, speaking to her in her dreams. And this was exactly the interpretation he stressed, in the questions and answers that followed, with an urgency which showed Cayce himself caught up in Frances' adventure into the land of death. He spoke with strong feeling: "Your mother *is* alive and happy." Then he contained himself and returned to a more objective style of speech:

> The entity may know that all force (both within and without the person) goes to show, to prove, to bring to the consciousness of the entity, that as ye live in Him, ye shall be made alive in Him at death! For there is no death. Only the transition from the physical to the spiritual plane. Then, as the birth into the physical is given as the time of the new life, just so, then, in physical (death seen properly) is the birth into the spiritual.

Frances had dreamed of her mother's death as a wedding. Cayce was telling her it was a birthday, too!

She asked a question: "Then, does my mother see me and love me as ever?" Cayce answered swiftly: "Sees thee and loves thee as ever. Just as those forces were manifest in the physical world." It was up to Frances, he said, how much reality that love would have, as she "entertains and desires, and places self in that (inward) attunement with those desires of that entity (the mother), the love exists—in that far, in that manner, see? For in spirit all sham is laid aside." The mother's love was there, he said. How free was Frances of guilt and grief and fear, so that she could accept it and return it?

Frances asked further, "Then, does she try to tell me, 'I am alive and happy'?"

Cayce's answer was clear, but again emphasized Frances' own role, and the source of the voice as her own: "*Tells* the entity 'I am alive and happy,' when entity will *attune* self to that at-oneness." He was making the proper vehicle of communication a deep inward turning in a spirit of prayer—not a seance.

Frances went on, somewhat hesitantly. "I feel her with me, particularly as I kissed her clay body—I felt she knew and responded—but did she, or do I fool myself?"

Cayce replied swiftly, telling Frances that in the same manner as she had "poured out self" to her mother, "the response came." "No, not fooling self," he went on, "for the soul liveth, and is at peace, and would that the daughter know that it liveth."

Then he turned again to Biblical passages, giving them an immediacy that often showed in his readings: "As has been given, 'In my Father's house are many mansions; were it not so, I would have told you' and 'I go to prepare a place for you, that where *I am,* there *ye* may be also.' This is as applicable to the daughter in this hour as was given by the Redeemer to those gathered about Him." He continued, "For as we entitites in the physical plane prepare that at-oneness (which could unite us with those in another plane), it is as He gave: 'Even as I be lifted up, I will draw *all* men unto me.' "

The doorway through death, Cayce was saying, lay in inward attunement to the One who could properly open it for communication between the living and the dead. He turned back to a teaching of Moses to develop the same theme once more: communication with the dead was not primarily to be found through an intermediary like Cayce, but in the dreamer's own inward experience.

> "Say not to thyself, who shall descend into depths to bring him up, or who shall fly into the heavens to bring him down, for the spirit of peace, truth, and love, is within thine own heart." As the spirit of oneself gives that (proper) attunement, there may be an at-oneness with those spirits in that other sphere, that each may know, may understand, may gather, that truth that makes one free.

Frances had, in Cayce's view, been given a memorable quickening on the night of her mother's death.

One more dream from that same night, summed up what had happened to her, in simple but forceful imagery.

> I saw an animal crawling over the ground, just sort of semiconscious, in a condition of half gray dawn.

Frances was, he said, seeing herself. She was seeing herself awakening. She was becoming conscious, however slowly, of the indwelling of the spirit within her—a spirit which could bear witness to the truth "of the Spirit of that one that gives and takes, and gives and takes—that we may become (alike through life and through death) one with Him."

The function of dreams, Cayce had told Frances many times, was not alone to solve problems. It was also to awaken the dreamer to his full stature as a person.

Frances was waking up.

Contact with the Dead

It was not long before the figure of Frances' mother began to appear in her dreams. Usually the figure came to further the inward stirrings that were occurring to Frances as a young woman. Occasionally it helped her with practical problems as well.

One of Frances' first needs was to handle the grief which she felt over not insisting that her mother receive precisely the medical care that Cayce had prescribed. The care had included (as was usual for Cayce in dealing with cancer patients) the application of a certain kind of ultra-violet light. It was a treatment which the doctor had neither understood nor sanctioned.

A few nights after her mother's death, Frances dreamed:

> Saw my mother with two lamps shining on the back of her neck. The lamps were administered by Dr. K.

This dream was not, Cayce said, a message to Frances from her mother. It was simply her own subconscious, trying to get at the truth of the medical situation. It was showing her exactly how the blood would have been affected, to bring relief to her mother. But, Cayce insisted, the point of the dream was not to bring her any sort of self-condemnation—just understanding, should she again someday have to make comparable judgments about doctors and treatments. She must understand that the treatment would not have saved her mother's life in any case, only stayed it awhile, and brought her some relief.

Several months later Frances again dreamed of her mother. Again Cayce said it was not a communication from her mother.

> This dream was very clear and seemed so realistic that my mind upon awakening remembered it and was impressed. I seemed about to have a baby, and was very sick—vomiting, etc. My mother was there and said it must be that I was sick, not pregnant. I asked for the doctor to be called, which my mother did. I seemed to have some sort of miscarriage— at any rate it ended that I was not pregnant but my sickness came from something else entirely, as the doctor informed me.

This dream, said Cayce, came because it was time for her to conceive again, to fulfill her vocation of motherhood—*symbolized* by the appearance of her mother in the dream. She would have to face the fears left by her miscarriage, and set about getting her body in shape for pregnancy. If she did so, she need have no fear of losing the child (she did not lose the baby this time), for as the dream showed, her problems lay only in her general health, not in her capacity for childbearing as such.

But Frances was hesitant. The disappointments of her miscarriage and her mother's death were still vivid to her, and she seemed to have repressed the whole question of pregnancy as well as put off getting the proper medical care. Then there came the first dream which indicated that her mother's help was available.

> I was paralyzed. I called to my mother and was frightened. Parts of me seemed to break or burst and I could not check this process, although I tried to desperately. Finally I suffered so that I wished to die.

Cayce told her bluntly that her dream showed her mental development at a standstill. She was letting herself become paralyzed as a person. The dream was not about her body, but about her consciousness, her growth as a person. She was going to have to quit fighting and denying the call to further development heard in her inner being—especially the call to motherhood. Then he added that she should note how in the dream "there is the call to that consciousness to whom . . . the body turns for the instruction, see?" It was her first hint that her mother could assume a helping role, in her dreams.

She did become pregnant. She did begin on the program of medical care which Cayce urged for her. Then she discontinued it, despite a constant backache. Aaron was frantic. Later he wrote to Cayce:

> I tried to persuade her, and she grew angry with me. . . . Night before last I prayed that (her mother), the psychic activity in the One Mind who was aware of the condition in her daughter's psyche, might appear and prevail upon her to do that which was best for herself and the forming child . . . I asked the Lord to join with me in this endeavor to better facilitate His creation. The wonderful response came as the dream indicates.

Frances dreamed that very night her first vivid contact with her mother.

> My mother appeared to me. I saw her distinctly. She said to me, "You should go to the doctor. You ought to be ashamed of yourself! If Aaron wants you to go the doctor, you should go."

The dream required little interpretation. Aaron reported that the effect of the dream on Frances had been so telling that "all the king's horses and all the king's men couldn't keep her away from the doctor." When Frances asked how her longing for her mother and her husband's prayer had contributed to the experience, Cayce answered: "The prayers of the righteous shall save many. 'Where two or three are joined together in one purpose, I am in the midst of same.' " The combination of the action of all, including the mother, had made the attunement possible.

Within two weeks Frances began to have frequent dreams in which her mother was present, either as an actor in a drama (which Cayce said was sometimes Frances dreaming under the influence of her mother and sometimes just dreaming of what her mother represented to her), or as a vivid personage, herself (which Cayce said was literally her mother, communicating with her).

The dreams were not an obsession with Frances. They were mixed in, from the first, with dreams such as she had been dreaming all along—a dream about trouble with her gums (which Cayce traced to circulatory problems in with her pregnancy), and a dream of lightning striking her (which Cayce said was a depicting of some of the fears current in her pregnancy), and a dream of success for the book her husband was writing (which Cayce said was an authentic preview of its potential).

Guidance from the Dead in Dreams

It was a practical matter which next brought the mother and her "guiding forces," as Cayce called them, into a dream:

> I was sick in a hospital and my mother was with me. It was either to have my baby or that I had a miscarriage again. Something wrong with my busts, and my mother said it should be remedied.

Nothing was physically wrong with Frances, according to Cayce. The dream came only to alert her to a need of the forthcoming child: it should be nursed at the breast, not bottle-fed.

A few nights later Frances had another dream that combined her mother's aid with Frances' own bent towards medical ESP (it is perhaps significant that concern for medical care was a feature of Frances' entire life: after her divorce she became a nurse). Her dream began:

> My mother appeared to me. She said to me: "I am alive."

Here Cayce interrupted with a note of happy urgency: "She is alive." The dream continued with the mother speaking further:

> "Something is wrong with your sister's leg, or shoulder." (Or both—I don't clearly remember.) "She ought to see a doctor about it."

Here, Cayce said, Frances could see her mother being mother to her whole household, through Frances' mind. For Frances' subconscious, when she was asleep, had been "in at-onement with the mother and the sister." There was in fact, Cayce said, a medical problem in the sister's limbs, an auto-intoxication through poisons from the system. The sister should be warned to seek medical care. And the cure, Cayce added, would involve an increase in her eliminations.

Both Frances and Aaron were immensely interested in this experience, which proved to have a sound medical basis—although one of which the sister was not conscious at the time of the dream. Their sense of high adventure in cooperation with the dead was apparent in their correspondence with Cayce.

Two months later there came another experience of the mother which was so vivid that it woke Frances up and sent her scurrying to her husband's bed.

> I dreamed of the play we saw . . . and then experienced my mother's presence right in my room with me. Her presence was so real, so pronounced and so close to me, the vision of her being there so vivid, that I jumped up in fright and ran from my bed to Aaron's.

But the dream experiences of the mother kept coming. One was a warning that an aunt was in a state of mind that made her accident-prone; it prompted Frances to visit her. Another was a warning regarding the danger of pneumonia to a much older aunt.

Then Frances reported a further set of dreams involving her mother and herself. These were not on practical matters at all, but on Frances' own depth and growth as a person, said Cayce.

> I beheld my mother. She was displeased with me because I was going out to theatres, etc. She said, "The least you could have done for me was to keep mourning for one year."

This was not a message from the mother, said Cayce, but Frances' own self reviewing her whole relation with her mother. It was not underscoring a duty (such as the Jewish custom of a year of *kaddish*, or prayers of mourning), but an orientation. For the experiences Frances had been through since her mother's death, "the appearances, the nearness, the feeling of the presence in the room, the full conditions (of concern and aid) as have been presented," were bringing out the best in Frances. Around these experiences, and the study of them, were developing a new and genuine spirituality which was native to Frances and should be cherished—even as one cherishes the memory of a loved-one dead.

The other dream made the point in a different way:

> Dreamed I was insane—my mind gone and my reason unbalanced. My mother was there and was having an awful time with me.

Here again, Cayce indicated, Frances could see how important to her total maturity were the awakenings of meaning and perspective coming to her from "the essence of the presence of the mother." The dream was showing Frances something she already knew about herself: "that there have been moments when the entity (Frances), in its attempting to belittle elements as pertaining to a spiritual understanding, has put its mentality into an unbalanced condition . . . creating barriers that have been hard to break, hard to be understood, even by self." The times she had mocked Aaron for his studies, since her miscarriage and her mother's death, were telling on her. She must, Cayce said, "keep self mentally, morally, physically, spiritually in that at-onement with the universal forces that give the better understanding to each and every entity."

Frances' next dream of her mother came through a correlation of Frances' mind and her mother's, as Cayce described it. The dream was memorable, both for its startling precognitive detail and for the bit of Jewish folk-mannerism used by her mother in the dream, giving it a tang of reality.

> I dreamed of my baby. It was just born and weighed eleven pounds and two ounces. It had blue eyes and blond hair, and was a boy. It had, however, a Jewish nose that I didn't like. I said to my mother, who was there: "It looks kikish—too Jewish." My mother, however, bit her finger in characteristic fashion and beamed upon the baby. She said it was grand.

Frances was only five months pregnant, yet her dream of the final features of the baby was substantially accurate, according to Cayce. He assured her that he would be a boy, that he would be blond, that his eyes would be blue; his weight, however, would be closer to nine pounds. (In every detail Cayce proved correct, when the baby was born.) Regarding the nose, Frances was only partly right, he said, for while there would be something of a Jewish nose, his features would be even and attractive (as they were). This part of the dream, he added, had come to underscore to the mother the boy's potential life work of religious teaching to his own people, and to prepare her for it (as a young man her son did indeed begin to turn towards the vocation of a rabbi, but crisis and illness intervened).

Dream material from later the same night underscored the same themes, and in addition previewed the delivery—a time which proved to be one of the highlights of Frances' entire adventure with her mother.

> I was on the obstetrical table, my mother there as before. I had a very easy time—so easy I could even get up and walk after the baby was delivered. I looked at my baby. It was then one or two days old as before, but instead of being partially homely it appeared to be a beautiful child with light hair, blue eyes and a healthy baby. It got up from the crib and came to me and said: "Here, I have a letter for you, Momsy!"

The dream came to urge Frances to make every preparation for the delivery in diet and rest and physiotherapy. And the part about the letter was just another way of saying that the baby could grow into a man with a special message to give.

Frances went right on dreaming during the months until the baby came. She dreamed of her husband's moneymaking, of the mental illness of a friend, of travel during pregnancy, of her husband's plans to join with others in building a hospital at Virginia Beach where Cayce's work could be better used and studied. She dreamed of her husband's talkativeness, of her own triviality, of the illness of her relatives. But she did not dream further of her mother.

Still fearful about the birth, she kept in close touch with Cayce. In January, he told her that the birth would be normal, and would come between March twenty-eighth and April sixth. It came April fourth. A few days before delivery, he told her all was well, and that the baby would arrive within ninety-six hours. It came in seventy-two.

With the baby came an unforgettable experience of Frances' mother.

Contact with the Dead beyond Dreams

What happened was best told in a letter to Cayce from Aaron:

> Now, as great an objective demonstration of spirit communication that I have ever seen or hope to witness occurred this afternoon between Frances and her mother, as I was holding her hand. It also indicates that anesthetic (as pointed out by Ousepensky) makes the mind subject, or opens it subconsciously, to communication. Frances' pains were so bad that they gave her an ether enema and it doped her. Hazily, she said to me: "My mother is with me. She has been with me since this morning. See, she is right there!" Then Frances pointed to the other side of the bed from which I was sitting, and indicating a little above her head, again said: "My mother is right there."

> "What is she saying?" I asked.

> "She is saying," replied Frances clearly and precisely, "not to worry—that everything is coming out all right!"

> "How do you know she is here with you?" I asked.

> "I feel her—I see her—she is praying for me—she is here right with me—right there," and again Frances pointed her hand to the same exact location.

Aaron went on, in his letter.

> Now I ask you, have you ever heard of anything so wonderful? Poor little kid; only her sister of her own kin with her, having lost her mother comparatively recently, longing for her on this day of suffering more than ever, feels and knows that her loved one is with her and hears from her. Her heart lonesome for that mother, bravely not complaining of her heartache, reaches for the mother, and glory be to the Almighty she reaches out not in vain!

> I tell you, when I came out and told five grown folks about this, including my very practical mother, every one of them cried like babies. Darn it, I am bawling as I write this. It sort of has me in a daze—I don't know just how to be grateful enough or what to do. It's so wonderful, so definite, so precise, so beautiful, that it is far beyond me. In some small way I hope to come somewhere near to appreciating such an experience, for I know it is bewildering and beyond me above and mightier than poor little me.

> Who cares for the opinions of those who call spirit communication bunk? What do their opinions amount to, anyway? What weight have they in the constructive field of knowledge-building?
>
> A little pain-wracked body, harboring a lonesome and aching heart, receives not only a response from the spirit mother that comforts the heart, but actually aids, encourages and sustains the physical strength of this body and does it in no uncertain manner. Is this, then, impractical? Is it illusionary? Well, then, make the most of it—I intend to in my lifetime, believe me!
>
> This is what I was trying to tell you over the phone, and I'm glad I couldn't. Must close and go to bed, as I am dead tired.

He asked Cayce to review the experience in a reading, explaining how it had all happened.

Evidently the force of the experience touched something in Cayce, himself, for during his reading there occurred something quite rare in his trances. Five different discarnates spoke through him—including the mother, herself. One was purportedly a well-known philosopher. Two were strangers to both Cayce and the dreamer. One was a family friend of Cayce's. Each spoke briefly and added a viewpoint on what had happened in the hospital; all were in agreement that the experience had been genuine.

Three confirmed what Aaron had suspected, that he, too, had experienced the mother in the hospital room, though in a different kind of psychic experience than Frances had been through. His had been an inner attunement, with no form or voice evident—only "an inner consciousness of the presence of another being." Frances, on the other hand, had found her "sensuous faculties" quickened in the experience, until the mother was "seen, felt, heard, known, by the subjugated consciousness," under drugs.

The unusual Cayce reading was not an instance of what investigators call "direct voice" mediumship (which happened to him in trance even more rarely), but one in which he was using his own language and consciousness to try to communicate the sense of what he felt another person, a discarnate, was saying.

When Cayce drew near to the end of the reading, the message came, as Aaron had hoped it would, from Frances' mother. Cayce expressed it in these words: "To Frances I have come, in that certain way that makes known the life after death." Then Cayce added his own assurance:

> And the willingness of the mother is to ever be present, in the mental attitude of the daughter, to shield every thought, every care.

The final words were again from the mother, as Cayce felt them. Not surprisingly, in the light of the views that Cayce and the dreamers held, there was a reference to reincarnatrion. "Be thou faithful, then, in those lessons I have given to you; be faithful to Aaron, and to the baby—who comes from among us, and whom

I have known before."

The reading was exciting for Frances. But she was not relying on it to carry the whole weight of assurance that she and her mother were reaching one another. Something else had happened in the hospital, a few days after the birth, which she reported to Cayce. She had been dozing when this occurred:

> Heard a rapping noise or knocks. I said to myself: "That is my mother."
> I sat up in bed to listen for the noise, and heard nothing. Again dozing,
> I heard the knocks, and again recognized them as being my mother.

This was an authentic experience, according to Cayce, coming to her not as a novelty but to stimulate her to a better awareness of the nature of love, between those alive or dead—"the living from plane to plane"—however encrusted love might become in the life and action of each. It had been the same kind of experience, he reminded her, that her husband had undergone when he had felt the bed trembling, months ago, while at her mother's side shortly after she died. The two of them, Frances and Aaron, should "keep these things—pondering them in the heart."

Now there began the final chapter in Frances' dreams of her mother. There was still to be a full year of varied experiences in dreams, before Frances' coaching by Cayce came to an end.

Varieties of Dream Sharing with the Dead

A motif that reached deeply into Frances' makeup, according to Cayce, appeared in the next dream where her mother appeared. In the dream, as often, Frances saw male intruders—but this time they did her no harm. While still in the hospital with her baby, she dreamed:

> My mother and I were in our old house in Mississippi, where we lived
> when I was a little girl. Mother and I were always afraid, and on this
> occasion heard men enter the house. Upon going to investigate, we found
> three men had broken in—but not to steal but to enquire about leaving
> liquor at our house. They said that they would give us several days to
> think it over and give our decision.

The heart of this dream, Cayce told her, was the shift from the theme of illegality—both of the breaking-in and the liquor (these were Prohibition days), to the theme of considerateness and helpfulness. It was, he said, a dramatization of Frances' own opportunity, now begun in the arrival of her son, to move from "the letter of the law" to "the law of grace."

The locale of the home showed her the seriousness of the dream, he suggested, for it represented—as he often said of loved childhood homes—her spiritual home, her "indwelling." How was it to be entered? As a lawbreaker, bringing on suffering and punishment? Or in the way of the mother, as a way of faith, and of giving to others?

Cayce had told Frances before that in past lives she had been a woman of much beauty, as lovely as Helen of Troy. Like Helen, she had been unfaithful, and willing to use her charms to get men to do her will. The result was that she entered this life with a deep fear of men—that they in turn would be unfaithful and would misuse her; this was the repeated dream motif of male intruders and pursuers.

If she were to live under "the letter of the law," she would have to experience from men the same hardship she had brought upon them, until her soul learned the lesson and she entered her "spiritual home" wiser, as a chastened lawbreaker. (In point of fact, Frances did find herself in deep distress with men, a few years later, when she divorced her husband. For a while she also drank heavily, as Cayce warned her this dream indicated.)

But her relation with the baby was presenting her with "the way of escape," he said , if she wished to choose it. By giving generously to this man-child, and to his father, she could quiet forever her own fears and hates, born of her own misdoings. On this course, she would come under "the law of grace, the law of mercy," and whatever events developed for her, she could meet them without fear of inner suffering. (Long after the divorce, when her son was a grown man and a troubled man, Frances nursed him and cared for him, faithfully, in just this way—fulfilling then the way of loving service that she could not earlier find in her heart for Aaron.)

In Cayce's view, this dream, coming with her mother's aid in the first fresh days of her baby's life, was showing to Frances two ways to grow to her true spiritual stature: the way of suffering, justly merited; and the way of grace, in which one received forgiveness and acceptance as freely as he gives it.

These two ways of growth formed a consistent theme in decades of readings that Cayce gave to hundreds of people. With or without the framework of reincarnation, it made sense to many who took the trouble to study what Cayce said, rather than stopping at the marvel at his psychic feats.

Five months later came another dream that related to Frances' basic value system. Like many dreams which came to those who were seriously studying their dreams with him, Cayce said that this was a "lesson" dream, meant to help Frances put her life journey in perspective. It was a dream of a close friend of hers who had recently died, in which his actual expiring was symbolically re-enacted.

> Regarding my mother and her pointing out a crowd to me; about David, who lay dying. He was in the last stage of the process. I saw his eyes glazed. My mother seemed to call attention to this. Then in a final effort, he tried to get up. Those about him would not permit. My mother showed me that of course they would not. Then he dropped back and died. I cried, at which my mother instructed me not to cry.

The dream was about David, according to Cayce, because he represented to Frances someone of notable wealth and social position—concerns that Frances was tempted to rate too highly. The dying showed her graphically how death puts everyone at one level—and no last-minute action can do anything about it.

David's effort to get up was a dramatization of the importance of will-power—what everyone must use to make life an unfolding, rather than a long indulgence which fails at last to yield the understanding and peace that should be there—from "the life well-lived and in service to others."

This dream preview of the exact events of dying was meant, as Cayce saw it, to give Frances more than arcane knowledge of life beyond the grave. It was meant to put her daily living into proper perspective, so that she might choose her proper working values. Such values were not a matter, he emphasized, of putting on a long face. Nor should Frances be always thinking of death and the future. Life was to be lived now.

"Yet it is not all of life to live, nor all of death to die," he continued. Living or dying, the soul must account to itself for all it has thought and done. For it is in the nature of the soul to return to the "Whole" which created it, yet to reserve in itself the power to know itself an individual, and all it has been and done.

Nobody escapes himself. What kind of Frances did Frances want to journey with, through time and death?

As though to emphasize that real values were known in the little things of life, a dream which came soon after was one which Cayce described as presented through the efforts of the mother, though she did not appear in it. Frances reported:

Saw the baby real sick—stomach upset and vomiting.

Seemed I should give it Milk of Magnesia.

The dream showed, as Cayce often said of health dreams, only the extremity of what could happen, if the baby's present need were neglected. The remedy of the dream, he said, was exactly right to counteract the baby's acidity, and should be taken at once—with his diet watched more carefully in the future.

Even more prosaic was a little dream fragment which Aaron reported to Cayce for Frances. *"Her mother told her that Frances was buying an evening dress."* Here Frances could see, said Cayce, that her mother was as completely aware of her daughter's "secular affairs" as of her "spiritual affairs." She was finding her daughter's whole life, including her social life "the same and as interesting as in physical life."

The underlying character of the mother's relation to her daughter was the theme of a dream that came a month later. This dream needed no interpretation by Cayce. It began with a reference to a sick relative.

Said my mother: "Your sister-in-law will be all right. We are all working for her recovery here." Then said someone else, or my mother, "Yes, that is the trouble. We cannot do what we want to do—go on and develop, because we still have dear ones on earth that need our help. This keeps us close to earth. We have to always be looking after you young people."

Later my mother showed me this latter in emblematical fashion, showing me how the mother love I have for my baby survives in the spiritual individuality of a cosmic entity, as for example it does in her for me.

Thus she gave me another lesson of the life after death, and of all life, love and close relationship of loved ones—of life's greater joy and glory depending upon service. It was as follows: I was preparing to go home to Mississippi, where I wanted to go. I was saying good-bye to all and my mother was packing my trunk. Seeing my baby, I changed my mind about going, and stayed with my baby.

Just so, my mother, loving me, her baby, stays close to earth with me, although the freedom of the universe holds an alluring invitation for the application of her present spirit power. Correct?

It was true, Cayce said, that her mother was "in physical plane or earth's sphere as yet, until that force leads on in its ever-developing, toward that oneness with the All-Force, see?" The time would come when the mother would move on, along her own soul's path of growth. For the present, Frances could count on her steady help, as was apparent in one of the last dreams Frances sent to Cayce for interpretation.

I saw my mother very distinctly. I was sending her a telegram that she was going to die.

This was no dream of warning or foreboding, according to Cayce. On the contrary, it showed Frances in a conscious act of acceptance of her mother's state. It signaled Frances' own deep awareness that her mother would give her all the guidance and protection she needed for her own life or for her baby, if she would rely from now on upon her own intuition and upon her mother's influence. Not even death could now take her by surprise.

When Frances next asked Cayce's counsel about proper care for the baby while she went on a six-week's trip, he gave her none. When she had such definite assurance of her mother's aid, he asked, and so many experiences of learning to work with her mother, why did she need Cayce?

Frances had found her way through the country of death.

She had found the thread of love that stretches from life beyond the grave.

Now she must weave her life of it.

Frances had her own view of the adventure on which her dreams had led her for four years. When the Cayce Hospital was at last completed at Virginia Beach, she mounted the speaker's platform on that windy Armistice Day of 1929, and shyly took her turn among the others who brought greetings. Her words were proper and formal, but they carried her thought:

May this institution so spread its teachings as to help and give guidance and understanding to all peoples of all lands—as the teachings have aided me to gain an understanding of the oneness of life and force.

PART II

How to Work With Dreams

CAYCE'S SKILL—AND THE DREAMER'S

THROUGH THE FORTY years in which Edgar Cayce exercised his puzzling gift, he often found his readings presenting as fact something his listeners considered unlikely.

The Cayce readings recommended osteopathy alongside of respectable drugs and surgery, when osteopathy was classified solely as quack medicine. They traced psychosomatic elements in illness—in perhaps a quarter of his readings—when only Viennese specialists considered psychogenic causes important. They described certain vitamins before these were isolated in the laboratory. They specified endocrine gland functions only discovered after Cayce's death.

In the 1930's, two decades before the discovery of the Dead Sea Scrolls at Qumran, the Cayce readings explained how ancient Essene and other centers of Covenanters were run, at the Dead Sea and elsewhere. In the 1940's, when France was occupied and faced a forlorn future, they predicted its post-war return as an independent European power. In the 1920's, long before the United Nations was founded, they insisted that the League of Nations had been the right proposal for mankind's outlawing of war.

Decades before Zen Buddhism and Hindu meditation were discussed on American campuses, they specified the procedures of deep meditation, and recommended it for everyone. They described earthquakes before they occurred, and noted the fault-lines involved. They produced a dissertation on the camber of airplane wings, a decade ahead of aeronautical research. They predicted the basic life patterns of newborn babies—and it required a generation to verify how incredibly accurate they were.

Those who studied the Cayce readings were staggered at the seeming range of their vision, which moved freely from microorganisms to life after death, from Persian history to stock market prices, from buried oil fields to buried musical genius in a child.

They also noted that the Cayce readings did not function as a psychic microscope or telescope. The readings were methodically engaged in building people, all through the forty years of his activity as the best-known psychic of modern times.

Edgar Cayce in trance presented every finding in terms of the difference it could make in someone's life. He refused to tell people whatever they could not constructively use. He would not give one person an unfair advantage over others. He turned every quest for aid into a quest for meaning, as well. When

51

people turned to him for medical counsel, he asked them, one way or another, "What will you do with your life if you recover?" He was evidently much more than a psychic oddity. He was a coach, an analyst, a teacher, a spiritual director, to those who sought his aid.

His total gift—both for information and for penetrating counsel on individual values—served to make his strangest claim of all seem this one: "I don't do anything you can't do."

He said it over and over again to visitors, the famed and the nobodies, who came to talk with him wherever he lived. He said it in a trance, again and again, explaining the processes at work.

He insisted that what people saw in Edgar Cayce was not unique in principle, though it might be striking. They were seeing the operation of laws, quite natural laws. They were seeing laws which they themselves could learn to use.

To be sure, not everyone who learned to understand and apply the laws would come out precisely where Cayce did. Some would have notably different gifts—for example, intellectual scholarship or administrative leadership—in which their psychic abilities and inward spirituality would help them as he was helped. Not everyone would have the same degree of gifts: there were geniuses in every field. Some—he said—would be better psychics than he: he was emphatic about the claim, and told one man he could learn to give a certain kind of readings awake, while he told another that he could learn (through a lifetime of disciplined work) even to raise the dead—capacities he said were far beyond Edgar Cayce in this lifetime.

The claim that anyone could do, in some measure, what Edgar Cayce did, may well have been the boldest claim he ever made.

But he did not let the claim hang in the air. He gave people a laboratory where they could investigate the claim for themselves. He urged them to recall and study their dreams. In dreams, he said, people could experience for themselves every important kind of psychic phenomenon, and every level of helpful psychological and religious counsel. What is more, they could, through dreams, learn the laws of these things and undergo a spontaneous and tailored dream-training program in the use of the laws—provided that in their waking life they put to constructive use everything they learned in the dreams.

It was an extraordinary claim for dreams.

When Cayce died, he left behind four complete cases of individuals whom he had trained, through the study of hundreds of their dreams by means of his readings, to broaden and deepen their natural gifts—psychic gifts, intellectual gifts, financial gifts, leadership gifts, artistic gifts, healing gifts, gifts of loving, gifts of wisdom, gifts of training others.

One of these cases was his own, a record of 106 dreams interpreted in sixty-nine readings, given in the years 1924 to 1940. He undertook the study of his own dreams because, shortly after he moved to Virginia Beach, he was told to do so by his own readings. Many who might not accept what he seemed to do in trance, he was told, would be willing to experiment with their own dreams, if he set them an example. In the systematic recording and study of their dreams there could unfold "much that may be worthwhile to the minds of many individuals, who will hearken and apply the same lessons and truths, as gained from same [study], to their individual lives."

The reading added a pregnant comment, indicating—as was always the emphasis over the years—that the right way to approach people about what Edgar Cayce did was *not* to try to sell them on Cayce's phenomena. Instead, others should be equipped with laws or "truths" which they could try out for themselves. It was not Cayce who mattered. "Not necessary to believe in the works of Edgar Cayce," the reading said bluntly. What was needful was for others to try out for themselves the "truths as manifested through same, see?" Dreams, it said, were an excellent way to do it.

The same reading drew a close parallel between Edgar Cayce's trance state and what occurs in sleep. "At the present," the reading began, describing his trance, "we find body and mind in that passive state, wherein the action of positive suggestion from physical mind"—this meant Cayce's own prayerful suggestion that put him in trance, reinforced by hypnotic suggestion from his wife—"directs toward the Universal Forces, as found in subconscious direction." It was the same process described for dreamers before, where their own subconscious could in dreams approach the Universal Forces, through superconscious tuning processes. This was all Edgar Cayce did in readings, except that he was also "capable of using physical faculties" to speak, and was simultaneously using resources which dreamers might approach singly or occasionally: "the cosmic and spiritual and superconscious forces all in action" at once.

Driving home its point about dream study, the reading went on, "Dreams, then, that come to the entity [Edgar Cayce] may be the correlation of any or all of these faculties, and should be made record of," if Cayce were to show people how their nighttime states reproduced his trance state.

Achieving a sleep state precisely like Edgar Cayce's trance became a reality to Frances—another one of the four dreamers he trained. She herself experienced in dreams not only telepathy, visions of the future, medical counsel, and insight into both relatives and strangers, but glimpses of stock movements and of life beyond death. Still, she found it hard to believe that she was using variations of the same process as Edgar Cayce used.

Then one afternoon during a nap, after she had been working on her dreams for two years, she had the following memorable experience:

> About 3:00 PM, just after getting to sleep, talking direct to myself (not seeing myself talking, but myself doing the talking, but aware of myself doing it), saying: "Now my body is assuming its normal forces, and will be able and will give such information as is desired of it at the present time. The physical body will be perfectly normal and will give that information now."

She was paraphrasing instructions she had heard given to Edgar Cayce as the prologue to each reading-period, shortly after his regular breathing indicated he was in deep trance. Frances continued by recording her thoughts at the time of her experience.

> "Now I am in the same condition that Cayce is in when he gives a reading.

Only my heart is beating, and higher organs (otherwise the body is still). Wouldn't my husband or the maid think it queer to hear me talking while in this condition? What would they think if they came in and heard me now?"

After a bit she found herself repeating the suggestion she had heard Mrs. Cayce employ, to bring her husband out of trance.

"Now the physical forces" . . . etc., etc. (right through the entire procedure of awakening, word for word as in a reading), until "Now perfectly normal and perfectly balanced, I will wake up." Then I did wake up. I jumped up, a little frightened and quite dizzy. I had a peculiar sensation at the back of my head. I felt hungry and after eating a little the dizziness passed away. The experience lasted about 25 minutes. Thereafter I went to sleep again, to sleep for quite a while—normally.

Frances asked, when she wrote to Cayce, "Was I in the same condition Cayce is in while giving a reading?" The answer from the sleeping Cayce was unequivocal: "The same."

When she asked how she had given herself the suggestion, when Cayce typically needed it given to him, she was told that her mother had helped her, from the next plane, though she had not realized it in the dream.

The experience had come to her, Cayce reported, for several reasons. She had been trying to grasp the nature of consciousness after death. So this dream experience had put her into a deathlike state, yet allowed her to keep in touch with her body. Further, she had sought to understand what Cayce did, and the dream came to help her do so, for "with the experience there comes the more reality" by understanding laws and processes at work; "in experience is the knowledge of conditions and the surrounding elements obtained."

Finally, the dream had occurred to show her one direction for the service to others, if she chose, and if she prepared herself correctly. Of course, Frances asked how she might do it again, taking up someone's physical disease, as she had seen Cayce do.

He cautioned her to move slowly, studying every such experience that happened to her, until she thoroughly grasped the processes at work. If she did this studying, and kept her waking life one of prayerful, loving service to others, she could then expect a series of such dream experiences—a kind of inward training program.

But she would have to face a most important question in seeking such development. Why was she doing it? If she sought it for fame or for power over others, or as compensation for failures or guilts in her life, she would get nowhere.

This warning, which Cayce repeated to everyone who sought serious psychic development, may have frightened Frances. Or she may have simply been distracted by the outward events in her life, which in two or three years pressed her hard. At any rate, she did not report achieving this state again, except in the modified form in which she sought attunement with her mother for guidance on her baby.

But she knew why Cayce claimed, over and over again, that anybody could do what he did—and could start doing it in dreams.

Dreams and Medical Readings

Edgar Cayce first received national attention in 1910, when a physician reported on him to a medical society, meeting in Boston. By then he had given medical counsel to doctors for several years.

Medical aid was the form in which his hypnotic abilities had first appeared, when a physician in his home town asked him to diagnose and prescribe for patients—as a few European hypnotic subjects had reportedly done.

The whole idea had seemed ridiculous to the young Edgar Cayce. He had no education beyond grade school, and his vocational experience was clerking in bookstores and assisting a photographer. Yet when unconscious he showed the capacity to go over a human body like a mental x-ray, using medical terms he had never heard, and then to prescribe complex medical treatments or refer patients to specialists.

The phenomenon of the "psychic diagnostician," as the newspapers called him, began as a novelty, a sort of natural wonder like a waterfall. But by the middle of Cayce's life his gift had become stable and respected enough to generate the "Cayce Hospital" at Virginia Beach, with a complete medical staff, and a university with a full faculty, administration, student body and football teams—Atlantic University at Virginia Beach, which operated until the Depression closed it.

Of the thirteen thousand or more readings recorded and kept in Cayce's lifetime (and thousands went unrecorded before he moved to Dayton, Ohio, in 1923), more than two-thirds were devoted to medical counsel for individuals, on a range of ailments that would equal the variety in a sizeable clinic.

Why was so much of his psychic effort medical? His own readings said it was because one of his best past lifetimes had found him as a dedicated healer, in ancient Persia, and that this inclination to aid people in pain had continued as part of his heritage as a soul. There was also the effect of his memorable prayer and vision as a boy of twelve, when he had asked, while studying the Bible, to be of service to his fellow man as had Biblical figures, and "especially to children." Perhaps there were other contributing elements. Cayce held high the figure of Jesus, whose ministry included healing. And in pragmatic American culture, a psychic would receive no hearing without a "useful" gift.

A typical medical reading, which Cayce called a "physical reading" rather than "medical" (out of determination that those he helped should work with their doctors, not using him in their stead), began by estimating the seriousness of the ailment that brought the person to him. Then the reading moved to the critical point of malfunction in the body—whether an infection or an injury or some other abnormality. Sometimes this point was different from what the patient or his doctor might expect—as Cayce located the critical point in epilepsy in the abdomen, and only secondarily in the brain. He would trace the fundamental pathology of the body he was looking at, as calmly as though he were studying a battery of x-rays and laboratory reports, instead of lying unconscious on a couch, often hundreds of miles from a patient he had never seen.

Usually he would next move through the major systems of the body, noting the history of each in the particular patient, as well as its present function—and even the precise symptoms and how they felt to the patient at particular times of day or night. He made a special point of noting how each system contributed to the malfunction or distortion of another system, and often insisted that the whole person had to be treated—not just a given disease-entity with a convenient medical name.

First came the circulatory systems, both blood and lymphatic. He seemed to be able to supply blood count statistics without difficulty, as well as toxins in the blood stream, blood pressure, and sources of infection, or constriction in the circulation. He examined endocrine function as it appeared in the blood, blood sugar, and microorganisms (he could even describe how one would look under magnification).

Then he went on to the nervous systems, cerebrospinal, and autonomic, describing impairment or irregularities. If any of the senses functioned abnormally, he might describe how and why, noting also reaction times, pain patterns, over-stimulation or under-stimulation to parts of the body. He singled out particular nerves and ganglia, where necessary, tracing their exact location and function in the body.

Next came the major organ systems of the body. He looked at the condition of the brain. Then he went on to the respiratory system, from nose to lungs, noting typical congestion patterns, history of TB, and—when necessary—what x-rays would show. Next came the heart and its pulmonary system for oxygenating the blood; he found no difficulty in indicating pulse, heart valve operation, deposits in or around the heart, and history of heart disease. Then it was time to examine the entire digestive system from mouth to excretory organs. He often commented on acid-alkaline balance, on peristalsis, on the secretions of liver and pancreas, on eliminations and kidney function. Sexual and childbearing organ systems were examined when appropriate, and throughout special attention was given to endocrine function—with the attendant questions of metabolism and of the body's patterns in growth and healing.

By this point in a reading, Cayce had been speaking in an unconscious state for over half an hour. It was time for him to move to the complicated question of treatment. He did it with equal thoroughness, for he insisted on mapping out a program to rebuild the patient and remove the cause of the ailment, not simply relieve symptoms.

He did not hesitate to prescribe sophisticated drugs, even narcotics, so long as these were given under a physician's supervision. Not infrequently he spelled out a compound in detailed grams and minims, for a pharmacist to follow. But he also singled out commercial products and used them by name—unless the manufacturer changed their formulas, which he promptly noted and corrected by suggesting a pharmacist's additions. Nor did he hesitate to recommend surgery, where he thought it was necessary, even when physicians were advising against it. He was quite capable of specifying the exact incision, procedure, and drainage.

But there was a heavier weight given to all types of physiotherapy, in his medical counsel, than one would find in the prescriptions and care of the typical family doctor. Behind this weight lay his insistence that the body should be helped to cure itself, as far as possible, and protected from the blows of needless chemicals or knife, which might accomplish a cure but weaken the system. So his readings contained baths, packs, colonics, exercises, manipulative therapy, electrotherapy, sweats, massages and oils.

They were also detailed in prescription of diet—both special diets and regular daily diets, as well as food supplements and tonics. His diets were not faddist, but comprised a part of his medical readings which early won wide recognition for their soundness. Handling food, he sometimes insisted, as he did with medication, that there were specific body cycles to be followed—a feature of medicine not as yet widely practiced, perhaps because the instrumentation to determine these cycles is not always available at the level of accuracy that the sleeping Cayce demonstrated.

Changes in attitude, habits, outlooks, recreation, life style and vocation, as well as religious orientation, came under discussion in his therapy—sometimes at the head of the list of treatments. Hypnosis and psychotherapy were at times recommended, as well as group therapy and even intercessory prayer by others. But most often the patient himself was told to rebuild his own inner life by examining its foundations and its impact on those around him, as well as on his health.

Perhaps the most striking feature in the medical readings was not the sleeping Cayce's diagnostic work; one could at least imagine him going out to look over a patient with x-ray vision (although in point of fact he claimed that the diagnosis came from the patient's own subconscious, which knew the body better than Cayce did). And it was not his encyclopedic knowledge of medical terms and a staggering variety of treatments; one could at least imagine a mind of superb memory, augmented by unseen medical counsel. What shocked observers as much as any feature of these readings was his seeming access to a complete directory of medical aids. He could instantly specify the best surgeon for treating a particular condition, and where he was located. He could specify where to order an unknown drug. He could identify where climate and altitude would be best for the patient—and even mention the local golf courses. Hearing this facility at work, and knowing of its accuracy in hundreds of readings, the listener was often driven to postulate some sort of a "universal consciousness," such as that which Cayce himself said he was tapping.

Yet Cayce insisted that all he did in his medical readings was capable of duplication in dreams—if the dreamer needed it and could understand it. At the very least, the dreamer who sought it would find himself directed where to get help, when, and why, for himself and his loved ones.

To be sure, those who had a natural bent towards medicine, as did Frances, would find more of such dream material than others whose major focus might be on art or history. But the body would make its needs known in dreams, and even suggest therapy.

Frances' husband, Aaron, dreamed of manipulative therapy for his ailing mother:

> I said to my mother, "Now I am going to give you this osteopath treatment

myself." I gave it more as Dr. H. (of Virginia) does, kneading and spreading cervicals gently, rather than roughly cracking them.

In his dream he was seeing exactly the care needed by his mother, Cayce reported, only it should be given by a doctor and not by the dreamer. To make things easier, Cayce then named a doctor in New York who would do it properly: "Marshall would be well with this, Dan Marshall." Since Aaron had never heard of him (very likely Cayce awake had never heard of him), he asked, "Will you give the address?" Cayce's reply was notable: "New York. Look in the telephone book—put self to some trouble."

Cayce's unending problem in training dreamers was to get them to rely on themselves, asleep or awake. He did not seek little Cayce-ites. He wanted capable, self-reliant people, using the talents with which they are endowed, and learning new laws to apply.

As a good coach, he had to keep encouraging his dreamers. He used all his medical skill to do it.

When women dreamed of pregnancy, he added the exact dates within which they should conceive. Then he challenged them to dream the sex of the baby, which he could confirm. It was up to them to learn to dream helpfully. If they dreamed the baby's formula was wrong, he corrected it, but pressed them to try for further leads to check with him.

When a man dreamed that his riding breeches were too large, Cayce was delighted with his progress in dreaming of medical care. The dream was noting, he said, that riding was good for the dreamer, but not too much of it. When another dreamer heard himself warned not to go to football games he loved, Cayce reinforced the warning, and asked the man to dream why the warning had come. He did. It was because of the danger of ear infection. Cayce agreed, and spelled out the treatment to free the dreamer to go to the games. And in a burst of encouragement he even told the dreamer which games his alma mater would win in the rest of the season—providing the starting lineup was not changed.

Dreams and Psychological Readings

Edgar Cayce was forty-five years old and had been using his gift for two decades when there first appeared the type of readings which was to become the second most numerous in his files: the psychological readings, which he called "life readings." There were, when he died, approximately twenty-five hundred of these, given for people of all ages and walks of life, beginning with his own family and relatives. The contents of these readings, too, he claimed, could be paralleled in dreams.

Similar in many ways to the medical readings, they examined the systems of the psyche instead of systems of the body.

At the very start of these readings the sleeping Cayce often spoke in a half-voice, as though to himself, while examining records. Going back year by year in the individual's life, he noted out loud the telling developments, the turning points, the traumas or stresses that had shaped the life—from one or two to a half-dozen items. Then he plunged into assessing an entire personality.

As in the medical readings, he began with a few sweeping comments to characterize what he was dealing with—the person's amplitude of spirit, the relative talents and potential for service, the kind of lessons most needed in the lifetime, the choices that must be made.

Then he began his systematic analysis of the person. First came the individual's temperament, talents, and tendencies of life style (how far outgoing, or an extremist, or reflective, etc.). He took up these questions, which he treated as the innate wiring and plumbing of the personality, however used or misused or ignored by the individual, in a novel fashion. Turning back to a sevenfold framework used by the ancient Greek Stoics, he employed the names of Olympian gods and goddesses, as emblems of trends in the personality. These same structures could, he said, also be correlated with traditions about planets in the Zodiac— though not in a mechanical way. In point of fact, he said, the seven emblems were ways of talking about tendencies of the person which he had developed and refined in interim periods *between* earth lives (a notion which the Stoics also shared).

In so approaching a personality, Cayce used his seven spotlights carefully to highlight trends in the personality. He dealt not only with the strength of individual endowments—for example, intellectual acumen, which he ascribed to "Mercury"—but with the way in which one endowment blended with another—as how "Mercury" might be affected by aggressiveness and force, which he called "Mars."

But in using this framework, Cayce set himself outside the terminology of modern psychology, which nowhere employs a similar typology—not even in the three panels of temperament types used by Sheldon, nor in the eight "functions and attitudes of consciousness" used by Carl Jung.

Sometimes Cayce only briefly discussed these innate structure patterns of the personality, because the individual, he said, was using his will to "set them all at naught." Other times he expanded on them at considerable length, linking them with the person's vocation, personality weaknesses, friendships, artistry, morality, philosophical interests, habits, and leadership capacities. These were the conduits down which the person's natural energy tended to flow, whatever the ends he sought. Often, he said, they were dramatized in abstract dreams, or dreams of structures and designs.

But then Cayce turned to the more dynamic side of personality—the goals and answers toward which the individual was moving, and the powerful drives and fascinations that were taking him there. These were elements which he said came from previous earth lives; they usually appeared, he noted, in dreams of strong sensory and emotional tone.

Cayce's method of taking up earth lives was a simple one. He selected from among the many he said he could see those which he felt were currently relevant for the individual. He warned that other past lives might have had their bearing at some previous point in the present biography, and passed on, while still other lives might come later into focus.

In Cayce's view one is, in some sense, living all his "lives" at the present. A past existence is not left behind like a closed book. It survives into the present much as psychoanalysis says childhood survives into adult life, coloring it in many ways. Cayce saw the full personalities developed in past lives as substructures of the present psyche, coloring all of life after adolescence, and constellated with different lives to the fore, depending on the individual's present behavior.

He insisted that dreams may recall actual scenes and memories from past lives, and that one is likely to dream of the personality drives and problems left as deposits by those lives.

In his "life readings" he sketched, as a rule, from four to six past lives bearing on the present. (When asked, he was able to go back and devote one or more entire reading to a particular life.) He frequently touched on the family and social standing of the individual in each past life as well as on his upbringing, education and talents. He caught the sense of whether the life had reached for clear goals or simply drifted. He singled out talents that might carry over to the present. He tried to convey the sense of belonging, what the main relationships were like and how they unfolded. He set the individual in the framework of the causes, institutions, and movements of his times—especially those that had struck deep chords in the person at that time. He spelled out the individual's name in an English transliteration from whatever language was appropriate—whether Hebrew, Chinese, Sanskrit, Egyptian, American Indian, or some other. And he summarized each life by tersely indicating how far "the entity gained" or "the entity lost."

He gave special attention to that lifetime in which he felt the individual had reached his highest spiritual development, his clearest ideal and greatest service to his fellowman. Often he told people they were already dreaming of this lifetime, in repeated fragments of which he reminded them, and he claimed that one of the main functions of dreaming of past lives was to quicken again the spiritual core of the person.

At the end of the reading, he came into the present, to summarize "the abilities of the entity, that to which it may attain, and how." Here he took up questions of vocation, education, marriage, public service, to suggest how the individual's heritage might be fitted into contemporary culture and into the web of his personal ties. He indicated where the person would find his greatest happiness, do the most good, feel the most alive, keep freshly growing. And he closed his analysis by putting the question of spiritual priorities to the fore: Where did the individual, in his heart, stand with his God?

Frequently there were also questions about practical matters, which Cayce took up one at a time: how to get along with certain relatives, how to decide between job offers, why certain failures kept daunting the person, how to begin a more disciplined life.

It was Cayce's claim, in the hundreds of dream readings he gave, that all of the important matters in his life readings were capable of investigation in the individual's dreams.

It would be no great surprise to a psychoanalyst, or to a modern student of dreams in sleep laboratories, to hear that dreams deal with all the *questions* about temperament, talents, style, drives, goals, commitments, and relationships which Cayce touched upon in his life readings. But it would be outrageous, in the views of most dream students, to expect dreams to present the same *structures* that Cayce described: past lives, and patterns from "interim" experiences. Yet

Cayce insisted that dreams, carefully studied, would be found to present both the present questions and the relevant past structures.

He used all of his life-reading skill in coaching dreamers.

When a financier dreamed of himself as a philosopher receiving a degree in academic robes, Cayce told him that he had the talent, from Egyptian and Chinese lives, and encouraged him to proceed. Within four years the man had published a meaty book on life after death, was lecturing monthly at a university, and received the honors he dreamed about.

When a sensitive and verbal young man dreamed of himself in the outfit of an ancient warrior, sword in hand, Cayce confirmed the dreamer's guess that he was glimpsing a past life. But Cayce also challenged the dreamer to discover, through dreams and self-study, how the warrior-self fitted into his present personality. The young man responded, in time, that he was now to use the old fierceness to keep him patient and dogged in serving others, rather than destroying them with his tongue and rebuffs. Cayce agreed, and insisted that the substructure of the warrior in his makeup would help him to develop controlled strength—as something surely did, in the years that followed.

An attractive, ambitious, power-driven woman, an executive in a New York business firm, dreamed of a man to whom she was drawn. He was in her apartment, where she could either seduce him or help him on a creative project in which he was engaged. Cayce suggested that the man in question had once been her son, at a time when she was genuinely self-sacrificing, though strong. By working with him now she could bring out her best side, rather than her predatory instincts.

When a stockbroker began to dream of stocks symbolically in number patterns that indicated their rise and fall, strengths and weaknesses, and even dates and quantities of purchase and sale, Cayce told the dreamer the name of a stranger whom he should consult on the symbology of numbers, and make into a good friend as well—for they had been associated in lifetimes before.

When a banker asked about the strange languages which others told him he spoke in his sleep, Cayce identified these as Egyptian and Celtic, which he indicated could be verified. In addition, he urged the dreamer to notice again the stone tablets which frequently appeared in his sleep (and which the dreamer had not mentioned to Cayce). He could learn to read these Egyptian tablets, Cayce said: "Study to read these up and down, not across."

Cayce told a woman that she could recall in her dreams a past life experience of being brought home from the Crusades as the Moorish wife of a Christian, and could write memorable stories on the conflicts and growth she had known.

In scores of dream readings he showed the dreamer how past life experience had precipitated a present pattern: the way a husband looked down on his wife as a child, the tendency of a dreamer who had once banished others to flee into self-imposed exile when things went wrong with him, the deafness now afflicting a man who too often had turned a "deaf ear" to the cries of others, the reason that classmates kept electing a student to leadership posts. Cayce took what he felt was an authentic bit of "life reading" in the dream, and added his own information and encouragement.

Whether Cayce's claims about reincarnation will ever be verified, by study of age-regression hypnosis, of claimed memories by the living, of dreams, of visions under drugs, and of structures of the psyche, remains problematic. Certainly if they are ever given stature by research, they may add weight of Freud's claim of sexuality in infants, to Rank's studies of the birth trauma, and to Jung's speculations on individual inheritances from a transpersonal or "collective" unconscious.

Dreams and Religious Readings

By the end of his life, Cayce had narrowed the variety of readings he gave to three kinds which together could give a profile of the individual. The "physical reading" could size up a person medically. The "life reading" could size him up psychologically. And what Cayce called a "mental and spiritual reading" could size him up in his relation to the divine.

There were fewer "mental and spiritual" readings than either physical or life readings, partly because they were not so immediately vital as the physical readings, nor as exotic as the life readings. Yet Edgar Cayce took particular joy in giving these straightforward little readings, because they touched on the questions that he felt mattered most in life.

These readings were an analysis of the composition of the whole "entity," the soul in its long journey, somewhat as the other readings had analyzed body and psyche.

To orient the individual receiving the reading, Cayce usually began by a review of what a soul was, and how it functioned in a human body in an earth life. All souls had been created in the beginning at the same time, he insisted and had been given free will to go out into creation, to adventure and experiment. Their destiny was to return to the divine by an informed and conscious act of will, entering into full partnership with the divine in aiding and advancing creation. However, it was their special contribution to the divine that they would remember all they had done and been, enriching the very Godhead itself.

Some of the souls, Cayce reported as calmly as he might report on the American Revolution in an episode of a life reading, had gone to the earth, to "be fruitful, multiply, and subdue it"—indeed to bring to earth's creation the possibility of consciously knowing its relation with the divine from which it had sprung. But these souls had attuned themselves so sharply to affairs of earth that they had become mired in its laws and processes—all elements good of themselves, but a different set of processes than were meant to guide the souls. The souls had lost their native attunement to the divine, and had to be given a way of growing back towards the divine, while experiencing the mysteries of creation and the Creator in the earth that they had chosen. The process of reincarnation was the result.

As each soul moved through life after life, and its interim experiences, it was to perfect its attunement to the divine, and its loving service to its fellows. The mental and spiritual reading was an examination of those two processes in the individual under question.

First was the matter of where the individual constantly turned his thoughts, in daily life. Cayce never tired of insisting that "mind is the builder," capable of bringing the soul into better and more productive relation with the divine lines of force, or taking the soul farther and farther away into its own dead ends.

Dreams, too, in Cayce's view, are often occupied with the question of the dreamer's habitual thoughts.

An inventor who dreamed that someone stole his invention was becoming so distracted with worry that he could no longer invent well. A pregnant woman dreaming of bills was so concerned about expenses that she was harming her health and the baby's, instead of leaving these matters to the husband who could handle them. A businessman was so suspicious of his partners, as his dreams mirrored, that he was alienating them and bringing on the betrayal he feared. On the other hand, a man who sought to bring out the best in people saw himself in a dream as having a great time fishing with friends—fishing for "spiritual food," Cayce said. A man praying for a desperately ill relative saw his prayers like a light in her hospital room, depicted in the dream as brighter or dimmer according to his constancy of focus and desire, and glowing with help for her.

Typically the mental and spiritual reading turned next to what the dreamer put forth in his life, through his vocation, his marriage, his friendships, his commitments to groups and institutions. In different ways Cayce would ask the same question: what is your ideal? In the long run there were only two kinds of ideals: self-serving goals, and the service of others. With a firm scalpel, Cayce cut open the individual's handling of fame, of wealth, of power, of wisdom, of love. He selected whatever was good in the person that could be built upon—motherhood, feeling for the underdog, courage under fire, capacity to take a long view, loyalty to friends—the best of the person's ideals. Then he compared the rest of the person's behavior and challenged him to bring them all into line. Ultimately, Cayce said, the one complete ideal for the human family, though many others were admirable, was the soul who had come to be known as Christ. He often asked the person before him to compare his life with that Life; despite the reality and usefulness of knowing about past lives, this was the Life that counted.

In Cayce's understanding of dreams, a comparison of the dreamer's life with his ideal was occurring in dreams almost every night, however symbolically portrayed, or however small the action examined.

A dreamer who recalled that the night before he was putting on peculiar shoes and shoestrings was told that he had been reminded to keep his feet on the upward path. A man who saw a wet street and streetlights being cleaned was told that his own "way" was being cleansed to receive more light, more truth about his life, which he could share with others. A man whose hobby was home movies saw a revolving light in a projector-like box in a darkroom; it was, said Cayce, a representation of "the Light within," and how the dreamer could, despite constrictions and darkness in his life, reach out to aid his fellowman through many channels. A dreamer who felt, in his dream, compassion for the children of shopclerks, who were waiting outside the store, was told that such compassion was the beginning of authentic sublimation of sexual fantasies such as had often crowded his mind about women clerks.

And a dreamer who heard in his dream only his name called aloud three times was told by Cayce that he had the same experience as the child Samuel in the temple. He should answer with the simple but whole-hearted response, "Use me!"

Whatever counsel or challenge Cayce might offer in his mental and spiritual readings was more than equaled, he felt, in dreams.

Dreams and Business Readings

Right alongside his readings about an individual's relations with the divine, Edgar Cayce gave readings about an individual's relations with his dollars. As he told a man who dreamed of great wealth, money, like learning or skill, "is made to serve its intent and purpose" in the scheme of things if kept in perspective.

Indeed, counsel on business matters was not infrequent in his medical readings and life readings, where vocation, employment and investment directly affected an individual's health and peace of mind. In his view, the divine was not only interested in man's religiousness, or moral propriety. As God could properly be called "the Creative Forces," so He could properly be described as interested in all levels of human creativity: making music, making love, making civilizations, making prayers, making medicines, making homes, and making money.

However, there was always human greed, which tended to appear when people saw that Cayce could deliver valuable information with his psychic gifts. On this question Cayce was firm. He considered his gift as rightly used for building people, not building fortunes. When it was appropriate to help someone build his income as part of his total growth, Cayce would give financial counsel as readily as he prescribed medicines. However, his stress was always upon what the individual could do for himself. When men of means came to him, as they often did, he questioned them as to what else they wanted to do with their lives besides grow rich; only as they showed a willingness to serve others with their means was he likely to give them sustained financial counsel.

When his own son and two relatives came to him for aid in locating a buried treasure, he told them they were on the right track, and proved it with details of the location and initial finds. But he insisted, in his readings, that they were not prepared for the notoriety and self-esteem which such a find would bring them, and he refused to give them further aid except as their own subconscious might give it to them in dreams—which he would then confirm.

The same values applied in all his business readings. When a dream showed how a group of financiers had taken steps to manipulate the market, he helped the dreamer to respond correctly in the manipulation. But he would give the dreamer no aid when the manipulators were only *contemplating* certain steps; at that point, he said, the men's thoughts remained their own property.

Relatively few sought business readings, and got them, because relatively few seemed to meet Cayce's qualifications. However, several dozen people did seek and receive such aid. And a few individuals secured a total of hundreds of readings on business affairs, chiefly as commentary on dreams.

A business reading was usually addressed to a specific problem: a real estate transaction, incorporation of a firm, consideration of specific employees or partners, stock trends, market opportunities, inventions to be developed. After the main problem was treated by Cayce, the individual or group who sought the reading might then ask questions about a variety of other business concerns. However, most of those who knew Cayce well knew also that in business readings they might come under Cayce's searching eye at any time, with their motives and methods of operation questioned or even rebuked. While he did not often expose people in front of others (he once gave a businessman a dressing down in German—a tongue that Cayce did not know but the businessman did—in order to make his point without embarrassing the man before his associates), he had a way of making clear that he knew where things were amiss in the individual's handling of funds, or handling of responsibilities or relationships. This discouraged many from seeking business counsel from him.

Besides, Cayce was insistent that one could discover through dreams all that he needed for business prosperity, if he was in the right vocation and operating with integrity, as well as using his means to help others less fortunate.

Two of the four dreamers whom he trained through the interpretation of hundreds of their dreams became millionaires over a period of four years, by adding their own dream study to their daily work. The other two were not in business nor seeking wealth as ardently as they sought to unfold other talents, though one achieved equal wealth through her husband.

Cayce used all of his psychic skill to coach his business dreamers.

When a woman dreamed of a coming stock rise in a coastal shipping line, he not only confirmed her dream and advised her to buy, but rewarded her with an extra by giving her the exact date, some ninety days off, when the market would prove best for her to sell (he was correct). When a stockbroker kept dreaming of steel stocks, although he was interested in rails and motors, Cayce helped him to see that the dreams were showing steel as the "criterion" of broad market moves for a certain period—and once even charted the movements of steel stock for an entire year ahead. When an investor dreamed he was riding a New York streetcar, which had in it a posted warning that he should not get off at a public building, Cayce not only showed him that this was a warning against New York subway stocks at the time, but how the dream had depicted the reason: Public officials were planning regulations which would cut the profit of the line. When a financier was planning to form a finance company, Cayce helped him to evaluate the proposed directors through his dreams. When a dreamer came up with a dream of trouble about a check for $150 in his office, Cayce showed him how he was in fact dreaming of two such checks—one that had come in and was improperly recorded, and one that the dreamer's wife ought to pay out, since she owed it. When a tired businessman went on vacation and dreamed that on his return his desk was shoved aside and his secretary installed in his place, he was simply seeing, Cayce remarked, the priority dictation would have on his return.

Over and over Cayce made clear how dreams could be helpful in business, and then added his own insights to encourage the dreamer and keep him growing. A banker dreamed of a stream of secretaries applying for the position he then had open; Cayce helped him identify what qualities he was seeking—and then added that he should hire the third in line. An entrepreneur saw correctly in his dream, Cayce said, how he could distribute and promote a new product for the care of gums—but the dream had also warned him not to use the relative he was considering to do the job.

Whatever factors influenced the business world—the collapse of a bank, orders to a firm from abroad, rumors, combines, labor troubles, government regulations, credit policies, salesmanship, bold decisionmaking, competition—Cayce proved hundreds of times over that he could correctly and instantly grasp them all. But more important, he proved to dreamers that they could grasp these matters as well, with one major difference: their insights were limited to what bore on their own affairs and on those of their associates. They were businessmen, and they got the business counsel they needed. Cayce was a counselor, and he got what his counselees needed.

Those with whom Cayce worked on dreams, to help them in business matters, were not greedy people—or he would not have helped them. But they did face the pressures of relatives and friends to maintain their wealth and the attendant social station; this brought them under severe Cayce scrutiny at times, exactly as it did in their dreams. There was nothing wrong with the making of money, Cayce insisted. Christ himself, he argued in one trenchant reading, could have made an excellent Wall Street broker while remaining wholly true to his Father. What counted was not dollars but motives. What was the soul trying to accomplish with money on its journey through earth lives?

Dreams and Readings on Hidden Resources

Because of his strange ability, Cayce was often approached to locate something hidden or lost. In earlier years he had tried a number of ventures of this sort, but towards the end of his life he was less inclined to get involved. In solving crimes, he had discovered his own psyche was touched and shocked by the violence of the criminal; his own readings told him that using his skill for the purpose was like cutting down trees with a razorblade. He could do it—but why?

When it came to mines and oil wells, he had helped others make fortunes. But he had also seen the investors fall apart as individuals and as a group, overcome with greed and jealousy of one another.

His readings told him that he could himself make legitimate money locating buried treasure, if he could handle his own motives and the consequences of his act. At one of the several times when he tried this, he was off on a journey to help a group of businessmen locate a treasure, with his wife and secretary along. The following dream sent him home:

> It seemed we were going to take a reading about my grandmother. We knew she was alive again and someone told us to go to a certain place and we would find her. It seemed like a storeroom, or an undertaking establishment. We found my grandmother with vines growing all around and over her. My wife and secretary and I were cutting them away, so there would be no trouble about the reading locating her. Then we started out, talking about how wonderful it would be if this could be proven to people. At the door we met three dogs of different kinds. We tried to get them out, but one got loose and ran back toward the dead body. We started running after him, but suddenly I realized it was all a dream and I knew the interpretation of it. It meant that we three were letting our work go to the dogs while we were trying to do something we had no business to do.

While Cayce felt reasonably sure he had the sense of his dream, he submitted it for a reading, anyway. The reading confirmed that the pulling away of vines represented what had engaged him in tramping with the treasure seekers; he was dreaming of the venture, which had for weeks crowded out his medical or vocational aid to others. But more important, it said, the three dogs were himself, his wife, and his secretary, who had started off as pleasant as tailwagging canines might be, but had developed under the strain dispositions that led to snapping and rending. In this circumstance what good Cayce might do was bound to be spoken poorly of, and he would not gain enough from the treasure nor the feat to be worth the price.

Then the dream commented on the theme of resurrection of the grandmother. His proper concern was with "awakening" people to their true natures and states; that was the purpose of his gift. But he had incorrectly felt that proving he could locate treasure with his gift would accomplish such awakening—certainly nothing of the depth and power of the New Testament resurrection motif with which he had invested the treasure hunt. People had to be awakened individually, with whatever they could use and apply in their own lives, not by the publicity of a psychic stunt.

His readings on the hidden or lost showed similar reserve when a woman came to him with a dream at the time of the Lindbergh kidnapping. He confirmed every detail in the dream, such as the roles of the nurse and of the gardener. He confirmed the use of a getaway boat on the Potomac, and even corrected her spelling of its name. The town of Arlington which she had somehow located in Germany, in the dream, was instead Arlington, Virginia, but approached by German-speaking principals in the dream. Still, he would not tell her exactly where the baby's body was located. Instead, he urged her to dream again and get the rest of the details, which he would gladly confirm. He even added that if she continued the chase in her dream she would go to Puget Sound. But he would not put her psyche under the stress of more notoriety, from the public solving of the crime, than her own subconscious would do. The next step remained with her and her motives and total strength as a person. She never returned with a further dream.

But she had seen, as did others, that whatever was lost or hidden and could rightfully be discovered by the dreamer, could be disclosed to him in a dream, provided he was ready to handle it. For example, a businessman felt he should invite his overbearing mother to live with him and his young wife. His dream told him emphatically otherwise, but then correctly supplied the address of an apartment building where he could place her not far away. Cayce was delighted to see his pupil making progress in practical use of his dreams.

Dreams and Readings on Social Change

An important body of readings which accumulated in Cayce's files over the years was a file on the progress of a small social movement, bent on changing certain aspects of American life. Its central concern was not civil rights, nor the rights of labor, nor birth control, nor international peace, nor psychoanalysis, nor health foods—though Cayce did give a limited number of readings on all of these matters.

The movement whose growth he coached through his readings, through years of changing personnel and programs and policies, was the activity of a small group of people who felt that Cayce's own work was significant, and representative of concerns that many would share if they understood them. They called this little movement simply "the Work," and readings on "the Work" remain some of the most interesting that Cayce gave.

These readings were astonishingly detached about the personal welfare and fame of Edgar Cayce. Cayce ought to be provided for, the "Work readings" made clear, but the right concern was not Cayce. It was the processes in which individuals could learn to help themselves, could undergo the "awakening" that had been symbolized, for example, in Cayce's dream of his grandmother. The awakening sought was not to some simple dogma, such as belief in life after death or in psychic phenomena, or in reincarnation. And certainly not to belief in Cayce. Nothing less than that each soul who came to them should awaken to his full creative stature as a son of "the Most High" would suffice as a goal for "the Work." But such awakening required starting where each man was, and building on his particular needs and talents. So they were going to have to deal in medicine, business, philosophy, psychology, physics, social justice, education—in a great many matters. And they were going to have to begin with what they had, right in the Cayce family and his closest associates, while waiting for others with different talents to join them.

Some of Cayce's associates were counseled on where to get an education, some on their vocations, some on their attitudes. As Cayce's life unfolded, the "Work" came to include the founding and operation of the hospital, and the university. When these were closed, the "Work" turned toward the development of spiritual depth and quality in a number of Virginia friends—ordinary people, who brought themselves under discipline and produced a little manual of the devotional life called *A Search for God*.

The history of the Cayce life and work was a microcosm of movements for serious social change. His readings dealt with every aspect of such a movement: its philosophy, its goals, its leadership, its covenants and corporations, its climate of daily work, its stages. Every lasting movement, they insisted, must proceed "first to the individual, then to the group, then to the classes, then to the masses." In this the Cayce sources were adamant, though many sought to promote Cayce by the usual advertising means. Social change had to be accomplished, his readings affirmed, by building and rebuilding one life at a time, supporting it with primary groupings at home and at work and in church and community, and then moving on to develop—over a period of years—exactly this same process with leaders in various professions and walks of life. Only then could something emerge so widespread, so well-understood and practiced, that it would touch masses of people.

In Cayce's view, every aspect of the growth of a social movement could be properly informed and guided by dreams. He used all of his skill to communicate this to the dreamers with whom he worked.

When they dreamed that the hospital could become reality, in times of doubt and difficulty, he showed them how their dreams were prophetic in quality, and not merely wishes. When the question of financing the hospital arrived at its last stages, he helped a dreamer to follow his dreams right to the office where the necessary mortgage could be placed. When the university was to be closed, he helped one dreamer see how the president was going on to new levels of personal and family growth, rather than stopping with present humiliation and defeat. When the study groups began their work, he showed the members how they could counsel each other through their own dreams, and could grow in grace to the point of true visions of Christ, through their dreams—if their lives were being spent for others. He coached dreamers to select board members through dreams, and then to improve attitudes on the board. He helped one dreamer encourage a hospital backer—to stop him from going off the deep end on a project.

The dream readings in the Cayce file showed every step of his "Work" previewed and guided in dreams, from 1924 until his death in 1945. The dreams even included one on Cayce's death, and the consequences for his life's labors—adding the little touch that his wife would die very shortly after him (which proved exactly true). They pointed to the possibility that anyone responsibly concerned in a movement of social change, social service, or social justice, might well seek nightly guidance in his dreams—precisely as had many Biblical figures.

Dreams and Topical Readings

From time to time a group of individuals interested in Cayce's work, or a researcher or writer on a particular topic, would secure one of a small number of readings not devoted to the needs of an individual or group, but to a body of subject matter. Once again, their ability to get the sleeping Cayce to supply such information was determined by what they intended to do with it. If they sought novelty, or recondite information about the soul's journey for their own amazement, or material on an ancient civilization with which to impress others, they might expect little or nothing from the sleeping Cayce, and perhaps a lecture on their spiritual growth instead. Still, on a number of occasions over the years topical readings were both sought and received.

An international YMCA leader, a man of much faith and good mind, secured information on the authorship of New Testament books—information previously refused to others, who were told that the biblical question for them was whether they could apply it in their own lives. Frances' husband, who was studying life after death, sought and received essays on conditions in the next plane, as well as readings on evolution, and the interplay of heredity and environment. A concerned group of Cayce's associates sought and received topical readings on international affairs, on the nature of Cayce's own gift, on the ancient and much-doubted civilization of Atlantis.

A reading was sought and secured on the causes and cure of the common cold. A small series was secured on the events leading up to and including the birth of Jesus. An entire series of topical readings, supplemented by analyses of how well a study group was understanding them, produced the little manual of spiritual growth, A Search for God, as well as a collection of studies of the book of Revelation. Yet another series was given to a group investigating healing by prayer.

Of all the varieties of Cayce readings, the topical reading must have seemed the least likely to be duplicated by dreams. But Cayce showed his dreamers, especially two of the four major subjects that he coached, that dreams were capable of producing extensive verbal essays—complete with diagrams and acted-out illustrations. Indeed, the serious students of their dreams learned to expect that kind of dream which combined a scene with an explanation of it—whether by a voice in their dreams or by a series of coherent thoughts.

Most of the essay dreams, in the Cayce view, originated in efforts of the dreamer's subconscious to teach him something he needed to understand in his daily life and in his studies; often such dreams had the setting of a school. Sometimes essay dreams originated with the dreamer's higher self, and sometimes the major part of the instruction came from a discarnate entity or guide who was helping the dreamer—according to Cayce.

Cayce used all of his skill at securing information to coach dreamers on their dreams of a topical nature.

When a stockbroker dreamed about how the "spirit" of a stock enters into predicting its future movements (and found the essay illustrated by the intentions of people going to a movie), Cayce confirmed the analysis and then showed the dreamer how to distinguish accurate stock leads in dreams from those which were only pictures of stock tendencies. When a Jew dreamed about the question of the work of Christ, Cayce encouraged him on the accuracy of the dream analysis, and added some illustrations of his own. When an American businessman dreamed about the forces breeding revolution in China, Cayce was quick to encourage the dreamer to put his concern into action—especially by studying Chinese affairs to write about them.

Cayce worked on dream-essays on how it feels to die, how the living and the dead communicate, how an individual reaches out to "Universal Forces," what souls can learn from animal creation, what suicide entails, how dreams work, how science and religion fit together, and how moral judgments are made.

In summary, the story of Cayce's forty years of trance counsel is a story of a cornucopia of information, some of it verified and some of it far from verified. It is also the story of the building of human beings, within a clear and cogent scheme of values which did not waver over the years. It is a staggering picture of the unknown potential of the human mind, in touch with some sort of More than itself.

But no claim in the entire Cayce story is more striking than the one he made for decades, right up until the end of his life: that others can do what he did—beginning with their dreams.

CHAPTER 6

GLIMPSES OF THE LAWS OF DREAMING

EDGAR CAYCE SHOWED his dreamers that the same laws which produced his readings also produced their dreams.

He did not spell out and name these laws, as a scientist might do. Whatever he explained, his readings said, had to be partly filtered through the capacity and terminology of his own psyche, and that of his listeners. Since none were scientists, he gave practical counsel on one dream and one life at a time. But occasionally he offered insights that lit up the landscape of dreaming. And then he urged the dreamers to "study, study, study."

Glimpses of Lawful Patterns in Dreaming

Whatever Cayce's mind was doing when he gave readings, it was not without lawful limits.

He had to be directed to his targets by hypnotic suggestions. For medical counsel he needed the address of the individual who sought aid. For psychological readings he needed the birth date of the individual. And for topical readings, or those on hidden resources, he had to be told both what was sought, and the names and location of those seeking.

Often those who wanted one type of counsel would request, in the quesiton period following the reading, counsel of another kind. When Cayce was especially keyed up, or relating deeply to the person seeking aid, they might get the desired medical information in a business reading, or counsel for a loved one in a dream reading. But more often they would be told, "We do not have this"; and instructed to seek a different type of reading.

Cayce explained to his dreamers that their dream-focus had similar limits. He coached them to set before their minds, by hard study, concentration, and activity, whatever they sought aid upon through dreams. Stock information would come in dreams to one who studied stocks, medical prescriptions to one charged with the health of others, spiritual counsel to one who straightened his paths before his Maker, past life information to one who tried to understand his urges. Dreams were limited by the conscious focus of the dreamer.

Cayce's readings were limited to the information and guidance which an individual could constructively use; it was the same with dreams, said Cayce. There was no point in resolving to dream of international affairs, or of ancient Egyptian times, or of policies of the Federal Reserve system, or of bacteria in a given disease, unless the dreamer were in a position to do something about these. Such information was available through the subconscious and the other resources it would tap, as Cayce felt his own readings showed. But the psyche protected its balance by feeding the dreamer limited material. It operated by laws of self-regulation.

Cayce's readings showed considerable variation in form, from day to day and year to year. As he spoke in trance of these variations, he said the laws at work also affected the form of dreams.

His readings varied in length, as do dreams. The shortest and most abrupt of his dream readings occupied two sentences; it was a reading given on one of his own dreams, which refused to interpret it, telling him he had done nothing about the last dreams interpreted for him. But there were also interpretations of dreams that occupied pages of transcribed notes. Other types of readings showed similar variations in length, from curt answers to long explanations.

His readings varied in clarity of communication, as do dreams. Some readings were direct and precise, while others rambled from clause to clause, trapping the meaning in a net of words.

His readings varied in detail. Some told the general state of a patient's circulation, while others specified blood count and blood pressure. Readings of a given day maintained about the same level of detail, much as dreams of a given night are general impressions, while those of another night are sharply etched.

His readings varied in level of discourse, as dreams vary from earthy material and even puns to poetic and spirited imagery. While most of Cayce's readings exhibited a stilted style, including the editorial "we," impersonal nouns such as "the entity" or "the body," and passive verb construction, some included bits of slang, or the jargon of a trade, or a homely expression of the person he was counseling. On the other hand, some readings were rhapsodic, and the hushed and cadenced phrases of others might be scanned as poetry. These levels of discourse, Cayce insisted, had a lawful base, as did the same levels in dreams.

The Cayce readings varied in the breadth of their focus—just as some dreams are capsules or cameos, while others sweep in widening circles of imagery and insight until the dreamer has a perspective of startling magnitude. Most of the readings simply addressed the person and matter in hand, but there were days when the readings would swing easily into extra spontaneous materials. Such comments might be brief, perhaps telling the individual that his widowed mother would soon marry someone she did not as yet know. The comments might be lengthy, explaining a Biblical parallel to the problem confronting the person before him. Or the spontaneous comments might be made as though from another perspective, warning all who heard that God would not forever endure "a wicked and adulterous generation."

There were still other variations in the readings which could be paralleled in dreams. There were variations in how swiftly Cayce addressed the subject matter at hand, sometimes without waiting for the usual instructions—as a dreamer may fall asleep and suddenly be dreaming so deeply that when awakened he is disoriented. There were variations in Cayce's interruptions of what was read to him, as a voice interrupts a dream with a comment, or a dream scene yields to another.

There were variations evident when Cayce gave a rare reading not yet requested, but needed by someone just then writing or telephoning him—much as dreams meet a need of others of which the dreamer is not yet consciously aware.

In all these variations, there were lawful modifiers at work, Cayce explained. For example, a whole series of modifiers within himself tended to affect his readings, just as the subjective state of the dreamer affects the form of his dream.

Cayce's health affected his readings. When he was ill he could not give them. When he was tired, they were less clear, detailed, or expansive. Similar factors, he said, affect dreams. Indeed, the effect of body processes on all types of dreaming is so real that one person's dreams over a period could be shown to vary according to whether he was on a vegetarian or a meat diet! Rest and physical fitness also constantly affect the recall, scope, depth, and clarity of dreams.

Cayce's state of mind affected his readings. When he was distraught and defensive with those about him, he experienced some of the few clear errors in a lifetime of giving readings: once in giving readings on oil wells, and once in giving readings on patients in his hospital. Neither time was a complete miss, but the distortions, as later pointed out, were dangerous; they contributed to his abandoning both the oil wells and the hospital.

His best readings came when he was buoyant, relaxed, humorous, secure. However, he also gave exceptional readings when in keen distress—as when he was twice jailed for giving readings, or when his university collapsed.

Dreams, too, he said, are conditioned subjectively. He urged his dreamers to get out and play, to take vacations, to balance up their wit and reason, to tease and to laugh and to enjoy children. But he also urged them to note the depth of dreams for the person confronted by death-loss, or by business failure, or by divorce, or by difficult vocational choices—all of which might call forth dreams of such depth and power as to make them "visions."

Cayce's readings were affected by what his own trance-products described as his relative "spirituality." When he was carried away by the ambitions of a treasure hunt, or temptations to seek notoriety with his gift and his considerable lecturing ability, he was reminded to notice how the quality of his readings suffered. On the other hand, when he was regular in his times of prayer and Bible study, as well as in his quiet fishing times, he was reminded to notice that his readings gained in quality, and that he even developed new types of gifts or capacities, both within his readings (for example, producing an entire series on a new subject), or awake (aiding the sick, through prayer).

Similar factors, his readings said, affect the quality of dreams. When his dreamers drove themselves for money or fame or power, they could see that their dreams brought up these very issues, and then began to deteriorate in clarity and helpfulness. When they were secure in their faith, their prayer times, and in their desire to serve others, they could find new vistas in their dreams—giving them glimpses into the world of the future or the past or the transcendent.

Besides the factors in Cayce's own personal life, there were more objective factors which influenced the form of his readings. While many people—perhaps almost anyone—could "conduct" a reading, the best guidance came with someone "passive"—not pushing for private ends. His wife fitted this role. In lesser degree, his readings were affected by the good spirits and spirituality of those in the room with him. The parallel in dreaming, as Cayce pointed out, lay in the effect on dreamers of their most intimate personal relationships. When husband and wife were bound in genuine love, dreams were facilitated by this bond and polarity, which often appeared in the dreams. Relations of brother with brother, or child with parent, would affect the stability and balance of the dreamer, and therefore the form and quality of his dreams. Such ties were not, he explained, matters of nice behavior, nor of duty, but of the weightiest significance to the soul itself.

Frequently, the Cayce source noted that the attitudes of those who sought information and guidance from Cayce affected what they got. Those who sought novelty, exploitation of others, a godlike guarantor for their lives, justification for their past mistakes, or anything but genuine aid and growth, received curt responses, or vague ones, or unexpected lectures on their motives. Those who failed to act on the counsel given them might find future counsel brief or even withheld.

Gullibility was as readily rejected as cynicism; adulation of Cayce accomplished as little as belittling or envy of him. "The real miracle," one reading said, "occurs in the seeker."

Similar factors, he said, govern the extent to which dreamers produce dream information helpful to those about them. Often a dreamer secures facts unavailable to a loved one because of his greater detachment toward the need or problem. Often, too, unconscious telepathy from a brother or sister or child shows dreamers how to reach the other's bad temper, or alcoholic habit, or despairing heart, or overbearing pride.

Glimpses of Lawful Patterns in Dream Interpretation

Just as there were lawful processes to color every reading Cayce gave, and every dream of every dreamer, so there were lawful processes of interpreting dreams.

Almost every dream reading, of the seven hundred that Edgar Cayce gave, began with a brief review of the progress of the dreamer. It examined how well he was recalling his dreams, how his waking experience of guidance and quickening paralleled his dreams, how the dreamer felt about his own progress, how far he had access to his own best self, what new gifts appeared in his dreams, how he handled old weaknesses, where he needed study or application, and how well he was interpreting his dreams without Cayce's aid.

All of these aspects of the dreamer's development, according to Cayce, can be reviewed for him in his own dreams. Indeed, one of the most frequent longer dream-types is the review dream, where one or more aspects of the dreamer's psyche or life is brought under scrutiny. Such dreams often go back to childhood, as their locale shows. Usually they involve many people, since the dreamer's identity and habits are bound up with particular people important to him. Or a dreamer might have an entire cycle of dreams, one every few nights, on the same theme—perhaps sex, or faith, or courage in adversity, or what to make of his talents. In general, as Cayce interpreted such review dreams, the endings indicate how the person is doing. A gloomy outcome and low spirits at the end underscore a warning, while adventure or discovery or attractive locales at the end underscore a promise.

As Cayce took up each dream in a typical dream reading, he first distinguished which levels of the psyche had produced that particular dream. The dreamer can also be taught by his own dreams, he said, to recognize the various levels working within him to produce each dream.

When a voice speaks in a dream, an aura of feelings and thoughts will show whether the voice is his best self or just his imagination. When a scene from the day flashes across his mind in sleep, he will be shown by nuances whether the scene represents merely worries from the day, or a prologue to helpful comments from the subconscious. When strange and outrageous material appears, his own subconscious will teach him to distinguish which is merely a dream caricature of his outrageous behavior, and which is instead a radical challenge to his being.

Dreamers should often ask in a dream, or immediately after it, he said, to be shown what part of their mentality has been at work in the dream, and why. Some of Cayce's dreamers were amazed at the colloquy which they were able to follow within them. Others were delighted to be able, they felt, to distinguish their own inner voice from the contribution of discarnates in dreams.

It was characteristic of Cayce's dream interpretation to set a small dream plot within a larger frame of meaning, when he felt that the dream intended it. A man who dreamed of the death of his brother, and was heartbroken, was shown the religious notes in the dream that distinguished it from a precognitive warning. The dreamer was seeing from his own superconscious, Cayce said, the meaning of the death of Christ, whom Cayce called the "elder Brother," for His fellows. A dreamer who saw himself escorting a strange young lady home from a dance was told to consider how service to others marked the full life. A businessman dreaming of a train trip was told it referred both to stock activity and to the question of the journey of the soul which he was studying at that time. In Cayce's view, dreams carry significant meaning on several levels at once, and should be interpreted accordingly.

Part of the art of interpreting dreams, according to Cayce, lies in the ancient art of "Urim," or recognizing symbols with relatively universal meaning. He emphasized the purely personal meaning of much dream contents, from articles of clothing to scenes of war. But he also challenged dreamers to see, in certain poetic and evocative dreams, the presence of symbols which have wide currency in myth and art. Fire often means anger. Light often means insight and help from the divine, as does movement upward. A child often means helpful beginnings, needing further aid from the dreamer. A horse and rider often mean a message from higher realms of consciousness. Pointed objects inserted in openings may well be sex symbols—although a key in a lock is more typically unlocking something in the dreamer.

Cayce used this kind of interpretation in less than twenty percent of the dreams he interpreted for most of his dream subjects, although more often in interpreting the dreams of his wife and a few others. The appropriateness of interpretation by Urim, he said, lay in the type of dreaming native to that dreamer.

In assigning to the term "Urim" the meaning of guidance by interpreting universal symbols in dream and vision, Cayce was incidentally solving a problem unresolved by Biblical scholars for generations—who have never agreed what sort of Old Testament divining it was.

One aspect of Cayce's dream interpretation was harder for dreamers to duplicate: the times he predicted their dreams, even the night and time of night. In the strange, wandering world of dreams, this bit of his skill seemed incredible—even allowing for the power of his suggestion upon the dreamer's unconscious. But he said he could do it because he could see factors in the dreamer's psyche which made the dreams inevitable, much as one on a high building could predict the collision of careening cars on separate streets below him. He added that dreamers would also learn to recognize when given dreams were signals of a new theme or series, and to predict for themselves how more would follow—as his dreamers did in lesser degree.

It was part of Cayce's skill in dream interpretation to devise analogies and illustrations for the point he said a dream sought to make. A dream scene on the simultaneous action of levels of consciousness is like seeing, he said, a pianist attending to sheet music and to finger action at the same time. The individuality of the soul, within its larger destiny, is like the individuality of a tree, coming from a seed and leaving one after it—true to pattern, yet a unique tree in itself. Cells sick in a body are like people who draw associates around them and start a movement with a mind of its own.

But this skill with images, a delightful part of the Cayce dream interpretation, is equally native to the dreamer, he insisted. This skill led to Frances' dream of canceling a trip to be with her baby, when she sought to understand her mother's care from the next plane of existence. It led another dreamer to see 1925 religious thought as a great hulk of a ship, foundering on a beach—beautifully built, but going nowhere.

In Cayce's view, determining the purpose of a dream is a major step in interpreting it. He explained that the psyche or total being tries to supply whatever the dreamer needs most. If the dreamer needs insight and understanding, it gives him lessons and even discourses. If he needs shaking up, it gives him experiences—beautiful or horrendous. If he needs information, it retrieves the facts for him. Dreams are part of a self-regulating, self-enhancing, self-training program, over which the dreamer's own soul ever presides.

An important step in interpreting a dream, then, is specifying what it came to accomplish—which the dreamer, according to Cayce, can learn to recognize for himself. A stock discussed by an acquaintance in a dream was a nudge to note and study the stock. But a stock seen in action, in actual figures, or described with instructions by a special kind of voice in his dream, was a signal for the dreamer to act, no longer to study.

Part of Cayce's training led dreamers to wake up after a vivid dream, review it in their minds so as to recall it later, and then return to sleep with the intention of having the dream interpreted for them—as it not infrequently was, whether by more episodes, or by essay-like passages, or by the voice of an interpreter or "interviewer," as one dreamer called it.

It is not surprising that those who studied hundreds of dreams with Edgar Cayce underwent major stress in their lives, and even marital or vocational crises. He showed them breath-taking vistas in their dreams, capacities for creativity which must have staggered them, and shaken their ego strength. He showed them that they could do whatever he did.

After the first few, Cayce never again trained dreamers as such. Instead, he trained people in an explicitly spiritual pilgrimage—one which included dreams but placed still greater weight on meditation, prayer, and daily service to others. Further, he trained people only in groups, where they could daily help one another in study, in love, in mutual intercession, in ways that his major dream subjects rarely knew.

But he insisted, whenever dreams or dream interpretation came up as part of this larger training, that dreamers could duplicate in the night—and sometimes in waking experiences—whatever he did in readings.

The Riddle of Outreach in Dreams

Cayce himself, when awake, wondered about the outreach that occurred in his readings and in his dreams. Accordingly, he dreamed about his question.

This dream, like a number he had, occurred while he was in trance, talking and concentrating on someone's need. A part of his mind was still available for a dream, even during a reading.

Shortly after the loss of this hospital, when he was asking himself the use of his gift after all, he reported the following:

> Saw myself fixing to give a reading, and the process through which a reading was gotten. Someone described it to me.

> There was a center or spot from which, on going into the trance state, I would radiate upward. It began as a spiral, except there were rings all around—commencing very small, and as they went on up they got bigger and bigger. The spaces in between the rings were the various places of development which individuals had attained, from which I would attempt to gain information. That was why a very low developed body [person] might be so low that no one even giving [psychic] information would be able to give anything that would be worthwhile.

> There were certain portions of the country that produced their own radiation. For instance, it would be very much easier to give a reading for an individual who was in the radiation that had to do with health, or healing—not necessarily a hospital, but in a healing radiation—than it would be for an individual who was in purely a commercial radiation. I might be able to give a much better reading (as the illustration was made) for a person in Rochester, New York, than one in Chicago, Ilinois, because the vibrations of Rochester were very much higher than the vibrations in Chicago. The closer the individual was to one of the rings, the easier it would be to get the information. An individual would, from any point in between, by their own desire to go toward the ring. If just curious (in seeking a reading), they would naturally draw down towards the center away from the ring, or in the spaces between the rings.

Cayce submitted this material for a reading, where he was told that it was an authentic vision of how his counsel was secured.

The vision had been correct in starting with Cayce as "a tiny speck, as it were, a mere grain of sand," for "in the affairs of the world" that was all Cayce was. Yet when he gave readings he was raising himself, or being raised, in a kind of funnel which stretched outwards and upwards until in its vast size it became all inclusive. He was being moved "direct to that which is felt by the experience of man as into the heavens itself." As he made his bodily activities "null" in trance, he was using only "as it were, (as seen in the cone), the trumpet of the universe—reaching out for that being sought." The answer to his reaching then came from the appropriate entity, some dot he had seen in its respective sphere, which "sent forth its note as a lute sends forth tones," to respond to his quest for information.

The reading was metaphoric, but its sense reached Cayce. It continued by assuring him that he had correctly seen how each individual, each group, each class or mass or nation, was found at some point on the vast spiral where its efforts had placed it, on the networks set by "an All Wise Creative Energy." Each speck was connected with the others, the reading said, as nerves connected each portion of a living organism to its center. Each could be instantly known or heard at the center.

He had also been correctly shown that the impact of readings varied as they were given to seekers from Rochester or Chicago. But the difference was not in healing counsel, for that could be given as freely to one place and station as to another. The difference lay in the resonating which occurred within the individual, in his locale, as he received information and aid from Cayce. Each heard and responded as his circumstance and development allowed him to hear and respond.

From this time on, especially in life readings, Cayce often murmured as he began a reading, "High on the spiral of vibrations," or "Low on the spiral of time," or "This city has the same point on the spiral as Allentown, Pennsylvania." Others about him were not able, in his lifetime, to see the structure which these comments implied, but the structure was real to the sleeping Edgar Cayce.

He took this reading as assurance that it was possible for a man with human limitations and weaknesses (which his readings let him know were many) to enter a state of consciousness where much more than himself came into play to meet someone's need.

His readings took the same tack in explaining outreach to a dreamer, one of Cayce's main dream subjects, who reported an unforgettable dream experience of a loved one who had died. Cayce assured him that the experience had been an actual meeting. Then he listened patiently while the dreamer explained a diagram which he had drawn for himself, to show how people from different planes meet, where the plane intersects. Although he was unconscious, Cayce followed the diagram as though he could see it, and then proceeded to modify it.

The man should draw a star, he said. The triangular points reaching out were like the total psyche of each individual. Out at the tip was consciousness, touching and resting upon the person's body—even partly emerging from the body's network of senses and drives. But as one moved away from the tip of the point, the psyche broadened. And as one approached the part of the circle where the triangular shafts touched their neighbors, one had a visualization of telepathy, or attunement to those near in thought or concern. And at the place where each pointed structure opened into the center body of the star, there was the soul of that person—uniquely oriented to its own point, yet also ever present with the center of the star. Then, said Cayce (and here his analogy was like that of the spiral), the dreamer should contemplate how each invididual might move in consciousness away from his own unique point towards the main body of the star, and into its center. The closer he got to the very center, then, the more he could enter completely into the consciousness and soul of each other person, or whatever plane of consciousness, represented by the other points of the stars.

There was a center in the universe, Cayce said. Indeed, a Center. Each man, each being, each creature and creation, was known and helped constantly from this Center.

He who, in dream or trance, drew near the Center, drew near to any other who needed him, or to any who could supply aid.

This was the answer to the riddle of outreach in dreams, however intricate the laws and processes involved.

To Edgar Cayce it seemed clear, however dubious to other serious men of his times, that man was not alone in the universe. And it seemed clear to him that the central Fact, bright as the center of a star, could be experienced as reality in dreams.

CHAPTER 7

HOW TO RECALL DREAMS

EDGAR CAYCE'S READINGS were tailored to the individual who sought each reading—especially his dream readings, where he took up each dream personage and activity in terms of their meaning to the dreamer.

One person's dream of his brother might represent his own undeveloped side, corresponding to something he did not like in his brother. However, when the same brother dreamed of *him,* he might see a literal warning of his brother's health problem, not a representation symbol at all.

When a woman dreamed of a doctor, it might signal that her body was ready for conception. When her husband dreamed of the same doctor, it might be a subconscious evaluation of the singlemindedness of a dedicated doctor.

If Cayce saw dreams as so personal, did he also point to processes that might be learned by dreamers today?

How far to generalize on the counsel Cayce gave to dreamers is a question for research. Only when the processes he described for particular dreamers are understood, and can be repeated and varied, will we know how far his dreamers, and his counsel to them, were like other dreamers and the counsel they need today.

Such research has hardly begun. Only in the middle 60's have Cayce's readings been indexed and duplicated so that all those referring to dreams could be isolated and studied, together with relevant correspondence and case records. However, the outlines of his dream theories and procedures were evident to his close associates as early as the late 1920's, and they have continued to record and study their dreams, as well as encourage others to do so, along lines representative of Cayce's thought about dreams.

In particular, Cayce's son, Hugh Lynn Cayce, has fostered the development of scores of study groups which often use dreams, in the national membership society called the Association for Research and Enlightenment, formed before his father's death to explore phenomena and processes such as were discussed in his father's readings. Hugh Lynn Cayce and others whom he has trained (including Elsie Sechrist, author of *Dreams, Your Magic Mirror*), have taught for over thirty years hundreds of ordinary people to work with their dreams. These lay-explorers of the inner continent of the unconscious have not conducted laboratory research, but they have been naturalists of the country of dreams. Among their discoveries has been evidence on a number of Cayce's claims about dreams: that they contain ESP of many types, that they present material suggestive of reincarnation, that they are affected by prayer patterns, that they may contain a high order of mystical experiences of the divine, that the style of each one's dreaming is unique, that dreams may be made the basis for self-analysis by laymen.

Systematic research on the Cayce dream materials is also under way. At least one psychotherapist has reviewed scores of client dreams to see how they embody processes which Cayce described. And students in an advanced psychology course in dreams have begun comparing his dream interpretations with those of Jung and Freud. Experiments have been held by Hugh Lynn Cayce to test the effect on dreams of stimuli which the readings described: drugs, fasting, meditation, certain colored lights, telepathic sending of targets, and systematic self-analysis.

All of the preliminary work suggests that modern dreamers may indeed find guidance on the recall, interpretation, and application of dream material, along lines Cayce suggested in his readings.

Question: How Can One Learn To Recall Dreams?

Many have not recalled a dream for years, and some can never remember dreaming. Does this mean that they do not dream, or are not recalling dreams?

Cayce was careful to distinguish the dreams of normal, healthy and growing individuals from those with damage to the brain or other parts of the endocrine systems. For the normal ones, as he saw it, there was no question that they were dreaming regularly, whether or not they recalled their dreams.

Long before modern sleep laboratories, where supposed non-dreamers were awakened when their eye muscles twitch, and helped to recall dreams at once, Cayce recalled for sleepers—on request—not only individual dreams but whole nights of dreams, and did so with such detail and force as to quicken the dreamer's own memory. After such experiences, the individual knew he was dreaming, and dreaming a great deal (as modern dream research shows about normal people).

Those whom Cayce coached had no great difficulty learning to recall dreams, once they set their minds to it. They had to be certain they were ready to confront whatever came forth in dreams, and to do something with it. Then they had to get across to their subconscious, one way or another, that they wanted dreams to be vivid enough to waken them, or to stay in consciousness in the morning. Some did it by telling themselves, just before dropping off to sleep, that they would dream and recall it—much as one tells himself to waken at five to go on a trip. Others did it by praying for guidance through their dreams. Others acquired the necessary first stimulus to recall dreams by reading and talking about them.

Cayce indicated, in one reading he gave on his own dreaming, that the body has a role in the recall of dreams. One can recover dreams better if he sets about remembering and recording them before he stirs his body, in the morning or when awakened at night. Evidently sufficient rest is also important, as Cayce repeatedly enjoined rest on those in dream-training with him—not only enough hours of rest, but the rest which comes easily with relaxation, exercise, fun, a change of pace, and committing one's life into God's hands.

He was firm with several dreamers that to recall their dreams they should record them—and go back over the records often. When he himself failed to record his dreams, Cayce was rebuked by readings for not using his mind on his dreams. (Part of the suggestion given him to secure dream interpretation included the "inquiring mind" of the dreamer; in one reading Cayce was himself told at the start that he was not "inquiring enough" about his dreams.) By the end of his life Cayce had made it a practice to discuss his more vivid dreams with his family, even if he did not write them out.

Cayce encouraged dreamers to start with whatever they could recall, even fragments. If they reported a hazy version, he corrected it. Yet he did less correcting for his systematic dreamers than a beginner might expect, for the dreamers soon learned that when doubtful, their own inclinations in recall were usually correct.

Starting with the moods on awakening could be useful, he reported. In his view, the individual's actions of the previous day, and of the current period of his life, are compared for him each night in sleep with his own deepest ideals. Accordingly, one who awakens grumpy and unrested ought to look into his life, as well as his dreams. And one who awakens in a clear and peaceful frame of mind may be sure that when he recalls his dreams they will not show him in serious inner conflict.

In Cayce's dream view, the processes of dreaming are not categorically different from those in waking life. While a dream may employ ESP to disclose the future or the distant or the unknown, so may a waking hunch or impression or inward voice. While a dream can unfold a dreamer's weaknesses of character, so can deep introspection. While a dream may offer an essay on the laws of consciousness so can a dreamer's hard study and incubation of them.

A dream may use a telltale image from the dreamer's past to convey a message, but so do waking memory-images and associations, as well as habitual word choices and slips of the tongue. So Cayce urged his dreamers to submit to him not only their dreams but also those happenings of daily life where the subconscious seemed to have the upper hand. And helping them with these, he also urged them to help themselves, by studying such waking products together with their dreams.

Finally, he saw it as important to the process of recalling dreams that dreamers act upon the dreams they recall. The very act of adding consciousness to the subconscious activity which produces the dream will set currents in motion within the total economy of the dreamer's mind—helpful currents to facilitate the recall of the next dreams, and eventually to aid in the interpretation of all dreams.

The simplest action is to record or tell a dream. This action is enhanced when the dreamer rehearses salient portions of the dream in his mind a number of times, whether he can interpret them or not. For if the dream reaches consciousness at all, it very likely has business with consciousness, and will profit from conscious attention. If the dream is a warning, going over it will strengthen the effect of the warning, however subtly. If an alerting, the effect of awaking and sensitizing the dreamer will be reinforced. If a lesson, rehearsing a dream will serve him as a drill.

Further, the remembered dream needs to be used, if possible. Not compulsively used, to be sure. But the subconscious is like a woodland spring to be dipped out and kept flowing, if it is best used. The dreamer may focus on some portion of the dream that strongly appeals to him, provided it is in keeping with his inmost ideal. For dreams, said Cayce, "are visions that can be crystallized." In dreams the real hopes and desires of the person, not idle wishes alone, are given body and force in the individual.

Trying to interpret the dream is better yet, for nothing facilitates recall like a direct conscious hit or connection with an important dream content.

Interpretation, Cayce explained, is a matter of "weighing" the dream content with more familiar aspects of the dreamer's life and thought. Understanding always proceeds by comparison. The two major steps of interpreting the contents of dreams are grasping what the dream *refers* to and sensing the *trend* of the dream—what it seeks to change or to invest with new meaning. To interpret a dream, one compares the dream with his outward affairs, as well as his inward thoughts and feelings and intents. Sometimes the same dream plot refers to both. Growth in dream interpretation is growth in ability to associate comparisons to dreams, readily and aptly, getting the sense of the reference, and of the trend of the message or stimulus; a great deal of the Cayce training was his coaching in just this process.

Beyond interpreting a dream, one can improve recall by giving the subconscious action of the dream an even greater boost from consciousness. Study is one way—study of laws and processes that seem to be at work in the dream or in a series of dreams, and at work in the dreamer and his affairs. Like using two stars of the Big Dipper to sight the North Star, one can line up two or more similar dreams, and perhaps some waking reflections and happenings, to sight clear through to important knowledge about living: how the levels of the mind interact, how love draws love, how fear and doubt cripple, how concentration quickens ESP, how tasks of demanding service draw the aid of both the living and the dead, how prayer brings consciousness to a Center not its own. Books may help, and Cayce both suggested books to his dreamers, although few of them, and added explanations of the difficult passages they were studying in such works as Ouspensky's *Tertium Organum* or James' *Varieties of Religious Experience*. Yet the essential study is not books but experience, and above all the steady, slow unfoldment of the dreamer's psyche—where one can see by careful comparisons (not morbid introspection) all of the creative patterns at work that also govern nature and the realms of the spirit around them. It can even be said, Cayce affirmed, that all an individual can understand of the workings of God is what he can find at work within himself, as he responds to the rest of creation.

While study is a major step in adding consciousness to dreams, and therefore important for stimulating clearer dreaming and clearer recall, study alone is not enough. A more active response to the dream, or to a series of dreams, is equally critical in improving dream recall. Cayce called such action "application," and he included a section on application in every dream reading. Study is a form of application, to be sure, but he often had something more definite in mind. The dreamer must put his dream insights, tips, and quickenings into motion with muscle and nerve, trying out truths by experiment, in order to gain the full understanding and guidance that dreams offer. Over and over Cayce pounded this into his dreamers: "Do, do, do," he said to a man bemused with dreams.

Two kinds of action on dreams comprise the Cayce repertoire of critical applications: attunement and service. One can use dream states and experiences as guides to attunement with his highest self, touched in dreams, and to attunement with God as found in dreams. Or one can work from dream impressions toward attunement with his fellows, and even with the spirit of stocks and markets. This form of application should be practiced daily with dream material one has interpreted.

The second major mode of application is giving, serving. Providing for oneself and one's family is important, whether one is a sailor or a philosopher. But even more important, once the basic needs are met, is giving a hand to others less fortunate. In Cayce's view, service is not a nicety in life, and not an onerous duty. It is the hallmark of reality, the way of the soul which seeks to live in its birthright, not merely to drag through its days. The universe is so constructed that service is the chief end of man while on earth—bringing out in others, however one can, something of their best potential to glorify God. If this is done properly, under the guidance of constant attunement before each new step (and Cayce insisted on this), one does not have to manufacture himself in ever-improved models. His next becomings will arrive right on schedule, whether these include the handling of wealth or of medicine, or ideas or of inventions, of family or of enemies, of beauty or of justice.

Finally, Cayce believed one can facilitate dream recall, even beyond study and planned programs of action, by deliberately repeating the type of response a dream initiates. A prayerful dream state can be carried forward by systematic prayers—and the readings sometimes dictated to his dreamers (including Cayce himself) little prayers or affirmations which could be reworded and often used in the day. If a dream initiates a more loving attitude towards one's wife, one can not only understand the need for such love and make some decisions about it, but one can carry forth the action by daily walks with his wife. Not just being busy, but a celebrating, stretching, growing into the full force of the dream, are further steps in adding consciousness to the dreams.

Each of these steps builds recall of dreams. They also build the depth and clarity of the dreams, for they serve to build the dreamer himself.

The alternative to recalling and interpreting dreams, said Cayce, is not always pleasant. Individuals cannot expect to drift forever. If they do not puzzle out their identity, and the direction of their lives by the aid of their dreams (which he said every normal person should try to do), then they may be brought, by the relentless action of their own pent-up souls, into some crisis which requires that they come to terms with themselves. It may be a medical crisis. It may be the end of a marriage or of a job. It may be depression or withdrawal. There are laws of this firm-handed disciplining, which he called part of "karma," or the process of sowing and reaping the harvest of one's deeds and thoughts, whether in one life or many.

Question: What Happens to Dreams Not Recalled?

Cayce made it clear, however, that even his most determined dream students were not recalling all of their dreams, and should not expect to do so. Many dreams are only meant to advance the dreamer's total growth, without reaching consciousness—nocturnal workouts which the psyche gives itself from the larger perspective of the subconscious, or from the yet larger perspective of the soul and of the Universal Forces. Such dreams do their work and go on.

Other dreams make a partial impression on consciousness, and are only partly recalled. If the dreamer is working at remembering and using his dreams, he need not be concerned about these fragments, for some are mere worry dreams, limited to consciousness and the levels of the mind closest to it, without helpful answers generated from the subconscious. Still other fragments, relatively few, serve to mask noise or body rhythms, and allowed the dreamer to keep on sleeping, as other such fragments do the opposite—wake him up when he should get up, without mysterious content. Further, there are food dreams not easy to recall, because while sometimes vivid, they have no "heads, tails, or points"—meandering nightmares, unlike those stark nightmares that certainly make their point and awaken the dreamer with it. In general, Cayce told his dreamers, a dream not fully recalled will repeat, with variations which do not change the reference or intent.

Cayce did not stress the "censor" effect in dreams, so much emphasized by Freud. It was obviously in operation in not a few of the dreams he interpreted, especially in dreams early in the study of a dreamer, before the dreamer had accepted the unpleasant or socially unacceptable sides of himself. Cayce preferred to point out that the petulance or lust or high-handedness often ascribed to another in the dream was really within the dreamer and projected onto others. But he did note a form of censoring that often occurred: his dreamers tended to forget or omit unpleasant or revealing parts of dreams more often than other parts; they also tended to forget happy endings, when the effect of such endings was to add to their sense of responsibility.

In addition to the question of dreams not recalled, Cayce addressed himself to the question of dreams known to the dreamer more by their actions on his body and emotions than on his mind. When the dreamer cries or screams or shouts in sleep, or walks or flails, he should be concerned for his general health, as he should when dreams are constantly and wildly unreal and unpleasant. In such cases, Cayce pointed out, the other imaginative processes of the dreamer are also likely to be affected: fantasy, daydreaming, and even the normal imaging of food or drink or companionship. Such distortion results from a physiological disability of the nervous system's sensory network, or of the autonomic nervous system that controls bodily emotions, or of both. Also, he commented in a score of readings on such dreams, the endocrine gland function of the dreamer is almost always involved and needs attention through action on poisons in the body, on failures in circulation, and on osteopathic lesions.

Dreams of the sick or fevered or damaged body, Cayce said, are not worth trying to recall and interpret. But most others which make their way to consciousness, leaving a clear plot and cast and mood, are worth the time to interpret. In 1924, when dream interpretation was used only by physicians for psychiatric purposes or by occultists for divination, Cayce was insisting that dreams are a normal aid by which the personality and body regulate themselves and advance the dreamer's affairs. They should be given, he emphasized, a larger place in the activities of "the human family."

Question: Are There Dangers In Recalling And Using Dreams?

Edgar Cayce saw dangers in *not* recalling and using dreams. Failure to do so might force the psyche to get in touch with itself by crisis or illness.

But he also saw dangers in recalling and using dreams.

The basic danger lies in the mind's powerful energies. These forces are not likely to be unleashed in the novice dreamer, nor in the person who keeps the levels within himself interacting by such non-dream processes as healthy prayer, artistic creation, honest loving, and hard work and play.

But one who seeks through dreams to arouse and tame the vigorous energies of the subconscious, without at the same time leading a sane and balanced, well-rounded life, puts himself in jeopardy.

Over and over Cayce warned his dreamers to keep their reason strong as they explored the land of dreams. They must continue responsible daily decisions, not relying on him or on dreams overmuch; on this he was adamant. They must continue to acquire skills and knowledge, the business of consciousness, as fast as they opened up the subconscious. A man must apply himself continuously to his work and thought, and a woman to her loving and relationships, however they were invited by dreams to new unfoldings.

As the farther reaches of dream experience opened up for his dreamers with experiences of ESP and of beauty and holiness, he told them even greater "equilibrium" was required of them, an "even keel," avoiding extremes of all sorts—whether of diet or thought or even of dream study. Otherwise, the same forces which operated so helpfully at one time would become destructive to the dreamer at another.

Dreamers might not only lose their capacity for guidance and growth by dreams—always a real possibility through narcissism, escapism, fanaticism, hypochondria, or messianism—but quicken dynamic energies within themselves which would not easily go away, seriously distorting and disturbing them if ignored or improperly used. In a revealing phrase, Cayce warned one dreamer that his selfish misuse of dream experiences, once they had begun to develop some stature and momentum in his psyche, would let loose "those disinterested forces" that could be harmful to the dreamer. The reference was not to discarnate entities, but to forces natural to the dreamer's psyche—as powerful as they were natural.

Yet dreams in general tailor their content to what the dreamer can effectively handle. They are self-regulatory and self-correcting. If the dreamer pays too much attention to dreaming, the dreams themselves draw his interest to daily affairs. If he lets himself become fascinated with one aspect of dreams, such as dream incursions into the land of death, he will find himself made foolish in just such dream settings until the point becomes obvious to him. But there is also a limit to the self-regulating in dreams. If the dreamer upsets his body or the balance of his whole psyche, he upsets the regulator function of dreams, and they run incoherently. Or he may impair this regulatory function by strenuous suggestion to himself, before sleep and during semi-waking intervals in sleep.

Cayce was firm in warning against "forcing" dream experiences of any particular type. One should not run before walking, he told an enthusiast. One should trust his soul and his Maker to supply what he needed in the night, he told others. Working responsibly with dreams is not the same as forcing them to substitute for living.

In spite of the warnings which ran like bright threads through his dream counsel, one of Cayce's major dream subjects lost his balance in a period of mental illness which also contributed to the loss of his employment and his marriage. Another also lost his vocation and his family. Both lost their gifts and gave up using their dreams, which had made them millionaires and at times happy and productive people. Frances, too, had her troubles, as we have seen. But all were warned, as was the man who asked, "Will I be able to foretell my own death?", which he had seen enacted in a dream. The reading that day came in a tone of unusual elevation, which included promises of great service by the dreamer, if he were faithful, and warnings as well:

> Then bind up thine feet, my son; keep thine ways aright, knowing there is the advocate with the Father . . . and when thou art called into account of those deeds done in the body, blessed will be found those that had come under the directing of thine endeavors! Keep—keep—the faith, the promise in thine self . . . keep in thee the guiding light to many a soul seeking the way.

But then the reading added:

> Be not overcome by much knowledge. Be not overdone nor undone by that as may be given [in dreams]. . . . Not of thine own power may these [prophesying] forces be done—for flesh and blood may manifest a spiritual truth, but may not order a spirit in any direction! Aid and succor may come through flesh and blood (in dreams or otherwise), even to those

near the pit—yet there is fixed that impassable gulf. Rather he that makes his will one with the Father may be committed a special care through His direction. Keep that . . . and err not in well doing. Keep thine self close to Him . . . for the stumbling block always lies in self-aggrandizement of power and ability, stored up in one's own self, and in the misuse of self in relation one to another. Keep the faith, my son, keep the faith.

The counsel did not take effect. The dreamer, who had for nearly five years plumbed every potential of dreams and been told that his abilities could exceed those of Cayce, was soon alienated from his family and reduced to selling trinkets for a living.

Working with dreams, like all human activities which at times engage one's every level—like loving and fighting and holding power and rearing children and espousing truths and creating paintings—holds in it peril. The peril is there because the peril is in the human being. His unfathomed potential is always matched by the unfathomed freedom of his will. This is the Cayce picture of the danger in using dreams.

CHAPTER 8

HOW TO START INTERPRETING DREAMS

AS EDGAR CAYCE counseled more than sixty persons on their dreams, over a period of two decades, he uniformly encouraged them to interpret their own dreams.

However strange the dream materials, they were not, in his view, coming from an alien intelligence. Even when a dreamer's production drew on greater wisdom than his own—on discarnates or on the Universal Forces—the dreamer was still viewing only what he could understand and was already beginning to live out. This meant there was always an inkling in the dreamer about each dream content, a little nudge of meaning that he could locate if he were patient.

But Cayce was less quick to encourage people to interpret dreams for others. To be sure, he told dreamers they could do whatever he did—and part of what he did was interpret dreams for others. But he treated this skill as unusual, and only encouraged one of his major dreamers in it—a man who dreamed of himself interpreting dreams for others! His interpretations, Cayce said, were in some cases quite sound, and could be even better, if he took the time to work on them.

Interpreting dreams, as Cayce described the process, is not looking up a symbol in a handy dream book and applying it to a dream. One interprets a *dreamer*, not a dream. That is why Cayce went to such trouble in every dream reading to specify which part of the dreamer's psyche was called into play by the dream, and what this part of the psyche sought to accomplish. If one grasps the dreamer in the dream, one can take the first important step in interpretation: determining which of the two major functions of dreams is to the fore in a particular dream—(a) problem-solving and adaptation to external affairs, or (b) awakening and alerting the dreamer to some new potential within him.

For most people, there is only one dreamer they grasp with the requisite depth: themselves. Accordingly, the proper study in dream interpretation is first of all oneself, at every level. Conscious plans, goals, interests, stances, decisions—all such elements need to be inventoried. The subconscious, too, should be studied, with its veiled habits, fears, longings, dependencies, defenses. Two more realms within call for study—the body, with its cycles, needs, habits, stresses, all of which might be mirrored in dreams; the soul, always present to the dreamer, and putting its imprint on him as his body does—but with its ideals, its searching questions, its burdensome memories hidden from direct view. Beyond the dreamer, yet resonating with him for his study and growth, is the realm of the Universal, with its energies and patterns reached by his superconscious.

"Study self, study self," was Cayce's first counsel on training to interpret dreams. He told people to search out memories, to list their working ideals in columns (physical, mental, spiritual), to decide what they honored in others and to compare this with themselves, to check their self-perception against what others perceived in them. He sent dreamers looking for laws, for the way X would appear whenever Y was present under Z conditions.

He was not fostering narcissism as he encouraged dream interpretation, for in later years when he trained people in groups, he specifically set them the task of talking over each other's dreams and visions—and then writing up the group's sense of what they had discovered. Working with others also working on dreams stimulated the psyche towards both helpful dreaming and helpful interpretation.

In these same groups he developed further the emphasis he had given to daily meditation on an affirmation, and deep silence. There is, he said, a frame of mind in which dream interpretation comes quickly and rings true. Often one can reach it by puzzling out a dream as far as consciousness would go—then praying about it and putting it down; when one picks up the dream again, in a quiet frame of mind, surprising clarity may emerge.

Bible study also stills the mind to a "oneness" with itself where dream meanings are transparent. Further, comparing dream incidents with specific Bible passages can awaken in a dreamer a sense of the big symbols, the "Urim" of the human family which repeats in dreams and myth, art and legend, of all ages. One of Cayce's most common coaching devices was to assign a dreamer a particular Bible passage to study with his dream. But he was also free, though he did it less frequently, to compare dreams with the experiences of Confucius, Moses, the Buddha, and Socrates, whom he treated with evident respect.

Whether a dreamer should also study books of dream theory seemed to Cayce to depend on the dreamer. He never discouraged it, and sometimes strongly enjoined it—especially on one dreamer with a sharp, curious mind. One of the strangest events in the entire body of Cayce readings occurred when this dreamer sought counsel on specific passages which he was reading—and got the comments immediately, although Cayce awake had never read the books. The experience may have somehow conveyed the thought of the books to the sleeping Cayce, for afterwards he occasionally illustrated points to other dreamers by referring to ideas from the same books—which he still had not read.

As when Cayce pulled from nowhere the names of medical specialists for physical readings, he also tapped, though less frequently—fields of scholarship. Explaining heredity and environment to one dreamer, he cited a study of scores of cases compared in hereditary chains, and encouraged the dreamer to read the book.

In all these ways, one can begin to train himself for the task of interpreting his own dreams.

But there was, of course, the question of interpreting dreams of a sick mind— which in Cayce's view always operated in a sick body. For these dreamers Cayce did not hesitate to recommend professional aid. He made it clear that professional aid had its limits, as when he told one dreamer that he was fixated on the idea of his own Oedipus complex, under the suggestion of his doctor. But he called for professional assistance to other dreamers promptly, in more than a dozen readings.

Question: Why Are Dreams So Confusing?

Edgar Cayce once dreamed that a watermelon was eating a pig. When he secured a reading on the dream, he was told that the ridiculous sight, just backwards from real life, was reflected the ridiculous way he was currently behaving. A plot that seemed meaningless made excellent satirical sense, once its purpose was established. In general, this is to be expected of dream material. All speech and thought, as Cayce described it, carries subtle nuances of association. A stranger will faintly resemble someone else. A predicament will be like one remembered, or one feared. A flag will carry a whole chain of half-recognized thoughts about one's country. In waking life these little associations are kept to the rear, so that communication occurs without distraction. In dreams, the associations come to the center of the stage.

Cayce told a broker that he dreamed of an old college friend because the friend was "bright" and studious—exactly the qualities the dreamer now had and needed in his work, studying a new phase of the market. He told a pregnant woman that she dreamed of a college girlfriend because of the girl's snobbish pride, representing her own airs about her forthcoming baby.

In waking life facts have association. In dreams, associations dictate the facts. Given this way of functioning, dreams are not so confusing after all.

Dreams originating with the subconscious, as it responds to the daily concerns of the dreamer, work up their plots and characters to present two things at the same time. They restate for the dreamer some conscious concern or interest of his, some decision or plan he is trying to make "deductively," based on all that he knows. At the same time they show him how that situation looks "inductively" when examined for the facts by the ESP of the subconscious. Given this complicated double task, it is surprising that dreams are not more confusing than they are. But sometimes even Cayce said of a dream episode, "Better let it go; it will come again" in a more intelligible version.

A dream of a talking spider taking over a man's house would seem absurd. Absurd, that is, unless one knew what Cayce saw instantly and the man's wife did not know, nor had the dreamer admitted to himself, that an extramarital relationship which had started on a small scale was moving to break up his home. Like a spider, it was spinning webs which were growing stronger and stronger. And the undermining comments of the paramour were doing deadly work, like the spider that talked. The only solution, Cayce told the dreamer, was the one in the dream: to cut the whole business out of his life, surgically and quickly. The dream went as follows:

> I was standing in the back yard of my home—had my coat on. I felt something inside the cloth on the cuff of my left hand coat sleeve. I worked it out, but it was fastened in the cloth and broke off as it came out, leaving part in. It proved to be a cocoon and where it broke a small black spider came out. The cocoon was black and left a great number of eggs—small ones—on my coat sleeve, which I began to break and pull off. The spider grew fast and ran away, speaking plain English as it ran, but that I do not remember, except that it was saying something about its mother.

> The next time I saw it, it was large black spider which I seemed to know was the same one grown up, almost as large as my fist—had a red spot on it, otherwise was a deep black. At this time it had gotten into my house and built a web all the way across the back, inside the house, and was comfortably watching me. I took a broom, knocked it down and out of the house, thinking I'd killed it, but it did more talking at that time. I remember putting my foot on it, and thought it was dead.

> The next time I saw it, it had built a long web from the ground on the outside of the house in the back yard, near where I first got it out of my sleeve—and it was running up toward the eave fast when it saw me. I couldn't reach it but threw my straw hat in front of it and cut the web, and the spider fell to the ground, talking again, and that time I hacked it to pieces with my knife.

Cayce ended his reading on this dream by warning that aspects of the relationship "have grown to such extent as may present a menace to the very heart and soul . . . Beware! Beware!" His counsel was ineffective. The dreamer got the reading and left home, never to return.

Such a dream is confusing if one tries to interpret the dream alone. It is not confusing if one knows and interprets the dreamer, whose situation must be symbolized by something insidious, complacent, talkative, and repugnant.

A very different situation called forth another spider dream, this time from Cayce himself. He saw a drunk kicked into oblivion, who turned into a menacing spider. When he sought a reading on the dream, he was told it was one of a series on how to handle the criticism he was experiencing from people who considered his readings the work of the devil. Cayce's impulse was to strike back just as heartily as the dream depicted. But the consequence of retaliation is always to increase opposition, making it more deadly, as the dream depicted with the irresponsible drunk turning into a bearer of venom.

Yet Cayce recognized that the interpretration of dreams is no simple matter, precisely because people are not simple. As he talked about dreams in hundreds of readings, he pointed to four kinds of dream imagery: nonsense, literal, symbolic and visionary.

Question: How Do Dream Images Differ?

Nonsensical or meaningless imagery—like that which accompanies a fever— occurs when the body is reacting to its own stresses, rather than using images for self-regulation and self-enhancement. Cayce saw such material as produced chemically, from the blood stream, whether from alcohol produced by too many sweets, or the endocrine secretions that might produce a sex dream to accompany an ejaculation in the night. Such imagery was rarely interspersed with meaningful imagery in the same dream, but appeared in dreams or fragments of its own. When an erotic dreamer reported a fragment where a girl's hair brushed pleasantly against his face, Cayce said it was "just physical" and needed neither interpretation nor anxiety from the dreamer. However, when the same dreamer reported a complete dream which included girls singing naughty songs in his ear, Cayce analyzed this segment as important—showing how little thoughts of erotic fantasy catch the ear of the subconscious and build tendencies difficult to control.

Second in Cayce's explanation of dream imagery is a category more common in dreams than the nonsense imagery: literal imagery. As Cayce saw the function of dreams in normal people not under great stress, much of their dreaming serves the same ends as their conscious thought: solving problems of outward circumstances. If the dreamer's business is tending machines, he will dream about handling those machines. If his job requires him to hire salesmen, he will dream about qualifications of salesmen. If a woman is concerned about her baby's walking, she will dream of how to get him to walk. If she feels overshadowed by her husband's airs of self-importance, she will dream about his airs. If she worries about helping him in his business, she may dream of offering a lovely dinner party for his associates, or about going on the board of his firm—whatever is appropriate for her.

Yet literal imagery rarely stands alone. Among Cayce's dreamers, an accurate picture of the death of a friend's mother was also accompanied by symbolic material, suggesting how to view death and how to be helpful to the friend when death came. A precise literal picture of tomorrow morning's quotations on a given stock was often accompanied with a scene such as a rising elevator, to suggest the coming climb but the danger of getting too far off the ground in that stock. The literal and the dramatic are woven together, as Cayce interpreted dreams.

How, then, may the literal be identified in the midst of fantasy elements? Again, by interpreting the dreamer, not the dream alone. One must know the dreamer's conscious thoughts and enterprises to pick out literal dream contents mirroring his conscious concerns. Someone worried about a sick relative ought to consider a dream of that sick relative for literal elements. But someone provided by a dream with an imaginary sick relative or with a relative's illness from an exotic ailment, has less cause to look for literal health guidance. A man investing in stocks may expect literal dream comments on stock movements, but one who makes his money trading horses should expect literal dream material on horses, not stocks.

Despite the surprisingly large place Cayce gave to literal pieces within dreams, a place far in excess of that assigned by any psychologist or analyst in the century which rediscovered dreams, he still saw *most* dream content as symbolic, or "emblematic." In this respect he came nearer to the experts of laboratory and couch.

As Cayce saw dreams, their chief imagery is like figures of speech, pictured and acted out. Feet and shoes often have to do with one's footing, or foundation, in what he is attempting. Dreams of mouth and teeth often have to do with that annoying function of the mouth—speech. A dream of a headless man was, in one case, a blunt warning from the dreamer's subconscious not to lose his head in worries at his job.

But dreams are made less of conventional figures of speech than of personal figures—in the way that a commonplace tune will be forgotten by one man but will for another quicken the pulse with memory of a loved one and "our song." Every dreamer, in Cayce's view, has his own repertoire of personal symbols or emblems, loaded with shades of meaning displayed in dreams. Men who are more than a little fascinated with women found their temptations and their talents dramatized as women. Dreamers delighted and mystified by radio, in its early days, found in broadcasting imagery for both their messianic tendencies and their attunement to the unseen divine. A man interested in Warner Brother's stock at the advent of sound movies found that dream imagery of "Vitaphone" represented not only the excellent prospects of the stock, but also his need to rely on his inner voice for stock guidance—his own "vital phone."

Why do dreams employ emblematic material, instead of providing explicit guidance to the dreamer? Cayce reported that dreams are charged with accomplishing more than providing information and guidance. Over and over he insisted that dreams come to provide an "experience" to the dreamer. They are meant to make his heart pound, his knees quake, his spirit sing. They are "happenings" for the dreamer, not simply picture language. Seeing a stubborn bull, as Cayce himself did in a dream, occurred not only to tell him that he was bull-headed, but to help him feel for himself all the blind energy which made him shrink in the dream. Dreams are intended to *change* the dreamer somehow, not only to inform him. To accomplish both informing and transforming, dreams had to use emblems—materials which both signified and sizzled.

A dream of Cayce's where he saw the floor of a house cave in, disclosing a cemetery below, was not alone a message that he was building a current effort on a poor foundation; he was meant to feel the foundation as repugnant as a cemetery, and as dead and useless to him. A husband older than his wife who saw her swim a difficult lake to bring a prize to the other shore was not merely told to respect her, but helped to feel like cheering her, for the progress towards maturity that she was making. A spot on the shirt of a man dishonest in business was not only in the dream to recall his soiled behavior, but to reawaken in him his tarnished self-respect.

The fourth type of dream material, which Cayce often called "vision" or "visionary," is as strongly devoted to changing the dreamer as literal imagery is to informing him. Like emblems, this material contains both sense and punch, but the punch is to the fore, and radical. Cayce saw ordinary people as capable of dreams of great poetic power, however rarely, provided they are truly seeking to grow. Among those busy scenes that crowd the night will come a dream, from time to time, that seems to step from the pages of mythology or of scripture.

Such a dream was one of his own. It came two years after the loss of his hospital and university, when he was still struggling to discover the meaning of his gift and how he would make his living. It was part of a series of dreams, stretching over several years, that led him to put his trust in his Maker, rather than in wealthy donors or in the splash created by his own clairvoyance. It also accurately represented his own inward sense of mission about his life, in the conflict of more than personal forces. Yet it drew him at the climax to an intensely personal affirmation which he could share with others in his work. Its richness of detail accurately expressed a psyche which had made him not only a competent photographer but a prize-winning artist in photography.

> I was on my way to a camp; had a strap over my shoulder with a little case which reminded me of a case for spyglasses, but I knew I had a message in it that I was to carry to whoever was the commander of the army where I was going.

The little box with a message was a symbol repeated in his dreams, representing his sense that he had something important to convey to people in the strange and awkward labor of speaking in trance. His dream continued:

> It was rough climbing over the mountain.

This symbol, too, often appeared, and his readings called it the sense of his life journey, climbing upwards to better attunement with his Master.

> I came down to the camp very early in the morning; it was just getting light. As I came down into the little ravine, I knew there was a stream of water not wider than a person could step over.

The symbol of fresh water repeated itself in his dreams, and he came to see it readily as what his readings called it—"the living water" of spirituality that must be offered to people by helping them where they needed it, as best he could.

> I saw a host of men dressed in white: white shoes, trousers, coat and helmet. They each had two straps over their shoulders, one a large canteen-looking container.

Beings clothed in white symbolized for Cayce, as for others, those who were pure in service of the divine. The image had even appeared to him in waking visions, several times in his life.

> And they were in groups of four, where they had a fire with a little skillet

of some kind over the fire. They made the fire from something they poured out of the canteen; it looked like sawdust, but it was red, green and brown, and might have been ground cork or sawdust. Out of the other can they poured something onto the pan, and when they stirred it together it looked like an omelette, or just something good to eat, but I didn't know what it was. I saw no arms, guns, swords, or anything of the kind, yet I knew it was an army.

The image of a warrior for the Lord was also one so strong for Cayce that it appeared to him at least once in a waking vision.

I didn't know anyone, but all up and down the ravine I could see the people preparing their breakfast in groups of four. And I asked them where the man in charge was. His tent was farther up or down the ravine. I could see a great white tent in the distance.

It was not the only time he dreamed of being led to the unseen person in charge.

One here and there joined in showing me the way to go. After a while I came to a place where, over to the right, there was another little ravine that turned off to the right. And as we got just opposite this (myself, and those that had come following me), we heard from out in the darkness someone walking on the sticks. We could hear the sticks break, and we stopped to listen.

There appeared a host of people dressed in dark; not dark skin, but their clothing was dark, not black but dark gray, browns, and the like. All their wrappings were dark.

It was typical of Cayce that he saw "the legions of darkness" not as black, but only darkly clad. Awake or asleep, conscious or in trance, he struggled with people whom he felt were wrong or misguided, but they were not for him monsters—only in the dark. His was not a black and white, paranoid cosmos, however genuine its divisions.

Then an angel of light stood between us, so that we could not see the crowd or group of dark people.

The angel symbol was as familiar to Cayce as his well-read Bible. Yet there was nothing trite for him about the concept, both because of a few intense visions he had experienced in his lifetime, and because of the awe that touched even his readings those few times when the subject of angels came to the fore.

Then there appeared the angel of darkness. The angels' figures were very much larger than ours as men—taller, heavier: of course, their countenance was very much brighter. When the angel of darkness appeared, he was dark like the people he was leading, but very much larger. His wings

were something like bat wings, yet I knew that they were neither feathers
nor just flesh, but the means of going fast wherever desired.

The imagination of an artistic photographer was clearly engaged. Cayce was
having an experience, not just contemplating an idea in his dream.

The wings appeared to be from the loins to the shoulders, rather than
just something growing out of the body—both in the angel of darkness
and the angel of light. The angel of light had wings something like doves'
wings, but extending from the loins to the shoulders, leaving his arms
and legs free.

Now the action began.

The angel of darkness insisted that he (the angel of light) should not
stand in the way, but demanded that there be a fight between someone
he would choose and one that the angel of darkness would choose. Then
there was between the two hosts a place cleared away, something like an
arena, and I was chosen as the one to fight with the hosts from darkness.
And we were wrestling.

I felt that I hadn't delivered my message and I didn't know just what I
would do about it—that I had waited so long and I hadn't told them what
I had come for, and I wondered why they had chosen me.

Cayce's poignant anxieties about his life, his gift, his message, showed here.
He could not guess that in less than two years he would be momentarily jailed
in Detroit for practicing medicine without a license. At the moment his waking
anxieties were more on money matters—even just getting enough for him and
his family to eat, as some of his dreams had shown.

I could still feel the strap and little package. I only had the one package,
and wondered why I hadn't been hungry, as the others seemed to have
to eat, but I only had the message to carry.

Then I began to wonder if my strength was to fail me—if the imp or
child of darkness was to put me down in the dirt. It would be an awful
thing.

Part of Cayce's experience under stress, as his dreams clearly showed, was
not only a tendency to depression, but a tendency to want to respond to the
attractive women who often surrounded him. It was a tendency he fought with
a lively sense of its reality and its potential danger, to both his family and his
work or "message."

But I knew if I could remember one word to say that he couldn't; and I
tried and tried to think and couldn't find it. I couldn't remember what

had been written in the message that I was to take.

Finally, as if just from out of the center of me, there came the words which I spoke aloud: "And Lo, I am with you always, even unto the end of the world!" As I said that, everyone of the darkness fell back, and there was a great shout that went up and down the ravine from the people in white. And as they fell back, the leader or angel of darkness (as the one that I was wrestling with fell away) reached out his left hand and struck me on my left hip.

That woke me; and I had an awful pain in my hip.

The closing flourish of his dream bore unmistakable resemblance to the biblical dream of Jacob wrestling with the angel. It also disclosed Cayce as aware that he was not, nor would be, a man of perfect behavior and virtue, but one touched and pained by darkness just as others were—an accurate estimate in his other dreams.

But the heart of the vision was the Biblical quotation which came as from the center of his being, defining his work as more than a psychic novelty: a means of awakening people to the unfailing presence of God. Yet to say it, to "deliver his message," by his words and his life, Cayce had to be conscious of his central thought, right in the middle of his own distresses. If his message did not apply to him in his own uncertainty and financial straits, how was he to give it to others?

In this vision, the central thought had not been so different from that which had struck him while awake, when two years previously he had lost his hospital and felt like dying—as his readings told him. Then one day, he reported, "While in church, the words in the song book spoke to me and danced right before my eyes. The words 'My grace is sufficient for thee' seemed to be impressed upon me."

Few of Cayce's dreams and few dreams of those he counseled were as stark as his symbolic dream of the legions of light and darkness, with his own small but sturdy case carrying the right thought for him and for those few who followed him. Yet such dreams occurred, and Cayce gave them weight.

Were such dreams the expression of mental illness?

One had to interpret the dreamer, not just the dream. If Cayce's life were organized around religious motifs, and if he felt under keen distress in vocation, perhaps such symbols were fitting, and not sick. In his life at another time, when he was a successful oilman staying in the best hotels, these symbols might have had a different and more ominous quality. Then he might have heard from his readings the kind of rebuke that one of his dreamers heard, who reported a dream experience that went, "Buy or sell five hundred shares of General Motors. I am the Lord your God."

That the dreamer was not receiving divine guidance, said Cayce in his reading, was obvious from the fact that the instructions on whether to buy or sell were not clear. He warned the dreamer that such a dream pointed to lack of balance in both understanding and actions in the dreamer's life. The line between divine aid and mental illness might be a fine one, but it was there. It was in fact—in the words already quoted on a dreamer's ambition to impress others by predicting his own death—"an impassable gulf." Not every vast symbolic content was meant to hearten the dreamer; it could also appear as a stark caricature of the dreamer's own pretentiousness.

Given the uncertainty about interpretation of every kind of dream content, can one ever be sure of dream interpretation?

Question: Is It Possible To Be Sure of Dream Interpretation?

Cayce's first answer to this question was in keeping with his emphasis on the role of "experience" in dreams. If the function of many dreams is to move the dreamer forward in his total life and growth, then such movement is an important function of interpretation, as well. A poor interpretation which gets only part of the dream's sense, but sets the dreamer thinking about an important aspect of his life, is not such a poor interpretation after all. Cayce set more store on advancement than announcement.

But of course those who tried to interpret their dreams with help wanted reliable means for validating their interpretations. He offered three such means.

The first is comparison within one's dream records as such. More often than not, several dreams of a given night focus on the same question or problem of awakening. What is clear about one dream ought to shed helpful light on others of the same night. Certainly the successive episodes of the same dream, however illogically connected on the surface, ought to be examined for the same motifs, whether shown over and over again, or expanded upon in segments. And interpretations for one dream ought to be compared with past interpretations for similar dreams. Frequently Cayce used in his readings the phrase "as has been seen," to refer to previous dreams, and to invite the dreamer to interpret in the light of his whole body of recorded dreams, rather than shooting at one dream at a time.

Dream interpretations can and should be validated in part by comparison with earlier dream materials for changes. If a theme is often repeated, it is likely that the dreamer hasn't yet caught the point—or acted on it. But if a theme shows a progression in successive dreams—for example a tempering of sexual rapacity with respect for the lover—then the dreamer might conclude that he is both interpreting the dream material effectively and making progress on the forces within himself that produces the dreams.

Secondly, a dreamer may validate his interpretations by comparing them with his subjective impressions about the interpretations. A feeling of release from inner panic may signal a sound interpretation, however unpleasant the truth the dreamer must face. A sense of heightened alertness, being keyed up without undue fear, may indicate that one has correctly come upon a warning of something untoward in outward affairs, foreshadowed in the dream. Relative certitude of interpretation may follow upon seeing how a given theme repeats itself in a series of dreams—for psychological certitude comes of stable repetition, from sensing lawful processes, according to Cayce. And the forceful quickening of new resolution or feelings, new stances in life, may also signal that one has struck upon the essential message of a dream.

Cayce encouraged his dreamers to rely on "the still small voice within," once they had learned to distinguish this voice from the clamor of conscience or anxiety or rationalization. It was a voice they could use, whether for guidance in dream interpretation, or guidance in driving a car or a bargain or an argument.

Thirdly, Cayce offered his dreamers a more comprehensive test of the validity of their interpretations. He told them to look at the quality of their lives. If they were growing, if they were functioning effectively in their rounds of life, the chances were that they were understanding and working with, rather than against, the mainstream of dream contents.

The test of their lives might be as simple as how grumpy they were. But better than examining their own lives, to approve or disapprove themselves, was to examine the quality of their relationships. Cayce never wearied of stressing the absolute importance of "the fruits of the spirit" in determining the forward-moving quality of a life. Patience, kindness, helpfulness, forbearance—these are not marks of a weakly feminine character according to Cayce, but of one who has found himself and his Maker, and does not project his fears onto others. The dreamer whose close associates—his family and his relatives and his business associates—give him their approval day by day is a dreamer who has the best overall test, however general, of the validity of his work with his dreams. These are the people who populate most dreams, Cayce said, just because they are the ones to whom a dreamer's being and behavior are most clearly known.

Nor are practical daily life skills to be ignored, in this way of estimating the validity of dream interpretations. When working well with his dreams, a dreamer ought to play golf better, Cayce said about one dream. He ought to make better business decisions, ought to make better speeches, ought to make better money—all other circumstances being the same. A woman ought to find herself more alert to danger and illnesses for those in her charge. She ought to dress with better taste, entertain better, reason better about politics or religions, shop better, and supervise employees better—all matters in which he showed dreamers they were helped by their dreams.

And finally, as part of his third type of validation by the thrust and quality of a dreamer's life, he told his dreamers they could rely on the evaluations made by those who covenanted with them in a spiritual-search group, such as Cayce encouraged for all dreamers in his post-hospital days. Those who met with a dreamer to talk honestly and deeply, week after week, about the real fabrics of their lives, would not be easily nor totally fooled about him, especially if they prayed for one another daily, as they should. Dream interpretations could be tried out on them, for group members could interpret his life, not just his dream.

Question: How Can The Usefulness Of Dreams Be Improved?

Few of Cayce's claims to the dreamers he coached were better verified than his claim that their dreams would change as they worked on them.

The dreams changed in length. First came snatches. Then for a while came long, rambling dreams, as though the dreamer were walking over the grounds of his inner estate. Then the dreams developed sharper definition. Partly this happened because the dreamers could sense the important dreams to recall and submit to Cayce. But partly their very psyches seemed to set forth the desired dream content and experience in sharper form, in terse comments, in scenes which carried with them interpretive thoughts.

The dreams also contained more religious experience, as they unfolded over a period of years. Part of this change may have reflected Cayce's own orientation. Part of it may have come from the stress under which a dreamer was placed by discovering that he could dream of stocks, or of meeting the dead, or of past lives, or of sickness and cures. To do this in American culture was strange, whatever it might reputedly be in Tibet, and raised questions of life's ultimates, for the dreamer. But part of the change may have come from the dreamer's own clarity of mind, and the ability of his soul or his superconscious to get through to him, after he had dealt with the pressures of more immediate subconscious material.

The dreams showed a tendency to go over familiar themes at deeper and deeper levels. A man whose early sex dreams largely emphasized controls found the theme of sex recurring in a series of dreams many months later which emphasized compassion along with passion. Then, still later, there were dreams followed by one searching review of his entire sex life, where a voice explained at the end that the crowning of masculinity was the giving of seed to others, seed for their total growth; it was the Greek idea of the Logos Spermatikos developed in the dreams of a twentieth century businessman without a classical education (but one who had, said Cayce, been a Greek in a past life).

The dreams showed cycles which analysts have noted, by alternating periods of weeks or months where they built up the dreamer, with other periods during which they took him apart. It was as though the psyche systematically raised him to new plateaus of maturity, and then relentlessly ground on his impurities until time to move him again.

A striking feature of one man's dream record was the emergence of a voice which spoke to him in dreams, making the major point of a dream, commenting on dream scenes, or simply instructing or rebuking him. Others also had this phenomenon, but never as dramatically as he.

Cayce insisted that each person's way of dreaming is as individual as his fingerprint—or as the markings of the soul in its long journey through many lives.

Yet another form of change lay in the closeness of dreams to waking impressions. One who dreamed of talking with the dead on another plane began to sense their presence and thoughts at moments of quiet while awake. A man who dreamed of stock movements before they occurred also began to sense, in hectic trading on the floor of the exchange, what would happen next to particular stocks. A mother who dreamed of her baby's health needs began to know awake and with accuracy when he was ill and when just fitful. A young man who was shy and argumentative with strangers came not only to dream about how to relate to each one in turn, but to feel spontaneous promptings on how to approach people and to listen to them.

A noteworthy change in dreams that occurred over several years of study was the shift to concerns larger than the dreamer's own personal affairs. Political questions, religious trends, the needs of undeveloped nations, the conflict of modern values, the long journey of the soul, the control of disease epidemics— these matters began to come into dream focus. It was as though the dreamer were making his way through his own layers, down to the strata that he shared with others in his time. To be sure, Cayce said that the issues which emerged in this fashion were colored by the dreamer's interests developed in past lives. But he did not minimize the importance of transpersonal dreaming, once the dreamer had taken firm hold upon his own life. On the contrary, he gave such dreams vigorous attention, for they fitted into his own insistence that no life was fully lived which was not lived for others.

Finally, the dreams of those Cayce coached offered them new experiences over the years. Some of these experiences were radical. When one dreamer first met in dream a parent who had died, the dreamer was shaken for weeks. The effect was even greater when the dreamers had their rare but decisive experiences of meeting Christ in dreams. But even the experience of inspecting the exact thoughts and feelings of someone living left its mark upon them.

Other new experiences were less startling and more adventurous: glimpsing a scene from a past life; getting a drawing of an invention; surveying a dream seascape of radiant beauty; discovering that two had dreamed the same dream on the same night; dreaming the location and type of trunk in which treasure was buried; dreaming of a friend just before he arrived.

Typically the "new experience" dream signaled the addition of this type of dream to the permanent repertoire of the dreamer. From then on, he might dream in these terms at any time. In fact, he was likely to. For once the psyche has opened the door to a particular type of dreaming, it seems to program a series of such dreams, to train the dreamer in the new type of dreaming—provided that the dreamer wants to dream in this way. Choice seems to be at work in dream types. Cayce told a woman who screamed in fright when she saw her dead brother in a dream that she need not be afraid, such dreams would not recur if she did not want them—or secretly seek them for their novelty and thrill, in some corner of her mind.

If dreams change so markedly, over the periods of time in which they are studied and used, can they be deliberately cultivated?

Cayce's first answer to the question of cultivating clearer and more helpful dreams was always the same: use the dreams. One lover of photography who saw himself entering his darkroom and finding his safety light shattered on the floor was told flatly that his guiding inner light would go out if he did not use it more faithfully. Among Cayce's earnestly repeated warnings was, "To know and not to do is sin." A dreamer who saw ancient warriors girded for battle, but feasting indolently on fruit delicacies, was told that his own inaction on dream promptings was making him look just as ridiculous to his own higher self.

Yet neither blind activity nor compulsive dream study, Cayce said, will improve the quality of dreams. Every person who seeks to grow, whether in dreams or awake, must find and assess his own working ideals. Words are not enough. One can profess love of God but only mean to flatter Him, said Cayce in a reading where he challenged a dreamer to distinguish between the deep cry, "As the hart panteth after the water brooks, so panteth my soul after Thee, O God" from the prudent affirmation "I know that Thou art a righteous God, rewarding them that seek Thy face." All the difference between a great ideal and a shabby one can be found in those two Biblical quotations. The ideals that matter are located in the tough pinches of life—in power, in wealth, in fame, in death, in sex; what did the dreamer really think and do about these things, and why? Was his ideal really his own, born of reflection and decision and more reflection? Or was it merely convention?

Once one clarifies his own deepest ideal, however hard to word and to picture, he must begin lining up his psyche in harmony with it, or his dreams will show him in constant conflict with himself. Part of lining up the psyche with its ideal, and ultimately with its Maker, is laying aside fear born of past mistakes. There is indeed a healthy fear that a soul should have, said Cayce, if it turns its back repeatedly on the best it knows. But morbid dwelling on past mistakes and excesses has no place in a program of improving dreams. Cayce was firm about this, resisting self-condemnation whenever he saw it, and insisting that guilt be replaced with present action. In one of his more startling sayings, he told a dreamer with unpleasant memories of sexual indulgence at the expense of the women in his life that "no condition is ever lost." Whatever the failing, even the cruelty, if the dreamer puts his life squarely in the hands of the best he knows, he will find his bitter fruits being turned, over the years, to the wine of under-standing for others. What has been one's "stumbling-block," he often said, can be made his very "stepping-stone" towards love and aid to others, because of deep sensitizing action—provided that the psyche is oriented to allow this trans-mutation to occur.

Cayce taught his dreamers other broad procedures. They were to work out their own philosophy of life, so that their whole minds might operate with conviction, right down through the subconscious to the soul. They were to carry forward the sense of dream symbols in the symbols they used in waking life—from the decor of an office to the symbolic "life seals" they might fashion for their walls as a kind of soul crest. They were to study new types of dreaming, soak in big symbols from ancient cultures, pray for guidance on particular dream contents, record their waking impressions on the same day they dreamed a certain theme. He also taught them knacks of interpretation by precept and by example. One should, as he did, seek first the overall thrust of a dream. Did it end happily or unpeasantly? What was the overall attitude or mood which it brought forth in the dreamer, and why might this be appropriate? A dreamer saw a Jewish friend forcing his wife to sing Christian hymns. Cayce told him that he should have little trouble seeing, in this dream, his own tendencies to force convictions on family members.

What choice did the dream present, if any? A man saw himself in a dream planning to shoot off fireworks to entertain the girls at the beach, but the fireworks were taken and set off by another, who won the applause of the onlookers, while the dreamer was disconsolate. Yet as the dreamer watched the fireworks, his attention was caught by the beauty of the sparks that lasted against the sky and were mirrored in the ancient ocean. The choice, Cayce said, was one which would occur often: to play for applause of his fellows, or to keep his eye on the sparks of the eternal which he could trace in his fellows and in all of creation. A husband found himself in a dream following an attractive girl as she swayed her hips in a suggestive walk down the street; yet he also noticed that when she called a cab, she knew exactly where she was going, and resisted advances made to her. Which way of relating to others was the dreamer going to follow, Cayce asked? A path of seduction, or a path of knowing his purposes so well that others were attracted rather than distracted?

Not all dream references need be complicated. Cayce himself dreamed of Solomon and was promptly told in a reading to seek Solomon's wisdom, but without his fondness for women. A woman who dreamed of herself on a ship in a fog was told that she was truly "all at sea" in her life. A businessman seeing two figures in a dream, one stout and one lean, was told he had dreamed a cartoon of two attitudes toward a situation in his work: fat optimism and lean pessimism.

But the note which recurred like a silver thread in Cayce's seven hundred dream readings, whenever he explained to others how to improve their dreaming and interpretation of dreams, was a familiar one in every type of Cayce reading— medical, life, business, topical. That note was service.

For some dreamers, service through dreaming meant literally dreaming for others and giving them aid and counsel. But such dreamers were few among those who consulted Cayce. Others were encouraged to draw or to write stories based on their dreams. Or to share stock tips secured from their dreams. Or to learn from their dreams the laws of human development, and teach these laws to classes of interested adults. Or to teach others to dream. Or to pray for those presented to them in their dreams. Each one's gifts were different.

Whatever the gift, Cayce said, there is a law about its development which applies alike to all gifts. Its first application must be to those closest to the dreamer. If one can't be loving to his wife, no dream can help him quicken love in others. If one cannot teach his children the fundamentals of living, there is no point in his preaching them further. If one cannot guide a partner in a business choice, through dreams, one cannot expect to guide the government. It is the way of growth. First the dreamer must change and grow. Then he must find a way to share his growth in unassuming service to those closest to him in everyday life. Only then may he find dreams that can occasionally help the leaders in his profession, or his social class, or his school of art, or his reform movement—by helping him to help them.

It is a law underscored by the failure of the early dreamers that Cayce trained to sustain the high potential which he saw for them, and which they realized at times in both their dreams and their lives. They fell away from one another in their families. This was a blow the straining psyche could not survive, said Cayce, while it was reaching for the heights of dreaming. With his next dreamers he put his first emphasis not on dreaming skill at all, but on loving and producing. There was loving and producing in the daily work, there was loving and producing in the gathered fellowship of those who met to study and pray. Only this course— the course of giving, giving, giving—would keep the flow of dreams clean and ever stronger.

His judgment proved sound. Under this kind of coaching, housewives became authors—and stayed good wives. A sea captain became an administrator of a research society—and stayed a good sea captain. A scoutmaster became a trainer in group dynamics—and kept his humor. A schoolteacher became a prayer leader—and a better teacher. A stenographer became a curator of ESP records—and learned to manage other stenographers. A mother became a psychic—and stayed a good mother. Each of these people worked with their dreams, and worked hard on them, for years. None of them tore the fabric of their lives.

If Cayce's dreamers were to grow in dreaming, they had to grow together.

PART III
ESP in Dreams

CHAPTER 9

DREAMS OF THE FUTURE AND THE UNKNOWN PRESENT

THE CENTURY OF the rediscovery of dreams has also been the century of scientific investigation of psychic phenomena.

Two kinds of investigation have filled library shelves with books and journals on telepathy, clairvoyance, mediumship, psychokinesis, survival of death, dowsing, drug-induced visions, and animal homing. One type has been the collecting of spontaneous experiences—the work of naturalists of the mind. The other type has been the establishment of lawful variations in the phenomena—the work of laboratory researchers. Both types have produced staggering amounts of data.

Yet psychic experience cannot be called a fact of science. The first and most important reason is lack of an adequate theory. Until it can be shown exactly how psychic phenomena work, how they start and vary and stop, the findings remain suggestive data. Theory is also needed to tie psychic happenings with better-known phenomena of the mind—with memory, emotion, perception, and learning.

A second reason for the dubious modern status of psychic phenomena is that they are often associated with a philosophy of dualism—of two basic substances called "matter" and "mind"—which is a philosophy uncongenial with modern scientific thought.

A third reason for their dubious status is the fact that they have not yet been sufficiently tamed to put them to practical use. Science can handle strange processes, provided it can show results—as the history of psychoanalysis shows.

But the cool reception accorded to psychic phenomena in modern times has not banished the report of them. Edgar Cayce was largely snubbed by scientists in his time, yet he went on giving his readings—whatever they were. And his readings kept insisting that psychic phenomena were lawful natural processes which could be studied, duplicated, and applied. Especially in dreams.

Dreaming of the Future

By the late 1920's, no dream of the future might have been more valued by an investor than advance aid on the great stock crash of October 1929, which initiated the Depression and wiped out fortunes. Since Cayce's major dreamers were at work during the years preceding this stock collapse, they had a firsthand opportunity to use dreams to protect themselves.

The first hint of the 1929 crash came in late 1927, when one of the dreamers reported to Cayce a type of dream that had now become familiar to him: a voice or "interviewer" from his own subconsious and superconscious talked with him.

> An interview in which I was told that something was taking place or would take place in Steel, that would lead to a two-year bear or liquidating market, in which U.S. Steel would go up only 5 points at the end of or during the course of 2 years.

While Cayce often called the counsel of the interviewer literal, he also reported that stock details could be symbolic—as in this dream. What the dreamer was seeing ahead for two years was his own chance to "liquidate" or make money on stock guidance from his "interviewer" or inner voice for that period. But with it went a warning, that if he did not use his ESP ability effectively for the coming two years, he would not have an opportunity to do so again until the "five-point" or "five-year" lapse had occurred. In other words, the dreamer had until 1929 to make extensive money on stocks through dreams, or he would find himself waiting until 1932 to again make significant gains.

A couple of weeks later, he dreamed further within this timetable of the future.

> Interviewer: "The conditions will last for one year and a half." My reply: "I don't find the conditions." Interviewer: "No, you don't see them now, but you will find them."

Interpreting the dream, Cayce urged the dreamer to think back to how he had been worrying about securing funds to establish the Cayce Hospital. The dream had followed with an answer to this concern. The substance of the assurance, Cayce said, was that for eighteeen months the dreamer would continue to be anxious about funds, and that at the end of that time (early in 1929), "great will be the inflow from many sources," for "in great numbers, great quantities, shall be the means to carry on." But Cayce was clear that the promise of much money did not extend beyond the period. As it turned out, the dreamer and Cayce were both correct. There were eighteen more months of hard work. Then, early in 1929, the money began to pour in. The dreamers were soon millionaires and Cayce had large stock accounts; the hospital was established that year and plans laid for the university. It was the time of greatest wealth in Cayce's career.

Then exactly a year before the crash, a dream about Montgomery Ward stock led the dreamer to ask about "the general slump" which he felt was coming.

Cayce confirmed that there would be a "general break" which would begin in rails, but that if the dreamer and his associates would continue to stick to their inner guidance, they would by then have "power and affluence."

In January of 1929, a dream of stock guidance from his dead father led one dreamer to ask, "Does this mean that we should sell out everything? What would be a good time to do it?" Cayce assured him that his father had only shown him the start of the break to come later that year. In the same night came a warning to the dreamer about messages he was seeking through a medium. The source was contrasted with the dreamer's father, whose dream messages he had learned to trust.

> I was sitting in school with my brother. The teacher was there. He asked us some questions. I answered a question and said, "I'm in partners with my brother on the Stock Exchange." My brother interrupted in irritable fashion, saying, "That's Pop." Then the teacher showed me a very ugly looking individual, rather ferocious-looking sort of person. All the others cleared away. The teacher gave me a glove turned inside out. Inside that glove was protection against the individual. We ran out into the hall trying to escape. It seemed to be a shrewd sort of individual—tried to misrepresent himself.

According to Cayce, the dreamer had correctly seen a lesson—as suggested by the school setting—that there were discarnates who would give questionable guidance through a medium, even though they might at times give factual guidance. He warned that the two brothers might be "led astray" by such "misrepresenting of the various phases of phenomena," and urged them seek protection or "covering" from "inside," represented by the glove—meaning inward attunement with the divine, not with discarnates alone.

It was mediumism which eventually led them into trouble in their stock activity, well after the stock crash of 1929. But there was no difficulty in their dreams.

In March of 1929, one of the brothers had a sharp dream.

> Got the impression regarding the market that we ought to sell everything, including the box stock. Dream concerning my wife and two business associates. A bull seemed to follow my red dress. I tried to catch the bull. Some special reference to Westinghouse and Wright Airplane.

The dreamer, said Cayce, was seeing a "parable" in which the bull represented bullish attitudes about the market among his associates, and their coming attempts, with his, to bolster the market. But, said Cayce, the reference to Westinghouse and Wright as stocks of one of the associates in the dream was a warning to the dreamer to protect the individual accounts in his keeping, just as he might protect his wife from peril. For there would soon be "turmoil as will come by these many changes, as will be seen in a downward movement of a long duration." He urged the dreamer to follow a course of "not allowing, then, those stocks that apparently even are *very* safe, too much latitude," and added that the dreamer's impression "that the body should dispose of all those held—even those in box—

would signify the great amount of change as would come."

In more than four years, the dreamer had never received such a dream warning.

In a follow-up reading given the same day, Cayce added that the red of the dress in the dream had indicated the danger in the bull market, and commented that "here is an expected long decline." However, he explained, there would not be "a real bear market" immediately, because "there has been in recent months a much greater tendency for larger combines than there has probably *ever* been before." These would slow the decline. There would also be a major division in financial circles, and—

> That fight has hardly begun. When this is an issue we may expect a considerable break and bear market, see? This [fiscal] issue being between those [who believe in using] the reserves of nations versus of individuals. And it will cause—unless another of the more stable banking conditions come to the relief—a great disturbance in financial circles.

Cayce was digging out the features of the forthcoming financial collapse, pointing to a decisive battle coming between the representatives of two different monetary policies: those who felt that government agencies should intervene, and those who felt that private financial enterprise could save the day.

In late March, Cayce commented on dream material about Macy's, that Macy's and certain other stocks would reach some peaks, but that there was to be "a long downward movement," given momentum by the proposed government "investigation of banking, Federal, and market speculations." He also urged the two dreaming brothers to dispose of an extra Stock Exchange seat which they held, for "these are near the peak for many days to come."

Just a few weeks later came a strange dream which led Cayce to extended comments on the stock market. The dreamer reported that he had fallen asleep after reading the Book of Ezekiel and "seeking aid from the divine." In the dream he was being blamed for a murder he had not committed; he was in seemingly desperate circumstances, yet he was not too frightened—a fairly accurate picture of how the coming crash would strike him before long. He noted especially the use of hypodermic injections in the dream. Cayce called these precognitive emblems of injections by financiers who would try to bolster the market. He went on:

> Materially, these are divided between those that would hold the Federal Reserve Board as the criterion for activity, and those who would use the moneys in the various centers for activity as related to the market. As individuals, these are members not so much of the Board—for the Federal Reserve Board is itself divided upon the issue: individuals who have had an ideal as to the functioning of the Board being on the one side, and those that would use the abilities of the Board on the other. And those are fostered—each side—by money powers. But, were these to be allowed to run without check in either direction, there must surely come a break where it would be panic in the money centers—not only of Wall Street's activity, but a closing of the Boards in many centers, and a readjustment

of the actual species and moneys in these centers.

Cayce and the dreamer were seeing, with prophetic accuracy, the details of the deadly struggle shown in the dream. They were viewing the coming loss of the gold standard, the closing of stock exchanges, and the actual panic that followed in October and November.

In July of 1929, one of the dreamers reported:

> Voice: "Hold only that which you are able to pay for outright." Saw Fleischman, 82, 83, 82. Big bank failure which precipitated a good deal of trouble on the market. Saw Western Union at 160. . . .

Cayce assured him that he was getting correct promptings to arm him for coming troubles on the market, including the accurate preview of a bank failure. But if the dreamer could keep listening to his inner voice without fear—and Cayce stressed the importance of acting without fear but in "simplicity of faith"—then he could get all the guidance he needed.

These dreamers and their close associates went safely through the crash on October 29. A few days later Cayce encouraged the chief dreamers of the group to take a vacation. They would, he said, continue to receive definite guidance "in no uncertain manner" on how to act on every major stock decision.

> Let not the minds be troubled. Let not the bodies become overwearied.
> Let not the mental become unbalanced by the clamor or the unsettledness
> as is arising at this time.

He urged them to take the next few days off, "that they may be able to get within themselves that stillness of purpose as comes from the constant prayer, with those that would aid or guide at this time." Then when they returned to the Stock Exchange, they would find help again, for "those that seek counsel at the Board, at His feet."

The dreamers weathered without severe loss the most trying financial storms of modern times. Their dreams kept them posted on each important stock movement in advance. As Cayce had told one of them five years previously, in first urging him to record his dreams, he was going to be able to see business conditions around him "before the manifestations begin."

Dreams of One's Personal Future

In Cayce's view, it was not only business details which would present themselves in advance to the dreamer. He had told Frances at the start of her dream recording: "any condition ever becoming reality is first dreamed." He meant, of course, major developments that were the outgrowth of the direction and habits of a life—or lifetimes.

He told her this when she was a bride of scarcely a week, dreaming of a weak-minded boy or child. He urged her not to dwell on such thoughts and fears—but the dream was reality for her twenty-five years later, when her only son became a mental case.

Frances also dreamed, early in her marriage, of the breakup that would one day come to her home. But she was not the only one who dreamed of it. On the morning he was to be married, her new husband recorded several dreams. One, which included a voice that warned him to pay close attention, showed him selecting six black veils for his face, at a store. The voice told him that the veils were obstructions to his better understanding and advancement. Cayce confirmed this, indicating that the dreamer was seeing six major ways in which he was going to have to change—either laying aside something or covering something with aid greater than his own—now that he was marrying (and incidentally marrying at a younger age than Cayce had advised him to do, although he was already thirty). On the same night he dreamed that he was back in New York with his bride, who was very serious and asking to be given a chance to adjust to Cayce and her husband's studies of the psychic field. Cayce warned the new husband against overseriousness toward his young bride—a seriousness which later dreams depicted as dogmatism.

A week later the new husband dreamed he and his wife were viewing a beautiful mountain-side, when she suddenly went off to see the other side and left him with a little notebook, where she had written, "this is good-bye." The dreamer was panic-stricken.

Again, Cayce told him he was seeing the peril in his *own* rushing ahead of his wife—giving her more than she would digest, and hurrying on to see the other side of the mountain of his interests. (Later personal involvements ended the marriage.) But there was more to the warning, for the notebook had been a stock-trader's notebook, and Cayce warned both dreamer and wife about their coming temptations to put money, position, and expensive possessions ahead of the real Kingdom of God that they must seek and share.

Marital relations were the subject of the dream of another young husband who divorced his wife some years later:

> Saw my father-in-law and myself walking in the court of Park Avenue apartment. Seemed to emphasize the fact that my father-in-law and I were there without our wives. We seemed completely alone, and the actions of mother-in-law and my wife seemed to be equally felt.

As Cayce looked at this dream, he told the dreamer he was short on seeing things from the point of view of his wife and his mother-in-law—qualities that later became critical when the mother-in-law came to live with them.

A man rebuked by relatives for his use of Cayce dreamed that his uncles warned him against a deadly poisonous scorpion. But then the dreamer and a helper drained some fluid from the scorpion that cured the disease of one uncle; everyone rejoiced. This dream, said Cayce, was showing the dreamer a time yet to come when the uncle would need Cayce's aid for a serious ailment, and get it—as he did.

A businessman dreamed of a woman who had been his bitter enemy for years. He was sitting near her in a theater, with tickets that cost more than thirteen dollars, and they were the best of friends. Cayce indicated that the friendship had been broken in the first place because of the actions of a busybody, and that in the thirteenth year of their alienation they would have a chance to reconcile, which the dreamer should take.

Dreams of one's personal future were also about the health and welfare of the dreamer or someone important to him.

Cayce's wife, who often dreamed of the future, and whose dreams were more poetic than most, reported a dream about a relative, which she submitted for a reading by her husband.

> I was at her house, with another relative showing me through the house. Especially noticing the white curtains at all the windows, then the going through underground passage—

Here the sleeping Cayce interrupted to say, "Someone to be buried here, you see, soon." She continued: "Of water coming in and me trying to—" He interrupted again to comment that water was, as he had often said in readings, the element from which all life had sprung, and that therefore death was the liberating of the person to the next plane, with the body returning to the first element from which it had come—seen in the flowing of the water. Mrs. Cayce went on: "Of me trying to help get the children to—" And Cayce again interrupted to indicate that the soul was returning to the state of a child, making a fresh beginning in its long journey, by dying. Then Mrs. Cayce finished: "Of seeing a tank of some explosive, and feeling afraid of same." He noted that she was dreaming of the woman's fear of death. But he reminded his wife that in the dream they had escaped the explosive; this depicted the correct attitude toward the coming death: nothing for the woman to fear, for "it is the Beginning." The woman died three weeks later. She died without the burden of needless anxiety from her close relative, Gertrude Cayce.

Not all of the glimpses into the future by Cayce's dreamers were so solemn. A father-to-be dreamed momentarily while he was praying, and he slipped into a dissociated state. A voice said to him, "Twenty-seventh to ninth." Although it was February, Cayce told him that the voice was giving him guidance on the concern about which he was praying—the welfare of his wife and coming child. The dates in question were March 27 to April 9, during which the baby would be born, safely and happily. Almost two months later, the baby was born right on dream schedule: April 4.

Not a few of the dreams of one's personal future were to be interpreted, according to Cayce, as dreams about one's talents—which for a man often appeared in a feminine form. A dreamer who had developed considerable psychic ability of his own, but was tempted to use it for purely personal advantage, as he was also tempted to use Cayce's readings, reported the following dream:

> Someone was paralyzed, by virtue of a stroke of apoplexy. It seemed to be my brother, yet, as I lifted the body to carry it to another place, it changed to a girl or woman—some friend of my mother's. I carried the body about, noticing how stiff the paralyzed side was—also that the head dropped peculiarly over my arm. I tried to readjust this as I engaged in conversation.

In Cayce's view, this dream was a serious warning, to which he devoted two readings. It was a warning to the dreamer that he could lose his own psychic ability, which would dismay him as much as paralysis of his brother or his mother's friend. It was also a warning that when readings were sought for personal gain through the sleeping Edgar Cayce, some of the selfish attitude seeped through and had physical consequences on Cayce's nervous system and circulation. There was no danger to Cayce, this reading explained, in dealing with stocks as part of training a dreamer to dream. But when someone sought stock counsel for dollars alone, under pressure to get ahead of others in the market, it was dangerous for Cayce.

The dream warning was only partly heeded, as later dream warnings showed. As a matter of record, the dreamer lost his own psychic ability within seven years. And Cayce, who two decades later pushed himself to give hundreds of readings to all needy seekers, after his biography was published, died after a stroke and paralysis, paralleling this warning dream.

Finally, there were dreams of one's personal future which only beckoned the dreamer to greater adventures. There were dreams of visitors coming, of an ocean voyage coming, of the coming reincarnation of a friend, of wealth coming, of public acclaim coming. When Cayce and his family were preparing to move from Dayton, Ohio, to Virginia Beach, Virginia, to carry out a long-standing directive from his readings, he was given a series of dreams that showed him the complete hospital which would someday be built there—and was. And he also had a dream about the family turmoil of moving.

> Regarding train with Gertrude as the engineer, running into a car, feathers
> flying, and turkeys in the tool box.

The reading assured him that all things were auspicious for the move; as in previous dreams where food was prominent—the solution to the family's larder problem was symbolized by the turkeys. And the "tools" for daily work would be found as well. Many of the family affairs would seem to be torn to pieces in the move, as was seen in the feathers flying. But Gertrude would provide the necessary driving force for the packing and traveling, and her husband should listen to her—provided she didn't try to "run right over him," as the dream had suggested she might.

Dreams of the Future in Work and Public Affairs

The dreams of the future in daily work submitted to Cayce ran into hundreds. Many were dreams of stock quotations, on scores of stocks and on the companies and industries they represented. Every aspect of a stock-broker's daily affairs turned up in the dreams—including his clerks, bookkeeping, phone calls, customers, competitors, models for success, legal procedures, law suits, leases, partners, and even the time of day for specific sales.

One of Cayce's dreamers was introduced to dreaming of the future at his work with the following scenario:

> Dreamed a man was trying to sell me a radio. Then someone put poison
> on the doorknob of my door and urged me to come and touch it. I was
> terribly frightened. He tried to force me to touch the poisoned knob.
> Struggling, I awakened in a cold sweat.

Cayce said the dream was precognitive. There would soon be offered to the
dreamer a deal in radio stocks or corporations, represented as "a wonderful
proposition." The poison was a graphic representation of the poisonous condition
that would follow if the dreamer took the deal. For sixteen to twenty days, Cayce
told him he should stay out of all stocks having to do with radio.

The prospects were more favorable, Cayce said, in the following dream of the
same broker:

> Heard L.M. talking in our apartment, but upon awakening found he
> hadn't even been in to see us. This was very clear and so real I actually
> thought it occurred even hours after awakening.

In Cayce's view the two business associates had experienced a meeting of minds
by telepathy, prior to a deal that would be presented to the dreamer by the other
man.

Still a different dream about business associates gave the same dreamer some
practical counsel.

> Saw a fire escape, which to me meant a way out, and seemed to refer to
> Pacific Gas and Electric stock we are now long on—own. Horace B. had
> given me an order to sell his stock, and I had that in mind. The fire
> escape seemed to be under a great strain, but was steady under the
> pressure. A man who was long of this Pacific Gas stock, and who is a
> member of the N.Y. Stock Exchange also, was jumping on the fire escape
> to test its strength. The fire escape withstood its test.

Cayce assured the dreamer that he was dreaming about that particular stock, and
that his dream was telling him to follow the leads of these men, for his own
sales. "That is, when the entity finds these various ones, members of Stock
Exchange, are long, be short with same, see?" Then Cayce added, as he often
did, that the stock in question would move to the dreamer's advantage one and
five-sixths points, very shortly.

The variety of business dreams of the future was striking. There was an accurate
preview of the failure of a brokerage firm. A dreamer saw a woman employee
leaving him, as she shortly did. One dream had the dreamer looking out over a
cemetery while still on a bus; it was, said Cayce, a dead stock rising—but
"Yellow Cab," not bus stock, which was going up the nine points indicated in
the dream.

Cayce himself had an anxiety dream about his own work, when he was out
of money, in which his wife hauled him up for trial as mentally incompetent.
In the dream he promptly gave life readings for everyone in the courtroom. The
reading which he gave on this dream pointed to a specific friend who had appeared

in the courtroom scene and indicated that this friend could foster the demand for life readings from Cayce—and thus provide him with the income he needed. It worked out as Cayce dreamed, for he got in touch with the friend, promptly.

But it was not only the work life of dreamers which crowded the stage at night, prompting previews of the future, usually under the management of the dreamer's subconscious. The dreamer could also be shown previews of social service and social action in which he was interested.

Cayce's dreamers were interested in the hospital and university they were trying to build, in order to study his work. Every major development of these institutions was previewed in their dreams. One of their practical problems was finding the right doctor to head the hospital staff; he had to be open to many schools of medicine, yet well-qualified. As it turned out, the one whom they first secured was soon unhappy, as a warning dream of Cayce's showed two years in advance.

> I thought that I went to New York to talk to the people up there about the institution, and they told me the doctor was already down here, so I came back. Several whom I knew well, and some other people whom I did not know all came with me, and we went down to this place where they said they had the institution. The doctor had Gertrude and my secretary in a great big pot of water boiling them, but it didn't seem to hurt them at all—they were just swimming around in the water without any clothes on. I tried to get them out and burnt my hand. When I woke up, I noticed a red streak or scratch on my hand.

The reading told Cayce that he would have to work with those in New York to achieve a clear understanding of the duties, abilities and supervision of the physician—or else they would all land in hot water. The scratch on his hand was something he had noted subliminally before falling asleep, and was the same kind of flaw in his body that the plans about the doctor were in his mind.

But not all the dreams of the future hospital were warning dreams. One of Cayce's dreamers saw it in dream a year and a half before it was built, complete with the recreation facilities and sterilizing equipment it eventually contained; he even got the name of one of its first patients.

But the same dreamer also saw in advance the nature of the breakup which one day came among the sponsors of the hospital. This dream occurred a year before the hospital opened.

> Was going over pictures of various things of Virginia Beach regarding the Hospital. Saw two trains; one was the champion, called the Pank-hurst—

Here Cayce corrected him, by reminding him that the *other* train in the dream had been called the Pankhurst. Then the dreamer continued: "Trains were running to Chicago and New York." Cayce interrupted again, with a note of urgency, and the rest of the dream was not read to him. The dream was on two levels, he said—a feature which he often noted in dreams. At one level it was a stock market dream, showing how rails would be the criterion of coming stock market action, preceding the big crash (which came a year later)—"the general *slump.*" He also referred to the national conflict of financial interests coming, in which one side would be the "champion" of truth, and the other a disturbing influence; and he pointed to the need for cooperation between large financial interests in Chicago and New York, as the dreamer had seen.

But then he added that the dream also dealt with another issue. There would come another crisis, when the "pictures" or views of how the hospital should be run would be laid out for everyone to examine. At that time the issue, too, would be whether individuals such as the dreamer would serve as the "champion" of truth and principle—or whether they would bring dissension by the severity of their demands that *others* live up to certain standards.

The hospital closed four years later in a climate of acrimony, where board members challenged each other's living up to principles, and challenged Cayce. Few questioned themselves, nor served as "champion of principle" alone—in the way the dream was urging. Small wonder that Cayce urged the dreamer to go over and over this dream, and recalled it to him in discussing later dreams!

Question: How Is The Future Symbolized In Dreams?

Cayce insisted that to the subconscious, which has the faculty of envisioning the future, time values are not as real as they are to the conscious mind. The subconscious sees things laid out endlessly, just as they are presently headed, until the dreamer uses his will to change them. There are, then, no special symbols set aside to signify the future, for the very idea of future is alien to the subconscious.

Still, Cayce said, there are ways of looking for the future in dreams. One can compare with dream material something about whose future he is consciously concerned—it should come up for comment in dreams.

Further, there are dynamic forces or "spirits" that one can find exemplified in dreams; these are the stuff of which the future was made. For example, the "spirit" of a corporation which wants its stock values high is one "spirit," while the "spirit" of investors who want at times to depress the stock for their own ends is another. Both of these forces need to be studied in dreams of future outcomes. Likewise, in one's personal affairs, there is the "spirit" of his own intentions, and the "spirit" of individuals and institutions with whom he is associated. A good marital or vocational decision ought to be enhanced by a glimpse of both kinds of "spirits" stretching into the future. Cayce used the term "spirit" in this sense to suggest the intent of such terms as "the spirit of '76" or "the Spirit of St. Louis" or "the spirit of a meeting"; he did not mean discarnates.

A different avenue to the future lies in glimpsing the past which has coded the problems of the future. One of Cayce's dreamers, a rebel, was one day going to land in a position where he would himself have to face holding authority. This would be true whether one were computing his future in terms of his having been a rebel in childhood, or a rebel in past lives.

Cayce himself had such a dream which warned him of his future. More than a year before his hospital opened, he saw a vivid scene of a priest being banished, in ancient Egypt. There were throngs gathered in the streets, some crying for the priest's banishment and some for his deliverance, while scourges drove him and his associates before them.

The reading he secured told Cayce he was seeing himself as the priest he had been in ancient Egypt, when marital infidelity had led to his exile, despite the genuine spiritual leadership he had offered his people for a period. Next, ominously, the reading told him that some of the same people who had been involved with him then would bring him similar experiences in this life—"disappointments, fears, railings." When it occurred, he was to do better than he had done in Egypt, by responding with "no malice" nor any other attitude that would hinder his best development as a soul.

Within five years his hospital and university were closed. He was banished to a house overlooking the hospital, where he had to watch it transformed to a night club. He went through agonies inwardly. But he also overcame bitterness as never before in his life, as his dreams showed. The result was that an entirely new group of people, mostly Virginians, now drew around him to replace the New York sponsors of his defunct institutions. And he himself developed, as had been promised to him, new gifts of counsel that enabled him to bring his associates into greater growth than he had ever been able to foster before.

One can look into the future by looking a long ways backwards.

More unlikely than reincarnation to the waking Cayce was numerology. But his readings insisted that numbers were old and familiar emblems to the human psyche, a natural way to dramatize the future. The readings showed his stock dreamers that the numbers in their dreams not only conveyed stock prices, but the days or weeks of stock rises and falls, and the relative strengths of given stocks (a figure of six, for example, was generally weaker than a five). One number or set of numbers might compress all of these indications into one dream image, just as dreams used the face of an individual to convey a variety of associations needed for the dream experience. As might be expected, one of his dreamers was more facile in handling the numbers in his dreams than were the others; in Cayce's view the phenomenon tended to vary with individuals.

Despite the relative indifference of the subconscious to conscious ideas of time and space, Cayce explained, it can pinpoint dates when necessary. For example, a stock movement after Thanksgiving was shown with a restaurant and much holiday eating. A stock development for the spring was accompanied by a glimpse of golfing clothes, to set the time with the opening of the golf season, while another dream offered a glimpse of Atlantic City to indicate that a certain stock action would coincide with the dreamer's trip to the resort city. Yet another dream showed ferries at work to indicate a stock movement after winter ices thawed.

It is noteworthy that where the important future developments were coming for the dreamer, these tended to appear in dreams of his close associates or family, as well. Whoever was involved with him, and especially involved without too much ego-concern, would be likely to receive relevant glimpses of the same events. It was as though the future could best be established by the intersection of the dreams of several—as Cayce showed in joint dreams not only on business developments, but on death, pregnancy, birth, illness, marriage, quarrels, and change of position in life.

Dreams of the Unknown Present

Much the same processes work in dreams of the unknown present, according to Cayce, as in dreams of the future. The dreamer's subconscious is using its native ESP, but is moving freely in space instead of time.

One of Cayce's businessmen dreamed of impure milk on the same night that his brother did.

> We were all out on a party with friends. I fell asleep at the table and we got home very late. My brother got out of the automobile and walked home and left us. First, however, my brother and I stopped to look at a bottle of milk that was marked "Undistilled Milk."

In the first part of the dream, Cayce told him, he was seeing how partying and late hours were tiring him, as shown in the falling asleep at the party. The solution was to see that these were "left off" until he was rested, just as his brother had "left" in the dream. As for the milk, about which he and his brother had both dreamed, it was adulterated and should be investigated, for the benefit of others as well as of the dreamers. Following the counsel of Cayce and their dreams, the brothers had the milk checked, with the result that the dairy firm was closed by the city Board of Health!

Because of the business interests of Cayce's dreamers, many of their dreams of unknown facts were about stocks. Cayce awake had early doubts that he could supply accurate stock information. So he had a dream of his own. In it he was giving a medical reading, the kind he knew best, and was doing a helpful job. However, he also saw into the body of the lad he described medically, and noted numbers on every bone. They were numbers of stock quotations in the railroad stock which had come up in the first part of the dream. The quotations proved correct, and Cayce was encouraged on the versatility of his readings.

A variety of symbols of unknown stocks appeared in dreams. American Express stock activity was symbolized for one by American Express checks. A subway ride meant subway stock to another. Two autos out of control warned the dreamer about a deal in motor stocks. A dream of a crowd in an uproar over a lost pair of rubbers was a tip on activity in rubber stock. This little dream took care of two stocks at once:

> I was drawing lines on the sidewalk. It seemed a combination of Sears Roebuck and Gimble. Had the impression that it was high enough now.

Cayce assured the dreamer that both stocks were at their high and should be sold. Then, with his characteristic encouragement for a dreamer doing well, he added information about Wabash Railroad and Missouri Pacific stocks, which the dreamer also held. An accurate dream of Havana Electric being split five for one, before public announcement was made, gave one dreamer "a great deal of money," as he wrote to Cayce. A dream of an obscure stock being pushed by an associate led the same dreamer to inquire of that associate the next day and again to make a killing.

In dozens of dreams, the exact details were given. For example—slowly and distinctly the following words: "Soo Railway 4% notes at 99 or 100." Here the dreamer was seeing that he should buy these bonds and hold them until they advanced to 99 or 100. The same dreamer, after some three hundred dream readings from Cayce, had a startling dream experience:

> It seemed I could ask any question about stocks that I chose to ask, and it was answered. I stood under a lighted lamp at about dusk. A man walked up and I asked him how U.S. Steel closed. He said, "It closed crazy, at 178." . . . "Well," I said, "then steel will go on up to around 188 or 190." . . . Then the whole market opened up to me. "Did that man who bought C and O make much money on the purchase?" "Not much," came the reply. The leather stocks seemed indicated for something, particularly Endicott Johnson. Then the others that I can't remember—all, everything I wanted, seemed to flow right to me or into my consciousness. Even as I awakened I seemed to be asking about Fleischman stock, and even after I awakened the voice said, "Use your own judgment on Fleischman."

In addition to the factual promptings in the dream, said Cayce, it contained a full promise that the dreamer could have guidance on every stock he desired, if he could keep his life and purposes straight. He had been through an experience of attunement like Cayce's dream of the mounting spiral. It is not surprising that this dreamer became a millionaire in the space of months.

A secret business deal was depicted in a dream as a fraternity having an initiation. An office boy trying to steal stocks was shown in a vision, but with a warning that he should be treated gently—helped to see that such temptations come to everyone. A poorly planned business deal was depicted as a defective baby. A dream of bandits looting travelers on a train was, said Cayce, a warning to an inventor that someone was trying to steal his new product. But a competitor seen lighting a fire under a table was only cause for care, as the dreamer should note that the fire never reached the table top. A dream of a holdup by a chauffeur led to Cayce's counsel that the man be released from employment. Cayce's own dream of a hog and a peacock helped him to see how those who hogged the show in his work were of as little value as those who strutted much and did nothing.

But the dreams showered facts about personal affairs, just as freely as about workaday life.

A father was tipped off that his small daughter's nursemaid was playing scary games with her, by a dream about a frightening beetle in his daughter's bed. A young woman seeing her boyfriend in a compromising situation with another girl was warned she had dreamed the facts correctly. A college student dreaming he was debating was shown his relationship with every one of his close associates, by the way they functioned in the dream. A woman who dreamed of her relatives discussing medical care for her invalid mother saw the essential life quality of each relative laid bare in the dream. A businessman was led by a dream to new friendships with two respected attorneys who shared his psychic interests but had never mentioned them.

What occupied the dreamer awake occupied him at night, as well, but with new facts added by dreams.

CHAPTER 10

DREAMS OF THE LIVING DEAD

IN THE OUTLOOK of the Edgar Cayce readings, death is a transition for the soul as a birth is a transition. But it is not an extermination.

How Cayce himself came to view death could be seen in a dream of his own. The dream, which came during a reading, presented its viewpoint with the charm and grace which were hallmarks of Cayce's own consciousness at his best.

> I was preparing to give a reading. As I went out [of consciousness], I realized that I had contacted Death—as a personality, as an individual, or as a being.
>
> Realizing this, I remarked to Death, "You are not as ordinarily pictured, with a black mask or hood, or as a skeleton, or like Father Time with a sickle. Instead, you are fair, rosy-cheeked, robust, and have a pair of shears or scissors."
>
> I had to look twice at his feet or limbs, or even at the body, to see it take shape.
>
> He replied, "Yes. Death is not what many seem to think. It is not the horrible thing that is so often pictured. Just a change. Just a visit. The shears or scissors indeed are the most representative implements to man of life and death. They indeed unite by dividing, and divide by uniting. The cord does not, as usually thought, extend from the center [of the body], but is broken from the head, the forehead—that soft portion you see pulsate in the infant.
>
> "Hence we see old people, unbeknownst to themselves, gain strength from Youth by kissing there, and Youth gains wisdom from Age by such kisses. Indeed, the vibrations may be raised to such an extent as to rekindle or connect the cord [there], even as the Master did for the son of the widow of Nain. For He took him not by the hand—which was bound to the body as the custom of the day—but rather stroked him on

> the head, and the body took of Life Itself. So you see, the silver cord
> may be broken, but vibration. . . ."

Here the experience ended.

A man in his mid-thirties, whose late father had been a strong influence in his life, dreamed his way through the death barrier in an unforgettable sequence. The dream began with girls, who were important in his life and dream symbols, and then moved to bed, where he had last seen his father dying:

> Now I beheld a vision of many beautiful women, all dressed in different
> colors—but they were not women after all, but lights, beautifully colored
> lights, which I interpreted as Spirit entities. They appeared before me in
> line. There seemed to be one particular shining light that I knew was my
> father.

Cayce confirmed that the dreamer had entered the "Border Plane."

> Then my brother said, "Why don't you turn out the lights?", meaning
> the electric lights in our room. This I did, and behold, my father appeared
> in bed with me. Now I was at the head, he at the foot of the bed, but
> although I seemed to recognize his physical form, yet it was not as I had
> previously seen him—instead in this same manner of a man, Light, the
> color of which was like the sun.

The light, Cayce said, represented the directing force from the dreamer's own superconscious realm; like an altar light, it could be trusted in what it showed him.

> I burst out crying, and wept bitterly at my father's nearness. The light
> flickered a bit, and many things flashed through my mind all at once. As
> this: it didn't do any good to cry—it didn't help my father; and why didn't
> I talk to him, instead of crying.
>
> I said to him, "I love you." The light flickered again, and I thought,
> "Maybe he cannot understand words," so I put my hands to my lips and
> childlike blew him a kiss. Motioning, with my lips whispering, "I love
> you." Then the light took the shape of my father's head, and out of his
> mouth came the words, "I love you too, Son!"
>
> The light came nearer to me—up towards my end of the bed, and
> unwrapped a package; on the inside of the paper wrapper I beheld my
> father's handwriting. I could distinguish the signature as my father wrote
> it, and although I could not make out any of the contents written, I
> recognized the handwriting.
>
> At this my emotions very nearly again overcame me—I was very close
> to my father indeed.

Cayce confirmed that the dreamer had entered into the "fourth dimension" of existence, beyond death, where his father would help him understand how things were, as the next portion indicated.

> Then the box inside the package came to my view, and being opened by my father, revealed four Chiclets—chewing gum pieces. "Take one," my father said. I did, and it tasted very good, and as I chewed he told me to take another. I did. There were still two left.

Here, in this homely sequence, the dreamer was being shown, Cayce said, that he would have to chew and digest four-dimension existence for himself, through such dream experiences, for he could never reason it out correctly otherwise.

> "Follow me," said my father. And I saw the light upon the wall. It was flat like a mirror reflection, yet not perfectly round as I first thought, but had shape. I cannot now in my conscious moments recall the symmetry of that light on the wall, but I do wish I could. It had shape, but how shall I describe it? What shape was it? I remained in bed, regarding the light, my father's spirit.

Then the dreamer heard a voice address him by name, a voice he had heard before as the call from his own superconscious being, or best self.

> "Follow your father." I got out of bed and followed the light. It traveled along the wall, sometimes leaving, taking shape in the air—from room to room, finally into the kitchen. Then I lost track of the light. I was left in darkness, seeking my father, seeking his spirit-light.

The dreamer would have to learn the truths about life beyond death little by little, Cayce said, emptying himself of "self." But then discovery would come, for "seek and ye shall find." The dream continued:

> I was then returning from some party—it seemed I was coming from the lawn of a fine estate. My brother and his wife and others were at the party. I was still seeking the spirit-light of my father and his guidance. Above all, I had in mind what had been given in my wife's dream, that my father would reveal four-dimension life to me. I sought that, as I yet do, above all.

Here the dreamer betrayed his fascination with the question of life after death—a fascination which would later bring dream rebukes and urgings that he keep a well-rounded life and pilgrimage. But at the moment something more immediate came into view.

> Then I emptied the contents of a bottle of whiskey I was carrying from the party, and I smelled the alcoholic fumes. The Voice: "Not in such an

atmosphere will you ever find your father." Again I was in the dark room
seeking my father's spirit-light.

In this incident, Cayce commented, the dreamer was experiencing for himself
how his heavy drinking deadened his psychic perception, and how his heavy
partying took his creative energies in another direction from the seeking in the
dream. He needed to look for something better to give others than the momentary
stimulus of social affairs—as the next portion showed him:

> But something happened then. Behold I was naked, and able to fly in
> graceful fashion through the air. Others, too, seemed able. First, I watched
> the others, gracefully traveling about, here, there, everywhere. "They
> are really spirit entities," I thought, "and their flights represent their
> universal energy; but my physical mind must see them as men, otherwise
> it can't understand." One of these men dropped upon his head, and got
> right up and gracefully flew again. "See," said the Voice, "not a sensuous
> being. He didn't hurt himself at all." Then I tried and started to fly. It
> was wonderful, gracefully floating through the air. But I had work to do,
> some purpose to perform, as had the others.

In the dream, as so often stressed in the Cayce readings, contact with the dead
had as its first purpose a transformation and quickening of the dreamer.

> I descended through the roof of a house to find men committing a burglary.
> "Oh," I cried at them, "Life up here is so wonderful—so much is in store
> for you! What you are doing is not worthwhile!" Then, pointing my finger
> at them from my position on a ladder, I said: "Thou shalt not steal. Thou
> shalt not commit murder, thou shalt not commit adultery, thou shalt not
> commit fornication, thou shalt not bear false witness, thou shalt love thy
> neighbor as thyself."

> They cried, "Hypocrite!" at me. "You have done these," they cried, and
> chased me out of the house. I ran panic-stricken to another house, where
> I found a gun, and hiding behind a table awaited their arrival. Someone
> entered, and I shot at him repeatedly. It was my friend who had died
> recently who entered. Approaching me, dressed in his tuxedo, he laughed
> as he said, "Here, try another shot—hit me here."

Now, Cayce said, the dreamer could see how a life not well lived brought fear
that blinded him to the realities of life both before and after the grave. Such fear
would make a man blindly shoot a dead man. But the dreamer must shoot, as
his friend was laughingly showing in the dream. However, he must "aim"—con-
centrate the energy of his whole life—toward worthy goals, not toward destroying
others in panic. Apparently the dreamer got the point, even in the dream, as the
next scene showed him in a different mood:

> My friend in the tuxedo and I sat down to a table and he told me a funny

story, at which we both laughed heartily.

The joke, Cayce said, was how ridiculous so many human actions—like shooting at a ghost—seemed when viewed from the perspective of eternity. It was time for the dreamer to laugh a bit. For it was necessary, Cayce added, that "laughter, gladness, be the message of each entity in every manner—not the long-faced fellow that gets his way, see?"

The journey into the realms of death had led far. It had led right back to the dreamer's daily life. And the last sequence placed it there firmly.

> Again I felt my father's presence—didn't see as before—but felt it. I was still seeking. The Voice: "Chicago Milwaukee, 69–75."

A very practical quotation on a railroad stock. It came, Cayce said, to show the dreamer that creativity in work life was not of a different order than the creativity which governed exploring through death. The laws of stock movements were ultimately the same in origin as spiritual law, physical law, moral law. It was all to be found from the same Source and Giver. Not from discarnates, but from the Lord of Life, Himself.

It was an affirmation that the Cayce readings never failed to make.

Dreams for the Sake of the Dead

Contrary to what the living may think, according to Cayce, not a few of the dreams where the living meet the dead are for the sake of the dead.

Sometimes the dead simply want to be known and recognized as still existent. The dreamer who reported the vivid experience of his father, above, had already dreamed a meeting with his dead grandmother. The dream began, as many such dreams of contact beyond the grave, with a note of beauty.

> We were in a room together, many of us enjoying ourselves and planning and trying to accomplish something. I heard beautiful music, and the rest seemed to vanish, and there lying before me on a trunk, which was in the room, was my grandmother, my mother's mother, who had died one day before my father. Happily I knelt beside her. I could only see her face and neck, and I put my arms about her neck. She seemed to be crying, or not exactly crying, but greatly distressed. She said "None of you want me to live." "How can you say such a thing, Grandma?", I answered, and attempted to kiss her. But she grew more distressed. "Your mother doesn't want, or care if I live," she said. I put my arms about her closer and tried to explain that Mother certainly did, but just didn't understand. The vision ended there.

Cayce confirmed that this had been an authentic contact, and warned again, as he had already told the dreamer, that to seek contact too often with a discarnate would bring distress to the discarnate, holding the dead back from their own full journey. Yet he added that there was also distress brought to them "by not understanding, by not hearing, the call"—just as the dreamer had seen.

Still more distressing was the dream of a young man about his father-in-law, who had recently taken his own life. In the dream a voice commented, "he is the most uncomfortable fellow in the world," and then the dreamer was shown his own baby crying for food. The image was to convey the dead man's hunger for guidance and spiritual sustenance, said Cayce. The next night the dreamer heard the man's own voice, together with "a wandering impression of restlessness." The voice said, "I seek rest. I want to leave and be with my family down there." Again Cayce said the dream contact had been authentic, showing the dreamer how much his prayers were needed for the father-in-law—who was still an "earthbound" discarnate. He added that the reason the discarnate was turning towards people in earthly life was that "the lessons *are learned from* that plane, see?" It was a point Cayce often made, that souls who had once entered the earth had to learn their final lessons in the earth, where will is called into play in a fashion different from existence on other planes.

Yet contact between the dead and the living can be joyous. Sometimes it occurs because the dead want to show the living what death is like, to take away their fear and grief. Exploring the possible reality of such contact, one dreamer had her side pinched by a discarnate friend, so vividly that she screamed in fright, while another had his toe pulled when he asked for it—and did not ask again. One dream took a man inside the brain of a woman dying of cancer, a relative, and showed him precisely what a relief death was, when it finally came. A later dream also showed him how a soul feels when awakening to consciousness after death and discovering he is with his body underground—and then bursting up through the dirt towards the light.

The startling fact, Cayce said, which all these dream experiences were making clear to the dreamers, is that the death-state is more nearly a normal one for a soul than is earthly existence. The usual human question of whether earthly consciousness survives death is backwards. The important question for a soul is how much of its normal awareness and creativity, and contact with the divine, will survive its birth into a body.

The fact of the normalcy of the death-state explains why Cayce, on entering his trance for readings—a trance much like a pre-death coma—was given the suggestion that "Now the body is assuming its normal forces," so that he could find and give the information needed for the reading. But life on earth, in this view, is also valuable. There are insights for the soul into creation and the Creator, which can be gained on earth as nowhere else. These are insights that "angels," whom Cayce described as beings that have not undertaken earth incarnation, will never know.

Discarnates are not only rewarded by recognition from the living, or even by the joy of teaching the living. They can also, in relatively unusual cases, work directly with the living for the fulfillment of worthy causes.

Because certain well-developed souls see more after death than do the living (except in the dreams of the living), these discarnates are in a position to bring to the dreamer guidance on many things: health, financial affairs, social causes, social service, relationships with the living. But they pay a price to do it, Cayce insisted, and warned that the dreamer who finds such aid has special responsibilities to stretch his own talents to the absolute maximum, while wide awake.

Cayce himself had sometimes recieved aid from discarnates. Such an experience occurred spontaneously some months before the opening of the hospital, when what seemed to be his dead mother spoke through Cayce at the start of a reading for someone else. Cayce remembered the contact later as a dream, but the others in the room heard the words spoken aloud. His mother, who called him "Brother," seemed to be talking to him about a fountain which Cayce had planned as a memorial to his mother at the entrance to the hospital. She felt he should let his sisters help, as well as his father who was still living (but not for long, as she correctly noted). The sleeping Cayce spoke with animation: "Mother!" Then he repeated her words aloud:

> "Mother is here. And you haven't written Sister yet, and told her—Sister wouldn't like it, Brother, and she'll feel hurt! Write to Sister, tell her, and Sarah and Ola and Mary—they'll all want to have a part, and they'll feel just as you do. And after a while when everything is straightened out, it will be so nice for you all to know that Mother will be right with you! Be a good boy. Write, Brother! Talk to Mother. Be good to Papa. He will be home before long. But write to Sister—and tell the children Mother loves them all."

Cayce did write, and the fountain was built as a joint effort. It was, of course, one of the harder things to lose when the hospital was later given back to its Depression-struck founders.

Meeting his mother was not Cayce's only experience of being guided from beyond death on how to raise money for his work. Years later, when he needed a fireproof vault to be built onto his modest home, as a safe place to house the records of his readings, he had an experience which he reported to friends as follows:

> On the evening of November 4th, I had this dream, vision, or experience.

> I was in our office "reading room," discussing with some of the family the necessity for protecting and preserving the records we already have, and the means for doing this. Suddenly a "master" (the Master, to me) appeared and said: "*Peace* be unto you! Ask all whom you have tried to help to *help* you save these records, for they are their experiences and are a part of *them!* Whether they contribute a shingle, a beam, a window, a door, or the entire vault for the records, give them all the opportunity to have a part in the work."

Cayce wrote to everyone who had ever had a reading recorded, and explained how they might contribute. Two years later the fireproof vault was dedicated—paid up.

Neither the dream of his mother nor of Christ seemed to Cayce experiences limited to him. He insisted to the dreamers he coached that wherever people were prayerfully engaged in some project of service, they would draw help from beyond the grave.

When one dreamer had seemed to secure dream aid for months on stocks, through the assistance of his discarnate father, so that he could amass funds to support the Cayce Hospital and Atlantic University, he had the following charming dream:

> My father in some way indicating something regarding a cigar I was smoking.

The father had been devoted to cigars, and Cayce commented on the "joy, satisfaction, contentment" seen in the dream, as father and son discussed the aroma of good cigars. It was an indication, Cayce said, of the good feeling in which the father and other discarnates were working cooperatively with the son—teamwork from both sides of the grave to accomplish a humanitarian work.

Dreams of Telling Others About the Living Dead

In later months the father appeared to assemble a team of discarnate financial experts, who aided the dreamer with promptings while asleep and awake. Cayce took this development as factual; he made his contribution by coaching the dreamer to keep a level head in the strange partnership. But the dreamer's relatives were skeptical and hostile, however wealthy his efforts were making him and his associates. Stinging with their rebukes, he had the following dream:

> It seemed I traveled to a place by boat, and there beheld the Master—Christ Jesus.
>
> I shouted to all about me as loud as I could: "We can be like Him—I have proved it! We can be like Him—I have proved it!" None would listen or believe me.
>
> I entered what seemed to be a grocery store, and there beheld a man who appeared as Christ—it may or may not have been He, but he was dressed as Christ would have been, but younger. A woman said to me, "Isn't He a wonderful God?" "You can be like Him," I answered her. "Oh," she replied, "you are not like Him. You are a soft, mushy human."
>
> I turned to show her Christ, and it may have been His picture on a box I showed her. But there He was, as I knew Him from pictures I had seen—an older Man, sympathetic, yet unyielding in His faith in the Truth, and its adherence, and propagation to His fellowman.
>
> I went up to the store counter and sat down. There behind the counter I saw the younger man, like Christ, kneeling down in prayer. He was thanking His Father for much.
>
> I leaned my head in my hands and cried bitterly. "It hurts in here," I

said, pointing to my heart, and it seemed this referred to my inability to make others understand—and also that He suffered just this way.

I said: "What is the use of the real, the true, if we are ridiculous to all here on earth?"—and I saw myself as ridiculously crying my message, "We can be as He—I have proved it." Then I saw Him again, kneeling down in thankful prayer, and crying, I said, "It hurts to my very soul."

Then the voice—it may have been His Voice—spoke and said, "They shall return again to earth to learn. They shall kneel down and worship. . . ."

It was a dream which mirrored the center of the Cayce message, as an experience for the dreamer: "We can be as He." Cayce often referred back to the crucial phrase of this dream.

But the dream also contained deadly peril of inflated self-importance for the dreamer, as later dreams showed. And Cayce interpreted it guardedly, commenting only at the end of his reading that the dream could be seen as a message from Christ. The dreamer had, he said almost entered into "the Holy of Holies, gaining strength and wisdom from Him who *is* strength and wisdom." He might through his dream begin to understand the cry of Christ on viewing the ancient capital city of Palestine: "O, Jerusalem, Jerusalem! How oft would I have gathered thee together, even as a hen gathereth her brood under her wings, and ye would not!" There was then but one course for someone determined to carry a difficult message to his fellows: to be "oft in prayer," for "those who seek Him, the Master, may find Him" as well as "strength and endurance in body, soul and mind."

In some ways the hardest lesson for Cayce to pound into his dreamers, when they became convinced of the reality of life beyond the grave, and of shared work with discarnates, was that they should not try to prove their view to others by psychic feats. No such proof should be attempted, he warned them over and over. People could be invited to explore for themselves, but demonstrations were out, exhortations were out. Exactly as Jesus had taught, no "sign" was to be given. Men's minds and hearts were to be won another way, by the quality of life shared with them.

The same issue lay in telling others about Cayce, as he commented on a later dream where he referred back to "I have proven it," in his interpretation. The dreamer reported:

I entered a room where there were many people and saw a man asleep—lying there asleep. It may have been Edgar Cayce.

I was worried about Pan Petroleum stocks, and the oil. Many were looking to me for advice at the same time. Then I said, "Oh, well, I can't converse with a sleeping man as easily as if (the way it is with my father) I could talk to him even though not a word is spoken—where I get my advice, from guide."

He was bragging in the dream about his stock and other counsel from his discarnate father, coming to him "direct" instead of through the sleeping Cayce. He also showed some scorn of the very people he was supposed to be helping: "Seems the others didn't ask the understanding to that advice."

But then the dream changed swiftly, to reach through to his better motives:

> Then a little boy dressed in rags entered. I felt sorry for him, and putting my hand on his head, said, "I'll take you in and love you." Then a man who seemed to be the child's father came in and the boy pointed him out to me. I said to him: "I want to take your son and care for him." Then the man answered: "I can support him and bring him up, if I had my health." Then he showed me a paralyzed arm. I felt terribly sorry, and thought I would like to use my power (of communicating with my guide) to convert the man, again with the sleeping man—and then talk with these people and explain in language they would understand what they could do.

> Then I saw the sleeping man in what appeared to be a department store window, and crowds of people there, looking through the glass window at this phenomenon.

As Cayce discussed the dream, he said the sleeping man represented both Cayce giving readings—in a state where mental and cosmic and spiritual forces were all combined to be helpful—*and* the sleep of onlookers themselves, where they might "through dream reach mental, spiritual, cosmic forces" that could be carefully correlated with waking experience to "gain knowledge through which the mental, the material, the moral, the *whole* being of man may be benefited, see?"

He was turning the dreamer's attention away from his dream feats to the question of what others could learn to do in their dreams.

But how were others to become interested? The dream dramatized two ways in which one might try to reach others.

One was the way represented by the man sleeping in the store window. This appealed to only a part of the mind of onlookers, not to their capacity for perfect understanding. It catered to the element of "mystery," to the "moment's understanding," to the sense of the "extravagant."

The other way lay in the episode of the child and the father, where the dreamer felt the prompting to compassion and helpfulness. It was the way of "education or knowledge for the young; assistance to those halt, maimed or in distress physically or mentally" which might far better "bring them in relation to those Universal Forces, in relation to God" through dreams and awake.

Besides, people who needed to understand life after death would find it in their own dreams, if they looked.

Among Cayce's dreamers, a dead husband came in dream to assist his widow to reclaim the estate from a crooked administrator. A mother-in-law spoke from the dead to warn a dreamer against poor companions. A father who had served as a dreamer's guide threatened to drop all assistance from the next plane if the son played around with women any longer. A dreamer who reported wrestling playfully with a dead uncle in a dream was told by Cayce he had slipped unknow-ingly in his dream into "the Borderland," where he and the uncle had enjoyed a happy time together.

Dreams came to Cayce's subjects to show them the kind of vehicle or body they might have after death, how they would know they were dead, how they would progress through various planes, and what sort of helpers they would find. Much was unfolded in their dreams about communication with the dead: how their perception was one sense seeming to be several, how they mustered energy for contacts with the living, how they gathered to listen where the living taught about death, how they longed to speak through a psychic, how some who were poorly developed would try to take over a living person left open to their influence by his attitudes or actions or poor health.

Question: When Is One Ready For Dreams Of The Living Dead?

In commenting on hundreds of such dreams, Cayce offered a number of answers.

First of all, one is ready for such dreams when he has them. His subconscious will not feed him experiences he can't handle if he chooses to do so. Secondly, one is ready for dream contact with the dead when he will not speak lightly of them. In Cayce's view, such dreams could mean dangerous escapism.

Thirdly, one is ready for dreams of the dead when he soundly loves and serves the living; such dreams always come for a personal reason, a personal growth of the dreamer, or some concrete service in the regular round of his daily life. Dream messages seeming to come for a general public are immediately suspect, for healthy contact with the dead was not designed to function for the living in this way.

Fourthly, one is ready for dreams of the dead when he is as ready to give aid to the dead as to receive it. When prayer for a discarnate comes freely and naturally to mind, then visions of them may follow. Any other approach tends to be exploitative. Fifthly, one is ready for dreams of dead loved ones when he has worked through his griefs and guilts regarding them, and has forgiven them for hurts to himself. Lack of this makes a nearly impenetrable barrier.

Finally, one may dream of the dead when his own full life draws to its natural close, and it is time for him to prepare for the next journey.

Dreaming of Reincarnation

One of the "dead" who will live, said Cayce, is the dreamer himself. In dreams he may meet himself as he has been in other lives.

There are two ways in which such dreams might occur. One, a relatively uncommon mode, is that of recalling a scene from a past life exactly as it once happened. The other is dreaming of a present scene, but with the plot supplied by forces from a past life.

In Cayce's view, one does not simply leave past lives behind; one lives all of them in the present, in some degree, and at varying times in the life. Consequently, dreams often carry forward the action of the past personality as it is called into play by events of the present life. Such dreams show the dreamer and his associates in modern dress, as Cayce explicitly indicated, but re-enact "karma," or the heritage of past-life themes and traumas and talents, just as other dreams re-enact similar motifs from childhood in this life — and still other dreams combine both.

Such a view made it difficult for Cayce's dreamer to distinguish dreams rooted in the present life from those which also had past-life roots. To Cayce this distinction was not particularly important. What matters, in his view, is that the dreamer act on the dream. Whether from one life or a dozen, selfishness must still be conquered, talent risked, love given and refused and given again. Unlike many fascinated by the idea of reincarnation, the sleeping Cayce brought it up only when it might specifically help a dreamer to understand himself or someone else. Otherwise, he stuck to the present choices before a dreamer.

But there were hints that all serious dreams may be read as embodying some degree of past-life themes. The life of the soul is woven of these many threads, however modern the present design.

When Cayce himself dreamed that a woman friend of his was used as a gunshield by bandits, whereupon he shot the leading gunman and rescued her, he was told by the reading that he should act as the woman's "protector, teacher, guide, director" in their present relationship, because of an association in a past life. The fact that all were in modern dress in the dream only accentuated the need for "modern defense" of her "activity, thought, or purpose." When he dreamed that he and one of his sons quarreled and the son left home, he was told that he was seeing the kind of stress they had known together in a time of Egyptian history, and that both he and his son would have to watch temper and tongue.

A woman who had in another lifetime controlled men with her beauty dreamed of competing with attractive women, to hold her husband in this one. A woman who had in another existence led her people as a female warrior was having in this lifetime to learn to control her power drives or alienate all who came close to her. A man who in a previous life had doubted the religious mission of his brother kept dreaming of his present brother turning on him. A young man who had been a king in another life was warned about his airs as a Southern gentleman in this life. A bright woman who had been the daughter of a philosopher dreamed of how to make her tongue yield to her heart. A man who in a past existence had used his power for the exile of a leader dreamed constantly of how it felt to be rejected by those in power and influence. A professional man who had been a rake in a life not too far past dreamed repeatedly of being caught and humiliated while making love to a woman not his wife. A woman who had been an actress dreamed of the choice between being a real artist and a show-off. A man who had used military power to humble others found himself belittled in his dreams by military figures.

At least this is how Edgar Cayce saw their dream plots and tangles. How could the dreamers achieve a perspective on such claims? By dreaming actual memories from past lives, he told them.

And dream they did. They dreamed of words, names, phrases in ancient Hebrew and Egyptian and Persian tongues. They dreamed of vivid foreign scenes: an oasis, a huge man in Arabian dress bending over the dreamer and threatening his life, tents of the Israelites encamped near Jerusalem on their return from Babylon, rays and machines from the ancient civilization of Atlantis, fishing on Galilee at the time of Jesus, the ceremonial dedication by thousands of a pyramid in Egypt, death by combat in a Greek arena, the landing of ships in early America, the conflicts of Israelities with Moabites, the Roman rule of Mediterranean countries, the spread of Hindu thought outside of India, and the moral force of ancient Chinese teachings.

Typically such dreams were not mere scenarios in the night, but episodes vividly focused on a present problem of the dreamer.

When Edgar Cayce was under stress amid the quarreling of backers of his hospital, shortly before it was closed and sold, he dreamed the following during a reading:

> I thought I was with Mr. and Mrs. Lot and their two daughters running out of Sodom, when it ws raining fire and brimstone. What had been called "she turned to a pillar of salt," because she looked back, was that they really passed through the heat—as came from the fire from heaven—and all were tried by that. I got through the fire.

To his surprise, Cayce was told by his own reading source that he had been there with Lot, as someone sent to warn of what was coming. He had actually accompanied the family in their frightening experience, which was reviewed for him now because he would have to pass through another kind of "fire" himself, in suffering with his associates. Whether he would again escape would depend on his "attitudes and activities." To prepare, he should study the life of each individual reported in the Bible story.

A practical Jewish businessman, weighing what to make of the figure of Christ, dreamed a startling vision:

> I fear to write—or as I write this I am still frightened from this vision. But it must have had its import in my life, and it is that which I seek.

> I visioned something pertaining to the Lord Almighty dying, and then something happened just one and a half years later.

> What happened, and how does it pertain to my present life?

> The death of the Lord and this subsequent happening one and one half years later reminded me of the death of the nineteen-year-old king, Tut-ankh-amen. What relationship does the Lord's death, and a following event (what was this event?) have to the death of the nineteen-year-old pharaoh?

In responding to this dream, Cayce told the dreamer, as he often told those who dreamed materials which he felt were out of past lives, that he could solve the riddle of this dream himself by turning his mind introspectively. One did not have to be asleep to get in touch with such memories.

The dreamer had once been very close to Jesus, even in his household, and experienced the immense shock of his death. He was only a young man then, and it took him a year and a half to make up his mind to acknowledge the place of Jesus as his "Master." It happened when he was just nineteen. He had been "a deep thinker" then, and a student of ancient cultures, on whom the helpful rule of the young Tut-ankh-amen had made a strong impression, especially the way he had knit together divided households. The young man of Palestine at nineteen had identified with the young monarch, and when the traumatic events and choices of his Palestinian lifetime came flooding back to him today, so did the associations with Egypt that were in his thoughts then. Now he was in a family divided by quarrels over the meaning of Christ for Jews, and he would have to look beyond surface appearance and loyalties for the deeper realities that applied. This was why his dream had taken him back through the centuries.

Cayce told those whom he coached on dreams that the study of reincarnation was just as important as the study of life after death. He put it to one woman this way: "For, if individuals were as mindful of what they have been as they are of what they are to be, this would become a much more interesting as well as a purposeful experience; for then, as He gave, those being on guard do not allow their houses, their own selves or their mental abilities, to be broken up."

PART IV
Self-Development Through Dreams

CHAPTER 11
THROUGH DREAMS TO A HEALTHY BODY

ALTHOUGH CAYCE EMPHASIZED the power of "mind the builder" to shape each person's life, he insisted that the body be reckoned with in every stage of growth. As he saw individual development, the mind is cradled snugly within the body, and deeply affected by endocrine gland function, as well as indirectly affected by diet, exercise, eliminations, posture, and other considerations. With this view Cayce took a position near to that of modern psychiatry.

Historically, he took a position about the role of the body in human growth which set him nearer to Judaism and the Bible than to Greek and Gnostic thought, which had alternated between worship of the human form and treatment of the body as a prison of the spirit. Cayce once commented in a reading that the body, for a human being, is as natural and intimate a structure for the soul as a fingernail is for a finger.

In this perspective, dreams of course deal with concerns of physical health.

To be sure, Cayce pointed out, many dreams deal with physical health and other concerns at the same time.

An associate who was slow in raising money for the Cayce Hospital dreamed that he was constipated. Cayce interpreted his dream to refer both to physical constipation, which needed attention, and to constipation of his money-raising, which was halted by the dreamer's holding back too much of the initiative for himself. Another dreamer saw himself falling in the wet snow of a street, where he lost his gloves and lost track of his brother. He was seeing, said Cayce, that he needed to prevent undue winter exposure, and he was also seeing that he ought to follow his brother's counsel more closely, both in health matters and in matters of business.

Dreaming of the Body

A businessman dreamed vividly of a relative who was just then leaving the hospital after major surgery.

> We were all out to the farmhouse, and she was coming home from the doctor, coming home alone. As she came in the room, I hid behind the door, so that she wouldn't see me. She was very pale and trembly, and was uttering something about another operation. Someone in the crowd said she was nearly hysterical.

This dream, said Cayce, was a serious warning to the relative to slow down during her postoperative period. The dream had been set in a farmhouse because it was "all feeling," as distinguished from a dream about mental activities. The dreamer had been shown hiding, because the dream was about a hidden complication developing, which would necessitate a second operation if the woman were not careful. And she herself was shown "trembly and hysterical" to indicate the warning, as well as her inward hope of recovery without repeating the pain of her first surgery—pain which would not be necessary, with care.

The warning was given serious attention, unlike some of the health warnings that came to the same dreamer. His wife opposed his use of osteopathy. This explained, said Cayce, his dream of going to meet somebody in a secluded hotel. The dream was indicating that he should get the care, even if he had to keep others from knowing about it!

Quite different was the dream of a woman soon to become pregnant:

> I was going in to swim from a rickety platform, very unsubstantial in its structure. As I jumped in, or tried to dive in, I made a belly-whapper—i.e., landed on my stomach. It hurt.

The entering into the water, a variation on Mother Sea or the mother of animal life in evolution, was here, he reported, a symbol of her preparing to enter into motherhood. But her body was not in shape, for it required physiotherapy and exercise to rearrange and strengthen some organs; thus the "rickety platform." She ought to get busy with the requisite medical care, for "this greatest of offices given to the sex—woman."

As often occurred to the dreamers being coached by Cayce, her second dream of the same night dealt also with the same question.

> Was back at college, and was going to room at the dormitory. I wanted two rooms to live with two other girls, and I wanted my own private bath. I wanted good meals. Decided not to stay because the food was poor.

Here the dream showed her need to prepare for the coming pregnancy—both physically, as shown by emblems of food and bath, and mentally, as shown by her desire for space and privacy in the dream.

Her husband had vastly different dream material about the body:

> I beheld a great advertisement in electric lights, shining out on Broadway.
> It said: "The substance of matter and mind is one and the same thing."

Cayce said, "This truth, and the understanding of same, should be emblazoned on the minds and hearts of people," as the lights had signified, over the "thoroughfare" of life.

In Cayce's view, matter and mind are two of the three original orders of creation (which he said are "matter, mind, and force"), and while different, each comes from and answers to the same Creator. For him there was never ground for dualism which disparaged matter.

The dreamer continued the report of his dream, which was typical of the philosophical or reflective type that appeared scores of times in the Cayce dream records.

> Then I added that the difference between matter and animal is that matter
> is a materialized-changed form of this one substance, whereas animal is
> this one substance organized to become materially manifested as mind.

The dreamer's view was much like Cayce's. For Cayce saw all subhuman creation moving slowly towards consciousness, with the mineral and vegetable and animal kingdoms successively ruling the earth in that order, and needing human consciousness to crown the progression. The dreamer went on with his dream:

> That the difference between animal and man is that the animal organiza-
> tion's development is confined to the section of the process of the one
> substance that becomes changed into a materialized form. Whereas the
> organization of a man-mind includes in the materialized form a develop-
> ment gained in all the other sections of the process of this one substance.

The dream was correct, Cayce said. Animal consciousness is limited to what develops out of its life span, whereas human consciousness, because of the role of the soul, also includes elements from vastly different realms of creation. Man is made to contain within himself all the patterns and modes of creativity yet devised by the Eternal (there could one day be more), for man's is "the highest created Creative Energy in the material plane."

Then Cayce spoke about death, where the separation of orders of creation becomes clear. At death "that of the material kingdom remains material. That of the spiritual kingdom remains spiritual. *Man* develops the soul, in that experience (or lifetime) along *its* plane of existence. Like the animal, the human body (at death) becomes as dust to dust. Like the body of the beast, all dust to dust moves in its accumulated forces, going on *its* . . . phase of the development, see? While the spirit force goes on *its* own sphere, see? Yet all of One Source, for we are brothers all." In Cayce's view, material creation has its own laws and destiny, just as the soul has its own laws and destiny. Souls now in earth lives have become disoriented, and too often try to live the way of the soul by the way of the animal—not an unworthy way, but wrong for them, in the appointed plan of creation. Reincarnation is a way of learning about animals, bodies, earthly creation, while still following the long destiny of the soul.

In a beautiful dream allegory of his own, Cayce saw the process dramatized. He saw himself living and dying in existences as various animals, alternating with incarnations as a human being. He was a snail, a fish, a cow, a dog, a bird. He was also a fisherman, a herdsman, a military guard, an Indian, and a Civil War soldier. His reading on this dream specifically told him that it was *not* literal, but emblematic—although touches of his real past lives as a human could be found woven into the fantasy. What he was seeing was what a human can learn of animal creation, from fear of extermination to mother love, with hate of other species and finally service of others—all symbolized in the animals of the dream. He was also seeing the greatness of human existence and companionship, yet how it was distorted by confusion with learnings from the animal kingdom.

Cayce's readings held unfailingly that men never incarnate in nonhuman bodies. But this dream had taken Cayce inside of animal existence in the most poignant way, to show him what humans learn in earthly lives about the manifestations of the One Force in its various orders of creation. All else but souls is appointed to endlessly disintegrate and reintegrate; souls, like their Maker whose eternal image they bear, are to endure.

Dreaming of the body's concerns takes many forms.

Dreams of Body Function

Cayce's dreamers submitted to him dream materials that touched each major system of the body.

There were dreams of circulation. A man dreamed that a rash broke out when he cut himself shaving, and Cayce said he was seeing evidence of poisons in his blood, which needed iron. When he dreamed later of gland trouble in the throat, he was, said Cayce, seeing endocrine malfunction, due to anemia. When he dreamed that his tonsils were removed, he was being warned of a different type of circulatory congestion. Another dreamer reported a dream in which eating refreshments at a family party led to hot words and a fist fight; he was seeing, according to Cayce, that some forms of alcohol were good for him in moderation, as in the party scene, but not the alcohol produced in the blood by too much sweets—which had dominated the party scene just before the fight.

There were gastrointestinal dreams. Cayce himself dreamed of a little wheel in his head that had stopped turning because of needing oil. The reading said he was seeing how his headaches derived from an intestinal need of lubrication to counteract constipation. A dreamer reported having a woman doctor treat a sore toe for him while in a store where many were eating ice cream and sodas. The helpful woman represented, as often in a man's dream, an element of guidance—in this case away from a sore point (Cayce said, "in common slang, a 'sore toe' to the entity"), which was the dreamer's overindulgence in sweets.

There were respiratory dreams. The impact of a cold was shown to a dreamer as sailors washed overboard into the sea. A bronchial infection was shown by choking. There were dreams of hypochondria, of sexual malfunction, of impaired metabolism, of nervous disorders.

Dreams of Bodily Care

When a dreamer reported how his legs had ached in a dream of a long train ride, Cayce pushed him to more exercise. When the dreamer reported seeing his brother paralyzed in a dream, Cayce said it had partly to do with danger to the brother's health, but mostly with the dreamer's own tendency to go stale, from lack of rest and play.

There were dreams of changes in diet. A man dreamed that tomatoes would be good for his wife—and Cayce concurred. Another saw himself brought a demitasse when he ordered a large cup of coffee; his subconscious was showing his taking too much caffeine for his nervous system, said Cayce. A dream of codliver oil led to dreamer's taking it, while another dream urged him not to bother his wife sexually while she was menstruating. A series of golf dreams sent one dreamer golfing, while another's dream that a trolley ran over his raincoat led him to dress better out-of-doors. As a result of dreams, a mother took better precautions to keep her baby from falling, and changed her habits to place him in the sunlight more.

Cayce had a vivid dream of being in church as the service was about to begin, when the floor suddenly caved in. His reading told him to avoid the "service" of others through his readings until his body was in better general shape for the strain. He took a vacation, for he and his family well remembered those frightening few times when his trance had turned to a coma from which he would not awaken, despite all the suggestions given him.

Dreams of Medical Care

More than a few dreams evaluated particular doctors, sometimes with approbation and sometimes with disapproval that led to a change of physician. Others evaluated the effect of particular drugs on the dreamer. Once Cayce himself dreamed a complete eight-part pharmacist's prescription for treating his cold—and found it helped. There were specific dream warnings of how to avoid danger from diphtheria and polio epidemics. There were dreams counseling sweat baths and fasting.

And of course there were dreams of the element of prayer as it could participate in healing. One woman dreamed of two doctors, but could only recall the name of one. Cayce reminded her that the other in the dream had been the "Great Physician," whose aid was much needed along with medical care for her dying mother. When a man sought to understand in a dream why his prayers for the healing of another had not been effective, he dreamed that "two plus two equals four" as part of the dream. Cayce explained that in such healing "there are two consciousnesses to be made manifest with the one psychic or spiritual law"; doubt and fear in the mind of either one could block the function of a law otherwise as real as mathematics.

Question: How May Dreams Of The Body Best Be Used?

Cayce never encouraged his dreamers to be their own physicians. He saw most of their dreams of the body as sensitizing them to concerns which they already had, but were neglecting. Or he saw such dreams as prompting them to consult their physicians.

He did not urge them to take dreams of death and severe illness as literal—for often, the subconscious might dramatize in such shocking imagery only tendencies that could in the long run lead to medical trouble. In those few cases where actual death was at hand, he pointed out that dream material often dealt less with bodily concerns than with psychological and emotional concerns, preparing the dreamer and others to handle the coming transition.

He noted the frequency of some dream element of actual body function when dreams are about the body. Food, or medicine, or pain, or a part of the body is set in focus, or a doctor or nurse is at hand. Bodily dreams are not obscurely symbolized. Nor are they isolated: if the warning is important, they are repeated, and not infrequently given to relatives, as well.

But the body may also appear emblematically in dreams, Cayce said. Feet can be one's stance or foundation; pain can stand for suffering. In the case of one dreamer, kinks in his hair were kinks in his reasoning.

A few of Cayce's dreamers had repeated dreams of animals, which he said dramatized both bodily function and—more significantly—psychological attitudes which such animals symbolized. To help them understand these symbols, he set some of his dreamers studying the imagery of mythology, and even of the Book of the Revelation in the Bible. He developed for them an entire theory of the function of endocrine glands, in response to psychological factors. It was a strange aspect of his interpretation of dreams and symbols, but to the sleeping Cayce all as matter of fact as a sore throat, a miscarriage, or the benefits of swimming for a sedentary financier.

CHAPTER 12

ORIENTING THE LIFE THROUGH DREAMS

IN THE VIEW of Cayce's readings, no man can or should invent his own life.

There are too many unknowns for consciousness to grasp. There are the impulses, talents, and problems from one's past lives. There are currents of social, political, and religious change moving beneath the surface of one's times, which require unforeseen responses from an individual. There are souls waiting to be born as one's children or grandchildren, if certain choices are made. There is a spark of the divine in every stranger, needing to be found and fanned into flame. There are discarnates clustered about men of good will and hard work, some waiting to learn and some waiting to help. There are even angels to be entertained unawares.

Given all these unknowns, no man can be expected to invent the best trajectory for his life — for his vocation, his marriage, his community, his causes, his people.

But it is enough for any man to begin with the best he knows.

Souls are not judged by absolute standards, Cayce said. They are judged by their fidelity to their own ideals, their own understanding. And they are not judged by their failures so much as by their willingness to get up and try again.

It is better, he often said, for an individual to be doing something with his life, even if it is wrong, than nothing at all — just drifting. For when a life is put in motion on the basis of the best one knows, however inadequate the vision, helpful forces are always called into play, both within and without the individual, which can straighten his course into an adventure of growth.

One does not need to invent his existence. He has only to "use what is in hand" and "the next will be supplied." For there are two helping forces always at work, to guide the unfolding and spending of a human life.

One force is a person's own original spark of creative energy, a force placed in him at creation, and bearing a potential for love and creativity as great as that of the Creator Itself. The other is a spirit "abroad in the universe" of helpfulness, of unending creativity, kindness, and wisdom, which was for Cayce typified by Christ, because He so fully exemplified it as a soul. This other force will "seek its own" within the individual when allowed to do so, and magnify whatever is good within the person.

In Cayce's view, dreams are of prime importance for the meeting of the ultimate creative force of a person with that other force which ever seeks to help him.

A stockbroker who was wrestling with the question of what God wants with human souls dreamed a bold and unforgettable vision, where God Himself came to his apartment. The dream began by focusing on the dreamer's daily work.

> I was in what seemed to be a railroad station and purchased a lot of candy. I paid $1 for each box, and anticipated selling them for $2 apiece.

The dreamer was seeing, said Cayce, his own vocation of buying and selling stocks, which often seemed to him luxuries like candy amid the world's needs, but were in fact necessities. He had told the dreamer before that God was God of "the Street" as much as of temple or hospital. The dream continued by highlighting the dreamer's desire to serve others:

> While carrying the candy out to the automobile, I saw a woman with children, also laden down with bundles. I felt I should like to help her with hers. "If I just could finish this work — get these out to the car, I'd help you," I said. "Oh, that is all right," she replied. "We have a car

outside, and it isn't so hard or far." I noticed that she was well-dressed,
had an automobile, and was burdened with what seemed radio batteries —
particularly the child was carrying such.

He was seeing his desire to be of more help than his present round allowed. But
her affirmation that she could help herself was a reminder to him that his best
service would always be to help others to find the best in themselves. Part of
this he could do by being a very good stockbroker. Then in time he would also
be able to teach and write, sending forth "messages" that were symbolized by
the hint of radio. He had to walk the road of duty in his daily life, and would
find this led to the promise of companionship with the divine, offered to every
soul as its destiny. This was the burden of the next part of the dream.

I returned to my work. It seemed menial, not pleasant. It was necessary
to work, and although I seemed reduced in position and the kind of work,
I remembered "the promise" [given in earlier dream] that I should be
"risen unto Him," and found happiness in that promise. I started to sing
as I worked, carrying the boxes out.

As if to underscore this thought, the dream now swung to practical stock
counsel, where the dreamer saw a business associate doing something ridiculous
at the Stock Exchange.

I was seated in a room upstairs with Wm. L. He seemed to be playing
a musical instrument. Then he asked me if I bought any Hupmobile stock.

The dreamer should note, said Cayce, that the incongruity of the scene was
already a warning to the dreamer about that particular stock.

"No," I replied. "I don't want any of that." "Then you won't be in on
the move we are in."

I saw loads of Hubmobile stock sell, reams of it coming out on the tape,
thousands of shares at the time. Hup is selling at around 21–22.

Again, said Cayce, the element of incongruity was a warning about this stock,
although it would soon be very active, as the dream suggested. The warning was
further emphasized by the dreamer's inability to place his order.

I rushed to buy 100 shares of stock, but couldn't get the order in. I reached
for the stock exchange phone to put the order in myself, to buy 100
shares of Hupmobile stock at market, when L's order clerk took the phone
from my hands, as though to say, "This isn't your affair." He said to me,
"I'll put the order in for you," and he did so. Then I went back and sat
down with L and noticed he started to play the guitar, or banjo.

Clearly, Cayce commented, the dreamer was being warned not to act on this stock at present. Instead, he should study it, using his conscious judgment. When the prospects looked good later, from a conscious viewpoint, then he could turn to the subconscious for confirmation, and "that as is necessary for the use as regarding same will be presented at that time."

Was the dreamer to check on such stocks only in dreams, or also while awake? Cayce said the next portion of the dream showed that he could have guidance both ways, if he worked at it:

> Then I was at home—our old living room, it seemed, in our Uptown home.

The setting of the old home and its associations was meant to indicate, Cayce observed, both the good values associated with home life there and the possibility of conscious guidance from the dreamer's now-dead father. The dreamer was already sensing that he could, by focusing his life on his highest values, and by the time and care spent in attunement, begin to call forth more guidance through telepathy than he had yet known—as the next part of the dream showed, with its hint of attunement across distance:

> The radio was going, and my mother and brother and I were enjoying it, the first two dancing to its tunes—I seated listening. Then it seemed we could not get any distance. I tried to tune in, and could not. I wrapped some wires around a spool, and attached this instrument to the machine, seeking thus to perfect and tune in, but it didn't work. Yet it should have, could have, might have. I gave it up, and we resumed listening to local stations.

The dreamer should on no account give up, Cayce insisted. Help was available.

> Then our maid came in and said, "You should be close to the front door, for God may come in. He will enter that way." My brother and mother paid little attention to her, but I perked up at once and started forward.

The maid was shown doing the announcing, said Cayce, because "he who would be master must be the servant of all," and "a little child shall lead them."

> Then the maid announced the distinguished visitor, that "God" was calling on us. I rushed out into the hall towards the door. Half way to the door I met God, and jumped for Him, throwing my arms around His neck, and hugging him. He embraced me.

The resemblance to the story of the Prodigal Son rested on the dreamer's deep regard for his own father, who had appeared in other dreams as his first glimmer of "the Heavenly Father."

> After that, I noticed God's appearance. He was a tall, well-built man, clean cut and clean shaven, wearing a brown suit and carrying a gray

derby hat. He had an intelligent look, an eye that was kindly but piercing. He had an expression that was firm and features clean cut. He was very healthy, robust, business-like and thorough, yet kindly, just, and sincere. Nothing slouchy, shuffling, maudlin, sentimental about Him—a man we might say we'd like to do business with. He was God in the flesh of today—a business or industrial man, not a clergyman, not dressed in black, not a weakling—a strong, healthy, intelligent Man, whom I recognized as the Man of today. And whom I welcomed and was glad to see, and recognized in this fine upright Man—not the ordinary—but God.

There had come to the dreamer, Cayce affirmed, a "vision as has been given of old, as even appeared to Father Abraham in the day of the destruction of the cities in the plains." The dream had shown God as a man, not as a servant but as "an equal in every way and manner—appearance, conversation, in dress" in order to burn into the dreamer's consciousness the realization that God desires to "make man, when man presents self in the fullness of self, equal *with* that Fullness. As has been given, 'We will make man in our own Image' " by "giving man that portion of the creation" within man's very soul, whose impulse would be "that man may become as God and One with Him."

It was a daring dream picture of the intent of creation itself, where man's destiny is to become an equal co-creator with the divine, and yet not the Whole. The pattern was not so strange, said Cayce, for it had been shown "even as the Son of Man in flesh appeared in the world, and made Himself one with man—yet His will, His force, His supply (drawn not from Himself) coming from the All-Powerful Force."

There is nothing automatic about the promise, Cayce affirmed. Each person must choose to put aside whatever blinds him, whatever distracts him—"that as is preventing man in the present from recognizing the force, power, manifestation, of the God that is presenting Self to man in everyday walks of life." The problem can be seen in the next sequence, set in Prohibition days.

> Then we passed my liquor closet—it was half open. God looked in; I showed Him the half-opened closet. But, I thought, I forget He is not the ordinary man he looks, but God and knows all. So I might as well show Him all, as pretend anything.

It was a response not out of keeping with repentance.

> So I opened the closet wide for Him to see. I showed Him my liquor, particularly the gin which I used for cocktails. "In case of sickness," I said to God. "You are well prepared," God replied sarcastically.

But it is not only lawbreaking, deception, indulgence, narcotism which shut man off from the divine, Cayce pointed out. The dream itself now turned to the deeper problem of "lack of thought, lack of quiet introspection," leading man to miss "the great love that is shown" and "the great force and power as is manifested," and "the great good as may be seen" shining right through and transforming "even those weaknesses, or that as is considered as of sin."

> We proceeded into the parlor, where the radio was still playing, and my brother and Ma amusing themselves with it. I wanted them to meet God, but they couldn't seem to recognize Him.
>
> "Of course they would not know Him," I thought. How could they recognize Him, when they have not the faith that He did appear in the flesh long ago in Christ, and that He could, might, may appear in the flesh again in just such a Man as was before me. If they don't understand how God appeared in the flesh Christ, how would they recognize a flesh God today?
>
> How could they understand that the true manifestation of the true perfection within us constituted the manifestation of God—whether of a man in one capacity or Another? So they did not see, or at least pay any attention to Him.

This portion of the dream called forth urgent response from Cayce, who said that each individual must "know that when they are in tune with the Infinite, how great must be that power which is set in motion, to bring about the manifestations of the divine that is within them"—with this purpose: "that men, others, thy brothers, may know that God *is,* and is the Rewarder of those who diligently seek Him." Such aid is not won by merit, nor found by abdicating selfhood. "Not as a gift that is bought, not as something that would take the place of the individual self. But as the natural consequence of the love of the Father for his creatures, for His Self in the soul, His portion in man, that would be One with Him."

God's aid to man, said Cayce, is not a vague, abstract assistance, but as concrete and immediate as the daily work or daily prayer, which the next dream scene showed. For this was He of Whom it was said, "Not one sparrow falls to the ground but what note is taken of same."

> I sat down on the sofa to converse with Him. "You could work harder," He said. I almost started to reply, yet bethought me that God knew all—no use. I meekly assented. "You could hardly do less," He continued.
>
> "How did you make out in Hup Motors?" he asked. I couldn't just say—not so well, it seemed. "That is L's purchase, L's recommendation, isn't it?" asked God. I knew that God knew before the asking. "Yes," I replied. "About all you have been doing lately is lifting capital, isn't it?" said God, motioning with his thumb towards my mother (from whom I had just borrowed). "Just about," I assented.
>
> God looked toward the radio. I was standing, studying the radio, as God disappeared.

The dreamer was being shown, said Cayce, "in that simple way and manner" where he must begin. As the radio made possible transmission from one human being to another "the things, the conditions, the good, the bad, that is taking place in one, how much more—through the infinite forces—must the cry, the pleading, of every individual come up to the Father on High!"

It was time, Cayce noted, for the dreamer to "take stock of self" in the light of this vision, to examine himself as a "servant of the One"—but as a servant who too often "sees not, because of the blinded eyes of self." Yet he should not despair, but attune himself as the radio suggested, "for the promise is to the faithful who do the biddings of Him, Who is the Giver of all good and perfect gifts." Stocks were His to give, but much more. He could bring an entire life to bloom, "for in Him we live and move and have our being."

The weight of such a dream not surprisingly tempted the dreamer to look down on others who had not received such dreams. Accordingly, he had another vision to correct his outlook. It was simple, but direct:

> I turned in bed, and beheld before me a statue in marble. It appeared as standing right next to me, or next to the bed right in the room. It was a headless statue, such as are represented in marble of the Greek God, Zeus. As usual, I became frightened (it was so vivid), but I felt assured when I reasoned that the statue was but an image or reflection of those lights that I now beheld on the ceiling. "Only an image of those lights," I reassured myself. But the statue remained, and so did the lights.

Cayce confirmed the dreamer's sense that the statue and the lights were connected, for he had seen a representation of spiritual force and material results, of the lights that bring forth men's products and creations. Each man, Cayce reminded the dreamer, is ultimately building his statue of the divine with the best he knows, whatever name he gives it, or no name. That he might not know the source of the One force is shown by the statue being headless. But each does what he can to bring into form what he believes is the "All-Powerful" in the universe, and no man can properly measure or condemn this effort in his brother.

Each individual must instead wrestle with his own evil, with those temptations which can hurt him and others. These are not so difficult to find, Cayce told the dreamer, "for as has been well given, three conditions prevent man in earthly plane from visualizing the spiritual elements in all phenomenized form in the physical world: pride of the eye, weakness of flesh, desire for fame." Each of these produce fear and doubt in the individual, making him lose his perspective, as the dreamer was shown in a startling vision:

> I was anywhere at any given time. I was contemplating the wonder of the inner power of all phenomena of the Lord.

> I was reflecting upon this power's direction of forms away from the One Self—hynpotizing its portion, as Bergson puts it, so as to appear in individual flesh form, and material phenomena.

Also saw my life experiences in this form, and I was very happy in my double vision of the outer form and the inner process.

Then a girl, seemingly representing the wisdom and consciousness of this inner power, and who seemed perfectly aware of my limited knowledge, threw a stone into space. It passed like a shooting star through the skies, and hit some animal there in space.

"He is going to get something he doesn't expect," said the girl, referring to me. And behold, it was so, for the stone, striking the animal in space, brought it to earth. There were two of them, and they were in cages. On earth they crawled along on their belly like a hideous snake, yet with head and neck upraised like powerful dragons. They moved around, dragging their cages with them.

Elsewhere Cayce described dragons as the sum of human passions and animal energies, as he discussed the symbology of the Book of Revelation.

They came close to the girl, close to other things: and although they looked dangerous, and I feared greatly for everything and everyone the animals came near, they seemed to do no harm—in fact helped matters. How, I cannot say, for I felt them a menace—i.e., viewed them with fear, but observed they did no harm.

The fear was in me, the hideous interpretation of what I recognized in me. But good seemed to be in them, for they suddenly changed from hideous animals to pretty little children, freely laughing, and dancing in glee.

Then, said the dreamer, the same point was made in a different way:

I was in a house with this girl who seemed to represent the power, the inner impetus, the Lord of creation—or as this power was represented in me, my subconscious self, which in a lower dimension is also present in all things.

I was in the material house, and knew my elusive pretty companion was also there. Yet I had much to learn about her, and she determined to give me a lesson. Mind, now, I knew she was there, saw in the vision the lesson she planned to surprise me with—that is, I was supposedly unaware of her plans.

I climbed the stairs of the house, and as I did so, the girl said to someone, "We'll give him a surprise and teach him." This all behind my back, so to speak. As I entered the room, instead of the beautiful girl I expected to find, I beheld a hideous black face, so ugly and so ferocious that I

fainted with fright! Upon awakening, I beheld the figure transformed
again into the pretty girl. She stood over me, winsome, smiling, and
encouraging. Happy—recognizing the spirit of her—I was yet afraid.

The dreamer himself guessed that the dream had shown him how fear distorts
human experiences, human energies. Cayce told him he was correct, and that
fear and selfishness are prominent in what men call hell, for "they are what first
separates an entity from God." The girl, as often in his dreams, was the force
of truth in his life, teaching him.

Human passions may be monsters or playful, hideous or winsome, depending
entirely on what human beings do with them. In themselves they are only power
or energy. Cayce pointed out this theme in many of the dreams submitted to him.

Dreams of Passions

There were many dreams of sex in the hundreds submitted to Cayce, employing
varied emblems. A dreamer interested in an illicit lover affair saw himself as
chasing a shiny white pig. In another dream he saw himself falling through
trapdoors and caught in a maze of wires around his legs—traps and entanglements,
according to the Cayce reading. One dreamer more than once saw himself playing
a game where spikes were placed in grooves. Another dreamed of himself in a
morass with his secretary trying to pull him out; when she couldn't make it, she
said, "Then pull me down." It was a dream not difficult for Cayce to interpret.
But Cayce did not devalue sexual energies, instead constantly urged his dreamers
to live well-rounded lives. A woman who withheld herself from her husband
was admonished to think the problem through for herself, not to call upon his
readings to justify her.

Anger, too, has its proper place in human affairs, as Cayce interpreted dreams
of hostility. One can, as Paul had said in the New Testament, "be angry but sin
not." However, anger mixed with cruelty, fear, and defensiveness has its own
way of poisoning the angry one, not only mentally but even physically. A dreamer
who found himself in a dream as a general, mercilessly slaying the enemy, was
seeing, said Cayce, his own vengefulness which so often led him to dream of
being persecuted by the Ku Klux Klan.

The peril of selfish fixation was underlined, said Cayce, in the dream of a
man too proud of his ancestry and clan; he clung to his wife desperately while
an "elevated" train swung dangerously on its tracks.

Part of the answer to the call of passions, in Cayce's view, is play and playful-
ness. One must take time to do many of the very things shown in dreams—go
to the theater, converse with friends, read, golf, take trips, read the comics—whatever one knows from experience worked best for him.

Dreams of Success Strivings

One of Cayce's dreamers had a memorable dream experience of Christ. But
in the dream, Palm Beach proved stronger than Christ, for the dreamer lost track
of Him as he name-dropped before wealthy associates in a resort hotel. The

dream warning was not one which Cayce had to labor. The same dreamer saw himself in another dream as coming to two bridges, a higher and a lower, and taking the lower, even though he had to crawl to traverse it, because it was more familiar to him. Cayce said the dream had set before him a choice of two ways of life.

But the choice that faced his dreamers was not between asceticism and tasteful surroundings. Cayce found nothing the matter with wealth and position, provided they weren't the ultimate goal. When a dreamer saw himself rebuked for having damaged the front of someone's fashionable New York brownstone, he was told by Cayce that his ideas were indeed going to embarrass some of his fashionable associates. But the damage would not be permanent, to him or to them, if he stuck by the truth, for "God is God, even of the brownstone house."

The lure of wealth came not only to others in dreams, but to Edgar Cayce himself. More than once he saw himself as eloping with a lovely girl, leaving his family behind. In addition to sex drives, his readings told him, he was seeing his own temptation to put wealth ahead of prior commitments. Nor did he escape dreams of illicit drives to fame, through lecturing to women's clubs, or locating treasures, or even contacting the dead. He would make his place in history, his readings assured him, but not by such performances—instead by the quality of his service to others.

A dreamer who was slight of build and emotional of temperament longed to be famous before his fellows, as his dreams kept showing him. The way of pomp was dramatized when he saw himself an officious ship's captain. A different and better way showed a boy named Tom doing creative things with radio antennae throughout an entire town. Showing people the way to attunement in their ordinary lives was a better service than being captain of an ocean liner.

The lure of psychic ability was often in the dreams of those who turned to Cayce, because of his example and their own experiences under his coaching. But the lure brought with it warnings. One man saw himself responsible for bringing Cayce out of trance, but leaving him there in grave personal danger, in order not to offend party guests with the strange sight of a hypnotized man. He would have to choose, said Cayce, between love of appearances and developing real ability.

Equally compelling to Cayce's dreamers was the call of wisdom, stimulated as they were by the range of knowledge on which Cayce drew. One man dreamed of knowledge as a dog which turned and bit him. Others dreamed of truth as a beautiful woman, coming down the stairs or even standing at a bar—but capable of appearing ugly, and of making imperious demands. Cayce himself dreamed of wisdom as a snake, after losing the hospital had cured him of some airs. In the dream the snake spoke to him, saying it would not harm him further, after he had chased it with a large stick—the "rod or staff of life" given to those who are faithful to God, said the reading of the dream.

It was difficult for Cayce to train those with newly found dream powers to place them in a balanced life. One man dreamed that he was getting help in his golf game from a discarnate who told him he couldn't help him if he hurried so much. The next day, after contemplating the dream, he played the best game of golf in his life. The same question had to be faced in business and home life, said Cayce, as well as in psychic development.

Dreams of Serving Others

A man given to many words found himself stirred in a dream, as he often was, to match wisdom with service. He saw a small child whom he wanted to take for a canoe ride. But the way was blocked by one event after another. He was seeing, said Cayce, the impossibility of service without devotion to the Source; without that, things had a way of never working out, however admirable the intentions.

A businessman dreamed that his brother was bored while he discussed his own hobby. It was, said Cayce, a reminder that if one wanted the interest of others, he had to be interested in them. Indeed, the ultimate worth of everything the dreamer said and did for others would be unconsciously weighed by others against the quality of his responsiveness to them in the little things of life.

A dreamer given to fantasies of his solitary grandeur as he pursued spiritual things was the subject of a dream where he saw chorus girls kicking in step. Unless he could learn to work with others at least as well as they could, said Cayce, his development would not go far. It was the same thought in a different setting which prompted Cayce to dream of a study group while he was giving a reading for them. He saw the face of Christ, and noticed how it changed as each member of the group was given a message in the reading. By reviewing those expressions, Cayce was told, he could help each member of the group to learn something about his own willingness or unwillingness to cooperate with the others in the studies before them.

The old tensions between Christian and Jew were often to the fore in dream material submitted to Cayce by his Jewish dreamers. One of them saw a resolution which Cayce commended. He was in a swanky dress shop which was running out of dresses, and told the proprietor he knew where to get the needed dresses "wholesale," from an East Side shop of lower status that carried excellent merchandise. The shops, said Cayce, were the Christian and Jewish establishments, respectively, and they needed to form a partnership because of what each could give the other.

But the changes that must occur to bring man closer to his full stature, in modern civilization, would not be accomplished primarily by the heads of religions or the heads of state. When a wealthy man dreamed of losing his job and his social status because of a book he was writing, Cayce told him to go right on with the book and the ideas it represented. In seeing himself poor, he was seeing that whoever would really serve must be "all things to all men." Moreover, he was seeing something else he intuitively understood, that what is "termed the mediocre class of individuals in the physical world bear the brunt of the whole nations, as a people"; so, from the ordinary folk "must come that balm, that leaven, that will leaven the whole lump." The key to lasting social change was helping ordinary people to help themselves.

All real service to others begins at home, Cayce told his dreamers. When a man dreamed that his pregnant wife had triplets, Cayce told him he was seeing that one and one make three—not only in the way two parents produce an offspring, but in the way husband and wife complement each other in many ways, and produce more good than the sum of their individual talents.

But family affairs were not absolutes. When a man saw his mother's face slapped in a dream, he was told he was sacrificing her well-being to the appearance of family harmony.

In Cayce's view, the service of others is central to human destiny. But it is subject to as much distortion of motive as are passion and success. In his view, service and attunement go hand in hand. Service without attunement leads to manipulation of others—doing good that never works out. But attunement without service leads to inflation of the dreamer and to his eventual paralysis, for "to know and not to do is sin."

Dreams of a Free Life

In Edgar Cayce's readings there is the promise of a way of life that offers a free and joyous spirit in the midst of the laws and contingencies that govern human existence.

Cayce himself reported that he had lost this sense of joyful freedom for many years, and then—after suffering and rededication—suddenly recovered it.

> While meditating in afternoon, the same exuberant feeling came over me
> that used to years ago, but which had been lost to me for twenty-five years.

When he submitted this experience for a reading, he was told he had been through "an experience of the inner self awakening to those potential forces as may become the more active . . . in those of the meditations." From this time on, Cayce gave silent meditation a larger place in his life, and urged it more often for those whom he trained.

The same reading added spontaneously, "As has been given, there shall be in the latter days, 'Your young men shall dream dreams, your old men shall see visions, your maidens shall prophesy.' These are coming to pass, with the upheavals as are just before the world [1932] in many a quarter!"

One of his dreamers reported a similar experience, after working on dreams for over a year.

> While reading James' Varieties of Religious Experience. I submit this,
> as I can't tell whether it is a religious experience of my own, or whether
> it was purely a case of nerves, i.e., physical or pathological.

Cayce interrupted him to say, "An experience—not nerves." Then the man reported:

> While reading, a sudden quivering came over me. I felt every pulsation
> of my heart, of the nerves, of the blood. I became conscious of a vibratory
> force moving everything within my body—even the chair upon which I
> was sitting seemed to be in motion. I was not asleep—

Again Cayce interrupted, and the report was not finished. He told the man he had experienced the physical effect of the "consecration of self, self's impulses, self's inner self" to the manifestation of the One Force in his life. He had undergone an authentic spiritual experience. In fact, Cayce added, it was an experience that could be traced "through the various ages of man's development," and he offered these illustrations:

Swedenborg, as he studied.

Socrates, as he meditated.

Paul, the apostle, as he meditated upon the happenings of the hour, with his inward purpose meeting that spiritual force in man which brought his self-conviction; the entity, then, being over-shadowed by the Force as seen, see?

And as was by Buddha, in that position when meditation in the forest brought to the consciousness of the entity the At-Oneness of *all force* manifested through physical aspect in a material world.

Cayce told the dreamer that in his moment of quickening he had seen and experienced the kind of personal baptism meant in the Bible—"My Spirit beareth witness with thy spirit, whether ye be the sons of God or not." This joy, this trembling sense of spiritual reality at work in human life, had been no deception. But it was meant to have concrete fruits. For Cayce told the man that from now on he would not only receive greater insights into the human lot, but he would have to counsel more people spontaneously seeking his aid regarding their daily lives. His prediction proved accurate.

Such lifting up would give a man a new sense of freedom. "But love is law and law is love," Cayce told him. The freedom came to put him in bondage—to those who needed him. Not painful bondage, not sad bondage, but grateful bondage.

Many months later, Cayce referred back to this experience while reading James, when the dreamer reported dreaming that his little baby was not afraid. This dream showed exactly the right outcome of such experiences, said Cayce. "Except as ye become little children, ye shall in no wise enter in." Such attunement could genuinely cleanse and renew a man, even when he had made drastic mistakes, until his spirit was as fresh as a child's.

The same dreamer had made a costly error of stock judgment, one which cost him and his associates thousands of dollars. It was the last he ever made of such magnitude, for he learned from it to better follow his inner guidance. But he berated himself for it, as seen in a little dream fragment which contained only two words "My fault." Commenting on this fragment, Cayce insisted that one should never be afraid of errors honestly made, if one's purposes were sound. One could and should walk free of self-condemnation, for such self-destroying was never intended for man.

A harassed businessman reported this dream, early in his work with Cayce:

A man approached many, including myself, in what seemed to be a hotel

lobby. When he first approached us, he had the appearance of a detective,
but as he drew near I had the feeling that he was Jesus Christ.

This little dream, said Cayce, had caught the whole force of God's ways with
man on earth. He would be found coming to each person as Man to man, coming
from out of the crowd in the hotel lobby. He would be as ordinary as the next
face seen but capable of changing each individual, each group, even the masses
and crowds, if taken seriously in one life at a time. His ways might seem
restrictive at first, but they were not. He came to set men free. The dreamer,
too, could walk among his fellows in this same manner and purpose, if only he
would choose.

In Cayce's view, the dreams which come to a seeking man can unfold to him
the very structures of creation, itself, if he needs to understand these. He interpreted dreams which he said were about destiny, about the One Force, about
evil, about the outer void, about Mother Sea and the Heavenly Father, about
laws, about grace, about the soul and its voyage in the ship of the psyche. These
matters are important, for they lead to understanding and conviction that can
reach to the farthest depths of the mind and heart.

But orienting the life through dreams means beginning much closer than these
far vistas.

Such a beginning was enacted in one of Cayce's own dreams—a quaint dream,
but pungent, that came when his hospital and university were being closed, and
when a number of dreams offered him encouragement.

About an old horse that in real life had died twenty years ago.

It was climbing up a hill. We turned it loose so it could pull itself up,
and we walked behind it in the tracks the horse made. I said it was a
good thing the horse had just been shod, so that the feet would make
tracks for us to step or climb by.

The reading on this dream interpreted the horse, as Cayce's readings often did,
as the bearer of a spiritual message. Cayce awake might feel his message was
spent, and his life of little account. But he should take one step at a time. Then,
if he looked, he would find that where he stepped there were tracks to walk in.
There would be places made not only by new horseshoes, but by the Messenger
Himself—Who goes before every man to lead him, "sure of step, but constantly
mounting."

Out of imagery as plain as the memory of an old horse, his dream had fashioned
for him a promise.

It was a promise fulfilled, for his best readings and most helpful training of
others were yet to come.

It was a dream where the eternal was hidden in the ordinary. This was the
promise Edgar Cayce's readings perceived in all dreaming, for all dreamers, in
the century which had rediscovered dreams.

EDGAR CAYCE

ON HEALING

*by Mary Ellen Carter
and William A. McGarey, M.D.*

All names have been changed except those of the Cayce family and their friends as they are mentioned; the Cayce Hospital Staff members; Mrs. Gladys Davis Turner, secretary to Edgar Cayce; and several doctors and practical nurses who are indicated by an asterisk.

M.E.C.

CONTENTS

INTRODUCTION

THE TWENTIETH-CENTURY history of parapsychology will probably catalogue Edgar Cayce, one of America's best-documented psychics, as a medical telepathist. The Association for Research and Enlightenment, Inc., a psychical research society, was formed in 1932 to preserve and experiment with his data. Its library in Virginia Beach, Virginia contains 14,246 copies of Edgar Cayce's psychic readings, stenographically recorded over a period of 43 years. Of this number 8,976, or about 64%, describe the physical disabilities of several thousand persons and suggest treatment for their ailments.

For a great many physicians, medical studies of treatment patterns for a number of major physical diseases seem to suggest the advisability of testing Edgar Cayce's theories. With this in mind, the physical readings have been made available to a clinic in Phoenix, Arizona staffed by four medical doctors. Through written reports and yearly conferences, information on results of treatments are being made available to more than 250 M.D.'s and osteopaths.

After two years of clinical work with the readings and ten years of study and testing in private practice, William McGarey, M.D., Director of the A.R.E. Clinic in Phoenix, agreed to collaborate with Mary Ellen Carter, a long time A.R.E. member and widely-known author on Edgar Cayce data, in bringing to print the human interest stories of a selection of original readings given by Edgar Cayce. For each one, Dr. McGarey has added an up-to-date medical commentary. Many of our readers have heard these stories told; here at last are the exciting details.

—Hugh Lynn Cayce

FOREWORD

Cases Cured in the Cayce Readings

THIS BOOK IS about a psychic and his work in suggesting methods by which healing might come to the human body. These suggestions centered on the field of medicine and spread out over osteopathy, chiropractic, physical therapy, herbal therapy, nutrition, spiritual therapy, hypnotherapy, dentistry, and what is best described as "other methods." As a waking individual, Edgar Cayce often looked into the future in flashes of insight or, at times, viewed a person's makeup from the appearance of his aura and commented on it, apparently seeing events in the past and in the future which dealt with that person's total life as an individual. His psychic ability was indeed unique while he was in the full waking state.

Asleep, however, Cayce apparently found the curtains pulled widely apart which for most of us usually obscure the past, the future, and the true nature of man as seen in the skein of time and space. He found himself giving information that, in his own unconscious state, he termed as arising from universal sources. He described events of the future with almost as great a clarity as he discussed the physiological functioning of an ailing human body that might be 2,000 miles away. In this state he apparently had communication with the unconscious minds of people everywhere but specifically with the mind of that person for whom he was giving a reading. Much has been written about this in numerous publications, and he has been adjudged the outstanding sensitive of the twentieth-century.

All of this activity at the unconscious level still allowed him to dream and, upon awakening from a reading, he was able to describe the dream experience. Even the dream, Cayce suggests, is a psychic experience which often participates in the past and the future and predicts for those who would study their dreams every important event destined to happen in their lives. Many important personal as well as world prophecies came to Cayce in dreams, both during the course of a reading and at the more normal dream times—at night while he slept.

At times during a reading, he would correct the shorthand notes made by his secretary who was sitting across the room and who had made an error in transcription of a word or a phrase. His mind, indeed, had many facets, and he has, after his death, become an object of study by interested researchers from many fields of scientific endeavor.

His discussion of an individual's travel through time led to the interweaving through all of the Cayce material of that theory which is called reincarnation, or the continuity of a soul's existence through all time.

His work with illnesses of the human body has provided for me the most fascinating and potentially important information that I have found in the 14,500 readings he gave over a period of some 40 years. Some 9,000 of these readings dealt with human illness and its correction. The manner in which he was able to describe conditions with such accuracy—illnesses and points of strength of which he had no conscious awareness—has within it implications that are not easily avoided to all those involved in the field of healing.

Since I enjoy a challenge, and since the nature of a researcher demands an open mind, this material then became a most exciting experience for me. It has gradually suggested the possibility that we, in our present state of knowledge and understanding, are far removed from the perfect comprehension of this amazing creation that we call the human body.

I realize that most physicians do not relish the idea of commenting publicly on the validity of psychic data—especially when this is dealt with in depth. But then most medical doctors have never either studied or experienced psychic happenings. Aside from the dream world, which most of us do not consider to be dealing with any manner of what is called ESP, we as physicians tend to stay away from the psychic event—especially in the practice of medicine—since it is so difficult to pin down with the current methodology of science. Also, if the truth be known, it scares us a bit.

When reincarnation with its concept of rebirth and karma—the law of cause and effect—is added to the picture, the gap for the physician then often grows wider. However, one studying the Cayce material must at some point deal with these concepts of the unusual qualities of the mind and the destiny of the soul as a timeless voyager in putting to rest the unique phenomenon that Mr. Cayce presents to us in his life and experiences.

Physicians with an oriental background do not have as much of a problem with the psychic as do occidentals, since the reality of the soul's voyage in continuity through many lifetimes is a portion of their heritage. Most orientals have accepted reincarnation as factual and not worth arguing about. This concept, they say, once accepted leads one away from a materialistic viewpoint and makes it easier to understand and accept psychic events and their implications.

Westerners for the most part are Judeo-Christian in their religious roots. There really should be no difficulty in accepting and understanding, to an extent, those things which we currently call "psychic" or what Shafica Karagulla, M.D., has called "higher sense perception." These religious teachings, based on the writings of the ancient Jews, are rich in psychic events. These include stories—often considered symbolic—such as Adam hearing God's words reverberating through a forest; the passage of the children of Israel through the divided Red Sea guided by an angel and a pillar of cloud by day and a pillar of fire by night; Elijah's restoring a boy's life at the behest of his mother; the dreams of Mary, Joseph, and the wise men guiding events in the life of the baby Jesus; healings of many kinds of afflictions by Jesus and his disciples; and the revelation of John, who did not know whether he was "in the spirit" or not—but saw some of the same symbols described much earlier by Ezekial, Jeremiah, and other Old Testament prophets.

Cayce's work, then, poses somewhat of a problem for those of us who are physicians and claim to be Jewish or Christian in our belief. For we can deny believing in psychic things only at the expense of divesting ourselves of some of our most precious religious concepts. To be a Jew or a Christian and to say that the psychic world is a myth is to introduce confusion into our methods of thinking and thus into our lives as a whole.

The Bible presents man as a spiritual being who is in that manner like unto God. Man as a physical creation with a mind capable of creative activity, even to the extent of denying his Creator, does not detract from his spiritual origin and existence. This spiritual reality, described rather explicitly in the Bible, is the basis—as Edgar Cayce sees man—for his inherent ability to perform in a manner which we call psychic. Thus, Cayce presents a challenge, not only to the physician—although he is perhaps primarily involved as far as this book is concerned—but to every reader, to evaluate the factual material which is present in the readings and to look at it with the degree of honesty and open mindedness that scientists must use in approaching a research problem.

This might lead one, then, to accept the implications in this mass of data and understand man's psychic capabilities as a part of one's daily life. Cayce would suggest that this then would bring all events of one's life into perspective as they relate to the activity of the soul and would lead one to see all events of life—even illness—as a necessary and perhaps a learning experience as man passes through time and space.

Leaving supposition, implication, philosophy, and other imponderables aside, I should point out that this book is written consistently in two parts. In the major structure of the writing, Mary Ellen Carter has created a picture of factual data revolving around the lives of several people (some critically ill) and who, through suggestions given by Mr. Cayce in his sleep-state, regained their health as well as a different perspective on life. The information in these stories is factual, and the details can be found in the library of the Association for Research and Enlightenment. People were interviewed, stories were substantiated, and the material from the readings was deliberately drawn upon to unfold the events in these people's lives.

Mrs. Carter has attempted to portray in these stories the human events that take place within a home and a family as sickness of a serious nature strikes. The doubts, the confusions that come about as people seek to find healing for their bodies in different manners is for each person, perhaps, a time of crisis in his life experience. For these same doubts and confusions and what one does about them may indeed shape and color one's total life accomplishments. These people are like most of us. They, however, asked for information from a source most people at the time considered to be really "way out"—a source that just could not be truly understood. For most people of that day, Cayce's information just "did not compute."

Each of Mrs. Carter's accounts is followed by the physiological concepts and the various therapeutic modalities which Cayce suggested and which were then a part of these various lives. I have tried to be factual and objective in my approach while adding to the discussion the concepts which seem to evolve out of this psychic data concerning the manner in which the human body functions, its nature as a physical-mental-spiritual entity, and the therapeutic approach which should be made to restore a body from a state of illness to its natural condition of health, I have drawn rather heavily on quotations from pertinent readings which illustrate how Cayce's concepts of man and his existence here on the earth vary from our present understanding of the body and utilization of therapy in treating disease.

I hope you enjoy reading this as much as I have enjoyed participating in writing it.

—*William A. McGarey, M.D.*

CHAPTER 1

THE LADY WHO WAS TURNING TO STONE

DISASTER OFTEN OVERTAKES us like a cat that steals upon its prey. For Florence Evans, 29, organist and choir director for the Toddesville Methodist Church on that chill November evening in 1937, the cat was about to spring.

She paused as she started up the church steps. There were only three of them, and yet her knees seemed to buckle a little and there was a strange shortness of breath accompanied by profuse perspiration in the palms of her hands. "I must be coming down with the flu again," she thought and swung the heavy door open with an effort.

Sunday's service was an ordeal for her. She was hardly able to play the hymns, the special anthem seemed to her to drag interminably, and the postlude was agony. At the end of the service she was aching throughout her body, perspiring, and near collapse. She managed to get herself out to her parents' Ford parked at the side of the church, and there she stayed until they came out to find her.

They rushed her home to the little house on Maple Street and put her to bed. She was so hot inside, she complained. And she wanted some aspirin!

After a day, when she was still in bed and had not improved, Dr. Harold Maddox was called in. He was certain, he said, that Florence had the flu. "Let her drink plenty of liquids, keep her in bed, and have her take the medicine I'll send around."

Every day she tried to get up; but the unrelenting ache engulfed her now, and she would fall back exhausted into bed.

Christmas came and went, and still she grew no better. Ten days before Christmas, she noticed an odd hardening of the flesh on her hips. "It's because I'm lying around so much," she thought. "I'm getting bedsores."

But the hardening grew worse. One day, she found that her flesh was hard throughout her body from her hips down to her knees.

By now, she had been examined by three doctors, all of whom were baffled by her symptoms.

Like a fresh breeze was her Aunt Stacy who lived in another town close by and who was her mother's sister. She was a tall, independent-minded soul who had married rather late in life and was not apologetic about it. Now she came swooping in upon the scene with a firm hand.

"Cara," said Aunt Stacy to her mother, "you are to get some sleep. You will let me make some of the decisions, and you are to let me help you with the housework. And, of course, I can nurse Florence as well as anybody."

Florence was taken by her mother and father to Nashville in January to enter the Haggard Clinic for tests. It was just after New Year's, the weather was cold, the trip dreary. When the tests were over, they assured her, they would know what to do.

But after all the examinations were done, the doctor who had greeted them now gave them little encouragement. Florence had a hardening and thickening of the skin, which they called "derma," or scleroderma.

"There have been only 400 cases like yours on record," Florence's father told her later. It was several days before Florence was told that very few such cases ever recovered.

"Florence Evans, the lady who's turning to stone," she thought as she lay in bed in her own room once more. It was a nightmare! One of pain and unnatural change through which she had been living for eight weeks. She had been pretty: grey eyes and chestnut hair. Now, when she looked into a mirror, the face of a stranger stared back at her, swollen and rigid. And it was hard, like her hips, now.

And the unspeakable word which no one had used, but which everybody understood, had filtered into her consciousness: the word *incurable*.

On January 6, Dr. Maddox came to visit her and said that he would obtain some information from a research laboratory about Florence's condition. Now her hopes soared, for she had faith in the science of her day. She still clung to the thought that some magic would be found to work for her.

But two days later, she awoke with the aching permeating her body more than ever, compounded by a burning sensation along her spine. Her mother came in, bringing aspirin and water. She took them gratefully, carefully propping herself up with a contrived smile. Her father came in and sat down on a chair by the bed.

"Florence, have you forgotten Cayce?" he asked, his head tilted inquisitively, his lean face gentle.

She was suddenly aware of the sun pouring into her room. And aware, too, more than she dared to admit even to herself, of her faith that a reading from Edgar Cayce, the clairvoyant "doctor" of Virginia Beach, would be the answer to her desperate need.

She was well informed of the unorthodox treatments he usually prescribed. She knew, also, that he had read for hundreds of people right there in Toddesville and the surrounding community, as well as people in many parts of the country. When medical doctors had failed, or found nothing could be done for their patients, Cayce had been called in to give readings, although he remained in his home miles away! Miraculous results had followed his diagnoses and treatments given for many people, and his fame was growing every day.

Three years ago she herself had been advised by him in a reading to "purify" her body by taking internally doses of a weird concoction containing essence of wild cherry, essence of poke-root, essence of yellow dock root, and several other ingredients. She had had to change her diet quite drastically, too: no fried foods, but a lot of fresh vegetables, no pork and not much beef; no bananas and no ice cream. But she had overcome her case of acne, and it had taken a mere seven or eight months.

Thinking back over that experience and recalling, too, that her mother, father, and Aunt Stacy all had had readings by Edgar Cayce that proved beneficial, she began to smile.

Her father said, "That's better!"

And her mother wept quietly as she sat at the foot of the bed. When Aunt Stacy was told on the telephone of the message they planned to send to Cayce that very day, she said, "*Now* we'll see some action!"

"Yes," began Florence's reading given a few days later, "we have the body here. This we have had before. As we find, it has been rather late in beginning with the disturbances that have arisen. . . ."

He went on to say that the distrubances were of a very subtle nature and that unless there could be something to help resist the inroads of a *tubercle* in Florence's body, the condition would rapidly become worse. He suggested that the tubercle was making inroads in the respiratory system and the muscles, as well as the red blood cells.

To throw off these conditions, castor oil packs should be applied over the abdominal area and also the lower part of the back up to the diaphragm. Also, Ventriculin in small quantity should be taken twice daily. She should have beef juice often and little or no starchy foods.

Specific details as to quantities and times were given for the application of these treatments. The packs, to begin immediately, were to be continued "until there has been stayed this tendency for the formation of knots or clots by the blood supply attempting to make for coagulations; and thus forming in the muscular forces, and drainings upon the system at the same time, those hardened places—not only in the spinal area, but in the abdominal area, also . . ."

The reading was translated later that very day into the following telegram, which Florence read with great elation as she sat propped up in bed: "Sponge off with saturated solution bicarbonate of soda, then apply hot castor oil packs heavy over abdomen and lower spine for three hours. Rest three hours, begin again. Also take Ventriculin without iron half teaspoonful twice daily. Small quantities of beef juice often with Ry-Krisp or whole wheat crackers. No other breads or starches. Use enemas body temperature rather than cathartics. Full information special. Consult Mrs. Stacia Holms for immediate application suggestions."

"Mrs. Stacia Holms" was, of course, Aunt Stacy, and she was delighted to supervise the treatments. She had nursed many of her relatives and friends as a practical nurse, and she was a welcomed presence now.

She stood silently by the door in the room and with Cara and Paul Evans listened while Florence read the telegram aloud. When she had finished, Stacy thumped the night stand. "I *knew* Cayce would know!" she exulted. "Let's start right in!"

"What do we do first?" Cara said breathlessly.

"We have to get a lot of castor oil," observed Paul quietly.

Florence giggled.

"Yes. And a box of bicarbonate of soda, and that Ventriculin from the drug store . . . without iron . . . Oh, I must write down a list!"

"We'll need a big piece of oil cloth," said Stacy.

When Paul returned a little later with the items on Cara's list, Stacy expertly began the ritual of bathing her in hot castor oil packs. Florence took her first dose of Ventriculin. They entered the treatment with rejoicing. Florence sensed that Stacy was going about her work, not mechanically, but as if she were indeed in league with the Higher Forces. Once, Florence would have seen no connection between scientific application of healing agents, and God. Now she told Stacy, "We're working with God!"

A little later, she looked up to see that Stacy's eyes were closed, as if in prayer. Florence said nothing, but closed her eyes and raised her own thoughts to ascend with those being offered up on her behalf. It proved to be a moment in which together they shared a healing Presence. Florence was to cling to that moment in the months to come.

"I've never had such a case before," Stacy told Paul later in the hallway, out of Florence's hearing, "nor seen such a pitiful condition. Frankly, it's going to be a long, uphill work."

The temperature and sweating which Florence was experiencing were due to the tubercle, said the reading which arrived in its entirety a few days later. This germ had attacked the blood stream. Florence was to remain in bed, yet she was to have "plenty of fresh air" in her room. Fumes from Oil of Pine burned in the room would help her chest as would fumes from equal portions of Eucalyptol and Tincture of Benzoin.

Five days after begining the treatment, color was reappearing in Florence's face. Her mother wrote Edgar Cayce, "I thank you so much for your interest in us and pray that there is some help for her. . ."

Always, Stacy seemed to apply the packs with a loving prayer in which Florence found it natural that she herself participate. With Cara, it was more verbal: "Oh, Father, please make our little girl well." She often said it at bedtime, just as she had when Florence was small.

But with Stacy, she *was* the prayer. She uttered it in her very step, in the way she put her head on one side and sized up a person or a situation from her own secret vantage point. Her strong hands moved through the myriad of services for her patient like the hands of a devout woman making the sign of the Cross or folding in prayer. There was about her a healing force that emanated to all who met her.

A few days after they removed the packs from Florence's regimen, they were dismayed to discover that she was becoming worse. On a Sunday evening, they sat near her bed, contemplating her plight. Florence lay with her eyes closed, her face pale, her body limp with fatigue. She had to be propped up on the pillows to get her breath.

They decided to call Dr. Maddox, because she was becoming distraught with the agony in her chest. When he arrived, he had little to say as he examined her. But he offered no hope and said merely, "Watch her carefully. I will be at home tonight and in my office tomorrow." He went out into the hall.

Then he added, "I'm sorry," to Cara and Paul. Paul nodded because there was nothing to say.

After he had left, Cara wept against Paul's shoulder. "She's dying!"

Stacy silently began to get out the castor oil and the oilcloth. Later, as Florence remained about the same though she was wrapped in the pack, they seemed to be back where they had started.

They decided to seek another reading from Cayce at once. Stacy insisted, "Don't send for this unless you are going to follow it!"

Injections given by the doctor had "caused disturbances to the heart's activity, to the coordination between the sympathetic and the cerebro-spinal system," said this reading.

The oil packs had been obtaining results, since they had been properly given. They were to be kept up now for several days at a time, then stopped for a rest period of a week. All other phases of the therapy were to be continued, particularly the starchless diet.

One new kind of treatment was added: application of a low electrical vibration by means of the "wet cell appliance" described by Cayce in previous readings for other illnesses. Substances which would be added to her body by this means would be Atomidine, Chloride of Gold, and Spirits of Camphor. The daily treatments would last for thirty minutes each. Cayce described how to make the attachments in detail: the plates were to be attached to various parts of Florence's body to allow the different solutions to impart their beneficial influences.

"Each solution carries to the circulation the vibrations of these properties to act upon the glandular system, as well as the circulation," said the reading.

For ten days she used the wet cell appliance as directed. There was never any sensation except that of well-being. Secretly, she wondered if the thing would really help her. Just as the packs were deceptively simple, so, too, were the low electrical vibrations that produced simply a pleasant relaxation and a predisposition to sleep.

Then, unaccountably, she experienced a rigor accompanied by severe aching. There was bleeding from the rectum. Another occurred, and she wired Cayce to ask if she was using the appliance correctly.

This was, she was told, "the system's attempting to adjust itself and eliminate those disturbances in the circulation that have caused the checking of the flow to the lymph circulation." The rigors arose from the attempts of her body to throw off the poisons in her system.

Changes were made in treatment. Alcohol rubs were added, and advice was given to continue with enemas using Glyco-Thymoline. It was now spring. Florence remained very ill, although improvement was noticeable.

On March 5, her mother wrote Cayce that Florence was not well and that her stomach trouble was something new. Strangely, on that very day Cayce volunteered a reading for Florence at the end of another person's physical check reading after Hugh Lynn Cayce, as conductor, had given the suggestion, "That is all."

Began this unsolicited advice: "Now the conditions are much on the improve, by the vibrations that have been set up through the system by the low electrical forces and the rub," and he identified this reading as being for Florence Evans, Toddesville, Kentucky!

"These should be kept," he went on. He gave further directions for the use of the wet cell and added that a charred keg of a gallon and a half be half-filled with pure apple brandy and that the fumes from this, heated, might be "inhaled whenever there is the tendency for a shaky or ague feeling or weakness."

Wrote Cara in reply: "The reading . . . was an answer to my prayers. We are so very grateful to you for this information. She has been so bright and cheerful all day. We felt that in some ways her condition was improved, yet she suffers so much from the aching. The hardness of her skin is less, though very evident yet, through the hips and limbs to knees. May God bless you and your wonderful work. . . ."

There had been a turning point. Her next reading now shifted from strictly physical healing to a high level of spiritual attitudes, particularly to be assumed during the wet cell treatments. Then she should be "in a meditative, prayerful mind," putting herself "into the hands, into the arms, into the care of the Savior. Not merely as trusting, not merely as hoping, but as relying upon the promises. And make them cooperative, co-active. Be used for something, not only good but good for something, that ye may bring into the experience of others—even by thine own ability to suffer—the glorious knowledge of the working of the Christ-Consciousness within the individual mind. . . ."

"For if these are adhered to," stated this reading, "if these are kept, we will find the helpful forces in every manner; not only with the patience to bear the cross of distress or anxiety but with the means and the friends and the hopes to *carry on* for Him!"

By May, she had improved so much that hardness was disappearing, her temperature was normal, and there were no more night sweats. But because she still suffered with the aching, she decided to go to the Mayo Clinic for tests and left off the castor oil packs once more. Soon she was suffering again with rigors and temperature, as well as the sweats. Now another reading put her back on the packs and other aids. In time her health returned to the point where she wanted to go back to her work of teaching music and conducting her choir.

In her next reading she asked, "Will you please tell me if you can when I can go back to work and if I should work at the church and teach also?"

She was told that she should do both. "These are a part of [your]self." She was to "Keep the constructive forces in much of the prayer and meditation, and especially in the periods when the appliance is used. Raise that vibration within self that there are within self the healing forces. For all healing of every nature comes only from the One Source, the Giver of all good and perfect gifts."

She was free now from the necessity of using the daily packs and was to take them only when she had a spell of "rigors." She was to use instead gentle olive oil rubs.

Cara was afraid she would pull her health down by going back to work. "Well, maybe Cayce can get me in such good health that I won't have any flu this winter," Florence told her.

Her aunt had gone home long before now, and when Florence told her the news that she was going back to work, Stacy was equally exuberant. "Don't get too frisky," she warned. "You're not out of the woods yet."

"I know. But just to get out of those packs is like heaven! In this heat they're not very funny."

But even at the end of the summer the aching did not leave her. "It's setting me wild," she reported to Cayce in late July.

She wrote him in August, "When I was taken with this trouble, the doctors called it flu. That was before we found the hardness, though. I was taken the same way as I have been with every spell of flu. I sometimes wonder if it hasn't been this trouble coming on for a long time. Would the flu shots do me any good? I would do anything to escape it. I dread the first cold spell until spring."

She was not to take flu shots, said her subsequent reading. She was to take halibut oil with Viosterol to help build muscular forces and to work with the enzymes in the Ventriculin. She was now for the first time to take osteopathic treatments: massage, rather than manipulation, however. If she was tired or weak or in pain, she was to have an oil pack followed by general massage. The electrical therapy was to be administered once a day or so.

The first Friday night in September she returned to her beloved choir. She opened the big heavy church door and walked into a waiting group that hugged her and congratulated her.

On the first Sunday morning, as she played the organ once again and led the choir and congregation through the musical part of the service, she was so nervous that she almost jumped up and ran from the choir loft. Members of the congregation could not resist coming up and speaking to her after church. She still ached with pain in her shoulders; and if she moved her head, it was worse. It was difficult now for her to speak with these well-wishers, but she made the effort, despite the perspiration that formed in her palms.

During the days of her recovery, Edgar Cayce wrote to her about a young girl who had been told in a life reading that she should play the organ. She lived right there in Toddesville and would Florence teach her, if he, Cayce, paid for the lessons?

Florence wrote him that she would be very happy to, and "I can't take money from you after what you have done for me. I'll never make enough money to pay you; in fact, money can't pay you for helping me the way you have."

Throughout the winter she persisted in the treatments which gradually led her to full recovery. By May she was considered fully cured except for a neuritic condition. Cayce now told her she was working too hard, and he said (in her reading) "Rest sufficiently, play sufficiently, work sufficiently—but think constructively!"

He was cognizant of her problems now with her new life, and had advice to heal and to nourish the soul, as well as the body: "Take into consideration more often the purposes of the activities, not as the outward appearances in thy choir practice but what do such activities stand for? What is the message that is to be given to the world through this channel of singing? The love of the Christ to the world!

"Then let it be a personal thing to thee, that He is thy strength, He is thy life! For in Him ye live and move and have thy being.

"There is too much work and too much worry to the amount of play and relaxation . . . Better divide it up! Did you find the Master worked continually or did He take time to play? And time to relax? He is a good example in *everyone's* life."

Florence Evans later completed her musical education, obtaining her Bachelor of Music degree. She married and has established herself as a very busy organist and choir director for three churches. She has only dim memories now of her long fight for life. She had once told her mother, "I won't stop fighting 'til I get well." And she didn't. The aching has long since gone, and she is completely well.

"People think I'm a curiosity," she once wrote to Hugh Lynn Cayce. She has smilingly told many people that she would have died if it hadn't been for Edgar Cayce. So it isn't surprising that she added in the same letter: "A girl from — came to see me . . . She is so pitiful with a different form of scleroderma from mine. The doctors at Vanderbilt Hospital in Nashville are at their 'row's end.' I told her how I was cured. I hope she will be as persistent as I was in the treatment if she gets a reading . . ."

Medical Commentary: Scleroderma

by William A. McGarey, M.D.

IN ORDER TO understand Mr. Cayce's approach to scleroderma as well as to any particular disease process, it would be well to establish some guidelines and principles as they are derived from the readings that Cayce himself gave from the unconscious state. These principles would be applicable in a discussion of all of the stories in this book—so they need be presented only once.

Cayce looks at the human being as a three-dimensional manifestation of a spiritual reality. He recognizes that we are in fact composed basically of atoms which are units of force and energy, and he attributes the quality of consciousness to these basic structural units. Thus he states, in effect, that man as we know him is composed of energy which is in a state of homeostasis, a balance and coordination that forms a structure which we can see and feel. This, of course, is in accord with present-day understanding of the atom—with the exception perhaps that we in the field of science have not yet attributed to the atom a specific consciousness. We do, however, see the oxygen atom as "doing its thing": quite differently from the iron atom, for instance. Perhaps Mr. Cayce is not too far afield even in that regard.

The body, then, from the Cayce viewpoint, is a unit made up of billions of cells, each with a consciousness, and each being composed in turn of billions of atoms, each of these also being points of consciousness or awareness of a type. All these, in their sum total and in their relationship with each other, make up the greater awareness which we individually call "I."

Cayce would have us believe that groups of cells—which we know as organs and systems—act as separate forces within the body which must coordinate with each other in their activity in a balanced homeostasis in order that we may experience what we call health.

Disturbance of these forces, then (in the viewpoint of the readings), creates the environment, the activities, and the imbalances or incoordinations which design the situations which we at the present time call disease.

On the other hand, a state of health within the human body is recovered when measures are taken which might encourage the gradual restoration of normal structure within cells themselves and a recovery of proper coordination between these activities, these energies—these forces, as Cayce would call them—which we call systems and organs of the body.

If the body is thus designed, as Cayce implies, a disease then is in the making of when something in the structure and relationship of the body-mind-soul unit becomes unbalanced or disturbed. Order and balance must once again be established before health is fully present, and those external factors are eliminated which our present-day medical understanding considers to be the true etiology. It certainly becomes more evident in such a physical body that etiology and therapy are often quite closely related.

To add further to the fascination of the situation, and perhaps also to the confusion, Cayce gave a number of readings which commented on the true nature of healing. Sometimes he related it to etiology or cause. The following extract from case 1472-14 was offered to explain why the administrations which were used for this individual who had sinus and digestive problems were not as effective as had been hoped.

> This does not imply, then, that these are incurable; but, as is the influence in ALL healing, whether the administrations be purely suggestive, of a vibratory nature, from the laying on of hands, of by the spoken word, the administration of medicinal properties or even the use of means to remove diseased tissue, we find that the same source of individuality in the cause must be attained. That is, that which has been dissenting in its nature through the physical forces of the body must be attuned to spiritual forces in itself as to become revitalized.
>
> This then, as we have indicated, does not mean that NO condition cannot be improved, or that no condition cannot be healed.
>
> As to what is that necessary influence to bring about curative or healing or life giving forces for that individuality and personality of the individual with same, as related to the spiritual forces, may be answered only within the individual itself. For, no source passes judgment. For, the spirituality, the individuality of the God-force in each entity's combined forces, must be its judge.

These preceding ideas, then, must be kept in mind if one desires to achieve an understanding of the position of the Cayce readings on: (1) the creative nature and the physiology of the human body and (2) the various factors and methods involved in producing a return to health.

We turn, then, to scleroderma and the story of Florence Evans, who was afflicted with one of the most severe manifestations of this disease—technically known as "progressive systemic sclerosis."

In today's medical-pathological understanding of this disease process, we find that scleroderma involves the collagenous connective tissues and may cause widespread symmetrical leathery induration of the skin followed by atrophy and pigmentation. The cutaneous lesions are believed to be the external manifestation of a systemic disease. The muscles, bones, mucous membranes, heart, lungs, intestinal tract, and other internal organs may be involved by the same process resulting in functional impairment such as heart failure or pulmonary insufficiency, and progressive, sometimes widespread organic pathology.

Its etiology is unknown. It may be related to other major connective tissue disorders, but the understanding of collagenous diseases is as yet incomplete.

The Cayce information describes scleroderma uniquely, using such concepts as coagulation, forces, and hardening of tissues. The autonomic nervous system becomes involved in the superficial circulation and its activities. Cayce describes how scleroderma affects not only the skin but also blood-forming structural areas such as bone and lung tissue in a process which produces a hardening or a clotting of the blood. This occurs mainly as a result of the blood attempting to bring about that creative activity which in the readings is called coagulation (the production of new cells as the old tissue normally dies).

Cayce has described coagulation in rather poetic terms as creating cellular structure from energy—the energy supplied from several sources including molecules of food and oxygen assimilated into the body from the intestinal tract and the lungs. In scleroderma, this process is seen most dramatically hindered in the superficial capillaries and lymph vessels in the various layers of the skin. As these structures atrophy, the nerve endings locally become deadened. Cayce implies that this neurological involvement in Florence Evans' case produced acute pain in addition to a reflex activity directly involving the autonomic nervous system in the disease process. The impulses to the organ of the body from the sympathetic and parasympathetic nervous systems then became disturbed and uncoordinated. This, Cayce stated, led first to a disturbed state of function in the organs and finally to a pathological condition.

Hormone-producing cells in the thyroid, adrenals, and liver are deficient in supplying elements which aid in keeping the skin normal. These elements are, I would suppose, hormones, which this source of information states flatly are needed to maintain a normal degree of the coagulation process described earlier.

One might say that the glandular deficiency creates a lack of essential nutrition in the circulatory structures of the skin, which in turn causes a decrease in the lymph and capillary flow. As the disease progresses, the nerves in these areas become involved as described earlier, and a swelling then occurs in the skin as an attempt on the part of the body to bring about better conditions. As the lymph flow is destroyed, the lymphatics become inflamed and create the germ or the tubercle bacillus which "consumes" the circulation of the skin, forming a hardened area or placque. In the more advanced cases of scleroderma, the respiration of the skin also becomes involved . . . destruction of the sweat glands. Without the normal perspiration, a gradual increase in acidosis comes into being within the body, which then becomes more susceptible to colds and to intercurrent infections.

Nearly all portions of the body are involved in advanced cases of scleroderma, including the lungs. Increasing oxygen needs of the body can scarcely be met by a malfunctioning respiratory system, and the entire body is thus put under a greater strain. As these conditions progress, assimilation becomes more difficult and less capable, and the lack of reconstructive activities in the body becomes progressively more acute.

Review of the above information points to the understanding that the endocrine glands of the body in their disturbed functioning become the primary cause of this disease process, with the collagenous changes being secondary to the inadequate restoration of circulatory structures within the skin. The tubercle bacillus is in this instance a product of the body itself, not a secondary invader. A few medical theorists have implied that viruses derive sometimes from still vital chromosomal material left over from cellular breakdowns. But nowhere has the idea been proposed that the body may produce an acid-fast bacillus, or any type of bacteria, for than matter.

It is interesting to note that such bacilli were never discovered in the skin of scleroderma patients until some years after Cayce's death. In 1968 Cantwell[1] published a report on these findings and suggested that the acid-fast bacilli that he demonstrated might be the cause of scleroderma. This series of events has been interpreted—rightly, I believe—as valid medical clairvoyance of a very unusual type on the part of the sleeping Mr. Cayce.

In the therapy program which Cayce designed for Florence Evans throughout the course of many readings, one finds perhaps more questions than answers relative to mode of action that might be operative here. If Florence had not responded to Cayce's recommendations they could have been dismissed. But she improved when she followed directions, worsened when she went off the therapy. It is uncanny to the practicing physician who must rely on his external powers of observation and what the laboratory facilities have to offer. It argues strongly that Cayce might indeed have been doing as he repeatedly said he did—actually communicating with the unconscious mind of the patient and relating while unconscious the state of affairs existing within that body. Even to the welfare of the individual red blood cells, or perhaps the blood forming organs.

Cayce's suggestions for Florence were almost legion in number. He seemed to view the body and its functions and abnormalities . . . reach into another psychic pocket, so to speak, and draw out a group of suggestions that would lead the ailing body back toward health, balancing these "forces" he spoke about so often and maintaining a homeostasis as it moved and changed.

Undoubtedly, in the case of scleroderma, Cayce saw so many systems and functions out of control that no therapy would be valuable unless it was designed to correct these functions in their relationship to each other. For instance, he frequently related the physiology of assimilation to that of elimination. He implied that adequate and normal assimilation of food taken into the upper intestinal tract

[1] A. R. Cantwell, Jr., Eugenia Craggs, J. W. Wilson, and F. Swatek, "Acid-Fast-Bacteria as a Possible Cause of Scleroderma," *Dermatologica*, 136: 141–150.

cannot really come about unless the body is eliminating fully and normally. He also described the lymphatic system as part of the emunctory forces of the body, which puts the lymph then into the category of an eliminatory activity. The lymph nodes, then, no matter where they are found throughout the body, would necessarily be associated in some manner with elimination. Physiologically, of course, these comments have no validity. The lymph does act as a drainage or eliminatory channel for individual cells and groups of cells throughout the body. The liver, which is the major detoxifier of the body, produces more lymph than any other single source.

Even with its "emunctory" activity, the lymph is also a part of the assimilatory apparatus of the body. We do not usually speak of assimilation today, but rather of digestion and metabolism. We are aware, however, that full assimilation means the process by which any substance is taken into the body and brought to its site of activity at the level of the cell. The many steps which are intermediary are all a part of this assimilatory process.

In the readings, it is also implied that in Florence's case the endocrine glands of the body as well as the blood were in a state that needed cleansing and purifying. He made suggestions as to how this would best be done.

But how would one understand the method by which the body is improved through the use of castor oil packs, for instance? What happens when soda is used to cleanse the skin first, and why does massage to the abdomen and to the back bring beneficial responses? What does Cayce mean by suggesting beef juice, for instance, or how valid is an alkaline diet? Why should brandy fumes coming from a charred oak keg be so beneficial to the respiratory system of the body? What value to the body comes from a very, very low voltage electrical energy that is brought to the body through the medium of the wet cell battery Cayce devised?

These and other questions obviously come to one's mind as he reads the story of how Cayce's suggestions gradually nursed this young lady back to a full and healthy life.

Leaving specific therapy aside, we can see that the primary objective contained in the suggestions Cayce gave in his readings was the elimination of the basic cause of scleroderma—which has already been described as a malfunction of the glandular structures of the body. He suggested and emphasized the need for persistence and patience in gradually establishing a normal function throughout all those areas of the body which had been disturbed. Perhaps, then, we could safely say that the primary aim of Florence's therapy was the gradual redirecting of the forces and energies of the body back toward what we know and consider to be normal function.

The question of why these specific therapies work and whether they would again be effective at a clinical level would properly lie in the realm of medical research.

In looking at Florence Evans' story, one is struck by the fact that these applications which took so much time to become effective (in a condition as chronic and deep-set as scleroderma always is) required a persistence that often taxes the patience of anyone faced with this particular disease—whether it is the one who suffers or the one who applies therapy.

That Florence Evans had scleroderma is factual, certainly. She recovered completely over a period of time, using therapeutic modalities which seem to be a mixture of old-fashioned folk remedies and methods utilizing energies of the body the existence of which has not yet even been accepted. Cayce, in giving suggestions for therapy, implied, for instance, that the balance of the autonomic nervous system and its control of the circulation to the periphery of the body can be enhanced by the application of castor oil packs over the abdomen, extending around to cover the back. It is probably not just fortuitous that the coeliac (solar) plexus—the largest collection of nerve cells outside the brain—lies within the abdomen in that area. From material derived from the readings in various conditions of the body, it becomes evident that Cayce "saw" an effect on the nervous system from the application of such packs. How does this effect come about? Cayce speaks about vibratory influences in the reading I quoted earlier. The implication is there that all substances have an influence on the human body in a vibratory manner.

These vibratory effects, which are assumed throughout the Cayce readings to be active as beneficial or detrimental influences on the physical body, must be clearly differentiated from the biochemical and physical reactions which take place in the body. To understand such effects even partially, I would assume one would have to agree first that they play a part in the normal functioning of the body. One would also have to understand that there is much activity of an electrical nature going on in and about the body that we have not satisfactorily demonstrated at the present time. He would naturally have to agree that our present understanding of the body is only partial and incomplete and that much more in unknown than we presently know.

Perhaps these therapies Cayce suggested for Florence had their major effect on what he called the vibratory body. Such an idea would not be original with Cayce, of course. In fact, he stated outright that he derived his information from other minds or from the akashic record, or the Universal mind. Homeopathy deals with finer vibrations of the body. Acupuncturists see much in Cayce which coincides with their theories of a finer vibratory flow of energies through the body which connect various organs and systems in a manner that is not strictly neurological in its pathways. Treatment by the homeopaths is through the use of high dilutions of medicine taken into the body orally. The acupuncturist uses steel needles, usually wound at the hilt with gold, and inserts them into the skin at sites that have been found over the ages to be effective in changing the vibrational nature of the body in a constructive way.

Cayce himself described a flow of energy in the body which is in the shape of a figure of eight, with the lines crossing at the solar plexus. Other psychics have seen the same energy patterns. Individuals who have this clairvoyant gift see a higher vibrational body in addition to the physical body. If we allow that all these individuals are not consistently hallucinating, then the impact of this bit of information is that we must learn to deal with the vibrational nature of the body if we are really to make progress in the therapy of the human body and in understanding its true nature.

Florence Evans experienced, indeed, an unusual recovery from a disease which would otherwise have taken her life. My training in the field of medicine does not explain why or how this came about. Frustrating, isn't it?

CHAPTER 2

"A FRIEND, SNATCHED FROM DEATH". . . .

by Mary Ellen Carter

"ROGER MCDERMOTT, WHAT'S ailing you?" Bill Calhoun, eyes narrowed at his friend, challenged.

Roger shook his head. "Can't seem to get myself together," he replied. "Sorry I snapped at you. Beth's after me, too. Says I'm working too hard."

"Wives know. She's been trying to get you to the beach. Why don't you go?"

"The factory . . ."

Bill waved a hand as if to dismiss the factory. "Just because you're singlehandedly responsible for this factory's success as our New York representative . . ."

"Well, it *is* the best of its kind . . ."

". . . doesn't mean you have to kill yourself. Why, you should be enjoying the fruits of your labors."

"And just because a man's 61 doesn't mean he's ready for pasture!"

By June (it was 1929) Roger was forced to cut his working day because of his increasing dis-ease. Finally, he was ordered by his physician to stay in bed for two or three days until his blood could be examined. When Bill went to see him, he found Roger languishing uncharacteristically among the pillows with only a flicker of his usual good spirits. Beth worried about, hushing Bill with, "He has a fever. Please don't upset him."

Roger fretted, of course, about the factory. But the crisis he had feared came about, not in his business but in his health. In the heat of July he went back to work, with nearly fatal consequences . . .

On a particularly close day, he loosened his tie to allow any stray breeze to touch his moist neck. The office fan rotating overhead did little to help. The papers in front of him blurred. A brief vision of his wife and daughter relaxing by the ocean passed before his eyes. An unaccountable weak, dizzy feeling gripped him, and a strange blackness descended.

Roger regained consciousness in the Tannhurst Hospital, under the care of Dr. Fred Galagher, a leading physician. Several specialists examined him. X-rays by Dr. Kern, a priminent Atlanta doctor, showed that, according to his diagnosis, he had advanced tuberculosis.

Unaware of all this, Bill had decided to write Edgar Cayce about Roger's

172

condition. Both men had previously sought information through the Virginia psychic on business and health matters. Bill had been the one, in fact, to introduce Roger to Cayce's work several years before. Bill's faith in Cayce stemmed from his own experience with the readings. From New York he now wrote: "I am writing this special request to ask you to get a check on these three questions for Mr. McDermott . . ." including his blood supply, fever, and cure. However, before Cayce received the letter, Bill received a call from Beth. "Roger's critically ill!" She said, "The doctors think there's no hope."

In response to a wire from Bill to Cayce, a reading was given on July 12. This was Roger's third, the last one had been given on April 1 for overactive kidneys due to poor eliminations. "Yes, we have the body, Roger McDermott," Cayce began now. "This we have had before.

"Now, we find the physical conditions are depleted with this body, as the result of the strain, both mental and physical, and as affect the heart and blood supply of the body.

"The temperature as arises in system is produced by that of the bacilli as is carried in the blood stream from that of poor eliminations, combined with those of uric acid reaction, though not wholly a condition of the uric acid: this is aiding the condition in raising temperature, and the weakness or faintness from same." (2579-3)

(Roger was to write later: "We work nearly one thousand men and owing to the stress of my duties, I was in a very run down condition.")

The reading recommended eliminations being properly set up: "To bring the better results for the body, we would change somewhat the *surroundings* of the body. Through the activities of those properities as will aid in eliminations being properly set up, that do not over strain the functioning of the kidneys with the normalcy of the liver functioning, will tend to reduce the cause of conditions. These may be brought about through many channels, dependent upon which ones would be used. *We* would suggest those of the homeopathic remedies. Do that."

On the fifteenth, the fourth reading said that he would ultimately recover if no complications occurred. This reading said that the doctor had not diagnosed his case entirely correctly, although he was receiving the right treatment, so it should be kept.

Roger was given a blood transfusion, according to his doctor's treatment; and was told by Cayce that he should add iodine to his system, plus iron and calcium, by means of a device first described in earlier readings which he called the radio-active appliance. Eliminations were important, for the drosses of the blood could easily bring about recurrent bacilli. But the appliance treatment would not be possible yet.

On July 26 Roger was told by Cayce that he could leave the hospital when he was able to walk in the open air. He would recuperate best in Virginia Beach, where he could benefit from the radium in sand packs "which carry both the gold and the iodine . . . and for the appliances that may be attached to the body that would aid in alleviating these conditions as seen in the thyroids."[1]

---

[1] It is difficult to think of the present headquarters building on 67th Street as a hospital: where once were hospital rooms and wards, there are now offices, apartments, and a library. The porches that

With Roger on his way to Virginia Beach, Bill wrote: "Mr. McDermott, I believe, will arrive with his nurse Friday or Saturday. Mrs. McDermott will probably come along. . . ." He asked that two connecting rooms be given them for easy access to the sun porch on the second floor. He pointed out with some satisfaction that when Roger's associates and friends back home heard how much the readings were helping him, new friends would be won for the hospital.

Roger was admitted on August 8 by Dr. Berger, to be treated for Streptocisis. (2596-5) He was to stay, said his reading, for three to four weeks.

He continued to improve but was warned against overtaxing himself under stress because of his heart's inability to store energy as yet. Cayce further warned that he might become too dependent on digitalis and if assimilations were to fail, the result would be a heart block. As the amount of digitalis was decreased, to prevent his circulation becoming taxed, pellets were recommended containing sulphate of quinine, muriated iron, and rhubarb, one a day. This would help him rest better, along with frequent massage of his cerebro-spinal system—first with tepid water, then cold water, then equal parts of olive oil and tincture of myrrh.

He was to get out in the open air as much as possible but was to have no crowds of people in his room, especially in the evening. Roger was still a very sick man.

He was too weak to walk yet, and it would be ten days before he could go into the water. Even the sand packs would be too hard on his heart. He was to take blood-building foods, especially those carrying iron, and all fruits except apples and bananas. The juices of meats rather than fleshy portions were best.

On August 22 he was told he could "add days, months, years to his life . . . thus enabling the body to accomplish mentally and physically and spiritually much as has been desired. (2597-7)"

Roger again worried that the factory might not run without him. Edgar found him on the porch with Beth, scheming how he would travel to New York and to the factory in Tannhurst. He would see about his business, then return to the hospital, he pointed out.

"We'll ask about it in tomorrow's reading," Edgar said.

surround the front and sides had been built with recuperation of patients in mind; once, indeed, patients had been wheeled out to catch the morning sun and the fresh salt breezes that was up from the ocean. Now the porches are enjoyed by visitors and staff members to whom the days of the hospital are somehow unreal and remote, and the drama of sickness and recovery but a twice-told tale.

The Cayce Hospital had been dedicated November 11, 1928, and was under the supervision of Thomas B. House, M.D., of Hopkinsville, Kentucky, until his death in October, 1929. He was succeeded by Lyman A. Lydic, D.O., of Dayton, Ohio. Gena L. Crews, D.O., took over supervision of patients after the departure of Dr. Lydic. Other staff physicians were: Grace Berger, D.O.; Robert W. Woodhouse, M.D.; and James M. Parker, M.D.

By 1930 the hospital was accepting patients from New York State and North Carolina, as well as Tidewater. A few were out-patients, not actually occupying beds in the hospital. When the hospital closed in February, 1930, Edgar Cayce had appointments six months in advance.

The institution had everything in its favor: a staff sympathetic to and knowledgeable of the Cayce concepts of healing; a beautiful, wholesome setting beside the ocean; proximity to Washington and New York. With the economic upset of the time, however, support was withdrawn by its prime benefactors and it was never reactivated.

The reading of August 28 told him that such a trip would actually be good for him, he had improved so much, provided he didn't overtax himself. But the worries of his well-meaning family would *cause* him to be anxious. (2597-8)

Sure enough, Beth pleaded, "Please don't try to go back to your business too soon."

"I won't overdo, I promise."

Cayce, in the middle, reiterated that such warnings were unnecessary: "The body *won't* overtax itself."

"The body" didn't. Eventually, he took the sand packs and the osteopathic treatments. Five weeks after arriving, he was released to return to New York to report to the president of his firm for duty.

In a report dated April 10, 1930, Roger wrote Edgar: "I have never felt better in my life than I have felt in the past eight months and I agree with Dr. S. who, in a letter to me, stated that I was out of the hands of the doctor and in the hands of God, and you no doubt have been the means for the information to come from God Himself to save my life and to you, again, I say, I owe my thanks. I certainly enjoyed the personal attention received from you, your doctors and nurses at the institution, and if at any time I can be of service to you or others, you have but to command . . ."

Some years later, Dr. S. wrote to Edgar Cayce: "At the request of Mrs. B. [an A.R.E. member] I am sending Mr. McDermott's medical statements to you at Virginia Beach. It is a real joy to see a man so useful, so big-hearted, so capable, and above all, a friend snatched from death, as it were, and apparently restored to health. I frankly confess that it was little short of a miracle, as *practically 95% of such cases of streptococcic infection do not survive* [Author's italics]. We doctors do not take the credit; I feel that a Higher Power directed the case.

"I am naturally extremely interested in Mr. Cayce and his work. Some of these days I hope to run up to Virginia Beach to see him and the Hospital . . ."

Such records of testimony to treatment and cures through psychic means say a great deal about the Cayce Hospital—that it was justified and that it did not exist, however briefly, in vain.

You could have asked Roger McDermott.

Medical Commentary: Streptococcus

by William A. McGarey

IN 1928, THE medical profession had little therapy for a streptococcus septicemia, which this case apparently turned out to be, despite an earlier diagnosis by x-ray of advanced tuberculosis. Today, therapy would have been given earlier, and undoubtedly adequately, in the form of antibiotics. It is interesting that Sir Arthur Fleming discovered penicillin at about the same time these readings were given, although it took fifteen years before clinical application of the discovery actually came about to any degree. But in 1928 and 1929, a strep infection was, indeed, a fearful thing.

The fact that the attending physician saw this 61-year-old man's recovery as such an unlikely event and attended by influences from a "Higher Power" still is not perhaps the most remarkable thing about this particular case. Cayce, while giving his first reading on this illness, stated himself that correction could be "brought about through many channels, dependent upon which ones would be used. *We* would suggest those of the homeopathic remedies." Cayce apparently saw that the doctors would probably not use homeopathy, although he saw that as being preferable in this case.

Actually, a blood transfusion—among other things—was one of the principal therapies in the acute stages. Cayce stated that there should be no fear of the outcome and recommended that the care and treatment being given at the time should be followed, as it was of course. McDermott was able to transfer from the Tannhurst Hospital to the Cayce Hospital in Virginia Beach.

Perhaps the most remarkable thing about this story is the host of questions and implications that arise from a serious study of the events as they took place in the course of this man's illness. More questions than answers, certainly; and more implications than evidence. Can a "sleeping" individual, for instance, foresee the outcome of a disease with accuracy, sufficiently to set at rest the worries of concerned family? What is the nature of a disease process? Is it found in the bacteria that enter the body in some manner; or does the body itself, through stresses and lack of balance within—created through improper use of life activities—bring about the disease condition, opening the way for bacteria to finish the job of complete disruption?

Let's trace the history of the septicemia and examine the explanation of things from Cayce's point of view, asking the questions and dealing with the implications as we go along. The human body, certainly, is one of the most fascinating subjects anyone can study, and we certainly know little about it at the present time. About its structure, maybe yes; but about its workings, its activities, the forces, the energies, the relationships, the coordinating activities, the coordinating intelligence—in other words, the function of the body—definitely no.

Cayce's very first reading for this man, given fifteen months before his severe illness began, pointed up a lack of coordination in the eliminating systems of the body which had established a chronicity that was apparently not fully corrected even though Cayce suggested at that point a manner in which it might be returned to normal. The kidneys apparently were not eliminating from the body the substances which they should due to their overstimulation from the very nature of the stresses this man was placing on himself in his work. This buildup of what Cayce often called "drosses" had to be eliminated in some manner, and the liver, the capillaries and lymphatics of the intestinal tract suffered as a result. This congestion then brought about a focal point of malfunction which Cayce called a "lesion," which in turn produced certain symptoms. He told his story like this:

> . . . There is seen that for some time back there has been the tendency
> towards the non-eliminations in the proper channel, and with the constant
> effect of an over-stimulation to the kidneys has brought that of the uremic
> forces to be active in an improper manner. Not that this is as uremia, or
> uremic poisoning, but an overactive kidney gives to the whole system

the improper distribution of eliminating forces in body to the excess of the liver and to the excess of capillary or lymphatic circulation, and eliminations. Hence we have the character of hindrance through congestion in the intestinal tract, and a form of lesion as produces stitch in side. Pressure produced on nerves of the limbs brings tautness and inactivity through the nerves *of* the limbs. Then the condition becoming acute, these are brought about in an acute form.

Cayce suggested at this point that McDermott take a three-day course of therapy that has similarities to treatments used thousands of years ago. A pint of sage tea and a pint of saffron tea, taken as hot as possible each day, followed by a steam bath to sweat the teas "through the body." Then, after a three-day rest, a series of osteopathic treatments. The sweats, Cayce said, would start proper eliminations through the alimentary canal, while the osteopathy would set up the proper coordination in the nervous system.

Both these herbs have anti-spasmodic activities. In addition, saffron (*Crocus sativus*) is a stimulant, gives tone to the stomach, and is used to promote the secretion of sweat and of urine. The sage (*Salvia officinalis*) tea, on the other hand, has been used in times past for nervous conditions, coughs and colds, and any condition where a sweat is desired. It also produces perspiration. Both are classed, therefore, among herbs as diaphoretics.

There is record made that McDermott took the teas but no evidence that he ever followed with the sweats or the osteopathic treatments. He did improve with the teas, recovering from a 24-hour syndrome which was progressively diagnosed as a stroke, then as blood poisoning, then as the gout. He was not hospitalized for this problem, but recovered rather promptly.

Then, working hard and encouraging what many call a severe stress syndrome, this man fell apart physically. Cayce stated that it was the strain rather than the infection which caused the heart and the circulation to be in such serious condition. The septicemia, he implied, came about because of poor elimination of an acute nature (probably affecting both the liver and the kidneys) added to a chronic imbalance in the organs of elimination, probably dating back to the inadequate therapy of more than a year previous. This imbalance, Cayce maintained, resulted in an increase in the blood uric acid and contributed in a large degree to the febrile condition of the body. Cayce agreed certainly with the anatomic and physiologic description of elimination in the body as coming about through the lymphatic system, the liver and intestines, the kidneys, the lungs, and the skin.

In the Cayce view of physiology, it can readily be seen why therapy of the first magnitude was to be elimination of the drosses in the system. Properly achieved, eliminations would protect the kidneys from serious damage and aid in restoring more of a normal function in the liver. Gradually, then, a balanced eliminatory system would be achieved which would "reduce the cause of conditions." This was where Cayce suggested homeopathy as his choice of therapy.

Assimilation apparently had become a serious problem here also. The ineffectiveness of the process of taking into the body the food which is needed and changing it sufficiently so that its energies may be utilized in all parts of the body in restoration and regeneration of body tissues—this ineffectiveness had brought about certain glandular changes, particularly in the thyroid, which in turn disturbed the distribution of these energies or forces into their proper channels. A complicated picture, to be sure.

A diet was important to the body, a diet designed so that it would not add to the wastes which needed to be eliminated . . . but which would help in keeping a balance.

The recuperating patient was then told, on the fourteenth day of his illness, that he would need three or four weeks of rest, preferably at Virginia Beach. There he could get "more of the applications as to meet the needs of conditions for the physical body."

These "applications" provide for us perhaps the most interesting part of the entire reading, not for what they *are* as much as for what they imply. Cayce suggested in once sentence that McDermott could take sand packs at Virginia Beach and receive beneficial vibrations to the functioning of his body from the radium, gold, and iodine found in the sand; and that by using what Cayce called a radio-active appliance, he could receive further benefits in a vibrational manner from iodine, calcium, and iron. These would aid the thyroid in its function and further balance and assist the assimilation of the body.

If Cayce was correct in what he talked about while asleep, we do indeed know little about the inner, secret workings of the human body!

A sand pack is a simple thing, certainly—one must allow himself to be covered and packed with sand up to his neck. Cayce said the Virginia Beach sand was unique in its content of gold in amounts which would be therapeutic. He advised against McDermott doing this too soon, before his recovery had gained to a certain point, for it might be a distress rather than an aid. But we seldom think of radium, gold, and iodine coming from such a pleasant interlude on the beach, at least as a therapeutic modality.

The radio-active appliance was described in many of the Cayce readings as being beneficial in a variety of ailments of the human body. Its value was seen as being, again, vibrational. A small cylindrical item when put together according to Cayce's specifications, it stands about six inches high and is two inches in diameter. It has two leads, like an ordinary battery, although it is not a battery; and plates from the two wire leads are attached to the body in a specified manner. In this particular reading, as in many others, Cayce implies that one of the wires should pass through a solution jar which would have in it a solution containing iron, calcium, and iodine.

The vibration of these elements, then, would be carried into the body through the wire by a flow of energy which Cayce stated was inherent in every living human being, and which, apparently, activated the appliance without external electrical energy being introduced. Engineers have puzzled over this device, and some testing has been done. But no definitive answers have really been arrived at.

The appliance, as described in many of Cayce's readings, is basically two five-inch bars of carbon steel drilled and tapped for copper wire leads at the top, a half-inch wide and a quarter-inch thick, separated by two one-eighth-inch-thick sections of glass the same length and width. These are surrounded completely by bars of carbon on all four sides, and the assembly is set in crushed hardwood charcoal inside a regular 16-ounce tin can, which is then sealed over the top. Small copper plates at the end of the wires are used to be applied to the body when the appliance is in operation. And Cayce insisted that the appliance be set in ice water when used. There is no known means of generating energy in this way at the present time, but Cayce saw this as a means of gentle, yet real therapy to the body.

Fascinating questions arise. And there are partial answers available. Is there a flow of energy in the human body which we have not yet discovered? Is there an energy field around the body? Is this what has been called the aura? Cayce described such a flow of energy, in the form of a figure-eight, crossed at the area of the solar plexus. He also described the aura of the human being as being a type of force field, visible only to those who can "see" it, but present in all individuals. Shafica Karagulla (*Breakthrough to Creativity*) told how the psychics she worked with saw the same figure-eight flow of energy, the same aura. Eemans described the same thing and reported a wealth of experiments using copper screens under the body and wires to bring about a therapeutic result. Similar reports and practices have been repeated down through the ages, from the time of ancient Egypt.

The ancient practice of acupuncture is based on the principle that there are specific points in the body where such a flow of energy is specifically contacted by inserting special needles. In recent years, using Kirlian photography, Russian scientists have photographed energies spurting out of these specific areas. They have also photographed the aura. In their minds, little doubt exists that these forces created by the human body are real and active. They are, in fact, observable and recordable in all living things.

As McDermott's recuperation continued, Cayce at one point foresaw an impending heart block plus a possible assimilatory failure of one type or another, due to the dependence of the body on the stimulation given to heart by the digitalis. He suggested in its place a small dosage of quinine sulfate, muriated iron, and rhubarb, to be phased in as the digitalis was phased out. We, of course, have no way of determining whether this man might in reality have developed a heart block. As his activities were gradually increased, however, as he obtained osteopathic treatments, special massages, the sand packs, a special diet, the treatments with the radio-active appliance, he recovered in fine style, following fully the suggestions Cayce gave while in a psychic state—what we now call an extended state of consciousness.

This case provokes a great number of questions which I shall pose, but not even attempt to answer. They constitute, in my mind, a challenge to the open-mindedness of the medical and scientific community, and to the government agencies which might encourage and support research into the nature of this wonderful thing that allows us to express ourselves in this three-dimensional consciousness— the human body. These questions all need reasonable answers:

1. Has diet been underestimated in its physiological effect on the human body?
2. Do herbs as used throughout the ages have a therapeutic effect that is measurable? And is the effect principally one to change the coordination of the body forces, perhaps? Or to aid an organ in its function?

3. Does elimination as a total body function really play this large role in the health of the body that Cayce suggests?

4. Is assimilation a recognizable entity in the body? Does it become an all-or-none phenomenon, or is it a force with a multitude of tasks, any one of which might become weakened or deficient?

5. Does physical therapy act only on the muscular structures of the body or does it perform a therapeutic duty to the uncoordinated functional organism?

6. Does osteopathy alter the physiological function of a human body in a therapeutic manner?

7. How does vibration work in relation to body functions?

8. Does a sand pack do more than introduce a tranquilizing effect into the body? What about related treatments from health spas around the world: mud packs, hot mineral baths, steam baths, uranium mine sitting, copper bracelets?

9. Does gold play a part in the normal function of the body?

10. Can the "vibration" of an element be carried into the energy field of a person so that the function of glands of the body is enhanced?

11. Can the flow of energy in the body itself activate an appliance which has no source of energy within itself?

How mankind may be healed is a subject which has stretched the imagination and ingenuity of men throughout the ages. It has not stopped today simply because we have achieved a degree of scientific accomplishment in the physical sciences. Cayce's suggestions given to a man with a serious disease offer to us more of that stretching of the mind. This, I think, is good.

CHAPTER 3

A MOTHER'S ORDEAL

by Mary Ellen Carter

FIVE-YEAR-OLD Suzy Paxton lifted the spoon to her mouth, but before she could take the morsel of oatmeal, her hand twisted and the spoon clattered to the table. Helen, her mother, watched with mild surprise. "You haven't forgotten how to feed yourself, have you?"

Again the child attempted to lift the spoon to her mouth, but it jammed an eye, instead. In an angry little storm of frustration she picked up the bowl and threw it to the floor, splattering the contents and broken pieces. "Dumb old bowl!"

Patiently, Helen, picked up the pieces and cleaned the linoleum. When the incident had been repeated, she resignedly fed Suzy, herself.

Soon afterward, Suzy was trying to draw her letters when her face suddenly twitched contortedly. The strange quirk became a habit. Puzzled, Helen tried to admonish her daughter. The time-honored command "Don't do that!" only served to frustrate Suzy further.

Now, she was increasingly unable to do the simple tasks she had learned readily. Her coordination was so bad that Helen was forced to do many chores for her, including dressing and undressing her. Suzy's temper tantrums became more frequent.

When she started to school, Suzy seemed to benefit from the change and the challenge. She had already learned her letters, numbers were no special problem. She was a good student, said her teacher. Until, that is, one day when the teacher, Miss Dresden, called to say, "I'm sorry, but Suzy has been very impudent these past few weeks. At first, I corrected her mildly. Now, she's worse. She has become disruptive and disobedient."

"What! . . . in what way?" Helen asked, her heart sinking.

"She called me 'an old cow,' and said she wasn't coming in when recess was over. I had to make her stay in the cloak room. She threw quite a tantrum."

"I am sorry. I'll try to talk to her."

Suzy's personality didn't improve. At home, at play with other children, she became a handful. One day, as she and Katey played with their dolls in the dining room, Suzy tore the head off Katey's beloved doll, then danced around the room in a frenzy. Her movements, Helen noted as she came in answer to Katey's cry, were a series of jerky steps.

"Don't cry, Katey," soothed Helen, as she picked up Wanda's head and cottony body, "we'll sew her back together, as good as new."

The doll was easy to deal with. Suzy was not.

In the years that followed, Suzy was taken to doctors for help. However, there seemed to be no one in the medical profession who could help her. Certainly, teachers and principals were at a loss as to how to handle the girl. Her condition worsened, even as she grew into her teens. At fifteen, she tried hard to seem normal, as though she realized that her problem was alienating her from her peers. A boy might come courting, but at her compulsive rudeness and jerky antics, he was soon discouraged.

One young man who came to the house tried to laugh off her strange ways. "Give me a chance," he said.

Billy did all the talking. He talked mostly about basketball, and Suzy seemed glad to be with him. But then she made a cutting remark and bolted into the house. Helen happened to be in the yard, raking leaves. She saw Billy's surprised expression and his frown.

He glanced at her, puzzled. "Mrs. Paxton," he asked, "what's wrong with Suzy?"

There was no answer. To all who asked the same question, Helen had no words. Her husband's people became quite critical of *her*, and she recalls even now the remarks they made. "Poor discipline," she was told.

"I know how *I* would handle that imp!" said another.

Helen began to avoid them. She kept her feelings to herself. She felt that even her husband didn't understand her frustration at coping with their child. They had other children, all normal and well-adjusted. Suzy remained an enigma.

When Helen once more confronted the child with her poor report card (she neglected her books, apt though she was), she pointed out her truancy record as well.

Suzy flew into a rage. She stomped the floor, yelling "Stop nagging me!"

By the time she was seventeen, in her third year at high school, the authorities were despaired. Her intolerable behavior marked by frequent outbursts in the classroom led to her dismissal. At home, Helen found her daughter increasingly irritable and helpless. She was obliged to bathe her and feed her and try to control her tantrums. When guests came to the house, the family was often embarrassed by the girl's unsocial behavior.

Physicians termed her condition a nervous disorder but could find little effective treatment for her; chiropractic was tried with no results.

Helen grew frantic. The burden of coping with her daughter all these years tested her endurance. To her horror, she found herself considering suicide. Peering into the gas oven one day, she thought that she might end her misery very easily—or else herself be committed to an asylum.

"I first heard of Edgar Cayce when I had trouble with my daughter," Helen told me. She spoke softly as she recalled her traumatic experience. The years had brought serenity to her fine features. She sat in the living room of another daughter in Chesapeake, Virginia. It was 1969, nearly 40 years later. A slender, greying woman, she has lived with this daughter and son-in-law since her husband died in 1968.

She spoke of her memories of Gertrude and Edgar Cayce and their influence on her and her family. "I was talking one day across my porch railing to a neighbor, Mrs. Bartlett. We were telling each other our troubles, particularly those concernning our children. I had only recently heard of Edgar Cayce. She didn't think much of him.

"He was giving lectures at Virginia Beach. Mrs. Bartlett telephoned down there and learned there was to be a lecture by a Mr. Morton Blumenthal."

They went to the lecture. "It was *Tertium Organum*. It was all so far above my head. I don't remember much except that he talked about the fourth dimension and its relationship to Mr. Cayce's ability."

After the lecture, Helen told her friend, "This is what I've been looking for alll my life."

"But I thought you couldn't understand the lecture."

"I understand a lot with my heart."

Even then, Helen was slow to get help from Edgar Cayce. She obtained a reading, however, for a friend's baby suffering from a spastic condition causing brain damage.

The Cayce Hospital had just opened its doors. Although many of her friends and acquaintances in Norfolk scoffed at the Cayce work, Helen persisted in learning more about it. She decided to have a reading for Suzy, who was now 20.

Suzy's first reading was given January 24, 1930. Helen was present with her, in addition to Gertrude, Edgar, Gladys Davis, a friend of Helen's (name withheld), and Dr. W. H. McChesney.*

Suzy's trouble, Helen told me, had started with diphtheria at the age of four. According to her reading at 20, the diphtheria antitoxin serum which was given to her had destroyed her assimilation. Her system could no longer take the amount of iodine necessary for balance. The thyroid was trying to provide a balance in the nerves, but it could not.

"There are deficiencies in the supply of nutriment through some of these channels," stated the reading, "and these, corrected, would bring better responses . . . These conditions have to do with the glands and the supply to the organs . . . Not that the body is not normal, save in this respect."

She needed iodine in her blood; she had an excess of potassium. There was an overactivity in her nerve system "and unless changes are brought about, the thyroids must suffer eventually . . . or there must be the reaction of same in the mental deficiency of the body . . ."

Her mental forces "as related to command, demand, and duty suffer from the loss of balance due to this deficiency." Her internal organs were normal.

She needed application of vibrations—low electrical—"that will cause the building up of the deficiencies and equalizing them through food values."

There was no mental unbalance but there was a lack of thyroid secretion to keep her equilibrium: ". . . not mental deficiency, no. Coordination deficiency." Treatment would best be conducted in the Cayce Hospital. She would recover completely if the readings were fully carried out, and it would take only six to nine weeks.

Her next reading, given after her admittance, instructed the use of the wet cell battery charged with iodine. The copper plate was to be applied first to her wrist and the larger, nickel plate or anode at the umbilicus. At first, it was not to be applied for longer than thirty minutes at a time.

The instructions were carried out. According to the further readings, the copper anode was placed at the base of her brain, or at the first and second cervical; the larger anode, at the ninth dorsal. Now the battery was applied for sixty minutes twice a day. Manipulations were given daily for her entire system, and corrections were given osteopathically. Her diet included quantities of shell fish, but no clams. She was to have no hog meat or bread. At least twice a week, she was given codliver oil and calves' liver. After two weeks, a reading said that she should have more body-, blood- and nerve-building material in her food, but not before changes had taken place in the glands through use of the battery. She needed more iodine. By March 3, suppressions causing her incoordination had been alleviated, said her reading. Particular attention should be given now to a local condition in the pelvic organs. Eliminations were to be corrected by osteopathy. This method was to be used for coordinations to the brain center—the pineal and adrenal—to be stimulated. The staff was to help Suzy in learning to coordinate her mental and physical bodies by guiding and controlling her reading, studying, and general activities. She was to have definite tasks to perform. Her reading explained that it was important that staff members make sure *their* activities and thoughts were in keeping with their attempt to bring about healing!

* His real name.

By March 24, said a reading, more improvements had occurred during the past week than had occurred up to then. There was relief in the pressure in the lumbar or pelvic regions. Coordinations had been effected through the ninth and tenth dorsal regions. The treatments were to continue.

As Suzy improved, Helen had time to collect her thoughts and to wonder what had brought about this painful relationship between herself and her daughter. She decided that a life reading would clarify matters. So in the next reading for Suzy, Helen asked at the end, "Would a life reading be a help?"

"Not at present," was the answer. "It's the physical forces that we must combat at the present." It explained that Suzy's condition was accentuated by influences in her past experience and also be the influence of the moon . . .

"This would be very interesting to the physician in charge—to watch the changes in the moon and watch the effect it has upon the body," was the volunteered comment. It added that following the new moon, she would exhibit "a wild, hilarious reaction." As the moon waned, her condition would become better. These, however, were merely influences which might be overcome by treatment in progress.

Here Cayce introduced for the first time the idea that the book of Revelation was related to the functions of the human body. It would be very good, he suggested, for the doctor attending Suzy to read it and understand it! "Especially in reference to this body." (2501-6) Just why this was so was not elaborated upon.

Less pressure on Suzy's solar plexus center had been brought about so that there was less incoordination through the pineal gland from the effects of the sympathetic system. The attitudes of the hospital staff were again pointed out as being particularly effective. they would help her even more if their attitudes were more positive, both physically and mentally.

Now that the pelvic and lumbar regions were more nearly aligned, said Cayce in the mid-April reading, principal emphasis should be given those centers where the cerebro-spinal and sympathetic were coordinant with the physical forces. Areas concerned were the third and fourth cervical, the second and third dorsal, the ninth and tenth dorsal plexus, and the fourth lumbar. Following stimulating (not deep) manipulations osteopathically, low electrical vibrations should be applied.

Again, Suzy's mental and spiritual environment should be planned for her welfare: "Well that due consideration be given to the environment of the mental activities—that is, as to *what* is read, *what* is said, to *whom,* and *where.* These not as suppressions, these not as hindrances. Rather as guiding and as counselling with that being created in the mental activities of the body."

In this reading, Helen asked for an explanation of the reference to The Revelation in connection with the patient. The Revelation, Cayce replied, contains the illustration of how the mental body is raised in consciousness to the "holy mount," such activity taking place through the glandular functions of the body. When Suzy was taken home, the best environment for her would be not that of any particular sect or "ism," but where the activities of individuals were sincere in their efforts. Where, she now asked, could the doctor study The Revelation in this new light?

". . . *any*one," said Cayce, "will they study that given in the Book and compare same to the anatomical conditions of a physical body, will learn the *spiritual* body, the *mental* body—not metaphysics, either!"

Study was undertaken by various persons of this subject, and today there are books and tapes available on The Revelation and the seven spiritual centers.

Helen had been sorely tried by her conflicts with her daughter for the past sixteen years. Suzy had developed toward her an attitude of rebellion. In return Helen had at times displayed the opposite of loving indifference, however much she attempted to control herself. Now, she wanted to begin again to reach her daughter and heal the breach. In asking how to begin, she was told that the young woman's physical healing must be accomplished first, and "both must, then, change" that there be no longer mere tolerance, "but a loving affection between each, that is not even akin to tolerance!"

After dismissal from the hospital, Suzy continued to improve; and, in a year's time, she was married. She had three children, all of whom are grown, married, and with families of their own. At 60, she has seven grandchildren and one great great grand-child.

And that makes Helen a very happy great, great grandmother!

Medical Commentary: Incoordination

By William A. McGarey, M.D.

INCOORDINATION AND NEURASTHENIA are two of the labels listed in the indexing system of the Cayce readings to describe the condition under which Helen's little daughter, Suzy, lived for over fifteen years of her life. We have no diagnoses in the medical literature to identify her specific condition today—if Cayce's clairvoyance was accurate—for incoordination of these nervous systems of ours is not at the present time a disease entity. It should be, for function is as real as is an organ of the body. And units of the body must function in coordination with other units or, obviously, an incoordination is present.

Incoordination of the voluntary muscular movement is described in medical dictionaries as an inability to bring into common, harmonious movement or action. But the other kind of incoordination is perhaps a new thought, although obviously, if it exists at all, it has had a part in the illnesses of mankind since mankind first appeared on the earth.

Neurasthenia, on the other hand, is an inaccurate diagnosis or description of Suzy's illness. The weaknesses, generalized fatigability, lack of energy, and general avoidance of activity of any kind found in true neurasthenia gives the condition its name, of course. But these are not the symptoms found in the little girl when she became ill, nor in the developing child and teen-ager as she found many difficulties in life.

Today, perhaps the best diagnosis we could offer for such a condition is that of the hyperactive child. This is still a name which is descriptive only of a clinical condition and which covers undoubtedly a multitude of underlying causative factors and apparent objective findings.

If such a child were brought into most doctors' offices, however, she would be termed a hyperactive child and be treated as such.

In a recent communication, Pecci describes some twenty factors as causative in the condition of so-called hyperactivity. Whether these are factual or not, there is no question but that the hyperactive syndrome finds its origins in many diverse causative factors. How the hyperactivity is produced in the living body of the individual, however, has never been fully understood, nor is it clear how some drugs have given an apparent beneficial effect.

Cayce's description of the illness present in this child is fascinating to follow for a number of reasons. First, it comes from a psychic source; second, it describes functions of the physiological organism as they bring about a diseased state; third, it pins down an antitoxin as the primary cause; fourth, it poses the possibility that there is an endocrine factor present in this case and probably other similar conditions; fifth, it suggests that there can be active in any human body a very real emotional change brought about by the phases of the moon; sixth, it states that the book of the Revelation in the New Testament deals with the function of the human body; and seventh, it implies that this factor of incoordination of the nervous systems could be etiologic in most of the conditions that we presently call hyperactivity.

At the age of four, Suzy contracted diphtheria. She was given antitoxin serum as part of her treatment, a standard and effective therapy of that day which dated back to the 1890's in its use. In 1914, the antiserum had more than twenty years of experience behind it, so was at that point a well developed therapeutic tool which had proved its effectiveness. Suzy, so ill that she required an airway in order to breathe, was given a series of injections of the antitoxin before she finally pulled through. It was after this episode that the young girl's symptoms began.

It is interesting that Cayce related the entire syndrome of 16 years' duration to the administration of the diphtheria antitoxin. He did not attribute symptoms of deficient physiological conditions to the diphtheria itself but saw the deficiency of iodine and the excess of potassium as coming directly from the antitoxin.

The development of the full clinical condition as Cayce seemed to reconstruct the event is not a biochemically-oriented etiologic process, but rather a sequential story of happenings which undoubtedly are associated with a variety of functions and chemical reactions.

First, Cayce implied that the antitoxin caused the body to be unable to assimilate iodine properly. Whatever the disruption that brought this about, it created at the same time an excess of potassium in the blood stream. The thyroid glands suffered from the lack of iodine in what must be considered to be a rather unique manner. Cayce saw that the lack of proper thyroid hormone secreted into the blood brought in turn an over-activity of certain nerve centers in the autonomic nervous system, especially as they related to the functioning of some of the organs of the body and—

> as seen in the activities of the mental forces as related to command, demand, and duty—and in this respect, the loss of the effect of the

balance is that which brings the effect of this deficiency in the system. (2501-1)

What this means in the final stabilized condition of the human body is that an incoordination was created between the cerebrospinal nervous system and the autonomic. In this case, Suzy's mother had then a major problem of child care on her hands: a severe case of hyperkinesis, maladaption, or whatever one might wish to call it. Cayce called it simply an incoordination which could be corrected with proper care.

As therapy was begun almost immediately after the first reading given for this twenty-year-old young lady, changes began inside the body; and they were carefully documented in subsequent psychic comments as further directions were given. I, at least, get a real thrill and sense of wonder when in the course of events in a story such as this something completely unexpected shows up in a simple, off-hand manner—an idea that leads one to a field of interest and study that seemingly has no end.

An example: does a book in the Bible have a place in the classroom of medical schools, demonstrating how subtle forces of the body play a part in health and disease? I would probably receive few affirmative answers to such a question from physiology professors, but Cayce would have this come about. In Suzy's sixth reading, he pointed out that there were pressures existing in the lumbar and sacral regions of the body which activated a force which, in Eastern religions, is called a kundalini energy. These forces rise up to and through the pineal gland,

> which corresponds to those forces as are spoken of, even in that of the Book of the Revelation. Be very good for the doctor here to read The Revelation and understand it! Especially in reference to this body! These forces as applied to this are the activities as are seen in the sympathetic nerve system, and *advance* in their activities as the force of same impel through the sympathetic and the cerebrospinal plexus from the 9th dorsal to the brain itself. (2501-6)

The Revelation, as a means of understanding the creative forces within the body and as a kind of textbook of endocrinologic study, was thus mentioned for the first time in the readings. A question was asked about this in the next readings, in which Cayce indicated that an illustration is given in the Revelation showing how the "mental body" is raised through various degrees of consciousness. The activity of this energy rises from the lower parts of the body through the correlated centers of an anatomical body, as consciousness in the autonomic nervous system is elevated "to the inner court, or in the holy mount, through the pineal gland—that coordinates with the sympathetic forces."

In answering a final question about how the doctor on the case could study the Revelation to obtain this information, Cayce briefly pointed out that "*anyone,* will they study that given in the Book and compare same to the anatomical conditions of a physical body, will *learn* the *spiritual* body, the *mental* body—*not* metaphysics either!" A fascinating statement which, if factual, might augment the projected study of the human body in the classrooms of our medical schools.

Astrology was still another area of subject material almost casually opened up to the interested reader in Suzy's sixth reading. Cayce's comments easily skipped over barriers and exceeded boundaries that man has carefully built up over the ages. The astrologer finds evidence that the moon, the closest of the other heavenly bodies, as well as the sun and the stars exert a material influence on the human being, his destiny and his very physical body. Medicine as a whole, however, finds lunar effects and the care of sick persons to be a combination not really compatible.

Cayce was not hampered, apparently, by prejudice toward any field of endeavor within the scope of man's interest and scientific study. He might comment easily—as he did here—that the moon and medicine are related, and almost let it go at that. But he didn't quite relinquish the idea. In describing how the doctor should use an electrically driven vibrator with a sponge applicator alongside the spinal column, he suggested that this quick vibratory motion would be especially effective with the double chain of sympathetic ganglia that lies deep in that area, and with the autonomic nervous system. The imbalance of the latter had "much to do with . . .the lunar conditions," or the emotional reactions to the waxing moon. Indeed, in Cayce's viewpoint, the body was an exceedingly intricate creation, sensitive to many influences, and capable of more than we presently suspect.

He was suggesting, apparently, that the manner in which the sympathetic-parasympathetic nervous system was unbalanced in its function and in its relationship to the rest of the nervous system was the primary reason for the moon to possibly have such an unusual effect on this person's emotions. The emotions are, after all, directly related to the unconscious portions of a person's makeup. They deal almost exclusively with the autonomic nervous system and the glandular functions of the body, at times seeming to be completely apart from any conscious (cerebrospinal) control.

This may be why Cayce suggested to the physician that it would be an instructive and interesting experience to observe and document Suzy's reactions to the phases of the moon. Had he been asked the question, it is quite likely that Mr. Cayce would also have suggested this as another course of study to be added to the medical schools' curricula.

The therapeutic program which Cayce outlined for this strange disorder of the body had several component parts. As a whole, however, it would seem best to call it a rehabilitation process, for it involved a number of therapeutic efforts. Osteopathy, physical therapy, low voltage electrotherapy, nutritional therapy, psychotherapy, a type of occupational therapy—all these were suggested. In addition, and perhaps overriding the entire therapeutic program, was the reaffirmed need for a physical-mental-spiritual coordination in treatment of the individual.

The staff of the hospital was instructed that their attitudes contributed in a very significant way to the healing process. The patient was informed—if she were to understand—that her acceptance of the various therapuetic modalities, her "response" to treatment, was a strong factor in the time-lapse during which healing might occur. In other words, if she responded in the most positive, creative, and constructive manner, her return to normal physical condition would be rapid. As events progressed, it appeared that she did not respond quite as expected, and the projected six to nine weeks that Cayce initially suggested lengthened out to six months. Why? "The manner in which the body responds to the applications that have been made." This was the answer Cayce gave to the questions.

As advice was given toward the rehabilitation of these physiologic processes, the doctors attending the patient were not left out of the picture. The osteopaths were told in what manner the treatments were to be administered, what spinal areas were to be paid special attention. In Suzy's case, it was the second and third cervical, the second and third dorsal, the eighth and ninth dorsal, and the fourth lumbar. The study of the girl's reactions to the phases of the moon, the attention to be paid to the Revelation and its relationship to this person's abnormality—these, too, became part of the therapy.

The only medication suggested for Suzy was iodine, which had to be administered in a vibratory manner through the mechanism of a battery. This was constructed in a special way, and according to a voluminous group of Cayce's readings, designed to create a low voltage flow of electricity which would be introduced into the body. As stated in the readings, this device would then bring into the body the iodine which Cayce maintained could not pass the assimilatory barrier of the body as food was regularly taken into the body—at least not in sufficient amounts to make for the health of the body.

The fact that these various suggestions, when followed, corrected the problem that was threatening to distort Suzy's entire life overshadows the knowledge that we do not know how such a battery could work or how essential a part it played in the curative process. But, then, we do not really know why one sperm cell out of thousands teeming around an ovum becomes the one which penetrates the cell-wall barrier and starts the process that eventually produces an individual. Whereas familiarity may not really breed contempt, certainly frequency breeds blind acceptance. We must be thankful for those who do ask the questions and work to find out the answers.

There were really two primary goals sought in Suzy's therapeutic program: one was the introduction of iodine into the system in such a manner that it could be used to aid the thyroid in its function; the second was the re-establishment of a coordination and a balance in the nervous systems of the body—the repair of an "incoordination" of functions within the human body. Thus we have a deficiency disease and resulting functional, physiological incoordination which is a disease entity in itself and which can produce other problems in the body as well.

In approaching such a problem, Cayce apparently utilized a balanced program which took into consideration all aspects of the human being, assuming that all parts of a person are contributory to health and well-being. He suggested a course of therapy which is best described as physiological rehabilitation, correcting the processes of the body rather than healing the organs. In this case, the organic condition of the body was good; only the functions were aberrant.

That Suzy recovered well is pointed out adequately in her story. It is an interesting fact that we have a reading for this woman some twelve years after she left the Cayce Hospital, when she had found her place in the world as a wife and as a mother. It points out the emphasis usually found in the readings when dealing with the physical body and provides us with an end to our story:

Mr. Cayce: Yes, we have the body here—this we have had before, you see.

> There are a great many changes that have taken place in the body since last we had same here. Most of these have been in the fulfilling or developing of the body and its activities, and in much bettered conditions in coordinating activities through the physical forces. (2501-12)

CHAPTER 4

THE TURNING POINT

by Mary Ellen Carter

LILA HAYNES SAT in the chair facing Dr. Merrill Dawson. She gripped her purse in her gloved hands and said, "Doctor, I'm a doctor, too—an osteopath. Tell me plainly what chances my boy has of coming through this?"

Dr. Dawson, large and kindly, shook his head. "I'm sorry, but all four of us physicians here have agreed his chances are very slight."

In her heart, Lila knew that this was the worst moment in her fifty-four years, and she did not trust herself to speak.

"A ruptured appendix is a dangerous thing to begin with," the man went on. "When he was operated on, his condition turned into peritonitis. There's even gangrene, now, I'm afraid. And he's contracted typhoid fever."

She stood up. "I must see him, please, if I may."

"Of course. You must realize he's very low. Only for a moment."

Phil Haynes, 28, lay drowsing under the sheet, only partly aware that his mother had entered the room. He was limp and still, and a pallor lay on his features, as though death had already drawn a veil over them. He was thin from the ordeal of his illness.

Phil, himself, was an osteopath.

As she stood gazing down at her son, she prayed, "Oh, dear God, tell me what to do. Dear Great Physician, help me to help this young man who had dedicated his life to healing others. Surely You have a plan for him, and surely You don't mean for him to die!"

She heard light steps advancing down the hall. They were those of her daughter-in-law, Vivian, who had gone to telephone her parents about Phil's crisis. Vivian appeared in the room, her face wan with the strain. Lila told her, "Dear, stay with him while I go to make a phone call of my own."

The young woman nodded and looked with frightened eyes at her husband, who had been only a while ago so full of life and hopes for the future. She touched his hand. Lila went out, saying, "Don't give up hope yet." Vivian's head was bent, but at those words her heart seemed to lift.

For Lila had remembered that only a few months ago she had had a reading from Edgar Cayce—a "life" reading telling her of her former incarnations. She had heard of his ability to diagnose physical ailments, however, and had learned something of his success in giving helpful suggestions for healing. As an osteopath, she knew of the power the body has to heal itself when manipulated and aligned properly, and she knew that Edgar Cayce had recommended her particular healing art to a large number of people. All that she had seen and learned of his ability and treatments had been acceptable to her. She had thought, upon recognizing his work as a valid step toward progress in healing, that if ever she herself or a loved one were in need of his help, that she would not hesitate to seek it.

Now, there was no time to lose. She passed by the elevator doors and went briskly down the stairs to the lobby to find a telephone. At this hour—6:15 in the evening—Mr. Cayce would doubtless be having dinner with his family. She hoped he would forgive her for the intrusion.

It had been a beautiful spring day at Virginia Beach. The Cayces had not yet sat down to eat dinner when the telephone rang. Edgar himself answered the ring. "Long distance," he told Gertrude, and waited.

A woman's soft voice began, "This is Lila Haynes. I'm so worried."

"What is it, Mrs. Haynes? I remember you. How is your son?"

"He's desperately ill, Mr. Cayce, in Murray Hill Hospital here in New York. He was operated on for ruptured appendix on Tuesday night, and it's turned into peritonitis. The doctors think there is only a slight chance he'll pull through!"

Cayce replied, "I'll give him a reading right away!" Then he added, "Call back in forty-five minutes!"

As she took the stairs once more to the second floor, Lila was almost smiling. At least, she felt a certain serenity she had not felt awhile ago. She thought that it would be wonderful to be able to tell Vivian that at this very moment, Mr. Cayce was preparing to give a reading for Phil. She would suggest that they pray together for the next half hour.

At the head of the stairs she met Dr. Tonner, one of Phil's attending physicians. He recognized her and stopped. "Did Dr. Dawson tell you about your son?" He added, "He's mighty bad off."

"Yes. But maybe there's hope for him yet."

Dr. Tonner looked at her sharply. Perhaps she was breaking under the strain. He would have to watch her.

"You see," Lila began, almost light-heartedly. But before she could explain, Vivian came out of Phil's room. The three of them walked to the waiting room and sat down. "Doctor," said Vivian, "please tell me what Phil was trying to say when you came in awhile ago."

Lila glanced inquiringly at the doctor. He was not as cautious as Dr. Dawson. He said, "I'll tell you, as I don't believe in holding back such things. He said that he did not want to live."

Lila gasped. "My Phil said *that?*"

"Those were his very words. He was not himself, of course. He hardly knew what he was saying."

Vivian and Lila looked at each other in disbelief. Vivian's young face was a white mask. Lila's sagged with the age she had not shown before. She thought, if he doesn't want to live, the reading will do him no good! One must *want* to live, to fight, or no treatment can help very much.

It was with all the strength she could muster that she stood up, remembering the "appointment" with Cayce and her intention to cooperate with him by keeping a time of prayer. It was this that kept her from sinking into utter despair.

"Vivian, come with me," she said. "Doctor, if we are quiet, may we sit in Phil's room for awhile?"

"Certainly. Just don't try to rouse him. He needs rest."

"We promise. We will be very quiet."

The doctor left them, and they returned to Phil's bedside. He was much as they had left him. He lay halfway between waking and sleeping, and they did nothing to disturb him.

In a low voice Lila told Vivian about her call to Cayce and of the reading he was to give this very hour. "We must keep our appointment with him, you see, in prayer." Vivian nodded and bowed her head gratefully.

At seven o'clock Lila left the room and telephoned Cayce once more. His voice was reassuring. "We can read it to you now. It was short, but very good, I think," he told her.

Now Gertrude's voice broke in and she said, "Mrs. Haynes, after the physical suggestions, Mr. Cayce said: "We have the body here. Conditions are serious. The sepses have advanced some. The vitality is low. The resistance is low. Yet we find the *will*, the determination are strong with the inner forces of the body, and that those administrations being made are very good. We would give that, as a stimulus—through tomorrow, especially—Golden Seal or Life Everlasting, in small quantities, will aid.

"The will, the attention, the prayers of many will have the greater effect. We are through." (102-1)

As the reading was repeated, Lila wrote it down word for word; when it was ended, she thanked Gertrude with all her heart. "I'll read it to him right away, as soon as they let me," she said.

With the precious notes in her hand, she went back up the stairs to Phil's room. He was somewhat awake and saw her. He lifted his hand in greeting. Vivian stood by, saying little but imploring Lila with her eyes to bring hope to them all. Lila took his hand. Dr. Dawson had come in. "You may talk to him a little."

"Hello, Phil. I want to read something to you."

"What is it, Mother?"

"I have received a reading about you and for you from Edgar Cayce in Virginia Beach. Would you like to hear it?"

"If you think it's good, go ahead."

"All right." In her low voice she recounted the message, and it seemed to Vivian that it sounded something like a poem. When Lila was through, Phil said with a flicker of vitality, "It sounds right. It's true. I know it's all true."

"Do you want to get well, Phil?" asked Vivian.

He almost lifted his head from the pillow. "You bet I do!" His glance locked with hers. *"Now I want to live!"*

The small quantities of Golden Seal or Life Everlasting prescribed as the sole medication in the brief reading were administered that evening and through the following day. By the next day he was able to retain food, which he had not done since the operation. He had been nauseated and had vomited a good deal, but now that was over.

At the same time, Lila determined to take the entire reading to heart. She would, she told Vivian, do just what it told them. Phil's response to the reading had been so plain. The response was so real! There should be many praying for him! They should be good church men, men of faith. She went to the telephone once more and called her good friend, the Reverend deBose, who had baptized Phil into the Methodist Church when he was two. Rev. deBose quickly agreed to telephone several other ministers, including the Rev. Garrett, pastor of the First Baptist Church. They would, he said, call others and come to Phil's side as soon as possible. Among their friends, said Mr. deBose, were a priest and a rabbi.

There strode from the elevator a few hours later a lean-faced rabbi with waving dark hair who wore heavy blackrimmed glasses and a grave air about him. He was perhaps 48. He did not smile, but there was a look on his face that invited confidence.

Lila met him in the hallway, saying, "Oh, Rabbi Steiner, I'm so grateful to you." She extended her hand, and he took it warmly.

"Where is your son?"

"In here. Oh, did Dr. Dawson tell you how ill he is?"

"Yes. But he is alive. We will begin our appeal to God who is Father of us all."

"He is truly that. And you are indeed our friend. Please come into the room."

Rabbi Steiner walked into the room quietly and took a stance by the window. He watched Phil for a long moment before he closed his eyes and began to pray softly in Hebrew. Lila bowed her head, not understanding the words, but joining her own prayers with his silently.

When the prayer was over, she heard footsteps down the hall. Someone was coming—slowly, regally. It seemed to take a long time. Lila left the room to await the newcomer, thinking, "I've never called on a Catholic priest to save me or my loved ones before. Nor a rabbi."

Then Father Martinelli emerged from the depths of the hall with great dignity, and she thought of the centuries of the Catholic Church that sat upon his broad shoulders. He approached with a beautiful look of benefaction for her, taking her hand in both of his own great palms. It was, she thought, like being sheltered if the heart of a massive cathedral. He said, "Dear Mrs. Haynes, I believe?"

"Yes, Father Martinelli. Phil, my son, is in this room." She led the way and he entered slowly, taking in the sleeping form on the bed, the barren walls, the rabbi who stood contemplatively by the window.

The two men stepped toward each other with outstretched hands and greeted each other as two people intent on saving a life by appealing to a common God. Phil slept on, unaware of them, and Lila thought that all of the world lay there, in Phil, waiting for the men of faith to meet in its behalf.

Presently, Rev. deBose and Rev. Garrett entered. The first was elderly, tall, lean, with greying hair and a merry look in his eyes that spoke of many Methodist fellowship dinners. There was, too, something of the circuit rider about him, as if he had just come in from a long trek across country and was expecting to conduct a tent meeting within the hour. He grasped her hand and said, "I guess we're all here now! What a wonderful thing! Rabbi Steiner, how are you? And

Father Martinelli—you beat us here!"

Young Rev. Garrett, looking ruddy-cheeked and gloriously calm, glanced often at Phil, who was about his own age. Only his eyes betrayed his inner concern. Lila's heart went out to him because of that, and because he was strong and healthy as Phil had once been. The youthful Baptist cleric was quick to sense the rapport among them and between himself and Lila. He looked into her face with earnest good will and said, "God bless you, Mrs. Haynes."

The six of them, including Vivian, now stood in a circle about the bed and bowed their heads. "Our Heavenly Father," began Reverend deBose solemnly, "we come to Thee from many paths this night, in order to ask your healing Presence here. Please be with young Phillip Haynes now as he takes on once more the will to live and to serve his fellow man. We know that he is only waiting thy loving touch and that if it is Thy will that he live, that he lives for a purpose. Be with his wife and his mother and strengthen them in this anxious time. In thy name we pray. Amen."

During this time, the prayer group led by Edgar Cayce was also praying for Phil.

From that night, Phil had progressed until at last he was able to leave the hospital. Now he was advised by later readings to recuperate at the Cayce Hospital in Virginia Beach, since his system still held the effects of the poisons from the original condition. He was admitted to the Cayce Hospital on May 29, 1930, nearly two months from the time he had been stricken. His reading that day stated that "There is a great deal of difference" in Phil's general condition from that of two months before. Although he had improved, it would be necessary to bring about proper blood coagulation and the building up of his system. He was to exercise cautiously in the open and to partake of a blood- and nerve-building diet. He was to take green vegetables in particular.

To the question, "What may be applied externally to the wound to aid healing?" Cayce replied: "We wouldn't apply anything as yet! Get the system properly adjusted and the healing will come, as has just been given, from the inside." (102-2)

Packs and antiseptics were used to heal the wound, of course. Several weeks later, Phil was well enough to ask when he could return to the work of practicing osteopathy.

"In a week or ten days. Do not attempt . . . to overtax self by too heavy work, for *osteopathy* is real work, if done properly." (102-3)

Movements involved in playing golf and tennis, which Phil asked about, would be good as long as he didn't deplete his energies. He was warned to take iodine- and calcium-containing foods and not too much potash or condiments which would put too much weight in certain places rather than in general area. Phil, said this message, would be "a pretty good size man."

On July 17, 1930, Phil wrote to Edgar Cayce: "I am now back in my office for the first time since March and I am so happy to be here again. My health is fine—I feel quite well in all respects and hope to regain my practice in a short while.

"I simply cannot express my thanks for all the wonderful things you have done for me. My stay at the Cayce Hospital was a Godsend—I picked up so much valuable strength . . ."

Later he wrote, "I will always be interested in Cayce Hospital and if your plans change and you need me down there I hope you will call on me."

In a letter several years later, he stated that he believed that his recovery "was due to osteopathic treatment and the ministrations coming through Mr. Cayce." During his lifetime he treated many people who went to him with Cayce readings, according to Gladys Davis Turner's note in the files. He always reported favorable results, she adds.

He wrote after recovery that he was taking care of his practice and recalled that Cayce had said that osteopathy was hard work! "But the most wonderful thing that the readings did for me was to turn the tide when I lay near death in the hospital . . . That was the turning point. And I have been going upward ever since."

Medical Commentary: Peritonitis, Gangrene

by William A. McGarey, M.D.

THE TURNING POINT in an illness is recognized as that timeless moment when—for one of many reasons—a sick person stops getting sicker ansd starts getting well. We tend to look at it as the progression of illness being stopped, when in reality it is what might best be called the revivification of a human being. Hope might be the instrument of change; today we depend on antibiotics more than hope. There is a restoration of balance within the body—in any event, the life force present within every one of us finds a resurgence of energy and power—and the sick person suddenly starts getting well. It is just that sudden and sometimes that simple.

No doctor who has dealt with the acutely ill has failed to see someone take a dramatic "turn" for the better, and then come rapidly alive again, gaining strength in a manner never expected. The opposite, of course, happens just as frequently, if not more so, when one who seems to be doing well suddenly changes and succumbs, leaving the physician often with the question in his mind: "What *really* happened inside that body—what *really* caused his death?" Answers to these questions are not easy to come by. We do not know, frankly, what occurs in the flow of life, the movement of all those wonderful forces within the body, that might trigger a sudden change in direction. Almost instantaneously, the dying patient suffuses with life, and his destination is obviously among those of us who are still physically present in this world rather than the other side of life—whatever that may be.

The story of this young osteopathic physician, Phil Haynes, and his peritonitis following a ruptured and apparently very septic appendicitis points out for us just this problem. That his course changed from a dismal and nearly hopeless prognosis to one of rapid recovery is the most interesting facet of this man's story. He needed care afterward, certainly, as the surgical site granulated in and closed—he was cared for in the Cayce Hospital in Virginia Beach and in time returned to his practice. These records are available and make interesting reading. The most intriguing question still remains however—what really did happen inside Phil Haynes as he passed the turning point?

Cayce was correct here, of course, in his analysis of the situation. He reassured the young man, told him he would get better, that he had the will to live, that he should take Golden Seal tea to quiet down the intestinal tract, and that he would benefit from the prayers of many. It is interesting that Cayce combined medical clairvoyance and precognition with therapeutic suggestions aimed at the mind (the suggestion that Phil wanted to live), the body (the Golden Seal tea), and the spirit (the prayers of many).

Perhaps it was the fact that Phil was given a message from an unconscious mind—something that many of us stand in awe of. He was told he had the will to live. He was already receptive, and he believed the statement, the suggestion. He *did* have the will—he *would* get well. This might have been the progression of events, and all the other factors might be of no real consequence. Suggestion is a powerful tool, and it would certainly work better coming from one like Cayce than from his own mother or wife. With the history of hypnosis to draw from, one cannot exclude this as a possibility, as the sole cause of recovery.

We must also look at the possibility that Phil in reality did have the will to live, even before Cayce pointed it out to him in the reading. Perhaps the reading came at a time when the change was starting anyway. Perhaps he would have gotten well without the reading. We cannot say otherwise, even though the prognosis was dark and the patient was not doing well. And the stomach might have quieted down without the tea. All these possibilities should be looked at and considered. To go back forty years and reconstruct a condition of illness is difficult at best.

In all fairness, however, one must also explore the obvious sequence of events, evaluating their individual influences on the total picture of the story Mrs. Carter has given us.

Let us suppose that Cayce clairvoyantly "saw"—as he stated—that Phil Haynes had a strong determination, a strong will to live. He also pointed out that the administrations being made by the doctors were very good. He did not seem to be making a point of suggesting anything to the patient except that this was the state of affairs, and that he was in actuality going to get better. This stimulus may have been all Phil needed to recognize within himself that he really *did* want to live, and thus activate the tremendous power of will that is within each of us. In other readings Cayce has much to say about will—its strength in the lives of people and how nothing in one's experience is stronger than his will. It seems to unlock spiritual strength which can bring one back from almost certain death. It can generate unbelievable changes in one's life, as it acts to supersede the laws of the physical body and its environment. The will, of course, is closely associated with the mind. In reading 416-2, Cayce said:

> Let the entity understand and know—there is no urge or influence that exceeds the will. . . . For, the WILL is that factor which is the birthright of each soul, each entity, through which choice is made, and by which the entity exercises that prerogative of showing itself to be a child of God with the abilities to apply spiritual influences rather than merely the exercising of natural or nature's laws in its relationships to Creative Forces.

Cayce's next suggestion was the only one having to do with the body. He suggested that Phil be given Golden Seal tea in small quantities as a stimulant, as an aid to the body. As he took the tea the vomiting and nausea ceased—certainly, in the early thirties, a necessary step in the recuperative process, even as it is today. Modern therapy, with antibiotics, drugs, and intravenous injections, would seldom leave a patient in as much distress as Phil found himself. These things, however, were not available.

Golden Seal is an herb, the root of the plant *Hydrastis canadensis*. It is known by a wide variety of other names, such as yellow paint root, orange root, Indian paint, yellow eye, and jaundice root. It is held in highest esteem by those who are knowledgeable about herbs. It has been used over the ages externally as a relief for skin problems and internally for a multitude of things, particularly for inflamed conditions of the stomach and small intestine. The root itself is classified medically as a hemostatic and astringent, but it is rarely employed as such. The alkaloids having similar hemostatic and astringent qualities, hydrastine, berberine, and canadine, are extracted from the *Hydrastis*.

The patient was given an ancient therapy and his intestinal tract responded, his nausea ceased, and he then was able once again to take nourishment so important to the recovery process.

We are told that prayer interceded for Phil. The mother in the case was not a hesitant woman. She covered the field—Baptist, Methodist, Catholic, Jew. Ministers, priest, and rabbi stood together with Phil's wife and mother, following the heritage of the Judeo-Christian faith of the ages, asking God for a physical healing. Is such a healing possible? Members of the medical profession have attested to sudden, miraculous healings that have occurred at Lourdes, France, for most of the decades of this century. So many documented recoveries have been recorded all over the world that it no longer is reasonable to comment until one has at least become familiar with the field. Kathryn Kuhlman has been an outstanding figure in this field since the middle 1940's. The relationship of prayer to healing of the physical body is a fact. We need to find out what happens.

In the case of Phil Haynes, the members of the clergy—and others—participated in what Cayce gave as the summation of his reading: "The will, the attention, the prayers of many will have the greater effect."

So what was it that actually brought about the turn of events which saw Phil move from illness toward recovery? As Cayce saw it, there are many channels through which healing might come. He saw all life as a oneness. No matter how an individual is able to bring to the cells within his body that they *are* one with Creative Energy which we call God, healing comes when that awareness is accomplished. Thus, healing could come through the mind, the body, the spirit of man, since they are one. The prayers, the awakening of the will, the administrations by the doctors—all might bring healing. Healing, Cayce said, is all of the same source, whether it be the laying on of hands, the use of medicine, herbs, surgery, or prayer—all healing comes from God.

A great many of us are skeptical. We need reasons and explanations. Cayce apparently had this in mind when he gave the following reading:

Let's analyze healing for a moment, for the benefit of those who, like this body, must consciously see and reason — see a material demonstration, occasionally, at least!

Each atomic force of a physical body is made up of its units of positive and negative forces, which bring it into a material plane. These are of the ether, or atomic forces, which are electrical in nature when they enter into materiality or become matter, with its ability to take on or throw off.

A group may thus raise those atomic vibrations which make for *positive* forces, which bring divine force into action in a material plane — *destructive* forces are broken down by the raising of that vibration! That's a "material explanation," see? And this is accomplished through Creative Forces, which are God in manifestation! (281-3)

Keeping things in context, then, Cayce was internally consistent in his readings as he unconsciously surveyed the situation, saw that only a few things were really needed. He suggested that these be done; and the sick man changed, turned the corner, and began to find health again.

CHAPTER 5

GRANDMOTHER TAKES A HAND

by Mary Ellen Carter

TEARS WELLED IN the eyes of 13-month-old Jane Marsh. She rubbed her ears fretfully, for the cold she had been having during the past week had settled in them.

Alicia, her mother, decided to take her to the family physician. Upon examining Jane, he thought it best to puncture both her ears in an attempt to cure the infection that had developed. But Jane grew worse, and he prescribed a new medicine.

It was the Sunday before Christmas, 1932, when Betty, her grandmother, took a hand in helping to care for her. In a letter to Edgar Cayce afterward, Betty wrote: "When I started to give her the second dose [of the presecribed medicine] she cried so hard that I only gave her half of it. I took the balance, myself, as a test. I found it contained something which burned terribly.

"In less than two hours from that time she began to break out in splotches on the lower limbs, and the bottoms of her feet had dark spots on them."

When Jane was touched on her legs, she cried. At midnight, when the doctor was again called in, he said that this was "a form of hives." When he learned that the medicine burned so severely, he ordered it discontinued.

"If that baby is living tomorrow morning," Betty told her husband that night, "I'm going to get Mr. Cayce to give a reading for her if possible." She added, "In all my years of child raising, I've never seen anything like those symptoms."

Jane now had dark circles around her ankles; her ears were black except for the lobes. Even the soles of her feet were black.

The next morning, they called in a specialist. He found her gums looked "mortified," to use the report in the readings from Betty's account.

The reading, 324-1, given immediately at Betty's request, was telephoned to her by Miss Gladys Davis, a personal friend of the Cayce family. Betty said nothing of the reading to the specialist, for it indicated, she said, that the treatments outlined wouldn't interfere with anything already being done.

With her daughter's grateful cooperation, Betty followed both the specialist's treatment and the reading. "The specialist prescribed only something to make a lining in her stomach where the medicine had destroyed the tissue to a certain extent; a sedative for making her sleep; and a mouth wash. The child's temperature registered 104 1/2 degrees, yet these were all the specialist ordered," according to Betty.

"As we find," began Jane's first reading, "there are the effects of cold and congestion, especially to the membranes of the throat and head; that is, the effect that produces such an amount of temperature.

"That to be prevented most is this causing too great a strain on the soft tissue, as to produce antrum or the ear trouble, or descending into the bronchi and lungs and making for the inflammation of the pleural cavity.

"While the temperature is high, as we find, some little changes in the ministrations would make for better conditions for the body."

The reading recommended the following treatment:

"First, we would massage as much camphorated oil in the spine, chest, and throat as the body will take up.

"We would massage the soles of the feet with mutton tallow, camphor, and turpentine. Keep these very warm. These would be mixed in proportions as about equal parts of each, see? Necessary, then, of course, to dissolve the mutton tallow. Two or three drops of the spirits of camphor and spirits of turpentine to about twice the amount of the mutton tallow dissolved. Of course, do not have this so hot as to burn, but have warm when applied and keep wrapped in hot flannels.

"We would take the syrup of squill, five to eight drops every three to four hours.

"Dissolve five grains of calcidin in ten ounces of water. Keep warm, and every few minutes when there is the choking or the irritating of the body give a few sips of this, see?

"These may be given without fear of hindering or being effective with any other applications.

"Do that.

"The oil and the squill, especially, will reduce the temperature.

"Be mindful of this, especially through the coming night and morning."

When the question about nourishment was asked, the answer came that nourishment was to be kept, but that they should not permit cold or congestion to settle in the lungs or upon the intestinal system as to cause colitis or any of the disorders from same. Hence, pre-digested foods would be better and natural fruit juices, with no sugar.

"Should all other treatments now being applied be kept up?"

"Only when necessary, for if these are applied properly, we will see—in four to six hours—a great deal of change for the better."

Later that day, a neighbor came over to see Jane. She looked at the tiny form in the crib and shook her head. "I've only seen two people in that condition," she said sadly.

"Did they get over it?" Betty asked, a bit shaken.

The mournful visitor hesitated uncomfortably. "No, they didn't."

Betty refused to be dismayed. "Here's one that is going to get well!" she smiled.

She followed the treatments scrupulously, massaging the little chest and spine and throat with the strong-smelling oil; rubbing the small feet with warm mutton tallow, camphor, turpentine; and following all the rest of the instructions. Just as the reading had promised, Jane's temperature began to drop at about 7 o'clock that evening! Betty and Alicia were overjoyed. Sharing their joy was Miss Davis, who had arrived for a visit to the little patient.

When the specialist came the next morning, Betty showed him the chart she had kept of Jane's temperature drop. He was amazed. "Well," he said, "I expected to find her *some* better . . ."

"As I never told him about the reading," Betty relates, "he never knew what brought it all about."

The sign of the "hives" had for the most part disappeared, and, with the temperature dropping, the outlook was much better. Grandmother Betty, in her exhileration over the improvement of her grandchild, became a little lax in her applications of the treatments Cayce had suggested. The result? The minute she relaxed the treatments, Jane's temperature would begin to rise! When she resumed them, it fell.

The specialist could not understand the fluctuation. A blood test which he took proved negative, so he called in another specialist who took a Malta fever test. This, too, was negative.

Within a week, Jane was out of danger. She recovered completely except for the right ear, which would start to discharge again whenever she got the least bit of a cold. This continued for the next three or four months. Her grandmother requested a second reading, given April 28, 1933, which answered questions about the infectious forces still present, especially in her right ear. For this, Cayce prescribed one drop of a mixture of St. Jacob's oil diluted with sweet oil, warmed, just before bedtime. The ear should be cleansed in the morning with an antiseptic solution, he added. Jane's system should be cleansed at this time with Fletcher's Castoria "with added senna." Her feet should be given daily massage with small quantities of olive oil and tincture of myrrh for an infection located on her foot.

The following September, Betty reported that Jane became completely well in response to the treatment faithfully carried out.

Medical Commentary: Ear Infection

by William A. McGarey, M.D.

THIS IS A rather simple story, but it does have certain implications and ramifications which should be explored. The response of the modern physician would most likely be that a simple antihistamine preparation and an antibiotic would have prevented the complications and rendered this a very mild infection, perhaps not *even* necessitating the surgical care to the eardrums. And certainly the recurring ear infection would not likely have come about. In 1943, however, antihistamines and antibiotics were a thing of the future, and the problem facing these people was a matter of life and death. A severe urticaria involving the entire body can be a frightful thing, and the problem facing the doctor at that point with the armamentarium at his command was a difficult one.

In his reading given for this child, Cayce saw the possibility of Jane's sickness being complicated by mastoid trouble, bronchitis, pneumonia, and possibly colitis, if the infection were not controlled. This is, in the medical mind, a reasonable—though psychic—insight on the part of Mr. Cayce.

The story of this very ill little infant highlights, in my mind, the question of the proper doctor-patient relationship. Why did the mother and the grandmother not tell the doctors about having a psychic reading done for the child's benefit? Were they afraid of being rebuffed and ridiculed because they asked the advice of someone with only Cayce's credentials? It seems reasonable to me that any physician worthy of the name should be willing to learn more about the nature of the body—knowing as we do so little about it. Should they have been hesitant?

A partial answer to these questions might be found in the life story of Edgar Cayce. Time and again he was scoffed at by the medical profession. This is unfortunate, but true. When Wesley Ketchum, M.D., for instance, actually worked with difficult patients who were given readings by Cayce and saw them improve and recover, he reported this to his fellow physicians. He, in turn, was laughed at, ridiculed, and finally threatened with expulsion from his medical society. Incidents such as this may have been influential here in the hesitancy shown in confiding the facts to the doctors.

Apparently Betty—the grandmother—did not really trust herself to tell them that she was doing other things than just what they ordered. She went ahead and did what Cayce instructed her to do, keeping this information from the family doctor and the pediatrician. Not the best relationship, this.

Perhaps this story is also an interesting little incident—vitally important to those involved in it, of course—to demonstrate that the healing of the body is not only the concern of the physician. It points up the fact that anyone who wants to be of assistance can be involved in the healing process; and that healing, which really comes from God, is not limited to the professional in the field.

This is not a new idea, of course. It is utilized every time a mother kisses the hurt on her child's knee or rubs away the pain when he bumps his elbow. It is the thought behind one person praying for another, and it underlies the love that motivates literally thousands of volunteers who help out in hospitals and clinics around the world.

Every time Cayce gave a reading, he demonstrated that one person's unconscious mind could reach out and contact the point of awareness in another person's body which knew what was wrong with that body. That was the nature of the physical readings as Cayce described them himself, repeated over and over again more than 9,000 times.

This repetitive and demonstrably accurate procedure provides us with the fascinating information that each of us—at some level of our unconscious mind—knows what is wrong with our own physical body when we are ill. This expands the realm of healing as we presently know it, for it indicates to us that perhaps there are no illnesses which cannot be diagnosed with an amazing accuracy. And it implies that were we to utilize this knowledge which is inherent within us, we might also come to know what needs to be done then to restore the body to health. Cayce apparently used the same capabilities in different ways to diagnose the problem and to prescribe for the illness. In some manner his mind reached out and contacted a source of knowledge which provided him with means to change the physiological functioning of the body more toward normal. This involves all of us in the healing act. Betty was not really astray, since she wanted to help her little granddaughter.

But what about the therapy which Cayce suggested—the treatments which apparently were instrumental in preventing complications of the infection and restoring the little girl back to a state of good health? Let's investigate these a bit more thoroughly. He suggested:

1. Massage the chest, throat, and spine with as much camphorated oil as the body will absorb. (I would imagine this was done two or three times a day.)
2. Massage the soles of the feet with equal parts of a warm mixture of mutton tallow, spirits of turpentine, and spirits of camphor, and keep the feet wrapped in hot flannel cloth. (Elsewhere in the readings, he stated that these substances should be made up beginning with heated mutton tallow, with the spirits of turpentine and camphor added in that order.)
3. Dietary advice: Eat only unsweetened, natural fruit juices and predigested foods.
4. Take syrup of squill, five to eight drops every three or four hours.

5. Take a few sips every few minutes of a mixture of five grains of calcidine in ten ounces of water as needed to relieve cough.

These procedures were obviously directed toward certain therapeutic objectives. Cayce wanted to protect the body from developing colitis while this infectious-allergic process was being dissipated. That was one of the functions of the diet prescribed. From my knowledge of these readings, I would understand the diet to be intended also to alkalinize the blood stream in the process, for natural fruit juice has that property—fruit and vegetables being the prime food substances providing an alkaline ash on analysis. Along with a number of other sources, Cayce laid great stress on an alkaline-reacting diet in infectious conditions of the body. He once stated that the body which is kept slightly alkaline in its reaction (primarily, he implied, through the diet) would not likely catch a cold. There are extremes in both acid and alkaline states of the human body, however, that are seriously detrimental.

Camphorated oil rubbed on the spine, chest and throat? This is a treatment used for years and years—not really anything new, of course. But Cayce said that this, plus the syrup of squill, would reduce the temperature. It—or something—did reduce the temperature, and in the time suggested. Why? Squill is described in the medical references as an expectorant and a diuretic and is prepared from the inner scales of the bulb of the white variety of *Urginea maritima*, a lilaceous plant. Does it have antipyretic qualities in addition?

What about the camphorated oil? It is a 20% weight solidus volume mixture of camphor oil in cottonseed oil, described as a counterirritant embrocation. This means that when it is applied to the body by rubbing, it tends to produce an inflammation of the skin for the relief of a more deep-seated irritation. We are not told *how* such a substance rubbed on the outside of the body affects irritation inside the body, but by its use over the ages, such a result has consistently come about. Thus its definition has developed while its methodology has remained unknown.

Thus, the combination of these two substances, one producing a carrying away of irritation deep in the tissues of the chest, throat, and spine, and the other acting as a diuretic—increasing certainly the elimination of substances from the body—brought about a relief of the high fever and apparently contributed to the resolution of the infection and the allergic condition which was present.

Calcidine is rarely used by the physician today. Calcidrine, as a cough preparation, is still available. The former, however, is a tablet which, when dissolved in water (adult dosage being 2 1/2 grains in four ounces of water taken every hour during the day for four to five days if needed), was indicated for dry cough and scant secretions. It is a compound containing 15% available iodine in combination with lime and starch. It is interesting that Cayce suggested that five grains be dissolved in ten ounces of water and the mixture be given in sips as needed. This manner of administration would pass muster with the best pediatric pharmacology standards of that day.

The remaining therapeutic measure Cayce suggested to bring some degree of balance to this little child was the mutton tallow spirits of turpentine and spirits of camphor mixture. This combination was suggested in literally dozens of readings given for respiratory conditions of the body. Consistently, advice was given to rub this either on the chest and throat or into the soles of the feet—sometimes after a hot foot bath and sometimes after a hot tub bath. One individual (585) was told to bring his fever down by bathing his feet in hot water every four hours and, following this, to take a rubdown from the hips to the feet. He was also told to massage the feet with the combination of mutton tallow, spirits of turpentine, and spirits of camphor.

In his reading given for the common cold (902-1) Cayce stated that the first remedy which should be applied in this condition is rest. Then treatment should be directed where the weakness lies. In most instances lack of eliminations is a major factor, and in many individuals the process of assimilation needs correction. Plenty of water is needed and, in most people, an alkalizer of the system would be in order. Something to stimulate eliminations seems to be almost a constant factor in Cayce's prescriptions.

While Jane's condition was not a cold, the respiratory system was highly affected, so Cayce's generalities in reference to colds probably were at least partially brought to bear on this problem. It may be that the unusual mixture was intended just to help bring down the fever, but its use so generally in respiratory conditions of the body in the Cayce readings would rather imply that there was something of a healing influence also brought to bear within the physiological processes of the body by the administration of this strange combination of substances.

Thus, the therapy which an alert grandmother was able to administer brought about a relief of the cough, an increase in the eliminations of the body, a resolution of irritations deep within the body, an antipyretic effect, an aid (or a "booster") to assimilation, an alkalinization of the body, and a probable healing effect of unknown quality and quantity. Quite a bit of change brought to the body, if indeed all these things are operative.

This child's experience provides a good example of the manner in which the Cayce readings directed healing to come about. Not by a medication designed to eliminate an illness, but rather a group of therapies aimed at restoring the equilibrium, the balance, and coordination of the forces within the body which, when full and normal, spell health for the body.

CHAPTER 6

TELL THEM THE LAME WALK

by Mary Ellen Carter

MID-JULY OF 1929 found Virginia Beach a haven for vacationers and visitors from out-of-town. It was a wonderful time and place to be young. At 19, Ginny Meades should have been at the beach with her husband Bart and their friends, as they had once been free to do. But for six months now, Ginny had been crippled and helpless from what doctors had told her was acute rheumatism. For her, especially, the joys of swimming in the surf and running on the beach were over.

Dr. Frank Johnson straightened up after examining Ginny and shook his head. She lay on the sofa, her once lovely body twisted beneath her cotton dress, her legs turned almost backward, her spine grotesquely bent. In her eyes was a mute plea for help.

He was shocked by what he had found. Her right leg had become at least ten inches shorter than the left! Her poor right knee had become so turned that the back almost faced forward.

"I'm afraid," he told Ginny's mother, who stood anxiously nearby, "that Ginny's spine is too twisted as a result of rheumatism for any hope it will ever be straight again."

At that moment Bart came in. Ginny knew from his expression that he had bad news. "Hello, Bart," she said, trying to hide the fear and anguish of that moment. When Dr. Johnson had left, she didn't at once tell him her own devastating news. Instead, she said, "You . . . didn't get the job?"

"No! But I'll try again tomorrow." He looked closely at Ginny. "What did the doctor tell you?"

When she had finished repeating Dr. Johnson's sad prediction, her lips trembled and she hid her face in the pillow. Bart put an arm around her and tried to comfort her. But the disappointment of his day had been topped by this; he could only offer an awkward kiss on the forehead. "Please don't cry," he said. But she did.

She had cried when the dull pain began in her legs last winter. The bitter damp winds that blew in from the Atlantic chilled the bones and sent one scurrying indoors. Grey clouds hovered overhead on that February day. As Ginny struggled to gather the wash from the line in her tiny backyard, she felt a pain in her legs she had never felt before. That night it became so severe that Bart called Dr. Radford, who agreed to examine Ginny in the morning. Following the examination, Dr. Radford advised that Ginny go to a hospital for treatment of acute rheumatism.

She exchanged glances with Bart. "Where will we get the money?" she asked. There seemed no answer.

Ginny suffered for a month at home before, with the help of friends and Dr. Radford, she was admitted to a Norfolk hospital. During the following weeks, she received all possible care. Three doctors attended her in addition to Dr. Radford. Her condition, however, gradually worsened. By May, her legs were beginning to swell, her spine was twisting, her right leg had grown five inches shorter than her left, she had lost her appetite.

Ginny was pronounced incurable. "I'm afraid there is nothing more we can do for you here, Ginny," Dr. Radford told her. "You may go home."

At home, Ginny's mother and two sisters nursed her, feeling certain that she would never recover. Ginny was by now so helpless that she couldn't feed herself; her appetite, however, returned as the rheumatism medicine was discontinued.

One day, Dr. Johnson came to the house to see one of Ginny's sisters. "Doctor, while you're here, would you look at our Ginny?" her mother requested. It was this visit that had led to the doctor's corroboration of the first doctor's prediction: Ginney would never walk again.

One evening shortly thereafter, Ginny and Bart discussed her plight. "Surely," said Ginny quietly, "there is somebody in this world who knows more about my problem and could tell me something to make me well again!"

As if in answer to her expression of faith, something happened soon that brought her hope. Her mother hired a painter to redecorate the house. As it was summertime, Ginny could be moved out of the house into the shade. Bill Langhorn stopped his work to ask her, "What are they doin' for you, if you don't mind my askin'?"

"Why, we don't know what to do. The doctors have given me up."

Bill's blue eyes lit up as he said slowly, "Well, ma'am, maybe there's a doctor here in town can help you."

"What do you mean?"

"A guy here claims he can help folks like you. I been doin' some work for him this past spring. He's a mighty fine man."

The day seemed to stand still. The birds had hushed, and in the distance there were the cries of children playing. "Tell me about him."

When Ginny's mother heard the story, she said, "There are many strange things in this world. And I'm going to find out about this one!"

That afternoon she made her way to the two-story house at 115 West 35th Street where she introduced herself and told Edgar Cayce her problem. The next day, Edgar came to see Ginny, accompanied by Dr. Thomas B. House, head of the Cayce Hospital. Dr. House examined her and said, "I can see why you were given up."

Ginny thought that she had never met two more kindly men. When they left, she had their assurance that Edgar would give her a reading. "But I don't know if I can help or not. I will try," Edgar cautioned.

Ginny's first reading was given the day following, July 19, at 3:30 in the afternoon. It was to be one of 45 physical readings she would receive over the next ten years. It referred to conditions stemming from two causes: one "of long standing" which brought to mind, Ginny later recalled, a fall four years before; and "disturbances in the structural portion of the system."

Trouble in her white blood leukocytes had "allowed the bone structure about the clavicle and fibre to form that of a seepage that has brought about enlarging of the bone, itself." (This was later called by other doctors "Osteochondritis or Perthe's disease," according to a notation by Gladys Davis Turner.) The condition was indicated by "the character of the plasm in the red blood cell," as well. It could be corrected, Cayce advised, by doses of carbon ash in distilled water; then ultra-violet ray on her body twice a week.

"First, we must stop the inroads of these conditions produced by this seepage. Then, we must create in the system, in the blood supply, that building force that will so build about it such cartilaginous forces as to aid the body in having sufficient strength" for the use of her shortened and twisted right leg. He promised that she would be able to walk, eventually, without the aid of crutches, depending on how her body responded to the treatment. (409-1)

Ginny was admitted to the Cayce Hospital on July 31 by Dr. Grace C. Berger,

D.O., to be treated for a dislocated hip. On August 15, a check reading suggested that as the swelling and seepage from the bone joint were allayed, and the soreness had left, she should now begin to force the use of her limbs as fast as possible. The treatments should be continued and osteopathic treatment should be given gently after the soreness was gone. (409-2) By September 23, she was to have, not merely gentle massage, but deep manipulations, especially in the lumbar and sacral region and in the lower dorsal to relieve pressure on her kidneys. "We would begin also with the gradual pushing down of the bone in the hip, so that the *muscular* forces—as they are relaxed through the sacral and lumbar—may be brought into play, near their normal or correct position." (409-3) She should continue the ultra-violet ray. It would relieve the tendency of inflammation from the manipulations. By October, she was to use a crutch and cane.

This was a great advancement from the pitiful condition she had presented upon her arrival five months before! Her first steps were hailed by the staff with joy. To her, it seemed a miracle.

Care had to be taken, she was warned in a reading, that there be little strain on her side muscles because these were directly connected with the errant bone. The lengthening of her leg, to be aided by exercise and manipulation, would be disconcerting at first.

Adjustments were now given involving weights on her right leg. In November, she was told that she should have oil and myrrh rubs. The bone was gradually taking its correct position and it would remain that way.

Before leaving for a few days' visit home, she hobbled about the hospital to practice walking with her cane. When she arrived at home, Bart and her mother watched anxiously. She laughed. "I can walk," she told them.

Ginny was, in fact, the hospital's "star patient." Edgar took a special interest in her, giving her moral support during the long months, having encouraging talks with Bart. Of course, they had at times been very depressed, with Ginny feeling that Bart was neglecting her if he didn't come to visit as often as she thought he should. Now, all that seemed to be passed. On November 29, Edgar wrote a friend: "It was very nice to see Mrs. Meades coming in from a visit home this a.m., walking into the hospital (with her crutch, of course) when we remember how it was when she was brought in first."

Like all hospitals, the Cayce Hospital depended upon the fees it charged its patients as well as upon donations. But Ginny had no money at all, so she was taken in as a charity patient. All she could give was her willingness to cooperate with the treatments. As her case is a triumphant one in the Cayce files, this proved to be a valuable contribution. Without her own valiant efforts, she would have remained a cripple.

She continued to heal. Her foot, she wrote later, "stretched a little each day until I was able to touch the floor."

After returning to the hospital, she was encouraged now in a reading to add the "deeper rays, or infra-red rays" to her system. She should precede this with hot packs or wet packs for five to ten minutes before the treatments of manipulation and rays. The packs would relax her body. She was warned that stiffness in her back and soreness in ankle and foot might result unless this was done properly. Oil rubs were to be given "more systematically and thoroughly, especially in the ends of sinews, or in the joints of the foot, ankle, knee, and hip." She was to persist in stretching her foot. She should take her exercises on the porch to benefit from the sparkling air and sunlight. At this point she began using two canes instead of a crutch and a cane. By early spring, 1930, she walked with only one cane.

By May, she was certain she could walk alone. Finally, the day came when the doctors told her she might walk without help. She had been tapping gamely about the premises, in her head bright pictures of Bart and herself running on the beach again like children, swimming and dancing. When the hour arrived for her to leave, the hospital staff and the ambulatory patients crowded around to see her off. With a smile she stood on the porch and handed her cane to Dr. Berger. A cheer went up from everyone! It was a time to remember, one which Edgar smilingly watched, no doubt seeing about Ginny just then an aura of gold.

Check readings every month thereafter until 1932 led her safely back to complete normalcy and freedom from pain. However, she had become overactive after leaving the hospital and was advised in a reading to go to Richmond for a surgical operation. She was there for three months, in a cast for eight weeks. At home, she resumed treatments suggested in the readings and attained full recovery by January, 1932, when she wrote: "I feel that I owe my life to the work of Mr. Edgar Cayce and all that I can ever say will express only in a small measure my deep appreciation and thankfulness that I was privileged to contact him in this time of dire need; for he showed me the way when all human agencies had apparently failed. I feel that this is a God-given gift worthy of consideration, and those who will follow his suggestions as I have followed them will reap the same wonderful results.

"I shall be glad to answer any questions about my case."

Ginny not only was cured of crippling rheumatism, she had gained new spiritual insight and knowledge of God's mercy. She wrote in January, 1932: "My last check reading informed me that I would be proud of myself in time, which I certainly am!"

In subsequent years, her devotion to the work was expressed by her influencing others among her family and friends to go to Edgar Cayce in times of stress. At least seven of these are on record. One day, she was at the hospital when a patient was waiting for his reading. "Be sure and follow it faithfully," she told him.

Ginny Meades died at the age of 30 of acute dropsy which apparently developed following pneumonia, according to her medical record. But for ten years, thanks to Edgar Cayce, she walked.

Medical Commentary: Perthe's Disease

by William A. McGarey, M.D.

IN TWENTY-FIVE years of practicing medicine, I have never seen a case of Legg-Calve-Perthes disease of this severity. The right leg was out of joint at the hip, foreshortened by a full ten inches and rotated so that the knee cap and toes pointed more backward than forward. There was apparently drainage from a chronic suppurative osteochondritis, and the patient had a scoliosis that rendered her—with the other deformities—completely unable to care for herself.

Today, in most instances, treatment of a surgical nature would intervene with this kind of a problem and bring about at least a partial resolution. Things do not often go as far as this case. *Osteochondritis deformans* still has a frustrating and disappointing outlook for the victim and the immediate family, however, since even reconstructive surgery has its limits on the one hand and its failures on the other.

This particular case is an excellent example of what medical care plus osteopathy plus physical therapy can do. Perhaps the most fascinating aspect of this whole series of readings is this simple illustration that more can be done with the physical body in the way of total rehabilitation than most of us really accept at the present time as being possible. Perhaps this is an ideal example of what happens when therapy is aimed at restoring, regenerating, and rebuilding the various functions of the body while maintaining a balance that we have come to know as homeostasis.

Homeostasis in the human body is that balance of energies, functions, and structures that allows the continuity of the life process. It fits into the Cayce concept of things in that homeostasis is the balance that the life force within the body creates so that the spiritual being that we call man might live in this three-dimensional sphere and fulfill the purpose for which he came into being.

Ginny—in this story—was a constant problem, however, in that she apparently had a major degree of difficulty in assisting the healing process from the standpoint of emotions and mental attitudes. The effect of emotional turmoil and negative attitudes was commented on again and again in the readings given for this young lady, since the balance of life forces was often difficult indeed to achieve within her body. She must have had a tumultuous unconscious mind with emotional patterns that would come unhinged at the slightest urging.

But the healing progressed, sometimes in spite of the emotions, and the patterns of therapy suggested through this unconscious source of information are like the weaving of a tapestry. A certain effect is achieved only after a period of time and effort. Ginny spent many months in the Cayce Hospital, received an inordinate amount of care it seems, but achieved a truly remarkable result.

It is not really an unheard of thing to see the regeneration of the bone and cartilage of the hip joint. Medical literature[1] records the case of a woman who underwent the almost complete regeneration of her hip joint over a four-year period when she had the sympathetic nerves to her hip joint and leg area sectioned. X-rays before and after revealed the results of the regenerative effort the body accomplished.

But to work with the adrenal-sympathetic complex still intact, with the femur out of joint at the hip—this is even more remarkable. It would have been most interesting to have seen x-ray progression of this series of events over the time period which elapsed between Cayce's visit to Ginny's home and Ginny's walk out of the hospital under her own steam, with the head of the femur back in its proper place.

The cause of Perthe's disease is not clear in the reference books of medical science. Neither did Cayce render the question crystal clear in his comments. He did give us a few ideas, however, which might be worth considering.

It seems that Ginny's white blood cells were inadequate in numbers—she had a leukopenia. There was also present what Cayce called an abnormal character of the red cell plasm. Perhaps this means that the red blood cells were not exactly healthy in their nature. At one point, there was apparently an injury, and the bone underwent injury which might be called an infraction, or perhaps incomplete fracture. And, in the process of repair, the body was unable, because of the cellular components of the blood and their inadequacies, to bring about a full callus formation.

Where the bone had failed to heal properly, there occurred a seepage or drainage; and this, in turn, caused the structural portion of the body to suffer:

> "This instability about the blood supply has allowed the bone struc-
> ture . . . and fibre to form that of a seepage that has brought about
> enlarging of the bone itself. This, then, is that as produces distress and
> creating in the system those conditions as bring abnormalities for the
> body." (53-1)

This "seepage," as Cayce called it, was a constant drain on the body energies and posed an ever-present problem in the therapeutic program. Ginny needed to stem this energy drain in order to bring about gradual repair.

The etiology, then, seemed to be an injury superimposed on an inadequate body repair system—the failure of union within the bone bringing about the toxic effect to the entire body that caused the progression of events that led to the

[1] W. H. Cammerer, and T. I. Hoen, "Unexpected Radiographic Changes of the Hip Joint Following Lumbar Sympathectomy for Arthritis," *Arthritis & Rheumatism,* Vol. 10, No. 3, p. 288, June 1967.

young lady's terrible plight at the time of her first reading.

In analyzing the measures suggested to bring about a restorative process within this girl's body, one is faced with the obvious fact that he must deal with general objectives rather than specifics and with the constant need to maintain a balance that will support a regenerative effort. This suits the objectives of a physical therapy department much more aptly than the desires of an internist—broad objectives rather than specific therapeutic results.

As I see it, there were five basic goals in Cayce's therapeutic program:

1. To stop the seepage from the injured bone
2. To build up the body generally, especially the formed elements of the blood stream, e.g., the white and red blood cells
3. To keep the balance of the body intact as much as possible as changes came about
4. To create in the system a "building force" that would in turn bring about the regeneration of the bone and cartilage of the joint and the strength for using the limb thus resuscitated
5. To use a variety of physical therapy modalities to bring about the gradual stretching of the tendons, the relocation of the femur in its hip socket, and the strengthening of the muscles and ligaments and tendons that are involved in the diseased area

Cayce's language is sometimes poetic in its expression but at other times a complete enigma—or so it seems. He states the therapeutic direction in a way, however, that bears repeating, since it relates the objectives sought for in a manner that gives them coherence and perhaps gives us a better understanding.

> First we must stop the *inroads* of those conditions prduced by this seepage. Then we must create in the system, in the blood supply, that building force that will so build about it such cartilaginous forces as to aid the body in having sufficient strength for the use of same through that limb, see? (409-1)

Cayce further stated that Ginny's condition might be materially aided if applications are made

> . . . for the correction of those conditions that will so build in the general physical forces those properties as will meet the needs of the condition and hinder or ward off, or encase, those conditions where seepage has occurred from this fracture as has existed, to such an extent as to allow the usage [of the limb]; as well as preventing the inroads and the creating of that condition in the structural portion itself as to create that as will build within itself the deficiencies for the normal action of the body. (409-1)

How did the actual therapy progress in the hospital, once started? The ultra-violet ray was used regularly for months. Later on, the infra-red lamp was used. She was taken out on the beach near the hospital where she absorbed the sunlight and received the benefit of the sands.

Massage was a constant therapy—designed gently at first to stretch the tendons and ease spasms, to bring about a better lymph flow and stimulate the healing process. Later on, the massage was deeper and stronger and osteopathic manipulation was added to the regimen. Traction was used in various forms to stretch the muscles and gradually make possible the replacing of the femur head into its socket.

Care was taken to prevent infections, such as respiratory problems, as these would hinder the progress of general repair. Diet was always a part of the treatment for those who were patients in the Cayce Hospital. The patient was given an alkaline-reacting diet, was kept from rich foods and was given those foods high in vitamins and similar food values.

Carbon ash was given through the mouth to this girl over a long period of time. This was the ash deposited on the globe of a carbon arc lamp burned in a partial vacuum. Cayce attributed to this fine dust or ash a value which he described as a power of oxygenation of the blood stream and tissues of the body, especially if given just before the use of the ultra-violet lamp. He said the use of the ash would tend to stop the seepage.

The program certainly was not one of bizarre therapies or unusual procedures. Aside from the ash, the treatments could have been given by any physician trained in his art. But it encompassed time and patience and demanded consistency and persistence. These qualities are hard to come by in one person, or, for that matter, in a group of persons. Ginny was making progress but felt after five months of continuous treatments that the hip should be getting back to normal soon. So she asked the question in her sixth reading given in November, still in the hospital:

Q. How long before it [the hip] will be normal?

A. Dependent upon the applications and how the body applied itself, and what accidents would or may happen to the body, and how the care is taken of the whole system. That's the same as to say when will a fly be swatted or when will it miss being hit!

Patience was apparently not one of her strong points. We are not given a clear picture of just how the mental-emotional pattern present here actually interfered with the therapy, or just what Ginny's emotional hang-up was. Apparently, however, there was such a hang-up. One night Cayce himself had to quiet down the sick girl from a crying and weeping episode when her husband had not come in to visit her for a time.

As her stay in the hospital wore on, the treatments continued under Cayce's unconscious guidance, but a warning crept into the very short reading given in April—after eight months of hospitalization. Ginny was told that the time had come when she could exercise more if she were to take proper precautions.

. . . but will the body be indiscreet in its actions, in its diet, in its moral and physical life, it may expect the latter condition worse than the first.

Now choose! We are through. (409-11)

In all the philosophy of health, illness, and healing that came through this very unusual source, there was always the bare fact that emotions are created by repetitive, directed conscious choice; that illnesses are brought into being by those same emotions, the energy patterns we have created as a distortion of that which God intended them to be. And thus it is no wonder that the personality structure of a girl with such a severe disability of the body would be replete with disturbances of a glandular-emotional nature. And her choosing was not always in a constructive direction despite Cayce's admonitions. This fact is evident in following the story through the events and the readings given her.

It was just a month after the last instruction and warning that Ginny received her twelfth reading. The hip was finally in place. She was ready to leave the hospital. The major therapy had been accomplished. She was undoubtedly feeling triumphant in many ways, and certainly those working with her must have felt a deep satisfaction in seeing a hopeless cripple come to active life once again. In his sleeping state Cayce saw that there was need, however, of caution and care still to be exercised, and he incorporated into his reading those necessary precautions. At the same time he saw the tendency of the girl to fall back into ways and habits that were destructive in their action on the body. And, perhaps with a great deal of unconscious patience, forgiveness, and understanding, he pointed out how the body would react if Ginny did not make certain changes of direction. It is interesting to compare his "refuses from the kidneys—causing blocking in the system" with the events that actually occurred ten years later— Ginny's death from acute dropsy which apparently developed following pneumonia. This is Cayce's comment:

> In the general condition of the body, we find there are *still* some of those conditions along the bone, where there is still some irritation. This ye should be mindful of, and the proper precautions taken as respecting this—or else we *will* have rheumatic conditions returning in the system, or either the return to those of the refuses from the kidneys—causing blocking in the system, or of other characters of poisoning; . . . but the moral and mental body *must* be in accord with that that has been attempted to be carried out, or to relieve it—or it had best not have been relieved. (409-12)

Ginny continued to make slow progress while at home, coming to the hospital for treatments. As the readings continued and the care progressed, other com- ments—almost unnoticed in their obscurity—were offered in the readings which strengthened the concept that Ginny's case was as any illness: an adventure in this dimension for a spiritual being who must at some time choose to obey God's laws and experience God's love. She found it difficult, but the theme in the readings was consistent:

> As had been given, there is much to be accomplished in the mental attitudes of the body, towards self and to things outside of itself, as in

> the material application—and unless those who apply, and those who receive, gain some conception of that being accomplished in a physical body, they are working very far wrong. (409-12)

Here Cayce gave the hint that, in all illnesses, there is a greater goal to be reached than simply the physical restoration. Attitudes, spiritual relationships, emotional expressions—all must be taken into account. For, as has been proven in a veriety of ways throughout man's history on the earth: that which one sows, he must reap. And certainly, if love is a factor in the relationship between man and God, then a directional change upward (of attitudes and emotions) made by one's own choice will bring about a response in the body that changes the outcome. This is called grace, but it is a physical result as well as a spiritual one.

Ginny was reminded in her next reading that "much is given; much is required." Responsibility is assumed when one accepts in this manner.

What really does go on inside a person? How much does that activity of mind, memory, emotion, attitudes, belief affect the outcome of a physical ailment? We would suspect from this case of a very unusual young lady that the answer is "much." The specifics will remain unknown, certainly, and we have only hints to give us understanding and help—if Cayce's readings are to be of assistance in the healing of the sick in this world of ours. But we are given to understand that the body, mind, and spirit are truly one. And we take from this story the concept that the healing of an illness is intended to be a healing experience for the whole man in time, in space, and in patience.

CHAPTER 7

NO SURGERY FOR KEN!

By Mary Ellen Carter

"WHICH SIDE," KENNETH Ives began, with a troubled look on his face, "is one's appendix?"

"Why, I get mixed up on that, myself," said Doris, his wife. She put down the dress she had been hemming and glanced at him sharply. "It's your right side. Why?"

Kenneth, a young man of 24, moved slowly across the living room. "I've been having these pains in my right side lately. I feel kind of loggish."

Doris frowned. "You'd better lie down. Don't go to work tomorrow."

"Got to. We're having a lot of lawnmowers and bikes to repair these days."

When he came home from work the next evening, he felt no better. The pain had persisted, and he had broken out in a rash. He was experiencing dizzy spells, and a vein in his leg had become swollen.

As he lay morosely on the sofa while Doris prepared dinner, they heard a step on the front porch. "Yoo-hoo, anybody home?" It was Doris' mother, Matilda

Derry, who had come over from her house across the street to bring them some of her preserves and to chat. "Not for supper. You go right ahead," she told them. "Why, what's wrong with Kenneth?"

"I'm worried about Ken. He's been having pains in his right side for the past several weeks. And they're getting worse!"

Kenneth groaned. "Chattering women!" he mumbled.

The pains became so severe that he could eat no food, the attacks of agonizing pain making him clutch his abdomen. As he started to bed at 8 o'clock, he suddenly doubled over, pain gripping him through the middle. He turned ashen and would have keeled over if Doris hadn't rushed to his side to support him.

Matilda went to the bedroom and turned down the covers. "That," she told Doris after they had gotten him gently into bed, "is a very sick boy."

Doris had grown up with Edgar Cayce's concepts of healing. She had heard her mother recount his successful cures many times to friends, had seen her sister cured of a long-standing illness, and she herself had been cured of an infection. Now, the two women exchanged glances.

"I think," said Matilda, "it's time to call Edgar Cayce."

Although Edgar Cayce generally gave only two scheduled readings a day, he was always willing to give one in an emergency. When Matilda had told him of the emergency for Kenneth Ives, he prepared to give a reading right away. It was given at 9 o'clock.

The disturbing conditions in Ken's body were of long standing, said the reading (1003-1), acute at present. "As we find, there are those conditions in the ascending colon that are in the form not only of an engorgement but in the way of producing— because of the position—toxic forces in the system."

The rash was due to the poisons being carried through the superficial circulation. It alternated at times with spots in various parts of his body. The engorged veins were due to pressure in the coccyx area produced by a lumbar disorder. They were to be mindful at present of the inflammation in the caecum area, "though with the corrections of the pressure in these areas, and with the adjustments in the lumbar and coccyx area, these conditions should disappear."

Treatment should begin with painting the lower caecum area and that of the ascending colon with three parts laudanum to one part aconite. "Then apply the castor oil packs over same. This should be kept up continually for four or five hours. Then give a soda enema, a colonic—using the high colonic irrigation, as far as may be attained; not to cause too great a quantity at a time, but a tablespoon-ful of baking soda to each quart of water used."

After repeating all this the next day, Ken should have an osteopathic adjustment "in the lumbar, sacral, and coccyx areas, coordinating this with the 9th dorsal and solar plexus and the brachial plexus area. . . .

"Do not allow temperature to arise. If so, inflammation will have set in sufficiently to necessitate operative forces."

However, if the procedure was followed "with the diet consisting of fruit juices, a little beef juice—and keeping the body quiet, these should—without irritation—relieve these pressures in the body."

What had caused his dizziness and the swollen veins?

"Toxic forces and the pressure on the area to the liver," was the answer, "and the lack of the secretions of the gall duct and gall area."

After the third day of this treatment, Ken should have large quantities of olive oil, half a cupful. The adjustments should be taken once each day for three days and three more on subsequent days as needed.

"Is this condition what is known as appendicitis?"

"Any inflammation [in that area] may be termed appendicitis. The condition in the present is *above* the appendix area, and may be seen or felt by the examination of the ascending colon—which lies between the lacteal ducts and the caecum on the right side, you see."

If the stoppage made for too great an inflammation, it would be necessary to take measures to prevent gangrene. "At the present, as we find, it is not indicated that the appendix is involved so much in the condition."

There was a practical nurse who happened to be present for this reading. Mrs. Jennie J. Jordan came to the Ives home and administered the treatment prescribed. She started with the laudanum and aconite solution on the lower caecum area. Doris helped with the castor oil packs and the soda water colonic, which was necessarily to be given under Mrs. Jordan's supervision. They repeated this routine the following day; by night time, Ken was out of pain and on the road to recovery!

He was, of course, very weak. Great care was taken that he didn't develop fever: he drank much beef juice and fruit juice. He slept and rested.

The next day, Kenneth began osteopathic adjustments by M. L. Richardson, D.O. Five days after his attack, he was back at work in the shop—a well man.

It is heartening to note that on September 14, 1964—29 years later—Kenneth reported that he never resorted to surgery and that he never had further trouble in his appendix region.

Medical Commentary: Appendicitis

by William A. McGarey, M.D.

APPENDICITIS IS STILL one of the most difficult diagnoses to make of all acute abdominal surgical conditions. The problem is solved if a surgical course is chosen: but when this is not the case, the problem of diagnosis often remains clouded.

Ken's predicament, then, despite the diagnosis of appendicitis which is carried in the Cayce readings index, will never be proved. He may have had a true case of acute appendicitis, or it may have been one of the other abdominal conditions which often fool the doctor prior to surgical intervention. His symptoms appeared rather typical.

Cayce himself, interestingly, never called the condition an inflammation of the appendix. He said that there was inflammation and engorgement of the tissues in the ascending colon, *above* the caecum and the appendix area, which, however, could get worse if proper care were not taken and could bring about a gangrenous appendicitis from an extension of the inflammation.

In the medical mind—at least the mind of the general practitioner, with which I am most familiar—a case of acute appendicitis is simply that. There is an irritated and swollen appendix, sometimes caused by a fecolith, sometimes by causes which we cannot discern. But when the appendix is removed, the person gets better. Apparently nothing else is wrong in the body or, at least, that is what we think. When inflammation progresses to the state of a gangrenous appendicitis with pus formation, we still give little thought to what the events were that perhaps led to the appendix becoming inflamed in the first place.

Cayce's evaluation of this particular man, with a long history of right lower quadrant trouble, who was having rather severe abdominal pain—a typical story of recurrent low grade appendiceal inflammation—is interesting in its complexity of physiological malfunction.

Let us suppose that Cayce was thorough and correctly clairvoyant in his evaluation of this man, as he apparently was in *so many* of the 9,000 times that he gave physical readings in illness of the human body. The picture that we get, then, has many ramifications.

In this reading, he does not state the relationship of the appendix to the other lymphoid structures, but in other instances, he does go to great lengths to discuss the lymphatic system. He relates it very intimately to the nervous system, in a way that is not recognized in the anatomy-physiology texts. He puts the appendix and the tonsils in the same family, never recommending the removal of either of the structures unless disease had progressed beyond the ability of normal treatment procedures to restore them reasonably. He relates all lymphoid structures—including the Peyers Patches of the small intestine—to the thymus gland and the emotional-hormonal-neurological impact of that gland on the life of its owner.

In the Cayce readings, the thymus is also known as one of the seven spiritual centers of the body, and is called the heart center. Psychics see vortices of energy in all areas where the spiritual centers are located, and the thymus is no exception. Thus, if there is anything at all to the psychic perceptions Cayce and a host of other people throughout the ages have demonstrated and talked about, then the appendix, as part of the lymphatic system, has a spiritual as well as a physical reality and implication. Interesting thought, isn't it?

In the intricate relationship of functions which create a normally active and healthy body, Cayce saw a group of problems existing which contributed individually toward the development of the symptoms which Ken brought to the psychic for evaluation.

In discussing this problem Cayce talked in terms of systemic malfunctions, old-fashioned (but meaningful) terms, common sense, and osteopathic concepts. He saw a condition existing in the body which, had it undergone surgery at that time, might have revealed to the surgeon a retrocaecal appendix, perhaps hung up a bit high in its retroperitoneal location, with perhaps the ascending colon ptosed a bit, or disfigured from its normal location. This is not too uncommon a finding and is most distressful to the preoperative diagnostician. The appendix at the point of surgery would not have been inflamed but would have been recognized as a potential source of real trouble.

But Cayce saw many things going on as he surveyed the situation with his psychic eye. They all contributed to or were involved in the process.

1. "Disturbances in the eliminations of the body." This would mean, I suppose, that constipation had existed in varying degrees for a long time; that perhaps the kidneys were not eliminating as they should. It may have meant for Ken that his poor diet had suppressed the function of the lymphatic system itself, which is the beginning of the eliminations at the cellular level.

2. Circulatory conditions resulting from the poor eliminations were set into motion and prepared the way for further trouble.

3. Engorgement of the vessels and tissues of the ascending colon developed into inflammation of the area and a degree of systemic toxemia affecting the entire body.

4. The superficial circulation carrying the toxins produced a tendency toward a rash, especially in the "emunctory" centers—the axilla, groin, knees, elbows, and neck.

5. The veins in the lower extremities became engorged as part of the circulatory disturbances and as a result of pressures (of an osteopathic nature) in the coccyx area. He indicated in an extension of his comments that lesions and subluxations in the coccyx, sacral, and lumbar parts of the spine were part of this man's primary problem.

6. Poisons brought about through the deviations from normal described above created then the pains and spasms and the acute syndrome, which was obviously called an appendicitis.

7. The circulating "drosses," as Cayce would call them, not only caused those conditions and problems listed above, but also created a toxic effect on the liver and a depression of function of the gall bladder.

The primary therapy needed to be directed toward the inflammation existing in the ascending colon because of its tendency to migrate toward the caecum and the appendix, which would then pose a serious problem.

Perhaps we as physicians cannot daily explore the details of the aberrant functions existing in the body as we survey a patient and try to decide what is wrong. However, I believe we will never understand the body until we understand and put into its proper place the function of the body as a whole, composed of its integral functions. Until we realize that the function of a part and not its structure is the essence of the life effect that it has, we are still walking in the dark.

Cayce's evaluation, then, may be more than a psychic observation of what is wrong: it may be a word picture of where the action really is.

Then, given a condition that was called appendicitis by those around the patient, and described as a group of failing functions by a sleeping psychic, let us follow the suggestions for the relief of the problem and see what rationale was behind Cayce's recommendations.

Some of the most important suggestions in a given reading are often put in a cryptic manner, almost as an aside—almost as if he were saying: "Listen carefully if you want the full import of what is being said." It was in this manner that Cayce recommended rest for Ken for three days: "keeping the body quiet."

Throughout this material collected for a period of over forty years, however, much was said about rest. For any ailing body, rest is a primary factor and apparently has no substitute because of the need within the body for a balanced function of the autonomic nervous system. During rest and sleep, balance of the autonomic is, to a great extent, restored. If the body is contracting an illness of any sort, it is understood that something within the body has been put through stress by the progression of events, and rest is usually one of the necessities in changing the status quo.

I have never painted an area of the body with laudanum and aconite, in any combination. Nowadays the former is not available, even by prescription, while aconite is seldom used. Both are prepared as a tincture, laudanum being a tincture of opium. Aconite as a tincture produces a local sensory paralysis when applied. I would assume Cayce's recommendation to use this combination was based on its efficacy in such situations, since perhaps local anaesthesia on the skin might well produce a relaxation of afferent impulses from the corresponding autonomically-innervated internal organs. This is not too unusual a physiological response and would indeed relieve the spasm and pain which was Ken's primary concern at that moment.

Cayce then told the patient to have a castor oil pack (a folded-over piece of flannel cloth saturated with hot castor oil) placed over the abdomen for four or five hours. A piece of plastic was to be placed over that and then a cloth such as a towel to hold both into place. Cayce did not say whether or not to use a heating pad over the pack in this instance, though most of the time he recommended such a pack, it was used with heat.

Several years ago I did an exhaustive search of the medical literature back to 1911. I was looking for castor oil references in preparing a monograph[1] on the use of castor oil packs as Cayce had suggested they be used and as I used them in 81 different cases. This search revealed a very few, but quite interesting data.

Douglas W. Montgomery, M.D., wrote in 1918[2] of the oil which he described as coming from a beautiful plant with large palmate leaves, often called Palma Christi, the palm of Christ. Somewhat facetiously, I suspect, he said: "If as a child, I had known this sonorous name, it might have mitigated the misery I often suffered in having to take the oil. A very determined and energetic Scotch auntie regarded 'a crumb o' oil,' as she used to call it, as a universal remedy of exceeding potency in both moral and physical contingencies; and indeed, there is no doubt of its efficiency as a cleaner."

Montgomery's observations are undoubtedly of interest and relate to Ken's use of the castor oil packs. He observed that in disease of the skin, the use of castor oil is of importance inasmuch as a clean alimentary canal is conducive to a clean

---

[1] William A. McGarey, *Edgar Cayce and the Palma Christi*, A.R.E. Press, Virginia Beach, Va.

[2] D. W. Montgomery, "Castor Oil," *J. Cutaneous Disease*, 36:466, 1918.

cutaneous surface. "It would appear that the medicine acts particularly on the ascending colon, and this is interesting, as it is undoubtedly a fact that many of the more active skin reactions are caused by poisons generated in the caput coli, a favorable location for the anaerobic proteolytic bacteria." He further pointed out that in the work of W. B. Cannon, in which castor oil was given to an animal with its food,[3] there was a serial sectioning of the food in the ascending colon followed each time by antiperistalsis which swept the food back—a type of action well fitted to clear out the haustra of the colon, "those pockets which in colonic sluggishness must tend to become especially dirty."

Schoch[4] later followed up on this information and noted some dramatic results in severe skin eruptions following the administration of often just a single dose of castor oil.

Ken took no castor oil by mouth, but he did have trouble with his ascending colon, certainly; there was a sluggishness and an engorgement of the tissues there, and his eliminations were not normal. My observations in the use of these packs revealed that abdominal administration of the pack often produced a cleansing reaction within the large intestine in a manner no one has yet been able to fully understand.

The packs may have started the elimination of the trouble in the ascending colon, which was then further retarded by the high enema given following the packs. Soda water used in the enema would aid in producing a more alkaline condition within the body which, in the case of acute infection, would bring about a more positive recuperative state of being, according to Cayce's reading.

This need for an alkalinity was emphasized by Cayce's suggestion that Ken take only fruit juice and beef juice at first. The latter is prepared by placing raw beef in a glass container, loosely capped, then placing the glass in a pot filled with water which is allowed to simmer three to four hours. The fluid collected in the glass jar is then strained off and taken a tablespoonful at a time, bringing strength to the body without the assimilation of the meat which would then have to be eliminated.

The second day, after being relieved of the pain and spasm, Ken was again given castor oil packs and the enema containing a solution of soda. Following the enema, he was given an osteopathic treatment concentrated on the coccyx, sacrum, the ninth dorsal area, and the brachial plexus area of the spine. This, according to the readings, was to bring about a balance in the nervous systems of the body and relieve pressures which had existed there for a long time.

After the third day's regimen identical with the second, Ken was given another remedy, aimed at the inactive and sluggish liver-gall bladder complex of organs. He took a half cup of olive oil. This certainly must have been the hardest part of the therapy.

Thus, the eliminations, the circulation, the local inflammation, the toxemia, the rash, the liver and gall bladder toxicity, and the symptom complex were all dealt with in Cayce's suggested therapeutic course. The suggestions were fol-

[3] W. B. Cannon, The Mechanical Factors of Digestion, New York: Longmans, Green & Co., 1911, p. 151.

[4] A. G. Schoch, "The Treatment of Dermatoses of Intestinal Origin with Castor oil and Sodium Ricinoleate," So. Med. J., 32:326-328 (No. 30), 1939.

lowed, including a third osteopathic treatment on the fourth day, and Ken was back to work and apparently healthy, hale, and hearty.

An interesting case, and one which I find very logical and reasonable. If I were to venture an opinion as to what was the most important part of the entire therapy, I would vote for the castor oil packs. It seems to have had most to do with his recovery, the others being aids, perhaps, the packs being the primary therapy. However, that's like diagnosing an appendicitis *after* surgical removal. The challenge, the question, is not there.

CHAPTER 8

TEENAGE ARTHRITIC

by Mary Ellen Carter

UNDER A LARGE maple tree that shielded her from the heat of the July sun, eighteen-year-old Sarah Blanding sat on a blanket and watched an ant lumber briskly over the mountainous folds. *I'll bet if your knee hurt, you wouldn't be traveling so fast!* she thought.

She heard the back screen door slam and the familiar step of her father. "There's my princess!" he called to her.

He took a lawn chair in the shade and accepted the glass of iced tea she offered him from a pitcher. He gave her a fond look. "How's the knee?"

Sarah adjusted the heavy, wet pack on her leg. "Dr. Frank told me to use hot salt packs. But I've been applying them for a week, now, and I'm actually worse!"

"Maybe we should try some other doctor."

"Oh, maybe. Then I'll beat you at a game of tennis, when I'm well."

"You'll have to look sharper than *that!*"

Sarah squirmed and grew pink, conscious of an eczema on her face and neck which had plagued her for years. Her father's idle remark had somehow touched off her sensitivity about it.

He seemed not to notice but said with belated tact, "You *are* looking brown and pretty these days. But maybe we'd better call the doctor about your contrary disposition."

"*Daddy!*"

As the days wore on, the pain in her knee was compounded by new aches in joints throughout her body. Now unable to bend her knees, she found she could hardly walk. At night she found the pain kept her from sleep.

In August she tried a series of diathermy treatments, but after these, she later testified, "I had eight afflicted joints instead of the six I had when I started."

Specialists x-rayed and examined her thoroughly, only to advise her that she had arthritis from some unknown source. Medicine they prescribed failed to help. "The only thing I can think might help at all," said the specialist in charge of her case, "is that you go to Arizona to live."

When Sarah and her mother told Hal Bolanding this, he said, "Well, if it will mean that Sarah can get well, then we'll move to Arizona!"

John Tydings, a real estate salesman, sat in their living room and talked about property values. With heavy hearts Ruth and Hal had shown him around. He had peered into corners, inspected the furnace. Sarah sat in her chair, a pale little bundle of aches and pains.

"Would you mind telling me why you're moving?" asked the salesman.

"Not at all," Hal replied. "Our daughter here is ill with arthritis. We're hoping the climate in Arizona will help her."

"Hm." John Tydings looked at Sarah with interest. "Mighty young to be having arthritis, aren't you?" He paused. "I hope you don't mind my being so personal, Miss Blanding. But it has occurred to me there might be someone who can help you . . . Of course, if he does, you might not want to move to Arizona, and then I'd have to let you folks keep your house . . ." He ended with a soft laugh.

Hal looked at the salesman curiously. "Just what do you mean? Who is this person?"

"His name's Edgar Cayce—a fellow who lives in Virginia Beach and gives diagnoses and treatment like a regular doctor, for people doctors can't help. He helped me and others I know."

It was October 15, 1932. Sarah herself wrote to Edgar Cayce: "My trouble is in my joints. Doctors have told me it is arthritis . . . I have considerable pain in all my joints, and am subject to severe night sweats."

Her reading was taken on the twenty-first. A few days later, her mother handed her a large envelope addressed to her. Sarah tremblingly opened it and read. It took a while, for the reading was three pages long, single-spaced typing. Ruth, growing impatient, said, "Well, what does it say, dear?"

Lying on the sofa, Sarah looked up with a smile. "It says a lot about diet."

"Is *that* all!"

"Not quite. It says I have to take something called Atomidine. Later, I have to have epsom salts baths."

"Why, that's simple."

When her father came home from work that evening, Sarah gave the reading aloud to her parents: "We have the body here, Sarah Blanding. Now, as we find, there are abnormal conditions in the physical functioning of this body. These conditions, as we find, would prove very interesting and worth while in considering a condition that in many portions of the country, and in all portions to some extent, is gradually becoming on the increase, and that has proven most unusually hard to cope with: for conditions are so often hidden that it is hard to find the source or the cause of that the professions have called 'the point of infection.'

"Were the pathological conditions studied in the proper light, taking some that may be given here as the basis for investigations, we find that this case would prove very helpful and beneficial in many other similar conditions; for in this body the point of infection is hidden, yet in the basic forces of the metabolism and katabolism of the system may it be located, as the lack of elements necessary for the developing of that which makes for the regeneration in the elemental forces of the living organism to function balancedly for the proper coordination and physical balance throughout the system.

"First, in the inception of this body, some nineteen years ago, —not what may be termed properly (as in old considerations) prenatal conditions, but as of prenatal *surroundings*—there were those elements taken by the body upon whom *this* body was dependent for that from which it drew its sustenance in the foetus or foetal forces of its inception. These made for first tendencies.

"Then, with the character of the surroundings of the body, the character of the water is assimilated, the general dispositions that made for the resuscitating forces in the assimilating system, in many portions of the body the glands have been deficient in some respects and over-active in others in supplying the elements necessary for the proper distribution of forces in the system.

"These are the points of infections, then, that make for tendencies in the structural portions of the body to become more active than other portions; not to the point that where the growth is turned into that position or manner where the elongation of bone itself begins, but rather the crystallization in the muscular· forces and tendons, so that the substance is lacking that should supply to the joints of the extremities that oil or that plasm in its activity about same to keep the functioning in a normal manner. Were this turned, as it were, in one more infectious point, then we would have rather the tendency of *Elephantiasis Proboscidis* in its inception; but as it is turned in the present—from those glands of first the lacteals in assimilation, from the activities from the spleen and those glands from the kidneys overactive, or the endrenal [adrenal?] and those in the lyden [Leydig] and those of the pancrean supplying, or carrying, or taking, or adding to the blood stream those forces that are as the chrysalis of the infectious forces from the adrenals—it makes for the stoppage, rather than the drainage from extremities, which must eventually turn into bone itself and become either Sleeping Paralysis or Stony Paralysis, or that more of the orthopedic nature that makes for a twisting and turning of the bones themselves, by the muscular forces becoming hardened into such conditions.

"Then, to meet the needs of such conditions, various stages of this particular disorder necessarily indicate that a different amount of elements are lacking or are excessive in portions of the functioning body; but in this particular body, at this particular period of the development:

"We would first be very mindful of the diet. Keep away from all forces that supply an over abundance of salines, limes, or silicon, or the like, in the system. Supply an overabundant amount of those foods that carry iron, iodine, and phosphorous in the system, for these will act against that already supplied to burn or destroy those tendencies of debarkation or demarcation in the activities of the glands. We would outline something as of this nature:

"One meal each day we would supply principally of citrus fruits, or nature's sugars, nature's laxatives in citrus fruits, figs, prunes, berries of most nature—any of the active principles in such; a great deal of those forces that may be found in the pie-plant, or the like; salsify, gooseberries in any of their preparations— whether those that are preserved or otherwise, provided they are without any of the preservatives; currants and their derivatives (that is, properties that are made from them, you see, *without pre*servatives); pomegranates and their derivatives; pears and their derivatives. Beware of apples and bananas among the fruits. Beware of any that would carry more of those that would add silicon in the system. One meal each day would consist of foods selected from such as these.

"Then there should be one meal almost entirely of nuts, and the oils of nuts; so that the activities from these in the system are such as to produce a different character of fermentation with the gastric forces of the stomach and the duodenum itself; so that the type of the lactics that are formed in the assimilation become entirely changed, so that the hydrochlorics that are formed in the system—or that are necessary to supply to the non-acid forces as they enter the system, or acid that make for turning of the system that which will gradually build in the pancreas, the spleen, the kidneys, the duodenum, those various folds themselves, more of those forces that will lessen the tendency for the accumulation of those conditions in extremities, where carried by the circulation itself.

"The evening meal may be of well balanced vegetables that are of the leafy nature, and that carry more of those properties as given. We will find much in turnips, eggplant (no cabbage of any nature, either cold or cooked), some characters of beans—provided they are well dried and grown in a soil that is different from that carrying iron, see? These will aid. The meats should be preferably (when taken at all) of wild game or fish, or oysters, or sea food.

"So much for the diet!

"Then we would take also, internally, those properties of Atomidine. This is iodine in a form that it may be assimilated in the system. In the beginning, if this is taken in large quantities, it would tend to make for a greater stiffness. Then, we would begin with small quantities. Twice a day take three minims in water, morning and evening. Each day increase the amount one minim, until there is being taken at least ten minims twice a day; then stop for five days, then begin over again.

"At the end of the third period of taking the Atomidine, we would begin with epsom salts baths (not until the third period of taking the iodine, see, or the Atomidine—which is iodine). These would be taken once a week; add five to eight pounds of the salts to sufficient water in the bath tub to cover the body up to the neck—which would be five to eight pounds to twenty or twenty-five gallons of water. The water should be just as hot as the body can well stand; as it cools add more hot water—and the body should lie in this for at least twenty-five to thirty minutes.

"After coming from this bath, the body should be rinsed off in plain water, then rubbed down thoroughly; massaging thoroughly into the whole of the body (that is, all of the cerebrospinal, all of the shoulder, head, neck, ribs, arms, lower limbs, toes, feet, hands, fingers) a solution of equal parts of olive oil, tincture of myrrh and Russian White Oil. Heat the olive oil first, then add the same amount of tincture of myrrh while the olive oil is hot, and while cooling stir in an equal amount of the Russian White Oil—and this doesn't mean any of those that are of the paraffin base, but rather that which has been *purified*, see? This should be massaged in thoroughly, all that the body will absorb. Following this (because it will make the body rather oily), a general rub off or sponge off with rub alcohol. After such treatments, of course, the body should rest.

"When this has been taken for a period of three to five weeks, then we will give further instructions. Remember, the diet must be kept up; remember, the Atomidine must be kept up for this full period, and then further instructions would be given.

"Ready for questions.

"Q-1. What causes severe night sweats, and what may be done to correct it?

"A-1. We have given what may be done, and we have given the cause; for with these conditions that are caused by the glands' functioning, and the attempts of the system to reject these conditions, it would make sweat break out on anyone!

"Do as we have outlined, and then when the period has passed as given, we will give further instructions.

"We are through for the present."

The Blandings listened in wonder, and Hal said, "Let's not waste any time!"

Taking a personal interest as always, Edgar Cayce wrote Sarah a few days later: "The information gotten at your appointment was mailed to you some days ago. I feel that I should write and insist that if possible you make a sincere attempt to carry out the suggestions given. From what you have said, and the reading, I feel that the medical profession has offered little or no hope for any permanent relief. If you can get the whole-hearted cooperation of a friend or nurse, there should be no necessity for your going to a medical man at all. I believe you will be able to see the results from carrying out these suggestions. As indicated, there may be one period in taking the first properties when you will feel even worse than you have heretofore, a little more stiff and sore, but this will be your first reaction from the Atomidine. Your druggist will be able to obtain the Atomidine from the address given, if he does not have it already in stock.

"I would like very much to hear from you, and to know just how you get along . . . Please understand that it is our whole desire to be of service. Sincerely, Edgar Cayce."

As soon as they had obtained the Atomidine—they were able to find it at the local drug store—Sarah began taking the prescribed dosage. Ruth made sure that her diet was changed to the letter to consist of the fruits recommended, nuts, and leafy vegetables. It was severely restricted fare for a teenager, but as Sarah staunchly abided by the strange regimen, she began almost at once to benefit.

"On the morning of the third day," she was to write afterward, "I awoke and could actually bend one knee!"

She added, "Our happiness knew no bounds, we were practically delirious with happiness."

It should be noted here that her improvement began even before the entire treatment had been in effect. Only diet and Atomidine had been introduced; the hot epsom salts baths were not yet scheduled for another month.

On November 1, Ruth Blanding wrote to Edgar Cayce: "We are following your advice. It seems too soon to say or think Sarah is better but she seems to be. The pain in her knees is gone, they are some stiff. Her elbows are better (not so painful). There is color creeping into her face. She has been so white. She has had one spell of palpitation of the heart, and a night sweat last night (one night in 3 or 4 or 5) as before it was every night. She is we believe permanently better. She was not clear down but close to it, some days. Of course we are happy beyond words. We feel she is going to get well. We will be glad to let you know how she is from time to time."

After resting for five days, as she was told, Sarah began her second series of drops and when she had ended this series, the pain and stiffness were gone throughout her body, except for her left elbow, according to her mother. Sometimes she had pain in her hands. The night sweats became less frequent, and her eczema cleared up about the first of December. Her heart palpitation, for which she had taken strychnine under her former doctors, was now better.

Edgar Cayce replied to Ruth's letter asking about foods with lime in them, and which were to be avoided. ". . . I certainly hope and believe that as she begins with the baths there will not be the recurrence of the distress in extremities. Too, I feel you will see a great difference in other ways. Some may be inclined to feel that such baths tend to reduce the body, but I do not think you will find this the case; that is, it has not been our experience that such baths—when followed according to instructions through the readings—have materially reduced the weight, and they have been most beneficial.

"I think you might be interested in how the Atomidine . . . originated. Many years ago the readings indicated that iodine would be very beneficial to the system if the poison could be taken out of it. Information was given to several individuals as to how kelp (from which iodine is obtained) might be treated to make iodine non-poisonous. It was rather an expensive process, and the lack of faith on the part of the individuals prevented them from undertaking it. Only a few years ago a scientist working on the same proposition succededed in preparing the product, which he called Atomidine. We know this man personally (Dr. Sunker A. Bisey). Many interested in the product feel it is good for practically everything, but the readings do not bear this out; however, wherever Atomidine has been used according to directions given in the readings it has been found to be most valuable.

"While the lime content of milk is quite high, the character of lime is quite different from that found in some vegetables, and many of the minerals that come from vegetables and fruits. It may be that if milk is to be part of the diet the pasteurized would be better, as it has less of the lime content; but to be sure, this again would have the tendency to produce constipation. Potato soup (which Sarah had found palatable) or the pie-plant would not have that tendency, though you know—as a starch—potatoes carry a great deal of lime, especially potatoes that would be grown in Ohio. I do not think the sweetening of the pie-plant would be detrimental, provided you are able to use beet sugar rather than the cane sugar.

"Thank you very much for letting us hear from you. I hope you will continue to write us every few days. Know that we are thinking of you and remembering you and Sarah in our prayers each day. . . ."

Contrary to expectations, Sarah's reaction to the first two epsom salts baths was more pain, lumps in her fingers, and a particularly severe night sweat. "The second bath was this past Tuesday night. Wednesday she ached all over and had a headache, her left thumb is still persisting (to be sore) and Wednesday was more acute, hurting into her hand and arm. Her right knee felt queer, rather creepy, like when she first took this . . .

"Her face and neck broke out badly this week even before the bath (per usual) about once a month and her period time came along Thursday; thus perhaps accounting for the aching on Wednesday. This is accompanied each time, it seems, with acute gas pains.

". . . her flesh seems flabby. We can feel a bump or lump along the right shin about two inches wide and three long. There are small lumps close against this shin bone at this spot. They are not sore . . ."

But several days after Christmas, Ruth reported: "We are glad to say at once this letter has a different message from the last one. Sarah's third bath was on last Tuesday and since Thursday her pain is all gone . . . She has stood the Holiday season very well. She has had a lot of extra work, trips up town for me as I was not so good myself. She is some tired, but no more than a well person would be."

Sarah continued to do "all the housework, cooking, and caring for" Ruth in January, evidently a time when Ruth herself became ill. Sarah steadily became better, although she had pain in her joints, which she was able to dispel with doses of Atomidine. She still had hard, sore lumps in her fingers and scaly spots on her face and neck.

A second reading given on January 20, 1933, found her much improved but full of encouragement to keep the diet and, when necessary, to take Atomidine and the baths. He still had much to say about diet. "As much of sea food as convenient will work *with* the balancing of the forces in system, for they create a character of element in the minutia, and supply to the blood and nerve forces of the system, to the active forces in the principles of the blood supply and the functioning organs, an assimilated character of force that works with the activities of the body. Also green vegetables; as lettuce, celery, spinach, mustard greens, and the like. Also those foods that carry sufficient elements of gold and phosphorous, which are found partially from sea food and partially from the characterization of vegetable forces—as in carrots, the oyster plant . . . Never any hog meat, very little of beef unless it is of the very lean (and the juices), but mutton and wild game—or the white meat of the fowl, or the like . . . provided they are not taken in excess for the system."

For a week to ten days, she should take olive oil in small amounts several times a day; rest for ten days, then begin again.

She should exercise in the open, but refrain from standing on her feet for long periods—especially before and after her menstrual periods.

The scaly, itching spots were due to impure circulation and would clear up from the internal changes taking place. This could be aided by use of the violet ray. A kernel at the base of her left ear was due to improper circulation and improper contribution of elements from various glands in the system. There was, said this reading, scarcely any organ in Sarah's system where there wasn't some kind of infection—"for the *natural* condition of the system is to involve all forces in the body." These infections would be eliminated if she followed the suggestions.

By July, 1934, two years after beginning treatment, Sarah had grown so well and strong that she was working as a playground instructress in the hot sun, said her mother, eighteen hours a week. "She has stood it very well and is looking fine."

"I seldom have even a touch of arthritis, but when I do, a dose of the medicine prescribed sets me on my feet again," Sarah told Edgar Cayce in her testimonial letter of August 14, 1934.

"We will never be able to express our thanks to Mr. Cayce for curing me and saving me from so horrible a death, as the reading stated that I would gradually die of sleeping or stony paralysis.

"My sincere regards to you and yours, Mr. Cayce, and I am proud to sign my name to this testimonial of you and your marvelous work."

Medical Commentary: Arthritis

by William A. McGarey, M.D.

ARTHRITIS IS A disease which probably affects fifty million people[1] in the United States alone. Sarah—the 18-year-old girl in this story—had the type of arthritis which we call rheumatoid or atrophic arthritis. It is also called proliferative arthritis or arthritis deformans. This type of disease process is characterized by inflammatory changes in the synovial membranes of the joints and in the periarticular structures and by atrophy and rarification of the bones.[2,3]

In the early stages, there is a migratory swelling and stiffness of the joints often with a rather typical fusiform swelling of the promixal interphalangeal joints of the fingers. Later on there is deformity with ankylosis and frequently an ulner deviation of the fingers as a sign of this disease. Subcutaneous nodules are frequent in these patients, and usually the disease is found beginning in young people, more commonly the male than the female. There is present anemia, chronic emaciation, loss of calcium in the bone structures, and the patient is rather severely and chronically ill.

Little has really been accomplished in establishing the etiology of the disease or in providing the physician with adequate tools with which to restore the patient back to full health. It is such an enigma that the Arthritis Foundation states categorically that there is no cure for the disease, and the sufferer from the condition is refrained from seeking such.

Sarah and her experiences give considerable food for thought when one considers the simplicity of the approach Cayce suggested and the manner in which he saw the disease process coming into being.

[1] *Arthritis—The Basic Facts,* Arthritis Foundation, N.Y. 1970.
[2] R. Cecil, "Diseases of the Joints," *R. Cecil's Textbook of Medicine,* 5th edition, Philadelphia and London: W. B. Saunders & Co., 1942, pp. 1408–1435.
[3] W. D. Robinson, "Diseases of the Joints," *Cecil & Loebe Textbook of Medicine,* 12th edition, Philadelphia and London: W. B. Saunders & Co., 1967, pp. 1390–1420.

Rheumatoid arthritis—in this instance, if Cayce was correct, came about not through an infectious organism or through any other similar process, but through a series of circumstances that put the body into a stress situation. This stress affected the abilities of the body to assimilate certain substances, and this in turn created glandular conditions over the entire body which were abnormal. The glands in turn became overactive in some respects, deficient in others, in supplying the elements necessary for the proper distribution of forces in the system.

Forces again! This seems to be such a recurrent theme in the Cayce readings. However, forces, vibrations, balances, and incoordinations are not current parts of the medical thinking processes. In Sarah we find the forces making for hardening or calcification in some areas *overactive,* the forces making for hardening in other areas *underactive.* Speaking strictly in terms of forces, this is a body just all goofed up.

In order to study etiology of atrophic arthritis, as Cayce suggested we might, we would necessarily have to adopt a different viewpoint relative to body-function and a different attitude toward what is disease. Here, in this case, disease again originates from within the body. Cayce's viewpoint on this is consistent. Even considering that the mother had an improper diet, Cayce points out in other instances how an entity chooses where he will be born. He picks his spot, so to speak, and thus fits himself even into the physical heredity which he has built in past lives. One may not agree with such a concept, but one must agree that Cayce is internally consistent in his readings. If he was correct, we have a lot to learn about diseases; and we also have a much more optimistic outlook relative to rheumatoid arthritis.

One of the truly leveling influences in these psychic readings is Cayce's unconscious recognition of the equality of all human beings in their nature as creatures designed in God's image. Degrees meant little to him in the unconscious state, and this spilled over a little into his conscious awareness.

He wrote to Sarah after the reading was given and encouraged her to follow the directions given her in the readings. He told her that if she got some good help at home, then "there should be no necessity for your going to a medical man at all." Now this sort of a comment might be ego-shattering if one took Cayce's words at face value and his own medical degree as the emblem of the source of all knowledge about the human body. But most physicians recognize that the mysteries of the human body and its function are truly beyond our present comprehension and that a spiritual being manifesting as a physical body must be a strange entity indeed. Our knowledge today is insufficient at best, and degrees give us most importantly the legal right to exercise in the active world that knowledge gained in our studies.

Cayce's comment about the lack of a need for medical assistance brings to my mind the story Dr. Kenneth Starz[4] told me about a young lady who had arthritis, not in the 1930's but in the 1960's, some 22 years after Cayce died. After seeking medical aid for five years, receiving a variety of pain medications, and being diagnosed as a rheumatoid arthritic with little hope of recovery, this 32-year-old woman found herself nearly incapacitated for normal living. Her left

---

[4] Kenneth Starz, M.D., Personal communication, August, 1971.

knee was locked in extension. She couldn't get in or out of a car without help. She could not get up from a chair without assistance. She found her outlook becoming more and more bleak and hopeless.

At this point she noticed a book in a five-and-dime store. It was Tom Sugrue's *There Is a River,* the story of Edgar Cayce's life. She resisted the urge to buy it, but the idea and fascination persisted. She came back later and did purchase the book and read it. In the back of the book a case of arthritis, probably rheumatoid, was discussed at length, as Cayce had prescribed for the afflicted person. The woman felt that the castor oil pack therapy described in the scleroderma readings might also apply to her stiff joints which seemed to her to be like "stone."

She decided she would apply the readings. After a struggle of several months, she succeeded in following the diet, which the readings said had to be begun first. She had always been overweight and compulsively ate sweets and starches which were hardly permitted at all in the diet. After she finally was on the diet, she took epsom salts baths once a week, massaged herself as recommended, took Atomidine in cycles of five days, and applied hot castor oil packs every other day. On and on she went. She achieved no real relief; but she persisted, week after week, month after month. Still no results.

The story told in Sugrue's book was so meaningful in this woman's life that she continued regularly, persistently, consistently for a full year without results. Finally, one morning she awoke, and her shoulder was no longer aching. This gave her renewed faith, if you want to call it that, and she continued her self-designed therapy program. Gradually, almost imperceptibly, her swelling subsided in all three joints, the knee became fully movable, and after two full years of treatments (and over a thousand pounds of epsom salts) only occasional aching still remained when the weather changed.

She still continued with the treatments. After three full years, she stopped. Her enlarged joints were normal, her swelling had disappeared, her activity was normal, and all her aches and pains were gone. No medication was needed at all.

It is humbling and inspiring to hear how a person on her own, with faith, persistence, and two Cayce readings helped her ailing body to re-establish more normal functions and a more health-giving coordination between the organs and systems of her body.

The woman in Dr. Starz' story exercised faith and persistence in following a course of physical therapy treatments which brought about changes in a physical body through physiological adjustments that are undoubtedly related to the mental-emotional-spiritual changes and activities in the whole person involved in the experience. This story is not unlike the one told by Mrs. Carter. The change in time and circumstance is interesting and makes us wonder, indeed, what is the arthritic process, and is it really incurable, as some would have us think?

CHAPTER 9

FOR LEONORE, "THE GLORY"

by Mary Ellen Carter

THE SMALL, RED-HAIRED girl with glasses sat herself down on the beautiful green velvet winged-back chair, being careful to place her candy bar on the arm. She watched intently as a chunk of mud from her left shoe fell to the rug.

Later, Harry Swann, who owned the chair, came home from work and sat down to read his paper. The smudges of chocolate caught his eye. "Who's been sitting here?" he wanted to know.

Leonore, his wife, came rushing in. "Little Cissy Duggan from next door. Why?"

"There's chocolate candy on the arm. See?"

"There is!" she peered about the chair. "And mud on the rug. Oh dear." Then she looked at her husband. "Cissy's such a cute little girl. I really don't mind."

"Kids are a lot of trouble."

Leonore sat down in her rocker, close to him. "That's the one kind of trouble I could use!"

He reached over and took her hand. "I know. Four years of marriage with no children, and no prospects of any. I wish . . ."

". . . that you had married a woman who could have children?"

"Stop that! Of course not. I just hope that someday, we will. I'm only 26, you're 24. There's lots of time."

"I'm sorry. You're right. There's lot of time." Then, "But I'm going to see the doctor tomorrow."

After examining Leonore, Dr. Fromm told her, "I find no reason for your infertility."

"I'm easily tired out," she told him, "and I break out frequently on my face. Would that have anything to do with it?"

"Well, you *are* underweight."

"And I have these pains in my head, neck, and lower abdomen . . . have had them for some time."

The doctor had no answer for this, but said, "Your underweight and tiredness are related."

"What?"

He had to repeat the statement.

231

"Oh, I also can't hear very well any more. I have a roaring in my ears! It's dreadful!"

Well, perhaps she should consult Edgar Cayce. She had been living by his readings since childhood, guided by her mother's interest in his work. She had not always followed her more recent readings as faithfully as she might have, but she felt that a reading now might get her on the right track.

"If Edgar Cayce can help me to get in shape to have a baby, I'll be happy," she told Harry.

On September 29, 1937, her sixth reading was given (578-6): "In some respects," it said, "we find conditions much improved and in others we find conditions have been retarded and are not as efficient as they should be in the reactions in the system. These particularly do we find in relationship to the pressures in the nerve system and their reaction upon the sensory organism."

In the previous reading, Edgar Cayce had recommended adjustments in the upper dorsal and cervical areas, with corrections in the lumbar, sacral, and coccyx areas. "These pressures *now* produce upon the nerve system *greater* strains than has been indicated heretofore . . .

"Unless there is a change in the manipulations by the one administering same, we would change from that one . . . ; and have those corrections made as has been indicated. For not only will the removal of these pressures bring about a better normal condition, and a closer relationship between the emotions and the nerve system and the activity to the organs of the body, but we will find better assimilations, the body would put on more weight, the body would be hungrier, the body would not tire so easily, the body would not find the pains through the head and the neck and those through even the lower portions of the abdomen that become so severe at times.

"*We* would change then [from the present osteopath] to Crews' reactions [Gena Lowndes Crews, D.O.], the only doctor in that area who used the lymph pump.

"Make *specific* adjustments in the coccyx, *raising* the lower end of same. Coordinate this with the fourth lumbar. This *gradually* done. Then coordinate same, of course (each time coordinating all of these), with the upper adjustments in the 3rd and 4th dorsal, 3rd and 4th cervical, 1st and 2nd cervical and in the head and neck and the vagus center, but with these adjustments going *up* the spine!

"The next specific would be in the 8th and 9th dorsal segment, then coordinating these with the lower portions."

These were to be taken twice a week for two or three weeks, left off for two weeks then taken again.

Asked about the deafness, he said that pressures in the coccyx area were not coordinating with those in the lumbar axis, deflecting from the ninth dorsal to the axis of the centers in the upper dorsal and cervical that make direct connection with her hearing. "Remove these pressures and these conditions will disappear!"

The breaking out on her face was due to poor lymph circulation from the areas where the nerve pressures in the upper dorsal area coordinated with her respiratory system. Hence, use of the lymph pump was recommended.

A blemish which had appeared on her left leg could be reduced to very little by rubbing castor oil on it for several weeks, daily; then, sweet oil.

Leonore had had an operation for removal of an ovarian cyst in January, 1936. When asked about this, Cayce said that this made for better conditions if the pressures were removed "so that there are still not those contractions during the period of gestation for the activity of the organs of the pelvis."

"Just what can I do to make myself susceptible to pregnancy?" she asked.

"It will be necessary first that the pressures in those areas . . . be removed before there will be the ability for the organs to retain their activity at time of conception."

"Is there any special time for me to have this baby?"

"Not until these corrections are made and there is a building up of the bodily system itself. Then it would be beneficial." This would be possible by the following fall.

"Keep constructive in the thinking," he added. "Do not let *little* reactions produce animosities."

Leonore found F. C. Hudgins, Jr., D.O., to be a doctor who worked willingly with the readings. During the following six months, she followed through with Cayce's instructions, and on May 5, 1938, he filled out a questionnaire sent him by the Association. In this he confirmed that in his opinion, the patient's condition was described in the reading. He called her condition "Sterility, Dysmenorrhea."

The questionnaire asked: "Were the suggestions for treatment in your opinion proper for this condition?"

"Yes," Dr. Hudgins replied, "possibly could be added local manipulative treatment to uterus in order to correct malposition if present. Possible study to determine virility of husband."

"What results have you observed?"

"Patient still not pregnant—dysmenorrhea cleared up, patient improved generally."

Another reading was given for Leonore, now 25, on October 18, 1938. This suggested for her specific exercises that would "make for a movement of the abdomen and the pelvic and the lower limbs." These, in addition to occasional manipulations, would now be sufficient to "attune" or "tone" her body. He said the exercises should be taken in the morning upon arising—the bicycle exercise in which she should lie down on her shoulders, making bicycle pedaling motions in the air with her legs.

Her condition was much improved, the treatments by Dr. Hudgins were "very good." She was still troubled by deafness. Cayce assured her that it was disappearing with the exercises and manipulations.

On December 2, 1938, she telephoned to Cayce the following questions: "1. Am I pregnant? If not, why don't I feel as I usually do near the period; and if so, what special precautions should I take to allow pregnancy to continue? How advanced is it?

"2. Would it be well to continue to wear the girdle for my back?

"3. Any further advice?"

Thus, at long last, the reading Leonore and Harry had hoped one day to be for them, began: "Yes, the glory of motherhood may be the part of the entity from the present experiences, if there is the care and precaution taken . . ."

Said this reading, osteopathic stimulation should be given to relax her tenseness but also to stimulate the retaining influences toward what may, without a disturbing force, become pregnancy. Such treatment should be given about once a week, "a quieting, through the manipulative forces" whenever there was too great an anxiety. Leonore should be careful not to get her feet damp or to take cold. She should keep wearing the girdle, which should be more an elastic for the abdomen.

"Has conception taken place?" she asked.

"As indicated, they may — it may not, dependent upon the conditions. The seed are present. The glory of such is present."

It had been one and one-half years since Leonore had begun treatment with Dr. Hudgins when he gave another report in answer to a second questionnaire. By now, he replied that results were "complete recovery." It was dated May 25, 1939.

The patient was now five or six months pregnant!

And on July 16, 1939, to Harry and Leonore was born a beautiful baby daughter.

Medical Commentary: Infertility

by William A. McGarey, M.D.

WHEN PREGNANCY COMES into the life of one who has previously been unable to have a child, it is a creative event that words cannot describe. The fact that children are born every moment of the day around the world does not lessen the miracle of new life to the individuals who had previously been denied the status of parenthood. The mystery of conception is most often pushed to the sidelines by the frequency of its occurrence, as if the simple statistics of the event explain how it happens. But for these two people, Leonore and Harry, the need to become mother and dad was a major factor in their lives, and they desperately wanted that miracle to happen.

In this story, it is not that Cayce was able to describe what Leonore needed to do to become pregnant that is to me the valuable data worthy of study. In our own private practices, Gladys and I, being man and wife, M.D.'s in general practice, have seen at least fifteen previously sterile marriages changed into parenthood situations by the simple administration of Vitamin E in one form or another. I am sure any physician working with sterility problems has seen the same thing happen through the use of nutrition, surgical means, physical clearing of the passages, hormones or the simple process of adopting a child. A professor of mine and his wife gave up on having a child as they entered their forties — they adopted a child and within several months, she became pregnant. This is not an unusual story.

Suggestion, hypnosis, unconscious mind activities play a large part in the sterility problem and its solution. Fear of pregnancy has been shown to prevent conception at times, at other times to cause tubal implantation of the pregnancy or to cause spontaneous abortion. So many factors unnamed, as well as those I have mentioned, can alter the picture in the case of women who cannot get pregnant.

The valuable data in this story—it seems to me—are some of the physiological factors that Cayce suggests are involved in promoting the possiblity of the continuation of pregnancy; the concept that the entire physical body needs to have a homeostasis that supports the possiblity of conception; the idea that there is a "glory" associated with motherhood that relates the child and the parents with their spiritual origin and heritage. These data are worthy of study and of implementation in every case of man and woman who desire to become parents and in every physician who counsels and cares for the mother during pregnancy and often before conception occurs.

Cayce told Leonore in her first reading for this condition that she should not try to become pregnant yet—and in fact could not—until her body was more balanced and in proper condition to support the pregnancy. He told her that there were pressures in the spine which could be removed through osteopathic treatments and corrective manipulation. He also suggested that if the lymph pump therapy were used in conjunction with this, the results would be more certain and would come about more quickly. The patient did not take Cayce's recommendation wholly—she did not change doctors and did not get lymph pump treatments from Dr. Crews as Cayce had suggested. It is interesting to note that whereas he had predicted she would have a child in the fall of 1938, under the circumstances of following his directions, she actually delivered in July, 1939.

The lymph pump is a manipulation of the chest which involves alternating pressures manually induced and which create an increased flow of the lymph through the chest cage—and probably, by extension, through other parts of the lymphatic system.

The actual problems of an osteopathic nature existing in Leonore's spine involved pressures and incoordinations in portions of the cervical, dorsal, lumbar, sacral, and coccygeal vertebrae, according to Cayce's insight. Relieving the patient of these conditions would have a profound effect on the body, physiologically speaking, if Cayce (as well as the osteopathic profession) is correct. A better functional relationship would come about between the emotions—or the endocrine system—and the entire nervous system; and the effect to the organs of the body would be enhanced as a result of this improved functional status. Cayce was implying, in other words, that the physical basis of emotions and thought—their proper relationship—would be bettered in all respects and the organs themselves would, as a result, function more normally.

With more normal liver, gall bladder, and pancreas activity, the assimilations of foods would be bettered; Leonore would put on more weight, her appetite would be improved because the utilization and metabolism of the food would be upgraded; her stamina and energy would be increased; and the symptoms of pains in the head, neck, and abdomen which had been so bothersome would disappear. "The removal of these pressures," as Cayce put it, "will bring about a better normal condition."

The skin rash which Leonore was experiencing had its etiology, according to these readings, in poor lymph circulation from areas where nerve pressures in the upper dorsal area coordinate with the respiratory system. I assume this means that those areas of skin rash were deficient in lymphatic drainage because of lack of adequate nerve impulse from the centers which direct and control lymphatic activity. These centers are apparently associated very closely with the chest and respiratory system, which would be Cayce's reasoning behind suggesting the lymph pump treatment. This would have a direct or indirect effect on the lymphatic drainage of the skin itself. Most textbooks of physiology do not recognize autonomic control of lymphatic vessels, but this has been demonstrated anatomically in some lymph vessels of the abdominal cavity. Perhaps nerve supply has as much to do with repair and regeneration of the lymphatic vessels—perhaps more—than the flow of the lymph.

It has been shown[1] that hemorrhage frequently occurs in the subendocardial area soon after lymphatic flow is obstructed in the hearts of dogs. Cardiologist working with lymphatic problems such as these reason that areas of hemorrhage might lead to fibrosis when the lymph drainage is chronically inadequate. These findings could lead one to postulate that insufficient lymph drainage of any area could produce pathology—a dermatitis in the skin, for instance. Lymphatic structures of the body and their function are at the present time poorly understood in their significance to the health of the body. That they do act as eliminating channels of the body is understood, however, and when such a function is not up to par, disturbance in the nature of illness follows.

The deafness which the patient complained of had its origin in the same pathology, apparently, that Cayce described as being part of the complex of pressures in the spine and spinal cord causing the other difficulties. It apparently did not need to be corrected in order that the body would be in good condition to bear a child, in the Cayce viewpoint, but Cayce did suggest that it would be better to clear it up once and for all. Leonore did improve, according to the records, but did not follow through on the directions given for this with consistency and persistence. Thus she was bothered with a recurrence and more acute loss of hearing later on.

When Leonore actually became pregnant, she was advised to have those things done which would "*stimulate* the *retaining* influences and the *development* of *all* influences *towards* what may—without a disturbing force—become pregnancy." This is a fascinating statement, for it recognizes that conception—the union of the sperm and the egg—has taken place; yet it implies that perhaps pregnancy—"being with child"—cannot be considered to be present until all forces of the body are proper to retain it: one might say, "until all systems are 'go'." Until, in fact, there is the proper homeostasis of the body.

At times Cayce apparently looked upon a situation with an ageless evaluation. Would the union of the sperm and the ovum produce that which would allow the woman to evaluate herself inwardly as a mother, carrying her child in her womb? Until the forces of the incoming entity, the physical condition of the uterus and its associated structures, the general condition and balance of the entire body physiology were coordinant in saying that this pregnancy would in fact be productive of a living child—then and then only did Cayce see an actual

---

[1] "Lymphatics' Role Stressed in Cardiovascular Disease," *Medical World News,* Vol. 7, Jan. 21, 1966, pp. 100–101.

pregnancy, a mother with child. "This may—it may not. Dependent upon the conditions," Cayce said in his reading to the young woman. The seed of conception was present, but the possibility of fulfillment was still to be determined.

Perhaps Leonore's position as a prospective mother can be better understood from the standpoint of the mind of Edgar Cayce if we were to look at a reading given for a 34-year-old woman (457-10) who was not yet pregnant but had been promised that she could become so. She asked many question about preparing for pregnancy and motherhood and did, in fact, become a mother about a year later. Cayce's philosophy about motherhood shines through:

> In giving information, or in answering questions respecting mental and spiritual attitudes, all of these should be approached from *this* basis of reasoning,—especially as preprations are made in body, mind and spirit for a soul's entrance into the material plane.

> While as an individual entity, [457] presents the fact of a body, a mind, a soul,—it has been given as a promise, as an opportunity to man through coition, to furnish, to create a channel through which the Creator, God, may give to individuals the opportunity of seeing, experiencing His handiwork.

> Thus the greater preparation that may be made, in earnest, in truth, in offering self as a channel, is first physical, then the mental attitude; knowing that God, the Creator, will supply that character, that nature may have its course in being and in bringing into material manifestation a soul. For, in being absent from a physical body a soul is in the presence of its Maker.

> Then, know the attitude of mind of self, of the companion, in creating the opportunity; for it depends upon the state of attitude as to the nature, the character that may be brought into material experience.

> Leave *then* the spiritual aspects to God. Prepare the mental and the physical body, according to the nature, the character of that soul being sought.

Isn't there, then, a challenge for Leonore and Harry, and for an opportunity for every practicing physician and for every prospective mother and father, in the implications suggested here, if indeed Cayce's work has a validity? Wouldn't it make a serious difference in a woman's life if she thought she were pregnant and received an admonition like this:

> The glory of motherhood may be the part of the entity from the present experiences, if there is the care and the precaution taken.

CHAPTER 10

MAYTIME MALADY

by Mary Ellen Carter

"ELEANOR BELMONT, I tell you, you have been taking terrible chances!" The short, little woman in a black straw hat settled herself on the rocker, her lined face wearing a dark look of disapproval. "At 74, you ought to have more sense!"

Eleanor passed a plate of little tea cakes and laughed. "Really, Glenda, you don't understand."

"I understand charlatan's work when I see it. Your daughter Joan has been completely taken in. I know she's sincere, so it must be that she's gone crazy!"

"Let me tell you the whole story, then say what you think."

Glenda shrugged. But there was a gleam of interest in her eyes.

"One morning back in 1926, just five years ago this past month of May, I started to walk out to my garden. The air was so sweet-smelling, up here in the mountains, that I felt I wanted to plant some seeds. Suddenly I jerked backward and collapsed in violent spasms on the steps. Joan rushed out to catch me, but I was stout then and she could hardly lift me."

"You're very thin now."

"Somehow she got me to the daybed in the back bedroom, and I lost consciousness, so I don't know just how . . ."

"Yes, I remember hearing about it. A convulsion, wasn't it?"

"That's right. When the doctor arrived, he examined me and found my heart was good, but he could find no cause for the spell. And I was so weak! Two years later, almost to the day, I had another. This left me even weaker. And in 1929—May again—I had still another attack. Each time I would be weaker than the time before, for these convulsions lasted all day."

"How did you hear about this Cayce fellow?"

"Through friends of Joan's. This spring of 1931 I was feeling very bad again, so Joan decided to write to Edgar Cayce. She told him that I had been under the weather for some time and told him about my vomiting, pressure in my chest, pains in my arms. She asked him if I'd ever had gall bladder trouble, and about my diet, and if my heart was all right.

"The reading was taken on June 10. On that day, I remember, I was feeling pretty low but I tried to tidy up the house: if Mr. Cayce was to pay a visit, I wanted everything looking nice . . ."

238

"If he was to . . . *what?*"

"Well, you see, while he's lying asleep there in Virginia Beach, he somehow comes to wherever you are to diagnose your case."

Glenda's eyes were full of alarm. "How can he do that, Eleanor?"

"Well, I don't *know,* exactly. Anyway, it was a warm, pretty day, and outside the mountains and the valley were still blue with mist. I dusted a bit around the living room. It's my favorite place . . ." and Eleanor indicated the time-browned photographs of her children and grandchildren on the wall over her roll-top desk. She had braided the rug herself, and she had tatted the doilies on the furniture.

"The time for the reading was set for 3:15 in the afternoon. I understood it was best to be in an attitude of prayer at the time of the reading. So I sat down at 3 o'clock. I felt at peace. I could look out over the valley far to the west where the mountains rise and fade into pale distances. I thought: *I will lift up mine eyes unto these hilles, from whence cometh my strength.*"

"Did you feel or see anything unusual?"

Eleanor grew quiet. "Only a peaceful feeling."

Glenda was more impressed now than she cared to admit. "What was the reading like?"

"Well, it told me to do a number of things. I was to have castor oil packs for four or five days, and after that, to take olive oil in small doses, as much as I could take . . ."

"Castor oil packs! Hmf!"

"Yes, over my liver area. You use heavy flannel dipped in the castor oil and wring out, and you apply them with hot salt packs. You keep them on for an hour or two each day."

"Go on."

"Then I took a high enema after several days of olive oil, then a cathartic made up from a prescription Mr. Cayce gave. I also took a pinch of elm in each glass of water I drank. I have to watch my diet—green vegetable salads at noon, fruit with rice or whole wheat bran cakes in the morning. Very little meat—only lean meat."

"What caused you to throw up?"

"My gall ducts not acting right." Eleanor smiled. "Edgar Cayce expressed better how I felt than I could. I can vouch for every line of that reading. Every bit is true. I'm following it to the letter."

"But, Eleanor, dear, how can you risk your life on the work of an untrained lay person?"

"Look at me!" Eleanor challenged.

"I have to admit," Glenda agreed, "you do look better than you did a few weeks ago." But she set her chin firmly and added, "But then, you would have gotten over your spell, anyway. You always do."

"Oh," Eleanor cried in exasperation. "Drink your lemonade."

Glenda ate her sixth little cake, put two more spoonsful of sugar in her lemonade, and winced.

"Why, what's the matter?" Eleanor asked concernedly.

"My arthritis again!"

On July 6, Eleanor's daughter, Joan, wrote to Edgar Cayce: ". . . Mother is giving your work the credit for her life. She feels like she would not be alive today except for the information and direction of the reading. She is improving every day and to say she is 'broadcasting' your work is expressing it mildly . . ."

To Joan, Eleanor said, "Keep track of the reading, and I'll follow the same course every year in the springtime."

The reading stated that "much might be given as respecting the history, or that as has brought about the disorders that at present exist." The condition must be "correlated *with* that which the body has *suffered* periodically in the past."

Pressure in the heart's action and a "heaviness" in the blood supply caused drosses in Eleanor's body, manifesting in pain in her shoulders, across both sides, under her arms, across the chest at times. Most of the heaviness around the heart was indigestion produced by functional and organic disorders in the eliminating system.

As the circulation attempted to be normal through the congested areas, "from poisons or accumulation in muscular tissue, as the intercostal, as in the brachial, as in the lumbar and locomotory plexuses of the system," even deep breathing at times gave catchy pains across her diaphragm.

At times, she had from the drosses acute use of her senses and, at other times, "dimness of vision, drumming in the ears, fullness in the throat, and a general tendency of a throbbing feeling in the pulsations, or the capillary circulation."

Her pulse was low, with pressure high in blood supply. Her respiration varied from faster than normal to below normal. Her digestive system was, said Cayce, who used slang if it best expressed what he wanted, "all out of kelter!" There was gallstone accumulation which produced sour stomach, tendency for constipation, or else temporary diarrhea. There was too-frequent activity of the kidneys at times and only abnormal elimination through the pores, with swelling in her feet as reflex from the kidney conditions.

"To meet the needs," the first suggestion was the use of the castor oil packs over the liver area. These were to be kept for four to five days, followed by the olive oil doses, the high enema, and the cathartic. If the pinch of elm in each glass of drinking water became offensive, producing belching, she was to discontinue this and take instead yellow saffron tea, made with twenty grains to one pint of water, steeped, strained, and cooled.

Her diet was to be mainly liquid, with the fruits and vegetables predominating.

She was to use enemas when necessary to relieve pains from the pressure in the intestinal system. The last water used should be that carrying Glyco-Thymoline, or boracic acid as an antiseptic (in a gallon and a half of water, two tablespoonsful of Glyco).

A year later in 1932, during that fateful month of May, Joan reported to Edgar Cayce that: "Mother had spoken about having another reading but she has been talked to so much (folks trying to get her to save me from insanity) that I don't know what she now intends to do. But she seem perfectly well . . ."

Eleanor decided to have her check reading, anyway. Joan's letter explained: "My mother is not so well and she asked me to write you for a reading, so give it at your earliest date—simply write her for the day and hour . . ." Questions asked were: "What causes breaking out with hives or itching bumps? Is the mineral oil now being used the right thing and should it be continued? Is she able to stand a trip soon to Virginia Beach?"

A few changes recommended now in Eleanor's check reading concerning diet and medicine brought about her continued gain in weight and strength. By early spring of 1934, Eleanor had been quite well for several years, but once more began to suffer some illness. She wanted another check reading.

"I owe the latter years of my life to the service Mr. Cayce has rendered me," she told Joan.

On the eleventh of April there was another reading. On the twentieth, Joan wrote: "When I wrote for the reading for Mother, I was very much disturbed about her condition. She had gotten so much worse. Her breathing was real laborious and panting, especially at night and when going up steps. She began at once on the new treatment and I can see a decided change already. While we were waiting for the reading our family physician chanced to come in here and, seeing how she was feeling, gave her an examination and told me that she had a leak, or I believe he said 'lesion' or something of the sort in her heart that was worth watching and to keep her absolutely quiet. Well, I was right much in hot water for I just did not know how the reading was going to sound to her, for she gets very blue and worried about her condition, but I knew I could not keep her from seeing the reading so you cannot know how relieved I was when the reading had no reference to a leak in her heart. In Feb. she had a pretty close shave with pneumonia and of course I was not surprised at a weakened heart condition. She still suffers with weakness, though her breathing is much easier. So I think she is responding very well considering her age. Where the reading says 'Many of the ministrations that have been outlined would be well to take or consider' etc. I had been wondering if that refers to the castor oil packs? If she keeps on feeling so weak I will try that again, for she received wonderful relief by it. Just at this time I have to be away and will not be able to give the vibrator treatment . . ."

Joan wrote once more on June 12 to say that "Mother was taken with one of her regular spring attacks on Apr. 25th and passed away on April 27th. I was not at home when she was first taken but hurried on as soon as I heard. She had not been able to react very well from the change in medicine, tho she was working faithfully and I believe had she been a little more careful of the diet it might have been different, I do not know; but if you remember the last rdg. was not at all encouraging, or not nearly so as the others. She had been gradually growing weaker all winter tho she made a brave fight . . . She said often the past few months that she owed the latter yrs. of her life to you."

In 1940 Joan stated: "The physician's analysis was heart weakness and gallstones. Her improvement was 100% when we followed the first rdg. I am sure that the Edgar Cayce treatment prolonged her life for 2 to 3 years."

Medical Commentary: Debilitation

by William A. McGarey, M.D.

WHEN A WOMAN has lived 74 years, she has experienced many things. Each experience undoubtedly contributes something to the quality of her physical health. Physical and psychological trauma, the ageing process, the residuals of previous illness, improper dietary habits, the stress and strain of life decision—all of these contribute to illness in a multitude of ways.

Eleanor's difficulty was a problem in the field that today we call geriatrics. In the older patient, there is an accumulation of minor problems—sometimes of major ones—and the duty of the physician is to keep the geriatric patient as healthy, hale, and hearty as possible. I would suppose it is really our responsiblity to help the older person to remain alive and vibrant and active until the change of environment that we call death comes about. It is a certainty that we can stem the tide only so long, then death must intervene.

Cayce gave several readings dealing with longevity. These comments would lead us to believe that length of life depends on a number of factors—one being how long one *believes* he can live, and another being how well one knows the laws of balance governing the physical body and how well he obeys them.

In the readings given this woman, a great variety of rather serious problems were identified, and one can almost sense Cayce's realization of the fact that a major rehabilitation was quite unlikely in this case. Actually, this is one type of evaluation done by every sensitive physician—the attempt to catch the degree of life potential present in a given patient and how much there is left to work with. Cayce "looked" psychically at her past history and said:

> . . . much might be given as respecting the history, or that as has brought
> about the disorders that at present exist. These, as we give then, will be
> rather that as exists which must be correlated *with* that as the body has
> *suffered* periodically in the past. (356-1)

In other words, as he had mentioned earlier in the reading, there were numerous abnormal conditions in the physical functioning of the body, as well as organic disturbances, but here he was giving specific suggestions to relieve the episodic springtime convulsive syndrome. He was not at this point—or even later—attempting a full rehabilitative effort.

The question arises in most minds, as this material is studied, whether Cayce

mimics the attitudes and procedures of a good physican or if some other explanation could be found for his basic excellent approaches in an unconscious state
to the problems of the sick individual. It was exciting reading for me when I
came across Cayce's own life reading that told about the time, many thousands
of years ago, when, in a past life experience, he was himself a physician and
apparently used these same methods of rebuilding the body that we find described
in the readings today. Undoubtedly a medical career in Persia 3000 years ago
does not qualify a man for a medical degree today, but the soundness and basic
quality of the advice given from this man with a probable Persian medical
background certainly makes the material worth looking at.

And, at the same time, it gives one the feeling that perhaps the medical advice
is based on more than information pulled out of a cosmic hat. Cayce had been
there—according to his trance information—and he knew how to handle the
tired, sick, often disgruntled patient. He knew how to keep a balance in the
function of the body as he helped it to regain health. He knew the meaning of
incoordination, and he knew the heartache that goes with the experience of illness
in one's own body and in the life of a dear one. Because he had been a physician,
he was aware of the sickness of the human body which needs relief.

With Eleanor, then, he gave suggestions that were designed to help out somewhat with the problem of cholelithiasis—the stones in her gall bladder had been
bringing about much distress. The eliminations from the system needed to be
improved in many ways. The intestinal tract needed soothing and balancing in
its action. The nervous system was under stress and strain due to improper
eliminations and the accumulation of normal waste products in the body muscu-
lature, the stress coming as the nervous system attempted to make the circulation
of the body normal under these trying circumstances.

In readings given for epilepsy, Cayce suggested most consistently the use of
castor oil packs over the abdomen and liver. These also were a regular therapy
program for nearly all gall bladder problems. In view of the history of periodic
convulsive episodes *and* gall stones with gall bladder irritation and congestion,
it is no wonder that the castor oil packs were recommended here.

An electrically-driven vibrator was used along her spinal column, to stimulate
better relationship and function between the cerebrospinal and the autonomic
nervous systems. A diet designed to supply simple nourishment to her body was
suggested. Elm water (or yellow saffron tea) to relieve the irritant within the
intestinal tract and enemas to relieve pain and to act as a cleansing agent completed
the first set of suggestions.

As these were carried out, Eleanor improved remarkably and apparently established a new basis of body balance which lasted the better part of three years.

This was good geriatric care, certainly. One wonders what would have happened
if Eleanor had consulted a physician with Cayce's insight and could have been
followed month by month. Would she have continued using some of these same
rehabilitative measures to build an even more vigorous body, or would she have
found such suggestions to be out of place in a doctor's office? Would she have
paid less attention to her doctor than she did to an unconscious man who had a
capability that has not yet been fully explained?

These questions cannot be answered, of course. It is quite apparent that the patient lived another three years, was greatly relieved for a period of time, and succumbed apparently to the same process that was going on when Cayce gave his first reading. All of which goes to substantiate a theory that illness *is* a process, probably set into motion by the thoughts, attitudes, emotions, and activities which a human being engenders throughout life; and it is most difficult to change 74 years' worth of patterns in a way that will bring about a major change in direction and thus a relief from the processes that create and shape the nature and activity of a disesase.

As a physician, I would not like to be responsible for the results brought about in a patient I would see in my office only three times in three years. That is a tough proposition. Cayce was in this position. But perhaps in the thousands of years and several incarnations that had passed since Cayce had been a physician in Persia, he had grown a bit more patient, a bit more philosophical, a bit more insightful than he was in those days. This would temper one's outlook. And a realization of the concept that death also often brings real healing would make one's position in relationship to an older patient's physical-mental condition much more tenable, much more liveable, much more creative.

CHAPTER 11

CALL THIS A MIRACLE

by Mary Ellen Carter

TONY CASTELLO WAS a skinny little six-year-old with large, dark eyes that held how many lifetimes of living and dying?

As his father, Ernesto, carried him up the steps of the Cayce Hospital, his mother followed close behind. "Don't be scared, Tony," she said. "Everything will be all right."

At the door there appeared a tall, lean man with a friendly, inclusive nod for the three of them. "Who have we here?" he greeted.

Puffing a little from the exertion of the climb with his burden, Ernesto replied with a smile, "We have my son, Tony Castello, Mr. Cayce . . . you are that man, aren't you?" He added, "You gave him a reading in March. It said he should be treated here."

"Oh, yes, we received your letter that you were coming. I hope we can be of help."

"Oh, Mr. Cayce, we have tried everything!" Rose Castello said plaintively. "Can you help him?"

"We will see," said Edgar Cayce.

Tony was admitted by Miss Gladys Davis, the pretty young secretary of Edgar Cayce, who smiled across her desk at the new little patient. His father gently put him down on one of the leather upholstered chairs in the lobby and gave a laugh of relief. Tony gurgled.

"You liked that climb, eh, Tony?" his father teased fondly.

"Especially the steps," Edgar Cayce rejoined.

The boy, anxious to join in the repartee, attempted to speak, but he could only jerk and writhe, his mouth opening wide, his head bobbing.

"He's really very intelligent," Rose hastened to explain. "He wants to talk. He likes you and he understands what you say."

"We've taken him to all kinds of doctors," Ernesto added. "All we can do is give him drugs. We try to help him walk every day, but it's no good. He still has to be carried everywhere."

"The doctors called this cerebral palsy, something that occurs at birth, isn't that right?" asked Cayce.

"That's right," Ernesto nodded. "But he's not retarded. We can tell he's learning a lot, he just can't make the physical movements to walk or talk. The doctors have said that all we can do is to train him to use whatever muscles and brains he has to function."

"What do they do for him?"

"There's nothing much they *can* do. We're supposed to get a walker to help him get around and to help him stand up." Ernesto sighed. "And there's muscle-relaxing drugs. But a lifetime of *that?*" And he gestured expressively.

The Castellos had obtained a reading for Tony on March 14, 1930. It told them that corrections could be made, that the results of treatment might prove "ideal." In many ways Tony was very special, the reading implied. The derangements in his body might be brought to normal by means of proper adjustments. "This particular condition would be an interesting study from the structural, anatomical condition, if studied from the application of the radiograph and the reactions made with the same," said this reading. The congenital nature of the condition had to do with the cerebrospinal system and those branches that lead from this to the locomotory centers.

"It will take patience, persistence, and some time," it continued, "but will be well worth the changes as may be wrought in the physical activities for this body."

Cayce then outlined a program of treatment: gentle manipulations, at first; use of the wet-cell battery carrying chloride of gold to the extremities and to the solar plexus; fresh air and sunshine that would "work wonders for the body;" body-building foods; and the use of the infra-red ray "to aid the bones' reaction in the system." (5568-1)

Changes would occur in ten days to two weeks after starting this program, but there would not be a permanent cure until there was the proper "rejuvenation" in the whole system.

The time required for a complete cure would depend upon how the body responded to treatment. A gentle approach would be needed in working with Tony. One should not use force but, instead, gain his confidence.

On the day following his admittance, Tony awoke in his room overlooking the ocean to see the panorama of long, rolling sand dunes and the wide sea itself. Treatments were begun with osteopathic manipulations, as recommended in the reading. These were done by Dr. Grace Berger.

"We're going to rig you up with a battery," Dr. Berger told him as she worked. "Then we're going to put a red light on you. That's called an infra-red ray. What do you think of that?"

Tony, lying still and obedient on the table, gurgled.

"We're going to do that every day: 30 minutes for the battery and 20 minutes for the light. Then we're going to take you to the beach. Think you'll like that?"

Another gutteral sound from Tony.

"We'll give you sand baths and you'll swim in the ocean, every day." As she worked she moved his legs and arms and massaged his torso.

That afternoon, Dr. Lydic began the wet-cell battery treatment. This was used with chloride of gold in the solution, which was to be carried to Tony's hands, feet, and solar plexus.

The weather was still cool, so after a half-hour on the beach in the pale April sun, Tony was brought back to his room. He had a supper of broiled lamb, carrots and peas, and tomato aspic, with ice cream for dessert.

When Edgar Cayce looked in on him a little after bedtime, he saw a tiny, distorted form beneath the covers. In sleep Tony's face was tranquil. He was at peace in whatever dream world that he walked, straight and strong.

As the days passed Tony was given more time on the beach, where he was immersed in "sand baths" or put into shallow pools made by the sea, where he remained for short periods. He soon acquired a tan and began to gain weight. As Cayce had predicted, he was improving ten days to two weeks after beginning his stay there.

After three-and-one-half weeks, a third reading (5568-3) was given on April 28 recommending "good sweats," but that these would be torture if not handled properly. They were to be followed by rub-downs with equal parts of olive oil and tincture of myrrh, with special attention to the spine. He was to take small doses of quinine "to stir the liver and rid the blood of those *effects* of poisons by congestions." Care was to be taken against cold and congestion from too much exposure outdoors. With warm weather he was to reduce the infra-red ray to once a week, since he was able to be on the beach almost daily.

On June 10 a reading reported his progress as "very good." A more vigorous manipulation along the spine was given "to stimulate the nerve ends as they function through the muscular portion of the body."

In July, a reading stated that if the staff kept up the program, making for the relaxing of the muscular ends and the tissue forces in the extremities and radial centers of the cerebrospinal system, these would make for a "straight body, for an active physical force in same." Now Tony was to have a rub-down every evening with cocoa butter and olive oil alternatively; or, it might be with olive oil and myrrh, then cocoa butter.

The seventh and final reading was given September 1, when he was told he might go home. In the five months he had been there, he had "improved in many ways," as the reading stated. Gladys Davis Turner attests to this improvement for she recalls that he had gained, he seemed more alert, and certainly his color had returned.

"A cure of this kind takes time," she points out in reporting to me on this case.

The record states that at that time, Tony had a tendency to be overactive as his system responded to treatment and became stronger. At home he was to continue treatments which could be given through the radioactive appliance containing spirits of camphor. He was to have osteopathy once a week and oil manipulations to stimulate capillary circulation. He was to continue his building diet.

He left on September 3. In November his father gratefully wrote Edgar Cayce that Tony was still improving and "wishes to be remembered, and also his mother, to everyone they knew at the hospital."

On December 13 he again wrote to say that Tony was having his osteopathic treatments and that "he is improving all the time."

This case is not listed in the files as officially "cured." No further reports were made on Tony's progress. Gladys Turner's efforts to get in touch with his parents were fruitless; more recent attempts on the part of this writer, 40 years later, were also negative.

However, the sleeping Cayce spoke so optimistically at the outset and in the final reading, regarding Tony's chances, that, knowing the *mind* of these readings, we are led to believe he recovered. Tony's marked improvement during eight-and-one-half months of treatment as suggested by Cayce was in itself a triumph. To Rose and Ernesto Castello, it was more than they had hoped.

Medical Commentary: Cerebral Palsy

by William A. McGarey, M.D.

TONY CASTELLO PRESENTED a rather typical picture of what we call cerebral palsy when he arrived at the Cayce Hospital back in 1930. His type of problem, from the information available, seems to fall into the category of choreo-athetosis. About one-fifth of all cerebral palsy victims have an athetotic difficulty. That is, they display writhing and jerking movements of the body and face when they try to speak or accomplish any voluntary movement. Athetosis is one of the so-called extra-pyramidal cerebral palsies.

Cerebral palsy as defined is not a disease entity with a known cause or characteristic course but is rather a term of clinical convenience covering any impairment or impairments of neurologic functions due to brain injury dating from birth or early infancy. There are broad groupings of the problem which serve as well as any medical classification to distinguish the different types. Tony had the choreo-athetotic type. From the readings which Cayce gave him, the cause may have actually developed before birth.

Because of the difficulty in determining the cause of the problem, therapy has been at loose ends. Thus the aim of treatment at the present time is to help the child achieve his maximum potential rather than to become normal. Cayce takes a point of view in this particular case that such a therapeutic objective falls far short of the ideal. He implies that Tony could, in reality, get well, or at least normal enough to be considered well—able to control his body, his voice, his actions.

I am fascinated by Cayce's description of the problem this young man is given to deal with. He does not say it in so many words, but he points out that the difficulty stems from an improper distribution of nerves. The condition is congenital, he says, but able to be changed. The cerebrospinal nervous system is defective in that the nerves have, in a sense, sought out an incorrect distribution throughout the locomotory centers of the body. That is, those centers of the nervous system which are primarily responsible for receiving impulses from higher and from autonomic centers and relaying the coordinated impulses to the muscles in order that they will contract properly are, in this case, innervating the wrong tissues. It is a condition similar to a fouled-up telephone switchboard.

The nerves from the higher centers also appear to be involved in finding the improper distribution, the result being that when the child desires to say something, nerve impulses go everywhere except where they are intended. The individual must deal with a writhing, contorted mass of muscles and tissues that are undoubtedly utterly frustrating.

Cayce's answer to such a problem once again refers back to his recurring concept that man is a spiritual being with a mind that builds living as a material entity in a three-dimensional world. Sometimes man builds in the wrong direction, and he has destruction as the result. Cayce states that the body may be rejuvenated, it may undergo constant rebuilding until it is normal. He implies that the nerve cells, given the proper impetus, may establish new channels, seeking out their proper distribution, and in the process bringing about a cure for the condition. The mind, he points out, works through the nervous system, and given the proper impetus, can re-map the pathways for the nerves, re-establish the proper connections with the muscles, and re-connect to the autonomic centers which bring about coordination to the entire body in its functioning.

Cayce, then, saw Tony as an individual who might be "with careful study, an *ideal* patient, an *ideal* result." (5568-1) He went on in the next reading to say that if "those suggestions be followed as have been outlined, in a consistent manner . . . *many* will call this a miracle." In other words, it is difficult to understand anything other than that cerebral palsy in this one patient could be cured—if Cayce was right.

It is indeed unfortunate that we do not have adequate follow-up data to see what did happen to this boy. From my own experience in working with people with a difficult and chronic condition where little change can be seen in a short period of time, I would expect that the Castellos stopped working with Tony after they got home. It is a bother to give massages or infra-red lamp treatments or to use a wet-cell battery that must be applied in a certain way and must be refilled with water and other ingredients every month. It is discouraging. The only thing that keeps people going on such a program of therapy is a vision of what could be, a faith that such a cure can come about. The Castellos here had only Cayce's words. They did not have an understanding of the body, nor did they have the advantage of knowing that anyone else had ever successfully done this type of therapy for cerebral palsy. Many things were working against them.

This group of disadvantages calls to mind the comment that Cayce made when they asked him how long it would be before Tony got well. He responded that it depends on the way and the manner in which the body responds. Does that mean that, in this case, Tony's will had a part to play? It probably means that if Tony were to rebel against the therapy, it would not work. Cayce also stated in the same reading that the speed of Tony's recovery would depend on how much confidence is built in him so that he does not feel forced in the application of his therapy.

However, there is no follow-up evaluation on this boy. Thus we cannot say whether the therapy would have been fully effective or not. In all of his readings, Cayce seemed to imply that the healing process, or the activity of regeneration or repair, involved not only the therapy that was given but the attitudes, emotions, and thoughts of the patient himself and those who were taking care of him. These factors, interposed into the picture, make the success of every therapy program dependent upon the individuals who are involved. Perhaps this factor applies more to the serious, chronic diseases but also, to a lesser extent, to everything that is treated in a doctor's office.

A little boy's bruise will heal quickly if his mother kisses it soon after the accident. A laceration will be restored to normal more efficiently if the person suffering the injury is not afraid and tense at the time of the suturing. The examples are virtually inexhaustible.

The actual series of treatments which were suggested in the seven readings given for this boy are all directed at a rehabilitative effort that Cayce calls regeneration and rebuilding. They were all aimed at the functions of the body, for Cayce assumed throughout his life that normalized and vital functions will bring about normal structures and a resultant full state of health.

Tony was told that the external applications of a therapeutic nature had to be coordinated with the internal. In this instance, the external were the massages with various oils (but particularly olive oil) which would act as food for the muscles and tissues of the extremities and for the tendons of the muscular apparatus. A patient of ours recently told us that, when she was a baby, she was vomiting so badly that no one could get any food into her body. In those days they did not have intravenous feeding. Her parents massaged olive oil over her entire body, using excessive amounts, and she responded and was able to survive on the food that the oil provided until she was able to take nourishment by mouth. So the idea of food or nourishment in this manner is not outlandish. We simply do not see it often and do not think of it as being a possibility.

The internal applications that Cayce had reference to were the wet-cell battery which was described somewhat in a previous chapter. Cayce visualized the vibrations of the gold chloride being carried into the body through the application of the low voltage battery which produces about 15 millivolts of electricity. The two leads were to be applied mainly to the abdomen and one of the extremities.

Gentle manipulations by an osteopath; sun, sand, and plenty of fresh air; infrared lamp treatments (especially when not out on the beach because of inclement weather); sweats, if properly handled; and 2½ to 3 grains of quinine for four or five doses "to stir the liver and *rid* the *blood* of those *effects* of poisons by congestion." These were other suggestions for therapy which Tony was supposed to be given in a consistent, patient, and persistent manner. The doctors and the parents were to keep a good rapport with him and work with him gently in a way to encourage his optimism and his trust. Diet was to be of a general building nature.

The massages, Cayce directed, along with the sun, sand, and open air would create within the systems of the body a building of the blood and tissue which needed regeneration. The massage would have further effect when done more vigorously in producing greater stimulation to nerve endings in the muscles of the body. When the olive oil and cocoa butter massages were alternated every other evening—that is, having one massage every night—it would make for better rest for his body and also for improved activity of the centers for autonomic coordination, which are located along the spinal cord. The massages would also improve his ability to be more active in walking and getting about.

Tony's problem is one experienced by thousands of people throughout the United States, perhaps by millions throughout the world. Cayce had something definitive to say about what was wrong inside the body, not too much about why or how the disease came into being. He commented at length on the possibilities of regeneration, at least in some cases, to the point where normalcy would be the design. If he proved to be an accurate prophet, our understanding of the body and its capabilities will undergo considerable change in the foreseeable future.

CHAPTER 12

"FOR LIFE ITSELF IS A SERVICE"

by Mary Ellen Carter

"ESTHER! MRS. GOODBOND'S here to see us!"

"I wonder what for. Yes, I see the limousine has stopped out front."

Gordon Worth, 22, leaned forward on his cot by the window and nodded. "He's a new man, the driver." Gordon moved with effort. In recent weeks his arms and legs were quite useless.

The stranger, an older man, opened the car door for the woman within. Gordon smiled wryly: there was a man, perhaps twice his age, agilely performing what only months before had been his duties.

"My former employers didn't waste much time replacing me," said Gordon. "Well, I can't blame them."

The new driver assisted Mrs. Eldora Goodbond, smiling and cool-looking despite the city's July heat, from the car. She spoke to him briefly, then came lightly up the walk.

Gordon pulled himself up as best as he could, legs drawn up as they were by the gradual paralysis that had benumbed his limbs. "Esther . . ." he began, and suddenly found that he had no voice. *"Esther . . ."* he whispered.

Lately, he had even suffered loss of sight and hearing at times. He covered his face with his hand in despair.

Outside, the man who had taken his place glanced at the sky with 20/20 vision and listened to the song of a sparrow.

After pleasant exchanges of greetings, Eldora Goodbond turned a steady gaze to Gordon. "I see you are no better, Worth."

"No, ma'am. Even the specialists have as much as said I'll never be well." He managed to speak hoarsely.

"He can't write anymore, can't straighten out his legs!" Esther exclaimed.

"And sometimes I can't even yell at my wife," said Gordon. "You'd better keep that new man out there. Looks as if I won't be chauffeuring for anybody, ever again."

"Worth, listen to me. You've heard us discussing the psychic readings of Edgar Cayce."

Respectful silence.

"Well, I've asked for a reading for you. It's scheduled for September 11."

Gordon sighed heavily. "Yes, ma'am."

"You don't seem very excited. He's helped *us* through several illnesses, as you know."

Esther moved closer and took his hand. "We have no money to pay for a reading," she said.

"I have arranged for Worth's expenses, including his transportation."

Doubt mixed with gratitude in Gordon. "Thank you, Mrs. Goodbond. I'll repay you if ever I can." Inwardly, he thought, *I just don't believe, I can't believe!*

Esther found work in a dress shop so that they could maintain their modest home. Gordon's mother, who lived nearby, had come in to help care for him. About all she could do, however, was to administer the sedatives prescribed by his doctors.

His reading was given on September 11, as planned. They received word from Miss Gladys Davis that he was to be admitted to the hospital on October 5.

At the train station two black porters stepped from the southbound train to the platform. One of them, a rather large man, spotted Gordon as he was being helped from the limousine by the new chauffeur and another porter. The concerned black man came over and said, "I b'lieve I can carry him right to his berth."

Like a mother, he then gathered Gordon into his long arms, and Gordon grinned. "Now *that's* service!" he said as he was hoisted from the platform onto the train. There was an awkward moment as they turned through the narrow passage into the waiting car. Then the porter was bearing Gordon, who weighed 140 pounds to a lower berth.

"Just let me know if I can be of any more service, sir," said the smiling fellow.

"Thanks," Gordon nodded. Esther tipped him. To himself, he said, *I wonder if Gordon Worth can be of any more service?*

As the train pulled out of the station and Esther slipped from view, he began to ponder what his reading had said at the end: something about service—that without service to others, one could gain little.

Then why had God taken away his very power to serve?

First, there had been his replacement, the "old man" who was now the Goodbonds' chauffeur. Now he had been obliged to be carried like a baby by the kindly black porter . . . How he envied them both!

He lay quietly, submitting to the lull of the train's motion. He remembered the time when his body was young and strong. He had been sure of everything, taking life itself for granted. But what had the reading said? It had said that life itself was a *service*.

The thought was sinking into his consciousness as he fell asleep.

The next day, he was whisked from the Norfolk station out to Virginia Beach and up to his room. As he was wheeled to his bed, he was reassured by the cheerfulness and tidiness of the staff and the hospital itself. Treatment was begun at once.

His condition was very good in some respects, his reading had stated. He was warned that further inroads into his system would be harder to combat if not checked. The pain relievers he had been taking were probably what Cayce was referring to by the phrase "outside influence" which had "caused derangements in his system which prevented proper distribution of that assimilated."

In studying Gordon's case Lyman Lydic, D.O., meticulously followed the prescribed treatment. Osteopathy, diet, and mental suggestion were foremost: "proper resuscitating forces as may be guided by the inner man itself, through that of the mental and physical coordinating together."

Before diagnosing Gordon's entire condition, Cayce began the reading with: "Now, we find the conditions are abstruse in some respects as respecting the physical forces of the body. While in many respects conditions are very good, there are those conditions in the physical that, taking warning of in the present, will prevent further inroads or later developments as would be much *harder* to combat than that as has been existent through this inactivity of that assimilated in its proper sphere or manner."

Characteristically, Cayce diagnosed Gordon's entire state, finding the blood to be below normal. In the nerves he found "impingements in the cerebrospinal system as produced by exterior influences and the result of the bacilli as has been active—or was active in the system, especially in those centers just below the solar plexus, or that of the 9th, 10th, and 11th dorsal—these not only being for a cold internal system, as related to the assimilating forces of the system, but to the locomotory system those of a disturbance between the sympathetic and cerebrospinal, in the lower lumbar plexus.

"This prevents proper coordination in the sympathetic and cerebrospinal and makes for the activities in the lower portion of the body, becoming those of voluntary-involuntary in their reflex."

Reflexes to the sensory system led to improper reflexes in throat, hearing, and eyes. "In the functioning of the organs, themselves—This as has been seen or given—these are very good, save as to the reflexes to the sensory system which, being in that position of incoordination between the sympathetic and cerebrospinal and in the lower portion—makes for, in the cervical and those of the hypogastric and pneumogastric plexus, as they cross in the upper portion of the body, those reflexes that make for the over-activity, or an accentuation of the functioning of the organs, as is seen at times from the throat—or in voice and speech; at others in the hearing, again as seen from the eyes. *All* of these, in their respective cycle, *have* had, or *do* have, their improper reflexes."

Dr. Lydic began a program of weekly osteopathic correction with massage as prescribed: two general treatments to one adjustment. The corrective one was in the cerebrospinal system, lumbar, and dorsal regions; the general from the solar plexus upward.

The sinusidal reaction, a form of electro-therapy, would make for the high, not the low, vibration. It was to be administered in specific areas "making same conjunctive with that of the brachial centers, or in the 2nd and 3rd dorsal, and those of the lower portion of the lumbar, or that in the 4th and in the 1st sacral. These would be changed, to be sure, for a *direct* reaction—after there has begun to be adjustments made, and the application then would be of the 3rd and 4th cervical, and to the umbilicus plexus—just *below* the umbilicus. These would make for a direct reaction, which will change for the vibrations through those of the intestinal system, so that assimilations are in accord with the vibrations of the body, so that the blood supply and the blood building becomes the nearer normal in its reaction; taking also, internally, those of the properties as would be in compound, as in this. . . ." There followed a prescription which included distilled water, ambrosia leaves, prickly ash bark, dog-fennel or Mayblossom, and wild ginseng. This was to be reduced by simmering to one-half the quantity, strained, and added to 35 per cent alcohol, balsam of tolu, and tincture of Capsici.

This was to be taken in very small doses: half a teaspoon four times a day, twenty minutes before meals.

Diet was particularly important in Gordon's case. He was to have citrus fruits often for breakfast, in addition to oat meal or Wheatena, although Cayce warned elsewhere they should not be taken in the same meal with citrus.

Noon meals were to consist principally of raw vegetables, especially celery, lettuce, and tomatoes. Oil dressings with tapioca would aid digestion.

Evening meals were to include fish or juices of meats; well-cooked vegetables, using the peelings of white potatoes; yams or turnips rather than the pulp usually served. Iron was to be gained from spinach and kale, well-cooked, without any grease except butter.

Eliminations were to be aided mainly by his diet.

Then Cayce urged coordinating mental and physical healing. The one administering to Gordon, Dr. Lydic, should do so "in a gentle, quiet, easy way and manner. Blustering about the individual will only irritate. To scold, or to be too much of the commanding nature, is to destroy the better portion of that that may be builded in the body. Learn, or train the body—not only to be good, but be good *for* something. Let there be known there is a duty to self, and hope in service—for without service to the other, one may gain little in this experience in life's forces; for Life Itself *is* a service. *Use,* not abuse."

Finding such words were meant for *him,* finding the staff, Dr. Lydic, and Edgar Cayce himself taking a personal interest in him, Gordon responded gratefully. As he was benefitted by the healing service of others, he opened his mind and heart to be healed. To Gordon's brother-in-law, Edgar Cayce was later to write, "We all came to love Mr. Worth when he was here . . ."

Within one week, Gordon began responding dramatically to his treatment. He felt once more that his hands and arms were a part of him; his command over them returned to such an extent he was able to write letters home telling the good news. He was elated.

Within that same week, he struggled one day from his bed and found he had the use of his legs, however weak; he tottered with some amazement to the bathroom.

On October 14, a second reading was given. "There are changes in the physical forces of the body, as is indicated by the better use of the limbs, of the changes in the eliminations, and in the distribution of that as is assimilated. In the releasing of the pressures as have been apparent in the lumbar, the sacral, and especially the coccyx, we will find that nerve energy to extremities will be more active in its activities in the physical functioning of the body."

Cayce now advised saturated solutions or packs of epsom salts; after osteopathic treatments, Gordon should be exposed to violet ray.

"How long before improvement will be notice in legs?" was asked.

"In eight to twelve days."

On October 19, Eldora Goodbond wrote: "We are so glad Worth is making such wonderful progress. I think his case is an interesting one for the Hospital. Doctors have admitted their inability to help and his cure will be a comparatively fast one."

Sure enough, three weeks from the time he was admitted to the hospital, he was well enough to leave. He still needed treatment. "I was not well," he wrote to this writer in 1970, "but the hospital was uncertain, everyone talked of closing. Dr. Lydic left before I did."

The hospital was indeed going through anxious days. It was only a matter of months before it closed, following the stock market failure and its aftermath.

When Gordon stepped off the train in the city, the same porter was there to meet him. The porter's eyes rounded in disbelief. Then he broke out in great smiles. "You're walking!"

"With a cane, but I'm walking!"

Treatment was continued under Theodore Berger, D.O., during the winter of 1930–31, under the Goodbond's sponsorship.

"I am glad to tell you I am still gaining," Gordon wrote Edgar Cayce. "I weigh 170 . . . I can walk about a mile in a day, but of course I get awful tired . . ."

In his third reading, given December 1, Cayce stated that Gordon was still showing improvement. He was to have only one general osteopathic treatment a week and one massage with balsam of sulphur in the lumbar and sacral regions, being rubbed thoroughly along the limbs to the knees and ankles, as well as the hips. The masseuse was to follow the course of the muscles rather than the nerves. "We will find that more of the greater strength will be gained by the body through this mode of application. This may be given by any masseuse, or by one at home—will it be *thoroughly* done, see?

"Keep up the general diet as has been outlined.

"Exercise in the open as much as possible, but do not overtax nor strain self, and it will be found that in an earlier period than expected the body will be able to return to daily labors—or work—as is desired."

On February 9, Gordon, having continued on this basis, wrote that he was sending for a mental, physical, and spiritual reading. "I can never thank you enough for all you have done for me and I am sure I will continue to gain. Also I can never repay Mrs. Goodbond for getting my first reading and telling me about you."

He still had some numbness in his limbs, too quick pulsation, dizziness, congestion of the liver. This last was due to the liver "adjusting itself to the manner in which administrations for aid have been given, with cold making it more acute at times." Cayce prescribed a vegetable compound such as Castoria or syrup of figs for stirring the liver. Increased manipulations would also help.

His circulation was improving constantly. He was actually concerned with gaining weight too fast, so that Cayce replied to this question that he should leave off starches and, for the next 30 to 40 days, keep a diet restricted to lamb, nerve-building fruits, pineapple. He was to have no butter, taking everything in as near its normal state as possible without the addition of sugar. He was to have no potatoes of any kind. He was to decrease the refill of his prescription until it was gone. Gordon was to follow the work he had found to be in keeping with his natural tendencies.

"Will body's health be so can safely have children, and when?" Gordon asked.

"This, we find, will be better, so that the body may *beget* children, in an early portion of the present year—or in the latter portion of present year."

"Any advice regarding mental or spiritual body?"

"As the body has builded in the mental forces, this recuperation has begun. Keep an ideal and work towards same."

Gordon now recommended Cayce to his brother-in-law, who wrote Cayce to thank him for helping both Gordon and his own mother. "He (Gordon) is fine, working every day, and always talking about you."

As soon as he could manage it (May 5, 1931) Gordon was back at work on the Goodbonds' estate, seven months after starting treatment with Cayce.

Dr. Berger wrote in June: ". . . .in my opinion it is the most spectacular cure that has ever been effected through the readings. He was a helpless, hopeless cripple and is now doing hard, physical labor on the Goodbond place . . ."

In his own report, Gordon wrote: "I am writing this letter in appreciation for all you did for me . . . have not laid off one day since [going back to work] . . . I tell everyone how Mr. Cayce helped me . . . You can show this letter to anyone to prove the good you can do by your readings. As you know, when people first hear about a reading they cannot believe in it. I did not at first and I hope others who are sick will let you help them before waiting too long."

Esther and Gordon had a son born to them in 1933 and another in 1937. Together, they have built a successful farming enterprise. Today, Gordon Worth looks back and calls his cure "a miracle."

Medical Commentary: Paralysis

by William A. McGarey, M.D.

GORDON WAS ONLY twenty-two years old when this strange paralysis began in his body. He must have wondered—as apparently his doctors did—just what in the world was causing him to become a hopeless cripple with spastic legs, useless arm, at times unable to see or hear or talk. For a young man in the prime years of his early manhood, having held down a responsible job as a chauffeur, the frustration, the fear of disability must have been intense.

Perhaps it was this underlying emotional pattern that caused Cayce to put such strong emphasis on the manner in which Gordon was to be handled psychologically by those caring for him and, likewise, on the attitudes which the patient himself was instructed to develop.

There is no question today that we can shape our emotional patterns; that these patterns, which activated, are wholly consistent with the hormonal activity of our endocrine glands; and that hormone levels have a vital, irreplaceable role to play in any normal regeneration activity within the basic cellular structure of the human body.

Gordon apparently was receptive to the advice given him and was also apparently what we would think of as a sensitive, retentive individual—the type of person who would respond best to suggestions of a constructive nature. The admonition to him that all of life is a service must have struck a responsive chord and probably made possible the full rehabilitation that eventually came about.

The part of this story, however, that catches my medical fancy most grippingly is the paralysis itself, the nature of its inception, as Cayce described it, and the manner in which the repair process might come about.

As a general practitioner, I have not seen a large number of severe neurological problems. Today they usually end up in the hands of the neurologist or neurosurgeon. It would have been very helpful, in my opinion and for my purposes, if Gordon could have had a neurological workup to establish just what type of lesion, in the medical world of nomenclature, Cayce was dealing with.

There are dozens of different syndromes described in the neurology textbooks in which a condition has been observed often enough and identified sufficiently that it has been given a name. Often the name is that of the person who first described it as an entity, but the exact cause and the curative therapy program both often remain a mystery. Some of these conditions recover in a manner we

256

call "spontaneous." This means that the body brings about its own healing process in a manner we do not understand, or we would have aided the body in its activity.

Several years ago, I treated a man whose paralysis of the legs was determined by my neurological consultant to be a Guillain-Barre's syndrome or disease. You can look this term up in a convenient neurological textbook or medical dictionary. This patient was in his fifties, and the problem developed gradually. He did not have any spasticity, however, and he had no real sensory symptoms. It was caught fairly early, and a vigorous program of physical therapy, massage, and diet brought about a gradual restoration to his continued activity as a college professor. Gordon's difficulty did not fit this picture.

The problem Gordon had might be diagnosed from the story by a good neurologist; but to me, at least, this was a syndrome which, without therapy, would have made of the patient a lifelong cripple, with life expectancy markedly reduced. There seems to be little question of that.

But Cayce looked inside the body, saw pressures on nerve structures, saw deficiencies in nerve plexuses that needed replenishing, and could identify forces of the body that control the locomotory system of the body. Cayce saw incoordination as an individual affect between the cerebrospinal and the autonomic nervous systems of the body. As a psychic who could lie down and enter what we call an extended state of consciousness, Cayce could clairvoyantly look at these functions and forces and deficiencies much as we look at noses and ears and abdomens.

If indeed some of these rare neurological conditions are related in their etiology or in their abnormal physiology; if incoordination, lack of proper assimilation, pressures, and deficiencies are part and parcel of each; and if Cayce's clairvoyant qualities were accurate, we would have a thesis and an hypothesis upon which to build a system of rehabilitation that could turn some of the Gordons of this world into active, contributing members of society rather than the cripples that they may find themselves.

What *did* Cayce see about this young fellow and his inner workings?

He pointed out that there had been in times past an infection—or bacilli—present in the blood stream. This, plus other undescribed "external influences," had created impingements on the nerves of the cerebrospinal system arising in the ninth, tenth, and eleventh dorsal segments. As in all disease processes, one thing leads to another. Cayce saw two abnormalities arising from these impingements:

1. A "cold internal system" as related to the entire process of assimiliation in the body. I would assume he meant here the actual temperature of the stomach, esophagus, duodenum, spleen, liver, pancreas, and small intestine was actually below normal. This produced in turn a lack of proper substances, necessary for normal body sustenance, taken from the food. In other words, the body was being partially or specifically starved. This needed to be alleviated or a worse condition would develop.

2. An incoordination between the functioning of the cerebrospinal and the autonomic nervous systems. In hundreds of other readings Cayce described this condition as arising because of pressures in those areas where the two systems have their channels of communication—the recurrent branches of nerves at each spinal segment which connect the spinal cord to the sympathetic ganglia. When

the impulses flowing through these nerves are disturbed in their nature, frequency, or force, an incoordination comes about which might bring into being a variety of conditions, dependent on the state of being of the rest of the body.

In this particular case, nervous system incoordination created again two conditions:

1. A lower lumbar plexus incoordination as it affected the locomotory system, or simple muscular action in the legs. Cayce said it like this: This incoordination "makes for the activities in the lower portion of the body becoming those of voluntary-involuntary in their reflex" (a beautiful description of the spasticity found throughout the lower part of the body).

2. An effect in the sensory apparatus in its reflexes, in the eyes, ears, voice. Cayce saw the sensory nervous system as a unit in itself—in a true sense apart from the autonomic or cerebrospinal. Thus the voice, as related to that which hears the voice, is also a part of the sensory nervous system. He also described the sensory system as being more closely related in its reflexes to the autonomic nervous system than to the brain itself. This attitude is upheld by our observations of the manner in which the sound of music, for instance, can have a quieting effect on the feelings of a sensitive person and how one using words can induce hypnotically far-reaching physiological effects throughout the body. The touchstone soothes a person's disturbed feelings. The erotic picture, through the visual apparatus, brings about a sudden conditioned autonomic response. The examples are almost numberless in their variety.

Cayce described the incoordination here as bringing about an effect which is better quoted for its full impact:

> In the functioning of the organs themselves—this, as has been seen or given—these are very good, save as to the reflexes to the *sensory* system, which—being in that position of incoordination between the sympathetic and cerebrospinal in the lower portion—makes for, in the cervical and those of the hypogastric and pneumogastric plexus, as they cross in the upper portion of the body, those reflexes that make for the over-activity, or an accentuation of the functioning of the organs, as is seen at times from the throat—or in voices and speech; at other in the hearing again as seen from the eyes. *All* of those, in their respective cycles, *have* had, or *do* have, their improper reflexes. (53-1)

Cayce also described certain activities within the body that we do not as yet relate to causation or therapy, probably because we have not yet accepted them at the conscious level.

From Gordon's reading comes the suggestion that there are radial forces within the body that supply from certain centers the replenishing in the nerve and blood forces of the limbs or the extremities "in their activity." These centers are the lumbar and solar plexuses, especially, and they apparently radiate their activity through locomotory centers existing in various parts of the spinal cord. Whether this radiation is through the nervous system pathways or by a vibratory route through the finer vibratory body of the individual was not clarified in this reading. In other data found in the readings, however, the nature of the "vibratory body" was more fully discussed.

The key to recovery from this strange complex of conditioning appeared to be the supplying to the body the "incentives" in order that certain portions might respond in a way that would build the defective portions of the body. Balance, coordination, health, and strength might once again be the experience of the afflicted person. Cayce realized that some dietary suggestions had been followed and some manipulative procedures had been accomplished. Nevertheless, he added:

> . . . both of these, as we find, have been neglected in part; for with the releasing of pressures, unless there are the incentives given as would cause or produce a resuscitation of the forces as regulate the activity of the extremities—especially in the lumbar or solar plexus centers, radiating through those of the locomotories—these will *not,* just because the pressure is taken off at times, build—*without* that as would stimulate same *to* the point where there may be resuscitation for those centers where impingements have existed, and where there is still the lack of proper filling or supplying of nutriment for the proper activities. (53-1)

We find Cayce's therapy program designed to bring about a regeneration of the nerve forces and centers, a reactivation of the assimilation, and a gradual restoration of the physical body through:

1. Manipulation and massage
2. Dietary regime
3. Incentives given to the body in various ways: sinusoidal electrotherapy; ultraviolet treatments; violet ray therapy; suggestion therapy; Ginsengherbal mixture; epsom salts packs to the sacrum; balsam of sulfur rubs to the sacral and lumbar areas and down over the muscular pathways of the extremities; and exercise.

It is a complex story of physiological balances to be maintained while building up the total functional capacity of the body, but isn't it fascinating? And does it not give one the feeling that we are on the threshhold of finding new ways (or are they actually regained out of the records of antiquity?) to bring healing to the body, hope to the mind, and direction to the spirit of man on the earth?

Gordon had a right to be enthusiastic about his recovery—much as we have a right to be enthusiastic about healing the ills of mankind. Gordon, learned, perhaps, the meaning of service.

EDGAR CAYCE

ON DIET *and HEALTH*

by Anne Read, Carol Ilstrup,
and Margaret Gammon

CONTENTS

INTRODUCTION

IN THIS VOLUME we have some of the most practical data to be found in the Edgar Cayce readings. Three people, Margaret Gammon, Carol Ilstrup and Anne Read, have cooperated to put together *Edgar Cayce on Diet and Health*. Diet, from Edgar Cayce's point of view, is one of the essential considerations for happiness in an experience on Earth. His central theme is "The body is the temple of the soul." In a healthy body the soul is capable of greater service in most instances. His ideas for the development of greater sensitivity (increased ESP capacities) should be considered also. After you have adjusted to these suggestions for a more balanced diet for six months to a year you may be interested in more detailed studies of the special diets for greater psychic awareness—at that point get in touch with the Association.

—*Hugh Lynn Cayce*

FOREWORD

THE ARRANGEMENT OF this material and commentaries on it have been made by one who has been in food work for over fifteen years, and closely associated with nutritionists as well as the body of literature which daily comes to their desks to keep their knowledge up to date. A wealth of material has been available for correlation with the Edgar Cayce dietary data, but only a small proportion could be included here.

Almost all who consulted Edgar Cayce for physical readings (indicated in the text by "P" followed by the number recorded in the files at Virginia Beach) were given dietary suggestions, voluntarily or by request. Many who requested Life Readings (indicated by "L" and a file number) were also given directions for proper food suitable to the individual. This fact confirms the extraordinary scope of wisdom by which the body-mind-soul is seen to be interrelated, and the food intake an important factor in the whole. All dietary suggestions from readings for people with disease or physical ailments—even that of constipation or over-weight, common as they are—have, however, been eliminated in this booklet. Instead, selections have been made from the large body of information about the normal diet, or diet for normal people. Other information is available to members of the Association for Research and Enlightenment, at Virginia Beach.

In compiling this material from the Edgar Cayce readings, one is immediately struck by the high degree of conformance with the best of modern dietetic opinion—if one includes *research* and *trends of research*.

There is, of course, some disagreement. There is also disagreement between various findings of modern research. One set may contradict another, yet in the overall view even the most dedicated scientist holds a faith that the truth will eventually emerge, that apparently contradictory information will eventually be harmonized if it contains truth. The scientific attitude is that of "wait and see."

Just so, we also are inclined to wait and see. Meantime, we accept the information from the Edgar Cayce readings because in thousands of instances it proved beneficial and practical.

CHAPTER 1

PHILOSOPHY

PSYCHOSOMATIC MEDICINE IS the new "discovery" by the medical profession, by which a connection between mental attitude and bodily health is now acknowledged and even made respectable.

In the readings by Edgar Cayce, this spiritual and mental life are not separated from the physical. All three are one, the readings gave. The importance of treating the body considerately, even reverently, since it is the temple of the spirit, is stressed over and over again in the readings.

> The body of each entity is the temple of the living God. To live—to be—and to maintain bodily activity unto the glory of the Creative Forces— is the purpose of the entrance of each entity into material consciousness.
>
> *2981-L-1*

> Study those charts pertaining to keeping well-balanced in the chemical forces of the body. Not in such a way as to become a human pillbox, but rather to know the law and to keep it. *2981-P-2*

> There is as much of God in the physical as there is in the spiritual or mental, for it should be one! *69-P*

> Each soul is the temple of the living God. Thus be more mindful of the body for the body's sake, that it may be a better channel for manifesting spiritual truths. *2938-L-1*

> Urges arise, then, not only from what one eats, but from what one thinks—and from what one does about what one thinks and eats! Also from what one digests mentally and spiritually. *2533-L-4*

> *Mind is ever the builder.* That which the body-mind feeds upon is what it gradually becomes, *providing assimilation takes place.* Just as in the physical body digestion does not necessarily mean assimilation; neither in the mental body does it mean that what is read, heard or spoken to the body is assimilated by the mental body. *3102-P-1*

Interrelationships of nutritional factors in the body, as they pertain to assimilation and digestion, constitute an area in which scientists themselves admit lack of information and need for more light.

W. H. Sebrell, Jr., M.D., Director of the National Institute of Health, U.S. Public Health Service, discussed the relationship of these factors in a welcoming address before the National Food and Nutrition Institute in Washington, D.C. Dr. Sebrell lists these questions which call for answers:

1. How do the more than 50 presently known essential nutrients work in the healthy and sick organism?
2. How well does the individual utilize his food?
3. What is the interrelationship of nutrients in the body?

Dr. Sebrell poses two more questions that relate to the preceding three:

4. When and to what extent is *appetite* reliable in the selection of a balanced diet?
5. How often should the body get specific nutrients and in what relation to one another? The time factor may be more important than is now realized.

The fourth question will remind the reader of the "Appestat," a control area for appetite, located in the brain; a term first used by Dr. Norman Jolliffe in his book, *Reduce and Stay Reduced*. In the psychosomatic approach to the problem of obesity, the reason given for overeating is to obtain emotional satisfaction. The Cayce Readings also have something to say on this point.

> The body should keep that diet which the physical *needs* through its inmost desires, and not override those conditions by the will of the individual. For the inmost desires of the individual would—and do lead this physical body correctly. . . . It is only when these are *overridden* by self-aggrandizement, or when self's motives are for carnal excess or success of the physical—that the body becomes *enamored* with things that hinder it. Hold steady along the lines which lead to understanding of self, and so present the physical body that it may be holy and acceptable unto Him. Remember that the physical is the earthly temple of God, to whom one should give the very best. It is only a reasonable service that this be done.   *257-P-3*

What effect have the emotions upon digestion and assimilation? A direct effect, the readings declared:

> Be mindful of the diet that it is kept proper. Take time to eat and to eat the right thing. Then give time for the digestive forces to act, before becoming so mentally and bodily active as to upset the digestion.   *243-P-17*

True, the body should eat, and should eat slowly; yet when worried, overtaxed, or when the body cannot make a business of eating but is eating merely to pass away the time, or just to fill up time—it is not good. For, the food will not digest, as the body sees.   *900-D-311,2*

Especially with this body, there should not be any food taken when the body is over-wrought in any way—whether caused from high-strung conditions, from wrath, or from depression of any kind. It is preferable at such times to take water or buttermilk. Never take sweet milk under such conditions.   *243-P-4,5*

It is a great detriment to better physical functioning to overload the stomach when the body is worried or under any general strain. Equally bad for the body is to take foods whether or not there is felt the need or desire for them.   *277-P-1*

Never when under strain, very tired, very excited, or very mad should the body take foods into the system. And never take any food that the body finds is not agreeing with same.   *137-D-15*

CHAPTER 2

"FROM THE READINGS"

"THE BODY IS the temple of the living God." This idea, told repeatedly in the Bible, is reiterated and enlarged upon throughout the Cayce readings. If we would keep that temple in such a condition as to glorify the Maker, it is imperative that we learn and adhere to certain laws, certain rules in regard to the nutritional needs of the body. For,

We are, physically and mentally, what we eat and what we think.   *288-38*

Vitamins and Minerals

The need for vitamins and minerals is now widely recognized, as is much concerning their functions and sources. The readings, however, add a great deal to our understanding of these and how they may be supplied. Vitamins, one reading explains, are

the Creative Forces working with body energies for the renewing of the body.   *3511-1*

Another explains that they are food for the glands, or

> that from which the glands take those necessary influences to supply the
> energies to enable the various organs of the body to reproduce themselves.
>
> *2072-9*

The glands, it is further explained, control the supply of materials for rebuilding
or reproducing the various tissues in the body, while vitamins are elements or
forces required for enabling each organ to carry on in its creative function or
generative activity.

The readings supply some little-recognized facts concerning functions of
various vitamins: for example, Vitamin A in addition to other functions, is
important for nerves, bone and the brain force; B, in addition to facilitating the
functioning of the nerves, also supplies

> to the chyle that ability for it to control the influence of fats, which is
> necessary . . . to carry on the reproducing of the oils that prevent the
> tenseness in the joints, or that prevent the joints from becoming atrophied
> or dry, or to creak. *2072-9*

They also say that a part of the function of C is to supply

> the necessary influences to the flexes of every nature throughout the body,
> whether of a muscular or tendon nature, or a heart reaction, or a kidney
> contraction, the batting of the eye or the supplying of the saliva and the
> muscular forces in face. *2072-9*

and that a C deficiency results in

> bad eliminations from the incoordination of the excretory functioning of
> the alimentary canal, as well as the heart, liver and lungs, through the
> expelling of those forces that are a part of the structural portion of the body.
>
> *2072-9*

From the foregoing it would seem that the vitamins may be even more important
than we had realized, but we are told also that vitamins are only a combination
of basic elements found in the body,

> give a name, mostly for confusion, by those who would tell you what
> to do for a price. *2533-6*

and we are then warned against taking supplementary vitamins over long periods
of time, lest the body, if it comes to rely upon these, cease to produce them in
the body, even though the food values are kept balanced. Conversely, there may
be an over-abundance of vitamins, and unless

> activities physical of the body are such as to put same into activity they
> become as drosses and set themselves to become operative irrespective
> of other conditions *341-31*

In such cases these unused vitamins act very much as bacilli and are destructive to tissue, affecting the plasma of the blood supply or the emunctory and lymph.

In most instances the readings agree with accepted dietary opinion as to which foods are rich in vitamins—and among the fruits and vegetables especially, those that are yellow in color—yellow peaches and apples, squashes, carrots, citrus fruits, etc. They add, however, some facts not generally recognized:

> Quite a dissertation might be given as to the effect of tomatoes upon the human system. Of all the vegetables, tomatoes carry most of the vitamins in a well-balanced assimilative manner for the activities in the system. Yet if these are not cared for properly, they may become very destructive to a physical organism, that is, if they ripen after being pulled, or if there is the contamination with other influences . . . The tomato is one vegetable that in most instances (because of the greater uniform activity) is preferable to be eaten after being canned, for it is then much more uniform.
>
> *584-5*

The value of gelatin in the diet is recognized, but the reasons for its benefits have been somewhat of a puzzle to nutritionists, since the amount of energy it supplies is out of proportion to the caloric value of its known elements. The readings give this explanation:

> It isn't the vitamin content [in gelatin] but it is ability to work with the activities of the glands, causing the glands to take from that absorbed or digested the vitamins that would not be active if there is not sufficient gelatin in the body . . . There may be mixed with any chemical, that which makes the rest of the system susceptible or able to call from the system that needed. It becomes, then, as it were, 'sensitive' to conditions. Without it [the gelatin] there is not that sensitivity.   *849-75*

Methods of preparing food may preserve or destroy much of the vitamin content. Thus fresh foods should, of course, be used as fresh as possible. Frozen vegetables, the readings say, have usually lost much of their vitamin content

> unless there is the reinforcement in them when they are either prepared for food or when frozen.

There is the possibility, of course, that this was true only of the slow-freezing methods of that time (year 1942) and may not hold true with the flash-freezing methods used commercially at present. Fruits, however, it is stated, lose little of their vitamin content by freezing. Cooking foods quickly by the steam pressure method, the readings relate, preserves the vitamins. (Contrary to some nutritional opinions.) (See 462-14 and 340-31.) Also recommended is cooking in Patapar paper, a parchment paper, in order to preserve the juices containing much of the vitamin value. (See 1963-2 and 1196-7.) One reading, emphasizing the need for more Vitamin B-1, said:

> All of the vegetables cooked in their own juices, and the body eating the
> juices with same. 2529-1

The need for certain minerals was given in numerous readings. Often mentioned are calcium, phosphorus, and iron. While all the minerals are undoubtedly of importance, these were evidently most often found to be insufficient in the diets of those for whom physical readings were given, and we may assume that they are often lacking in the average diet.

> Keep plenty of those foods that supply calcium to the body. These we
> would find especially in raw carrots, cooked turnips and turnip greens,
> all characters of salads—especially as of water cress, mustard and the
> like—these especially taken raw. 1968-6

When there is fowl taken—that is of chicken, goose, duck, turkey or the like—chew the bony pieces or make broths of them (808-15). Milk and milk products rich in calcium are highly recommended.
One individual was told:

> Preferably the raw milk, if it is certified milk. 275-25

Another reading, given 1/17/44, for a two-year-old child, warned, however:

> Raw milk—provided it is from cows that don't eat certain characters of
> food. If they eat dry food, it is well. If they eat certain types of weeds
> or grass grown this time of year, it won't be so good for the body. 2752-3

> The phosphorus forming foods are principally carrots, lettuce (rather
> the leaf lettuce, which has more soporific activity than the head lettuce),
> shell fish, salsify, the peelings of Irish potatoes, and things of such
> natures . . . Citrus fruit juices, plenty of milk, the Bulgarian buttermilk
> (Yogurt) is the better . . . or the fresh milk that is warm with animal
> heat, which carries more of the phosphorus. 560-2

> Let the iron be rather taken in the foods (instead of from medicinal
> sources) as it is more easily assimilated from the vegetable forces. 1187-9

Foods high in iron are spinach, lentils, red cabbage, berries, raisins, liver, grapes, pears, onions and asparagus.

> Concerning sources of minerals in general, or in combination, these are given:

> Cereals that carry the heart of the grain, vegetables of the leafy kind,
> fruit and nuts. 1131-2

Rolled or cracked wheat, not cooked too long, is recommended to add to the body the proper proportions of iron, silicon and vitamins necessary to build up the blood supply that makes for resistance in the system.   *840-1*

And the almond (recommended in several readings to guard against or counteract a tendency toward cancer)

carries more phosphorus and iron in a combination easily assimilated than any other nut.   *1131-2*

Physiological Effects of Foods

In recommending specific foods, the readings attributed to them certain physiological effects. Some of these may be due to little-understood effects of the vitamins they contain; others apparently have effects aside from vitamin or mineral content.

Raw green peppers are better in combinations than by themselves. Their tendency is for an activity to the pylorus: not the activity in the pylorus itself, but more in the activity from the flow of the pylorus to the churning effect upon the duodenum in its digestion. Hence it is an activity for digestive forces. Peppers, then, taken with green cabbage, lettuce, are very good for this body, taken in moderation.   *404-6*

Beef juice taken in small sips, more than one person was told,

will work toward producing the gastric flow through the intestinal system; first, in the salivary reactions to the very nature of the properties themselves; second, with the gastric flow from the upper portions of the stomach or through the cardiac reaction at the end of the esophagus that produces the first of the lacteal's reaction to the gastric flows in the stomach or digestive forces themselves; thirdly, making for an activity through the pylorus and the duodenum that becomes stimulating to the activity of the flows without producing the tendencies for accumulation of gases.   *1100-10*

Meats, especially glandular meats such as calf's liver, brains and tripe, were advised for their "blood-building properties." More often, however, "Fish, fowl, and lamb, never fried," were recommended. Fowl prepared in such a way that "more of the bone structure itself" is used was given, not only for the actual calcium content of the bones but also "that better reaction for the assimilation of calcium through the system is obtained."   *1523-8*

Another reading (5069-1) also stated that "chewing the bones will be worth more to the body in strengthening and in the eliminations" and added that when these are stewed the lid should be kept on so that "the boiling will not carry off that which is best to be taken."

Cooked long enough in a pressure cooker, the bones become dissolved.

Certain vegetables were recommended for their effect in protecting the body against communicable diseases.

> Plenty of lettuce should always be eaten by almost everybody; for this supplies an effluvium in the blood stream itself that is a destructive force to most of those influences that attack the blood stream. It's a purifier.
>
> *404-6*

Raw vegetables, such as tomatoes, lettuce, celery, spinach, carrots, beet tops, mustard greens and onions were said to

> make for the purifying of the humour in the lymph blood—as this is absorbed by the lacteal ducts as it is digested.   *340-1*

Cooked onions and beets were also said to be blood purifiers.

A food which can be used to "cleanse all toxic forces from any system" is "raw apples when taken alone, no other food for three days, then followed with olive oil. (Half a cup)"   *820-2*

Raw apples, under other circumstances, however, were advised against, unless eaten, say, between meals with no other food. (See 830-2 & 567-7.)

That portion of carrots close to the top carries "the vital energies which stimulate the optic reactions between kidneys and the optics."   *3051-6*

Peelings of potatoes are said to be "strengthening, carrying those influences that are active with the glands of the system."   *820-2*

These influences or "vital energies" referred to may also be the vitamins, minerals, or both.

"Vegetables," one reading notes, "will build gray matter faster than will meats or sweets."   *900-386*

Jerusalem artichokes were recommended for a number of individuals with diabetes with the explanation that they carry those properties that have

> an insulin reaction that will produce a cleansing for the kidneys as well as producing the tendency for the reduction of the excess sugar.   *480-39*

One individual was also told that these would

tend to correct those inclinations for the incoordination between the
activities of the pancreas as related to the kidney and bladder.   *1523-7*

These were never recommended in large amounts, but one about the size of a
hen's egg at a time; in some cases once a day, in others once or twice a week,
and alternately raw and cooked.

Perhaps the strangest or least understood physiological effect of foods spoken
of, and one repeated in many readings, is the effect of eating foods grown in
the vicinity where the body resides, rather than those shipped in. This "prepares
the system to acclimate itself to any given territory (3542-1). And will more
quickly adjust a body to a particular area or climate than any other thing." Further,
this is more important than "any specific set of fruit, vegetables . . . or what not.
4047-1

Acid and Alkaline Balance

Readings frequently emphasized the importance of maintaining the correct
balance of acid and alkaline reactions in the body through the kinds and combinations of foods taken. Though "an over-alkalinity is much more harmful than
a little tendency occasionally for acidity" (808-3), apparently it is much more
rare, the emphasis throughout being on more of alkaline-reacting foods.

In response to a question asked concerning common contagious diseases, this
answer was given:

> If an alkalinity is maintained in the system—especially with the lettuce,
> carrots, and celery, these in the blood supply will maintain such a condition
> as to immunize a person.   *480-19*

Colds are often the result, according to the readings, of an unbalancing of the
alkalinity of the system:

> Cold cannot—does not exist in alkalines.   *808-3*

How to maintain the correct balance, "about 20% acid to 80% alkaline-producing," (1523-3), sufficiently alkaline yet not too much so?

> The less activities there are in physical exercise or manual activity, the
> greater should be the alkaline reacting foods taken. Energies or activities
> may burn acids;—but those who lead the sedentary life or the non-active
> life can't go on sweets or too much starches . . . these should be well
> balanced.   *798-1*

An over-acidity may be produced by overeating of sweets, especially before
sufficient food has been taken at meals.

> The acidity is produced by taking too much sugar in the system in candies,

and in those properties as were taken before the stomach was filled with foods, and then overloading the system at such times (294-86), or by combining sweets and starches (340-32), or several starches at the same meal.   *416-18*

An abundance of vegetables and fruits, especially citrus fruits, helps to maintain the alkalinity of the system. Lemons especially are a good alkalizer, and the readings consistently recommend adding a little lemon juice (or lime) to orange juice. (See 2072-3.) Vegetables should be in the proportions of three that grow above the ground to one that grows below the ground, and one leafy vegetable to every one of the pod vegetables.

Sweets and Chocolate

Although warning is frequently given against an excess of sweets in the diet, some are said to be necessary "to form sufficient alcohol for the system" (487-11). Or, as stated in one reading:

the forces in sweets to make for the proper activity through the action of the gastric flows are as necessary as body-building [elements], for these become body-building in making for the proper fermentation (if it may be called so) in the digestive activities.   *808-3*

The kind of sweets is important, as well as the amounts. Those sweets recommended were grape sugars, beet sugars, raw cane sugars and honey, especially in the honeycomb. Date sugar too is now available, another natural sweetening. One reading recommended:

Chocolates that are plain, not those of any brand that carry corn starches, should be taken—or not those that carry too much of the cane sugar.
                                                                    487-11

Several later readings, however, warned against chocolates during the war years. Said one, given in 1944, "Chocolate that is prepared in the present is not best for any diet." (4047-1)

The "Do Not's"

One individual was advised, "then, it is well that the body not become as one that couldn't do this, that or the other; or as a slave to an idea of a set diet" (1568-2). Nevertheless, the readings frequently recommended that certain foods and combinations of foods be avoided.

Starches and sweets except in small amounts, should not be taken at the same meal, nor should there be several starchy foods taken together, since this produces too much acidity in the system. Neither should bread and other starches that grow above the ground be taken with meats. Potatoes, especially the peelings of same, are preferable to breads with meats.

That citrus fruits should not be taken with cereals was a consistent warning. One reading gave this explanation:

> for this changes the acidity of the stomach to a detrimental condition. For citrus fruits will act as an eliminant when taken alone, but when taken with cereals they become as weight, rather than as an active force in the gastric forces of the stomach itself.   *481-1*

> Coffee or tea should not be taken with milk or cream, for this is hard on the digestion.   *5097-1*

From the information given in different readings, apparently the effect of coffee or tea alone varies—for some individuals being harmful, but not for others.

Onions and radishes (raw) should not be taken at the same meal with celery and lettuce, one individual was told, though either might be taken at different times. (See 2732-1.)

> Oysters should never be taken with whiskey, as this produces a chemical reaction that is bad for most stomachs.   *2583-1*

Fried foods should never be eaten, according to the readings, nor vegetables cooked with bacon or fats. Canned foods containing superficial or artificial preservatives should be avoided. Benzoate of soda was specifically mentioned as one of these. Carbonated drinks in most cases were warned against, being referred to as "slop" (5545-2), nor should cane sugar in quantities be used.

Warning is given against using some foods cooked in aluminum, especially where a "disturbed hepatic eliminating force" exists. (1196-7). For this "produces a hardship upon the activities of the kidneys as related to the lower hepatic circulation, or [affects] the uric acid that is a part of the activity of the kidneys in eliminating same from the system" (843-7).

Specifically mentioned were tomatoes, or cabbage:

> There are some foods that are affected in their activity by aluminum, especially in the preparation of certain fruits, or tomatoes, or cabbage. But most others it is very well.   *1852-1*

Many readings recommended that bananas not be eaten, unless, like raw apples, alone, uncombined with other food.

When rabbits are cleaned, "be sure the tendon in both left legs is removed, or that might cause a fever" (2514-4).

Warnings were repeatedly given against eating pork, except for a little crisp breakfast bacon occasionally. One individual was told of the result, in his or her case, of eating pork:

> The character of dross it makes in the body-functioning causes a fungi that produces in the system a crystallization of the muscles and nerves in portions of the body . . . These distresses began as acute pain, rheumatic or neuritis . . . This is pork—the effect of same.   *294-41*

Red meats, or heavy meats not well cooked, were frequently warned against— while fish, fowl, and lamb were recommended, and wild game, properly prepared, was said to be preferable to other meats. (See 2514-4.)

Meat—To Eat or Not To Eat

Whether an individual should eat meat or abstain has long been a disputed question among health-minded and spiritual-minded individuals. The attitude of the readings on this subject was definite and consistent. One individual was told:

> Meats of certain characters are necessary in the body building forces in this system and should not be wholly abstained from in the present. Spiritualize those influences, those activities, rather than abstaining.
>
> *295-6*

Another reading had this to say:

> This, to be sure, is not an attempt to tell the body to go back to eating meat. But do supply, then, through the body forces, supplements, either in vitamins or in substitutes. This is necessary for those who would hold to these [vegetarian] influences . . .
>
> But purifying of mind is of the mind, not of the body. For, as the Master gave, it is not that which entereth in the body, but that which cometh out, that causes sin. It is what one does with the purpose; for all things are pure in themselves and are for the sustenance of man—body, mind and soul. And remember, these must work together.   *5401-1*

Attitudes and Emotions

What importance do attitudes and emotions have in relation to foods? Much, according to the readings. That strong emotions such as anger, fear, or worry have an adverse effect upon the digestive system is well known, and confirmed in the readings to the extent that they advise, "Never when under strain, very tired, very excited or very mad, should the body take foods into the system" (137-30).

But the readings go further concerning the effect of attitude upon the assimilation of food and what mind "as a builder" accomplishes in constructing the body. Thus,

As to what you eat, see it doing what you would have it do.

Now the question is often considered as to why there are different effects under different conditions, from use of vegetable, mineral, or combination compounds. The difference is in the consciousness of the individual body. Give one a dose of clear water, with the impression that it will act as salts—and how often will the water act in that manner. It is the same with impressions to the whole organism. For each cell of the blood stream, each corpuscle, is a whole universe in itself.

One who fills the mind, the very being, with an expectancy of God will see His movement, His manifestation, in the mind and sun, the earth and flowers—the inhabitants of the earth. And so, as the body is built, is the food taken just to gratify an appetite? Or to fulfill a purpose, make it better able to magnify what the body-mind-soul has chosen to stand for?

Thus it will not matter so much what is eaten, or where or when; but just knowing it is consistent with what is desired to be accomplished through the body—that does matter!

As has been given of old—(Daniel 1:5-17). The children of Israel stood with the sons of the heathen, and all ate from the king's table; and that which was taken exercised the imagination of the body in physical desires; strong drink, strong meats, condiments that magnify desires within the body. And these, as Daniel well understood, built not for God's service. He chose, rather, that the everyday common food would be given, so that the body and mind might be a more perfect channel for the manifestations of God. For the Creator's forces are in every force and made manifest in the earth.   *341-31*

May we, as Daniel, choose that which will build such a temple to serve, magnify, and glorify God!

CHAPTER 3

THE NORMAL DIET

WHAT IS A good everyday diet to follow, which will promote good health and keep the individual as a body-mind-spirit *unit* functioning on a high level? We are not born with this knowledge; we must learn it. The Edgar Cayce readings contribute a great deal of information to enlarge our understanding.

For purposes of comparison, let us first consider the *Basic 7* Food Groups which have been established as a guide for a normal daily diet by the Bureau of Human Nutrition and Home Economics, Agricultural Administration of the U.S. Department of Agriculture.

In the leaflet, *National Food Guide,* the *Basic 7* food groups are outlined, and people are advised to eat foods daily from all seven categories. By doing this, we obtain food elements that (1) yield energy; (2) supply materials for growth and upkeep; and (3) keep the body in good running order.

Here is the list of *Basic 7;*

1. Leafy, Green and Yellow Vegetables—One or more servings daily.
2. Citrus Fruit, tomatoes, raw cabbage and other high Vitamin C foods—One or more servings daily.
3. Potatoes and other vegetables and fruit—Two or more servings daily.
4. Milk, Cheese and ice cream:
    Children through teen ages—3 to 4 cups of milk daily.
    Adults—2 or more cups of milk daily.
    Pregnant woman—At least 1 quart of milk daily.
    Nursing mother—About 1-1/2 quarts of milk daily.
5. Meat, Poultry, Fish—One serving daily.
    Eggs—4 or more a week.
    Dried beans, peas, nuts, peanut butter—2 or more servings a week.
6. Bread, flour, cereals—whole-grain enriched or restored—every day.
7. Butter and fortified margarine—some daily.

The Edgar Cayce readings do not of course classify foods into such a *Basic 7* scheme, yet they do agree with the ideal of variety and balance in daily food elements needed. The readings emphasize certain ideas in regard to daily food selections, from which we might put together these seven points:

1. Eat more fruits and vegetables
2. Watch the Acid-Alkaline balance in the body
3. Avoid certain food combinations
4. Keep a balance between foods grown above and below ground
5. Eat lightly of heavy meats; use fish, fowl and lamb plus eggs and milk
6. Use whole-grain cereals and such products exclusively
7. Avoid fried foods; use fat sparingly

Before citing extracts from the readings to illustrate the above points and compare with the *Basic 7,* we wish to have the reader realize that each reading covered a wide scope. Thus there is a "spillover" of subject matter which is interesting for correlation, and more helpful than if points were isolated.

Fruits and Vegetables

The readings placed the greatest emphasis upon foods in the first three categories of the *Basic 7:* fruits and leafy, green, yellow tomatoes, citrus fruits, etc.

Do *include* often in the diet raw vegetables, prepared in various ways, not merely as a salad, but scraped or grated and combined with gelatin.

3445-P-1

Often have raw vegetables such as celery, lettuce, carrots and watercress. Prepare these often with gelatin. Do not throw away the juices when grating or preparing any of these, but include the juices in the gelatin, to obtain a greater amount of necessary vitamins.   *3413-P-1*

Eat plenty of raw as well as cooked carrots. Have plenty of lettuce, and tomatoes in moderation—also raw cabbage occasionally . . . Do not eat too much potatoes, but more of the skins. Eat plenty of onions, raw as well as cooked; and plenty of the legumes such as peas and beans.

480-P-47

Eat more vegetables! The leafy variety would be preferable to those of the pod nature such as dried beans or peas, or the like.   *1657-P-1*

The Acid-Alkaline Balance

The readings recognized the fact that a normal diet may vary with individuals. Some are more active than others. In adjusting the diet to greater or less activity, it is very important to consider striking a balance between foods that produce acid and foods that produce alkaline. Most vegetables are alkaline-reacting; so are most fruits except prunes and cranberries. The readings give the ideal balance, as follows:

Question: What should the diet be?

Answer: It should consist of those foods which will not create too much of an acid nor too much of an alkaline condition throughout the system. It would be better (for this body) to have more of the alkaline-producing than of the acid-producing foods.   *140-P-5*

In all bodies, the less activity in respect to physical exercise or manual activity, the greater should be the amount of alkaline-reacting foods taken. Energies or activities may burn acids; but those who lead a sedentary or nonactive life cannot go on sweets or too many starches. These foods (alkaline and acid-producing) should be carefully balanced.   *798-P-1*

Question: What foods are acid-forming for this body?

Answer: All of those that combine fats with sugars. Starches naturally incline toward an acid reaction. But a normal diet is about 20 percent of acid-producing foods to 80 percent of alkaline-producing.   *1523-P-3*

Have a percentage of 80 percent alkaline-producing to 20 percent acid-producing foods in the diet. It is well, however, that the body not become as one who can't ever do this, that or the other—or as a slave to an idea of a set diet! But do not take citrus fruit juices and cereals at the same meal. Do not take milk or cream in coffee or in tea. Do not eat fried foods of any kind. Do not combine white bread, potatoes, spaghetti, or any two foods of such natures, in the same meal.   *1458-P*

As indicated, keep the tendency toward alkalinity in the diet. This does not mean there should never be any acid-forming foods in the diet—for over-alkalinity is much more harmful than a little tendency toward acidity occasionally. But remember that there are tendencies in this system toward cold and congestion . . . and cold cannot, does not exist in alkalines.   *808-P-3*

The diet should be more body-building; that is, contain less of the acid foods and more of the alkaline-reacting foods. Milk and all its products should be a portion of the body's diet now; also those food values making for an easy assimilation of iron, silicon, and those elements or chemicals found in all kinds of berries, almost all kinds of vegetables that grow under the ground, almost all of the vegetables of a leafy nature. Fruits and vegetables, nuts and the like should form a greater part of the regular diet in the present . . . Keep closer to the alkaline diet; using fruits, berries and vegetables—particularly those carrying iron, silicon, phosphorus and the like.   *480-P-17*

In an alkaline system there is less effect of cold and congestion.   *270*

Food Combinations

On the question of food combinations as such—some good, some bad—we come to a debatable or controversial point in respect to opinions held by authorities in the nutrition field. Medical and scientific opinion at the present time seems to be divided: some authorities scoff, others are violently *pro.* The pendulum appears to swing to and fro in this matter. The reader will probably recall a number of widely publicized books on diets for arthritis, etc. which are based primarily on the use of food combinations.

The Edgar Cayce readings greatly stress the value of some food combinations, and the harm of others. We believe that as research proceeds to discover how the human body uses the foods given it, the basic soundness of the Edgar Cayce approach will be verified.

As we find, there . . . an unbalancing in the alkalinity of the system. Not an unbalancing produced by the foods themselves, but rather by the manner of their combination. For as indicated, starches and sweets should not be taken at the same meal—or at least, not so much taken together. That's why it is that ice cream is so much better for a body than pie which combines starches and sweets.   *340-P-31*

Question: What foods can be used with citrus fruits to make a complete meal?

Answer: Any foods that may be eaten at any time, save whole-grain cereals.

2072-P-9

Question: Are a quart of milk a day and orange juice every day helpful?

Answer: Orange juice and milk are helpful, but these should be taken at opposite ends of the day and not together.   *274-P-6*

Question: What foods should I avoid?

Answer: It is rather the *combination* of foods that makes for disturbance with most physical bodies, as with this one.

In its office activities in its present surroundings, preferably use those foods which tend toward greater alkaline reaction. Hence avoid combinations where corn, potatoes, rice, spaghetti or the like are all taken at the same meal . . . all of which tend to make for too great a quantity of starch—especially (undesirable) if any meat is taken at such a meal. If no meat is taken, the reaction of these starches is quite different. For the gastric flow in the digestive system is of such kinds that one reaction of the gastric flow is required for starch and another for proteins—and still another for digesting carbohydrates combined with starches of such kinds. In the combinations, then, do not eat great quantities of starch along with proteins or meats. Sweets and meats taken at the same meal are preferable to starches and meats. Of course, small quantities of breads are all right with sweets, but not in large quantities.

Also do not combine acid-reacting fruits with starches other than whole wheat bread! That is: citrus fruits, oranges, apples, grapefruit, limes or lemons—or even tomato juice. And do not have cereals—which contain a greater quantity of starch than most—at the same meal with citrus fruits.   *416-B*

A comment on the preceding extract is in order, since it is a rule given by most reducing diets not to eat two starches at the same meal. Another reason for not "filling up with starches" is of course that we should not crowd out of the meal the leafy green and yellow vegetables and fruits which we need. The normal diet is thus one which nourishes the body properly but does not overbalance it towards overweight or underweight.

On the subject of food combinations, here is an idea which is probably new to those working in the science of modern dietetics and food research. At least, we believe so for we have never seen any allusion to it. It is that lemon or lime juice be added to other citrus fruit juices.

> It will be much better if you add a little lime juice to the orange juice, and a little lemon juice to the grapefruit juice. Not too much, but a little. It will be much better and act much better with the body. For many of these are hybrids, you see.   3525-P-1

> When orange juice is taken, add lime or lemon juice to it: four parts orange juice to one part lime or lemon.   3823-P-2

> Take plenty of citrus fruit juices. . . . With the orange juice, put a little lemon juice—that is, for a glass of orange juice put about two squeezes from a good lemon . . . so that there is up to a half teaspoonful of lemon juice added. And with grapefruit juice, put a liitle lime juice—about eight to ten drops. Stir these together well before taking, of course.   2072-P-2

> Take whole grain cereals or citrus fruits juices, though not at the same meal. When using orange juice, combine lime with it. When using grapefruit juice, combine lemon with it—just a little.   1523

Here is another idea involving food combinations which is emphasized in the Edgar Cayce readings but not found elsewhere: a judicious use of vegetables growing above the ground versus those growing below the ground. The readings gave no explanation for this distinction; perhaps no one asked for it. At any rate, it seems to be an important point to be considered for normal diets as well as diets recommended in the readings for various bodily ailments.

> A normal diet . . . use at least three vegetables that grow above the ground to one that grows under the ground.   3373-P-1

> Have at least one meal each day that includes a quantity of raw vegetables such as cabbage, lettuce, celery, carrots, onions and the like. Tomatoes may be used in their season. Do have plenty of vegetables grown above the ground—at least three of these to one grown below the ground. Have at least one leafy vegetable to every one of the pod vegetables taken.
> 2602-P-1

Meats

Whether or not to eat meat was one of the questions often asked in the question period of a reading. The answers showed insight into the purposes and ideals of the questioners; at the same time pointing out the need of the body for protein.

> This, to be sure, is not an attempt to tell the body to go back to eating meat. But then do supply to the body forces either vitamin supplements or meat substitutes. This is necessary for those who hold to vegetarian

influences. . . . But purifying of the mind is *of the mind,* not *of the body.* For as the Master gave, it is not that which entereth into the body but that which cometh out that causes sin. It is what one does with the purpose that matters. For all things are pure in themselves and are for the sustenance of man—for his body, mind and soul. Remember, these must be allowed to work together . . .   *5401-P-1*

Question: Should the body abstain from meats for its best spiritual development?

Answer: Meats of certain kinds are necessary for the body-building forces in this system and should not be wholly abstained from in the present. Spiritualize those influences and those activities, rather than abstaining from meat. For as He gave, that which cometh out, rather than that which goeth in, defileth the spiritual body.   *295-P-6*

Scientific opinion is definitely in favor of eating meat for body-building, repair and maintenance of repair functions; and to obtain vitamins, especially vitamin B; for minerals, especially phosphorus and iron; and for the important amino acids which are now being intensively investigated and fitted into the dietary pattern.

Meat is a "complete protein" as are poultry, fish and eggs mentioned in No. 5 of the *Basic 7* food divisions. A "complete protein" is one that contains all the *essential* amino acids (needed by the body to manufacture others) in quantities readily usable by the body.

The Edgar Cayce readings stress the use of meat in moderation, especially certain kinds of meat; also fish and fowl.

Question: Please outline the proper diet, suggesting things to avoid.

Answer: Avoid too many heavy meats, not well cooked. Eat plenty of vegetables of all kinds. Meats taken should preferably be fish, fowl and lamb; others not so often. Breakfast bacon, crisp, may be taken occasionally.   *1710-P-3*

Keep away from red meats, ham, or rare steaks or roasts. Rather use fish, fowl and lamb.   *3596-P-1*

Question: What should the diet be for this body?

Answer: Not too much of meats of any kind. Rather take fowl or fish, and vegetables that clarify the blood. These would be cooked onions, beets, carrots, salsify, raw carrots, celery or lettuce. These will act well with the mental and spiritual forces in the body.   *288-P-4*

And in the matter of diet, keep away from too much grease or too much of any foods cooked in quantities of grease—whether of hog, sheep, beef or fowl! Rather use the lean portions and those meats which will make for body-building forces throughout. Fish and fowl are the preferred meats. No raw meat, and very little *ever* of hog meat—only bacon. Do not use bacon or fats in cooking the vegetables.   *303-P-7*

Use plenty of fowl, but prepared in such a way that more of the bone structure itself is used . . . in its reaction through the system; so that assimilation of calcium is obtained. Chew chicken necks, then! Chew the bones of the thigh! Also have the marrow of beef or such as a part of the diet, and eat foods such as vegetables soups rich in the beef which carries the bone marrow . . . and eat the marrow!   *1523-P-6*

In the diet, keep away from heavy foods. Use those which are body-building; such as beef juice, beef broth, liver, fish, lamb. All of these may be taken but never fried foods.   *5269-P-1*

Surprisingly, we find high praise in the readings for wild game which is seldom mentioned in tables of nutritional values. The readings caution about preparing rabbit or hare:

Question: Is it all right for me to eat rabbit and squirrel, baked or stewed?

Answer: Any wild game is preferable to other meats, if it is prepared properly. In cooking rabbit, be sure that the tendon in both left legs is removed, for this is the part which might cause a fever, being what is called at times "the wolf" in the rabbit. Prepared in some ways, this might be excellent for some specific disturbance in a body, but it is never well for it to be eaten in a hare.

In preparing squirrel, of course, the same is not true. When squirrel is stewed or well cooked, it is really preferable for the body; but rabbit is all right if that part indicated is removed.   *2514-P-4*

Eggs, Cheese and Milk

Eggs and cheese are also "complete proteins" valuable in the diet. According to *USDA Bulletins,* the important nutrients in eggs are: protein, vitamin A (in the yolk), iron, vitamin B-1 and B-2. The readings also have good things to say about eggs and cheese; and eggs were frequently recommended for breakfasts, as will be seen in the *Menu* Section.

Eggs may be taken two or three times a week, and cooked in any manner except fried.   *257-P-15*

Some elements in eggs are not found in other foods—particularly sulphur. Egg whites cause other elements in the diet to be bad; yet we would take them occasionally. Do not necessarily eat meat if you are that-minded.

But remember, it is not what goes in the mouth but what comes out of the mouth that defiles the body.   *5399*

Take in food values those foods which carry iron and silicon, such as beets, celery and radishes. These cleanse the system. Eat spinach and eggs. . . . Do not eat too heavily of meats except fish, fowl or game. Never use fried meats of any kind for this body, but rather broiled, boiled or baked—and not with much grease. Eat olives of every kind. Cheese and cream are good for this system.   *257-P-7*

Most of us know—or should know—the importance of drinking enough milk every day. Nutritionists of the United States Department of Agriculture recommend drinking at least 3 cups or 1-1/2 pints of milk a day, for the population as a whole. According to these nutritionists, the national average is less than a pint of milk a day, taken in fluid form. They say that regardless of age, the calcium in milk and dairy products is vital for good health.

The readings recommended milk as a beverage for meals, as will be seen in the *Menu* Section, and gave milk as a source of calcium for those who needed more calcium in the diet. In addition, we have these sidelights on the value of milk:

Irradiated or dried milk, as a rule, is much more healthful for most individuals than raw milk.   *480-P-39*

Milk in all its forms, and the products of milk, should be a portion of the diet.   *903-P-14*

It would be well for the general strength to be built up with beef juices, egg and milk drinks, and easily assimilated foods.   *265-P-7*

Question: Is buttermilk good?

Answer: This depends upon the way in which it is made. If it is the ordinary kind, it would tend to produce gas; but that made by the use of the Bulgarian tablets is good in moderation. Not too much!   *404-P-5*

Milk and milk products, and leafy green vegetables are rich in calcium and contain little starch.   *382-P-6*

Whole-Grain Cereals

As the next point in our parallel study of the *Basic 7* we come to #6: Bread flour, cereals—"whole grain, enriched or restored." The readings advocated only whole-grain cereals, used for breakfast or made into bread. In the *Menu* Section of this book, we find several mentions of buckwheat cakes and whole grain cereals prepared for breakfast, as well as whole wheat toast (Readings No. 1523-P-9; 3224-P-2 and 3823-P-2). In Section 4, under Vitamins and Minerals, will also be found references to food values found in cereals and breads. The two extracts given below may be considered merely an introduction to this whole body of information detailed elsewhere.

> Rolled or cracked-whole-wheat that is not cooked so long as to destroy the whole vitamin force—this will add to the body the proper portions of iron, silicon and vitamins necessary for building up the blood supply which makes for resistance in the system . . .   *840-P-1*

Question: What is particularly wrong with my diet?

Answer: The tendency for eating too much starch, pastries, white bread. These should be almost entirely eliminated. Not that you shouldn't eat ice cream, but don't eat cake too! White potatoes, such foods as macaroni or the like, with cheese—eliminate these. They are not very good for the body of this individual, in any form.   *416-MS-4*

It sounds to us as if No. 416 were worried about overweight. Certainly the advice given him is good from a dietetic standpoint. Starches and sweets not burnt up by activities are deposited as fat. Yet the Cayce emphasis is not upon obesity as such; but upon keeping the body healthy that it may be a fit temple. The Laws of Balance and Moderation hold true here as in all other aspects of living.

Sweets

Some of us have more of a "sweet tooth" than others. The readings recognized the fact that we have a desire for sweets, and gave this advice:

Question: Please suggest the best sugar for this body.

Answer: Beet sugars are the best for everyone; or cane sugars that are not clarified.   *1131-P-2*

Keep away from too much sweets, though honey may be taken.   *3053-P-3*

Keep the body from too much sweets, though have sufficient . . . to form enough alcohol for the system. That is: watch the *kind* of sweets, rather than just taking sweets. Grape sugars would be good—hence grape jellies or sweets of that nature.   *487-P-7*

Do be careful that there are not quantities of pastries, pies or candies taken; especially chocolates and carbonated-water drinks. These sweets, we find, will be hard on the body.   *5218-P-1*

Saccharin may be used. Brown sugar is not harmful. Best of all would be to use beet sugar for sweetening.   *307-P-3*

Question: What type of sweets may be eaten by the body?

Answer: Honey, especially in the honeycomb; or preserves made with beet sugar rather than cane sugar. Not too great a quantity of any of these . . . but enough so that the forces in sweets make for proper activity through the action of gastric flows. . . . For these [sweets] become body-building by producing proper fermentation [if it may be so called] in the digestive activity. Hence two or three times a week, honey used on bread . . . would furnish that activity necessary in the whole system.   *808-P-3*

Energies or activites may burn acids but those who lead a sedentary or non-active life can't go on sweets or too much starchy food. Yet these should be well-balanced.   *798-P-1*

The diet also should be considered. There shouldn't be an excess of acids or sweets—or even an excess of alkalinity. . . . There should be maintained a normal, well-balanced diet that has been proved right for the individual body.
                                                                                    902-1

We come finally to point 7 of the *Basic 7*, butter and fortified margarine. The modern trend in dietetics is away from the use of much fat in the diet. The Edgar Cayce readings (1901 through 1944) de-emphasized the use of fat throughout all items of the diet. Meats were not to be fried; vegetables were not to be cooked with fat meats; the lean portions of meats instead of the fat portions were nearly always suggested; and butter was mentioned as a light seasoning, along with salt, for vegetables.

CHAPTER 4

FRUITS AND VEGETABLES

"BALANCE" SEEMS TO be a key word in the Cayce readings. We should strive to keep a balance of activities, attitudes, and additionally the chemical composition or balance of our bodies. One of the most important of these physical (or chemical) balances is that of acidity and alkalinity. (See Chapter 1.)

Bernard Jensen, D.C., N.D., author, lecturer and Director of Hidden Valley Health Ranch at Escondido, California, is in complete agreement with the Cayce readings, both as to the importance of maintaining this balance and the proportions of different types of foods necessary to do so—that is, 80% alkaline-producing and 20% acid-producing. The correct proportions would be four vegetables and two fruits to one protein and one starch, he says, though he does not recommend keeping these exact proportions each day, but rather approximating them over a period of time.

Dr. Jensen relates two experiments which were performed in relation to the effect of low acidity of the body. In one, turpentine was injected into the leg of a rabbit while it was alkalinized, with very slight damage resulting to the leg. The same amount of turpentine injected into the leg when the rabbit was acidized, however, resulted in inflammation, tissue sloughing and death. In the other experiment it was discovered that among a number of scarlet fever patients two-thirds of those with high acidity developed nephritis, though this complication occurred in only 3% of the cases in which the acidity was low.

When citrus fruits (which are strongly alkaline-producing) cause distress, Dr. Jensen states, it may be due to their tendency to stir up acids already accumulated in the body, giving the mistaken impression that they are having a bad effect. ("Vital Foods for Total Health"—Dr. Bernard Jensen Enterprises, Los Angeles, California.)

In general, starchy foods, fatty foods, sugar (either white or raw) and proteins are acid-forming, while fruits and vegetables are alkaline-forming (with a few exceptions). Also, Dr. Jensen points out, vegetables which are alkaline-forming when fresh may be acid-forming within a few days after being picked. Incorrect combinations of foods, according to the readings, become a factor in producing an over-acid condition.

Alkaline-Forming Foods

ALL FRUITS, Fresh and Dried, *except* large Prunes, Plums and Cranberries.

Apples	Grapefruit	Peaches
Apricots	Honey	Pears
Berries	Lemons	Pineapples
Dates	Limes	Raisins
Figs (unsulphured)	Oranges	Small Prunes

ALL VEGETABLES, Fresh and Dehydrated; *except* Legumes (Dried Peas, Beans and Lentils) and Rhubarb.

Asparagus	Green Peas	Radishes
Beets	Kohlrabi	Rutabaga
Cabbage	Lettuce	Spinach
Carob	Mushrooms	Sprouts
Carrots	Olives (ripe)	String Beans
Cauliflower	Onions	Sweet Potatoes
Celery	Oyster Plant	Tomatoes
Egg Plant	Parsnips	Turnips

MILK
All forms; Buttermilk, Clabber, Sour Milk, Cottage Cheese, Cheese.

Acid-Forming Foods

ANIMAL FATS & VEGETABLE OILS
Large Prunes, Plums, Cranberries, Rhubarb.
ALL CEREAL GRAINS
And other such products, as, Bread, Breakfast Foods, etc., Rolled Oats, Corn Flakes, Corn Meal Mush, Polished Rice, etc. (Brown Rice is less acid forming).
ALL HIGH STARCH AND PROTEIN FOODS—White Sugar, Syrups made from White Sugar. (Starchy foods in combination with fruits or proteins are acid combinations and should be avoided.)
NUTS
Peanuts, English Walnuts, Pecans, Filberts, Coconut.
LEGUMES
Dried Beans, Dried Peas, Lentils.
MEATS
Beef, Pork, Lamb, Veal.
POULTRY
Chicken, Turkey, Duck, Goose, Guinea Hen, Game.
VISCERAL MEATS
Heart, Brains, Kidney, Liver, Sweetbreads, Thymus.
EGG WHITES
(Yolks are not acid forming.)

Fruits

Fresh ripe fruits may be served raw in a variety of combinations as salads and juices, and are so satisfyingly delicious "as is" that except for apples there seems little reason for cooking them. Raw apples were often advised against in the readings, and never, to our knowledge, recommended as part of the regular diet, other than in "the Apple Diet":

> 3 days of raw apples only, and then olive oil (1/2 cup), and we will cleanse all toxic forces from any system. *820-2*

Fully ripe fruits, especially when ripened on the tree or vine, have a greater vitamin content as well as better flavor. In order to preserve the nutritive value they should be chilled as soon as ripened and picked, handled carefully to avoid bruising—washed quickly and peeled or cut just before using. Berries should be washed before being stemmed, rather than after, but should not be washed before storing, as they bruise easily. If it is unavoidable that fruits should stand for some time after being peeled or cut, discoloration and vitamin loss may be lessened by having them chilled before peeling, by mixing cut fruit with a little lemon juice to retard enzyme activity—returning them to the refrigerator as quickly as possible. The same precautions apply to the squeezing of orange juice—the juice should be extracted just before being used, but there is less loss of vitamin C if the oranges are chilled before being squeezed, and the juice kept refrigerated with air excluded.

Stewed Dried Fruit

Dried fruits should be washed quickly and if soaked, cooked in the water used for soaking. They may be cooked without soaking, or may be tenderized by soaking in hot (boiling) water with no further cooking, but with either method, the water or juice should not be disturbed, as it will contain much nutritive value.

> Method #1 - Cover fruit with water and bring to a boil. Remove from heat and allow to stand overnight.

> Method #2 - Bring 2 cups of water to a boil. Add 1 pound of fruit (dried), cover utensil, reduce heat and simmer until fruit is tender (about 12 to 15 minutes).

Dried fruits contain a large proportion of sugar and usually require no added sweetening. For variety, bits of lemon or orange rind may be added to prunes, apples, pears or figs during cooking, or small amounts of cloves and cassia buds, or stick cinnamon to prunes, pears, peaches or apples.

Stewed dried fruits may be served with cereal, or sprinkled with ground nuts or grated coconut, or served with cream as a breakfast dish or healthful dessert; stewed or raw dried fruits may be used in cakes, cookies, confections and puddings. For the latter, see the chapter on Desserts & Sweets.

BAKED APRICOTS

1/2 pound dried apricots	1/2 cup honey
1 cup seeded raisins	Juice of 1 lemon
2 cups water	1 orange

Wash apricots, add raisins and water and place in baking dish. Cover and bake at 325° for 2-1/2 hrs. Remove from oven, add honey and lemon juice, stir and chill. Before serving, top with sliced peeled orange.

Mummy Food

For those not familiar with the origin of the recipe for "Mummy Food"—Edgar Cayce had a dream (December 2, 1937) concerning the discovery of ancient records in Egypt in which a mummy came to life and helped to translate these records. The mummy, he dreamed, gave directions for the preparation of a food which she required. (See 294-189 Supplement.) Thus the name, "mummy food."

Other readings for particular individuals recommended this same combination. One such was as follows:

> and for this especial body, a mixture of dates and figs that are dried, cooked with a little corn meal—very little sprinkled in—then this taken with milk, should be almost a spiritual food for the body.   275-46

More detailed instructions were:

> . . . Equal portions of black figs or Assyrian figs and Assyrian dates—
> these ground together or cut very fine, and to a pint of such a combination
> put half a handful of corn meal or crushed wheat. These cooked together.
>
> *274-46*

"Half a handful" is, of course, a rather indefinite amount and the amount of water is not given. The following has been tried and found satisfactory:

MUMMY FOOD

1/2 cup chopped pitted dates	1 to 1-1/2 cups water
1/2 cup chopped dried black figs	1 rounded tbsp. corn meal

Cook over low heat, stirring frequently, for ten minutes or longer. Serve with milk or cream. Serves 2 to 4.

BAKED APPLES

Wash and core large red or yellow apples, one for each person to be served. Set in baking dish and stuff center of each with a mixture of chopped raisins and nuts. Honey may be added to this mixture if desired. Sprinkle with cinnamon, nutmeg, or grated lemon rind. Put piece of butter on top and add 1/4 cup boiling water. Cover and bake in hot oven until tender; 20 min. or longer, depending on variety of apples.

Serve hot or cold, with top milk, cream or yogurt.

BAKED PEARS

4 medium sized pears	1/4 cup honey
1/4 cup boiling water	1 tbsp. lemon juice

Scrub pears, remove blossom end and put stem side up in baking dish. Mix honey, boiling water and lemon juice and pour around pears. Add 2 tsp. butter if desired. Cover and bake at 375° for 1 hr., basting occasionally.

If large pears are used they may be cut in half, lengthwise, the cut surface brushed with lemon juice, then cooked as above.

BAKED PEACHES

Cut unpeeled, scrubbed peaches in half and remove seed. Place in baking dish, pour 1/4 cup water around them. In center of each peach put 1 tsp. or more of honey, top with a small chunk of butter, sprinkle lightly with cinnamon or cloves. Cover and bake at 350° to 375° just until tender.

BAKED BANANAS

Place peeled bananas in shallow baking dish, sprinkle with lemon juice, and add 1 tsp. honey for each banana if desired. Bake 10 to 15 min. at 375°.

APPLE SAUCE

Bring to boil 1/2 cup water in saucepan. Drop in 2 lbs. of cooking apples, washed and quartered but not peeled or cored. Cover, reduce heat and steam until soft, about 15 min. Press apples through a collander or food mill, chill, and sweeten to taste with raw sugar or honey. Flavor if desired with cinnamon, nutmeg, or grated lemon or orange rind.

STEWED WHOLE APPLES

Peel washed and cored apple 1/4 of the way down and put peeled side down in saucepan containing 1/2 cup boiling water. Cover, boil for 1 min. then reduce heat and simmer until tender when tested with a toothpick. Turn peeled side up, sprinkle with raw sugar and cinnamon or nutmeg and top with butter. Brown under broiler.

Appetizers

ORANGE-APRICOT

Combine in each serving glass
2/3 cup orange juice   1/3 cup apricot juice or thin purée

Stir, garnish with sprig of fresh mint. Serve cold.

BLACK RASPBERRY-PEACH

Mix directly in each serving glass
1/3 cup black raspberries   1/3 cup unsweetened pineapple juice
1/3 cup diced yellow peaches

Set in refrigerator until time to serve.

PEAR-PERSIMMON

1 medium-size fresh pear, washed,   1-1/3 cups pineapple or grapefruit juice
   unpeeled
2 large unpeeled California persimmons

Dice pear and soak in juice for 1/2 hr. Have persimmons frozen solid and just before serving cut them in small cubes and combine with pears and juice.

DECORATIVE JUICE CUBES

Use any clear light-colored juice. Half fill ice cube trays with juice and set into freezing compartment until ice crystals form over top. Quickly arrange small fresh raspberries, strawberries, or bits of orange or lemon peel with small mint leaves, to simulate flower arrangement, in center of each cube. Freeze until solid, then add enough juice to fill the tray and complete freezing. Add these cubes to glasses of chilled juice just before serving.

FROZEN FRUIT PURÉES

Beat or mash through collander or food mill, soft stewed apricots, plums, peaches, or other fruit. Add honey to taste. Freeze in freezing compartment, stirring or beating 2 or 3 times. May be served in sherbet glasses with meat course or as dessert, or stored in freezer in plastic containers for use when fresh fruit is not available.

FRUIT ASPICS

Combine in saucepan 1/2 cup fruit juice and 1 tbsp. gelatin, and soak for 5 min. Heat slowly until gelatin is dissolved and add 1-1/2 cups fruit purée. Add 1 or 2 tbsp. lemon juice if purée is not tart. Pour into mold, chill until firm. Unmold and serve with meat.

SUNNY COMPOTE

In a covered dish, slice bananas and plump moist figs. Mix together, then sprinkle chopped sunflower seeds over them. Keep the dish covered until time to serve.

BERRY BOWL

1 cup fresh strawberries
1 cup raw blueberries

1 cup black raspberries
1 cup cherries

Blend fruits in a bowl and keep covered until time for serving. Add honey and nuts or sunflower seeds if desired.

RAW WINTER PEARS

Pare, core and slice winter pears into a serving dish. Dribble with honey or maple syrup and season with 1/4 tsp. of ginger. Cover until time to serve.

APRICOT CONSERVE

Pit and mash fresh apricots. Stir in the desired amount of honey and thicken with blanched ground almonds.

STRAWBERRY SHERBET

1 pkg. Polar frosted strawberries

1 cup orange juice
1 cup water

Mash strawberries, add orange juice and water. Pour into refrigerator tray and freeze. Serve with heavy whipped cream.

FRESH PEACH MOUSSE

5 peaches, mashed
1/2 pint whipped cream

2 tbsp. maple syrup
1/3 cup almonds, ground

Mash fine either fresh peaches or soaked dried peaches, and chill. Then combine with whipped cream. Add maple syrup and nuts. Chill before serving.

BANANA DELIGHT

Stem 2 cups dried figs. Chop fine and put in covered dish, cover with hot water. Cover and let stand over night or several hours. Then mash fine. Slice 4 bananas in a casserole-type dish, pour the mashed figs over them. Sprinkle with chopped English walnuts or peanuts. Keep covered, unchilled, until serving time.

Vegetables

If eighty percent of our food is to be alkaline-producing, as recommended, probably at least fifty percent will be in the form of vegetables. Certainly it is worth while to use considerable care in their selection and preparation.

Vegetables should be freshly gathered if possible. Frozen vegetables, however, are preferable to those which have been several days in shipment, or to commercially canned foods which have added chemical preservatives.

Bright yellow and intensely green vegetables provide the greatest concentration of minerals and vitamins. Green leafy vegetables also contain an anti-stress factor as yet unidentified[1]: perhaps this is why the readings advised at least one leafy vegetable with each one of the pod variety.

Nutritive value may be lost by peeling, since most of the minerals are concentrated just under the skin; by boiling, which leaches out the minerals, sugars, and water-soluble vitamins; and by destruction of vitamins through the action of enzymes in the presence of oxygen and light.

Vegetables, except for potatoes and dry onions, should be washed, dried and returned to the refrigerator, and then when cooked, heated rapidly, as enzymes are inactive when cold and are killed by heat. Having the cooking utensils heated and filled with steam, plus leaving the lid on during cooking are important, as vitamin B is destroyed by heating in the presence of light. Alkali destroys vitamin C; thus, soda should never be used in cooking vegetables. Minerals in hard water

---

[1] "Let's Get Well," By Adelle Davis.

are another offender in this respect. Contact with copper or iron also destroys vitamin C and should be carefully avoided.

Cooking vegetables by the steam pressure method helps to retain the vitamins, so the readings point out (462-14) but care must be taken to avoid over-cooking when using this method. Cooking time should be checked precisely and the utensil cooled immediately when cooking time has expired. Cooking in Patapar paper (trade name of Paterson Parchment Co., Bristol, Pa.) was recommended. (1196-6) Note: Cooking parchment, available in most Health Food stores, also meets the requirement for preserving nutrients, retaining the juices of the vegetable which contain the vitamins and minerals, and excluding oxygen and light. The paper should be tied tightly around the vegetable to eliminate dead air space, and put into rapidly boiling water. Time-tables must be relied on to indicate when sufficiently cooked.

Timetable for Steaming Vegetables

	Minutes		Minutes
Artichokes, Globe	20–30	Kale	8–10
Artichokes, Jerusalem	6–10	Kohlrabi	9–10
Asparagus	10–15	Leek, sliced	8–10
Beans, Green or Wax	15–20	Mushrooms, chopped	8–10
Beans, fresh Limas	15–20	Mustard Greens, shredded	5–8
Beets, whole small	30–35	Okra	5–8
Beets, grated	5–8	Onions, sliced	5–8
Beet Leaves	3–5	Onions, whole	20–25
Broccoli	8–10	Parsley	5
Brussels Sprouts	10–12	Parsnips, sliced	10–15
Cabbage, Chinese	4–7	Parsnips, whole	20
Cabbage, quartered	4–7	Peas, fresh Green	8–10
Cabbage, shredded	3	Peppers, Green	8–10
Carrots, small whole	20–25	Potatoes, halved Sweet	30–35
Carrots, grated	5–8	Potatoes, halved White	30–35
Cauliflower, in pieces	8–10	Rutabagas, cubed	25–30
Celery	8–10	Spinach	3–5
Celery root	20–25	Squash, Summer	8–10
Corn, fresh	3–5	Swiss Chard	8
Dandelion Greens	3–5	Turnips	20–25
Endive	3–5	Turnip Greens, shredded	5
Eggplant, cubed	8–10	Tomatoes	3–5
Garbanzo Peas	180		

LEMON BROCCOLI

1-1/2 lbs. broccoli   2 tbsp. honey
1 tbsp. lemon juice

Trim outer leaves and tough ends of broccoli, split any thick stalks, then cut stalks and flowerets into about 3 in. lengths.

Steam, covered, in a small amount of salted water in a medium size saucepan, 10 min., or just until crisply tender. Drain carefully, retaining water, and spoon into heated serving bowl. Mix lemon juice, water drained from broccoli, and honey, and drizzle over broccoli.

STEAMED CELERY CABBAGE

1 medium size head Chinese cabbage   1 tsp. celery seeds
1 tsp. salt

Shred cabbage fine, wash well and drain. Place in a large frying pan (no need to add any water), sprinkle with salt and celery seeds, and cover. Steam 3 min. or just until crisply tender. Serve with cooking juices.

ASPARAGUS WITH CITRUS SAUCE

1-1/2 lbs. asparagus, steamed   4 tbsp. orange juice
2 tbsp. butter   Grated rind of 1/2 orange
2 egg yolks, well beaten   1/4 tsp. paprika
1 tbsp. lemon juice   Dash of salt

Set steamed asparagus aside. To make sauce: combine butter, salt, egg yolks, paprika and grated orange rind. Cook over hot water, stirring constantly until thick and smooth. Add orange and lemon juice and beat until smooth. Serve over asparagus.

SLICED BAKED BEETS

8 small beets, sliced   1-1/2 tbsp. butter
1 tbsp. honey   1-1/2 tsp. lemon juice
3/8 tsp. salt   2-1/2 tbsp. water
1/8 tsp. nutmeg   1 small onion, chopped

Place beets in layers in greased baking dish. Season with honey, salt and nutmeg. Dot with butter, add lemon juice, water and onions. Bake in moderate oven 30 min. or until tender. Sprinkle with parsley and serve. Serves 4-5.

Note: for those who object to onions, substituting celery wherever recipes call for onions has been found altogether satisfactory.

BAKED ACORN SQUASH WITH PINEAPPLE

3 acorn squash, halved
1/2 cup crushed pineapple,
  unsweetened, drained
2 tbsp. honey

4 tbsp. butter
1/4 tsp. ground nutmeg
1 tsp. salt
4 tbsp. butter

Place cleaned and halved squash in greased baking dish and divide honey and butter mixture into center of each half. Cover and bake at 400° for 30 min. or until tender. Scoop cooked squash out of shells leaving about 1/4 in. remaining in shells. Mash squash and combine with 4 tbsp. butter and remaining ingredients that have been heated until well blended. Spoon back into shells and return to hot oven for 15 min.

BAKED CARROTS

Mix 1 lb. coarsely shredded carrots with 1/4 cup minced onions, 1/4 cup water, 2 tbsp. butter, 1-1/4 tsp. salt, 1/4 tsp. celery salt. Bake covered at 375° for 45 min. or until tender.

GREEN PEAS WITH CELERY AND RIPE OLIVES

2 cups celery, sliced at angle into
  2-in. pieces
2 tbsp. vegetable oil
2 pkgs. frozen peas, partly thawed

20 pitted ripe olives, halved
1/2 tsp. salt
1/4 tsp. pepper

Use large frying pan, on low heat. Stir celery in oil thoroughly until all cut surfaces are coated. Cover and cook celery in oil for 10 min., shaking occasionally; add peas, cover and continue cooking at same temperature for 6 min., shaking several times. Add 1 tbsp. water if necessary during cooking. Stir in olives, salt and pepper. Serves 6-8.

RAW CARROTS AND PEAS

2 cups raw peas

2 cups raw baby carrots

Top and wash baby carrots. Cut them into chunks not much larger than the peas and put both in a covered dish. Serve raw. Neither dressing nor seasoning is needed. They are delicious "as is."

GARBANZOS CREOLE

2 cups cooked garbanzos
1/2 Spanish onion, chopped

1 cup home-canned tomatoes

Simmer these ingredients together until the onion is tender. Serve hot. 1/4 tsp. honey may be added, if desired.

SUCCOTASH

Open one package each of frozen sweet corn and green lima beans (or home-canned ones) and simmer together gently, seasoning with sea kelp, dried marjoram and 1 tbsp. of salad oil. Add a shake of black pepper and garnish with green peppers cut in fancy shapes. Serve hot in a heavy utensil.

YOUNG BEETS AND GREENS

Wash and cook young beets gently until tender, probably 10 min. Cut the little beets off the tops and skin them. Chop the beet tops and place in a serving dish, with the baby beets nested in the center. Dress with oil, vinegar and honey and a faint dusting of cinnamon.

Jerusalem Artichokes

Jerusalem artichokes, frequently recommended in the readings for individuals with diabetes or a tendency to same, were also said to

> "produce a cleansing for the kidneys" (480-39), and to "correct those inclinations for the incoordination between the activities of the pancreas as related to the kidneys and bladder" (1523-7).

There is no indication whether they are advisable in the normal diet, but they have been used by many as a vegetable rather than as a medicine with no apparent negative effects.

The Jerusalem artichoke has been referred to as the "starchless potato." It is a nutty-flavored tuber containing unulin (not insulin) and levulose, and good amounts of potassium and thiamine. They are good steamed (in Patapar paper, the readings advised) or raw, in salads, grated or thinly sliced. They are planted like potatoes, says an article in *Prevention Magazine,* yield better than potatoes, and are handled and harvested in the same way, except that they are perennials and should be planted in a permanent place. Also, they will not keep well for any length of time out of the ground, so should be left in the ground, under a heavy mulch, during the winter and dug up as needed. The blossoms, similar to small sunflowers, reach a height of from 6 to 12 feet, so they should be planted in a place where these will not be undesirable.

Seed Sprouts

The section on sprouts is included not because of specific recommendations as such in the readings, but for the fact that they offer an excellent way of obtaining a fresh supply of alkaline-producing vegetables with all the vitamins and minerals.

In many sections of the country it is difficult to obtain fresh salad greens or vegetables during large parts of the year, and impossible in most areas to have them year round, grown ("in the vicinity in which the body resides").

Sprouting seeds increases their vitamin content and changes their starch into a simple sugar, easy to digest. The cooking time of beans, such as navy beans, red beans, etc., which ordinarily require two to three hours may be shortened to 10-15 min. by sprouting, giving the double advantage of saving fuel and avoiding the destruction of food values which takes place during long cooking.

Many different seeds may be used. Almost every kind of bean, especially mung and soy beans, peas, lentils, wheat, rye, oats, corn, barley, millet, alfalfa, clover and parsley are among those which produce tasty and nutritious sprouts.

They may be used as soon as the sprout is seen, and the vitamin content continues to increase as the sprout grows. However, many kinds of sprouts become less tasty if allowed to grow too long.

Catharyn Elwood, in her book, "Feel Like a Million," states her preference for the length of the different sprouts thus:

Wheat sprouts—length of the seed.
Mung bean sprouts—1-1/2 to 2 inches
Alfalfa sprouts—1 to 2 inches
Pea and Soy Bean sprouts—good either short or long
Lentil sprouts—1 inch
Sunflower seed sprouts—length of seed.

How to Sprout Seeds

There are several methods of sprouting seeds, some of which seem to work better than others. Probably the more satisfactory method depends on seed size. You may have to experiment to find the method that suits you best, but the principle of all is the same: the seeds must be kept warm and moist, must get enough oxygen, and should be kept in the dark.

 # 1—Put soy beans in an earthenware pot with the hole in the bottom covered by a piece of crockery. For 1/4 lb. of beans use a 2-qt. pot. Pour water over them and make sure it drains off. Keep beans warm and moist, sprinkling them about twice each day (more often if necessary). The beans may be soaked for about 6 hours, before being placed in the pot.

 # 2—Wash wheat, soak over night, drain and rinse in the morning, add fresh water and put in a dark place. Repeat draining and rinsing 3 times a day for 3 days. The evening of the 3rd day drain wheat thoroughly, put in a shallow pan in a dark place until morning, when sprouts should be of the proper length.

 # 3—Place about 1 tablespoon of alfalfa seed in a widemouth jar, cover with water; place a piece of nylon stocking or fine nylon net over the mouth of the jar and secure with a rubber band. Let stand over night or eight hours, out of light. When time is complete, drain well, rinse slowly and easily and place jar on its side out of light. At least 3 times a day cover with water and drain again. After each draining, return the jar to its side. If the humidity is low, there is danger of the seeds drying out. To avoid this, sprinkle them occasionally throughout the day with water. In 3 to 5 days the sprouts will reach a length of 1 to 2 inches and are ready for use. Remove the sprouts from the jar, place in

large bowl and rinse carefully to remove the brown hulls, using a collander.

4—Scatter seed on damp bath towel. Roll towel loosely, sprinkle towel whenever necessary to keep damp. This method may be most successful with small seeds.

When sprouts are of the desired length put in large bowl, wash thoroughly to remove hulls if necessary, and store in refrigerator in crisper or plastic bag.

Using Sprouts

Sprouts may be eaten by themselves with your favorite seasoning, in sandwiches, salads, or many cooked dishes. Sprouted wheat may be added to bread dough for an interesting variation. Soy and mung bean sprouts may be served as a cooked vegetable.

MUSHROOM CHOP SUEY

2 tbsp. vegetable oil
3 cups onion, diced
3 cups celery, diced
1 cup beef stock or
   chicken broth
1 can mushrooms, broken
   or sliced

2 tbsp. soy sauce
2 tsp. Bead molasses
1 tsp. salt
2 tbsp. corn starch
1 lb. mung or soy bean
   sprouts

Sauté onion and celery slowly in vegetable oil for a few minutes, add 3/4 cup stock or broth and simmer for 10 min., add mushrooms. Mix remaining broth with corn starch, soy sauce, Bead molasses and salt. Add to vegetables and cook, stirring constantly until thickened. Add bean sprouts and simmer 5 min. Serve with cooked brown rice.

Chinese chestnuts and bamboo sprouts may be added if available. If raw Chinese chestnuts are used, slice thin and add with sauce.

CHICKEN-BEAN SPROUT CHOP SUEY

1 lb. bean sprouts
1/2 cup onion slices
2 tbsp. butter
2 cups diced chicken or turkey
1 cup celery, diced
1 can water chestnut slices
1/2 cup chicken bouillon or
   turkey broth

2 tbsp. arrowroot (corn starch)
1/4 tsp. salt
1/4 cup water
2 tbsp. soy sauce
1/2 cup slivered almonds

Cook onions in butter until tender, but not brown. Add chicken or turkey, celery, water chestnuts, broth, and heat to boiling point. Combine arrow-root, seasonings, water and soy sauce. Stir into poultry mixture. Cook until thickened. Add sprouts and nuts. Serves 8.

EGG FOO YOUNG

2 med. onions
3 med. green peppers
4 eggs, beaten whole

2 tbsp. vegetable oil
1/2 tsp. salt
1 lb. fresh bean sprouts

Chop or cut fine onions and peppers, add other ingredients, and mix well. Spoon onto a hot oiled grill and sauté until light brown on both sides.

SOY BEAN SPROUT OMELET

1 egg, separated
1 tbsp. water
1 tsp. vegetized salt

2 tbsp. soy bean sprouts
1 tsp. butter, sweet

Beat egg white until frothy. Add water and salt. Continue beating until stiff, then fold in the well-beaten yolk and the bean sprouts. Pour into a hot, buttered omelet pan and cook over the fire for 2 min. Bake in moderate oven, 350°, for 3 min. or until done.

BEAN SPROUT OMELET

3 eggs
1 cup bean sprouts, cooked
1/2 cup raw sweet cream

Salt
Radishes to garnish

Beat eggs until light, add bean sprouts, cream and salt. Cook in double boiler until eggs are set. Garnish with thin slices of crisp red radishes.

MUNG BEAN SPROUTS

1 tbsp. butter
1/2 cup onion, chopped

2 cups mung bean sprouts

Sauté chopped onion in a pan. Remove from heat and add mung beans. Shake or carefully stir the mixture until sprouts are well covered.

ALFALFA SPROUTS RAREBIT

Put the following ingredients in blender and blend well:

2 cups water
3 tbsp. raw cashews
1 tsp. salt
1 tbsp. whole wheat pastry
  flour

1 tsp. onion powder
3 tbsp. arrowroot powder

Pour liquid into pan, on low heat, and stir constantly until sauce thickens. Remove from fire and add the following ingredients, mix well:

3/8 cup sesame tahini or raw nut butter
2 tsp. Chef Bonneau's
Aminotone (optional)—
obtainable at Health Food
Stores

Then add 1-1/2 cups alfalfa sprouts. Serve over whole wheat toast, garnish with pimento strips and ripe olives.

Salads

Of all the recommendations on diet in the Cayce readings one of the most invariable, it seems, is for raw fresh vegetables, as a salad, for the noon meal. Sometimes it was recommended that fruit salads be alternated with these (935-1). Frequently individuals were advised to prepare the raw vegetables with gelatin (3429-1). Some were told not to use any acetic acid or synthetic vinegar with them, "but use that vinegar which would be made from apples, that is apple cider vinegar" (935-1).

Oil dressings, such as olive oil with paprika with the yolk of a hard boiled egg worked in, were recommended.

All the nutritionists we know agree on the value of an abundance of raw fresh vegetables, with deep-green leaves being especially rich in vitamins A, C, E, K, P, B2, folic acid, eight or more B vitamins, iron, copper, magnesium, calcium and other minerals.

Fresh salad greens are, or should be, the basis for most salads. There are a larger number of these than many people realize, and variety may be obtained by different combinations of these as well as from the other ingredients of the salad. Greens which may be used raw for salads include the following:

Kale	Beet Greens	Chicory
Spinach	Finocchi	Bibb Lettuce
Dandelion Greens	Chinese Cabbage	Savoy Cabbage
Field Salad	Iceberg Lettuce	Escarole
Water Cress	Mustard Greens	Celery
Boston Lettuce	Nasturtium Leaves	Romaine
Sour Grass	Green Cabbage	Leaf Lettuce
Turnip Greens	French Endive	

EGGPLANT SALAD

1 medium-size eggplant
1 medium-size onion, grated
Juice of one onion

2 tbsp. salad oil
2 tbsp. minced parsley

Bake eggplant, whole, in moderate oven (300°-350°) for 30-45 min. in glass dish. Cool and peel. Cut into cubes. Mix other ingredients and chill thoroughly before serving.

JERUSALEM ARTICHOKE SALAD

2 cups scrubbed artichokes,
  cubed

1 onion
Parsley sprigs

Grind or chop parsley and serve on bed of Romaine. Dressing may be added if desired.

LETTUCE AND WATERCRESS SALAD

2/3 cup nut meats
1 cup watercress

1/4 cup lemon juice
2 cups shredded lettuce

On a bed of watercress and shredded lettuce, serve nut meats (walnuts, pecans, almonds) which have been dipped in lemon juice.

GREEN AND GOLD VEGETABLE BOWL

1 lb. cut green beans, cooked,
  drained
1 cup sliced celery
2 lbs. sliced carrots, cooked,
  drained
1/4 cup salad oil

2 tbsp. lemon juice
1 tsp. minced onion
1 tsp. dried parsley flakes
1 tsp. brown sugar
1/2 tsp. salt
Lettuce

Toss beans with celery in small bowl, place carrots in a second bowl. Mix salad oil, lemon juice, onion, parsley flakes, sugar and salt in a cup, drizzle half over carrots and remaining half over beans; toss each lightly. Chill. Spoon carrot and bean mixture in separate piles in a lettuce-lined shallow serving bowl. Serve with mayonnaise or salad dressing as desired.

RIVIERA GREEN BEANS

2 cups tender green beans cut
  in inch lengths
1 tbsp. green onions, chopped
1 young carrot, sliced thin on
  a grater

1 cup tiny red or yellow vine-
  ripened tomatoes
1/2 cup shelled peas
Salad greens and fresh herbs

All ingredients are raw. Line a salad bowl with the salad greens. Dice the fresh herbs over them. Toss the other ingredients together with your favorite dressing and pour them into the salad greens. Garnish with rose hips and paprika. Keep covered in refrigerator until serving time.

RAW VEGETABLE SALAD

1 bunch spinach
2 green onions
1 vine-ripened tomato
4 sprigs watercress

1 small cucumber
1 carrot
Radishes to garnish

Chop spinach, onions, watercress, cucumber. Dice tomato and grate carrot. Combine all in mixing bowl and toss with mayonnaise. Make radish roses for garnish.

COOKED VEGETABLE SALAD

1 cup carrots, cooked and cut
  in strips
1 cup string beans, cooked

1 cup lima beans, cooked
1 cup peas, cooked
Ripe olives for garnish

Cut the string beans through the center, lengthwise. Place all vegetables in 3/4 cup lemon honey dressing. Place combined vegetables in individual salad bowls and garnish with ripe olives.

CRISP ALFALFA SPROUT TOSS

2 cups finely cut celery
1 cup sprouted alfalfa

1 cup raisins
2 carrots, grated

Mix ingredients thoroughly and when ready to serve, make a "dent" in top of salad to fill with generous amounts of thick yogurt or sour cream.

BEAN SPROUT TOMATO SALAD

1 head Romaine lettuce
1 cucumber, sliced
3 tomatoes, vine-ripened

2 cups bean sprouts
Radishes
Ripe olives

Place Romaine leaves on salad plates. Place a layer of bean sprouts on the leaves. Slice alternate layers of cucumber and tomato over them, tapering up to a peak. Garnish with ripe olives and radishes. Serve with sour cream dressing.

REFRESHING ALFALFA SPROUT SLAW

3/4 cup crushed pineapple,
  unsweetened

3 cups cabbage, chopped
1 cup alfalfa sprouts

Mix ingredients and serve with remaining pineapple juice, unsweetened, as dressing.

ALFALFA SPROUT SALAD

2 cups alfalfa sprouts   1 cup sliced okra
3/4 cup avocado, cubed   3/4 cup green soy beans

Place lettuce leaves on salad plates. Mix above ingredients together and place mixture on the leaves. Top with slices of vine-ripened tomatoes. Serve with your favorite dressing.

BASIC RECIPE FOR GELATIN FOR VEGETABLE SALADS

1 tbsp. gelatin   2 to 4 tbsp. honey
1/2 cup cold water   1/4 tsp. salt, if water is used
1 cup boiling water or light-   1/4 cup lemon juice
   colored stock   2 cups diced vegetables, cooked
1 tbsp. onion, grated   or raw

Soak gelatin in cold water and dissolve thoroughly in boiling water or stock. Add honey, salt, lemon juice, and onion if desired. Chill. When about set, add vegetables, and chill until set firmly. Serve on lettuce leaves with mayonnaise.

GELATIN AND ALFALFA SPROUT SALAD

4 tbsp. unflavored gelatin   1 cup alfalfa sprouts, chopped
1/2 cup warm water   3/4 cup diced avocado
1-1/2 cups pineapple juice   2 tbsp. honey
3/4 cup crushed pineapple,
   unsweetened

Soften gelatin in warm water for five minutes. Liquefy with 1 cup unsweetened pineapple juice. Cook for a few minutes, until gelatin is completely dissolved. Add remaining pineapple juice and honey. Let stand a few minutes, add chopped sprouts, avocado and pineapple. Pour into mold, chill, and serve topped with mayonnaise.

ALFALFA SPROUT-GELATIN SALAD

1 envelope unflavored gelatin   1 cup cabbage, finely shredded
1/2 cup cold water   1 cup celery, cut fine
1 pint boiling water   1/4 cup green pepper,
1 lemon, juiced   chopped
1/2 cup honey   1 cup alfalfa sprouts

Soak gelatin in cold water for five minutes. Add lemon juice, boiling water, honey and seasoning. Pour into mold. When beginning to set, add remaining ingredients. When firmly set, cut into squares and serve on lettuce leaves.

ALFALFA SPROUT-VEGETABLE GELATIN SALAD

1 envelope unflavored gelatin
1/2 cup cold water
1 pint boiling water
Juice of 1 lemon
1 cup carrots, shredded
1/2 cup green pepper,
  chopped

1/2 cup cucumber, thinly
  sliced
1/2 cup radishes, thinly sliced
1 cup alfalfa sprouts
1 teaspoon seasoning
1/2 cup honey

Soak gelatin in cold water for 5 minutes. Add lemon juice, boiling water, honey and seasoning. Pour into mold. When beginning to set, add remaining ingredients. Chill. Serve on lettuce.

FRESH VEGETABLE-GELATIN SALAD

2 envelopes unflavored gelatin
1/2 cup cold water
2 cups hot water
1/3 cup honey
1-1/4 tsp. salt
1/4 cup lemon juice
2/3 cup ripe olives, pitted and
  diced

1-1/2 cups cabbage, shredded
3/4 cup celery, diced
3/4 cup carrots, shredded
1/4 cup green pepper,
  chopped
2 tbsp. pimiento, diced

Soften gelatin in cold water, add hot water and stir until dissolved. Stir in honey and next 2 ingredients; cool. Add olives and remaining ingredients; mix well. Pour into 1-1/4 qt. ring mold or 8x8x2 cake pan. Chill until firm. Cut into squares. Garnish with crisp greens and serve with mayonnaise. Serves 10-12.

FRESH FRUIT SALAD OR DESSERT

Use all your favorite fresh fruits (except pineapple and apples) with unflavored gelatin, for delicious flavor and Nature's own vitamin content.

1 envelope unflavored gelatin
1/4 cup cold water
1 cup hot water
1/4 cup honey

1/2 cup grapefruit juice
1/8 tsp. salt
1 tbsp. lemon juice
Fresh fruit, cut up

Soften gelatin in cold water, add honey, salt and hot water. Stir until dissolved. Add grapefruit and lemon juice. Mix well. Pour 1 cup mixture into mold that has been rinsed in cold water. When it begins to thicken, arrange fruit in it. Chill remaining gelatin until it begins to thicken, then whip until frothy and thick and pour on the gelatin mixture. Chill until firm. Serves 6.

GELATIN FRUIT SALAD

1 envelope unflavored gelatin
1-1/2 cups pineapple juice,
   unsweetened
1 tbsp. lemon juice

1 tbsp. coconut, finely grated
2 tbsp. banana, cut fine
2 tbsp. pineapple, unsweetened
1 tbsp. orange, cut fine

Dissolve gelatin in 1/2 cup boiling water. Place on stove and let boil for 1 minute, stirring constantly. Add pineapple and lemon juice. Set aside to cool and when it is half set, add the mixed fruit and coconut. Pour into molds; it will set in approx. 20 min.

TOMATO ASPIC

4 pkgs. unflavored gelatin
2 cups cold tomato juice
5 cups hot tomato juice

1 tsp. salt
1/4 tsp. Tabasco
4 tbsp. lemon juice

Soften gelatin in cold tomato juice. Dissolve thoroughly in very hot tomato juice, stirring well. Season with salt, Tabasco and lemon juice. Pour into individual molds. When set, unmold on salad greens. Serve with salad dressing or plain. Serves 12.

TOMATO-SHRIMP ASPIC

2 pkgs. gelatin, unflavored
1/2 cup cold water
2 cups tomato juice
3 tsp. lemon juice

Salt and pepper
1 cup celery, chopped
1/2 cup green olives, chopped
1/2 cup shrimp

Sprinkle gelatin on 1/2 cup water to soften. Place over very low heat and stir until dissolved. Remove from heat and stir in tomato juice and seasoning. Chill mixture to unbeaten egg-white consistency. Fold in celery, olives and shrimp. Turn into a 6-cup mold.

SHRIMP TOSSED SALAD

1/4 cup salad oil
1-1/2 tbsp. lemon juice
1 tsp. salt
1/8 tsp. pepper
1/8 tsp. dry mustard
1/8 tsp. celery seeds
1/4 tsp. onion, grated

1/2 cup ripe olives, sliced
1 vine-ripened tomato, medium
   size, diced
1 cup cleaned, cooked fresh
   shrimp, crab meat or lobster
1 qt. crisp lettuce, coarsely
   shredded

Combine oil and next 6 ingredients. Mix well with fork. Place with remaining ingredients in salad bowl, pour dressing over all and toss. Serves 4-6.

TUNA FISH-GELATIN SALAD

3 7-oz. cans tuna fish	1 cup celery, diced
4 hard boiled eggs, chopped	2 pkgs. unflavored gelatin
1 cup ripe olives, chopped	1/2 cup cold water
1 small onion, minced	3 cups mayonnaise

Combine first 5 ingredients. Soften gelatin in cold water and set over hot water and stir until dissolved. Stir in mayonnaise. Add to tuna mixture and blend well. Turn into mold. Chill until firm. Unmold and garnish with parsley and celery curls. Serves 12.

CRAB-STUFFED AVOCADO

1/2 cup mayonnaise	1-1/2 cups chilled cooked or
1/2 cup celery, minced	canned crab or lobster meat
1/4 cup pimiento, minced	2 ripe avocados
2 tsp. lemon juice	Salt
1/8 tsp. Worcestershire	Lemon juice
Dash Tabasco—(optional)	

Combine first 6 ingredients. Halve avocados lengthwise and remove pits, peel. Sprinkle with lemon juice and salt. Arrange on bed of crisp greens and fill halves with crab meat. Top with dressing. Serves 4.

Salad Dressings

Salad dressings should all be homemade rather than the commercial variety. They are used to enhance the salad but should also contribute to health. There is some question as to the advisability of using vinegar, though the number of readings prohibiting this is too small to be really conclusive. (Apple cider vinegar is recommended.) We prefer lemon juice where acidity is desired. Oil used may be olive oil, frequently recommended in the readings, or vegetable oils. Adelle Davis ("Let's Cook It Right" and "Let's Get Well") recommends using a mixture of vegetable oils, peanut, soy and sunflower, as each is high in a different essential fatty acid.

Avocados, used either in salad dressings or otherwise in the salad, are a nutritionally valuable addition. They are rich in protein, in a highly digestible oil, and in vitamins A and C. Mineral contents include an ample amount of calcium, potassium, magnesium and sodium, considerable iron and phosphorus, and smaller amounts of manganese and copper, essential to the assimilation of iron.

AVOCADO DRESSING

1 avocado	Juice of 1 orange or 1 lemon

Whip the avocado pulp to the consistency of whipped ceam. Add citrus juice very gradually, then whip with a rotary beater until light and frothy.

MAYONNAISE #1

Mayonnaise is a great favorite, not only as a dressing but for combining with other foods. Care must be used in storing all mayonnaise combinations in refrigerator, as they are subject to bacterial activity which may be very toxic without showing any evidence of spoilage.

Use chilled ingredients. Place in a medium-sized bowl and beat with a wire whisk: Beat in

2 egg yolks	1/4 to 1/2 tsp. dry mustard
1/2 tsp. salt	1/2 tsp. lemon juice
Few grains cayenne	

Then beat in very slowly, 1/2 tsp. at a time—1/2 cup salad oil—soy, safflower, peanut, etc. Add 3-1/2 tbsp. lemon juice.

Beat into dressing, 1/2 tsp. at a time—1/2 cup salad oil.

Alternate the oil with a few drops of lemon juice. If the ingredients are cold and are added slowly during constant beating this will make a good thick dressing. Should the dressing separate, place 1 egg yolk in a bowl, stir constantly and add the dressing very slowly. If the dressing is too heavy, thin it with cream or whipped cream.
When making mayonnaise with an electric beater, beat the egg yolks at medium speed for 4 min. Combine the dry ingredients and add them. Add 1-1/2 tbsp. cold water. Add 1/2 of the oil, drop by drop. When the dressing begins to thicken, add the lemon juice. Add the remaining oil more freely, beating constantly at medium speed. Time required, 20 min.

MAYONNAISE #2

2 egg yolks	2 tbsp. lemon juice
1/2 tsp. salt	

Put above ingredients in electric blender or use electric mixer. Slowly add 3/4 cup oil while machine is running, until desired consistency. Add 2 tsp. honey for use on fruit salads.

MAYONNAISE #3

2 egg yolks	1 tsp. honey
2 tbsp. lemon juice	Dash red pepper
1/2 tsp. salt	3/4 cup salad oil
1/2 tsp. dry mustard	

Blend all ingredients, except oil, in blender or mixer. Add salad oil very slowly, blending until thick.

FRENCH DRESSING

1 cup salad oil
1/3 cup lemon juice
1/4 tsp. pepper

1 tsp. salt
1/4 tsp. garlic salt

Put above ingredients into blender or mixer, and blend for 1 minute.

ALMOND NUT DRESSING

2 tbsp. almond butter

4 tbsp. raw cream or milk

Beat together with an egg beater. This is an excellent dressing for fruits as well as vegetable salads.

TOMATO DRESSING

1 pt. canned tomatoes
3/4 cup lemon juice
1/2 cup salad oil
1/4 cup honey
1 tbsp. soy sauce

2 tbsp. onion, grated
1 tsp. vegetable broth powder
1 tsp. paprika
2 cloves garlic

Sieve tomatoes and add next 7 ingredients. Place in quart jar, shake well, and add 2 whole cloves of garlic. This will keep indefinitely in your refrigerator. Yield: about 1 quart.

PEANUT BUTTER DRESSING

2 tbsp., cold pressed,
  unhydrogenated peanut
  butter

1 tbsp. salad oil
1-1/2 tbsp. lemon juice
1 cup mayonnaise

Mix all ingredients together.

YOGURT OR SOUR CREAM DRESSING

1 cup sour cream or yogurt

1/2 cup lemon juice

Mix together. This dressing is best with fruit salads, but may be used on vegetable salads also.

YOGURT AND HONEY DRESSING

1 cup yogurt   Honey to taste

Mix and use as dressing on fruit salads.

Carob, Soy and Peanut Flours

Carob, soy and peanut flours are all alkaline-producing in the body. In most cases they would be used in combination with wheat flour which, being a starch, has an acid reaction. Cakes, cookies, etc. made with these are therefore not likely to be alkaline-producing, but would be less acid-producing than those made with the starchy flour alone.

Besides their alkaline-producing characteristics, these flours have much to recommend them, as their use provides another way of obtaining those properties recommended, or avoiding those warned against in the readings.

Carob flour is produced from the pod of the carob tree, or honey locust, and is thought by some to have been the "locust" that John the Baptist ate in the wilderness, thus called "St. John's Bread." It has a sweet taste and pleasant flavor, somewhat like chocolate, and may be used as substitute for both sugar and chocolate. It is low in starch and very high in natural sugars. It contains a large amount of minerals and a fair amount of several of the vitamins.

Soy flour is more than 33% protein, is extremely high in calcium (200 mg. per cup), has more iron, thiamin, riboflavin and niacin than whole wheat flour, and is high in pantothenic acid, another important part of the Vitamin-B complex.

Peanut flour is higher yet in protein, one cup of flour (113 gm.) having 59 gm. of protein. It is also higher in calcium and thiamin than whole wheat flour, and has twice the amount of iron and riboflavin and more than 3 times the amount of niacin as does whole wheat. Peanut flour has the added advantage that it can be used raw, and has a flavor very pleasing to most people.

CHAPTER 5

MEATS AND MEAT SUBSTITUTES

NO REASON SEEMS to be given in the Cayce readings for the frequent recommendation of fish, fowl and lamb, rather than of red meats. However, since beef juice was often advised in cases of illness, it seems most likely that the reason is one of digestibility, rather than that of "vibrations" or such. It is recognized by nutritionists that fish, fowl and lamb are easily digested meats and that they are a good source of complete proteins. Fish, especially ocean varieties, also contain valuable minerals, particularly phosphorus and iodine, either not found in other meats, or occurring in smaller quantities.

The readings, likewise, give no reason for the statement that "any wild game is preferable even to other meats" (2514-4). J.I. Rodale, in "The Health Finder" states in support of his opinion that fish is an especially good food, "First of all there has been no tampering with it. Commercial fertilizers and insecticides play no part in the fish business . . . Ocean fish cannot be doped, chemicalized or processed." The same things, of course, could be said of wild game, and may have resulted in that preference in the readings.

Glandular meats, as tripe, calf's liver, brains, and the like were referred to and recommended as "of the blood-building type" (275-25). Here we have the full agreement of the nutritionists. The vitamins found more abundantly in the glandular meats than in muscle are those needed to enable the bone marrow to produce red blood cells.

All meats should be cooked at low temperatures for maximum nutritive value, digestibility and flavor. High temperatures toughen the protein and cause contraction of the fibers, squeezing out the meat juices. Fish and glandular meats especially should be cooked at very low temperatures. These have very thin sheets of connective tissue which begin breaking down around 150°, and when they are cooked above 150° much of the juices will have been lost. Adding salt during cooking also results in juices being drawn out.

Meats should usually be roasted, baked, or broiled—never fried. Stewing is permissible if the broth is to be used, in which case a closely covered utensil should be used, and the meat should be simmered rather than boiled.

Temperatures and Time for Broiling

	Broiling Temp.	Thickness or cut	Time (Min.)
Fish steaks or fillets	Very Low	1 to 1-1/2 inches	15-18
Chicken, fryer or broiler	Low	Quartered or halved	45-50
Kidneys	Very Low	1/2 in.	12-16
Lamb chops, patties	Low	1 in.	20-30
or steaks	Low	2 in.	40-45
Milt	Low	Uncut	15-18
Rabbit, young fryer, 2 lbs.	Low	Quartered	45-50
Liver	Low	3/4 in.	12-18
Brains	Low	3/4 in.	15-20

Temperatures and Time for Baking or Roasting

	Oven Temp.	Internal Temp. at which served	Time (Min. per lb.)
Whole fish or fillets	300°	140°	1 in. thick-20
			2 in. thick-30
			3 in. thick-35
Chicken, roasting	300°	185°	35-40
Chicken, stewing	225°	185°	60-70
Duck, young	300°	185°	25-30
Goose, young	300°	185°	25-30
Lamb, leg	300°	155°-160°	25-30
Lamb, shoulder	275°	155°-160°	40-45
Rabbit	300°	180°	30-35
Turkey, large	300°	180°-185°	15-18
Turkey, small	300°	180°-185°	20-25
Liver, uncut	300°	145°-160°	15-20

CURRIED COD BAKE

2 lbs. frozen cod, partly thawed
2 large onions, chopped
(2 cups)
1 clove garlic, minced
2 tbsp. butter
3 med. size apples, pared,

cored, quartered and sliced
6 oz. tomato paste
3/4 cup water
2 tsp. salt
1 tsp. curry powder
1/8 tsp. pepper

Cut cod into 6 serving pieces, place in a 6-cup shallow baking dish. Sauté onions and garlic in butter or margarine until soft in a medium-size frying pan; stir in remaining ingredients. Heat, stirring constantly, to boiling; spoon over fish and cover. Bake in moderate oven (350°) 1-1/2 hours, or until fish flakes easily.

POACHED EGGS AND BROILED FISH

For a treat, the eggs may be poached in muffin tins which have been well oiled so that the eggs come out easily. Arrange the muffin-shaped eggs on a platter and surround them with chunks of broiled fish. This is a rare protein treat, as broiled fish is one of the highest sources of protein obtainable, and eggs are a fine source of minerals and vitamins as well as protein. Garnish with paprika.

SALMON LOAF

1 can salmon	3 tsp. green pepper, chopped
1 tsp. lemon juice	1 cup cooked peas
1 can celery soup	Dash nutmeg
3 tsp. parsley, chopped	

Bake in moderate oven (350°) for 30 min.

QUICK-BAKED FROZEN FISH FILLETS

This exception to the rule that fish is better when fresh, or thawed before cooking, is inserted for the benefit of the hurry-up cook.

Cut into quarters 1 lb.—block frozen fillets.
Combine 1/4 cup unbleached flour
        3/4 tsp. salt
        1/8 tsp. pepper

Roll the fish in this until well coated, then place in a well-greased oven-proof dish.

Sauté lightly 1 tsp. grated onion in 3 tbsp. melted butter and add 1/2 cup vegetable stock.

Pour the sauce over the fish, cover closely and bake in 300° oven for 20 to 25 min.

RED SNAPPER FISH FILLETS

1-1/4 lb. red snapper fillets	1 tbsp. onion, minced
2 cans tomato sauce, Spanish	1 tbsp. parsley, minced
style	Dash Cayenne

Place the fillets in oiled baking dish. Pour tomato sauce over them. Sprinkle with onion, parsley and cayenne. Place in preheated 300° oven for about 25 min. or until fillets are done. Serves 5.

FILLET OF SOLE WITH TOMATO HERB DRESSING

Rub a warm skillet lightly with butter. Then slowly sauté 3 tbsp. finely minced onion and 1 tbsp. finely chopped green pepper until tender. Stir in:

Juice of 1 lime	1/2 tsp. oregano
2 tbsp. tomato paste	Pinch of savory
1 cup homemade mayonnaise	

Place 4 sole fillets on a broiler pan, sprinkle with lime juice, salt and cracked pepper and broil until just heated through (about 5 min.). Serve topped with some of the sauce and the remainder in separate bowl. Makes 4 servings.

BAKED FISH WITH SOUR CREAM

Split and remove bones from—
 4 lb. whitefish

Flatten it out and rub inside and out with
 paprika and butter

Place it on an oven-proof dish or shallow baking pan under a flame until it is lightly browned. Cover with
 2 cups sour cream

Place a lid over it and bake in 300° oven for 25 to 35 min. Remove from oven and season with salt.

CELERY BROILED CHICKEN

Rub 2 young broilers, split lengthwise, all over with lemon juice, then sprinkle with cracked pepper. Place skin side down on a broiler pan, lay strips of celery in the cavities and broil for 10 to 12 min. Turn skin side up, lay fresh celery strips over all and broil until browned and tender. Makes 4 servings.

BROILED CHICKEN FRYERS

Have the chicken cut in serving pieces. Rub the outside with a mixture of salt and poultry seasoning and place the pieces on the broiler rack. Broil low in the oven until browned, turn and finish broiling.

STEWED CHICKEN

Select a young chicken which has a small amount of fat, and stew it with a big handful of celery tops, plus salt. Use a small amount of water, cook it gently, letting the water nearly cook away. Serve hot. It is a most delightful meat when prepared this way.

CHINESE TURKEY

15 lb. turkey	1 cup honey
Soy sauce	3/4 cup butter, unsalted

Dress the turkey, wiping the interior with soy sauce, and stuff with dressing (below). Preheat oven to 450°. Make a paste of honey and butter and completely plaster the bird with this mixture, being careful to get it in under the wings. Place the turkey in a large pan and into the hot oven for 1/2 hr. until it is evenly colored. Turn it several times with wooden spoons, being careful not to break the skin. Continue to brown until it is evenly crusted to a blackish brown. The honey turns black and in carbonizing completely seals the skin. Reduce the heat to 300° and roast for 3 to 4 hours. Baste with drippings after the first hour of cooking and every 20 min. afterward.

DRESSING

16 ribs celery, leaves and stem
   cut up
1 cup parsley, chopped
24 Julienne strips tangerine
   rind

1 cup onion, lightly sautéed
1 cup mushrooms, lightly
   sautéed

ROAST DUCK

3-1/2 to 4 lb. domestic duck
1 orange, unsprayed
1/2 cup boiling consommé
3 tsp. brown sugar

1/2 tsp. salt
1 tsp. honey
1 tsp. lemon juice
Currant jelly

Prepare the duck for cooking. Place it unstuffed on a rack in a pan in a moderate oven (350°). Roast the duck uncovered, allowing 20 to 30 min. to the pound. Skin the orange and scrape the white pulp from the skin with a spoon and discard it. Cut the yellow peel into very thin strips. Add a cupful of boiling water and simmer the peel for 15 min. Drain it. Reserve the liquid. Remove all membrane from the orange sections and discard it. Fifteen minutes before the duck is done, pour the drippings from the pan and replace with the consommé. Continue to cook the duck and add to the drippings the orange liquid, salt, honey and lemon juice. Simmer these ingredients for 10 min. Add the currant jelly and stir until dissolved. Add the orange peel and simmer 10 min. longer. Add the consommé from the pan. Sprinkle the orange sections with the brown sugar and broil them for 3 min. Cut the duck into individual servings. Arrange on a hot platter and garnish with orange sections and dabs of currant jelly. Pour the sauce over it.

ROAST GOOSE WITH APPLE DRESSING

Prepare an 8 lb. goose for cooking. (This weight is for a bird dressed but not drawn). Rub the inside with salt and fill with following dressing:

Peel, quarter and core cooking apples and combine them with currants or raisins, about 1 cup to 6 cups apples. Steam the currants or raisins in 2 tbsp. water in top of double boiler for 15 min. before combining.

Allow a cupful of dressing to each pound of bird. If the bird is very fat, prick through the skin into the fat layer around the legs and wings. Truss the goose. Roast in moderate oven (325°) allowing 25 min. to the pound, on a rack in an uncovered pan.

CHICKEN CANTONESE

2 frying chickens, disjointed
1/4 cup honey
1/4 cup soy sauce

1/2 cup catsup
1/4 cup lemon juice

Arrange chicken pieces in single layer in large baking dish. Mix honey, soy sauce, catsup and lemon juice. Pour over chicken pieces. Allow chicken to stand in marinade several hours or over night. Cover pan and bake in 325° oven 1 hr. Remove cover and baste with sauce. Return to oven and bake uncovered until tender.

ROAST LEG OF LAMB

Place the leg of lamb on a roaster rack with the fat side up. Rub it heavily with sea kelp. If you like mint with lamb, then cut through the fat at intervals and pack mint leaves in the cuts. If you prefer other herbs, use them instead of the mint. Bake in a 300° oven, allowing 25 to 30 min. per lb.

BROILED LAMB CHOPS AND POTATOES

Prepare the chops in the morning and keep refrigerated in a covered dish. If you leave any fat on, cut every 1/2 in. to prevent curling. Brush each chop with cooking oil, then sprinkle with either dried mint leaves or dried herbs and sea kelp. A suitable herb is marjoram. Stack the chops so that they are seasoned from both top and bottom through the day. Later, place them on the broiler rack at room temperature while you prepare the potatoes. Scrub, but do not peel the potatoes and cut in thin slices. Arrange them on the broiler rack around the lamb chops; then brush with cooking oil and sprinkle with sea kelp. Broil the chops and potatoes slowly, turning the chops when browned on one side. Just before turning off the broiler, sprinkle the potato slices with sesame seeds and let them toast slightly. Serve chops and potatoes very hot.

LIVER DUMPLINGS AND DILL SAUCE

Put 2 cups of liver through a food grinder. Add the following ingredients:

2 heaping tbsp. corn meal
2 eggs, beaten
1 tsp. minced onion

1 tsp. fresh or dried marjoram
2 tsp. sea kelp

This will make a stiff dumpling dough. In a large kettle, put cups of meat and vegetable stock and place over medium heat. When it boils, dip a large tablespoon into the broth, then dip up a heaping spoonful of the dumpling batter, shaping it into a round ball with the spoon. Drop it into the boiling broth; dip the spoon in the broth again and repeat until you have 8 or 9 round liver dumplings distributed evenly in the boiling broth. Cover tightly and cook gently for 15 min. without lifting the cover.

Lift the dumplings out with a slotted spoon and place them in a rather deep serving dish. Keep warm. Put 2 tbsp. of fat green dill seed (from the freezer if they aren't available in the garden as yet) in the broth. Thicken it with 2 rounded tbsp. of arrowroot flour moistened in cold water. Pour this dill gravy over the liver dumplings and serve very hot.

This is an excellent way to serve liver. The dumplings are very tender and can be eaten by small children and elderly people.

BRAISED LIVER

2 lb. liver (1 thick piece)	2 tbsp. catsup
2 tsp. cooking oil	1 tbsp. green pepper, chopped
1 onion, sliced	Salt and pepper
2 tsp. Worcestershire sauce	Hot water

Place liver in greased baking dish and brush sides with oil. Add remaining ingredients, using enough hot water to nearly cover liver. Place lid on and cook at 300° for about 1-1/2 hrs. Remove lid for last 15 min. Serves 6.

CHICKEN-LIVERS MOLD

Boil chicken livers in water to which a handful of celery leaves and sea kelp has been added. Strain the broth and keep it for use as liquid for a molded or pressed meat dish later. Chop livers fine and add your own mayonnaise. Place in a mold and chill. Serve with a sprinkling of chopped egg and onion rings.

BAKED BRAINS

1 pair lamb or beef brains	1 tbsp. lemon juice
3 tbsp. water	

Place all ingredients in saucepan and simmer for 15 min., to prepare brains for recipe.

1 pair prepared brains, chopped coarsely	4 tbsp. cream
	1 tbsp. catsup
1/4 cup bread crumbs, whole wheat	1/2 tbsp. lemon juice
	1/3 tsp. salt
2 hard-cooked eggs, chopped	1/8 tsp. pepper or paprika

Place all ingredients in a greased baking dish or in individual dishes. Sprinkle the top with additional whole wheat bread crumbs. Dot generously with butter. Bake for 15 min. at 400°.

BROILED CALF BRAINS ON TOMATOES

Prepare brains according to directions in preceding recipe.

2 sets of calf brains, spread
  with butter
8 thick slices of vine-ripened
  tomatoes

Seasoning of salt, pepper,
  brown sugar and whole
  wheat bread crumbs

Place prepared butter-spread brains on the greased rack of broiler pan. Broil them for 5 min. on one side. Place tomato slices on an oven-proof plate; season tomato slices with salt, pepper and brown sugar and cover one side with buttered whole wheat bread crumbs. Place the brains, cooked side down, on the tomatoes. Broil them for 5 min. longer, and serve at once.

WILD GAME, RABBIT, PHEASANT

Cut rabbit into serving pieces, after tendons of left legs have been removed; season with salt, flour and brown quickly in oil. Arrange pieces in roaster pan and spread with sauce made with the following:

1/2 cup sour cream
Juice of 1 lemon

1/2 cup water

Bake uncovered at 300° allowing 35 to 45 min. per lb. In the meantime, sauté 1/2 lb. mushrooms in 1/4 cup butter for about 5 min. Remove rabbit from pan and arrange on large platter. Add about 1 cup water to pan and heat in order to get all the juices from the meat. In a bowl mix 1 cup sour cream, 1/2 cup water and 2 tbsp. whole wheat flour and add this to the meat juices to make a light gravy. Add mushrooms to the gravy and season to taste.

Meat Substitutes

Complete proteins, that is, those containing all the essential amino acids, are necessary for building body tissue and thus maintaining health. Also, many of the vitamins necessary to health can be produced in the body itself only if a sufficient supply of these amino acids is obtained. It is rather difficult to obtain a sufficient amount of complete proteins without including meat or at least eggs and dairy products in the diet. The following table gives the approximate amounts of complete proteins from animal and vegetable sources:

Animal—	Amount	Gms. Protein
Milk, whole, skim, buttermilk	1 qt.	32 to 35
Cottage cheese	½ cup	20
American or Swiss cheese	1 oz.	7
Meat, fish or fowl, boned	¼ lb.	18 to 22
Egg	1	6

Vegetable—	Amount	Gms. Protein
Soybean flour	1 cup	60
Cottonseed flour	1 cup	60
Wheat germ	1 cup	48
Brewer's yeast, powdered	¼ cup	25
Soybeans, cooked	½ cup	20
Nuts	½ cup	14 to 22

The protein of some nuts is incomplete; others are either complete or on the borderline. Peanuts, for example, can support growth and maintenance, according to Adelle Davis,[1] but not reproduction.

It is possible to obtain all the essential amino acids from incomplete proteins by combining foods which together have all the essentials. If these are taken at the same meal they may be used by the body as complete proteins. Baked beans and brown bread, for instance, together supply all the essential amino acids, but the amount of protein supplied by the quantity of these normally eaten would not be very large. Also, considerable study would be required concerning the composition of the various protein foods—that is, which amino acids each contained—in order to have any degree of certainty as to the amount of complete protein obtained in this way. Therefore it is very important that as much as possible of the complete protein foods be included in any meatless diet.

CARROT LOAF

1 cup mashed cooked carrots
1 small grated onion
2 tbsp. oil or butter
1/2 cup peanut butter

2 cups cooked rice
1/2 can tomato paste
2 eggs

Combine all above ingredients as you would for a meat loaf. Do not overcook the rice. Reserve the other portion of the tomato paste to make the sauce to serve with the loaf. Bake at 350° for 1 hr.

SAUCE

2 tbsp. butter
2 tbsp. flour (or cornstarch)
1/2 tsp. salt

Dash pepper
1 cup cold water
1/2 can tomato paste

You can also add 2 tbsp. chopped parsley if you have it, or just garnish it with parsley for color.

[1] "Let's Eat Right To Keep Fit"

CARROT BURGERS

1 cup raw carrot, grated
1 cup walnuts, ground, or your
  local variety
1 cup sunflower seeds, ground

1 tbsp. fresh herbs, coarsely
  chopped
2 egg yolks, raw
Raw peanut flour

Blend all ingredients together, shape into patties and roll in raw peanut flour. Keep in tightly covered dish until served.

ASPARAGUS SOUFFLÉ

1 pt. canned asparagus or equal
  amount fresh cooked
3 egg yolks

Salt
1 cup cream
2 tbsp. butter

Put asparagus through collander. Blend pulp and liquid with well-beaten egg yolks and cream. Salt to taste and place in individual oiled molds. Place molds in pan to which 1/4 in. water has been added and bake in moderate oven until custard is set. Add butter to each mold. Serve hot.

SWEET POTATO SOUFFLÉ

2 cups sweet potato, baked
2 eggs, separated

1 tsp. salt
2/3 cup cream

Mash baked sweet potato and blend with beaten egg yolks, salt and cream. Fold in stiffly beaten egg whites and bake 30 min. in moderate oven.

VEGETABLE LOAF

2 lbs. raw spinach
1-1/2 cups raw carrots, grated
1 onion, chopped
1 cup celery, diced

1 green pepper, chopped
1/2 cup nut meats
2 eggs, beaten
1/2 cup vegetable oil

Mix vegetables and steam together, then add 1/2 cup nut meats, chopped well. Mix beaten eggs and oil and add to mixture. Bake in moderate oven approximately 1/2 hr. Serve with tomato juice.

WALNUT LENTIL LOAF

1 cup lentils
1 cup walnuts, chopped
1/2 cup celery, chopped
1 small onion, cut fine

1 tsp. vegetized salt
1 egg
1/2 cup milk

Combine lentils, walnuts, celery, onion and salt. Over these pour milk to which has been added beaten egg. Mix lightly. Bake in oiled casserole in moderate oven for 1 hr.

ALMOND NUT LOAF

1 cup celery tops
1 cup celery
1 cup almonds

1 cup apples
1 egg
1/2 cup milk

Chop finely and blend the first four ingredients. Beat egg and add milk and mix lightly with other ingredients. Bake in oiled loaf pan in moderate oven for 1 hr.

NUT LOAF SURPRISE

1 onion, chopped
1 cup nut meats, chopped
1/4 tsp. paprika
1-1/2 tsp. lemon juice

1 tsp. soy sauce
Cottage cheese for desired
   consistency

Combine ingredients and form into loaf. Pack firmly and chill. Cut into slices and serve.

NUT PATTIES

2 cups cooked grated carrots
2 tbsp. minced parsley
1 tsp. vegetable broth powder

1/4 cup pecan butter (or
   other nut butter) thinned
   with water

Thin nut butter with water to the consistency of a very thick sauce. Mix well with other ingredients and shape into patties. Roll in whole wheat toast crumbs, place on buttered tin and bake in moderate oven until brown.

NUT LOAF

1 cup walnut meats, chopped
   fine
1 cup whole wheat bread
   crumbs, dried
1/2 cup wheat germ

1 onion, chopped fine
1 egg
1/2 cup celery, chopped fine
1 clove garlic
1/2 cup milk

Beat egg and add to milk. Pour this over the other ingredients and mix well. Bake in oiled loaf pan 1-1/2 hrs. in moderate oven.

LARGE NUT ROAST

2 eggs
1 cup milk
1/2 cup onion, minced
2 cups walnuts or pecans
  ground
1 cup whole wheat bread
  crumbs

1 cup wheat germ
1/2 cup celery, chopped
4 tbsp. butter
1/2 tsp. powdered sage
1 tbsp. parsley, chopped
Salt and dash of garlic

Pour 1/2 cup water in skillet and cook onion for 5 min. Beat eggs well, adding milk, then add to onion and remaining ingredients. Mix well and put in oiled baking dish. Cook 1/2 to 3/4 hr., basting with equal parts hot water and melted butter.

SPINACH NUT LOAF

3 bunches cleaned spinach, cut
  up
1 cup nut meats, chopped
2 eggs, well beaten
1 tsp. salt
1 small onion, diced finely

1 bunch parsley, small,
  chopped finely
1/2 cup wheat germ
3/4 cup whole wheat bread
  crumbs

Mix all but 1/2 cup bread crumbs. Place in oiled loaf pan. Sprinkle remaining bread crumbs over top, dot with butter and bake in moderate oven about 30 min. Serve with tomato juice sauce.

LIMA BEAN LOAF

2 cups cooked lima beans
  (fresh or dried)
1 cup whole wheat bread
  crumbs
2 tbsp. melted butter, or oil
1/2 cup green peppers,
  chopped

1/2 cup onions, chopped
1/2 cup nuts, chopped
2 eggs, well beaten
1/2 cup milk or cream
Vegetable salt to taste

Mix all ingredients together thoroughly, place in well-buttered loaf pan and bake in a moderate oven for about 30 min. or until done. Baste with melted butter.

SOYBEAN LOAF #1

3 cups cooked soybeans,
  seasoned
1/2 tsp. dry mustard

2 tsp. sorghum
2 tsp. raw sugar
1/2 cup hot water

Mash cooked soybeans and mold into loaf pan. Pour mixture of remaining ingredients over loaf. Bake uncovered in moderate oven until browned.

SOYBEAN NOODLES WITH CHEESE

3 cups cooked soy noodles
2 tbsp. vegetable broth powder
1/2 cup cooked tomatoes

1/3 cup American cheese, grated

Place noodles in oiled baking dish and pour tomatoes over them. Sprinkle broth powder over noodles and then cheese. Bake in moderate oven for 35 min.

SOYBEAN EGG LOAF

1/2 lb. soybeans, cooked
2 eggs
2 tbsp. parsley, chopped

1/2 cup thinly sliced celery
1 small onion
2 tsp. salt

Put soybeans through grinder. Beat eggs well. Mix all ingredients and mold into loaf pan. Bake in moderate oven for 30 min.

SOYBEAN LOAF #2

3 cups soybeans, cooked
1 small onion, chopped
1 tbsp. salad oil

1/2 cup cooked tomatoes
1/2 cup green pepper, chopped

Mash cooked soybeans and mix with remaining ingredients. Season to taste and bake in oiled loaf pan for 1 hr. in moderate oven. Serve with tomato sauce.

EGGS IN A NEST

1 egg
1/3 cup milk
4 slices whole wheat bread, slightly dry

2 tbsp. butter or margarine
1 pkg. (10 oz.) frozen spinach cooked, drained and seasoned
4 eggs, poached

Beat egg slightly with milk in a pie plate. Dip bread slices in mixture, turning to soak both sides well. Sauté slowly in butter in a large frying pan until golden, turning once. Top each slice with a ring of spinach, place poached egg in center. Serve hot.

COTTAGE CHEESE PATTIES

1 small onion, finely chopped
1 lb. cottage cheese
3/4 cup whole wheat bread crumbs

1/3 cup wheat germ

Mix ingredients and form into small patties and bake on greased baking sheet in moderate oven 20 min.

CHEESE LOAF

2 tbsp. onion, chopped
2 tbsp. butter
1 cup walnuts or pecans, chopped
1/2 cup whole wheat bread crumbs

1/2 cup wheat germ
1 cup cheese, grated
2/3 cup hot water
2 tbsp. lemon juice
2 beaten eggs
Salt to taste

Cook onions in a little water for 5 min. Add all ingredients, then mix well. Put in well-oiled loaf pan and bake for 30 min. Serve with tomato juice sauce, if desired.

CHAPTER 6

WHOLE GRAIN BREADS AND CEREALS

WHEAT IS, AT least in the United States, the most popular grain for bread making, largely because its protein has the proper texture for forming gas bubbles, thereby making a light loaf. However, there are also nutritional advantages, provided whole wheat grain is used, including both the bran and germ. Wheat, unlike other grains, such as rye, will not grow on soil low in phosphorus, so all wheat has a fairly high content of this bone-building mineral, as well as silicon and iron. It is also an excellent source of the vitamin B complex, and wheat germ is the richest known source of vitamin E, so important in maintaining a healthy cardio-vascular system. There is considerable evidence of other factors in wheat, as yet unnamed, which play important parts in health and vitality.

Many diet outlines in the readings included whole grain cereals and bread. "Rolled or cracked whole wheat," one recommended, "not cooked too long so as to destroy the whole vitamin force—this will add to the body the proper portions of iron, silicon, and the vitamins necessary to build up the blood supply that makes resistance in the system" (840-1). Buckwheat cakes, rice cakes and graham (whole wheat) cakes were also frequently recommended.

It is of importance that whole wheat flour be freshly ground in order to protect the vitamin content. Deterioration of vitamins begins almost immediately after grinding, due to oxidation, and it is estimated that at least half the vitamin content may be lost within a few days' time, especially if the flour is not refrigerated. The oil of the wheat germ also becomes rancid in a short time, impairing the flavor. Cracked wheat used for cereal should also, of course, be cracked as shortly before use as possible. We recommend the purchase of a small hand mill for this purpose.

Bread Making

There are only two important secrets to making good whole wheat bread. The first is the type of flour used. Hard wheat should be used, and there is no substitute for fresh stone-ground flour for flavor, texture and nutritional value of the finished product.* Flour ground by roller mills contains larger particles of bran, which may be irritating to the digestive tract, makes bread of coarser texture, and the difference in flavor of freshly ground flour, as compared to that left standing for some time in warehouses and grocers' shelves, can hardly be imagined.

The second important secret is in allowing sufficient time after mixing and before baking for the bran particles to absorb the moisture and become soft. This requires at least four hours, preferably longer, and is necessary to prevent the bread from being crumbly and dry.

Other points are of lesser importance. The exact amount of flour needed to make dough of proper consistency for handling may vary if measured by volume, as it may be packed more in some cases than others (measurements in bread recipes are for unsifted flour) and the best degree of stiffness must be learned from experience. Weighing the flour, if possible, may give more uniform results.

The exact temperature at which bread rises (80° to 85°), is important only if you wish rising time to be as short as possible. If you have plently of time, room temperature is usually quite satisfactory, and you avoid the danger of accidentally killing the yeast, which is possible from setting dough in too warm a place, as in an oven.

The exact amount of kneading can only be learned by experience. (It may vary with different flours). Time is important for the *best* possible texture in bread, but not essential for *good* bread. In short, it is difficult if good ingredients are used with a reasonable amount of care, not to have bread superior in flavor and nutrition, so don't hesitate to try because of lack of experience.

WHOLE WHEAT BREAD

5-1/3 cups lukewarm water
1 pkg. or cake yeast
2 tbsp. salt
1/3 cup vegetable oil

1/2 cup honey
3-1/2 lbs. (12 cups) unsifted
　whole wheat flour

Dissolve yeast in water, add salt, oil and honey, and stir. Add flour all at once and stir until thoroughly mixed, then let stand for 20 min. or longer before kneading. Knead on floured board until smooth and elastic and place in well-oiled bowl or pan (at least 6-qt. size). Cover (plastic wrap or a thin sheet of plastic is good for this) and let rise to double its bulk. Punch down well to remove all gas bubbles. Continue to let rise, punching down each time as soon as double in bulk until ready to make into loaves, preferably about 5 hrs. from time of

---

* If this kind of flour is not available, a small family size stone grinding mill would be a worthwhile investment. For information write to: Lee Engineering Company, 2023 W. Wisconsin Avenue, Milwaukee, Wisconsin, 53201

mixing. It should rise at least twice in this time. Turn out on floured board, knead a few minutes and divide into 4 equal portions. Knead and form into loaves, place in well-greased medium size loaf pans, lightly grease top surface with vegetable oil, and cover loosely with plastic wrap. Let rise until not quite double in bulk and bake at 325° about 45 min.

VARIATIONS

#1 Dough may be mixed in the evening, using cold rather than lukewarm water and doubling the amount of yeast. Leave in the refrigerator over night. In the morning remove from refrigerator and let stand at room temperature one-half hr., then knead and shape into loaves. Let rise and bake as in basic recipe.

#2 Mix in the evening, omitting yeast, and let stand at room temperature over night. In morning, soften two yeast cakes or two packages dry yeast in 2 to 4 tbsp. warm water and add to dough mixture, working it in well with hands. Let dough rest 10 to 20 min., then knead, allowing to rise until double in bulk and then shape into loaves as above.

#3 If time does not allow for any of above methods, yeast may be increased to 2 or 3 cakes, dough left in warm place to rise (be sure temperature is not above 85°) and kneaded and shaped into loaves after rising once to double in bulk, about 45 min. or less. Bread will be less moist than in other methods.

#4 When bread has been formed into loaves, brush with water rather than oil and sprinkle with sesame seed. This adds a delightful flavor as well as nutrition.

#5 For increasing nutritive value, milk may be substituted for water (if fresh milk is used it must be scalded), soy flour substituted for part of the whole wheat flour (not more than one-fourth the quantity, or 2 to 4 tbsp.) Brewer's yeast may be added, but bread will probably not be as light, as the addition of substances not containing gluten decreases the elasticity. Blackstrap molasses, which is extremely high in calcium, iron, and some of the B vitamins, may be substituted for all or part of the honey.

WHOLE WHEAT BUNS AND ROLLS

Buns and rolls may be made from the dough for whole wheat bread.

Hamburger Buns: Take pieces of dough the size of an egg. Roll into a ball and flatten to 3/4 in. thickness. Place on oiled cookie sheet or shallow pan, allowing at least 1 in. between buns; brush with vegetable oil, cover with plastic wrap and allow to rise until double or triple in size. Bake in moderate oven about 20 min.

Rolls: Roll out on floured board to 1/2 in. thickness. Cut with biscuit cutter, dip in vegetable oil and place close together in baking pan. Cover, let rise and bake as above.

Parker House Rolls are shaped by holding left forefinger across center of round, bringing far side of dough over and pressing edges together.

REFRIGERATOR ROLLS

1-1/2 cups lukewarm water
2 pkgs. or cakes yeast
2 tsp. salt
1/3 cup honey

1/3 cup vegetable oil
2 eggs, well beaten
4-1/2 to 5 cups unsifted whole
   wheat flour

Dissolve yeast, salt and honey in lukewarm water. Add oil and eggs and mix well, then stir in flour. Set in refrigerator over night. Take dough from refrigerator about 2 hrs. before time for serving rolls, let stand at room temperature about 1/2 hr. Knead on floured board, shape, and let rise as above. Bake 15 to 20 min. at 375°.

Scalded fresh milk or reconstituted powdered skim milk may be substituted for 1 cup of the water in this recipe, in which case the yeast and honey should be dissolved in the water (1/2 cup) and allowed to stand 20 min. before adding other ingredients.

WHEAT GERM ROLLS

1 cup warm water or milk
1 cake or pkg. yeast
1-1/2 tsp. salt
3 tbsp. blackstrap molasses
1 egg

1/4 cup vegetable oil
3/4 cup toasted wheat germ
1/3 cup powdered milk
2-1/2 cups whole wheat flour

Dissolve yeast in liquid, add other ingredients and stir to mix, then beat 200 strokes by hand or 10 min. with electric mixer. Cover bowl, set in warm place (not over 85°) until double in bulk. Make into rolls, kneading thoroughly and shaping as desired. When double or triple in bulk, bake at 350° for 20 to 25 min. or until brown.

If time allows, this dough may be placed in refrigerator over night as in recipe for Refrigerator Rolls, or after rising may be stirred down and left in refrigerator for 1 to 8 hrs. before using.

POTATO ROLLS

1-1/2 cups milk
1/2 cup potato water
2 pkgs. or cakes yeast
4 tbsp. honey
2 tsp. salt

2 eggs, beaten
1/3 cup mashed potato
4 tbsp. vegetable oil
6 to 7 cups sifted whole wheat
   flour

Dissolve yeast in liquids, add honey, salt, eggs, oil and mashed potatoes. Mix well, and stir in 2-1/2 cups flour to make a sponge. Let rise 1/2 hr. Add about 3-1/2 cups flour to make a medium stiff dough. Knead well and let rise until double in bulk. Knead again and shape into rolls. Put on well-greased pans, let rise 1 to 1-1/2 hrs. and bake for 20 min. at 400°.

CINNAMON ROLLS

Make dough as in either of foregoing recipes. Roll 1/4 in. thick, brush with mixture of melted butter and vegetable oil and dribble honey over surface. Sprinkle with cinnamon, and with raisins or pecans or walnuts if desired. Roll like jelly roll, cut in 1-in. pieces and set close together in baking pan. Let rise and bake in moderate oven.

COFFEE CAKE

Add 1/4 cup raw sugar or extra honey and 1/2 cup raisins to roll dough. After dough rises roll it 1/3 in. thick, brush surface with molasses or honey, sprinkle with cinnamon, nutmeg, 1/2 cup nuts, pressing nuts into dough. Let rise in refrigerator over night. Bake in moderate oven 18 to 20 min.

SALAD STICKS

Use any roll dough desired. Roll or pat dough to 1/2 in. thickness, cut into narrow strips, brush with oil on all sides. Place 1 in. apart on greased baking sheet. Cover and let rise and bake in moderate oven 10 min.

RAISED MUFFINS

1 cup warm water or milk
1 pkg. or cake yeast
3 tbsp. honey or blackstrap
   molasses
1 tsp. salt

3 tbsp. vegetable oil
1 cup whole wheat pastry flour
1/3 cup powdered milk
1/2 cup wheat germ flour

Dissolve yeast in water or milk and let stand while gathering other ingredients. Add honey or blackstrap, oil and salt, and stir. Sift in flour, wheat germ flour and powdered milk. (Wheat germ may be substituted for wheat germ flour, but of course can not be sifted. Add with flour.) Stir just enough to mix. Do not beat. Drop from tablespoon into oiled muffin pans until half full. Let rise until double in bulk. Bake at 350° for 20 min. Makes 12 large muffins.

RYE BREAD #1

2 cups warm potato water
1 pkg. or cake yeast
1 tbsp. salt
1 cup mashed potatoes

4 cups rye flour
2 cups whole wheat flour
1 tsp. caraway seed

Dissolve yeast in potato water, add other ingredients, stir to mix and knead until smooth and elastic. Let rise in warm place until double in bulk. Form into loaves, place in pans, let rise. Bake at 350° to 375° one hour or longer.

RYE BREAD #2

1 cup whole wheat flour
3 cups rye flour
1 tbsp. salt
Hot water

1 cake yeast
1/4 cup honey
1/4 cup lukewarm water

Mix dry ingredients. Pour in, while beating, sufficient hot water to make a stiff batter. Cover and let stand until lukewarm. Add yeast and honey dissoloved in lukewarm water, and enough whole wheat flour to make a dough. Let stand until double in bulk, shape into loaves. Let rise until double in bulk. Bake at 375° one hour or longer.

RYE BREAD #3

1-1/2 cups cold water
3/4 cup corn meal (yellow)
1-1/2 cups boiling water
1-1/2 tbsp. salt
1 tbsp. honey
2 cups whole wheat flour

1 pkg. or cake yeast
1/4 cup lukewarm water
1 tbsp. caraway seed
2 cups mashed potatoes
6 cups rye flour
2 tbsp. vegetable oil

Mix cornmeal with cold water in saucepan, add the boiling water, stirring constantly, and cook about 2 min. to a mush. Stir in salt, honey and oil and let cool to lukewarm. Dissolve yeast in lukewarm water, add this, the potatoes, caraway seed and flour. Mix well, knead on floured board to a smooth stiff dough. Cover and let rise in a warm place until doubled in bulk. Divide into 3 or 4 parts, shape into loaves, place in oiled pans. Let rise and bake 1 hr. at 375°.

PUMPERNICKEL

Follow directions of above recipe, substituting rye meal for the rye flour. Make into small loaves and bake until very well done.

Quick Breads

Quick breads are usually made light with baking powder. Since double acting baking powder is made with an aluminum compound we doubt the wisdom of using it, even though it may make breads and cakes lighter and is more convenient to use. We recommend Royal Baking Powder, which is made with Cream of Tartar, a product of grapes, as its acid constituent. A mixture of Cream of Tartar and soda (2-1/2 tsp. of Cream of Tartar to 1 tsp. of soda for each quart of flour) may be used for baking powder. Since once the gas bubbles released by the combination of these have escaped from the dough or batter no more are formed, or released during cooking, breads made with this type of baking powder must be handled quickly after liquid is added and stirred as little as possible. If extra lightness is desired, more baking powder may be used, as an extra quantity of this type does not result in a bitter taste as with baking powder made with aluminum.

The elasticity of gluten is developed in breads made with wheat flour by stirring or kneading. This is desirable in yeast breads but it is not necessary in quick breads and will make them less tender—another reason for handling as little as possible. Quick breads will be more tender if made from soft wheat flour which contains less gluten. Pastry flours are usually of this type. Hard wheat flour, as is used for yeast bread, may be used, however, and is probably slightly more nutritious.

BUTTERMILK BISCUITS

2 cups whole wheat flour
1 tsp. salt
3 tsp. Royal Baking Powder

1/3 cup vegetable oil
3/4 cup buttermilk
1/4 tsp. soda

Sift dry ingredients and mix in oil. Add buttermilk all at once and stir quickly, only enough to mix. Pat out 1/2 in. thick on floured board and cut. Brush with vegetable oil and bake at 400° for 15 min.

BAKING POWDER BISCUITS

2 cups sifted whole wheat flour
1 tsp. salt
4 tsp. baking powder

6 tbsp. vegetable oil
2/3 cup milk

Sift dry ingredients together. Mix in oil thoroughly. Stir in milk to make a soft dough. Pat out on floured board, handling as little as possible. Cut with biscuit cutter, or in squares with knife. Bake at 375° to 400° for 15 min.

Butter may be substituted for a part of the oil in either of these recipes for better flavor, and 1/2 cup wheat germ or wheat germ flour used in place of 1/2 cup flour for extra nutrients. 1/4 cup powdered milk may be added if desired.

DROP BISCUITS

Follow above recipe using 1-1/4 cup milk. Drop by spoonfuls onto oiled baking sheet or well-greased muffin tins.

CHEESE BISCUITS

Reduce oil to 2 tbsp. and blend in 3/4 cup sharp Cheddar cheese.

WHEAT GERM MUFFINS

Sift together:
1 cup whole wheat flour
1/2 tsp. salt
3 tsp. baking powder
Add: 1-1/2 cups wheat germ

Mix together:
1 cup milk
1/2 cup powdered milk
1 egg
1/4 cup (each) oil and honey

Combine the two mixtures. Stir quickly and spoon into buttered muffin tins. Bake 20 min. at 400°. Makes 1 dozen large muffins. Raisins, chopped dates, or nuts may be added if desired.

DRIED FRUIT MUFFINS

2 eggs, separated
2 tbsp. oil
1 tbsp. maple syrup
1 tsp. sea kelp

1 cup figs, prunes and raisins
    chopped together
1/2 cup wheat germ
1/2 cup peanut flour

Beat the egg whites stiff and set aside. Blend the other ingredients and fold in the egg whites last. Pour batter in oiled muffin tins and bake about 25 min. at 350°. The cup of dried fruit may be of any variety, just so there is a cup of packed dried fruit after chopping. This recipe makes 6 large muffins and can be enlarged to fit the crowd. These are fine breakfast muffins.

CORN-CARAWAY GEMS

2 eggs, separated
1 tbsp. honey
1 tsp. caraway seeds
1 tsp. sea kelp

2 tbsp. cooking oil
1/2 cup wheat germ
1/2 cup coconut or nut milk
3/4 cup yellow corn flour

Blend all ingredients except the egg whites, to be added last, beaten stiff and folded in. Bake in tiny muffin tins if possible, or in small custard cups. Have baking dishes well oiled and bake about 10 min. at 400° or until brown and done in the middle. These are crunchy and very good.

HOT CAKES

1-1/2 cups unsifted whole
  wheat flour
3 tsp. baking powder
1/2 tsp. salt

1-1/4 cups milk
1 egg
2 tbsp. honey or raw sugar
3 or 4 tbsp. oil

Sift dry ingredients together. Combine other ingredients in blender or beat eggs and then other ingredients. Combine the two mixtures, stirring just enough to mix. Bake on slightly oiled hot griddle.

BUCKWHEAT CAKES

3/4 cup buckwheat flour
1 tsp. Royal Baking Powder
1/2 tsp. salt
1 cup milk

2 eggs, separated
1 tbsp. melted butter
1 cup cooked brown rice

Blend milk with rice, add well-beaten egg yolk. Combine dry ingredients into this mixture and add butter. Whip egg whites until stiff and fold into above mixture. Bake on oiled griddle and serve with butter and maple syrup.

WHEAT GERM PANCAKES

2 cups nut milk*
4 eggs, separated
2 tbsp. cooking oil
1-1/2 tsp. sea kelp

1 tsp. honey (optional)
2 cups wheat germ
1 cup brown rice flour

Beat the egg yolks, then add the milk and flour. Beat well, adding other ingredients, and fold in the stiffly beaten whites of the 4 eggs just before baking. This recipe makes about 16 nutritious pancakes.

WAFFLES

1 cup sifted whole wheat flour
3 tsp. baking powder
1/2 tsp. salt
2 eggs, separated

1-1/4 cups milk
1/4 cup oil
2 tsp. raw sugar

Sift dry ingredients 3 times. Add egg yolks, milk and oil, beaten together, and beat 2 min. with electric mixer on low speed. Fold in beaten egg whites and bake in preheated waffle iron.

* See Chapter 8, Beverages

BUCKWHEAT WAFFLES

2 cups water
1 tsp. lemon juice
1/4 cup raw almonds
3 tbsp. vegetable oil
Blend in blender, then add:
1/4 cup soy flour or powder

1-1/4 cups buckwheat flour
2 tbsp. honey
2 tbsp. molasses
3/4 tsp. sea salt
1/4 cup oatmeal
3/4 cup whole wheat flour

Blend thoroughly and bake in preheated waffle iron.

NUT WAFFLES

1 cup whole wheat flour
1/4 cup soy flour
3/4 tsp. salt
3 tsp. baking powder
1/4 to 1/2 cup chopped
    pecans or other nuts

1-1/4 cups sweet milk or
    almond milk*
2 eggs, separated
2 tbsp. raw sugar or honey
5 tbsp. oil

Sift dry ingredients twice. Add egg yolks, milk, sugar and oil, beaten together, and blend. Add chopped nuts and fold in egg whites.

SPICY APPLE BREAD

1 cup unsifted whole wheat
    flour
1 tsp. soda
1 tsp. salt
1 tsp. cinnamon
1/2 tsp. nutmeg
1/2 tsp. cloves
1/2 cup butter
3/4 cup dark brown sugar

2 eggs, beaten
1 cup coarsely grated sour
    apples
1 cup unsifted whole wheat
    flour
1/4 cup sour milk or
    buttermilk
1/2 cup chopped nuts

Sift together first six ingredients; set aside. In mixing bowl combine butter, sugar and eggs and beat well. Stir in apples and second cup of flour. Add sour milk and blend well; add sifted ingredients and stir just until well mixed. Add nuts and bake in greased 9x5x3 loaf pan at 350° for 55 to 60 min. Slices best after cooling for several hours or over night.

* See Chapter 8, Beverages

DATE-NUT BREAD

2 cups chopped dates
2 cups boiling water
1 tsp. soda
2 eggs
1/2 tsp. salt
2 tsp. cinnamon
2 tsp. butter

2 cups raw sugar
4 cups sifted whole wheat flour
1 cup chopped nuts
   (preferably pecans)
2 tsp. vanilla
3 tsp. baking powder

Combine boiling water and soda, then add dates and butter. Combine beaten eggs and sugar and add to first mixture. Add flour, spices, and baking powder which have been sifted together twice. Add nuts and vanilla. A cup of raisins may be added if desired. Pour into loaf pans, let stand for 5 min. Bake 1-1/4 hrs. at 325° to 350°. Loaf pans should be greased and the bottom lined with waxed paper.

NUT BREAD

1 cup warm potato water
1 pkg. dry yeast

2 tsp. honey
1 cup corn flour

Blend together and let rise until very light, probably around 45 min. Then add the following to make a stiff loaf:

1/2 cup sunflower seed meal
1 cup chopped nuts
1 cup raisins
1 egg, beaten

1 tbsp. oil
1 cup peanut flour
1 cup wheat germ flour
1 tsp. sea kelp

Don't bother to knead this bread because there is no gluten in it. Stir it with a big spoon, then put it into an oiled bread tin. Let it rise while the oven heats, and bake 10 min. at 400°, then about 50 min. at 350°.

STEAMED DATE-NUT BREAD

1 cup whole wheat flour
1 cup soy sauce
1 cup wheat germ
3 tsp. bone meal
3 tbsp. Tortula yeast
1-1/2 tsp. soda

2 cups buttermilk
3/4 cup blackstrap molasses
1 tbsp. vegetable oil
1 cup dates
1/2 cup pecans

Sift together dry ingredients, except wheat germ. Add wheat germ, dates, and pecans, then other ingredients mixed together, and mix quickly, stirring as little as possible. Pour into greased molds, filling about 2/3 full, cover and steam for 2 hrs. Five #2 cans serve well as molds.

This bread is extremely high in protein, calcium, iron, and the B vitamins.

STEAMED BROWN BREAD

1 cup all-bran	1/2 cup sugar
1 cup sour milk	1 cup whole wheat flour
1/2 cup raisins	1 tsp. soda
1 tbsp. molasses	1/4 tsp. salt

Mix all-bran, sour milk and raisins. Let it absorb the milk, then add molasses, then dry ingredients. Put into a greased coffee can (tall). Cover tightly and steam 3 hrs.

DIXIE CORN BREAD

4 cups soy milk	2 tbsp. cooking oil
2 cups yellow corn meal	1 tsp. sea kelp
4 eggs, separated	

Heat the milk hot, add the corn meal gradually, stirring constantly. Sir and cook until very thick. Remove from fire and cool to warm.

Beat the 4 egg whites stiff, then put the corn meal mixture, the egg yolks, oil and sea kelp under the beaters and blend them thoroughly. Fold in whites and pour the batter into an oiled oblong cake tin. Bake at 375° until done, about 45 min.

WHOLE WHEAT CORN MEAL BREAD

1 cup corn meal	2/3 cup shortening
1 cup whole wheat flour	1 cup milk
2 tsp. baking powder	1 egg
1 tsp. salt	1/4 cup sugar

Combine ingredients in each of the columns above, separately, then mix or blend together and bake as in preceding recipe.

PEANUT BREAD

2 cups raw peanut flour	1 cup ground nuts
2 egg yolks	(preferably black walnuts)
2 rounded tbsp. homemade (or unhydrogenated) peanut butter	

Blend ingredients, adding peanut butter if too dry, or peanut flour if too sticky. Shape into thin wafers and lay them on a cooky sheet. Dry in the sun for 30 min., then store in a covered dish. These raw slices of nut bread are just delightful in flavor and high in nutrition. Made very tiny, they can be served as hors d'oeuvres. They are wonderful to munch on as between-meal snacks, or for the children's afternoon treats.

OATMEAL CRACKERS

1 cup cold potato water
1/2 cup cooking oil, safflower

1 tsp. sea kelp
4 cups quick-cooking oatmeal

Mix ingredients into stiff dough and chill it in refrigerator. Lightly flour a board and roll thin. Sprinkle with Seseman (sesame) seeds and roll these in. Cut in squares and bake on oiled cookie sheet at 350° for 25 min.

WHOLE WHEAT CRACKERS

3 cups sifted whole wheat
  pastry flour
1/2 cup vegetable oil

1 tsp. (scant) sea salt
1/3 cup, plus 3 tbsp. soy milk

Sift flour and salt together, add oil and mix well. Add soy milk and mix to stiff dough. Roll thin, cut in desired shapes and prick with a fork. Bake at 350° until brown.

HEALTH CRACKERS

2 cups whole wheat pastry
  flour
1 cup millet meal
1/2 cup rice polishings
1/4 cup sunflower seed meal

3/4 tsp. sea salt
3/4 cup vegetable oil
2 tbsp. honey
3/4 cup water

Mix dry ingredients, add oil and blend in well with fingers or pastry cutter. Add honey dissolved in water, mix and knead very lightly. Roll to thickness of piecrust. Cut into squares and prick with fork. Bake at 350° until brown.

Cereals

WHOLE WHEAT

1 cup clean whole wheat
1 tsp. salt

2 cups water

Bring water to a boil and add salt and wheat. Remove from direct heat as soon as water reaches second boil, pour in casserole dish and place, uncovered, on adapter ring or shelf of steamer or deep well cooker. Have boiling water in bottom of steamer to within 1 in. of shelf. Cover steamer tightly, and cook over low heat to keep water in steamer just simmering for 8 to 10 hrs. Serve with butter or cream and honey.

CRACKED WHEAT

1 cup cracked wheat   1 tsp. salt
4 cups water

Add salt and cracked wheat to boiling water and cook over direct heat for about 30 min. or in double boiler for 1 hr. or more. This may be started in double boiler at night and cooked for 30 min. then finished cooking in the morning.

Another method of cooking, which would retain more of the vitamins but perhaps make the wheat less easily digested, is as follows:
Add 1 cup cracked wheat to 3 cups boiling salted water. Boil for 5 min., then put into quart thermos to retain heat and leave for 8 hrs. before serving.

MULTI-GRAIN DRY CEREAL

3 cups whole wheat flour   1-1/2 cups dry malt
3 cups corn meal   3-1/2 cups milk or soy milk
3 cups millet flour   4 tbsp. honey
3 cups oatmeal   1 tbsp. salt or sea salt

Blend dry ingredients together. Mix milk, malt and honey and add to dry ingredients to make a stiff dough. Roll very thin, prick and bake at 300° until golden brown. Put through food chopper to crumble it.

DRY CEREAL #2

1 cup whole wheat flour   1 tbsp. sea salt
1/2 cup rye flour   1/2 cup water
1 cup soy flour   1/2 cup honey
1/2 cup corn meal   1/2 cup oil
1 cup oatmeal   3 tsp. toasted sesame seeds
1/2 cup rice bran

Mix dry ingredients. Add water, honey and oil mixed together, and stir to form granules. Bake on a sheet pan at 325° until lightly browned, stirring frequently. Turn out fire, and allow to stay in oven, stirring occasionally until cool. How long your oven retains enough heat to cook will determine the degree of brownness before fire is turned off.

CHAPTER 7

DESSERTS AND SWEETS

WHILE WE CAN find no corroboration from scientific sources of the statement in the Cayce readings that beet sugar is preferable to cane sugar (or, in fact, that there is any difference, from a chemical standpoint), the deleterious effects of refined sugars and an excess of concentrated sweets are widely recognized.

According to Adelle Davis, one of the country's best known nutritionists,* excessive eating of sweets, especially refined sugar, increases the need for choline, a deficiency of which has been found to produce nephritis and liver damage, and interferes with the absorption of calcium by increasing the production of alkaline digestive juices, thus counteracting the acidity of the digestive juices of the stomach necessary to dissolve calcium. She also notes that persons suffering from atherosclerosis often show a particularly high intake of refined sugar.

J.I. Rodale, Editor of *Prevention Magazine,* relates the consumption of refined sugars to susceptibility to insect bites, sinus trouble, stomach trouble, arthritis, pyorrhea, dental decay and cancer. He stresses the price we pay in vitamin B for eating refined sugar, stating that B vitamins, occurring in the natural sweets, fruits, and sugar cane, are necessary for the assimilation of sugars, and when refined sugars are eaten these vitamins are drawn from the organs and tissues of the body, leaving them deficient in these important food substances.

The relation of sugar consumption to dental decay is generally recognized. In an article in the *Journal of the American Dental Association* for July 1, 1947, Isaac Schour, D.D.S., Ph.D., and Maury Massler, D.D.S., M.S., in discussing the low incidence of tooth decay among children of post-war Italy, as compared to the enormously higher rate (several times as high) among children of the same ages in this country, point out that the diet of the Italian children included very little refined sugar, although it was high in starches and the children were not especially well nourished.

Melvin Page, D.D.S., in his book, "Degeneration—Regeneration," states that sugar is indirectly a cause of dental decay, pyorrhea and arthritis by disturbing the calcium-phosphorus balance. Sugar disturbs this balance, he says, more than any other single factor. The amounts of these materials, he believes, is not as important as their proportions to each other. He also states that he does not

* "Let's Eat Right to Keep Fit"
"Let's Get Well"—Harcourt, Brace and World, Inc., N.Y.

remember seeing a single cancer case that showed correct sugar level of the blood.

Michael H. Walsh, M.Sc., F.R.I.C., Instructor of Clinical Nutrition at the University of California, stated in a speech in April, 1950,* that there is evidence of a dietary relationship between high sugar consumption and polio, rheumatic fever, arthritis and many degenerative diseases.

According to J. I. Rodale,[1] Dr. Sandler brought to a standstill a polio epidemic in North Carolina several years ago, by means of a diet the essence of which was a sharp reduction in the consumption of sugar. Apparently large numbers of residents were sufficiently frightened by the proportions of the epidemic to be willing to try the diet he recommended. His theory was that low blood sugar, brought about by eating too much sugar and thus triggering an overproduction of insulin, can increase the susceptibility to polio.

Dr. E. M. Abrahamson, in his book, "Body, Mind and Sugar," not only agrees with Dr. Sandler, but relates low blood sugar to such a wide variety of ills as asthma, alcoholism, neuroses, fatigue, rheumatic fever, ulcers, epilepsy, depression, and so forth, and explains how consumption of concentrated sweets produces low blood sugar through stimulating the pancreas to excessive production of insulin.

All sweets, save natural sweets such as found in most fruits, maple syrups, and honey, are acid producing, another reason why the consumption of them should be strictly limited. Fruits (fresh, stewed or dried), confections and desserts made with dried fruits and honey as the only sweetening agent, and honey used on bread and cereals, can supply the sugars necessary to form the alcohol needed for a proper digestion and assimilation, and are most to be recommended from a nutritional standpoint, although an excess even of these can produce an unhealthy imbalance.

Raw sugar was among those sweets recommended by the Cayce readings. Real raw sugar, we have been told (that is, sugar which has not gone through the refining process), is now impractical to obtain in this country. That which is sold as raw sugar at the present time is produced by adding molasses to refined white sugar, thereby replacing the vitamins and minerals which have been removed in the refining process.

Whether factors as yet unknown have been altered by this process, making this inferior to raw sugar, we have no way of knowing, but it is certainly preferable to cane sugar without the addition of the mineral-rich molasses. Therefore, since most people will eat some cookies, cakes, puddings, and such, we have included here some recipes for these, which use raw sugar and other natural sweets. However, we would remind the reader of the warning in the readings against the combination of starches and sweets.

---

* "Sugar and Dental Caries"—*Journal of the California State Dental Association,* 1950.
[1] "The Health Finder"—The Rodale Press, 123 New Bond St., London.

PROTEIN CAKE

1/2 lb. nut meats, ground fine	1 cup raw or brown sugar or
7 eggs, separated	1/2 of each
Pinch of salt	1 tsp. vanilla

Beat egg whites until very stiff and dry. Set aside. Beat egg yolks and sugar together until creamy, add nut meats gradually, then salt and vanilla. Fold this mixture into the egg whites carefully, and bake in an ungreased tube pan for 1 hr. at 325°. Invert pan to cool.

CARAMEL SAUCE

2/3 cup maple syrup	4 tbsp. cream
2/3 cup brown sugar	

Simmer a couple of minutes, partly cool, and add 1 tbsp. butter; finish cooling.

CAROB CAKE

1/2 cup butter	1-1/2 tsp. cinnamon
1 cup raw sugar	1/2 tsp. baking powder
2 eggs	1/2 tsp. baking soda
1 cup sifted whole wheat pastry	1/2 tsp. salt
flour	1/2 cup buttermilk
1/2 cup carob powder	1 tsp. vanilla

Cream butter and sugar. Add eggs and beat well. Combine all dry ingredients and sift together three times. Add sifted dry ingredients to creamed mixture, alternating with buttermilk, beating well. Pour into an oiled 8x8 baking pan. Bake at 350° for 25-30 min. Frost with Carob Fudge Frosting.

CAROB FUDGE FROSTING

3/4 cup rich milk	1/4 cup butter
1/4 cup carob powder	2 cups raw sugar

Place first three ingredients in saucepan over medium heat, stir constantly until smooth and thick. Add sugar and stir until completely dissolved. Without stirring, cook until the "soft ball" stage when tested in cold water. Frost cooled cake.

OATMEAL CAKE

1 cup oatmeal
1/2 cup chopped dates or
    raisins
1/2 cup butter
2 cups brown sugar

2 eggs
1 tsp. vanilla
1/2 tsp. salt
1 tsp. baking soda
1-1/2 cups whole wheat flour

Pour 1/2 cup boiling water over oatmeal and fruit. Stir well and cool. After it is cooled, mix and add remaining ingredients to oatmeal and fruit mixture. Bake at 375° for 30 min.

TOPPING

1/2 cup brown sugar
1/4 cup whole wheat flour
1/4 cup butter

2 tbsp. water
3/4 cup nuts or coconut

Melt butter, add water, flour, sugar and coconut. Spread over cake and return to oven for about 10 min.

DELUXE SPICE CUP CAKES

1 cup uncooked prunes or
    dates, pitted and chopped
    (may substitute 2 cans of
    thick applesauce)
1 cup boiling water
2 cups unsifted whole wheat
    flour
1-1/2 cups dark brown sugar

1 tsp. salt
1-1/4 tsp. soda
1 tsp. each: cinnamon, nutmeg,
    cloves, ginger, allspice
3 eggs
1 cup raisins (optional)
1/2 cup vegetable oil

Pour cup of boiling water over dried fruit. Let stand a minimum of 2 hrs. (omit this step if using applesauce). Place fruit mixture and all other ingredients (except raisins) in small bowl of mixer. Blend for 1 min. on low speed. Beat 2 min. on medium speed. Add raisins. Stir in. Makes 2 dozen medium cup cakes. (Use liners.) Bake 25 min. at 350°. When cold, sift over top of cakes, 1 part dried milk to 1 part powdered sugar.

PEANUT COOKIES

1 cup chopped organically
    grown peanuts
1-1/2 cups peanut flour

1/2 cup homemade (or
    unhydrogenated) peanut
    butter

Mix the ingredients together. If too dry, add drops of salad oil. If too sticky, add soy milk powder. Shape into small cookies and roll in sunflower seed meal. Store in the refrigerator. These cookies satisfy the peanut lover's taste for peanuts, and are easily digested. Even children and the aged can eat them safely and they are a high protein dessert or snack.

Nutty Confections

Put 1/4 lb. of brick carob to melt. Meanwhile, chop the following ingredients and form the mixture into thin cookies:

1 cup locally grown nuts	1-1/2 cups pitted dates,
1 cup shelled peanuts	chopped
1/2 cup sunflower seeds	1 cup grated coconut

Dip the thin cookies into the warm carob mixture, on both sides, then lay on an oiled pan until the carob is reset. Serve as cookies.

Health Cookies

2 cups raw sugar (yellow D)	3-1/2 cups whole wheat flour
1/2 lb. (2 sticks) butter,	2 tsp. soda
softened	1-1/2 tsp. cream of tartar
3 eggs	1 cup sunflower seeds, shelled
2 cups coconut, fine,	
unsweetened	

Cream together sugar, butter, and eggs. Add coconut. Blend. Combine flour, soda and cream of tartar, and add to first mixture, mix, and add sunflower seeds. Let stand 1 hr. in refrigerator, if possible, as the mixture is then easier to handle. Pinch off teaspoonfuls and flatten almost to paper thin, using a wet cloth over a flat-bottom jar or wide glass. Bake at 375° about 7–8 min. Makes about 75 cookies.

Fig Fandangos

3 eggs, separated	1 tsp. sea kelp
2/3 cup honey	1/2 tsp. cinnamon
1 tsp. pure vanilla extract	1 cup peanut flour
1 cup nut meats, chopped	1/2 cup wheat germ flour
1 cup figs, chopped	

Beat the egg whites and set aside. Blend the other items and fold the egg whites in last. Bake in a 9x9-in. tin about 45 min. at 350°. Try with a toothpick, making sure it is done before removing from oven. Cool and cut in squares. This is very light; take out with a pancake turner or slanting spatula.

COCONUT MACAROONS

1/2 cup raw sugar
2 egg whites
1/2 tsp. cider vinegar

1/8 tsp. salt
1/2 tsp. vanilla
1/2 cup coconut, shredded

Beat whites until foamy, then add vinegar and salt. Beat until peaks hold, gradually add sugar, a tablespoon at a time, beating well after each addition. Lightly fold in vanilla and coconut. Drop by tablespoon on brown paper or cookie sheet. Sprinkle top of cookies with coconut. Bake at 275°.

UNCOOKED TAFFY

1/2 cup homemade (or
unhydrogenated) peanut
butter
1/2 cup honey

1 cup peanuts—shelled from
whole unroasted peanuts
Instant soy milk powder

Blend the first three ingredients together (the peanuts may be chopped if desired). Then use only enough of the soy milk powder to make a stiff dough. Roll it in a long roll, place on a cookie sheet, and chill over night. In the morning, whack off inch pieces for the lunch pail, or for the children for special treats.

LOLLIPOPS

1 cup raisins
1 cup dried prunes
1 cup locally grown nut meats

1 cup coconut chunks
1 cup figs

Put the above ingredients through the food grinder and shape into balls, then flatten into oblongs. Roll each one in either ground coconut meal, ground nuts, or ground sunflower seeds, and put a wooden paddle in each lollipop. A treat for the children.

DATE CAROB BARS

4 eggs, separated, whites beaten
stiff
1/3 cup honey
3/4 cup dates, pitted and
chopped

3/4 cup almonds, ground
3/4 cup wheat germ
1/3 cup carob powder

Blend egg yolks with other ingredients, fold in the whites last and bake in a small cake tin about 45 min. at about 325°, or until done. Cut in bars while warm. This recipe may be varied by changing the fruit and nuts and by adding different spices with the various combinations.

CANDY

1 cup "Grandma's Molasses"   1 cup raw sugar
1 tbsp. butter

Cook slowly for 10 min. (270° candy thermometer) and pull until candy becomes light in color.

Dried Fruits and Nuts

DATE PATTIES

Press 1 cup dates and 1 cup pecans through food chopper, mix thoroughly. Form into patties and roll in coconut or Mal-ba nuts.

NATURAL CANDY BARS

Press 1 lb. black Mission figs with 2 cups almonds through food chopper. Roll out 1/2 in. thickness on wax paper to prevent sticking to board. Cut in bars 3 in. long and 1 in. wide. Cover each bar with Mal-ba nuts and wrap in wax paper.

RAISIN BALLS

Raisins ground and formed into balls and rolled in freshly grated coconut.

FIG CANDY

Take desired number of white figs, cut off 3/4 in. of stem end and open fig for stuffing. Put equal parts of fresh coconut and sesame seeds through food chopper. Add a little Mal-ba nuts and stuff each fig fully. Garnish each fig with a pine nut.

CARROT PUDDING

1/2 cup butter   2 tbsp. lemon peel, finely
3/4 cup brown sugar   chopped
1 egg   1-1/4 cups whole wheat flour
2 tbsp. water   1 tsp. baking powder
3/4 cup raw carrots, grated   1/2 tsp. salt
1/3 cup dates, chopped   1/3 tsp. cinnamon
1/2 cup seedless raisins   1/2 tsp. nutmeg
1/2 cup nuts, chopped   1/8 tsp. allspice

Cream together butter and sugar until light and fluffy, add egg and water and beat thoroughly. Add carrots, dates, raisins, nuts, and lemon peel, blend well. Sift together flour, baking powder, salt, cinnamon, nutmeg and allspice, and gradually add to creamed mixture. Turn into buttered 5-cup mold.

Bake for 1-1/4 to 1-1/2 hrs. at 325°. Allow to stand for 5 min. Remove from mold. Serve warm. Serve 8 to 10. Pudding may be prepared ahead of time and refrigerated or frozen. To reheat, wrap in foil and place in oven until heated through.

FRUIT CRUMB PUDDING

Mix 1 pt. whole wheat crumbs in pt. hot milk and let stand for 10 min. Steam 1-1/2 cups mixed raisins, dates, and figs for 5 min. Add to bread crumbs. Then add 1 egg, beaten. Mix thoroughly and bake for 30 min.

DATE CREAM

1 cup dates, pitted
1 cup applesauce

1-1/2 cup whipped cream

Mash dates and mix with applesauce to which add whipped cream. Pile into sherbet glasses and chill.

DATE COCONUT CREAM

1 cup dates, pitted and ground
1/2 cup fresh coconut

2 cups whipped cream

Combine ingredients and chill thoroughly.

VANILLA RICE CUSTARD

3 tbsp. natural brown rice,
   unpolished
1 cup milk, skim or whole
1 egg, beaten slightly

3 tbsp. dark brown sugar
1 tsp. vanilla
1/2 cup raisins (optional)

Nutmeg to sprinkle over top when ingredients are well mixed. Bake in 325° oven for about 1 hr. or until silver knife comes out clean after testing.

COCONUT CUSTARD

3 eggs, beaten
1/3 cup honey
1 tsp. pure vanilla

2 cups coconut milk
1/4 tsp. mace

Beat well and pour into a small baking dish. Set this in a pan of hot water and bake until the custard is set in the center. Cool, then grate fresh coconut over the top and serve.

COCONUT RICE

1 cup boiling hot brown rice	1/2 cup almonds, chopped
1 egg yolk	1/2 cup coconut milk
1 tsp. honey	
1/2 cup fresh-shredded	
coconut	

Blend these ingredients and stir into the boiling rice, then remove from the fire and cool.

GLORIFIED RICE

1 cup brown rice, cooked	1/3 cup honey
1 cup crushed pineapple,	1/2 tsp. salt
drained	1 cup whipped cream

Mix ingredients, and fold in whipped cream.

DRIED APRICOTS IN GELATIN

3/4 cup dried apricots	Hot water to cover apricots
1 pkg. (small) peach gelatin	1 cup boiling water to dissolve gelatin
1/4 cup yogurt	

Allow apricots to soak and cool a few hours or over night. Purée in blender and add peach gelatin made with only 1 cup water. Put 1/2 mixture from blender in bowl or mold and let stand until it sets—10 min.—then either mix in the yogurt or stand it on top of mixture in bowl. Then cover with remaining blender mixture.

LEMON CREAM GELATIN DESSERT OR SALAD

1 pkg. gelatin. Sweeten and flavor with 1 cup natural sugar and the juice of 1 lemon (about 2 tbsp. lemon juice)
1 cup crushed unsweetened pineapple, drained
2 cups hot water (Use the juice drained from the pineapple and also count the liquid from the lemon to amount to a portion of the liquid, then add enough hot water to make up to the 2 cups.)
1/2 cup Cheddar cheese, grated   1/2 pt. whipping cream

Dissolve the gelatin. Add all the liquid. Chill until just set. Then add the crushed pineapple, grated cheese, and fold in the whipped cream. Serves 4 to 6.

STRAWBERRY ICE

2 cups fresh hulled strawberries	1/2 cup honey
2 egg yolks	1 cup fresh pineapple juice

Put all the above in a blender. (If you have no fresh raw pineapple juice, use a heaping tablespoon of chopped raw pineapple and 3/4 cup cold water.) Pour this mixture into a freezing-tray and stir it several times while it freezes.

HONEY FREEZE

6 eggs, separated
1/2 tsp. salt
1-1/2 cups honey

1 envelope unflavored gelatin
Whipped cream
Pistachio nuts, chopped

Beat egg yolks until thick and lemon colored. Combine with salt, honey and gelatin in the top of a double boiler. Cook over boiling water, stirring constantly, until mixture is somewhat thickened and smooth. Cool mixture in a pan of ice water until throughly chilled. Beat egg whites until soft peaks form. Gently fold egg yolk mixture into egg whites. Pour mixture into freezer trays or individual molds. Freeze 2 hrs. Serve with garnish of whipped cream and nuts. Makes about 1-1/2 qts.

FRENCH STRAWBERRY PIE

2 baskets strawberries
1 (3 oz.) pkg. cream cheese
1 baked pie shell
1-1/4 cups sugar, unrefined

3-1/2 tbsp. corn starch
1 tbsp. lemon juice
1/3 cup whipping cream

Spread softened cream cheese in bottom of pie shell and press 1/2 of the choicest berries whole into the cheese, tips up. Mash remaining berries. Measure to make 1-1/2 cups berries and juice (add water if necessary). Mix corn starch and sugar. Add berries and lemon juice and cook until thick. Add a few drops food coloring and cool. Pour over pie shell containing creamed cheese and strawberries. Chill 4 hrs. Serve garnished with whipping cream.

CHAPTER 8

BEVERAGES

MILK WAS FREQUENTLY recommended in the readings, especially certified raw milk. The use of raw milk is contrary to opinions stated in many health magazines and books, but most nutritionists recognize the nutritional importance of milk itself as the most nearly complete single food known. Soy and nut milk recipes are included here, primarily for the benefit of those who may be allergic to cow's milk, since these furnish most of the nutritional elements of the natural milk.

Since chocolate is now deemed generally detrimental to health, recipes are given using carob, a chocolate substitute, and other ingredients both pleasing to the taste and healthful from the viewpoint of the readings.

Raw vegetable juices have most of the nutritional value of the vegetables from which they are prepared and can be taken in much larger quantities than would be possible with the whole vegetable. Since roughage is important in the diet we suggest adding these, rather than substituting juice for the raw fresh vegetables. One individual was advised by the readings to take vegetable juices, either separately or in combination, once or twice a week. (1709-10) Another was told to take an ounce of raw carrot juice at least once a day. Vegetable juices may be obtained at health food stores, or can be prepared at home with a vegetable juicer.

Fruit juices as beverages, likewise, add more of the values of fresh fruit to the diet, but should not be substituted for fresh fruit. Citrus fruit juices were those most often recommended in the readings, and it was suggested that lime or lemon juice be added to orange or grapefruit juice; (2072-3), (3525-1) also that lemon and lime juice be combined.

Milk Drinks

CAROB MILK DRINK #1

2 cups certified raw milk
2 tbsp. carob powder

2 tbsp. honey
1/4 cup water

Heat milk, don't boil, and pour over remaining ingredients.

CAROB MILK DRINK #2

1 small carob candy bar

2 cups certified raw milk

Melt carob candy in top of double boiler, add milk and warm to desired temperature. Don't boil. Sweeten with honey if desired.

CARROT MILK

1 cup certified raw milk
2 med. size carrots, cut in
   pieces

Place ingredients in blender and liquefy. This drink has an attractive pale-carrot tint and a coconut-like flavor.

APRICOT MILK

1 cup ripe raw apricots or
1/2 cup cooked dried apricots

3 cups certified raw milk
Honey to taste

Place ingredients in blender and liquefy.

MAPLE-EGG MILK

3 tbsp. pure maple syrup
1 egg yolk
2 cups certified raw milk

1/4 tsp. pure vanilla
Dash of salt

Blend ingredients 15 to 20 sec.

Yogurt (Bulgarian Buttermilk)

Bulgarian buttermilk, recommended by the Cayce readings, and more commonly known in this country as yogurt, has been one of the principal foods of the Bulgarians for a long period of time, and is considered by many to be largely responsible for their unusual health, vigor and virility. The 1930 census showed that there were more than 1600 Bulgarians over 100 years old per million population, compared with only 9 persons in America. Baldness and white hair are said to be almost unknown in Bulgaria.

The health-giving properties of yogurt are primarily due to the fact that the bacteria in yogurt, Lactobacillus bulgarius, streptococcus lactis, thermobacterium yogurt, thrive in the intestines and are capable of synthesizing large amounts of the entire group of B vitamins, as well as destroying or inhibiting the action of putrefactive bacteria. The bacteria also partially break down the proteins of the milk, making it more easy to digest, and the acid produced in the milk dissolves some of the calcium, making it more available to the body.

Yogurt may be beaten and served as a beverage, having a flavor very similar to buttermilk. If the taste is not enjoyed at first, as is frequently the case, a taste for it may be cultivated gradually by taking it frequently in very small amounts. It may also be served with fruit or berries or as an ingredient in salad dressings.

PREPARING YOGURT AT HOME

Basic recipe: Combine 1 quart pasteurized whole or skim milk and 1/4 cup commercial yogurt. Warm slowly in oven or top of double boiler or in glasses set in a pan of warm water over simmer burner until milk reaches temperature of 100° to 120°. Maintain at temperature between 90° and 120° until milk becomes the consistency of junket, or from 3 to 5 hrs. If temperature is kept lower than 90° lactic acid bacteria, rather than the yogurt culture, will grow; and while these will thicken the milk and are not harmful, they cannot live in the intestinal tract to produce B vitamins. If temperature rises above 120° the bacteria will be killed and milk will not thicken.

Thick yogurt: Combine 3 cups pasteurized milk, 1-1/2 cups evaporated milk and 1/4 cup commercial yogurt, or combine 1 quart pasteurized milk, 1 cup powdered skim milk, and 1/4 cup yogurt. Proceed as above.

If raw milk is used instead of pasteurized, heat to simmering and cool to 120° before adding yogurt starter.

As soon as yogurt has thickened to custard consistency, it should be refrigerated, and may be kept for several days. 1/4 cup of this home-made yogurt may be used to start the next batch instead of commercial yogurt. Yogurt culture may be used, instead, as a starter. It can be obtained from International Yogurt Co., 8478 Melrose Place, Los Angeles 46, California.

GRAPE BUTTERMILK (OR YOGURT) DRINK

1/4 cup grape juice
2 tbsp. lemon juice
1 pt. Bulgarian buttermilk or
   yogurt

2 tbsp. honey

Blend about 15 sec.

BUTTERMILK (OR YOGURT) DRINK

2 tbsp. honey
1 egg
1 pt. Bulgarian buttermilk, or
   yogurt

1 tbsp. lemon juice
1/2 tsp. lemon rind, grated

Blend for about 20 sec.

ORANGE BUTTERMILK (OR YOGURT) DRINK

1/2 cup orange juice
1-1/2 cups Bulgarian
   buttermilk or yogurt

2 tbsp. honey
1/2 tsp. orange rind, grated

Blend about 20 sec. Delicious, even for those who do not care for buttermilk or yogurt.

PINEAPPLE BUTTERMILK (OR YOGURT)

1 cup Bulgarian buttermilk (or
   yogurt)
1/2 cup pineapple juice,
   unsweetened

1/2 cup fresh papaya, diced

Place all ingredients in blender, and blend until papaya is liquefied.

Baby Formulas

EVAPORATED MILK (NEWBORN)

Carnation evaporated milk,
   10 oz.

Water, 20 oz.
Unpasteurized honey, 2 tbsp.

This will make 30 oz. of formula, which will probably be more than the average newborn will need in 24 hrs., until he weighs 9 or 10 lbs.

FULL-STRENGTH FORMULA, EVAPORATED MILK

Carnation evaporated milk,
　13 oz.

Water, 19 oz.
Unpasteurized honey, 3 tbsp.

This will make about 5-1/4 oz. in 6 bottles; 6-1/2 oz. in 5 bottles; 8 oz. in 4 bottles.

RAW MILK FORMULA (NEWBORN)

Certified raw milk, preferably goat milk, 15 oz.; unpasteurized honey, 3 tbsp.: "Mineral Cocktail" water (see below), 15 oz.

This will make 30 oz. of formula. When the child is 2 or 3 months, half the quantity of water would be sufficient for the dilution of the milk. After 3 months, the milk can be taken straight.

"MINERAL COCKTAIL"

Boil Irish potato skins in water (used above) for about 15–20 min.

SOY MILK MADE FROM SOYA POWDER

1 cup soya powder
4 cups cold water
1 tbsp. honey

1 tsp. liquid lecithin or
　1 tbsp. salad oil
1/4 tsp. salt

Liquefy the soya powder in cold water. Let stand for 2 hrs. Then cook over double boiler for 1 hr. When cool, add to other ingredients. This milk is very rich and may be liquefied with seed milks for a wholesome palatable milk: 1 cup soy milk to 1 cup almond, cashew, etc. nut milk.

SOY MILK MADE FROM SOY FLOUR

1 cup soy flour
2 cups water
1/4 cup honey

1 tbsp. liquid lecithin, or
　1/4 cup salad oil
1/2 tsp. salt

Liquefy the soy flour in water and cook in double boiler for 1 hr. When cool, liquefy again with the remaining ingredients. Pour the oil in gradually, while other ingredients are blending. Add enough water to make 2-1/2 qts. of liquid. This milk may be used in any recipe calling for liquid soy milk.

SOY BEAN MILK MADE FROM WHOLE SOY BEANS

Soak 1 cup raw soy beans for 3 days in the refrigerator, pouring water off each day and adding fresh water. On the 3rd day, pour off water and liquefy the beans with 4–5 cups fresh water. Extract all milk by running liquefied beans through a juice press, a fine strainer or cloth bag. Put the milk in double boiler and cook for 1 hr. Liquefy again.

CAROB SHAKE

2 cups soy milk
  (see previous recipe)
2 rounded tbsp. carob powder
2 tbsp. honey

5 pitted dates
4 rounded tbsp. raw almond or
  cashew butter
2 tbsp. pure vanilla

Liquefy ingredients together. Chill and liquefy again.

ALMOND MILK
(BASIC NUT MILK RECIPE)

1/2 cup blanched almonds
2 cups water
Honey to taste

Salt to taste
1 tsp. liquid lecithin

Liquefy nuts and water, add remaining ingredients. Almonds are a perfect protein food. This recipe may be used for raw peanuts, pine nuts, sunflower seeds, sesame seeds, brazil and hazel nuts, pecans, etc.

CAROB AND NUT MILK DRINK

1/2 cup raw cashews, or
  almonds
2 cups water

1/4 cup water
2 tbsp. honey
2 tbsp. carob powder

Liquefy the nuts with the 2 cups of water. Heat, but do not boil the milk. Pour the milk over mixture of remaining ingredients, stirring until blended.

Fruit and Vegetable Beverages

PINEAPPLE-WATERCRESS COCKTAIL

2 cups pineapple juice
1 bunch watercress, washed
3 tbsp. honey

1 thick slice peeled lemon or
  2 tbsp. lemon juice
1 cup cracked ice

Blend until cress is reduced to drinkability. Serves 4.

VEGETABLE COCKTAIL

2 cups tomato juice
1 small stalk celery, with
   leaves, cut up
2 or 3 sprigs parsley
2 slices lemon, with peel

1 slice green pepper
1 slice onion
1/4 tsp. salt
1/2 tsp. honey
1 cup cracked ice

Blend until vegetables are completely liquefied. Serves 4-5.

PINEAPPLE & ALFALFA-SPROUTS DRINK

2 cups unsweetened pineapple
   juice or orange juice
1 cup alfalfa sprouts

2 tbsp. almond butter
Honey to taste

Place ingredients in blender and liquefy.

CRANBERRY COCKTAIL

2 cups raw cranberries,
   unsprayed
1 cup water
1 cup orange juice

1/2 cup honey
Dash of salt
Juice of 1 lime

Blend until liquefied. Strain and chill before serving.

ORANGE-COCONUT DRINK

1-1/2 cups shredded coconut
3 cups water
1 can frozen orange juice

Juice of 1 lime
1 cup cracked ice

Simmer coconut and water for 10 min. Cool, strain and add remaining ingredients. Blend about 15 sec. Pour over more cracked ice in tall glasses.

RASPBERRY PUNCH

1-1/2 cups raspberry juice
1/4 cup lemon juice
1 cup orange juice
1/4 cup lime juice

1/2 cup honey
1/2 small cucumber, diced
1 qt. water

Blend all ingredients, except water, until cucumber is liquefied. Let stand in refrigerator several hrs. Strain and add water.

Fruit and Vegetable Juice Combinations (1 pint)

Celery juice . . . . 10 oz.
Spinach juice . . . . 4 oz.
Parsley juice . . . . 2 oz.

Carrot juice . . . . 11 oz.
Coconut juice . . . . 2 oz.
Beet juice . . . . 3 oz.

Carrot juice . . . . 10 oz.
Beet juice . . . . 3 oz.
Spinach juice . . . . 3 oz.

Carrot juice . . . . 10 oz.
Spinach juice . . . . 3 oz.
Mustard greens juice . . . 3 oz.

Carrot juice . . . . 7 oz.
Celery juice . . . . 5 oz.
Lettuce juice . . . . 4 oz.

Cucumber juice . . . . . . 6 oz.
Radish juice . . . . 5 oz.
Green pepper juice . . . . 5 oz.

Coconut milk . . . . 8 oz.
Fig juice . . . . 8 oz.

Dandelion greens juice . 8 oz.
Pineapple juice . . . . . . 8 oz.

Pineapple juice . . . . . . 8 oz.
Cabbage juice . . . . 8 oz.
Almond butter . . . . . . 4 tsp.

Celery juice . . . . 7 oz.
Lettuce juice . . . . 5 oz.
Spinach juice . . . . 4 oz.

Carrot juice . . . . 13 oz.
Coconut juice . . . . . . 3 oz.

Carrot juice . . . . 9 oz.
Beet juice . . . . 3 oz.
Lettuce juice . . . . 4 oz.

Carrot juice . . . . 7 oz.
Celery juice . . . . 4 oz.
Parsley juice . . . . 2 oz.
Spinach juice . . . . 3 oz.

Carrot juice . . . . 9 oz.
Celery juice . . . . 5 oz.
Endive juice . . . . 2 oz.

Cucumber juice . . . . . 3 oz.
Watercress juice . . . . . 3 oz.
Celery juice . . . . 3 oz.
Tomato juice . . . . 4 oz.
Parsley juice . . . . 3 oz.

Orange juice . . . . 7 oz.
Lime juice . . . . 1 oz.
Pomegranate juice . . . . 8 oz.
4 egg yolks
Honey . . . . 4 tsp.

Strawberry juice . . . . . 5 oz.
Rhubarb juice . . . . . . 5 oz.
Pineapple juice . . . . . . 6 oz.

Orange juice	8 oz.	Grapefruit juice	8 oz.
Lime juice	1 oz.	Lemon juice	1 oz.
Celery juice	7 oz.	Spinach juice	3 oz.
Almond butter	4 tsp.	Pineapple juice	4 oz.

Boysenberry-Coconut Drink

1-1/2 cups boysenberry juice
3/4 cup coconut juice
1/2 cup orange juice

1 tsp. lime juice
2 tbsp. honey

Liquefy together.

Prune-Coconut Drink

1-1/2 cups prune juice
1/2 cup orange juice

1 tsp. lime juice
1 cup fresh coconut juice

Liquefy together.

CHAPTER 9

Soups and Broths

IT IS NOT difficult to understand, from a nutritional standpoint, why soups and broths were recommended in the readings in almost every case where advice was given concerning the menu. They are easily digested and when properly prepared contain an abundance of minerals and vitamins in easily assimilated form. The readings particularly recommended broths of the bony pieces of fowl for their calcium content (808-15) and vegetable soups carrying the marrow of beef bones (1523-8). Gelatin, which is needed to enable the body to utilize vitamins (849-75) is also extracted by boiling bones for stock. Vegetable parings boiled along with the bones add extra important minerals to the stock, and fresh vegetables may be utilized in soups with little loss of vitamins or minerals.

In making soup stock, bones having bits of meat clinging to them should be browned slowly to develop a more enjoyable flavor, then boiled for 3 to 4 hrs. or cooked in water in a pressure cooker for 1/2 hr. or longer. Since it is desirable to break down the connective tissue as much as possible, thereby extracting the greatest possible amount of gelatin and calcium, cooking at high temperatures is preferable to simmering. Adding a small amount of vinegar also hastens the breakdown of connective tissue and increases the amount of calcium and gelatin obtained. The calcium combines with and counteracts the acid. Salt should be added with the water, as this aids in drawing out the juices in the scraps of meat and bones. Vegetable parings should be added only during the last 15 min. of cooking, and vegetables (added after straining the stock to remove bones and parings) should be finely chopped and cooked quickly in the stock, only as long as necessary for tenderness.

The following recipe for Beef Juice was given in reading 1343-2 and advised for several people receiving readings. It was referred to "as medicine" (5374-1) or "almost as medicine" (1100-10). Instructions for eating were explicit:

> Take at least a tablespoon during a day, or two tablespoonfuls. But not as spoonfuls, rather sips of same. This sipped, in this manner, will work towards producing the gastric flow through the intestinal system.   *1100-10*

Pure Beef Juice

Take a pound to a pound and a half of beef, preferably of the round steak. No fat and no portions other than that which is of the muscle or tendon for strength; no fatty or skin portions. Dice this into half-inch cubes, as it were, or practically so. Put same in a glass jar without water . . . Put the jar into a boiler or container with the water coming to about half or three-fourths toward the top of the jar. Put a cloth in the container to prevent the jar from cracking. Do not seal the jar tight, but cover the top. Let this boil (the water, with the jar in same) for 3 to 4 hrs.

Then strain off the juice. The refuse may be pressed somewhat. It will be found that the meat or flesh itself will be worthless. Place the juice in a cool place, but do not keep too long; never longer than 3 days. Hence the quantity made up at the time depends upon how much or how often the body will take this.

1343-2

Soups

Delightful, nutritious soups may be made by adding cooked natural brown unpolished rice to chicken broth, beef broth or bouillon cubes with fine slivered onions. Just before serving add toasted, buttered croutons.

CHICKEN SOUP WITH RICE OR NOODLES

1-3/4 lb. stewing chicken cut into quarters	2 tsp. salt
1 carrot	1/4 tsp. pepper
2 qts. cold water	1/4 cup uncooked brown rice or whole wheat noodles
1 stalk celery	2 tbsp. parsley, minced
1 med. onion	

Place chicken, carrot, water, celery, onion, salt and pepper in a 4-1/2 qt. pot. Cover and simmer approx. 2 hrs., or until meat is tender. Remove chicken from pot, strain the liquid and remove all possible fat. Return the stock to pot, bring to boil, add rice or noodles, cover and cook until tender. Add parsley. Serves 4-6.

CHICKEN SOUP

2 cups chicken broth
1 cup chicken meat
1 small can tomatoes
1/2 pkg. frozen peas or
  leftovers

4 stalks celery, diced
1 cup cashews, raw
Dash salt

Boil bony pieces of chicken in water to cover, to which 1 medium size onion has been added. When chicken is tender, remove from heat, cool and remove meat from bones. Place first 5 ingredients in blender, blending well. Add more broth, if desired. Place in saucepan, heat, add salt and serve.

TURKEY-POTATO SOUP

2 cups turkey or chicken broth
  prepared as above recipe
1 cup turkey or chicken meat
1 Irish potato, with skin

1 small onion, diced
1 small can mushrooms
Dash salt

Place first 5 ingredients in blender, blending well. Place in saucepan, add salt, heat, and serve.

FISH BROTH

Keep the fish head, tail, fins, skin and bones for stock. Partly cover with cold water. Add cut-up vegetables suitable for soup:

1 onion
1/2 carrot

Celery stalk with leaves
Seasonings to taste

Simmer the stock for about 1/2 hr. Strain. Serve as soup, or use it in aspic or sauces. The stock may be kept for several days in tightly closed container in the refrigerator.

ROMAN EGG SOUP

1 qt. chicken broth
4 eggs, beaten until thick
1-1/2 tbsp. whole wheat flour
1-1/2 tbsp. parmesan cheese,
  grated

1/8 tsp. salt
1/8 tsp. pepper

Bring chicken broth to boiling point, add egg slowly, until well blended. Continue stirring and add remaining ingredients. Let simmer for about 5 min.

HOT MUSHROOM SOUP

2 cups meat or vegetable stock
2 cups mushrooms
1 small onion

2 med. potatoes, scrubbed and
    cubed
1 tsp. marjoram

Put all ingredients in blender or food grinder; whip or chop fine. Put 1 tbsp. cooking oil in a heavy saucepan, add the soup mixture, season with sea kelp and simmer about 5 min. Put in thermos bottle for the lunch, if need be.

CREAMED ALFALFA SPROUT SOUP

1 qt. water
3/4 cup raw cashew nuts
2 tbsp. arrowroot powder
1 tbsp. whole wheat pastry
    flour

2 tsp. salt
1 tsp. onion powder
1/2 tsp. celery seed powder
2 tbsp. Energy broth
1 cup alfalfa sprouts

Liquefy first 8 ingredients, then bring to a boil and cook until it thickens. Chop alfalfa sprouts, approx. 1/4 cup to each bowl, and add just before serving. Serves 3-4.

PARSLEY VEGETABLE BROTH

1 bunch parsley
1 small onion
1 tbsp. butter
1/4 cup vegetable broth
    powder

1 bunch spinach
1 small carrot
2 cups celery, chopped
Parsley sprigs

Wash spinach and celery, chop very fine. Grate onion and carrot. Combine and cover with water. Cook slowly for 20 min. Season with butter and broth powder, sprinkle with chopped parsley and serve.

TOMATO SOY BEAN BROTH

1 cup cooked soy beans
1 small onion, cut fine

4 cups tomato juice
2 small green pepper, cut fine

Steam onion and green pepper 10 min. Add mashed soy beans and tomato juice. Heat, but do not boil. Dot with butter and serve.

TOMATO-ALMOND-ASPARAGUS SOUP

4 to 6 cooked asparagus spears
1 No. 2 can tomatoes
1 cup raw almonds
1 vine-ripened tomato, if
    desired

Dash onion salt
Dash vegetable salt

Place first 4 ingredients in blender, blending well. Add salts and heat, but do not boil.

TOMATO-CASHEW SOUP

1 No. 2 can tomatoes
1/2 bunch parsley
1 tsp. minced onion

1/2 cup raw cashews
Dash vegetable salt

Place first 4 ingredients in blender and blend well. Add salt and heat, serving immediately.

SWEDISH CUCUMBER SOUP

4 cups buttermilk
1 cup sour cream
1 cup cucumber, diced
1/2 cup cooked beet greens,
    finely chopped

1 tbsp. raw carrot, grated
1 tbsp. onion, finely chopped
1 tbsp. dill
1/4 tsp. pepper
1 tsp. salt

Beat buttermilk and sour cream until smooth, add vegetables and seasonings. Simmer gently until vegetables are tender. Do not boil. Serves 6-8. In summer chill this soup without simmering, and serve very cold.

FROZEN PEA-TOMATO SOUP

4 med. vine-ripened tomatoes
2 stalks celery, large
1/2 cup almonds, raw
1/2 tsp. onion, grated

Dash of salt
1 pkg. frozen peas
1/2 tsp. butter
1/2 cup water

Defrost peas until they separate. Place all ingredients, except butter and salt, in blender, blending well. Add salt and butter and heat. Do not boil. Serve immediately.

CHAPTER 10

MENUS

SPECIAL BREAKFAST, LUNCHEON and dinner suggestions have been given separately in the readings. Following these, readings giving a whole day's menus will be given. At the conclusion of this section, we will give a few menus prepared for the average daily diet by nutritional authorities.

Before considering the readings' breakfast suggestions, remember that in recent years nutritionists have become very much concerned with the bad breakfast patterns in this country. They point out that breakfast is extremely important, and that a toast-coffee-and-orange juice breakfast can have a bad effect upon the body's capacity for morning energy. Researchers at Marquette University say that temperatures inside the stomach drop when one is hungry, but are quickly restored to normal after eating. At 11 o'clock, they say, the poor breakfasters first feel hungry. The temperature drops, and this leads to a lowering of metabolism in the stomach. Doctors believe that this means lower body fires. Accordingly, 11 A.M. is the hour of lowered vitality for many, many people.

> In the mornings, eat a whole-grain cereal, well cooked, with milk or cream; or citrus fruits. Do not take the citrus fruits and the cereals at the same meal. Rather, alternate these from day to day. Rice cakes, corn cakes or the like, with syrup or honey, are well to be taken occasionally.   *2693-P-1*

> In the mornings, eat citrus fruits, preferably with the pulp—having oranges at times, lemons at times, and grapefruit at other times. Then have whole wheat toast or cakes with milk, and use honey as the sweetening. At other times, eat cooked whole wheat cereal or Wheaties, Grape Nuts or any of those that carry a great deal of iron and vitamins for the system. But do not give cereals and fruit juices or citrus fruit at the same meal.
>   *318-P-5*

> In the mornings, eat citrus fruit or stewed fruits such as figs, apples, peaches or the like. But do not serve the stewed fruits with the citrus fruit juices, nor the citrus fruits with a dry cereal . . . when cereals are taken, there may be added buckwheat cakes, rice cakes, or a coddled egg, and a cereal drink. It would be well for these to be altered or changed occasionally.   *623-P-1*

Don't be satisfied with just taking a sandwich for lunch. Use only green vegetables or fresh green vegetables in the lunch period. Don't just eat a scrap of bread and a scrap of meat, or a chocolate soda, or a milk shake. These are poisons for the system at such periods.   *243-P-11*

At noon, eat a green vegetable diet, without too much bread. Eat brown bread at such times. These vegetables may be seasoned with oils or dressings. Eat vegetable soups, mostly made with green vegetables. Or eat meat soups, but none of the heavier foods.   *943-P-8*

For lunch, eat rather lightly. For sweets, take the fruit juices or pies with milk.   *781-P-1*

At noon, eat some raw vegetables such as lettuce, celery, carrots or the like; with some soup, preferably vegetable soup.   *2693-P-1*

At noon, eat green vegetables, such as carrots, cabbage, slaw, lettuce, celery, spinach and the like. These should be taken preferably with oil dressings. At this meal, there may also be taken at times . . . meat juices but no meats.   *623-P-1*

In the evenings, eat meat in moderation, but no red meat, and no hog meats at any time, although very crisp bacon may be eaten at times with eggs. But do not have any grease in it . . . Drink plenty of water during the whole day.   *943-P-8*

In the evenings, do not eat too heavily. Eat fish, fowl or lamb—although they should never be fried. Have well-cooked vegetables. This is not all that may be eaten, but it is an outline.   *2693-P-1*

In the evening, eat meat but not too much; and a well-balanced vegetable diet of those that grow above the ground.   *781-P-1*

This would be given as an outline [of the day's foods]; not as the only foods, but as an outline:

Mornings: Whole grain cereals or citrus fruit juices though not at the same meal. When using orange juice, combine lime with it. When using grapefruit juice, combine lemon with it. Have an egg, preferably only the yolk; or rice or buckwheat cakes; or toast. Any one of these would be well in the mornings.

Noons: A raw salad, including tomatoes, radishes, carrots, celery, lettuce, watercress—any or all of these; with a soup or vegetable broth; or sea foods.

Evenings: Fruits, such as cooked apples; potatoes, tomatoes; fish, fowl or lamb—and occasionally beef but not too often. Keep these as the main part of a well-balanced diet.   *1523-P-9*

In the matter of diet, we would have this as an outline; though, to be sure, this may be alternated from time to time to suit the tastes of the body. At least 3 mornings each week, we would have rolled or cracked whole wheat that is not cooked too long so that the whole vitamin force is destroyed. This will add to the body the proper portions of iron, silicon and the vitamins necessary to build up the blood supply that makes for resistance in the system.

We at other times would have citrus fruits, citrus fruit juices, the yolk of eggs, preferably soft-boiled or coddled—not the white portions; browned bread with butter; Ovaltine or milk or coffee (provided there is no milk or cream in same). Occasionally have stewed figs, stewed raisins, prunes or apricots. But do not eat citrus fruits at the same meal with cereals, or gruels, or any of the breakfast foods.

Noons: Preferably eat raw fresh vegetables, none cooked at this meal . . . tomatoes, lettuce, celery, spinach, carrots, beet tops, mustard, onions, or the like that make for purifying in the lymph blood. We would not take any quantity of soups or broths at noon.

Evenings: Broths or soups may be taken in a small measure; but let it consist principally of vegetables that are well cooked; and a little of meats such as lamb, fish, fowl. These are preferable. No fried foods.   *840-P-1*

This is not all that is to be taken, but is given as an outline:

Mornings: Citrus fruit juices. When orange juice is taken, add lime or lemon juice to it, four parts orange juice to one part lime or lemon. When other citrus fruits are taken, such as pineapple or grapefruit, they may be taken as they are from the fresh fruit . . . a little salt added, if preferable. Take whole wheat bread, toasted, with butter. Coddled egg, only the yolk of same. A small piece of very crisp bacon, if so desired. Any or all of these may be taken. But when cereals are taken, do not have citrus fruits at the same meal! Such a combination produces just what we are trying to prevent in the system. When cereals are used, have either cracked wheat or whole wheat, or a combination of barley and wheat as in Maltex, if these are desired. Or Puffed Wheat, Puffed Rice, or Puffed Corn—any of these. And these may be taken with certain kinds of fresh fruits, such as berries of any nature—even strawberries if desired—no, they won't cause any rash if they are taken properly! Or peaches. The sugar used should be saccharin or honey. A cereal drink may be had if desired.

Noons: Only raw, fresh vegetables. All of these may be combined, but grate them and don't eat them so hurriedly that they would make for that unbalanced condition (resulting from) improper mastication. Each time you take a mouthful, it should be chewed at least 4 to 20 times . . . each should be chewed so that there is the opportunity for the flow of the gastric forces from the salivary glands to be well mixed with same. Then we will find that these foods will make for bettered conditions in the body.

Evenings: Vegetables that are cooked in their own juices; each cooked alone, then combined afterward if so desired by the body. These may include any of the leafy vegetables or any of the bulbar vegetables; but cook them in their own juices! There may be meats, if so desired, or there may be added—if preferred—the proteins that come from the combination of other vegetables . . . in the forms of a certain character of pulse, or of grains.   *No. 3823-P-2*

Mornings: Citrus fruits, either cereals or fruits . . . or have citrus fruits and a little later have rice cakes or buckwheat or graham cakes, with honey in the honeycomb; and with milk—preferably the raw milk if it is certified milk!

Noons: Rather vegetable juices than meat juices; with raw vegetables—a salad or the like.

Evenings: Vegetables, with such as carrots, peas, salsify, red cabbage, yams or white potatoes. These potatoes should be the smaller variety and if eaten with the jackets it will be better. Then the finishing, or dessert . . . blanc mange, or jello, or jellies with fruits such as peaches, apricots, fresh pineapple or the like.
These foods, as we find, with the occasional eating of sufficient meat for strength, would bring a well-balanced diet. Occasionally we would add those foods of a blood-building type, once or twice a week: the pig knuckles, tripe, calves' liver, or such meats as brains and the like.

                                        275-P-21

Question: Outline diet for 3 meals a day that would be best for this body.

Answer: Mornings: Citrus fruit juices or cereals, but not both at the same meal. [Use with] other cereals at times, dried fruits or figs combined with dates and raisins—these chopped very well together. And, for this special body, mixture of dates and figs that are dried, cooked with a little corn meal (a very little sprinkled in—) then this taken with milk . . . should be almost a spiritual food for this body. Whether it's taken one, two, three or four meals a day. This is to be left to the body itself to decide.

Noons: Foods such as vegetable juices . . . and a combination of raw vegetables. But not ever any acetic acid or vinegar or the like with same. Oils, if they are olive oil or vegetable oils, may be used with same.

Evenings: Vegetables that are of the leafy nature; fish, fowl or lamb preferably, as meats—or their combinations. These of course are not to be all the foods, but this is the general outline for the three meals for the body. *275-P-34*

Mornings: Whole wheat toast, brown bread; cereals with fresh fruits. The citrus fruit juices occasionally. But do not mix the citrus fruit juices and cereals at the same meal.

Noons: Principally (very seldom deviating from these) raw vegetables or raw fruits made into a salad. Not having the fruits and vegetables combined, but these may be varied. Use such vegetables as cabbage cut very fine; carrots, spinach, celery, onions, tomatoes, radishes; any or all of these. It is preferable that they all be grated, but when they are grated, do not discard the juices. These should be used upon the salad itself (from the fruits, on the fruit salad; from the vegetables on the vegetable salad). . . .

Preferably use oil dressings, such as olive oil with paprika. Even egg—that is, the yolk—may be included in these same dressings. Work the yolk of a hard-boiled egg into the oil as a portion of the dressing. . . . Use in fruit salad such fruits as bananas, papaya, guava, grapes, all kinds of fruits except apples. Apples should only be eaten when cooked, preferably baked and served with butter or hard sauce on same, topped with cinnamon and spice.

Evenings: A well-balanced cooked vegetable diet, including principally those things that will make for iron to be assimilated in the system.

935-P-1

For the purposes of comparison, let us consider a day's menu suggested in the booklet, *Recommended Dietary Allowances,* National Research Council, Number 129, page 26. This menu fulfills recommended dietary allowances for a "physically active man."

Breakfast

Menu 1

Orange Juice
Cooked cereal, milk
Eggs
Toast, butter or margarine
Beverage

Menu 2

Tomato Juice
Ready-to-eat cereal, milk
Eggs
Hot biscuits, butter or
   fortified margarine
Jelly
Beverage ·

Lunch

Baked macaroni and
   tomatoes
Green beans

Baked sweet potato
Turnip greens or collards
Sliced onions with vinegar

Rolls, butter or
  fortified margarine
Fruit in season
Milk

Corn bread or muffins,
  butter or fortified
  margarine
Molasses
Beverage

Dinner

Menu 1

Broiled chopped steak
Creamed potatoes, carrots
Head lettuce,
  French dressing
Bread, butter or
  fortified margarine
Apple pie and cheese
Beverage

Menu 2

Fried fish
Hominy grits, cole slaw
Bread, butter or
  fortified margarine
Stewed prunes or fruit in
  season
Cookies
Beverage

Some Menus Suggested for Children

Question: I would appreciate an outline of an ideal daily diet for this child's age (6 years) and for the near future.

Answer: Mornings—Whole grain cereals or citrus fruits, but these never taken at the same meal. Rather, alternate these, using one on one day and the other the next, and so on. Any form of rice cakes or the like; the yolk of eggs and the like.

Noons—Some fresh raw vegetable salad, including many types. Soups with brown bread, or broths or such.

Evenings—A fairly well-coordinated vegetable diet, with three vegetables above the ground to one below the ground. Sea food, fowl or lamb; not other types of meats. Gelatin may be prepared with any of the vegetables—as in the salads for the noon meal—or with milk and cream dishes. These would be well for the body.   3224-P-2

For a nine-year-old:

In the evenings, eat a great deal of whole vegetables, well balanced with meats. Eat all the leafy vegetables that agree with the body. And let several of the evening meals each week contain calf's liver, hog tripe, beef tripe, or the like. Do not give the body hog meats. . . . Drink as much milk as the body may well take at such meals. . . . At noon, eat a great deal of butter and bread, or those foods that carry a high calorie content in carbohydrates, or sweets, provided they are honey-based. For

honey will act with the digestive forces in the system much better than
corn or cane sweets.   *318-P-5*

For a six-month-old baby:

Do not overcrowd the stomach or be over-anxious as to the amount [of
food] taken, especially through the hot months. . . . Have plenty of fruit
juices—that is, orange juice, preferably, then other juices as the body
develops. But do not overcrowd these through the hot months. Make the
changes more in the early fall, but not . . . too much in the present.

Also have plenty of strained oatmeal, but not on the same days when the
orange juice is given. Use preferably the steel-cut oats, strained, and
with plenty of milk.

Yes, owing to the general strength and tendency of the body in the bone
structure, there is the inclination for not sufficient calcium. Thus it would
be well for the body to have the Haliver Oil rather than the cod liver oil.
This . . . in the form of pellets. . . . The body will be able to take it
without choking, provided it is given at meals.   *2289-P-1*

For all growing bodies:

In general conditions, you must know that there is a growing body and
that there is necessarily . . . (much) activity and that the energies must
be supplied. Also, there is a drain upon the whole of the nerve and blood
supply of the body. Hence, meat should be a portion of the diet each
day, though it should not be the greater portion, and it need not be eaten
at every meal.   *759-P-7*

CHAPTER 11

QUESTIONS ABOUT SPECIFIC FOODS AND COOKERY—FOOD ELEMENTS

STEAM PRESSURE AND waterless cooking are the modern methods advised nowadays for preservation of maximum vitamin and mineral content. The use of
Patapar paper accomplishes the same end. This is not now manufactured, we
understand, but a similar paper may be obtained from the Kalamazoo Vegetable
Parchment Co., Kalamazoo, Michigan.

Keep away from heavy foods. Use those which are body-building, such
as beef broth, beef juices, liver, fish and lamb. Never eat fried foods.

Include butter and milk and raw vegetables; preparing the latter often with gelatin. Eat only the yolk of the egg. Leafy vegetables are all right—raw cabbage and cooked red cabbage, spinach and string beans. But not dry beans, nor white potatoes, and only a few sweet potatoes and yams. Artichokes are all right in season, but prepare them in Patapar paper, so that the juices mix with the pulp.   7059-P-1

Question: How about steam pressure for cooking foods quickly? Does it destroy any of the vitamins of the vegetables and fruits?

Answer: No, it preserves rather than destroys them.   462-P-5-

Question: Does Steam Pressure cooking at 15 pounds temperature destroy food values in vegetables?

Answer: No. [Retention of food values] depends upon preparation, the age and how long since gathered. All these are factors affecting food values. Just as it is so well advertised that coffee loses its value in fifteen to twenty or twenty-five days after being roasted; so do foods or vegetables lose their food values after being gathered—in the same proportion in hours, as coffee does in days.   340-P-30

In the matter of the diet throughout the periods of convalescence, we would constantly add more and more of Vitamin B-1, in every form in which it may be taken: in bread, in cereals, in types of vegetables . . . in fruits, etc. Be sure that there is sufficient each day of B-1 for adding to the vital energies. These vitamins are not stored in the body as A, D, and O, but it is necessary to add these daily. All of those fruits and vegetables that are yellow in color should be taken: oranges, lemons, grapefruit, yellow squash, yellow corn, yellow peaches—also beets. *But all of the vegetables should be cooked in their own juices, and the body should eat the juices with same.*   2529-P-1

On the subject of tomatoes, which many people say are too "acid" for their particular systems, the readings shed considerable light.

Question: What is the effect on my system of eating so many tomatoes?

Answer: Quite a dissertation might be given as to the effect of tomatoes upon the human system.

Of all the vegetables, tomatoes carry most of the vitamins, in a well-balanced assimilable manner suitable for the activities in the system. Yet if these tomatoes are not cared for properly, they may become very destructive to a physical organism. That is, if they ripen after being pulled, or if there is contamination with other influences or substances.

In this particular body, as we find, the reactions from tomatoes have not always been the best. Neither has there been a normal reaction from eating same. For here there is a tendency to make for irritation or humour. Nominally, though, tomatoes should form at least a portion of a meal three or four days out of every week, and they will be found most helpful. . . . The tomato is one vegetable that in most instances . . . is preferable to be eaten after being canned, for it is then much more uniform. The reaction from non-canned tomatoes in this body, then, has been to form an acid of its own; though the tomato is among those foods which may be termed non-acid forming.

584-P-5 (10/4/1935)

Question: Would it be well for me to eat vegetables such as corn, tomatoes, and the like?

Answer: Corn and tomatoes are excellent. More of the vitamins are obtained from tomatoes than from any other growing vegetable.   *180-P (5/26/1928)*

It will be very interesting and instructive to compare the food values attributed by the readings to certain foods with a similar listing given by any textbook on nutrition or leaflets obtainable from the National Research Council; Metropolitan Life Insurance Company; National Livestock and Meat Board; and the U.S. Department of Agriculture. Verification will be found for the information given in the Edgar Cayce readings — in many instances, many years before food facts were established by modern research.

Question: Should plenty of lettuce be eaten?

Answer: Plenty of lettuce should always be eaten by almost everybody, for this supplies an effluvium in the blood stream that is a destructive force for most of those influences that attack the blood stream. It's a purifier.   *404-P-4*

Keep plenty of those foods that supply calcium to the body. These we would find especially in raw carrots, cooked turnips and turnip greens, and all kinds of salads — especially of watercress, mustard greens and the like; these especially taken raw, though turnip greens cooked, but cooked in their own juices and not with fat meats.   *1968-P-2*

Often use the raw vegetables which are prepared with gelatin. Use them at least three times each week. Those which grow more above the ground than those which grow below the ground. Do include, when they are prepared, the carrots with that portion especially close to the top. It may appear the harder and less desirable, but it carries the vital energies (which) stimulate the optic reactions between kidneys and the optics.   *3051-P*

Keep away from sweets, especially chocolates at this period; also foods prepared with coconut. Other kinds of nuts are well, and almonds are especially good. An almond a day is much more in accord with keeping the doctor away, especially certain types of doctors, than apples! . . . For the apple was the fall . . . remember, the almond blossomed when everything else died.

3180-P-2

In connection with almonds, which have food values little considered even by those in the field of nutrition, it is quite interesting to note how the readings' information tallies with the latest research and investigation. In *Recommended Dietary Allowances* by the National Research Council, page 17, it is stated that "In the case of other adults the phosphorus allowances should be approximately 1.5 times those for calcium." According to the USDA Handbook No. 8, *Composition of Food, Raw, Processed and Prepared,* almonds are at the top of the list of foods having such a proportion of phosphorus and calcium. Almonds contain 475 Mg. of Phosphorus, 254 Mg. of Calcium—and in addition 4.4 Mg. of iron. *Almonds rank highest in iron of all foods having the proportion of 1.5 phosphorus to amount of calcium.*

Question: Please give foods that supply iron, calcium and phosphorus.

Answer: Cereals that carry the heart of the grain; vegetables of the leafy kinds, fruits and nuts. *The almond carries more phosphorus and iron in a combination easily assimilated, than any other nut.*

1131-P-2

For supplying the system with calcium and other elements, such as phosphorus and salts . . . eat sea foods at least once or twice a week, especially clams, oysters, shrimp or lobster. The oyster or clam often taken raw; the others roasted or boiled, seasoned with butter.

275-P-21

The phosphorus-forming foods are principally carrots, lettuce (rather the leaf lettuce, which has more soporific activity than the head lettuce), shell fish, salsify, the peelings of white potatoes (if they are not too large potatoes).

560-P-1

Vitamins—should we take them separately or in foods? The Edgar Cayce readings varied in their advice, apparently according to the individual's body capacities. In the majority of readings, however, the position was taken that it is better to obtain the vitamins from foods.

So keep an excess of foods that carry vitamins, especially Vitamin B, iron and such. Do not take the concentrated form of vitamins, you see, but obtain these from foods. These foods would include all fruits, all vegetables that are yellow . . . thus lemon and orange juice combined; all citrus fruit juices, pineapple as well as grapefruit. Some of these should be a part of the diet each day. Squash, especially the yellow; carrots, cooked and raw; yellow peaches; yellow apples—preferably have the apples cooked. All of these carry an excess of the greater quantity of the necessary elements for supply of energies for the body and are more easily assimilated by the body. Yellow corn, yellow corn meal, buckwheat—all are especially good; also red cabbage. Such vegetables, such fruits, are especially needed for the body of this individual.   *1968-P-3*

Knowing the tendencies (toward weakness in your body), supply in the vital energies that which ye call vitamins or elements. For remember, though we may give many combinations (for treatments), there are only four elements in your body: water, salt, soda and iodine. These are the basic elements; they make all the rest! Each vitamin, as a component part of an element, is simply a combination of these other influences— given a name, mostly for confusion, by those who would tell you what to do, for a price!   2533-L-4

All such properties as vitamins that add to the system are more efficacious if they are given for periods, left off for periods, and then begun again. For if the system comes to rely upon such influences wholly, it ceases to produce the vitamins, even though the food values are kept normally balanced. It is much better for these vitamins to be produced in the body from the normal development than supplied mechanically, for nature is much better, still, than science! As we find, then, these vitamins should be given twice a day for two to three weeks; left off for a week, and then begun again, especially through the winter months. This method would be much more effective with the body.   *759-P-10*

Question: What relationships do vitamins bear to the glands? Give specific vitamins affecting specific glands.

Answer: You want a book written on this subject! They—the vitamins—are good for the glands. Vitamins are that from which glands take those influences necessary to supply energies, to enable various organs of the body to reproduce themselves. Would you ever consider it likely that the toenails would reproduce themselves by the influences of the same gland which supplies the breast—or head, or face? Or that the cuticle would be supplied from the same source which supplies the organ of the heart itself?

These [building substances] *are taken from glands* controlling assimilated foods; hence foods require elements or vitamins to supply various forces enabling each organ and function of organ, in the whole body, to carry on its creative and generating force, see?

In discussing the vitamins, let us begin with A. It supplies portions of the nerves—to the bone and to the brain itself. It is not all of the supply to this area, but this is a part of the function of A vitamin.

Then vitamin B and B-1 supply energies, or the moving forces of the nerve and white blood supply, for itself, and the brain for itself. These [vitamins] supply the sympathetic or involuntary reflexes through the body. And this [energy] includes all kind—whether you are wriggling your toes, or ears, or batting your eyes, or whatever!

In these [B vitamins] we also have that influence which supplies the chyle with its ability to control the use of fats. —This body has never had enough of it; and this [control of use of fats] is necessary for carrying on the reproducing of oils which prevent tenseness in joints, or prevent joints from becoming dry or atrophied—seeming to creak. At times, the body has had some creaks!

In vitamin C we find that which supplies influences necessary for the flexes of every nature throughout the body: of a muscular or tendon nature; a heart reaction; a kidney contraction; a liver contraction or the opening or shutting of your mouth or batting of the eye, or supplying of the saliva, and the muscular forces in the face. These are all supplied by vitamin C. Not that C is the only supply, but it forms a part of it.

C is that from which the [necessary supplies for] structural portions of the body are [taken and] stored; then drawn upon when it becomes necessary. And when [lack of C] has become detrimental to the body—which has been the case for this body—it is necessary to supply vitamin C in such proportions as to aid. Else conditions become such that bad eliminations result, because of incoordination between excretory functions of the alimentary canal—as well as functioning of the heart, liver and lungs—through the expelling of forces that are a part of the structural portion of the body.

Vitamin G supplies the general energies, or the sympathetic forces of the body itself. These are some of the principles.   2072-P-5

Question: What foods carry most of the Vitamin B?

Answer: All those that are of the yellow variety, especially, and whole-grain cereals or bread.   457-P-4

In the matter of diet throughout the periods of [convalescence], we would constantly add more and more of vitamin B-1, in every form in which it may be taken: in bread, in cereals, in types of vegetables . . . fruits, etc. Be sure that each day there is sufficient vitamin B-1 to add vital energies, for B vitamins are not stored in the body, as are A, D, and G. It is necessary to add these daily. All those fruits and vegetables, then, that are yellow should be taken: oranges, lemons, grapefruit, yellow squash, yellow corn, yellow peaches . . . beets. But all of the vegetables should be cooked in their own juices, and the body should take the juices along with vegetables. 2529-P-1

What are vitamins? One scientist of note has said that a vitamin is a unit of ignorance—nobody knows what it is, only what it does. Listen to the Cayce reading:

> Have ye not read that in Him ye live and move and have thy being? What are those elements in food or in drink that give growth or strength to the body? Vitamins? What are vitamins? The Creative Forces working with

body-energies for the renewing of the body!   *3511-P-1*

And again:

Know that the body must function as a unit. One person may get his feet
wet and have a cold in the head. Another may get his head wet and have
a cold. The same is true in any relationship. For in the body, the circulation
carries within the corpuscles such elements or vitamins as may be needed
for assimilation in each organ. Each organ has within itself a special
ability to create from what is assimilated the elements needed to build
itself . . . Hence it may be said that the adding of vitamins to the system
is merely a precautionary measure at seasons when the body is the most
susceptible to colds—either by contact, by exposure, or from unsettled
conditions.   *7046-L-1*

Remember your high school days in chemistry class, when you added a
"catalyst" to the chemicals with which you were working, and their reaction was
speeded up amazingly? The newly emphasized *amino acids,* with which scientific
literature is filled now, seem—at least to an informed layman—to be such
catalysts. The various kinds of amino acids, when isolated and tested, always
seem to be needed by certain vitamins so that the action of the vitamins can be
more fully realized by the body.

This new emphasis on amino acids takes on new significance in the light of
the Cayce reading on diet, especially with regard to gelatin. You have noticed
how often gelatin was mentioned and recommended. Over ten years ago, someone
asked the sleeping Cayce:

*Question: Please explain the vitamin content of gelatin. There is no reference
to vitamin content on the package.*

Answer: It isn't the vitamin content in gelatin (which is important), but its
ability to *work with* the activities of the glands. It enables the glands to take
from what has been absorbed or digested the vitamins—otherwise inactive if
it were not for sufficient gelatin in the body. There may be mixed with any
chemical, you see, that which would make the system able to use what is
present and needed. The system becomes, then, as it were, "sensitive" to
conditions. Without it [the gelatin] there is not that sensitivity [to vitamins].

                                                    849-P-6

We quote from the *Gelatin Guide—What Gelatin Is and How to Use It,* obtained
from the Knox Gelatine Company:

"No one food article supplies all of the types of amino acids that make
up the complete protein . . . Real gelatin and several of the cereal and
vegetable proteins are in this class. Unflavored gelatin which contains 9
of the 10 essential amino acids takes its place as a useful supplementary

protein. . . . The protein of real gelatin contains amino acids that have special value in the production of hemoglobin. . . . Protein must also serve as material for the precursors of essential biological catalysts such as enzymes and hormones."

Food and Nutrition News, published by the National Live Stock and Meat Board, stated as far back as October 1952: "Research indicates that the requirement or metabolism of all vitamins is interrelated with that for protein or specific amino acids. One nutrient can no longer be considered apart from all other nutrients."

Not too heavy a diet; that is, not too much meats, more vegetables. Fruits and nuts may be included . . . raw vegetables prepared oft with gelatin. Gelatin, ices, ice cream: all of these may be taken.   *3395-P-1*

Do not leave off the gelatin. Do keep the vitamins that will add strength to the body.   *3389-P-1*

Do have raw vegetables oft. These not as to cause too great a relaxation, but [to obtain] those energies as with the nerve-building forces from celery, lettuce, tomatoes, carrots . . . but grated or chopped fine. Oft prepare these with gelatin.   *5246*

In the diet of this body, keep plenty of raw vegetables such as watercress, celery, lettuce, tomatoes and carrots. Change the manner of preparation of these, but do have some of these each day. They may be prepared rather often with gelatin, such as lime or lemon gelatin, or Jello. These will not only taste good but be good for you.   *3429-P-1*

Have a great deal of such foods as liver, tripe, pig's knuckle, pig's feet and the like; a great deal of okra and its products; a great deal of any kind of desserts carrying quantities of gelatin. Any of the gelatin products, though they may carry sugars at times, should be had often in the diet.
2520-P-1

In building up the body with foods, preferably have a great deal of raw vegetables for this body: as lettuce, celery, carrots, watercress. All should be taken raw, with dressing, and often with gelatin. The vegetables should be grated or cut very fine—even ground; but do preserve all of the juice with them, when they are prepared in this manner with gelatin.   *5394-P-1*

CHAPTER 12

MISCELLANEOUS HEALTH INFORMATION

SO FAR AS we know, the science of modern dietetics has done no research on the subject of acclimatization by means of using foods grown in the specific locality to which the individual wishes to become quickly adjusted. Acclimatization itself has not been defined, nor have any difficulties or diseases been traced to the lack of it. Those who travel to other sections of the country—or even a few miles beyond home territory—are commonly heard to complain of the upset caused by a change of drinking water. Such an upset may just as easily be caused by change of food grown in another locality, reacting differently in the body.

The Edgar Cayce readings have very definite advice to give on the subject of acclimatization. The reader may find a fertile and fascinating subject for speculation in the fact that frozen foods, vegetables, meats and sea foods native to specific sections are widely used in many other sections of the country. Is there any connection between this fact and the enormous trek to Florida, California and adjacent parts of the country? Is the consumption of such foods helping to make us more national minded? Is it sweeping away some of the sectional prejudices? Is it making us more nomadic?

Question: Is the climate of Austin, Texas, satisfactory and should I remain here?

Answer: The climatic conditions here are not the basis of the trouble. The body can adjust itself. As we have indicated, bodies can usually adjust themselves to climatic conditions if they adhere to the proper diet and activities, or eat all characters of foods that are produced in the area where they reside. This will more quickly adjust a body to any particular area or climate than any other thing.

Question: Is a diet composed mainly of fruits, vegetables, eggs and milk the best diet for me?

Answer: As indicated, use more of the products of the soil that are grown in the immediate vicinity. These are better for the body than any specific set of fruits, vegetables, grasses, or what not. We should add more of the original sources of proteins.   *4047-P-1*

379

Have vegetables that are fresh and especially those grown in the vicinity where the body resides. Shipped vegetables are never very good. *2-P-14*

Have raw vegetables also, but not a great quantity of melons of any kind, though cantaloupes may be taken if grown in the neighborhood where the body resides. If a cantaloupe is shipped, don't eat it. Fruits that may be taken are plums, pears, and apples—not raw apples but plenty of roasted apples.

5097-P-1

Do not have large quantities of any fruits, vegetables or meats that are not grown in or come from the area where the body is at the time it partakes of such foods. This will be found to be a good rule to be followed by all. This prepares the system to acclimate itself to any given territory. *3542-P-1*

Body's Need for Water

Do you drink enough water? Most people do not drink as much as they think—or say—they do. Some health information sources say to drink six to eight glasses of water a day, exclusive of juices, tea, coffee, etc.; others lower this to four to six glasses. The practice of giving babies water in addition to milk is frowned upon nowadays—milk is mostly water, pediatricians explain. Is drinking water important and why? The Edgar Cayce readings say it is.

There should be more water taken into the system in a more consistent manner, so that the system—especially in the hepatics and kidneys—may function normally, thus producing . . . correct elimination of drosses in the system, and for this reason each channel should be kept in equilibrium (with the other channels) so that there is not an . . . accentuated condition in any one of the eliminating functions. There should not be an overtaxing of the lungs, kidneys, liver nor respiratory, but all should be kept in an equal manner. . . . Lack of this water in the system creates an excess of such eliminations which normally should be cleansed through the alimentary canal and the kidneys; so that drosses are forced back into the capillary circulation. *257-P-7*

Always drink plenty of water, before meals and after meals. For, as has often been given, when any food value enters the stomach, it immediately becomes a storehouse or a medicine chest that may create all the elements necessary for proper digestion within the system. If foods are first acted upon by pure water, the reactions are nearly normal. Also, therefore, each morning upon arising, first take a half to three-quarters of a glass of hot water . . . Not so hot that it is objectionable. Not so tepid that it makes for sickening [reactions], but this will clarify the system of poisons.

311-MS-3

Question: How much water should I drink daily?

Answer: From six to eight tumblers full. *574-P-1*

Sleep

Few of us get enough sleep; or, as much as we think or suspect we need, in order to feel at our best. If we deliberately deprive ourselves of enough sleep, this will be added to our sins of neglect, or omission. The readings say, "Take Time to Sleep!"

> Take time to sleep! It is the exercising of a faculty—it is a condition meant to be a part of the experience of each soul. . . . It is but the shadow of life, or lives, or experiences. Just as each day of experience is a part of the whole life that is being builded by an entity . . . [so] each night is but a period of putting away—a storing up into the superconscious or the unconsciousness of the soul itself. *2067-P-1*

> Seven and a half to eight hours' sleep should be taken for most bodies.
> *816-P-1*

> Sedatives and hypnotics are destructive forces to brain and nerve reflexes.
> *343l-P-1*

Question: Why can't I sleep at night?

Answer: This is from nervousness and over-anxiety. Of course, keep away from any drugs if possible—though a sedative at times may be necessary. Drink a glass of warm milk with a teaspoonful of honey stirred into it. *2514-P*

Question: What may be done to enable me to sleep through the night?

Answer: Purifying of the system in the manner indicated will relieve the tension upon the nervous system. . . . For, if the body takes time for thought: physical rest is the natural means whereby the mental and spiritual forces find the means of coordination with mental-physical activities of the body. Hence rest is necessary; but that which is *induced*—unless it becomes necessary because of pain—is not a *natural rest,* nor does it produce regeneration of activities of the physical body. *1711-P-1*

Question: Why am I so dependent upon sleep, and what do I do during my physical sleep?

Answer: Sleep is a *sense,* as we have given heretofore. It is that which is needed for the physical body to recuperate—or to draw from the mental and spiritual powers or forces what has been held as ideals for the body. . . . Don't think that the body is a haphazard machine, or that the things which happen to individuals are chance!

Then, what happens to a body in sleep? This depends upon what it has thought and what it has set as its ideal. For when one considers, one may find these to be facts: there are some individuals who in their sleep gain strength, power and might, because of their thoughts, their manner of living. There are others who find that when any harm, any illness, any dejection comes to them, it is following sleep! Again, it is a law. What happens to this body? That is dependent upon the manner in which it has *applied* itself during the periods of its waking state.   *2067-P*

Smoking, Coffee and Tea

Is smoking permitted, or compatible with everyday living in which a strong effort is made to apply ideals? What about alcoholic drinks? Coffee and tea? Are they harmful? Information given in the readings is extremely helpful.

Question: Have personal vices such as tobacco and whiskey any influence upon one's health or longevity?

Answer: You are suffering from the use of some of these in the present, but it is over-indulgence. In moderation, these stimulants are not too bad, but man so seldom will be moderate. Or as most would say: those who indulge will make pigs of themselves. This over-indulgence, of course, makes for conditions which are to be met. For what one sows, that must one reap. This is unchangeable law.   *5233*

Question: Does smoking hurt the body?

Answer: Moderate smoking is not so harmful as would be the nervous and mental reaction to total abstinence from it. Six or eight (cigarettes) a day then, in moderation.   *1568-P*

Question: Would smoking be detrimental to me or beneficial?

Answer: This depends very much upon self. In moderation, smoking is not harmful; but to a body that holds such as being out of line with its best mental or spiritual unfoldment, do not smoke.   *2981-P-1*

Question: Is the moderate use of liquor, tobacco and meat a bar to spiritual growth?

Answer: For this entity, yes. For some, no.   *2981-L-1*

Wine taken in excess, of course, is harmful. Wine taken with brown, black, rye or whole wheat bread is body-building.   *821-P-1*

No beer, no strong drink, though occasionally red wine may be taken as a *food*—for this is blood building, and blood forces are carried in same, such as iron and plasms that make for proper activity in the system. But never more than two or two-and-a-half ounces of same—and this only with black or brown bread, not with sweets.   *1308-P-1*

Question: Are too much coffee and smoking dangerous for nerves and stomach?

Answer: Not necessarily. Depends upon how the coffee is prepared—with milk or cream it can be (bad for him). Smoking in moderation is not harmful.
                                                                                          3477-P-1

In *Food and Nutrition News* December 1956 issue, we find this statement about coffee: "The presence of relatively large amounts of niacin, one of the B vitamins, in coffee has been confirmed by animal tests. This is relatively unimportant to Americans since their diet usually contains adequate amounts of niacin. However, among some populations abroad, the drinking of coffee may help prevent niacin deficiency."

Question: Will coffee hurt the body?

Answer: Coffee without cream or milk is not so harmful. Preferably the G. Washington Coffee for this body, because of the manner in which it is brewed.
                                                                                          1568-P-2

Question: Is coffee good for the body? If so, how often taken?

Answer: Coffee taken properly is a food. For many kinds of physical conditions, as with this body, caffeine in coffee is hard on the digestion—especially when there is a tendency for a plethoric condition in the lower end of the stomach. Hence the use of coffee or chicory . . . with combinations where breads, meats or sweets are taken is helpful. But for this body it is preferable that tannin (in tea) be mostly removed. Then it can be taken two or three times a day, but without milk or cream.   *404-P-5*

Coffee is a stimulant to the nerve system. The dross from coffee is caffeine, which is not digestible in the system and must necessarily be eliminated. Thus when caffeine is allowed to remain in the colon, poisons are thrown off from it. If it is eliminated—as it is in this system—*coffee is a food* and is preferable to many stimulants that might be taken.   *294-P-37*

Question: Does it hurt me to use sugar in my coffee?

Answer: Sugar is not nearly so harmful as cream. You may use sugar in moderation.   *243-P-16*

Coffee taken properly is a food—taken, that is, without cream or milk.   *303-P*

Question: Are tea and coffee harmful?

Answer: For this body, tea is preferable to coffee, but tea in excess is hard on the digestive system; to be sure, it should never be taken with milk.   *1622-P-1*

Question: Are tea and coffee harmful to this body?

Answer: Tea is more harmful than coffee. Any nerve reaction is more susceptible to the kind of tea that is usually found in this country, though in some ways in which it is produced, it would be well. Coffee, taken properly, is a food—that is, without cream or milk.   *303-P-1*

Recreation

Work, rest, recreation, exercise, eliminations, food and drink—all these are the physical factors of life having mental and spiritual effects, which must be properly balanced with time we take for the purely spiritual. The difficulties of reaching this proper balance—each for himself—are reflected in the following questions put to Edgar Cayce, and the wonderfully constructive answers.

> We find that these conditions arose as a result of what might be called occupational disturbances: not enough in the sun, nor enough of hard work. [There has been] plenty of brain work, but the body is supposed to coordinate the spiritual, mental and physical. He who does not give recreation a place in his life—and the proper tone to each phase—well, he just fools himself. . . . There must be certain amounts of sleep. Didn't God make man to sleep at least a third of his life? Then consider! These are physical, mental and spiritual necessities. This is what the Master meant when He said, "Consider the lilies of the field, how they grow." Do they grow all the while, bloom all the while—or look mighty messy and dirty at times? It is well for people, individuals, as this entity, to get their hands dirty in the dirt at times, and not be the white-collared man all the time! . . . From whence was man made? Don't be afraid to get a little dirt on you once in a while. . . . And take time to play a while with others. There are children growing. Have you added anything constructive to any child's life? You'll not be in heaven if you're not leaning on the arm of someone you have helped. . .   *3552-P-1*

Question: Do you advise the use of colonics or Epsom Salts baths for the body?

Answer: When these are necessary, yes. For everyone, everybody, should take an internal bath occasionally, as well as external baths. People would be better off if they would!   *440-3*

Clear the body as you do the mind of those things that have hindered. The things that hinder physically are poor eliminations. Set up better eliminations in the body. This is why osteopathy and hydrotherapy come nearer to being the basis of all needed treatments for physical disabilities.   *2524-MS-2*

For hydrotherapy and massage are preventive as well as curative measures. The cleansing of the system allows the bodyforces themselves to function normally and thus to eliminate poisons, congestions, and conditions that would become acute throughout the body.   *257-P-51*

Question: What physical and mental exercises will be beneficial?

Answer: Of course, meditation is always well—for the mental attitude has much to do with the general physical forces. As for the physical exercise: walking is the best of any exercise—and swimming now for the next three or four [warm] months.   *2823-P-1*

The best exercise for this body would be to stretch in the manner of a cat, or panther. Stretching the muscles but not straining them causes the tendons and muscles to be put into positions natural for the building of a strong and graceful body.   *4003-P-1*

Question: Is there any special exercise I should take, other than the head and neck exercise?

Answer: Walking is the best exercise, but don't take it spasmodically. Have a regular time and do it rain or shine.   *No. 1968-P-4*

Question: Has lack of setting-up exercises in these last months been detrimental to the body?

Answer: Whenever something is begun and then left off, it becomes detrimental—anything, that is, which should have been kept up!   *457-P-7*

Fasting means what the Master gave: Laying aside our own concept of *how* and *what* should be done at any period, and letting the Spirit guide. Understand the *truth* of fasting! To be sure, overindulgence in bodily appetites brings shame to self, as overindulgence in anything. True fasting is casting out of self any thought of what we would like done, and becoming *channels* for what He, the Lord, would have done in the earth through us.   *395-L-2*

Take time to be holy, but take time also to play. Take time to rest, time to recuperate; for thy Master, even the pattern in the earth, took time to rest. He took time to attend a wedding, took time to be apart from others, took time to attend a funeral. He took time to attend those who were awakening from death. . . . He took time to minister to all.   *5246*

EDGAR CAYCE

ON ESP

by Doris Agee

CONTENTS

INTRODUCTION

THIS BOOK WAS designed to discuss the question, "What are the varieties of ESP which can be found in the records of Edgar Cayce's work?"

Doris Agee has brought to this material not only a writing style of clarity and directness of a good reporter but also the intellectual intensity of a research-minded seeker. She is obviously fascinated by the mechanics of the Edgar Cayce readings. Her opening chapters will help answer for many readers the oft heard questions, "Why was *he* able to do it?" and "How were the readings given?"

Presenting new cases for the most part, Mrs. Agee opens up a bewildering area of ESP capacities in the Edgar Cayce data. She uses the physical and life readings as sources of telepathic-clairvoyant insight. Her section on missing persons presents some cases which have never been examined before. Her treatment of scientific confirmation of many of the prophecies is very well handled.

In all this is a welcome addition to the books on the Edgar Cayce readings.

—Hugh Lynn Cayce

CHAPTER 1

"THE UNIVERSAL MIND"

UNTIL A FEW years ago, only the most foolhardy of men would openly acknowledge his belief in the existence of "sixth sense," that enigmatic something we now generally call extrasensory perception, or ESP. To admit acceptance of such an idea was to court criticism, derision and in some extreme cases a suspicion that one had lost his reason.

For the unconscious mind is a dark, mysterious place. Many centuries passed before man became convinced that he *had* an unconscious mind, operating on many different levels; and then many more years went by before he began to feel that he had a right to investigate its workings.

Not that humanity has ever suffered a dearth of psychic phenomena! How many "witches" were drowned or burned at the stake before man came to understand that just because something could not be explained by established scientific law, it wasn't necessarily evil? How many people who experienced true psychic phenomena were judged insane and put behind locked doors, simply because other people couldn't accept the truth of what had happened?

We've come a long way in the past few decades. We've now reached the point where individuals are publicly discussing ESP and psychic phenomena and asking questions about the subject. It is no longer a question of, "Do I believe in ESP?" Rather, more and more people are asking, "Now that I know that ESP exists, how can I learn more about it? How does it work? Do I have it? If I develop my own ability to use it, will it harm me or help me?"

Many of the answers to these and other questions may be found in the remarkable collection of psychic readings given by an outstanding clairvoyant, Edgar Cayce, during the more than forty years of his adult life. Although much has been written about Cayce, the scope of his psychic ability and of the subjects he treated while in a self-imposed hypnotic sleep are so vast that great portions of the knowledge they contain are still, as yet, untapped.

It is the purpose of this book to present to the reader, mainly through use of the readings themselves, material which may aid his understanding of psychic phenomena as well as the individual's own place and value in today's troubled world.

Cayce's own psychic abilities enabled him to help many thousands of people; but in many ways they brought terrible burdens to his own life. Often misunderstood by his contemporaries, he went out of his way to make his "waking" hours seem as ordinary and commonplace as those of every other man. Throughout his life he was constantly being tested and challenged, sometimes under severe physical pain, because people simply couldn't believe he could do the things they'd heard he could do. On several occasions he was jailed as a fraud, accused of cheap showmanship or of practicing medicine without a license. None of these claims were valid; he was a quiet, humble man who supported a wife and children more on faith than money.

A common reaction, upon first learning of the work of Edgar Cayce, is to think of his clairvoyant abilities as something in the nature of magic. Edgar Cayce's own description of it, as shown in the many readings he gave on the subject, is much more down to earth. Later chapters will go into this in more detail, but a general explanation might be in order here.

As the readings explained it, the knowledge gained while Cayce was in a self-induced sleep came principally from the subject's *own* unconscious mind. He was, in effect, simply "tuning in" to the correct frequency.

He described the levels or degrees of an individual's unconscious mind, and he talked about the collective unconscious in which the individual unconscious has its origin. This collective, or universal, unconscious he described as a vast "river" of thought flowing through eternity, fed by the collective mental activity of mankind since its beginning. According to Cayce, this collective unconscious is accessible to anyone who develops his own psychic faculties to such a degree as to be able to draw from, as well as feed into, this river of thought.

This was nothing new, really. Scholars and philosophers since ancient times have advanced similar theories about the unconscious mind. But Edgar Cayce didn't just *tell* about it; he *performed* it. His highly developed psychic abilities put theory into practice, with information that has been proved accurate again and again.

The story of Edgar Cayce is remarkable in two important ways. First, of course, is the extraordinary scope of his psychic powers, his extrasensory perception. Second, and equally important, is the fact that meticulous records were kept of the readings he gave during his lifetime, and these have been carefully maintained and *used* in the more than two decades since his death. Over 14,000 readings, and a large number of studies based on their contents, are completely indexed and available to interested researchers. These are living files in every sense of the word, for they contain vast amounts of knowledge that may be used by this generation, and many generations to come, in man's never-ceasing struggle to understand himself and the world he inhabits.

Edgar Cayce has been called the Miracle Man of Virginia Beach. It is an understandable and apt title. Although the readings reflect, at first glance, the realization of Cayce's boyhood dream to someday help people, as he certainly did with the thousands of physical and life readings he gave, they contain much, much more.

They contain, for example, a great deal of history of man—some of which may have passed, for the moment, out of the realm of accepted knowledge. If so, future archaeological findings may confirm many of the events Cayce spoke of in his readings. This has already happened in some instances.

One such example followed the discovery of the Dead Sea Scrolls in 1947 by two shepherd boys grazing their goats in the vicinity of Khirbet Qumran. Cayce, in giving a life reading for a woman in 1936, had referred to her having been, in a previous incarnation, a Sister Superior in an Essene community. At the time of the reading it was believed that only men had inhabited such communities. But in 1951 excavations into ruins near the coast of the Dead Sea established the fact that an Essene monastery had existed just where Cayce had placed it in his reading. And when graves surrounding the community were opened, skeletons of many women were found!

Cayce was a deeply religious man. Thus it was a moving experience for him when, in the course of a reading given spontaneously, he seemed to "attend" the Last Supper. He described it in detail, and it will be presented, just as he told it, in a later chapter.

Edgar Cayce "read" the past, but he also read the future, both for individuals and for mankind as a whole. For instance, he predicted both world wars, and furnished the dates of beginning and ending. He predicted the stock market crash of 1929, the gradual lifting of the depression beginning in 1933, racial violence in America (pinpointed with absolute accuracy as to the time it would begin), and talked of the death in office of two presidents (Roosevelt and Kennedy, although he did not name them). These and other Cayce prophecies will be discussed in a separate chapter on the subject.

He read the present. As will be illustrated throughout the following pages, Cayce's ability to put his own unconscious mind in complete communication with the unconscious minds of others was, by accepted definition, telepathic in nature; that is, he read the conscious or unconscious thoughts and ideas of others. But much of it was also clairvoyant; he was able to acquire knowledge of physical objects or events (apart from mental ones) without the use of any of the recognized channels of communication. These were abilities within his power to control. Although some of his psychic experiences were spontaneous, most of them occurred because he *willed* them to occur. For example, he might experience a dream during the course of a normal night's sleep. What set him apart, however, was that he could later put himself to sleep deliberately and ask for, and receive, an interpretation of what he had dreamed! Even more remarkable, if his conscious memory of the dream was dim, his unconscious memory of it would fill in any missing details at the time the interpretation was going on! Some of his dream interpretations, as well as his explanation of what might be considered universal dream symbols, will be explored in a later chapter.

Edgar Cayce also, at times, participated in *conscious* phenomena. Visions came to him all through his life; he experienced his first one at the age of six. As with his dreams, he was able to gain, via the psychic readings, interpretations of his visions; and often his source of information would supply the answer to the question, "Was the experience had by Edgar Cayce on such-and-such a date a dream, or a vision?"

Another interesting talent of his was the ability to see, when looking at any individual, an aura: a kind of halo of light and color which told him much about the mental and physical well-being of the person he was consciously viewing. This will be discussed later in this book, together with some special color charts developed by Cayce: a sort of do-it-yourself-analyze-your-friends kit.

When giving a reading, he seemed actually to put himself where the subject of the reading was situated—even if that person was halfway around the world. The Cayce files are full of indications of his awareness, during the readings, of physical surroundings and actions of the person receiving the reading.

Once a Hopkinsville, Kentucky, businessman, doubting Cayce's ability to do all the things he'd heard about, challenged Cayce to trace his steps as he went from his home to his office on a particular day. Cayce, who had a high regard for skeptics, accepted the challenge. At the appointed hour, in the office of the local newspaper, Cayce put himself to sleep.

The man went out of his way to trick him. He altered his usual route. Instead of buying the single cigar in the tobacco store at which he stopped each morning, this time he purchased two. He took the stairway to his second floor office instead of the elevator. But when he arrived at his office, he put the "test" out of his mind and went about his daily business, beginning with opening and reading the morning mail.

Many people in Hopkinsville were highly amused to learn that Cayce had "seen" him every step of the way. But he was amazed, and a little disconcerted, to discover that Cayce had also read his mail!

Once, at the beginning of a reading, Cayce exclaimed, "Yes, not bad looking pajamas!" A check with the patient later got the response that he had wanted to make sure Edgar Cayce would be able to "find" him, so he had deliberately put on a pair of new pajamas—bright red ones at that.

Another time, after repeating the location of the subject in an undertone, Cayce said, "Yes, we have had this place before." A check through the files showed that, although this particular subject had not had a reading previously, his brother-in-law had, several months before. Both men had been at the home of the brother-in-law when their readings were given.

One day Cayce put himself into trance easily enough, but then seemed a little reluctant to begin the reading; he showed signs of having been distracted by something. Then he said, "1075 Park Avenue. Very unusual in some of these halls, isn't it? What funny paintings!" He then went on with the reading as if there were nothing out of the ordinary. A query about this to the subject brought the response that there were some very unusual wall adornments in the hall, including some wood plaques from Central America. At the time of the reading, however, she had been neither looking at them nor thinking about them.

Often the readings would begin with such statements as, "Yes, little stream there . . ." or, "That's a right pretty tree on the corner!"

It seems that Cayce, while giving a reading, was always aware of what the person was doing at the time. Once he began with the usual, "Yes, we have the body here." Then he raised his voice a little, saying, "It would be better if he would keep quiet a minute. No use bawling *that* man out!" A check with the subject later brought a somewhat chastened admission that he had been shouting at one of his employees at the time set for the reading.

Normally, only one physical reading was given at a session. However, follow-up readings—called check readings—were usually brief, and often they were scheduled so that Cayce could do several while in the same hypnotic sleep. He wasn't told the names of the subjects in advance; these were given only at the beginning of each individual reading. John Brewer, scheduled for a reading at nine thirty, stayed in his Baltimore apartment until ten o'clock, as he'd told the Cayce office he would do. At that time, he began making preparations to leave for his office. At precisely the same time, at Virginia Beach, Edgar Cayce was being given the suggestion to read for a San Francisco man. Suddenly he interrupted the proceedings. "Better take John Brewer first. He's going out!" The readings were switched. A follow-up with Brewer later confirmed that this is exactly what had happened.

Throughout the files, there are many indications that Edgar Cayce not only "saw" the subjects of his readings and their surroundings but knew, as well, what people were doing. Thus we find a great many statements such as:

"Come back here and sit down!"

"Yes, we have the body here. The body is just leaving, going down in the elevator now."

Once he located the subject of a reading on a Fifth Avenue bus. The man had been held up in traffic, and was still en route to the appointed location. Edgar Cayce, giving the reading from his home in Virginia Beach, mentioned that the subject was not at the New York location given in the reading suggestion, and then proceeded to do a little psychic detective work by tracking down the man. Once the subject was in Cayce's "view," the reading went off without a hitch.

Often Cayce would correct information given to him at the beginning of the reading. Once Gertrude Cayce identified the subject by her nickname, rather than her given name as used in an earlier reading. Edgar Cayce said, "Yes, we have the body here. This we have had before. Different names, same body." (This, incidentally, is a striking example of the phenomenal memory shown by Cayce when in the sleeping state. No matter how many years elapsed between readings, he never seemed to forget anything and simply picked up where the other reading had left off!)

Another time, after the location of the subject had been furnished by him, Edgar Cayce said, "We do not find the body here, but rather at the office—11th and Virginia Street." The subject, when asked about this later, replied that at the time of the reading she had been in her office, at the address Cayce had supplied, rather than at home as originally planned.

In addition to the readings given for diagnosing and prescribing treatment for physical problems, Edgar Cayce gave many of the type called "life readings." These dealt mainly with psychological problems, vocational talents, personal characteristics, and so forth, examined in the light of what Edgar Cayce called the "karmic patterns," arising out of previous lives spent on the earth by the individual soul (called, by Cayce, "the entity").

The life reading began with a suggestion different from that used in the physical reading. That is, instead of identifying the individual by name and present location, as used in obtaining physical readings, the conductor of the life reading furnished Cayce with the name, birth date and location of birth of the subject. (The hour of birth was also helpful to Cayce; if the subject couldn't supply this, Cayce often would.) To get his psychic information on the subject, the sleeping Cayce would consult what he referred to as "the book." When he found what he was looking for, he'd say, "Yes, we have the record."

Apparently subjects could keep no secrets from Cayce. One day a life reading suggestion was given for a young woman born January 23, 1919, at Mount Sinai Hospital in New York City. This information had been supplied by the subject before the reading. When Cayce began, however, he said, "We don't find it here. Yes, we have the record here (looks like it's the wrong place and date) of that entity now known as or called Martha Smith." The subject's mother finally got things straightened out by advising the Cayce office that her daughter didn't have it exactly right; she had been born, in fact, on January 24, 1919, in Cleveland, Ohio. The subject was quite dismayed to learn that Cayce knew about this, when she herself did not!

One striking example of Cayce's clairvoyant powers is shown in a life reading he gave for a man born in a town in Texas on February 25, 1906. In locating the "record" for this man, Cayce said of the town, "Quaint place! Not too nice a day, either, is it?" This reading was given on August 21, 1944. A check with the weather bureau in the Texas town showed that the weather, pleasant for several days just prior to February 25, 1906, had suddenly turned extremely warm and uncomfortable that day. Cayce had not only located the town in question, he'd gone back in time some thirty-eight years and given a weather report on it!

Whenever a statement of this type was made by Cayce during the course of a reading, the Cayce office would contact the subject for confirmation or denial of its accuracy. Not all the subjects responded, of course, but in some forty-three years of readings, no one ever notified the office that such a statement "just wasn't so."

Now let's examine, in detail, the way Edgar Cayce went about his business of "helping people."

A Kind of Miracle

Outside, at four o'clock in the afternoon of a day in October, 1940, the air was cold and crisp. Inside, in the small examining room of a Kentucky hospital, the air was stifling, and filled with the terrible sound of a child's screaming.

The cause of the screaming was all too apparent. The child, a little girl just one year old, lay naked on the white table. From her blonde hairline to her toes, nearly every inch of skin that could be seen was deeply scalded, the result of a container of boiling water she'd pulled down on herself half an hour earlier. With over fifty percent of her skin surface involved, the doctors didn't hold out much hope for her survival. Even if she lived, they admitted to each other—although not yet to the young parents—she'd most likely be badly scarred, and quite possibly blind.

They waited, now, for the results of a telephone call the child's father had just made to Edgar Cayce's home at Virginia Beach. The answers would come soon. Because the doctors had experienced such telephone calls in the past, and knew the good that could come from them, they'd agreed to go along with whatever they were instructed to do.

The parents waited, too, in the small hospital room. The child's father looked at his watch and said softly, "It's time." Then he took his wife's hand, and together they moved away from the child and sat down in the two straight chairs by the window. Silently, they lowered their heads in prayer.

Eight hundred miles away, Edgar Cayce was getting ready to perform what some called a kind of miracle. He was going to put himself to sleep, and while he was asleep he was going to describe in detail what was wrong with the child, and what to do for her—this child he had never seen. He didn't even know it *was* a child. All he knew was that a telephone call had just come in, requesting an emergency reading for someone, and that he was going to try to get "the information"—he always called it this—necessary to help that person.

In truth, he didn't look like the sort of man who could perform miracles. He was thin and quite tall, which probably accounted for the slight stoop to his shoulders. He was sixty-three years old and his hairline, as well as his chin, receded a little. If there was anything mystical about his appearance, it was in the large, blue-gray eyes that peered from behind rimless spectacles with a brilliant intensity.

Now he sat on the edge of the couch and untied his shoes, removed his tie, and unbuttoned his collar and cuffs; it was important that there be nothing binding. He swung his long legs onto the couch and lay back quietly. He smiled at his wife, Gertrude, who was to "conduct" the reading, and at his secretary of many years, Gladys Davis, who would note in shorthand precisely what he said, for he would remember none of it afterwards. He placed his hands on his forehead and closed his eyes. His breathing gradually deepened. He moved his hands to his abdomen, and began to breathe normally. Now he seemed to be simply taking an afternoon nap.

Gertrude said the words to begin the reading, just as she had said them so many times before. She told him only the name and present location of the patient, leaving out any mention of age, sex, or physical problem. Then she said, "You will give the physical condition of this body at the present time, with suggestions for further corrective measures, answering the questions as I ask them."

Edgar Cayce lay silent for several moments. Then he began to mumble, in a strange, faraway voice, repeating the name and location of the child to himself several times. Suddenly he cleared his throat, and spoke in a voice that was clear and forceful, that carried more authority than his waking voice.

"Yes," he said. "We have the body here. While these appear very serious in the present, because of the blister or the water, we do not find the injury to the eyes, but rather to the lids."

He then proceeded to outline, step by step, the treatment to be used by the doctors to heal the skin. "We would cleanse and use the tannic acid, followed with the Unguentine and the camphorated oil to prevent or remove scars, as the tissue heals.

"Be very mindful that eliminations are kept above the normal. Use *both* the Podophyllum and the calomel as a base for eliminants, at various times, not together. But under the direction of the physician. While these would not be used under most circumstances for a child, these would be the better in this case—because of the poisons from so much area covered with the burn, and the shock to the system, as well as the kind of poisons to be eliminated, and the need for the excess lymph.

"Ready for questions."

Gertrude Cayce asked, "Apply tannic acid?"

The answer came quickly. "Tannic acid; the light, to be sure. This is understood by the physician. Cleanse it first, then apply the tannic acid."

"How should it be cleansed?"

With a note of scorn, Edgar Cayce replied, "Would you ask how to tell a doctor to cleanse a thing!"

"Are they using the tannic acid in the way suggested here?"

"Not using it as yet, but it should be a part of the bandages."

The strange dialogue continued between the sleeping man and his wife.

"Then after the tannic acid apply the Unguentine?"

"As it heals. Not, of course, while the tannic acid is being used, but as it heals. See, this cuts away air, produces dead skin, and leaves a scar. Then the oils from the Unguentine, and the camphorated oil, are to take away scar tissue, see? These are to follow within ten days to two weeks, see?"

"The eyes themselves are not injured?"

"As indicated, the lids; though there will be, of course, some inflammation. But keep down the excesses of poisons by increasing the eliminations, to remove these poisons that are as natural accumulations from such an area burned."

"Any suggestions for relieving the pain?"

"As just given, this will relieve the pain when it cuts off the air!"

Gertrude needed no further clarification, and Edgar Cayce ended the reading as he always did, by saying, "We are through for the present."

Doctors caring for the girl applied the tannic acid bandages as prescribed by Cayce. They had never used this method before, but as a result of this case and its outcome, added it to the regimen for many such burn cases with excellent results. They balked, at first, at the idea of administering such strong eliminants for a baby, but finally agreed to go along with Cayce's reading on an "all or nothing" basis.

Twelve days later, a second reading was given for the child. Cayce announced that ". . . improvements have been rather phenomenal . . ." as far as healing of the skin was concerned. This time, his major concerns were lowering the fever and helping the body get rid of excess fluids and toxic substances that were accumulating faster than the kidneys could dispose of them—often a cause of death in severe burn cases. His instructions dealt with removing these fluids with certain eliminants; on this occasion he gave exact dosages to be used. He also prescribed gentle spinal massages twice a day with a mixture of one part grain alcohol to two parts water to reduce the fever; this was possible because the child's back was practically the only portion of her body not burned in the accident. He gave specific advice on the diet, and repeated his earlier instructions for applying Unguentine and camphorated oil to prevent the formation of scar tissue.

The child's recovery was complete. However, when she was three years old she was given another reading in which Cayce was asked to prescribe something to remove, or lessen, the one scar remaining on her arm. He recommended frequent massage with a mixture of two ounces of camphorated oil, one-half teaspoon dissolved lanolin, and one ounce peanut oil. (This, incidentally, is a

Cayce "invention" which was prescribed in a number of cases. It has been used by many people, with various types of scars, who have found it quite effective.)

Now twenty-eight, this young woman is walking proof of what Cayce's readings could do when followed in every detail. She has no scars from a burn so severe it could have killed her. Indeed, she is exceptionally beautiful, and only the fact that she is married, and the mother of three handsome sons, keeps her from working as a photographer's model, which she has often been invited to do. Her eyesight? She doesn't need glasses even for reading!

CHAPTER 2

WHAT IS A READING?

IT IS MOST fortunate that, among the many thousands of readings given by Edgar Cayce during his lifetime, a large number were devoted to the subject of psychic phenomena. People—including Cayce himself—wanted to know what, exactly, he did when he put himself into trance. And how he got the information he got. And from what source. And why. So they asked him, and the sleeping Cayce replied.

We live in a world that demands scientific proof of such phenomena before any of it may be accepted. So Cayce's answers, for the time being at least, must be considered theory, rather than fact.

But what an interesting theory they form!

Cayce's Conscious Description

One of the clearest statements on the Cayce work was made by Edgar Cayce himself in an address to a study group on February 6, 1933. He began:

"What is a reading?

"It is rather hard to describe something which has become so much a part of me—almost like trying to describe what my face looks like. I can show you, but I can't tell you. I might tell you some of my experiences and thoughts concerning the readings; but as to what a reading is I can only tell you what others have said about them and what has come to me as I have studied the effect created in the minds of those receiving readings.

"It would not be an exaggeration to say that I have been in the unconscious state (during which the readings are given) perhaps twenty-five thousand times in the last thirty-one years; yet I myself have never heard a single reading. How can I describe one to you?

"Many people who have never heard a reading have asked me just how I knew I could give one. I never did know it—don't know it yet—except by taking another person's word for it.

"The first step in giving a reading is this: I loosen my clothes—my shoelaces, my necktie, my shirtcuffs, and my belt—in order to have a perfectly free-flowing circulation.

"Then I lie down on the couch in my office. If the reading is to be a physical one, I lie with my head to the south and my feet to the north. If it is to be a life reading, it is just the opposite: my feet are to the south, my head to the north. The reason for this difference is 'polarization' as the readings themselves call it. I do not know.

"Once lying comfortably, I put both hands up to my forehead, on the spot where observers have told me that the third eye is located, and pray. Interestingly enough, I have unconsciously and instinctively, from the very beginning, adopted the practices used by initiates in meditation. This instinctive putting of my hands to the point midway between my two eyes on my forehead is a case of what I mean.

"Then I wait for a few minutes, until I receive what might be called the 'go signal'—a flash of brilliant white light, sometimes tending towards the golden in color. This light is to me the sign that I have made contact. When I do not see it, I know I cannot give the reading.

"After seeing the light I move my two hands down to the solar plexus, and—I'm told—my breathing now becomes very deep and rhythmic, from the diaphragm. This goes on for several minutes. When my eyes begin to flutter closed (up until now they have been open, but glazed) the conductor knows I am ready to receive the suggestion, which he proceeds to give me, slowly and distinctly. If it is a physical reading, for example, the name of the individual to receive the reading is given me, together with the address where he will be located during that period of time. There is a pause—sometimes so long a pause, they tell me, that it seems I haven't heard the directions, so they give them to me again—after which I repeat the name and address very slowly, until the body is located, and a description of its condition is begun.

"This, then, is how I give a reading. I am entirely unconscious throughout the whole procedure. When I wake up I feel as if I had slept a little bit too long. And frequently I feel slightly hungry—just hungry enough for a cracker and a glass of milk, perhaps.

"As to the validity of the information that comes through me when I sleep—this, naturally, is the question that occurs to everyone. Personally, I feel that its validity depends largely on how much faith or confidence the one seeking has in the source of information. Of course its validity has been objectively proved many hundreds of times by the results that have come from applying the advice.

"With regard to the source of information, I have some ideas, naturally; but even though I have been doing this work for thirty-one years I know very little about it. Whatever I could say would be largely a matter of conjecture. I can make no claim whatsoever to great knowledge. I, too, am only groping.

"But then, we all learn only by experience. We come to have faith or understanding by taking one step at a time. We don't all have the experience of getting religion all at once, like the man who got it halfway between the bottom of the well and the top when he was blown out by an explosion of dynamite. We all have to have our experiences and arrive at conclusions by weighing the evidence with something that responds from deep within our inner selves.

"As a matter of fact, there would seem to be not only one, but several sources of information that I tap when in this sleeping condition.

"One source is, apparently, the record that an individual or entity makes in all its experiences through what we call time. The sum total of the experiences of that soul is 'written,' so to speak, in the subconscious of that individual as well as in what is known as the akashic records. Anyone may read these records if he can attune himself properly.

"Apparently I am one of the few who can lay aside their own personalities sufficiently to allow their souls to make this attunement to this universal source of knowledge—but I say this without any desire to brag about it. In fact, I cannot claim to possess anything that other individuals do not inherently possess. Really and truly, I do not believe there is a single individual who doesn't possess this same ability I have. I am certain that all human beings have much greater powers than they are ever conscious of—if they would only be willing to pay the price of detachment from self-interest that it takes to develop those abilities. Would you be willing, even once a year, to put aside, pass out entirely from, your own personality?

"Some people think that the information coming through me is given by some departed personality who wants to communicate with them, or some benevolent spirit or physician from the other side. This may sometimes be the case, though in general I am not a 'medium' in that sense of the term. However, if a person comes seeking that kind of contact and information, I believe he receives it.

"Many people ask me how I prevent undesirable influences entering the work I do. In order to answer that question, let me relate an experience I had as a child.

"When I was between eleven and twelve years of age I had read the Bible through three times. I have now read it fifty-six times. No doubt many people have read it more times than that, but I have tried to read it through once for each year of my life. Well, as a child I prayed that I might be able to do something for the other fellow, to aid others in understanding themselves, and especially to aid children in their ills. I had a vision one day which convinced me that my prayer had been heard and would be answered.

"I still believe that my prayer is being answered and as I go into the unconscious condition I do so with that faith. So I believe that if the source is not wavered by the desires of the individual seeking the reading, it will be from the universal.

"Of course if an individual's desire is very intense to have a communication from Grandpa, Uncle, or some great soul, the contact is directed that way, and that becomes the source. Do not think that I am discrediting those who seek in that way. If you're willing to receive what Uncle Joe has to say, that's what you get. If you're willing to depend on a more universal source, that's what you get. 'What ye ask ye shall receive' is a two-edged sword. It cuts both ways."

Thus we have Cayce's own conscious description of his work. Many of the points he touched on in his talk will be expanded in succeeding chapters.

Earlier, in a reading given in 1923, Edgar Cayce reported that psychic readings were not new. "Among the Chaldeans they were first used as the means of assistance to physical bodies—not in the same manner as they are given today. They came as the *natural* means of expression of an unseen force; the soul and spirit of an earthly individual, manifesting through the physical body, enabled that life-giving flow of such revelations to appear—nearly four thousand years before the Prince of Peace came."

Language of the Readings

Before we embark on what Edgar Cayce, in his readings, had to say about psychic matters in general, and his own psychic work in particular, we must pause for a moment and consider the peculiar language he spoke while in the sleeping state. It is, at times, difficult.

Anyone who has researched the readings to any degree has been frustrated, sooner or later, by the strange phraseology, the complicated sentence structure, the allusions and circumlocutions of the Cayce language. Gina Cerminara, who has written so much about Edgar Cayce, authored a witty treatise on this subject in the April, 1966, A.R.E. *Journal.*

"Why," she wondered, "did he have to engage in psychic double talk? Why, instead of saying, 'This is a spade,' did he have to say something such as, 'This as we find has to do with not the consciousness in spirituality (as commonly conceived) but rather the consciousness of materiality, as condensed in what is known as, or called, in the present, an implement of spading, or a spade.' "

Portions of the readings do sound as obscure as Dr. Cerminara's made-up example—although we will not boggle your mind with them in this book, but will paraphrase when necessary.

At times, no doubt the people working closest to Edgar Cayce were frustrated by the language, too. A gentle hint of this is found in a reading given in April, 1934, wherein Cayce was asked, "Are there any suggestions or counsel that may be given at this time that will aid in securing clearer, more valuable information?"

Cayce seems to have evaded them rather neatly. He replied, "Seek and ye shall find. As given, that which may be helpful and hopeful on any subject that pertains to the welfare of the souls and bodies of individuals may be sought through these channels . . . "

Even earlier than that, however, those working with Cayce asked him outright, in a reading given in April, 1932, "How can the language used in the readings be made clearer, more concise and more direct?"

"Be able to understand it better!" he said.

There is much valuable and interesting material in what Cayce had to say, however awkwardly some of it may seem to be worded. If you would "be able to understand it better," then, do take time to read and reread difficult portions. Just as you found when you first encountered Shakespeare or Chaucer, familiarity with the particular "shape" of the language will make you more comfortable with it.

CHAPTER 3

SOURCES OF EDGAR CAYCE'S INFORMATION

AS WE MENTIONED, the readings themselves named two major sources of information available to the sleeping Cayce. There are indications of other sources as well.

The First Source

This was the unconscious mind of the person for whom the reading was being given. Edgar Cayce, in putting his conscious mind out of the way and letting his unconscious mind take over, by means of self-induced hypnosis, was able to "tune in" on the unconscious mind of the individual.

In view of what we now know about the workings of the unconscious mind, this seems quite acceptable. No one pretends to understand the mechanics of such an accomplishment, but there are many thousands of Cayce readings, dealing with the diagnosis and suggested treatment for physical disorders of all types, that can hardly be explained in any other way. One thing is certainly clear: whatever it was that Cayce was doing, it worked—and it worked extremely well.

What *are* some of the things we know about the unconscious mind? Well, for one thing, we know that it is fed by the conscious mind, which has in its turn been fed by the five recognized senses of sight, hearing, taste, touch and smell. We know that the unconscious mind never forgets. And we know that it can receive messages given so quickly that the conscious mind is not even aware of them; experiments with subliminal advertising have shown this to be true. We know that a hypnotherapist can say to a receptive subject under hypnosis, "I am burning your arm with a red hot poker," and touch the arm with any object at all, and a blister will form in that spot. We know, then, that the subconscious mind exerts tremendous control over the physical body. We know that the hypnotherapist can put his subject into varying levels of sleep all the way from an almost-conscious state to a sleep so deep that the subject will respond to no stimulus whatsoever. We know that each level of sleep seems to have its own memory track. Something told the subject at Level A, for example, might not be recalled at Level D, but will be recalled verbatim when the subject is brought back to Level A again.

We know that the subconscious mind speaks a literal language. The hypnotherapist can say, "Can you give me your date of birth?" and the unconscious mind, speaking through the subject, will reply, "Yes." The unconscious mind will not reply to such a question with the birthdate, but will merely indicate that it *can* reply if it wants to!

Yes, we know a lot about the unconscious mind. But there's a great deal we don't know about it. We don't know, as yet, just how deep it may go, and we still don't know quite how it works. We don't know what principle governs the peculiar tie-up between the will of the hypnotherapist and the willingness of the unconscious mind of a receptive subject to comply with correctly worded commands. Most of what we now know of the unconscious mind has come directly from experimentation with the process of hypnosis.

But the subject of a Cayce reading was not under hypnosis. He might have been half a world away when Cayce reached out psychically and put his unconscious mind in tune with that of his subject. And while today's hypnotherapist, working within the framework of accepted medical procedure, is concerned only with taking the subject's unconscious mind back as far as earliest childhood, Cayce went much further. He went deep into the subject's unconscious and "read" the history of that person's past lives!

Cayce's first experience with this phenomenon, in a reading given in 1923, shocked and dismayed him, for it seemed to be in direct opposition to his orthodox Christian beliefs and training. Over a period of more than twenty years, he had given many thousands of psychic readings dealing with physical problems. Now the same informational source was indicating that people spend many lifetimes on earth. Even more startling was the indication that they carry the unconscious memory of these lifetimes with them into each new appearance on the earth—and Edgar Cayce had been given the means of telling them about it! This seemed incredible to Cayce, and he wanted no part of it.

Had his physical readings not been proven accurate and useful in all the years he had been giving them, he probably would have turned from this new development in his psychic work and never have given another reading of any kind. Fortunately, however, he decided—after much soul-searching and listening to the arguments of those around him—to continue. The more than 2,500 life readings he gave in the years between 1923 and his death in 1945 form some of the most engrossing and compelling "testimony" on the subject of reincarnation ever recorded.

Suddenly, then, there was a new and fantastic wealth of information—having to do with ancient religions, philosophy, universal laws, the whole history of mankind—available through the unconscious mind of Edgar Cayce. For it seemed that there was almost no question that could be put to the sleeping man that would not elicit some kind of answer. Sometimes the information confirmed and expanded knowledge of certain subjects, and sometimes it refuted it. Often, questions put to Cayce months—or even years—apart would receive the same answer, in almost identical wording.

As this new material began to pile up, more and more questions were raised in the minds of Edgar Cayce and those associated with him concerning the source of his information. Consequently, a great many readings were devoted to this subject alone.

One of the best statements in this regard was given during the course of a physical reading for a young man. After repeating the suggestion to begin the reading, Cayce opened with one of his frequent demonstrations of clairvoyance by reciting the time of day and describing the actions of the subject.

"Yes, we have the body here, John Hanson. 11:47. He has just laid aside the paper he was reading.

"In giving information concerning this body, it would be well that the body understand or have an idea of how such information may be given that there may be credence put in that which may be supplied as helpful information in the experience of this body, entity, soul, at the present.

"Then, in seeking information there are certain factors in the experience of the seeker [John Hanson] and in the channel through which such information might come [Edgar Cayce]. Desire on the part of the seeker to be shown. And, as an honest seeker, such will not be too gullible; neither will such be so encased in prejudices as to doubt that which is applicable in the experience of such seeker. Hence the information must not only be practical, but it must be rather in accord with the desires of the seeker also.

"This desire, then, is such that it must not only hold on that which is primarily the basis of all material manifestation of spiritual things, but must also have its inception in a well-balanced desire for the use of such information not only for self but for others.

"Then there may come, as for this body in the present, that which if applied may be helpful in the present experience.

"On the part of that channel [Cayce] through whom such information may come, there must be the unselfish desire to be of aid to a fellow man. Not as for self-exaltation because of being a channel. Not for self-glorification that such a channel may be well spoken of. But rather as one desirous of being a channel through which the highest spiritual forces may manifest in bringing to the material consciousness of the seeker those things that may be beneficial in a spiritual and material sense to the seeker.

"What, then, is the hypothesis of the activity that takes place during such an experience? Not merely that word telepathy, that has been coined by some untutored individuals; neither that a beneficent spirit seeking to do a service seeks out those ones and in an unseeming manner gives that from its sphere which makes for those experiences in the mind of the seeker, as some have suggested. For, if such were true at all times, there would never be a fault—if real developed spirits were in control. But rather in *this* instance is *this* the case:

"The soul of the seeker [John Hanson] is passive. The soul of the individual through whom information comes [Edgar Cayce] is positive—as the physical is subjugated into unconsciousness—and goes out on the forces that are activated by suggestion given [by the conductor of the reading] and locates the place of the seeker. And the souls commune one with another.

"Then, it is asked, what prevents the information from always being accurate, or being wholly of unquestionable nature? The fact that such information must be interpreted in material things. And that then depends upon how well the training of the physical-mental self is in such a communion."

The importance of desire on the part of the recipient was emphasized for the author by a discussion with a close relative who had received a number of Cayce readings over the years. She indicated that all her readings were personal, warm communications from the sleeping Cayce, with the exception of the very first one.

"I don't like to say this," she remarked, "but I never felt it was *my* reading. Oh, I could recognize many things in it that surely applied to my life and my way of thinking, but somehow that one reading seemed somehow remote and impersonal. And then several years ago it dawned on me what might have happened.

"You see, I was only nineteen years old at the time the reading was given. My fiance and his friend had both received life readings, and they kept urging me to have one then. I wanted to wait a few years. I never admitted to them that I just went along with the idea as a favor to them, and that secretly I resented, a bit, the pressure they had put on me. Probably I wasn't cooperating as fully as I should have been, and Cayce sensed my reluctance."

Edgar Cayce was once asked to supply a term that could be used in referring to his ability to give psychic readings, for use in some literature that was being prepared for publication. He replied, "Application of the harmonious triune; or that as may be determined by those who may 'make' a word or term to designate the various phases of the activities presented through such information.

"To be sure, it is psychic—or of the soul. As is stated, this is confusing to many whose knowledge or awareness is only of some mediumistic seance or of some activities founded upon an experience of individuals that has led to such a train of thought.

"It is the harmony of the triune—of body, mind and soul—towards the purpose of being a help, an assistance, and aid to others."

This harmonious triune was elaborated on in another Cayce reading.

"First, there is the body-physical, with all its attributes for the functioning of the body in a three-dimensional or a manifested earth plane.

"Also there is the body-mental, which is that directing influence of the physical, the mental and the spiritual emotions and manifestations of the body; or the way, the manner, in which conduct is related to self, to individuals, as well as to things, conditions and circumstances. While the mind may not be seen by the physical senses, it can be sensed by others. That is, others may sense the conclusions that have been drawn by the body-mind of an individual by the manner in which such an individual conducts himself in relationship to things, conditions or people.

"Then there is the body-spiritual, or soul-body—that eternal something that is invisible. It is only visible to that consciousness in which the individual entity in patience becomes aware of its relationships to the mental and the physical being.

"All of these, then, are one—in an entity."

Therefore, we see that, according to Cayce, the physical body is housing for the mind and the soul for purposes of existence in the earth plane.

Mind, to Cayce, is the active principle which governs man: the active force in an animate object—the spark or image of the Maker. Therefore, mind is in control of the will—that which makes one individual when we reach the earth plane. Further, said Cayce, it is mind which reasons the impressions from the senses as they manifest before the individual. Just as the psychic force is a manifestation of the soul and spirit, the mind is a manifestation of the physical.

Cayce defined the mind as being made up of many parts. First, of course, is the conscious mind, which depends upon the recognized senses of sight, hearing, smell, taste and touch to feed it material necessary for conscious reasoning.

Then there is the unconscious mind—an area in which the Cayce readings part company, at times, with accepted scientific belief. Two broad divisions of the unconscious mind, according to Cayce, are the subconscious and the superconscious minds. The readings and science agree that the subconscious stores messages received from the conscious mind through the five senses and exerts, as well, enormous influence over the well-being of the physical body. But Cayce goes further than orthodox scientific beliefs. To Cayce, the subconscious stores full memory of all past lives which are not available to the individual's own conscious mind—although, as Cayce demonstrated in his psychic readings, these memories may be "read" by one who is able to "tune in" on them.

It is suggested by the readings that it is this part of the mind, the subconscious, that becomes, in effect, the conscious mind at the time of death of the body. You most probably will not find *this* suggestion in any psychology textbook!

Another division of the mind, according to Cayce, is the superconscious mind—another word not likely to be used by today's psychologist. It is the superconscious mind, says Cayce, which has not come into physical expression at all. *And, he continues, man's development depends upon his ability to release spiritual energy from the superconscious and bring it into conscious expression.* Mind, then, is a part of the soul.

Somewhere in the unconscious mind, too, there seems to be a mechanism which establishes contact, or attunement, between minds—as in the phenomenon of telephathy.

About the soul, Cayce once had this to say in a reading: "What, then, is a soul? What does it look like? What is its plane of experience or activity? How may ye find one?

"It may not be separated in the material world from its own place of abode in the physical body. The soul looks through the eyes of the body; it feels with the emotions; it develops awareness through the faculties in every sense—and thus adds to its body, just as food has produced a growing physical body."

Of soul memory, Cayce once said, "For know: all that the entity may know of God, or even of law or international relationships, already exists in the consciousness for the entity to be made aware of . . .

"Then, for this information to become knowledge or understanding, there must be application of self to those sources of material knowledge, yes—but with faith and trust in universal knowledge. For, as indicated by the Lawgiver, think not who will come from over the sea that a message may be brought; for, lo, it is within thine own self. For the mind and the soul are from the beginning. Thus there must come within the entity's own consciousness the awareness of how the application is to be made."

Stating the relationship between body, mind and soul, Edgar Cayce said in one reading, "When the body-physical lays aside the material body, that which, in the physical, is called the soul becomes the body of the entity; and that called the superconscious becomes the consiousness of the entity, as the subconscious is to the physical body. The subconscious becomes the mind or intellect of the body [after death]."

As an amusing example of the singleness of purpose with which Cayce's unconscious mind attuned itself to the unconscious mind of his subject, there is the case of a 23-year-old man who was given a physical reading in 1943, following his medical discharge from the service.

According to the reading, a recurrent and serious problem of amnesia had as its cause an injury to the spine, and treatment was outlined accordingly. One question submitted by this young man prior to the reading, and asked of Cayce while he was giving it was, "Can you tell me what the government records show in my trouble and what became of all my papers that were lost?"

Cayce responded immediately. "We haven't the government records; we have the body!"

The Second Source

The second major source of Cayce's information, as described by many readings, was in the collective, or universal, unconscious. According to the readings, it is in this collective unconscious that the individual unconscious has its origin.

Because of similiarity of terms, we should pause here and note the distinction between Cayce's "collective unconscious" and that defined by Carl Jung.

According to Jung, the collective unconscious is that part of the unconsious born with the individual—containing inherited patterns of instinctual behavior—that links it with all other minds in that all have a common substratum or foundation. Jung's collective unconscious is often erroneously thought of as being a group mind. "Personal unconscious" was Jung's term for that part of the mind which contains the products of individual experience.

The Cayce readings explained that every thought, every action of mankind since its beginning has been incorporated into a universal "record." Sometimes referred to in the readings as "God's Book of Remembrance," or "The Book of Life," it was most often called "the akashic records." This is the adjective form of the Sanskrit word *akasha,* and refers to the fundamental etheric substance of the universe, electro-spiritual in composition.

According to Cayce, this universal record, the akasha, is available to anyone who has developed the ability to read it. Edgar Cayce was one of many—including Socrates, Plato, Noah and Jesus—who could do this.

Cayce's ability, said the readings, had developed as a result of the experiences of many previous lives spent on earth. These included an incarnation as a high priest in pre-history Egypt, when he possessed great occult powers; as a physician and leader in Persia; as a chemist during the Trojan war; as a guard in the court of Louis XV of France; and as the British soldier, John Bainbridge, during the colonization of the United States.

One of his own life readings carries an interesting remark concerning this appearance as Bainbridge. "In the developing upon the present plane, we have much of the personality as shown in present spheres, as from that of the ability to take cognizance of detail, especially in following instructions as given from other minds or sources of information."

In the Persian incarnation, he had been wounded in desert warfare and left to die. For three days he lay on the sand, alone, without shelter, food or water. To relieve his physical suffering, he had willed consciousness to leave his body—a step in the direction of his present ability, as Edgar Cayce, to set aside his conscious mind, through trance, and make contact between his own unconscious mind and that of another individual or with the akashic records. His own readings indicated that it was this experience, coupled with the earlier experiences as a high priest in Egypt, that had begun his development as a psychic.

In a reading concerning the akashic records, Cayce was asked, "What is meant by the Book of Life?"

He replied, "That record that the individual entity writes upon the skein of time and space, through patience. [It] is opened when self has attuned to the infinite, and may be read by those attuning to that consciousness."

"The skein of time and space" appears frequently in the readings. In one reading we find, "Conditions, thoughts, activities of men in *every* clime are things; as thoughts are things. They make their impressions upon the skein of time and space. Thus, as they make for their activity, they become as records that may be read by those in accord or *attuned* to such a condition. This may be illustrated in the wave length of the radio or of such an activity. [These activities, etc.] go upon the waves of light, upon that of space. And those instruments that are *attuned* to same may hear, may experience, that which is being transmitted."

At another time, Cayce stated, "For the light moves on in time, in space; and upon that skein between them are the records written by each soul in its activity through eternity—through its awareness—not only in matter but in thought, in whatever realm the entity builds for itself in its experience, in its journey, in its activity. The physicist builds in the field of mathematics, the artist in the field of demonstration and color, the musician in sound, and so on. All are a part of the soul's ability, according to that field in which it has developed."

In another reading, he stated, "Activity of any nature, as of a voice, as of a light, produces in the natural forces a motion, which passes on, or is upon the record of time. This may be illustrated in the atomic vibrations as set in motion for those in that called the audition, the radio in its activity. Hence, light forces pass much faster; but the records are upon the esoteric, or etheric, or the akashic forces, as they go along upon the wheels of time, the wings of time, or in whatever dimension we may signify as a matter of its momentum or movements. Hence, the forces that are attuned to those various incidents, periods, times, places, may be accorded to the record, the contact, as of the needle upon the record, as to how clear a rendition or audition is received, or how clear or how perfect the attunement of the instrument used, as the reproducer of same is attuned to those keepers—as may be termed—of these records. What would be indicated by the keepers? That just given; that they are the records upon the wings or the wheels of time itself."

The readings were careful to point out, however, that there is no such thing as time and space; these have been developed by man as necessary means of measurement. "Time and space are the elements of man's own concept of the infinite, and are not realities as would be any bodily element in the earth—as a tree, a rose, a bird, an animal, or even a fellow being."

The following case seems to illustrate, quite well, Cayce's ability to read the akashic record.

In giving a life reading for a woman in May, 1939, Edgar Cayce said of one of her earlier incarnations that she had been "among those spoken of as 'holy women,' first the entity coming in contact with those activities at the death and raising of Lazarus and later with Mary, Elizabeth, Mary Magdalene, Martha. All of those were a part of the experiences of the entity, as Salome."

Seemingly, Cayce's reading was in error. Of the four Gospels, only one, St. John, incorporated the story of Lazarus, and in it there is no mention of Salome.

But more than twenty years after the reading, on December 30, 1960, the Long Island *Newsday* carried an Associated Press dispatch announcing the discovery of an ancient letter which did, indeed, place Salome at the raising of Lazarus. According to the news story, Dr. Morton Smith, associate professor of history at Columbia University, had found the letter two years earlier while studying ancient manuscripts at the Monastery of Mar Saba near Jerusalem. He had just presented it at a meeting of the Society of Biblical Literature and Exegesis, together with evidence indicating that the letter had been written by Clement of Alexandria, an author who wrote between 180 and 202 A.D., and who is generally considered to be either the creator or to have laid the foundation of Christian theology.

The letter by Clement of Alexandria contained the story of Jesus' raising Lazarus from the dead, but attributed the account to St. Mark, rather than to St. John.

It is interesting that Cayce, who read the Bible once for every year of his life, would, in trance, depart from the accepted version of the story of Lazarus. It is also most interesting that he talked of the presence of Salome at the resurrection so many years before evidence supporting this was discovered. Otherwise, we might suspect that he was receiving the information telepathically from some living person who knew of such documents.

How, then, did Edgar Cayce "know" that Salome had been present? To understand this, in line with what the readings had to say on the subject, you must consider the theory of reincarnation, together with the theory that a living person has an unconscious memory that goes back through each of his appearances on the earth plane. You must also consider it possible that Edgar Cayce could call upon this history by putting his own unconscious in time with the unconscious of the reincarnated Salome and with the akashic records, which contain every thought and every action of mankind since its beginning.

That's quite a lot to consider; but can you think of a *better* explanation?

Other Sources?

We have now considered the two major sources of Cayce's information: the subconscious mind of his subject, and the akashic, or universal, records. Could there have been other sources as well?

The readings tell us that there may well have been others. Edgar Cayce mentioned this possibility in his talk, "What Is a Reading?" which was quoted earlier.

You will recall Cayce's statement that, although he did not operate as a "medium" in the usual sense of that word, he thought that at times he might be receiving contact from "some benevolent spirit or physician from the other side."

There were a number of readings devoted to exploring this possibility. In one of them, the question was asked, "While in the state of unconsciousness in which readings were given, could Edgar Cayce communicate with entities in the spirit plane?"

He replied, "The spirits of all that have passed from the physical plane remain about the plane until their developments carry them onward, or they are returned for their development here. When they are in the plane of communication, or remain with this sphere, any may be communicated with."

In another reading, he said, "First let it be understood that, in the material or physical plane, there is a pattern of every condition which exists in the cosmic or spiritual plane. For things spiritual and things material are but the same conditions of the same element, raised to different vibrations. For all force is *one* force.

"Remember, conditions are not changed [by death]. We find individuals, while living, at times communicative; at other times uncommunicative. There are moods . . . there are conditions under which such communications are easily attained. There are other conditions that are difficult, as it were, to meet or cope with. Just so . . . in that distant sphere."

And still another reading carried the statement, "The information as obtained and given by this body [Edgar Cayce] is gathered from the sources from which the suggestion may derive its information. In this state [self-induced hypnosis] the conscious mind becomes subjugated to the subconscious, the superconscious or soul mind, and may and does communicate with like minds, and the subconscious or soul force becomes universal. *From any subconscious mind information may be obtained either from this plane or from the impression as left by the individuals that have gone before.* [Author's italics.] As we see a mirror directly reflecting that which is before it—it is not the object itself, but that reflected. The suggestion that reaches through to the subconscious, or soul, in this state, gathers information from that as reflected from what has been or is called real or material . . .

"Through the forces of the soul, through the minds of others as presented, or that have gone on before; before the subjugation of the physical forces in this manner, the body [Edgar Cayce] obtains the information."

In this same reading, given in 1923, Edgar Cayce was asked if the thoughts of one person could affect another person, either mentally or physically. The sleeping man answered, "Depending upon the development of the person to whom the thought may be directed. The possibilities of developing thought transference are first being shown—evolution, you see. The individuals of this plane are developing and will develop this as the senses are developed."

Cayce was once asked to describe how thought transference or telepathy might be accomplished, or learned. His answer was simple. "First, begin between selves. Set a definite time and each at that moment put down what the other is doing. Do this twenty days. And ye shall find ye have the key to telepathy."

Normally, in the trance state, Cayce did not receive his information via a "control," such as Arthur Ford's "Fletcher." And yet an extraordinary occurrence, on October 9, 1933, seems to indicate that at times a discarnate entity may have spoken through him.

The first paragraph of the waking suggestion had been given to Cayce following a reading concerning his own psychic work. Suddenly he announced, "Some good information here!"

Gertrude Cayce, who was conducting the reading, said, "May we have it at this time?"

For the next ten minutes, Cayce spoke on the subject of the personality of discarnate entities and their influence on our thinking—particularly in connection with great movements in political, economic, social or religious thought. This included the statement, "So we begin to see how the thought, or mental movement that produces thought in the minds of souls in the earth may be influenced by that movement outside of self."

The topic of the reading was interesting, if difficult to comprehend because of the intricate wording. Most interesting, though, is the fact that it was delivered by Cayce in a distinctly British voice, unlike any accent he had ever used before or would use again in a reading! The secretary reported, "It sounded like Edgar Cayce, but more as if he were acting the part of an Englishman—trying to repeat the tone of voice and comments of an Englishman standing by; not at all as if the Englishman had taken over."

In 1934, at the end of a routine physical reading, Cayce was given the suggestion to wake up. Instead of doing so, he began to speak. "There are some here that would speak with those that are present, if they desire to so communicate with them."

There were four people in the room in addition to Cayce: his wife, Gertrude; his secretary, Gladys Davis; Mildred Davis; and Cayce's father, Leslie B. Cayce.

After a long pause, Edgar Cayce began a strange monologue. "Don't all speak at once!" Then another pause. "Yes, I knew you would be waiting." There followed a one-sided conversation which included such comments as, "All together now, huh? Uncle Porter too? He was able to ease it right away, huh? Who? Dr. House. No. Oh, no—no, she is all right. Yes, lot's better. . . . Tell Tommy what? Yes! Lynn? Yes, he's at home . . . Oh, you knew that! . . . Well, how about the weather? Oh, the weather doesn't affect you now—doesn't change—Oh, you have what you want . . . depends on where you go. . . . For Gertrude? Yes, she is here . . . she hears you. Oh, yes."

Mrs. Cayce didn't hear anyone but Edgar Cayce, and said so.

Edgar Cayce continued. "Sure, she hears you; don't you hear her talking?"

Again Gertrude Cayce asked for the message. This time she received some interpretation of what Cayce had been discussing. It included an explanation that " . . . Mama and Dr. House and Uncle Porter and the baby [possibly the child born to Edgar and Gertrude Cayce some years before, who lived only a few weeks] . . . we are all here. . . . We have reached, together, that place where we see the light and know the pathway to the Savior is along the narrow way that leads to His Throne. We are on that plane where you have heard it said that the body and the mind are one with those things we have built. . . . Well, we will be waiting for you!"

Naturally, there was much interest in the source and meaning of this message, and so a reading was given on July 17, 1934, for the purpose of finding out more about it. In part, the reading went as follows.

The suggestion was given, "You will have before you the body and inquiring mind of Edgar Cayce and all present in this room, in regard to the experience following the reading Monday afternoon, July 9, 1934, explaining to us what happened . . . and why at that particular time, answering the questions that may be asked."

Cayce said, "Yes, we have the body, and the inquiring mind, Edgar Cayce, and those present in the room July 9, 1934.

"In giving that which may be helpful, for the moment turn to that known as the body of self and by those present in the room respecting what is ordinarily termed spirit communication or . . . should be (and that which has caused much of the dissension) . . . *soul* communication. For the soul lives on and is released from a house of clay. The activities in the world of matter are only changed in their relationships to that which produces them and that which the physical body sees in material or three-dimensional form.

"There were those that were in attune . . . through the vibrations from that sounded in the room at that particular period . . . and these sought (many—even many that spoke not) to communicate that there might be known not only their continued existence in a world of matter but of finer matter. They sought, through those channels through which the soul-force of the body was passing at the particular time, to produce that which would make their presence known.

"Although the various communications given at the time were from those thought to be dead (from the physical viewpoint) or in other realms, yet their souls, their personalities, their individualities live on. The personalities are lost gradually . . . [as they develop in the other plane]."

Cayce was asked, "Why did we hear only one side of the conversation?"

"Denseness of matter to the spirit realm," he replied. "All who attuned themselves *felt* the presence of those influences. The Master said, 'They that have ears to hear, let them hear.' There be none so deaf as those who do not *want* to hear. All could hear if they would attune themselves to the realm of the activity during such an experience. The conversation dealt with matters that were to them, are to them, very vital in their experiences in the present plane.

"How, some would ask, did the body, Edgar Cayce, or soul, attune self at that particular period and yet not remember in the physical consciousness? This is because *the soul passes from the body* into those realms where information may be obtained. Help was sought on the ninth of July for the physical condition of a body [referring to the physical reading given just before Cayce began to "converse" with several departed relatives]. This realm from which such information is obtainable is either from those that passed into the realm of subconscious activity or from the subconscious and superconscious activity of the one through whom information is being sought. This particular body, Edgar Cayce, was able to attune self to the varied realms of activity by laying aside the physical consciousness. If the body, from its material and mental development, were to be wholly conscious of that through which it passes in its soul's activity in such realms, the strain would be too great. Material activity could be unbalanced and the body become demented. And he is thought crazy enough anyway!"

Humor was ever-present in the Cayce readings. This last comment undoubtedly alluded to the many people who were unable to accept the validity of clair-voyance—even when it was demonstrated by Edgar Cayce so well, and for so many years—and thought of him as "some kind of a nut."

A Visit From an Old Friend

Edgar Cayce experienced visions throughout his lifetime. Often they were symbolic in nature, and special readings were given to gain interpretation of them.

One such vision occurred on October 22, 1933. This is the way Edgar Cayce described it in a report given in 1936.

"Some years ago I had a very warm personal friend who was an executive of the Western Union Telegraph Company in Chicago. We met quite often, and in our discussions of various subjects the question frequently arose between us as to whether or not there was a survival of personality. It usually ended jokingly with one of us saying, "Well, whichever one goes first will communicate with the other.'

"During the last few years of my friend's life, we did not meet, but we corresponded intermittently. Then I was notified of his death in April, 1933.

"Several months afterwards I was sitting alone in my living room, listening to the radio. The program was Seth Parker's. Members of the group had decided they would sing songs which their loved ones had been fond of during their lifetime. One lady asked that they sing, 'Sweet Hour of Prayer.' Another asked her which one of her husbands had liked that song. I remember that I was very much amused, and leaned back in my chair, smiling to myself.

"Suddenly I felt as if there was a presence in the room. I was cold, and felt something uncanny or unusual taking place. The program was still on.

"When I looked toward the radio, I realized that my friend, who had died several months before, was sitting in front of the radio listening to the program. He turned and smiled at me, saying, 'Cayce, there IS the survival of personality. I KNOW! And a life of service and prayer is the only one to live.'

"I was shaking all over. He said nothing more, and just seemed to disappear.

"The program finished, I turned off the radio. It still appeared as if the room was full of some presence. As I switched off the light and climbed the stairs, I could hear many voices coming from the darkened room.

"Jumping in bed and shivering from cold, I aroused my wife. She asked me why I hadn't turned off the radio. I assured her that I had. She opened the door, and said, 'I hear it—I hear voices.' We both did.

"What was it?"

CHAPTER 4

OUT OF BODY

THE FOLLOWING IS an excerpt from a talk given by Edgar Cayce in August, 1931.

"Let me tell you of an experience of my own. I feel that it was a very real experience, and as near an illustration of what happens at death as it would be possible to put into words. On going into the unconscious state one time to obtain information for an individual, I recognized that I was leaving my body. There was just a direct, straight, and narrow line in front of me, like a shaft of white light. On either side was fog and smoke, and many shadowy figures who seemed to be crying to me for help, and begging me to come aside to the state they occupied.

"As I followed along the shaft of light, the way began to clear. The figures on either side grew more distinct; they took on clearer form. But there was a continual beckoning back, or the attempt to sidetrack me and bring me aside from my purpose. Yet with the narrow way in front of me I kept going straight ahead. After a bit I passed to where the figures were merely shadows attempting to assist; they urged me on rather than attempted to stop me. Then they took on more form, and they seemed to be occupied with their own activities. When they paid any attention to me at all it was rather to urge me on.

"Finally I came to a hill, where there was a mount and a temple. I entered this temple and found in it a very large room, very much like a library. They were the books of people's lives, for each person's activities were a matter of actual record, it seemed, and I merely had to pull down a record of the individual for whom I was seeking information.

"I have to say as Paul did, 'Whether I was in the spirit or out of the spirit, I cannot tell.' "

This experience indicates, we think, the delicate balance of Edgar Cayce's being while he was in trance. Many readings confirm this and serve, as well, to amplify our understanding of the condition known as "out of body."

In this state, Cayce's body remained on the couch with the unconscious mind in control. Suspended above him, at a height of about eighteen inches, lay the conscious mind which had been temporarily set aside.

The readings explained that in this state, Cayce operated much in the manner of a radio receiver, tuned to the proper channel for receiving the information sought in the reading. Any interference—such as the asking of irrelevant questions, antagonistic thoughts on the part of anyone connected with getting the reading, and so on—could disrupt the process by creating a sort of psychic static.

Any physical interference with Cayce's body, or with his conscious mind, or "personality," suspended above it, could have alarming consequences. Once, during a public session, someone who didn't understand this out of body state passed a sheet of paper to Hugh Lynn Cayce across the form of his sleeping father. Cayce immediately stopped talking, and went into a cataleptic silence which lasted for several hours. This had never happened before, and no one knew what to do about it. When Cayce *did* wake up, he did so with alarming speed—jackknifing himself to a standing position at the foot of the couch.

Needless to say, precautions were taken to see that this sort of thing never happened again!

In a reading given April 30, 1934, the question was asked, "What has caused the jerking and twitching movement of Edgar Cayce's physical body during readings given within the last few months?"

His answer serves to further our understanding of out-of-body experiences. "Not perfect accord in the physical body of Edgar Cayce, partially," he said. "Not perfect accord in the minds of those present as to the purpose of seeking in each instance.

"For, where lack of harmony prevails and a soul enters into the veil where there may be the realm of those influences that become so impelling in their activity in material things, *what* a strain! The wonder may ever be that there isn't and has not been much greater contortion, save that—as given—the body-mind, the body-consciousness, the soul-consciousness has been attuned to much that to many would have been a breaking point.

"Not that the body is to be pampered, nor to be shown other than that deference which each individual present does hold. But know, all that draw near, what they are dealing with: that the soul is very *near* at all times to *being away from* the body, seeking. Hence the care, the caution, that should be taken by those that feel they have any interest in the body, life, or in the *greater* life of the entity in its seeking and its desire to serve."

As one further illustration of this, there was the morning on which apparently a few too many questions were asked of the sleeping Cayce. Showing some irritation, he abruptly ended the reading by saying, "We are through."

And then an extraordinary thing happened. As Cayce was being given the normal suggestion to awaken, his body nearly turned a somersault. His head bent over to almost touch his feet, and he stayed in that strange position until the waking suggestion was completed. He awoke normally, then, and remarked that he felt "exuberant—*fine!*"

Later that day, another reading was given on the subject of the Cayce work. He was asked to explain why he had demonstrated such a strange physical reaction at the close of the morning's reading.

He answered, "As was seen, through the seeking of irrelevant questions there was antagonism manifested. This made for a contraction of those channels through which the activity of the psychic forces operates in the material body. . . . The natural reactions are for sudden contraction when changing suddenly from the mental-spiritual to material [from the hypnotic to the conscious state].

"For, as evidenced by that which has been given, there is the touching—with the mental beings of those present in the room or at such manifestations—of the most delicate mechanism that may be imagined."

Levels of Consciousness

Apparently, in seeking certain information about an individual or an event, Cayce's unconscious mind operated on many levels, or in various dimensions.

There are many indications, in the readings, of his "seeing" certain activities at the various levels on his way to the eventual source of much of his information: an old man who handed him a large book containing the data he wanted. He described, for example, what appeared to be classrooms in which teachers were preparing souls for their next return to earth.

Many readings point to the existence of various planes within what Cayce called his "sphere of communication," peopled by entities on the various planes according to their levels of development in the long, hard struggle toward ultimate perfection. Mental attunement with any of these entities was possible.

One reading stated, "Each and every soul entity, or earthly entity passing through the earth's plane, leaves in that plane those conditions that are impressions from the soul or spiritual entity of the individual. This, then, becomes the fact, the real fact, in the material world.

"The body, Edgar Cayce, in the psychic or subconscious condition, is able to reach all subconscious minds, when directed to such by suggestion—whether in the material world or in the spiritual world, provided the spiritual entity has not passed entirely into another level. Then we reach only those radiations left in the earth's plane. These are taken on again when re-entering the earth's plane, whether the entity is conscious of the same or not. The consciousness of this movement and development must eventually be reached by all."

This is the way Edgar Cayce once recalled the experience of getting his information:

"I see myself as a tiny dot out of my physical body, which lies inert before me. I find myself oppressed by darkness and there is a feeling of terrific loneliness. Suddenly, I am conscious of a beam of white light. I move upward in the light, knowing that I must follow it or be lost.

"As I move along this path of light, I gradually become conscious of various levels upon which there is movement. Upon the first levels there are vague, horrible shapes, grotesque forms such as one sees in nightmares. Passing on, there begin to appear on either side misshapen forms of human beings with some part of the body magnified. Again there is change and I become conscious of gray-hooded forms moving downward. Gradually, these become lighter in color. Then the direction changes and these forms move upward and the color of the robes grows rapidly lighter.

"Next, there begin to appear on either side vague outlines of houses, walls, trees, etc., but everything is motionless. As I pass on, there is more light and movement in what appear to be normal cities and towns. With the growth of movement I become conscious of sounds, at first indistinct rumblings, then music, laughter, and singing of birds. There is more and more light, the colors become very beautiful, and there is only a blending of sound and color. Quite suddenly, I come upon a hall of records. It is a hall without walls, without a ceiling, but I am conscious of seeing an old man who hands me a large book, a record of the individual for whom I seek information."

Keeper of the Records

"My! What a large volume!" said Cayce at the beginning of a reading for a seven-year-old girl in 1936.

"The cleanest record I've ever experienced. The book is the cleanest. And yet I had never thought of any of them not being perfectly clean before." Thus Cayce ended a reading, also in 1936, for a three-year-old boy.

What did Cayce mean by "record," by "book"? Why, at the beginning of each life reading, did Cayce seem to be thumbing back through some sort of soul diary—not only to the birth date of the person for whom the reading was being given, but further, still, back into the history of previous lives spent on the earth by the individual? For it was always the same in a Cayce life reading: he put himself into trance and then "took himself" to the "old man with the books." There he got his information.

In a reading given in September, 1933, Cayce explained this. "To bring from one realm to another those experiences through which an entity, a soul, may pass in obtaining those reflections that are necessary for transmission of the information sought, it becomes necessary (for the understanding of those in that realm seeking) to have that which is to the mental being put in the language of that being, as near as it is possible to do justice to the subject."

Cayce, then, was using symbology when he referred to "books." Now he explained why. "[The information is given] in the form of pictures or expressions, that there may be the conveying to the mind of the seeker something in his own type of experience, as to how the transmission of the activity takes place. Of what forces? The psychic or soul forces, that are akin to what? The Creative Forces, or that called God.

"So the body [of Edgar Cayce] arrives at a place in which there is kept the records of all; as signified in speaking of the Book of Life, or to indicate or symbolize that each entity, each soul in its growth, may find its way back to the Creative Influences that are promised in and through Him that gives—and is—Life; and finds this as a separate, a definite, an integral part of the very soul."

Thus Cayce explained that each soul, in each experience of assuming bodily form, makes a record. It gains in development; it loses. It exercises its free will, given by God, for good or for evil in each earthly appearance. " . . . Hence, symbolized as being in books; and the man the keeper, as the keeper of the records . . .

"So, in the materializations for the concept of those that seek to know, to be enlightened; to the world, long has there been sought that as in books. To many the question naturally arises, then: are there literally books? To a mind that thinks books, literally *books!* As it would be for the mind that in its passage from the material plane into rest would require Elysian fields with birds, with flowers; it must find the materialized form of that portion of the Maker in that realm wherein that entity, that soul, would enjoy such in *that* sphere of activity. As houses built in their essence, are what? What is the more real, the book with its printed pages, its gilt edges, or the essence of that manifested in the Son, the Savior, for His brethren, or the essence of love that may be seen even in the vilest of passion? They are one."

CHAPTER 5

EDGAR CAYCE'S DEVELOPMENT AS A PSYCHIC

AS WE HAVE mentioned, it was not until 1923 that the subject of reincarnation entered the Cayce readings. And yet there is a hint of things to come in a reading given the day after Cayce's forty-second birthday, on March 19, 1919. It is one of the most fascinating readings in the Cayce files, in terms of the clear and concise way it explains his psychic work.

Background for the reading was furnished by Cayce as follows: "In December, 1918, I received a request from a Mr. Thrash, who was editor of a newspaper in Cleburne, Texas, for a physical reading. He also wanted to ask some questions about business. Among these letters was one in which he asked for my birthdate; he said he wanted to have my horoscope cast. Soon after this I received several communications from astrologers telling me that on March 19, 1919, I would be able to give a reading that would be of more interest to mankind as a whole than any I would be able to give during that year. I was asked to make this reading public. I did not care for notoriety, which I felt this would give, yet I was curious and desired to know what the reading would give at this time. I attempted it—and the following reading is the result. The questions asked in this reading were prepared by myself."

Reading: March 19, 1919

> *Conductor:* You will have before you the body and the inquiring mind of Edgar Cayce, and you will tell us how the psychic work is accomplished through this body and will answer any other questions that I will ask you respecting this work.

> *Cayce:* We have the body, Edgar Cayce. We have had it before. In this state the conscious mind is under subjugation of the subconscious or soul mind. The information obtained and given by this body is obtained through the power of mind over mind, or power of mind over physical matter, or obtained by the suggestion as given to the active part of the subconscious mind. It obtains its information from that which it has gathered, either from other subconscious minds—put in touch with the power of the

suggestion of the mind controlling the speaking faculties of this body—or from minds that have passed into the Beyond, which leave their impressions and are brought in touch by the power of the suggestion.

What is known to one subconscious mind or soul is known to another, whether conscious of the fact or not. The subjugation of the conscious mind putting the subconscious mind in action in this manner or in one of the other of the manners as directed, this body obtains its information when in the subconscious state.

Conductor: Is this information always correct?

Cayce: Correct in so far as the suggestion is in the proper channel or in accord with the action of subconscious or soul matter.

Conductor: Do the planets have anything to do with the ruling of the destiny of men? If so, what? And what do they have to do with this body?

Cayce: They do. In the beginning, as our own planet, Earth, was set in motion, the placing of other planets began the ruling of the destiny of all matter as created, just as the division of waters was and is ruled by the moon in its path about the Earth; just so as in the higher creation, as it began, is ruled by the action of the planets about the Earth.

The strongest power in the destiny of man is the sun, first; then the closer planets, or those that are coming in ascendency at the time of the birth of the individual. But let it be understood here, no action of any planet or any of the phases of the sun, moon, or any of the heavenly bodies surpass the rule of man's individual will power—the power given by the Creator of man in the beginning, when he became a living soul, with the power of choosing for himself.

The inclination of man is ruled by the planets under which he is born; for the destiny of man lies within the sphere or scope of the planets. With the given position of the solar system at the time of the birth of an individual, it can be worked out—that is, the inclinations and actions without the will power taken into consideration.

As in this body [Edgar Cayce] born March 18, 1877, three minutes past three o'clock, with the sun descending, on the wane, the moon in the opposite side of the earth (old moon), Uranus at its zenith, hence the body is ultra in its actions. Neptune closest in conjunction, or Neptune as it is termed in astrological survey, in the ninth house; Jupiter, the higher force of all the planets, save the sun, in descendency, Venus just coming to horizon, Mars just set, Saturn—to whom all insufficient matter is cast at its decay—opposite the face of the moon. Hence the inclination as the body is controlled by the astrological survey at the time of the birth of this body, either (no middle ground for this body) very good or very bad, very religious or very wicked, very rich or always losing, very much in love or hate, very much given to good works or always doing wrong, governed entirely by the will of the body. Will is the educational factor of the body; thence the patience, the persistence, the ever-faithful attention that should be given to the child when it is young.

As to the forces of this body, the psychical is obtained through the action of Uranus and of Neptune. Always it has been to this body and always will, just outside the action of firearms, yet ever within them, just saved financially and spiritually by the action of great amounts of water. The body should live close to the sea, should always have done so. The body is strange to other bodies in all of its actions, in the psychical life, in all of its ideas as expressed in the spiritual life as to its position on all matters pertaining to political, religious or economical positions. This body will either be very rich or very poor.

Conductor: Will this work hurt the body?

Cayce: Only through the action of power of suggestion over the body. This body is controlled in its work through the psychical or the mystic or spiritual. It is governed by the life that is led by the person who is guiding the subconscious when in this state, or by the line of thought that is given to create ideas of expression to the subconscious.

As the ideas given the subconscious to obtain its information are good, the body becomes better; if bad or wicked, it becomes under the same control. Then the body should not be held responsible save through the body controlling the body at such times.

Conductor: Can this power be used to be of assistance to humanity and also to obtain financial gain?

Cayce: There are many channels through which information obtained from this body in this state would be of assistance to humanity. To obtain financial gain from these is to obtain that which is just and right to those dependent upon this body for the things of life. Not those that would be destructive to the bodies themselves, physically or mentally, but that which is theirs by right should be obtained for such information.

As to which is the best channel, it depends as to whether the information desired is in accord with the ideas of the body from which they are attempting to obtain them.

When credence is given to the work in a material way, anyone is willing to pay in a financial way for such information; but without credence there can be nothing obtained.

Conductor: Is there any other information that this body should have now?

Cayce: The body should keep close in touch with the spiritual side of life—with sincerity to the spiritual side of life—if he is to be successful mentally, physically, psychically and financially.

The safest brace is the spiritual nature of the body; sincerity of the work done or obtained through any channel with which this body is connected is governed by the masses through the action of the body towards the spiritual.

We call particular attention to the statement in this reading, "The body . . . is governed by the life that is led by the person who is guiding the subconscious when in this state, or by the line of thought that is given to create ideas of expression to the subconscious."

In giving this reading, at the specific request of a man interested in astrology, Cayce had referred to the role of the planets in determining the destiny of man. Cayce's own psychic abilities were explained in the light of planetary influences, with no mention of past lives. Perhaps this was because Mr. Thrash had no apparent interest in, or knowledge of, theories concerning reincarnation. Or perhaps it was simply because Cayce himself, and those around him, were not yet ready to accept this new expansion in the scope of information received through Cayce's unconscious mind. None of the information given in this reading was later refuted by other readings. It simply went so far and no farther.

But in 1923 a man named Arthur Lammers, a wealthy printer of Dayton, Ohio, heard of Edgar Cayce and made a special trip to Selma, Alabama, to visit him and watch him work. He persuaded Cayce to return with him to Dayton for a special series of readings, since he was unable to remain in Selma long enough to get the answers to some of his questions.

Lammers' intention was to try to obtain, through the readings, information concerning matters of universal significance. Why was a man born? What was his reason for living? What happened to him when he died? He was impressed by the accuracy with which Cayce could "see" within the human body, tell what was wrong with it and how to repair it. But Lammers sensed that there were areas of knowledge available to Cayce that so far had not been touched. An intelligent, well-educated man, Lammers had long been a student of astrology, theology and philosophy. Here, possibly, were answers to questions that had puzzled him for years.

So it was into a new climate of interest that Cayce's remarkable statement, at the end of a reading given for Lammers, was made: "He was once a monk." With these five simple words, Cayce opened the door to an entirely new aspect in his work. The reading had been set up for the purpose of casting a horoscope for Lammers. Cayce had volunteered this new and startling information at the end of an otherwise unremarkable reading.

A series of readings followed, so positive in their statements concerning the *reality* of reincarnation, that Lammers now persuaded Cayce to move his family to Dayton. He paid their train fares and furnished housing to enable them to do this.

Soon after the move to Dayton, Cayce discussed, in one reading, the influence of the planets on the destinies of individuals. This portion of the reading, given four years after the one quoted earlier in this chapter, matched the earlier one almost word for word. Cayce said, "Just as the division of waters was ruled and is ruled by the moon in its path about the Earth, just so is the higher creation . . . ruled by its action in conjunction with the planets about the Earth. The strongest force used in the destiny of man is the sun first, then the closer planets to the Earth, or those that are coming to ascension at the time of the birth of the individual . . .

"The inclinations of man are ruled by the planets under which he is born, for the destiny of man lies within the sphere or scope of the planets . . .

"But let it be understood here, no action of any planet or the phases of the sun, moon or any of the heavenly bodies surpasses the rule of man's WILL POWER!—the power given by the Creator of man in the beginning, when he became a living soul with the power of choosing for himself."

Cayce contrasted horoscopes and life readings in the following reading given at the request of Arthur Lammers:

Reading: February, 1925

> *Conductor:* You will have before you the psychic work as done by Edgar Cayce. You will answer the following questions as I ask them regarding this work.
>
> *Cayce:* Yes, we have this work here, with all of its modifications, and the various channels through which it may manifest in the various phenomena of the psychic forces. Ready for questions.
>
> *Conductor:* Is this body when in this state able to give a horoscope reading?
>
> *Cayce:* Able. But would not be worth very much to anyone.
>
> *Conductor:* What is a horoscope reading?
>
> *Cayce:* That in which the planets and their relative forces having to do with the planets that control the actions without respect of will, or without respect of the earthly existences through which the body has passed.
>
> *Conductor:* Do horoscope readings include former appearances in the earth plane?
>
> *Cayce:* Not at all. The former appearances and the relation of the solar forces in the universe have their relations to what might be termed life readings, or experiences. For, as has been shown and given, horoscope, the science of the solar system and its relation to various phases of earth's existence, may mean for anyone.
>
> In life existence in earth's plane and the entity's relation to other spheres, there is a different condition. For the sojourn in other spheres than earth's plane controls more the conditions or the *urge* of the individual. Just as we see in the earth plane an individual is controlled by the surroundings, or by the circumstances that have to do with the individual, yet we find the urge, the latent forces, that would give an individual, or two groups, or two individuals raised under the same environ-

ment, of the same blood, different urges. These are received from experiences the spirit entity gains in other spheres, correlated with its present circumstance and condition.

These should never be confused. For, to gain a horoscope is only the mathematical calculation of earth's position in the universe at any given time, while in the life reading would be the correlation of the individual with a given time and place, with its relative force as applied and received through other spheres and manifested in earth's sphere in other flesh, and the development being the extenuation of the soul's development manifested in the earth plane through subconscious forces of a body or entity.

Conductor: Give the words that should be given to this body to obtain a reading of this kind, a life reading, with the former appearances and their effect in the present life on an individual.

Cayce: "You will have before you the body—(giving name and place of the individual at birth, the name at birth as given) and you will give the relation of this entity and the universe, and the universal forces, giving the conditions that are as personalities latent, and exhibited, in the present life. Also the former appearances in the earth's plane, giving time, place, name and that in that life which built or retarded the development for the entity, giving the abilities of the present entity and that to which it may attain, and how."

In this, you see, we will find the effect not only of the present environment, as it has been, as it may be, but the effect of the past experiences and through what sphere these were obtained.

We are through for the present.

Compare this information with that given in the 1919 reading, and you can see the ever-broadening scope of Cayce's information.

But it wasn't just the information that was expanding; Cayce's ability to receive it was expanding as well. Just as the experiences of his earlier incarnations, according to the readings, had prepared him for the work he was able to do in *this* lifetime, so the ability itself developed during the forty-three years it was utilized.

An example of this is shown in a reading given in November, 1932, in which Cayce was asked to explain a conscious vision he had experienced while engaged in teaching a Sunday school class. In the vision, he had seen a number of people of the Jewish faith enter the church and stand about, listening to Cayce's words.

Said the reading, "As should be understood by the body, this was an experience, real, literal, in the sense that we as individuals are ever encompassed about by those that are drawn to us by the vibration or attitude concerning conditions that are existent in the experience of entities or souls seeking their way to their Maker." Explaining this further, the reading told Cayce that, since the subject of his lesson had been certain activities of the Jews, "so there was gathered mostly those that had held in common a faith and desire in this particular phase of experience. The carnal eye was then lifted for Cayce, so that he saw; even as the servant of Elisha saw those that camped between those that would hinder Elisha in his service to his people.

"As the visions as a child, then, Cayce is again entering that phase of development or experience where there may be in the physical consciousness periods when there may be visioned those that are seeking in the spirit realm for that which will aid them to understand their relations with the Whole. [Author's italics.]

"As has been given to this body Cayce, to this peculiar people has he been sent; as one—one—that may aid many to come to a better understanding of their relationships to the Creator and their relationships to their fellow man . . .

"Know that the body is being given more and more the opportunity to minister to not only those in the material things in the material life, but these as seen who are seeking in the Borderland, those that are to many a loved one in the spirit land they are seeking—seeking."

So, according to the reading, Cayce was now to serve as a help to those in the spirit world, as well as to those on earth! Can you imagine the responsibility he must have felt when this information was given to him?

The reading carried a warning to Cayce. "Do not become self-important, nor self-exalting. Be rather selfless, that there may come to all who come under the sound of thy voice, to all that come in thy presence, as they look upon thine countenance, the knowledge and feeling that, indeed, this man has been in the presence of his Maker; he has seen the visions of those expanses we all seek—to pull the veil aside that we may peer into the future. As ye may become a teacher to those that are 'beyond the veil' also, how glorious must be thy words even then to those that falter in their steps day by day!"

In June, 1936, a reading asked, "Is there any special preparation necessary for [Cayce] to make, consciously, for his psychic work as it will develop within the next few years?"

The sleeping Cayce answered, "There are many experiences that remain as those promises that are a portion of the entity's development in this material plane. These are the stepping-stones, the milestones along the path of efficiency or of the abilities in the experience of the entity to become more and more *efficient*—as would be termed.

"But as for preparation, is a sound apple prepared at once or does it *grow* that way? Is the sun's light all of a glow or has it *grown* that way? The consciousness of the ability to serve is only by service, not by just wishing. But how has it been given? Desire of such a nature as to act, as to will, and act with the fusion of will and desire towards that purpose! *Fear* being cast aside by the very abilities of the self-submerging of the physical consciousness through those influences as has so oft been indicated, makes for an attunement to those sources sought by the individual seeker.

"The preparations, the *desire* ever, the will to do, are ever present. Then the variations are only according to that purpose for which and through which the seeker is making the attunement for self.

"As to those influences for greater preservation, greater abilities; as those promises have come, and there are the fulfillments in the experience to that voice from within and that meeting constantly within the temples of the physical forces where there has been the consecrating of self for service, there comes that growth that may be more and more helpful. But keep the faith!"

This particular reading, by the way, indicated that Edgar Cayce was doing a fine job of working out his karma. By being of service to his fellow man, through his chosen work, he was making great progress in atoning for the weaknesses of the flesh of some of his earlier lives.

"The abilities of this entity, then, arise from those experiences [in past incarnations] when the ego, the self, was submerged in a service for the fellow man. The *confusion* [disturbances in Cayce's present life caused by some tendency toward being too critical of others, as well as a terrible temper which bothered him throughout his lifetime] arises from those experiences when self-indulgence, self-aggrandizement, made for the purposes as with desire and will in its association with circumstance or conditions in the experience of the entity."

As so often happened in readings, this one gave Cayce some advice toward controlling his temper, with the statement, "Easy is the way of those that would find fault; greater is the sounding of the cymbal than the coo of the dove. Or as has been manifested in those of old, indeed in the storm, in the thunder, in the lightning is the *power* shown, but the activity is rather in the still, small voice that speaks from within." And again came the warning against letting anyone use Cayce's abilities for selfish purposes: "Oft there is confusion in the minds of those that may seek or may study, in that there is the lack of understanding that *psychic is of the soul;* whether of groups or whether of individuals that manifest in any given experience."

Such advice was important to Cayce, for his psychic abilities were always dependent upon his mental and physical health. There were times, throughout his life, when he would put himself into hypnotic sleep but no reading would come. Often the problem stemmed from worry; and worry, in turn, usually stemmed from finances. For the giving of psychic readings—particularly during the dark years of the depression—was far from a lucrative occupation. Any emotional disturbance could affect his ability to do his work, as could any physical ailment. Usually, however, the reading would be obtained at a later time.

Occasionally—especially during the early years of Cayce's career—unscrupulous people would try to take advantage of his abilities, to use them in money-making ventures. Even if they gained by it, Cayce always lost. Whenever this sort of thing happened, he suffered afterwards from severe headaches or other physical problems. In surrendering his conscious mind to his unconscious mind, he was completely at the mercy of those attending him. It was for this reason that the readings were generally conducted by Cayce's father, by his wife, or by his son. Even with these precautions, it required much courage to do the work he did.

CHAPTER 6

UNUSUAL CLAIRVOYANCE

IT HAS BEEN estimated that during his lifetime Edgar Cayce spoke in some two dozen different languages while giving readings, although he had conscious knowledge only of English. Here are two examples.

Cayce was living in Selma, Alabama in 1917 when a woman in Palermo, Sicily, heard of him and wrote to request proper diagnosis and treatment for an abdominal illness. Her letter was in Italian, so Cayce sent it off to a friend in Tuscaloosa for translation.

The reading, when it was given on January 27, 1918, was entirely in Italian. An Italian fruit dealer, hastily summoned to Cayce's studio from his stand nearby, was able to take it down in longhand and dictate the translation to the stenographer afterwards.

And here's another case. On July 11, 1933, Edgar Cayce began to give a life reading for Hans Mueller of New York, who had been born 53 years earlier in Frankfort, Germany.

The customary reading suggestion was made. Cayce repeated it to himself and then began his usual custom of going back over the dates from the present until he reached the subject's date of birth. Then he said, "Yes, we have the entity and those relations with the universe and universal forces, that are latent and manifested in the personality of the present entity, known as Hans Mueller."

Now, however, he became silent. After a long pause, he began to utter a series of German words. Cayce, as we've mentioned, had no knowledge of the German language; nor did his wife, who was conducting the reading; nor did his secretary, Gladys Davis (Turner), who could only take down the words phonetically. (Mr. Mueller later translated these to a group of exclamations, including, "Little corner place! Little one! Little child! I make one speech; I speak German! Oh, my, I speak German! Oh, my, no!" Mueller thought that some of the expressions, such as "little one" and "little child" might have been words used by his grandparents to express their delight at his birth. This seems plausible when we consider that Cayce always seemed to take himself back in time and be psychically "present" at the events and places he described in his life readings.)

After completing the series of German expressions, Cayce said abruptly, "We are through."

The reading was attempted again the next day. Cayce had no trouble getting it, for it was wholly in English.

In September of that year, a day was set aside for readings in which special questions about Cayce's work could be answered. During the morning session, Cayce was asked to explain why Hans Mueller's reading had been disrupted so strangely.

There was no hesitation on Cayce's part; his unconscious memory, functioning perfectly as always, immediately recalled the event. He explained that the one who had been attempting to guide him in obtaining the information spoke only German. As soon as it was clear that no one in the room could understand the language, the communication was cut off.

Then he was asked, "What is the interpretation of the German words given?"

Cayce's answer carried some rebuke. "This is simply curiosity," he said. "Learn German!"

One of the most remarkable examples of Cayce's clairvoyance can be found in a reading given on October 9, 1933. Four questions and answers, appearing in the readings exactly in the order in which they appear below, illustrate how rapidly and clearly Cayce's unconscious mind could analyze objects brought to his attention.

The first question concerned a dark brown liquid used for treating various gum disorders. It was recommended so often in the readings that eventually it was produced under the brand name "Ipsab."

> *Conductor:* I hold in my hand a bottle of Ipsab recently prepared according to a formula given through this channel. Is this correctly prepared, and will it in this form do what is expected of it?
>
> *Cayce:* It will.
>
> *Conductor:* It is correctly prepared, then?
>
> *Cayce:* Good.
>
> *Conductor:* Would you suggest any changes which would benefit it?
>
> *Cayce:* Deeper clarification only, or clearer of contamination of the water used, where there's not so much matter that has made—or does make—for a concentration of same.

By way of the next question, Cayce turned from being a sleeping "druggist" to a sleeping "editor." Some pamphlets based on the readings had just been completed, and the writer wanted to know if they accurately represented the material.

> *Conductor:* "I hold in my hand copies of two papers, *Oneness of All Force* and *Meditation*—"
>
> *Cayce:* (interrupting) "They are very good, both of 'em. Use them as they are! Very good looking papers!"

CHAPTER 7

AURAS

"AURAS" IS THE name of the last A.R.E. booklet authored by Edgar Cayce. Written in collaboration with his biographer and friend, Thomas Sugrue, and published just after Cayce's death in January, 1945, it begins:

"Ever since I can remember, I have seen colors in connection with people. I do not remember a time when the human beings I encountered did not register on my retina with blues and greens and reds gently pouring from their heads and shoulders. It was a long time before I realized that other people did not see these colors; it was a long time before I heard the word 'aura,' and learned to apply it to this phenomenon which to me was commonplace. I do not ever think of people except in connection with their auras; I see them change in my friends and loved ones as time goes by—sickness, dejection, love, fulfillment—these are all reflected in the aura, and for me the aura is the weathervane of the soul. It shows which way the winds of destiny are blowing."

Once Cayce realized that this phenomenon was unusual, but in no way peculiar to him, he began comparing his own impressions with those of other people. He found them surprisingly in accord. "We only differ with regard to the colors which are in our own auras," he said. "This is curious, for it shows how universal are nature's laws. We know that opposites attract and likes repel. Well, I have a lot of blue in my aura and my interpretation of this color does not always jibe with that of a person whose aura does not contain it and who therefore interprets it objectively. One lady I know has a great deal of green in her aura, and she is inclined to dislike green in the aura of others, and place a disagreeable interpretation on it, whereas it is the color of healing and a fine one to have."

Cayce was able to see personal characteristics of perfect strangers reflected in their auras. But he found it best, in terms of being helpful, to know the individual. "Then I can tell him when I see the twinkling lights of success and achievement, or warn him when melancholy or illness threaten. Of course I do not do this professionally. I would not think of such a thing. But I believe it is an ability which all people will someday possess, and therefore I want to do what I can to get folks used to the idea of auras, so they will think in terms of them, so they will begin to attempt to see auras themselves.

"Where do the colors come from, and what makes them shift and change? Well, color seems to be a characteristic of the vibration of matter, and our souls seem to reflect it in this three-dimensional world through atomic patterns. We are patterns, and we project colors, which are there for those who can see them."

Cayce had been asked, during the course of a reading ten years earlier, to give the nature and source of an individual's aura.

"Auras are twofold," the reading said. "That which indicates the physical emanations, and that which indicates the spiritual development. These, when they are kept more in accord with the experience of individuals, make for greater unification of purpose and ideal.

"The aura, then, is the emanation that arises from the very vibratory influences of an individual, mentally and spiritually—especially from the spiritual forces."

Even earlier, the sleeping Cayce had described the aura as "not a cause, but a result—the result of a condition existing within the entity. By 'entity' we mean not just the physical being or body, but the whole being, including the mental and spiritual being."

Elaborating on this, he had said, "As we react to various conditions, we emanate or send out certain vibrations. . . . We ourselves throw off energy, since we are constantly building and have built within ourselves. Our reactions are radiations which form themselves into color. That which we as individuals radiate, or throw off as energy, is the aura."

Over the years, Cayce worked out a kind of color chart to explain the meanings of colors as seen in a person's aura. These are based on his own experience with reading the auras of those around him, comparing what he saw with what other people who shared this particular talent saw, and noting the relationship between colors seen in a person's aura and events and conditions in this person's life that seemed to match the aura patterns.

As an example, he told of a man he'd known from boyhood who had always worn blue. "Frequently," Cayce said, "I have seen him with a blue shirt, blue tie, and even blue socks. One day he went into a store to buy some ties. He was surprised to find that he had selected several which were maroon in color. He was even more surprised when as time went on, he began to choose shirts with garnet stripes and ties and pocket handkerchief sets in various shades of scarlet. This went on for several years, during which time he became more nervous and more tired. He was working too hard and eventually he had a nervous breakdown.

"During this time the red had grown in prominence in his aura. Now gray, the color of illness, began to creep into the red, but as he recovered, the gray disappeared and then blue began to eat up the red. Eventually all the red was consumed and he was well. Nor did he ever afterward wear anything red, scarlet, or maroon." Apparently, then, a person reacts to his own aura by the choice of his clothing colors, even if he is not aware that he *has* an aura!

Cayce felt this was not at all uncommon. "The majority of people do see auras, I believe, but do not realize it. I believe anyone can figure out what another person's aura is in a general way, if he will take note of the colors which a person habitually uses in the matter of clothing and decoration. How many times have you said of a woman, 'Why does she wear that color? It does not suit her at all.' How many times have you said, 'How beautiful she looks in that dress. The color is just right for her. She was made to wear it.' In both cases you have been reading an aura. The first woman was wearing a color which clashed with her aura. The second woman was wearing a color which harmonized with her aura. All of you know what colors are helpful to your friends, and bring out the best in them. They are the colors that beat with the same vibrations as the aura, and thus strengthen and heighten it. By watching closely you can even discover changes in your friends as they are reflected in a shift in the color predominating in their wardrobe."

Here, in an abbreviated version, is the color chart developed by Edgar Cayce.

Red

Red indicates force, vigor and energy. Its interpretation depends upon the shade and, as with all colors, upon the relationship of other colors. Dark red indicates high temper, and it is a symbol of nervous turmoil. A person with dark red in his aura may not be weak outwardly, but he is suffering in some way, and it is reflected in his nervous system. Such a person is apt to be domineering and quick to act. If the shade of red is light it indicates a nervous, impulsive, very active person, one who is probably self-centered. Scarlet indicates an overdose of ego. Pink, or coral, is the color of immaturity. It is seen usually in young people, and if it shows up in the aura of one who is grown it indicates delayed adolescence, a childish concern with self. In all cases of red there is a tendency to nervous troubles, and such people ought to take time to be quiet and to get outside themselves.

Orange

Orange is the color of the sun. It is vital, and a good color generally, indicating thoughtfulness and consideration of others. Again, however, it is a matter of shade. Golden orange is vital and indicates self-control, whereas brownish orange shows a lack of ambition and a don't- care attitude. Such people may be repressed, but usually they are just lazy.

Yellow

Golden yellow indicates health and well-being. Such people take good care of themselves, don't worry, and learn easily. Good mentality is natural to them. They are happy, friendly, and helpful. If the yellow is ruddy, they are timid. If they are redheads they are apt to have an inferiority complex. They are thus apt often to be indecisive and weak in will, inclined to let others lead them.

Green

Pure emerald green, particularly if it has a dash of blue, is the color of healing. It is helpful, strong, friendly. It is the color of doctors and nurses, who invariably have a lot of it in their auras. However, it is seldom a dominating color, usually being overshadowed by one of its neighbors. As it tends toward blue it is more helpful and trustworthy. As it tends toward yellow it is weakened. A lemony green, with a lot of yellow, is deceitful. As a rule the deep, healing green is seen in small amounts, but it is good to have a little of it in your aura.

Blue

Blue has always been the color of the spirit, the symbol of contemplation, prayer, and heaven. Almost any kind of blue is good, but the deeper shades are the best. Pale blue indicates little depth, but a struggle toward maturity. The person may not be talented, but he tries. He will have many heartaches and many headaches, but he will keep going in the right direction. The middle blue, or aqua, belongs to a person who will work harder and get more done than the fellow with light blue, though there may be little difference between them in talent. Those with the deep blue have found their work and are immersed in it. They are apt to be moody and are almost always unusual persons, but they have a mission and they steadfastly go about fulfilling it. They are spiritual-minded for the most part, and their life is usually dedicated to an unselfish cause, such as science, art, or social service.

Indigo and Violet

Indigo and violet indicate seekers of all types, people who are searching for a cause or a religious experience. As these people get settled in their careers and in their beliefs, however, these colors usually settle back into deep blue. It seems that once the purpose is set in the right direction, blue is a natural emanation of the soul. Those who have purple are inclined to be overbearing, for here there is an infiltration of pink.

White

The perfect color, of course, is white, and this is what we are all striving for. If our souls were in perfect balance then all our color vibrations would blend and we would have an aura of pure white. Christ had this aura, and it is shown in many paintings of Him, particularly those which depict Him after the resurrection.

These are handy guidelines for those of us who now see, or hope to see, colors in connection with people we know. As one who has always experienced this phenomenon, I can assure you that it is most helpful to be able to detect, in a loved one, the warning signs of impending illness (always gray), or that flash of red that says, "Tread softly; this person is upset about something!"

As might be expected from one so psychically talented as Cayce, however, his view of an aura was a great deal more complex. He was able to study the aura in terms of position of the colors contained in it, their intensity, and how they were distributed. As Cayce saw it, "The aura emanates from the whole body, but usually it is most heavy and most easily seen around the shoulders and head, probably because of the many glandular and nervous centers located in those parts of the body."

He saw the aura in specific shapes. "In children, for instance, it is possible to tell whether a great deal of training by example will be needed, or whether precept will do as well. If the child is reasonable and will accept instruction on this basis, the aura will be like a rolling crown. If example is needed, the aura will be a more definite figure, with sharp points and a variety of colors. If the child intends to be a law unto himself, the aura will be like a rolling chain, lower than the position of a crown, going about the shoulders as well as the head."

Cayce went on to say that several times he had seen little hooks of light dotted through a person's aura. "In each case, the man had a job as overseer of large groups of other men, a director and a leader."

To Edgar Cayce, the perception of color and light around each person he met was a natural phenomenon—so natural, in fact, that the absence of an aura meant one thing: imminent death. But to most of us, such perception is not natural at all, although Cayce felt it could be developed. "You can become color-conscious," he said, "and you can learn to read auras from people's clothes and the colors you see predominant in their surroundings.

"It can be a fascinating game, noticing how any person with vitality and vigor will have a little splash of red in a costume, in a room, or in a garden; noticing how persons who are quiet, dependable, sure of themselves, and spiritual, never are seen without deep blues—it is almost as if they turn things blue by being near them. Notice how bright and sunny people, who like to laugh and play, and who are never tired or down-hearted, will wear golden yellow and seem to color things yellow, like a buttercup held under the chin.

"Colors reflect the soul and the spirit, the mind and the body, but remember they indicate lack of perfection, incompleteness. If we were all we should be, pure white would emanate from us. Strive toward that, and when you see it in others, follow it as if it were a star. It is. But we who must take solace from smaller things can draw comfort from blue, get strength from red and be happy in the laughter and sunshine of golden yellow."

CHAPTER 8

PSYCHIC DEVELOPMENT IN OTHERS

WHO AMONG US, at one time or another, has not wished for the power to see into tomorrow? Who among us, at one time or another, has not wished for the power to understand what lies beyond that mysterious condition we call death? Who among us, at one time or another, has not wished for the power to know, as clearly as if spoken aloud, the thoughts and desires of another person? And, through knowing, to be able to *will* the thoughts and desires of another to conform to our own?

Who among us has not, at one time or another, experienced what seemed to be a genuine manifestation of ESP? A dream that later comes true; a statement by one person "heard" by another person moments before it is spoken; a positive kind of feeling that something is going to happen, that does happen, just the way we knew it would—all these things, and many more, convince us of the reality of ESP and psychic phenomena.

Now, suddenly, it seems that everyone is talking about ESP, and haunted houses, and the significance of dreams. A scientist writes an article for a national magazine concerning his discovery that plants can be affected by the emotions of human beings, and appears on the Johnny Carson television show to explain this, and demonstrates the elaborate equipment by which he learned this to be so—and wonder of wonders, this man is not laughed off the stage! A famous clergyman and an equally famous psychic medium appear in a nationally televised seance in which contact may have been made with the clergyman's dead son—and if the results of the seance are not fully understood or accepted by all, at least they are accorded respectful attention.

Suddenly, everyone wants to know more about this kind of thing. Maybe, just maybe, there is something in it after all!

Certainly there is no longer a lack of printed information about the subject. Hundreds of books and articles are being published every year, including the book you now hold in your hands, in which people tell about their own psychic experiences or those of others. Many of these books go further: they tell the reader how to develop psychic ability in himself.

We who have long studied psychic phenomena are gratified that at last we can talk openly about our subject without too much fear of ridicule. We welcome careful and thoughtful experimentation in the field. At the same time, we are somewhat alarmed by some of the advice being given on the subject of developing psychic ability. People are being taught the principles of automatic writing, of self-hypnosis, and more; indeed, many well-meaning individuals are *urging* them to learn these things. But we wonder if such matters are not being grabbed up a little too enthusiastically for the good of some of the people involved.

Perhaps we should pause, then, and consider what the Cayce readings—and Cayce consciously—had to say on some aspects of psychic phenomena.

Clairvoyance and Telepathy

Funk & Wagnalls Standard Dictionary defines telepathy as "the supposed communication of one mind with another at a distance by other than normal sensory means; thought-transference."

Edgar Cayce, in one reading, stated, "Be sure of this fact; be assured of this: thought-transference occurs when both bodies, or entities, are in the subconscious condition—whether for a moment or whether for ages. For time in spiritual forces is not as it is in material forces."

Funk & Wagnalls Standard Dictionary defines clairvoyance as "the ability to see things not visible to the normal human eye; second sight . . . "

Edgar Cayce, in one reading, stated, "*Every* entity has clairvoyant, mystic, psychic powers." This theory was advanced in many Cayce readings.

At another time he said, "In the study of phenomena of this nature there should be, first, the analysis as to purpose. . . . What is the source of the information . . . that goes beyond . . . ordinary . . . guessing? What is the basis of telepathic or clairvoyant communication? What are these in their elemental activity?

"To be sure, this experience is [in] a portion of the mind; but mind, as we have given, is both material and spiritual . . .

"It is not, then, to be a calling upon, a depending upon, a seeking for, that which is without, outside of self; but rather the attuning of self to the divine within, which is a universal, or the universal, consciousness . . .

"As to making practical application—it is what you do with the abilities that are developed by this attunement in coordinating, cooperating one with another in such experiment. For the universal consciousness is constructive, not destructive in any manner, but ever constructive in its activity with the elements that make up an entity's experience in the physical consciousness . . .

"The more each is impelled by that which is intuitive, or the relying upon the soul force within, the greater, the farther, the deeper, the broader, the more constructive may be the result.

"More and more, then, turn to those experiments that are not only helpful but that give hope to others, that make for the activity of the fruits of the Spirit.

"Wait on the Lord; not making for a show, an activity of any kind that would be for self-glorification, self-exaltation, but rather that which is helpful, hopeful for others."

Edgar Cayce discussed this in a public address on February 15, 1931. In part, this is what he had to say:

"Mind reading, or mental telepathy, does exist; we know that. We experience it ourselves every day. Many of us have had the experience of thinking about someone—and that person calls us on the phone. Again, we may have been speaking about certain people, and they walk in the door.

"This kind of thing happened to me just a few days ago. We were discussing a subject. As far as I knew, there was no reason on earth for the person involved to come to my home; but as we were speaking of him and his abilities, it happened that he appeared right then.

"What caused this? Was it chance—just an everyday occurrence? Or was it that the thought-vibrations between our minds and his mind brought about the conversation?

"My experiences have taught me that practically every phase of [psychic] phenomena may be explained by activities of the subconscious mind." [Author's italics.]

Cayce then related an experiment in mental telepathy which he had carried out some years before, while he was still working as a photographer. He told his assistant, a young woman who had discussed various phases of psychic phenomena with him on many occasions, that he could will a person to come to him. She thought this would be impossible, and said so. Cayce then challenged her to name two people she felt could not be influenced in this way.

"You couldn't get my brother to come up here," she said. "And I know you couldn't get Mr. B to come here, either, because he dislikes you."

"I told her," Cayce related, "that before twelve o'clock the next day her brother not only would come up to the studio, but he would ask me to do something for him. And the day after that, before two o'clock, Mr. B would come, too."

At about ten o'clock the next morning, Cayce entered the studio and sat quietly thinking about his assistant's brother. "I felt sure he would come," he said. "I did wonder, though, if I hadn't overstepped myself in saying he was going to ask me to do something for him, because his sister had told me he didn't have any patience with the work I did."

After thirty minutes of meditation, Cayce looked out the window and saw the boy passing by on the street below. "He stood there a few seconds, looking up the steps—then walked away. In a few minutes, he turned in again and came up the steps to the second floor."

The sister looked around and said, "What are you doing here?"

The boy sat on the edge of the table, turning his hat around in his hands. Then he blurted out, "Well, I hardly know—but I had some trouble last night at the shop, and you've been talking so much about Mr. Cayce, I just wondered if he couldn't help me out."

The next day, Cayce repeated the experiment with Mr. B as the target of his thoughts. He sat quietly for about half an hour and then left, telling his assistant that he preferred not to be in when Mr.B arrived, " . . . because he dislikes me so much."

Afterwards, the young woman reported that at twelve-thirty, Mr. B had indeed come into the studio. She had asked him if there was anything she could do for him. "No," he snapped. "I don't know what I'm doing here. I just came up!" Looking puzzled, he turned and marched out.

Cayce then told his audience that he had never repeated the experiment, and never would. "Now, to my way of thinking these are examples of mental telepathy, or mind reading—but they show a forcing of yourself upon someone else. That's dangerous business! It pertains to the black arts; it's one of those things none of us has a right to do unless we are very sure of what we're doing, and of our motives. Sometimes it might be used well, perhaps at times to control our children in that way. Yet even then it might be dangerous, for, as our information says, anyone who would force another to submit to his will is a tyrant! Even God does not force His will upon us. Either we make our will one with His, or we are opposed to Him. Each person has an individual choice.

"Then what part may mental telepathy play in our lives—that is the big question. For anything good can also be dangerous. I could mention nothing good but what it also has its misapplication, its misuse. How, then, may we use mind reading or mental telepathy constructively?

"The best rule I can give is this: don't ask another person to do something you wouldn't do yourself. The Master never asked such a thing; and let us never ask it."

Once, in giving a reading, Cayce addressed himself to whether or not the combined thought power of many individuals could change the course of physical events. He stated, "We find that when the thought of many individuals is directed to one focusing point, the condition becomes accentuated by force of thought manifested . . .

"As thoughts are directed, the transmission of thought waves gradually becomes the reality—just as light and heat waves in the material world are now used by man. Just so in the spiritual planes the elements of thought transmission, or transference, may become real."

Automatic Writing

The practice of automatic writing has long been of interest to students of psychic phenomena. Often Cayce was asked, during the course of the reading, to advise on this subject.

Once he was asked if it is possible to communicate with entities in the spirit plane by means of automatic writing. He replied, "Yes. By practice. Sit alone with pencil and paper and let that guide that may be sought, or may come in, direct. It will come. Anyone may do this—*but is it the better way?* It may oft be questioned."

Cayce always cautioned against possible dangers to the individual when engaging in automatic writing. In a reading given in 1938 he said, "We would not, from here, counsel *anyone* to be guided by influences from without. For the Kingdom is from within! If these come as (automatic) inspirational writings from within, and not as guidance from others—that is different."

In 1936 he urged another, "As has been indicated, rather than automatic writing or a medium, turn to the voice within! If this then finds expression in that which may be given to self in hand—by writing—it is well. But not that the hand be guided by an influence outside of self. For the Universe—God—is within. Thou art His. Thy communion with the cosmic forces of nature, thy communion with thy Creator, is thy birthright! Be satisfied with nothing less than walking with Him."

Hypnosis

Hypnosis, in the hands of a responsible therapist, can be one of medicine's greatest allies. In spite of all the stage demonstrations, and attendant hilarity, it continues to be studied seriously as a safe and efficient means of relieving both physical and emotional pain.

It should be pointed out, here, that *all* hypnosis is, in effect, self-hypnosis. No one can control the subconscious mind of another. What happens is that a receptive subject will accept the suggestion of a skilled therapist and hypnotize himself. At no time is the subject "taken over" by the therapist.

I once witnessed a dreadful demonstration of unthinking hypnosis that illustrates how dangerous it can be under the wrong conditions. The hypnotist, an amateur who had nevertheless worked many times with the subject of this experiment, was showing the process to a number of us following a dinner party. We were sitting around the living room in a friend's house in Mount Clemens, Michigan. The hypnotist put his subject "under," and gave her the suggestion that she was in a room in a Swiss chalet. If she would go the the window, he said, she would see the skiers getting ready for their day on the slopes. He described the scene outside the window, as well as within the room; his subject indicated that she saw everything he described. She seemed to be having a thoroughly enjoyable time; looking through the window at Michigan's September-red hills, she exclaimed over the beauty of the snow.

The hypnotist said, "If you'd like to join them, go get your skis from the bedroom."

His subject turned immediately, and with some excitement started for the door to the hall. Just as she stepped across the threshold, she sank to the floor and began crying hysterically.

It took us some time to figure out what had happened. But the answer was simple. The hypnotist, you'll recall, had said, "You are in a *room* in a Swiss chalet." The moment she stepped through the door she was back in the house in Mount Clemens, and her disappointment was crushing. It was several days before she completely recovered from the experience.

Hypnosis is discussed in a great many Cayce readings. Cayce's first concern, in prescribing it, was the person who would be administering it. Most often it was not a professional hypnotist, but a member of the patient's own family who was to give the suggestion.

Once he was asked, in connection with a 13-year-old boy who was a deaf-mute afflicted with epilepsy, "Could hypnotism be used in this case?" He answered, "It might be used, but be mindful of who would use same!" He advised that autosuggestion would best be given by the boy's mother.

He was asked, then, to give the form of suggestion to be used. He replied, "That as is desired to be awakened. Work with one applying the manipulative [osteopathy] forces in this, but appeal always to the inner being—that being awakened in this formative period of the development of the body, mentally and physically. This may be as a form, but should be put in the words of the individual making such suggestions. [Say,] as the body sinks into slumber, 'May the self, the ego, awaken to its possibilities, its responsibilities, that, as I speak to you, in the normal waking state you will respond in that same loving, careful manner that is given to you.' See?"

In a reading for a young woman suffering from insanity, Cayce indicated that the suggestion should be given by "one of the people that have a clean mind themselves. The body is good to look at and it would not be well to put under the influence of one with ulterior motives or desires." [Note the clairvoyance indicated by the expression "good to look at." Cayce had never, consciously, seen this patient.]

For a man who had been suffering from constant hiccoughs for six days, Cayce prescribed hypnosis. "Let this be done by suggestion, through such as Kahn."

And finally, this general statement on hypnosis. "Many an individual, many a personage has given his all for the demonstrating of a truth.

"As it has been indicated from the first—through this channel, there should ever be that ideal, 'What does such information which may come through such a channel produce in the experience of individuals? Does such make them better parents, better children, better husbands, better wives, better neighbors, better friends, better citizens?' And if and when it does not, *leave it alone!*"

Possession

We have discussed several areas in which people are experimenting with what we might term "do-it-yourself psychic development," and we have given you a general summary of Cayce's advice concerning them. Hugh Lynn Cayce, in his book *Venture Inward,* has told of his personal observations of people who got themselves into trouble as a result of injudicious experimentation along these lines.

We now come to the most startling concept of all: the possibility that there can be such a thing as possession.

Does this idea—yes, in the old-fashioned sense of the word, meaning that a human being has been "taken over" by the spirit of some discarnate entity—bring a smile to your lips? It may well do so. After all, a lot of gripping suspense stories have been built around this subject. It is such a far-out idea, with such exciting ramifications, that it makes good fiction. Therefore, it is difficult to consider it seriously.

The sleeping Cayce, however, did consider it seriously. We have no way of knowing whether or not he was correct in his statements about it, but the subject came up in many readings. Bearing in mind the high rate of accuracy of his physical readings—which will be discussed a little later in this book—we can only offer you the following examples and invite you to make of them what you will.

Once, reading for a 72-year-old woman, Cayce said, "Yes, we have the body here." He paused for a long moment, and then said in an undertone, "We have possession here."

Reading for a woman who had questions for Cayce regarding the problems of her alcoholic husband, he was asked, "What causes my husband to lose control of himself?"

Cayce answered immediately, "Possession!"

"What is meant by possession?"

"Means POSSESSION!"

To the next question, "Is he crazy or mentally deranged?" he replied, "If possession isn't crazy, what is it?"

"Does possession mean by other entities, while under the influence of liquor?"

"By other entities while under the influence of liquor," replied the sleeping man. "For this body, the husband, if there could be a sufficient period of refraining from the use of alcoholic stimulants, and the diathermy electrical treatments used, such treatments would drive these entities out! But do not use electrical treatments with the effects of alcohol in the system; it would be detrimental."

We have given these examples to show that, to Cayce, possession was something that might happen to anyone. For those experimenting with such activities as automatic writing and self-hypnosis, however, the need for special caution was indicated throughout the Cayce readings.

Here are three cases dealing with the consequences of careless experimentation with certain Yoga techniques. [This does not, by the way, include Yoga exercises used to improve physical health; Cayce often recommended these in his readings.]

In a reading for a 50-year-old woman, Cayce said, "While those activities that have been taken by the body produce some conditions that are beneficial . . . they have caused and do assist in producing the exciting of the glandular forces in their activity, as related to the genital system. This, combined with pressures upon the nerve system, [causes] distorted and disturbing conditions for this body."

"What causes the burning sensation which comes over me, as if someone has [put] the power on me?" he was asked.

"This is the incoordination between the cerebrospinal and the sympathetic nervous systems. And as the glandular system is affected—as related to the genitive system, and especially affecting directly the center above the puba—there is produced (with the toxic forces in the system) this burning, and the *effect of possession!*"

"Should anything be taken for the glands?"

"As has been indicated, there has already been too much taken!"

In a reading for a woman of 53, Cayce said, "The body is a supersensitive individual who has allowed itself—through study—through opening the gland centers of the body, to become possessed with activities outside of itself . . . "

"How did I happen to pick this up?"

"The body—in its study—opened the gland centers, and allowed self to become sensitive to outside influences."

What is it exactly that assails me?"

"Outside influences. Discarnate entities."

And finally, for a 39-year-old woman, Cayce said, "There has been the opening of the lyden gland, so that the kundaline forces move along the spine to the various centers that open—with the activities of the mental and spiritual forces of the body. The psychological reaction is much like that which may be illustrated in one gaining much knowledge, without making practical application of it. . . . Now combine these two and we have that indicated here as a possession of the body—a gnawing, as it were, on all of the seven centers of the body, causing the inability to rest or even [engage in] a concerted activity, unless the body finds itself needed for someone else. Then the body finds, as this occurs, the disturbance is retarded or fades, as the body exercises itself in giving help to others."

We know this sounds fantastic. But we do not apologize for offering it here. After all, who's to say Cayce *didn't* know what he was talking about?

We should take a moment to explain some of the terminology used in the above readings, or connected with it in some way, for it may be completely unfamiliar to you.

Kundalini is a Sanskrit word for an activity connected with Yoga. By concentrating on nerve centers, and through exercise and breathing, kundalini, a fundamental power of electrical force, may be awakened in the body. Unless done under expert supervision, it is considered a dangerous practice. Probably some of the people mentioned in the above readings had been experimenting with this activity without utilizing proper controls.

Kundalini is believed to lie at the base of the spine, coiled like a serpent, until deliberately raised up through the various chakras in order to radiate from the top of the head.

Chakras (another Sanskrit word) are seven vortices of psychic energy. They are said to be situated along the spine and in the head, and are considered, in Yoga, to serve as points of reception for "pranic forces" (vital energies) which rouse the individual to action. They are psychic in nature, not physical. Beginning at the base of the spine and working up to the head, their corresponding glands— which *are* physical, of course—are the adrenals, the sex glands, the pancreas, the thymus, the thyroid, the pituitary and the pineal glands.

In the last-mentioned reading above, for the 39-year-old woman, Cayce mentioned that there had been "the opening of the lyden gland, so that the kundaline forces move along the spine to the various centers that open. . . . " *Lyden gland* was a term used often by Edgar Cayce in his readings, to designate the source of Leydig cells. These are interstitial cells which secrete the androgens or male hormones.

In a reading given in September, 1928, Cayce stated, "The basis or seat of the soul is in the lyden (Leydig) gland."

This is a confusing statement. "Lyden gland" does not appear in any dictionary or in any of the endocrine charts I consulted, and I examined many of them. Leydig cells *are* recognized, of course—and accepted scientific knowledge seems to agree with what Edgar Cayce had to say on the subject. Did Edgar Cayce suffer a slip of the tongue *on the great many occasions* when he mentioned the lyden gland, or did he have access to some very special information—information just waiting to be discovered, or rediscovered?

In one reading, Cayce stated, "Lyden, meaning sealed, is that gland from which gestation takes place when body is created . . . located in and above the genital glands." Here, too, he said, "The base or seat of the soul is in the lyden (cells of Leydig)."

So the readings indicate that the soul enters the body through the cells of Leydig, or the lyden gland. They also suggest that the soul continues to function through a network connecting gland tissue in various portions of the body. As one reading explained this, "The spiritual contact is through the glandular forces of creative energies; not encased only within the lyden gland of reproduction, for this is ever—so long as life exists—in contact with the brain cells through which there is the constant reaction through the pineal."

In the early 17th Century, the French mathematician and philosopher, Rene Descartes, identified the pineal gland as "the seat of the soul." He based this theory on the belief that the pineal was found only in humans. When it was discovered to exist among other other vertebrates—sometimes proportionately larger than in humans—Descartes' theory was pretty much laid to rest. However, many Cayce readings refer to the pineal gland in just these words; and in one reading it was referred to as "a channel through which psychic or spiritual forces may manifest."

If there has ever been an orphan among glands, it is certainly the pineal. A tiny organ attached, like the pituitary, to the base of the brain, it lost its status as a "gland" when—after intense research failed to locate a pineal hormone—scientists began to refer to it as the "pineal body." Indeed, the pineal seemed of no value at all to the human body.

Then in 1958, a hormone, melatonin, was isolated from the pineal. Scientists connected with this advance were quoted as saying, "It is possible that the pineal gland has a function not yet discovered." With the discovery of melatonin, the word "gland" was restored to the pineal.

Somewhat later, experiments were conducted at Harvard Medical School with a protein-free extract from the pineal glands of beef cattle. Administered by injection to a group of fifty-five chronic schizophrenics, there was improvement in each case—and results in some cases were said to be "spectacular."

In a reading given in 1932, replying to a question concerning the source of his information, Edgar Cayce said, "There must be, in the physical or material world, a channel through which psychic or spiritual forces may manifest. . . . In this particular body [Edgar Cayce] through which this at present is emanating, the gland known as the pineal gland, with its thread, is the channel along which same operates. With the subjugation of the consciousness—physical consciousness—there arises, as it were, a cell from the creative forces with the body to the entrance of the conscious mind, or brain, operating along, or traveling along, that of the thread or cord [called by Cayce, at times, the silver cord] as, when severed, separates the physical, the soul, or the spiritual body."

In another reading he said, "Pituitary forces become manifest in intuition.

"In the body we find that which connects the pineal, the pituitary, the lyden, may be truly called the silver cord . . . which is the Creative Essence in physical, mental and spiritual life; for the destruction wholly of either will make for the disintegration of the soul from its house of clay."

And, at another time, "It [the pituitary] is the door . . . through which phys-ically all of the reflex actions [penetrate] through the various forces of the nerve system. It is that to and through which the mental activities come that produce the influences in the imaginative system as well as the racial predominating influences—or the blood force itself.

"In the spiritual it is that in the adult which brings the awakening to its capabilities, its possibilities, its ultimate hope and desire.

"In the mental it is that which gives judgment and understanding, tolerance and relationships to the determining factors . . . "

"Why Do They Doubt?"

In a general reading, given for the purpose of getting information about psychic phenomena, Edgar Cayce was asked the question that has plagued all who seriously study the subject, "Why do so many people ridicule the idea that useful information can be obtained through this source of psychic data?"

He replied, "Lack of understanding of the law governing so-called psychic powers; lack of consciousness being brought to the individual of the potential powers which are manifested in and through the psychic or occult forces.

"Much of this misunderstanding is caused by the lack of proper use of the knowledge obtained through such sources. For the incorrect use of such knowledge may, and would, bring destructive elements . . .

"The only real life is that which, in the material or physical plane, is called psychic. . . . Those who ridicule such forces are to be pitied rather than con-demned, for they must eventually reach that condition (adversity, frustrations, etc.) wherein the soul awakens to the elements necessary for the developing.

"For without the psychic force in the world, the physical would be in that condition of 'hit or miss,' or as a ship without a rudder or pilot. For that element which is the guiding force in each and every condition is the spirit or soul of that condition—which is the psychic or occult force."

CHAPTER 9

TELEPATHY AND/OR CLAIRVOYANCE AS SHOWN IN THE PHYSICAL READINGS

THE SLEEPING CAYCE "practiced" a strange kind of medicine, in that it recognized no boundaries. If osteopathy was indicated as being best for the particular body, and for the particular ailment, then an osteopath—often specified by name in the reading—was recommended. If surgery seemed the only solution, then surgery it was—and again, the M.D. to perform the operation might be named. Odd medicaments were often recommended; so odd, in fact, that many times they had to be specially compounded of ingredients named in the reading. Occasionally the dose seemed poisonous in nature or in proportion. Then the druggist filling the "prescription" might quietly substitute another ingredient for the one called for in the reading. (In such cases, the next reading would confirm what had happened, as an explanation for the patient's not having improved or become completely well.) Often, in the case of a psychosomatic disorder, Cayce offered a special prescription for cure: that of getting the mental and emotional house in order.

The Cayce physical readings, in short, form a curious amalgamation of naturopathy-osteopathy-surgery-drugs-psychology-diet therapy. The only limits, it seems, were dictated by the needs of the patient. Since Cayce, in trance, was constrained by the dictates of no particular order or school of medicine, he was free to suggest whatever each patient required to get well.

However, before others—and Cayce himself—could become convinced that what he was doing in his readings was not only harmless, but actually beneficial, they were used almost exclusively on people closest to Cayce, and then only as a last resort. Indeed, an examination of the family history almost makes it appear that desperate situations were thrust on Cayce as a means of forcing him to use his psychic ability. Each time he tried to turn his back on the power that had been given him, he was impelled by circumstances to return to it once again.

One of many such instances was the case of his wife, Gertrude, who contracted tuberculosis soon after the birth, and death, of their second son. The physicians attending her gave her up to die, just as her brother had died from the same disease.

Cayce, still trying to make a career as a photographer, and still questioning the value and safety of the information that was coming to him when he went into the unconscious state, gave a reading for her. The diagnosis, according to the physicians, was excellent. So was the general statement of her condition. However, they said, the suggested treatment was truly ridiculous. They admitted that the diet matched the one customarily used for TB patients. But she was to take drugs—including heroin, mixed to make a liquid and administered in capsule form—which were normally used to make up prescriptions; never should they be taken in the form Cayce had specified in the reading. Hardest of all to take seriously, though, was the recommendation that Gertrude inhale the fumes of apple brandy contained in a charred oak keg!

So the doctors refused to have anything to do with it. The local druggist risked jail by making up the compounds called for in the reading without benefit of a doctor's prescription. The apple brandy keg was procured, and treatment was begun in August, 1910. By January, Gertrude was well on her way to complete recovery.

Edgar Cayce "Cures" Edgar Cayce

Probably it was the strain of this period in their lives that resulted in a reading given on December 1, 1910, for Edgar Cayce himself. It dealt with the vocal paralysis which afflicted him periodically throughout his adult life. Whenever emotional or physical strain proved to be too much for his body to tolerate, Cayce would become unable to speak above a whisper.

The reading was conducted by Al C. Layne, the Hopkinsville, Kentucky, amateur hypnotist (and correspondence school osteopathy student) who had discovered, in 1900, that although Cayce would not respond to the posthypnotic suggestions of others, he was capable of following his own when in a self-induced trance. (It was Layne, too, who had discovered that Cayce could also prescribe treatment for the ills of others. Layne gave the name "readings" to this activity of Cayce's unconscious mind.)

In the reading, Cayce was asked to examine the throat of the body, Edgar Cayce, and ". . . tell what is the matter with it, if anything."

Cayce replied, "The muscles of the vocal cords here, you see, produce a partial paralysis to the vocal cord, especially to the left side of the vocal box. You see, the cords are taut from the box or sound here, as the air is expelled from the lungs . . . We have a nervous effect of the nerves and muscles all over the whole body; we have a tightening or a sensation in the nerve force to contract it and of the muscles of the vocal cord or box here.

"All along in the front part of the body along the larynx to the vocal cord, to the right end here in front, this muscle is taut; then the voice sounds as if it is loose here, or not contracted by the nerve forces and muscles. Together, this leaves one side that does not sound and produces a whispering sound. This comes from the same trouble we have had before from the pelvis."

"What will we do to remove that now?" asked Layne.

"Just circulation here will remove it; that is the only thing that will do it. Suggestion to the body forces the circulation through it here, and as the circulation passes along it takes that away—puts new life to it—makes the supply to the nerve force go, you see."

Layne gave the suggestion, as he had done in the past: "Increase the circulation and watch that and see the condition removed; that congested condition. Increase the circulation. Is that removing now?"

"Circulation is beginning to increase," said Cayce. [It should be noted that while this was going on, his voice was normal. Without the procedure being followed in the reading, however, it would have reverted to a mere whisper upon awakening.]

Layne continued the suggestion. "Watch it increase, now. Watch that remove. All that congested condition will be removed away by the circulation. Passing off now, is it not?"

"Passing off now," said Cayce.

"Watch it move clear on; it will become normal. Will be in its normal condition. Watch it now and when that becomes perfectly normal, tell me."

Cayce replied, "Have to remove the trouble first."

"What is the trouble now? You see the trouble is away. Now the trouble is gone. Now the vocal cords are perfectly normal, are they not?"

"They are perfectly normal now."

"That is all right now," said Layne. "They will continue to work perfectly. Now at times in the past, he [Edgar Cayce] has suffered with severe headaches. What causes the headache?"

"In the pelvis."

"How will we remove that?"

"To operate on it."

"In what way?"

"Here, from the side here."

"Cannot it be done by manipulation?"

"Cannot absorb it. It has hardened at times past, you see; it is hard. See here the testicle comes—here at the upper end of the pelvis—comes in contact with a lesion at the second lumbar, and there you see it forms a lesion. Now between this lesion and into the pelvic region here—right opposite to the left side and about two inches from the pelvis bone—has formed a clot or a knot at the time of cold or extreme excitement or anything [that affects] the nervous organism of the system. It produces then the pains that revert to the head, at the top, in the center. Produce cold all along the spine and heat on top of the head. When we reverse this it settles in the organs; that is, in the weakest point in the system. These come together again from these troubles in sympathy with the sympathetic system here at the stomach. We have at times, at the same time, a filling up of gases in the stomach; pains in the lower part, in the intestinal tract. We have a reverse and produces the condition in the intestinal tract itself. That is the aftereffects and not the cause of the trouble. The trouble is from the clot that formed here from this accident we have had here in the testicle.

"It will have to be here. Roll the intestines to the side; we have here at the lower part a clot formed and when that is cut loose it makes a reaction to the nerve supply and makes it rebuild instead of forming this clot on the nerve force here."

Layne gave the final suggestion before the one to wake Cayce. "Your circulation is going to continue perfect."

Now, what do we find in this reading? Many things.

First, there is the information that Cayce's vocal paralysis was principally of psychological origin. He described the condition, and requested that Layne make the suggestion that the circulation increase to the affected portion. Cayce, amenable to such a suggestion, then proceeded to do so!

Gladys Davis (Turner), Cayce's secretary for many years, witnessed this phenomenon many times. Upon being given the suggestion, she has reported, Cayce's face and throat would change in color from normal to deep pink, as the circulation was increased. After the skin color had returned to normal, Cayce would announce, "The condition is removed." When he came out of the trance, his voice would be perfectly normal again.

There is also, in this reading, information concerning Cayce's headaches and intestinal pain. It was stated that the pain resulted from an accident involving a testicle, which had caused a clot to form in the intestinal tract—causing, in turn, an obstruction which must be removed by surgery.

Cayce, when this reading was complete, reported that he *had* suffered such an accident; in childhood, he had fallen on a stick which had gone completely through the testicle. It was a serious injury and healing was painfully slow.

The condition was completely verified a few years later, when Cayce was operated on for appendicitis. The surgeon reported that he had never seen a worse case. Cayce's intestines were terribly twisted and obstructed, just as the reading had indicated.

The Aime Dietrich Case

As we have mentioned, the first readings, with a few exceptions, were given for members of the Cayce family.

One of these exceptions concerned Aime Dietrich, and it occurred in August, 1902. Edgar Cayce, who was then working in a bookstore in Bowling Green, Kentucky, was summoned to his home town of Hopkinsville one Sunday to deal with the seemingly incurable case of a little five-year-old girl.

According to her father, the child had been perfectly normal up until the age of two, when, following an attack of influenza, her mind had simply stopped developing. A great many specialists had been consulted, but none had been able to provide the answer or even stop the convulsions which were coming in increasing numbers—sometimes as many as twenty a day. Her father had heard of Cayce through Al Layne, and was now turning to him as a last resort.

Cayce found, when he entered the Dietrich nursery, a beautiful child with an absolutely blank mind. A nurse stood by, watching Aime's every move. Edgar Cayce wondered if he had a right to tamper with this child's life by asking for information from a source he couldn't begin to understand. It was not an easy decision. However, he reasoned, what *other* chance did she have?

So he gave the reading. It indicated that, a few days prior to coming down with influenza, Aime had suffered a fall which had injured her spine. (Her mother later confirmed this. Aime had slipped when getting out of the family carriage and fallen to the street. But she had jumped right up, seemingly unhurt, so her mother had thought no more of the accident.) The flu germs had settled at the site of the injury, said the reading. It was this, and this alone, that had caused the trouble. Instructions were given for some osteopathic adjustments, which Layne would administer.

For Layne, a "mail order" osteopath without benefit of diploma, some additional readings were needed to be sure that he was giving the proper adjustments. He did make some mistakes, and the readings were careful to point these out and suggest correct procedures.

Within a matter of weeks the child's mind had begun to pick up where it had left off three years before. Within three months she had managed to make up for most of the time lost to illness and had caught up with children of her own age. She recovered completely, and developed just as normally as if nothing serious had ever touched her life.

The case of Aime Dietrich has been reported by many of Cayce's biographers, and is therefore well known. So we have not disguised her name or any of the circumstances. However, in discussing other cases in this book, fictitious names will be used to protect the identities of the people for whom readings were given. This is in accordance with A.R.E. policies; although the files are open to the public, they have been carefully coded for this purpose.

The Strange Pregnancies of Wilma Franklin

Some warnings concerning possible future trouble were given in a reading for Wilma Franklin on September 3, 1937. She was twenty-six years old, and had been married just under a year. Her doctor had assured her that she was not pregnant, and she had taken some pills to bring on her overdue menstrual period.

Severe abdominal pains, fever and hemorrhage followed. Her mother-in-law, utilizing an old family remedy of some kind, applied a large quantity of iodine to Wilma's abdomen in the belief that it would relieve the pain. Wilma's husband called Edgar Cayce's office, several hundred miles away, and requested an emergency reading.

Cayce began it with one of his frequent demonstrations of clairvoyance. "We find the odor of iodine about the body."

He then proceeded to outline the case in full, explaining, ". . . as we find, conditions that disturb in the present are acute, arising from the organs of the pelvis, or more specific the sac, there being produced or caused spasm in same— by the active principles of orris and ergot—and an expulsion of the activities of the system from normalcy." In other words, it was the pills that had caused the trouble—and Cayce had named a couple of ingredients. Unfortunately, we are unable to attest to the accuracy of this.

"For it is as serious as an abortion would be," he continued. "Unless there are great precautions taken in the activities of the body, it will be very hard for the body to have the period of gestation without a great deal of trouble, and the inability to carry through the full periods." (From the events that later occurred, as we shall see, it seems that Wilma may well have been pregnant, after all, and that the drug had caused an unwanted abortion.)

Wilma was told, in the reading, to keep off her feet for at least ten days, to keep her hands out of cold water (a frequent and somewhat mystifying Cayce warning in such cases), to have some osteopathic manipulations "to correct adjustments in pressures from the lumbar, sacral and coccyx area," and to watch her diet and eliminations. Cayce cautioned that the uterus "dropped down" and must be allowed to return to its proper position, principally through sufficient rest and reclining, in order that future pregnancies might come to term.

Two check readings were given during the next several days. On September 7, Cayce urged Wilma to remain off her feet. On September 14, he stated that improvements were being made and that Wilma might begin to be a little more active, "but not too strenuous for the next several days."

On September 19, a reading stated, "Conditions are not so well as we last had same. Too much activity has caused a bruising through the pelvic area and thus brought on the flow again." Cayce suggested that curettage might be required, and upon a request to do so, named the doctor to perform it. It was done the next day by the physician named in the reading.

On September 27, Cayce began another check reading with a psychic weather report, "It is raining there!" [Wilma later confirmed this.]

The reading indicated that "conditions are progressing, in the main, very satisfactorily." Again he suggested more attention to proper eliminations, the use of a specifically named tonic, and "two or three more osteopathic adjustments . . . not so much now for the pelvic organs as for the head and neck and the drainings from same to the alimentary canal." [Wilma was also having trouble with her ears at this time, although Cayce's office had not been told of this.]

On April 5, 1938, a Cayce reading for Wilma Franklin indicated that she was pregnant. However, said the reading, "Conditions are not yet wholly normal.

Then, there will be the necessity of being very careful during this period; keeping off the feet most of the time, hands out of water to any great extent, keeping the feet very warm—and most of the time when resting, the lower limbs should be a little bit elevated, see?"

Menstrual periods had continued in spite of the pregnancy, and the reading indicated that, should this continue after the third period, hospitalization would be required. Also, said the reading, the womb had dropped—a serious complication. Osteopathic adjustments were recommended, and were outlined specifically.

In a reading on April 20, Cayce said, "Conditions as respecting the attempt to save the body-developments are rather serious. . . . The organs of the pelvis are out of position and in such a state of strain that the fetus forces are causing a drainage that produces irritations, as well as a great deal of pain. It is, of course, close to the third month, as indicated. Hence it becomes the more serious for all conditions."

Wilma was advised to contact Dr. G, a surgeon, and be hospitalized immediately. This was done.

On May 7, Wilma's husband wrote to Edgar Cayce. "Wilma has been getting along fine since Dr. G fixed her up. I was pretty much worried about her for a while. Thanks a million times for the readings."

On May 24, Wilma wrote to Cayce, expressing her own gratitude. She added, "Needless to say, I'm so excited about this coming event of ours that I can hardly realize that it is actually true. I think I'm about straightened out now. . . ."

On June 6, another reading was given. It stated, "While there are disturbing conditions at times, especially at the periods, gestation is being carried on in near to a normal way and manner. . . ." Caution was ordered; Wilma was to walk a great deal, but avoid any strenuous activity. A specific cod liver oil and iron tonic was recommended. In the reading, upon request, Cayce supplied the name of the physician to see Wilma through her confinement, Dr. H.

A letter dated July 21 from Wilma to her mother, who lived in another state, indicated that some rather peculiar things were going on. In the first place, although according to the Cayce readings Wilma was now in her sixth month of pregnancy, no one—including any of the doctors—was convinced she was really pregnant. She continued to have her menstrual periods on schedule, didn't "look pregnant at all," and felt fine, she said.

"Even Dr. H isn't positive," she went on. "He is very interested in the information from 'that fellow Cayce,' as he calls him. He practically asked me to get another reading to 'see what he'll have to say about it. He's done some wonderful things; maybe he can throw some light upon this case.' The quotations are his. He's funny—terribly interested in the readings but doesn't want to appear too much so. He was completely flabbergasted when I told him that I had come to him through advice from a reading from Mr. Cayce. I didn't say anything about my reading the first time I went to him, since I didn't know his ideas on the subject. But during the second visit, while he was trying to make me understand, in a very diplomatic manner, that I was more than likely mistaken about being pregnant and was giving me that pregnancy test to top off his opinion, the conversation gradually came around to the point where I could introduce the subject.

"He remembered Dr. M [a doctor who had worked closely with Cayce in the past] and in that way, finally, I got to the point I wanted. I let him do the talking and he was going strong. He said, 'You know that fellow has really got something; I don't know what, but something.' Said he met him only once, years ago, and knew of several things about him. Says he has been interested for a long time in such subjects and liked to talk about them, but that you just couldn't talk about such things, 'because people will think you're nutty.' He expressed it just that way and it just seemed so odd to hear Dr. H talk like that. He doesn't strike you as a person interested in psychic matters. Anyway, he's interested in my next reading . . ."

In a letter to Edgar Cayce a few days later, Wilma told of her experiences with Dr. H and his attitude toward the readings. "It was while we were waiting for the results from a pregnancy test (an injection in my arm) that I told him I'd had a reading and that it said I was pregnant. He was very much interested and waited enthusiastically for the results of the test. The test *agreed* with what the reading said and he pulled on his nose several times real hard and said, 'Well, it looks like the ole boy is right.' That was the second visit to him. I've been several times since, and he still isn't convinced in his own mind about it. He said, 'Well, if Cayce says you are pregnant, I suppose you are. But you couldn't prove it by me!' "

On July 29, another reading was given for Wilma, in which some questions she had included in her letter to Edgar Cayce were asked. The reading indicated that Wilma's condition seemed good "in many directions. However, if there is the continued strain produced upon the system, as well as upon the fetus—through the drainages from the system through the [menstrual] periods, there will not be allowed normal or nominal developments. . . ." X-rays were suggested, with extreme care to protect the fetus, in order to determine the safety of allowing the pregnancy to continue. "The conditions and the test, from the very natures that have existed, would show that there are not normal conditions, not a normal pregnancy."

In answer to the question concerning how far advanced Wilma's pregnancy was at this time, Cayce said, "The condition is advanced as has been indicated [about six months] but the development of same—as to the proportions and all—is less than a month in size or form, or not more than two months." Rather alarming news for Wilma in *that* reading, we'd say!

Her letter to Edgar Cayce, on August 8, informed him that she had taken the reading to Dr. H. "It was the first one he'd ever seen, and the expression on his face as he read it was an experience! He has felt all along that I'm not pregnant—but allowed for the possibility that he might be wrong. He read it over and over and said finally, 'I just don't know what to make of it. It sounds logical, but I can't understand why I can't locate this evidence if it's there.' "

X-rays, according to Wilma, had been made; they showed nothing. "He gave me a thorough examination, too, and he couldn't find any symptoms of pregnancy. He said, though, that there was only one thing to do and that was to wait and see what developments took place. . . . Dr. H gave me the enclosed questions to ask in my next reading. He admits the possibility of the fetus removing itself in a natural manner if it is not to develop normally. He said that he believes that is what will happen if I really am pregnant, if it hasn't happened already.

"This is the strangest sort of experience. We never dream such things can happen to *us*. And I feel so good physically. Naturally I'm worried, and I tire much more quickly than usual—but aside from that I still feel grand."

The next reading took place on August 11, 1938. It began, "Now, as we find, conditions have not changed since that as last we had here. Under the existing conditions, we find that the interpretation should be rather first by those handling the condition [Wilma's doctors]. For to interpret and then not be assured by their own indications or findings will only make for confusions.

"Conditions are much as has been indicated, as we find. There has been inception, not once but more than once—as has been and is indicated by the blood test, as well as the character and the profusion of activity of the glandular system.

"That there have continued to be first conception, then abortion, then conception and then abortion, has made for the abnormal developments.

"But the construction and the developments must be followed by those handling same [the doctors].

"Ready for questions."

The conductor asked the questions, speaking for Wilma. "Am I still pregnant at this time?"

"At this time still pregnant—about six to ten weeks; and this added to others makes for this shadow that is indicated."

"What is the cause of continual menstruation?"

"Continual abortion!"

"Will the fetus develop in the normal manner?"

"Not until some changes have been made—and there is a retaining and a normal development of the flows of the system for nominal or normal developments."

"How shall we interpret the X-ray picture which we have made?"

"Use the common sense!" Cayce paused for a moment, and then ended the reading with the usual phrase, "We are through."

Wilma wrote to Cayce on August 14: "Thank you again. It is very upsetting, all this, in view of the fact that the doctors think I'm not pregnant. Nothing else showed up in the X-ray. The two shadows I asked him about when I first saw them were, he says, a little gas in the intestines! It shows a shadow about the size of a silver dollar, and a much smaller one a little distance from the larger one. 'Gas in the intestines' it *is*, as far as they're concerned. They think I've tried to *think* myself into a state of pregnancy! Can you imagine?

"I haven't had a chance to show this latest reading to Dr. H. I hope to see him today. It may make a difference in his opinion . . .

"The abortions the reading described were the two very unusual [menstrual] periods which I've experienced, evidently. Dr. H didn't think it important. But I've been in bed each time never less than a week; sometimes ten days to two weeks. That was taking place and I didn't know it!"

Wilma Franklin was indeed pregnant, in spite of what her doctors had to say about it. She miscarried a few weeks later, and there was no question that it was a true miscarriage.

After all her trouble, we are happy to report that, in a letter to Edgar Cayce dated April 3, 1939, Wilma stated, "I have beautiful news. We're expecting a baby in early fall, and are so happy about it. I'm getting on fine and feel grand and am sure there won't be any trouble. However, I'd like to be positive about it and will sincerely appreciate it if you will [give me] a check reading when you can arrange it.

"I haven't been to a doctor yet. I can't help feeling hesitant about them after my experience last summer. I just don't feel very confident about any of them and am sincerely in a quandary as to whether or not to go back to Dr. H. I'd like to ask that in the check reading."

The reading, given on May 9, stated, "As we find, conditions are developing normally.

"There should not be any hindrance towards full, normal development, if there is plenty of exercise taken . . ."

A few osteopathic manipulations were recommended, "not for corrections, other than assisting the body in correcting its new positions—but for relaxing of the system, for the bodily forces to adjust themselves to the development of those conditions with the body." A special cod liver oil and iron supplement was recommended, as well as a calcium preparation.

Concerning Wilma's reluctance to consult the doctor who had attended her before, Cayce said, "The physician we would continue; Dr. H should care for same. While this in some respects offers—mentally—some disturbing conditions, we find that as to abilities, other than Dr. T—there's not a better one in this vicinity; and one that may be relied upon, if all conditions are thoroughly understood."

In answer to specific questions, Cayce replied that the baby was developing normally, and that a maternity supporter should be worn "when the time comes. Fitted by the [osteopath] would be advisable." As to a question about exercise, "Do as has been indicated. Do not overdo, but keep plenty of exercise. Don't try to jump or dance or the like, nor kick up the heels, but plenty of walking, plenty of keeping in the open. . . ."

In a letter dated May 21, Wilma thanked Cayce for the reading. "I'm so grateful to know that I'm getting on so well. Of course I knew, as far as it's possible to know, that everything was progressing normally, but the readings *see* things that the rest of us can't know. . . .

"That's funny, the reading sending me back to Dr. H. He'll like that. He was very pleased at being recommended last summer. I'll explain to him, too, what [the reading] meant by 'disturbing conditions' regarding him. I *do* have confidence in him; I was just peeved at his attitude!"

A check reading was given on August 26. Conditions, said Cayce, were quite normal. "There should be the expectancy, as we find, between the first and the eighteenth of September."

Cayce then gave a weather forecast! "Owing to circumstances as will arise, not of the physical but of natural forces—the weather—it would be better if the body would be in the hospital rather than at home. . . ."

Actually, he missed the date of delivery by some two weeks. The baby, a girl, was born on September 29 with no complications. The weather forecast, however, was completely accurate. The sudden cold snap that occurred while Wilma was in the hospital proved too much for her home heating system, and it broke down!

Wilma's second child, a boy, was also a "Cayce" baby. The reading, given on November 30,1942, indicated that delivery could be expected on July 10 or 11. Cayce's batting average improved with this one; the baby was born on July 16!

It is interesting to note that Wilma had suffered a miscarriage only a month before conceiving this child, who was born eight and half months after the reading was given. So perhaps Cayce's earlier readings, indicating that Wilma's miscarriages were followed almost immediately by other conceptions—a highly unusual situation—were not nearly so farfetched as they might have seemed at the time.

The Case of the Missing Light Ray

Alice Marshall was suffering from a severe mastoid infection. A reading was given on April 21, 1928, which supplied the diagnosis and recommended treatments. Three days later, a check reading was given.

Cayce began, "Yes, we have the body here. This we have had before. Now we find in many ways the body shows improvement from that we have had before; yet there is the indication of reinfection, especially in the area about the soft tissue in the inner ear, and that in the portion just back of ear. Would there have been applied the light ray—that affects the nerve and blood—we would have found a different condition, as we see it."

A letter from the person attending the patient carried the confession that the light ray had indeed been omitted from the treatment because of fear that it would burn the skin. Following the second reading, the light ray was applied. The patient's recovery was swift and complete!

A Case of Poisoning

Janet Baylor, at 8:20 in the morning of January 21, 1940, was extremely sick.

It had begun at about 8:30 the night before, with all the signs of acute indigestion or food poisoning. The first attack of pain and diarrhea had resulted in fainting. About ten o'clock the family physician had been called; he had administered a hypodermic injection which had relieved Janet for a few hours. The second attack had then come, worse than the first, and the doctor had returned to give her a second injection. At that time he had advised immediate surgery for what he felt was locked bowels. A third attack, he said, might prove fatal.

Janet had refused surgery—at least for the time being. But since six o'clock that morning she had been vomiting about every twenty minutes. Her father went to the Cayce home to sit in on the emergency reading, which was given at 8:20 A.M.

Mrs. Cayce, conducting the reading, said, "You will give the physical condition of this body at the present time; giving the cause of existing conditions, also suggestions for help and relief of this body, answering questions that may be asked."

"Yes," said Cayce. "We have the body. This we have had before.

"As we find, the acute conditions arise from the effects of a poison—Pyrene.

"From this activity the acute indigestion as produced through the alimentary canal has caused an expansion of, and a blocking in, the colon areas.

"As we find in the present, we would apply hot castor oil packs continuously for two and a half to three hours.

"Then have an enema, gently given. It would be well that some oil be in the first enema; that is, the oil alone given first, see? Olive oil would be better for this; about half a pint; so that there may be the relaxing.

"And then give the enema with body temperature water, using a heaping teaspoonful of salt and a level teaspoonful of baking soda to the quart and a half of water. Give this gently at first, but eventually—that is, after the period when there has been the ability for a movement—use the colon tube.

"Then we would take internally—after the oil packs and the enema—a tablespoonful of olive oil.

"This, as we find, should relieve the tensions and relax the body sufficiently to remove the disturbing conditions. . . ."

At the end of Cayce's instructions, he was asked to supply the source of the poison. "Pyrene," he said. "Pyrene—on the beans!"

This was later explained by Janet. She had been visiting her mother the day before the reading, a few hours before the illness struck. In late afternoon she had fixed herself a raw vegetable cocktail, using her mother's new juicer, and one of the ingredients was a handful of "some beautiful green string beans."

There were no laboratory tests to confirm that Pyrene had been the cause. And it is not clear how Pyrene—trade name for a carbon tetrachloride preparation used in fire extinguishers—might have found its way to the green beans consumed by Janet Baylor. Possibly it was through some industrial accident, or an accident during shipping of the vegetables.

At any rate, if Cayce was correct in his reading, it had been enough of a dose to make Janet a very sick girl. From her symptoms, there was little doubt that it was a true poison, and the lengthy recuperative period indicates that it was a serious one. But she did avoid surgery, and she did get well.

"Treat the Cause, Not the Effect"

The case of Mary Lewis is one of the most extraordinary, and one of the best-documented, to be found in the Cayce files.

To fully appreciate the value of Cayce's clairvoyance in this instance, it is necessary to know a little of Mary's case history.

A schoolteacher in New York City, Mary had gone to Florida in the fall of 1935, at the age of thrity-two. In March, 1936, she was discovered to be suffering from advanced tuberculosis. She spent the next three months in a Miami hospital, during which time pneumothorax surgery (artificial collapse of the lung by the injection of air into the pleural cavity) was performed on each lung. In June, 1936, she returned to New York and entered Bellevue Hospital. Pneumothorax treatments were continued. Sputum tests indicated the tuberculosis was still active. An X-ray report in July indicated, according to the attending physician, "about twenty-five percent collapse of upper lobe of right lung. Adhesions at the apex. The cavity below clavical not collapsed. The uncollapsed portion of the lung shows nodular infiltration, fibrosis and coalescence of the lesions, most marked in the middle third of the lung. Similar changes in lower half of the left lung."

In September, Mary was transferred to Sea View Hospital in Long Island. Pneumothorax continued; surgery was considered by several of the specialists attending the case. An X-ray report on September 2 indicated, "Bilateral pneumothorax present. There is a nominal amount of fluid in the right base and extensive collapse of the lung, the apex of which is still suspended from the upper chest by numerous band adhesions. There is a large cavity in upper lobe, immediately beneath site of adhesions. There is a peripheral collapse of left lung which shows no definite excavated lesion, but there does appear to be an acinous nodose seeding throughout the lower two-thirds."

At the end of September, Mary entered Manhattan General Hospital in New York City, where surgery, intrapleural pneumolysis on the right lung, was performed. She remained there, confined to bed, for six weeks. Pneumothorax treatments were discontinued in the left lung but continued in the right. X-rays following surgery indicated that the cavity, due to pressure, was closed to some extent. Adhesions and extreme pressure on the right lung had pushed the sternum and heart toward the left side of Mary's body, crowding the left lung. Breathing was extremely difficult, and any movement of the body was nearly impossible.

By November, Mary's finances were exhausted, and her emotional state was poor. She returned to her parents' home in Virginia. Placed immediately in a tuberculosis sanitarium nearby, she remained there until a few days before the Cayce reading was given on March 12, 1938. At the time of her release from the sanitarium she was told that her tuberculosis had been arrested, but that she would have to continue pneumothorax in the right lung indefinitely. She was to spend nearly all her time in bed; and the doctor attending her warned her parents that Mary would most likely be bedridden for the rest of her life. He expected to have her back in the sanitarium soon—possibly to stay for good.

Her parents had heard of Edgar Cayce, and arranged for a reading. Mary was allowed to attend the session; but she asked specifically that Cayce not be told anything about her case before the reading.

He began the reading by getting immediately to the point. "Now, as we find, the conditions and the causes of same are rather specific. The *effects* of the disturbances have been the more often called the *causes*, rather than that which is producing same.

"These are affectations to the pulmonary circulation and the associations of the activities of the disturbances there upon the rest of the system.

"However, as we find, the causes arise from pressures which exist in the cerebrospinal system; and—through the deflected nerve portions of the system—have thickened tissue, producing pressure upon the capsule of the lung.

"Thus we find the disturbance and inflammation caused, rather than infectious forces arising *only* through being predisposed to disturbance through the pressures. . . ."

Cayce then proceeded to give a complete rundown of Mary's condition, including information about the blood, the nerve system and, finally, clinical details concerning the state of her throat, bronchi, larynx and lungs.

One of the most important statements in the reading, however, was, "This was caused first by the inhalation of foreign substance, dust and the like. Then with the pressure produced by an injury in the area indicated, there was caused—or begun—the disturbance there."

Detailed instructions were given regarding diet, exercise, osteopathic manipulations and rest. In addition, Mary was to use the apple brandy keg so often specified in Cayce readings for TB.

"First, have prepared a cask or keg—gallon or gallon and half, oak, charred inside. If it is a gallon keg, put in same half a gallon of apple brandy. Not apple jack but *pure apple brandy*. Keep this tightly corked but close to where it will produce evaporation. Prepare so that the gases may be inhaled; not the brandy but the gas *from* the brandy; inhaled through the mouth into the bronchi, larynx and lungs. Do this at least two or three or four times a day."

With faithful attention to all the instructions given in the reading, said Cayce, "We should, within six to eight months, be entirely free of the disturbance for this body."

When the reading was over, Mary talked for a while with Gladys Davis, who had taken stenographic notes of all that had been said by Cayce.

"It's incredible!" she exclaimed. "I haven't thought of it for years, but I know exactly what injury Mr. Cayce was referring to—the one that led to my TB. You see, about fifteen years ago I fell from a tree and hurt my back, up near the shoulders. For over a week I was in such pain that I had to stop teaching. I went to an osteopath and had a couple of treatments. The pain left, and I returned to my job. I was bothered by it for some time afterwards, but after about a year and a half, the trouble seemed to clear up."

She paused, and began to tick off some dates. "Yes. Eleven years after that accident, I was in charge of a settlement house in New York City. I worked outdoors in the recreational field a lot of the time. I was exposed to the dusts of the playground, changing weather conditions and poorly ventilated classrooms.

"That's probably when I breathed in the foreign substance, like dust, that Cayce talked about in the reading. I was in that job for two years. Then I went to Florida, where I found out that I had TB."

Finding the apple brandy keg required a month; it is, after all, a rather unique item! However, one was procured, and the treatments began. On June 6, a second reading was given, in which Cayce stated that much improvement in the general condition had been made. He altered his instructions somewhat; due to the excellence of osteopathic manipulations that had been made, he said, these could now be cut down from twice a week to about twice a month.

Following this check reading, no further pneumothorax treatments were ever required for Mary Lewis—after only two months of actual treatment under the Cayce regime!

In August, a third reading cautioned against too much activity; by now, Mary was feeling so well that she actually had to be restrained from overdoing things!

In December, Cayce gave a fourth reading for Mary, in which he said that "conditions are much improved. Much lung tissue has now been renewed, and is working well—even aids [the body] rather than being a detriment to it."

Continuing, he said, "The keg is as life itself. When it is prepared again, rinse it out first, you see, before it is refilled again. Rinse with warm—not hot, but warm—water, so that the accumulations from the distillation or evaporation of the properties are removed, and there is less of that influence or force which arises from the acids that come from such infusions." As always, there was no detail of treatment too unimportant to be fully explained.

The next reading was given on January 4, 1940, less than two years after Mary's first reading. Cayce reported that although "to be sure, the weaknesses and the inclinations as yet exist, as indicated by the tendencies of portions of the right lung to settle . . ." there were no "live tubercular forces through the system, or through the lung area. There are no more adhesions of the pleura."

At this time, Mary reported that she had seen the doctor who had released her from the sanitarium a year and a half earlier, expecting to have her back as a bed patient within a matter of weeks. His reaction to her appearance, she said, was one of amazement. "He asked if I had got religion, since that would be the only explanation he could find for the continued and marked improvement!" X-rays and tests, of course, confirmed the conditions Cayce had described in his reading.

In November, 1941, the final reading was given for Mary Lewis. "The conditions are good," reported Cayce. "While there are still indications of affected areas, there are not indications of the areas being active."

Mrs. Cayce, conducting the reading, said, "Please read the last X-ray, which I hold in my hand."

Cayce unhesitatingly did so. "We find that this indicates there is not active tissue in the area that *has* been the disturbing center; that there is not *any* adherence in any of the wall of the pleura; that there is a good flow of circulation throughout all portions of the lungs themselves save in that one particular area." [Accuracy of Cayce's clairvoyant reading of this X-ray: 100 percent, according to the attending physician.]

Cayce reported that Mary would now be able to return to work—so long as it did not overtire her body; preferably she should work out-of-doors.

Reports from relatives to A.R.E. tell what has happened to Mary in the years since her readings were given.

In 1952, her mother reported that, during 1942, Mary had used the keg ". . . mostly on those occasions when she had a cold. Her health was pretty good and she was enthusiastic about her progress. At about this time she met Mr. Andrews, and was instrumental in getting a reading for him. As suggested in his reading, he took one or two osteopathic treatments. After that, he discredited the value of both the treatments and their source.

"In 1943 they were married. By that time, my daughter had discontinued all treatments outlined in her readings. I was very much concerned about her, because I had heard that she and her husband drank occasionally. Financial difficulties gradually developed, and by 1945, my daughter had turned to strenuous outdoor work to help with the income. As the strain of their marriage relationship increased, they both resorted more frequently to alcohol. My daughter became very nervous, irritable and neurotic.

"In 1947 she had a cyst removed from her rectum. About two years later, a second operation was performed for the same condition. She became extremely thin and her face looked pale and drawn. Eventually her marriage ended in a separation. And yet, none of these hardships caused TB to return.

"Today, while she is still a neurotic addicted to drink, she has nevertheless good resistance. She has gained weight and looks well. I am indeed grateful that, all things considered, at present she is free from tuberculosis."

Later reports to A.R.E. from Mary's sister indicate that, although other illnesses have been experienced through the years, there has been no recurrence of tuberculosis. In 1967, she said Mary is quite well. She is no longer bothered by a drinking problem, and her mental attitude is excellent.

A Question Not Asked, But Answered

Kim Albright, just two years old, had been sick for the past week. Her parents wrote to Edgar Cayce, requesting a reading. They volunteered no information concerning her condition, and submitted only two questions: (1) What is causing the digestive disturbances, and (2) How can we protect her from the infantile paralysis epidemic now raging in this area?

Cayce, in his reading, stated, "From outside influences we find that pressures have been caused in the cerebrospinal system; especially in the areas of the second and third dorsal and third cervical, which has caused some deflection to the activity of the stomach, as well as a deflection in the auditory forces—which is indicated in the speaking voice.

"This should be corrected, else we may find—while it may be corrected in a manner by the body's own growth—it would leave weaknesses and tendencies to be met later on, in the digestive system as well as in the abilities of enunciation. . . ."

So Cayce had detected, at a distance of some nine hundred miles, that this child—who had been talking quite well since the age of eighteen months—had suddenly developed a severe case of stuttering!

Cayce was asked, in the reading, "Was this pressure from an injury, or just what?"

He replied, "From the outside, apparently from a wrenching or hitting—or wrenching of the spine. Of course, it was very slight, but it has been sufficient to deflect even the emptying of the duodenum."

This reading was given in September, 1941. Upon seeing it, the child's aunt recalled that in June, while visiting friends in another town, Kim had fallen off a couch, "right on her head. She didn't seem badly hurt, so we didn't pay any particular attention to possible injury. Probably that's what jammed all those vertebrae mentioned in the reading."

Osteopathic treatments were started at once, and the child recovered completely.

Too Long a Wait

Much more than telepathy was at work when Edgar Cayce, at Virginia Beach, gave a reading for Don Collier, a small boy in an Ohio hospital, in October, 1942.

The case had been diagnosed as polio. This seemed the most probable answer to the doctors, who had noted some paralysis on the right side of the boy's body for about a month.

Cayce, however, said, "These are very serious disturbances; a form of strep that, unless this is allayed, will attack the brain or nerve [spinal] cord structure itself."

The child's temperature at the time of the reading, said Cayce, was 103° [This was confirmed as being exactly right.]

Cayce gave his instructions, which included—of all things—a crushed grape poultice to be applied over the abdomen.

Apparently a good deal of precognition was involved in this reading. In addition to the remark about the strep eventually attacking the brain or nerve cord, Cayce said, "*If* there is improvement, then we may give further instructions on Friday or Saturday." Unfortunately, the child died later that day, too soon for Cayce's "prescriptions" to be tried.

The postmortem disclosed that the case was not polio. It was a form of strep that led to meningitis—in other words, the germ did attack the spinal cord and brain. Perhaps, if the doctors had known what the disease really was, if the reading had just been requested a little sooner. . . .

A Word for the Skeptics

It is easy to find reasons for the high percentage of "cures" among the Cayce files. Certainly there were some people who were suffering from psychosomatic ailments, or even overactive imaginations, who needed only to believe that Cayce could make them well in order to *become* well. The readings themselves, over and over, indicated the importance of mental attitudes and emotions as they relate to bodily health.

But then you come across correspondence such as this, a report from a woman given to A.R.E. in 1952, referring to her husband's physical reading in July, 1943, and you begin to wonder.

The reading began, "As we find, these conditions have gradually grown to be of a very serious nature. The crystallization of the segments, or the cartilaginous forces in the segments of the spine, have become gradually so taut, from the accumulations because of lack of eliminations from the body, that this stiffness in the lumbar and lower dorsal area is almost static. . . ."

Although the reading was five pages long, no name was given to the ailment. As so often appears in the Cayce readings, it was not names that mattered, but manners of treatment. These Cayce gave in this reading, in complete detail, with some criticism of the way the case had been handled by others.

At any rate, this is how it all came out, in the words of the wife. "The doctors said there was a parathyroid tumor and tuberculosis of the kidneys. Later X-rays revealed that this was not correct. [The doctors] indicated that there was no hope, and that my husband would eventually turn to jelly. There was nothing they could do, they said. They suggested that he take aspirin.

"I knew that the things Mr. Cayce gave would work, but my husband did not. I literally overrode his objections in carrying out the treatments.

"My husband was not at all keen on the treatments, but I continued to give them to him just as outlined, for I was sure they would work.

"He continued to improve, although after 1945 he only kept up the treatments occasionally and paid attention to the general diet that had been outlined for him in the readings.

"When the doctors would meet him on the street, later, they would turn white with the shock of realizing that he had not died. They asked him to come in so they could check him and see what the changes were. He did not want to do this, and I did not encourage him to do so, because there were so many unpleasant memories connected with his previous illness.

"He is now enjoying the best of health—boating, swimming, dancing and carrying on his business."

At the time of this report, this man—who didn't really believe the Cayce readings could do much for him—was sixty-four years old and still going strong, nine years after he'd been given up for nearly dead.

This brings up a thought-provoking question. If he had no faith in Cayce's work, and followed the readings only because his wife insisted on it—then what, pray tell, made him well?

It's the Attitude . . .

Leona Masters, after reading Tom Sugrue's biography of Edgar Cayce, *There Is A River,* in June, 1944, wrote to Cayce for help. "I have been in three hospitals and treated by many doctors, but only one doctor has made a suggestion as to what he thinks it may be. He said that my symptoms came nearer to indicating disseminated lupus erythematosus than anything else, and that if such is the case, the only thing that medical science can propose is rest, and keep out of the sun. I've been resting and keeping out of the sun ever since I went to the hospital in November, but the disease is still with me. At the last hosptial the doctor said that I did not have that disease, but they didn't have any idea what disease I *did* have.

"The illness began in October, and I was in bed from November to April, and then spent the month of May in bed. I am stronger now and have no fever at present, but the disfiguring eruption is all over my face and neck. . . ."

The letter, of course, was not given to Edgar Cayce prior to his reading. Nevertheless, he gave a complete and accurate description of Leona Masters' affliction, and added much that was not implied by anything stated in her letter.

One statement in particular is worth noting. At the end of the prescribed treatment, he added, "These, as we find, offer the better prospects. It's the attitude the body takes. Don't attempt to shield self from anxieties but know there are truths, there are conditions one must conform to for bettered improvements through the body, as well as the applications to bring better conditions."

Now, why would Edgar Cayce give advice such as this?

A clue to the desperate need for it came with Leona's next letter to him. She sent a detailed description of what she had been through, emotionally, over the past several months. Her husband had been in a prison camp. She had finally been able to get him back home, but he was not normal mentally.

She said, "The worry, the strain, the constant watching resulted, I am sure, in my becoming ill with what the doctors considered an unknown disease. Can you believe that not one doctor, of all those who have treated me in three hospitals, has ever asked me if I were worried or had any problems? Since I'd covered up in front of my own family for my husband, I couldn't reveal his condition to a doctor, even though I felt that by talking about the conditions I'd give them a clue that would lead to my recovery. Each time I went to the hospital it was after a fresh shock supplied by my husband. Your reading did take into consideration the mental strain that I was living under—although, as I've said, no doctor ever thought of that angle."

The treatments that Cayce recommended, and the release this woman gained in having someone, somewhere, understand her problems led to a complete cure.

Always the Attitude . . .

Leona Masters was grateful to Edgar Cayce, and profited by his spiritual as well as his physical advice. In contrast we offer the case of Alma Long.

Alma also was troubled by a skin condition. She lived near the Cayce offices, and thus was able to sit in the reading room and listen to what Cayce had to say.

Cayce's secretary reported, "The girl made her appointment for the reading by phone and only appeared at the A.R.E. office a few minutes before the appointed time, talked to me a few moments concerning questions and was ushered into the 'reading room.' It was the first and only time Edgar Cayce saw her. Of course, as usual, he made no conscious 'examination' of the patient."

The problem was clearly outlined in the reading. "There has been a subluxation produced in the eighth and ninth dorsal center, by a strain or a wrench or a hurt. This has caused poor circulation through the areas of the pelvis and from the activities these infectious forces have arisen. These have produced in the lymph circulation a nerve tension and then the body-mind has indicated an unfavorable reaction here. These have brought about nerve tensions which produce, on various portions of the body, a rash, which causes great irritation to the body . . ."

After a full description of treatments to be followed, he added, "Keep as constructive as possible. Don't ever condemn self; don't condemn others! Forgive as you would be forgiven. Keep sweet!"

The readings for Leona Masters and for Alma Long were both given during the month of July, 1944. Both women had come to him as a result of reading *There Is A River*. Their attitudes, however, were quite dissimilar.

There is evidence, in the note from the osteopath who treated Alma, that not much attention was paid to Cayce's spiritual advice. Said the doctor, "My provisional diagnosis was cystitis, pyelitis, dermatitis. I gave her six treatments and had poor cooperation. I am unable to contact her for results. . . . The subluxations were found in the eighth and ninth dorsal." (This, you will recall, is exactly as Cayce had described the situation.)

Precognition — Or What?

In January, 1925, the Cayces were living in Dayton, Ohio. However, on January 16 they were visiting friends in New York City. Around midnight, Cayce was giving a series of readings before a group of people who had assembled to watch him work.

At 12:15 A.M., which would make it early morning of January 17, he finished the readings, and was being given the suggestion to awaken. Instead, he began to speak with unusual urgency.

"Lorraine Whittier. Chicago, Illinois. Now, in this condition that has arisen in the body from the disarrangement in the pelvic organs, especially those in the false pelvis, we find these need attention at once, through that condition as given, for the operation on the body, else there will be in nineteen days the setting up of an infection that will bring destructive forces to the whole system. The alleviation of the pressure has been effective to the body, but this attempt to lift that heavier than the body should have attempted, under the existing conditions, has brought about this condition, or falling more of the organs in the pelvis, and the rupture of the left Fallopian tube, and these conditions should be attended to at once.

"We are through for the present."

This was not the first reading he had given for Lorraine Whittier. However, this was the first one he had given for her *without a specific request!*

The Cayces did not return to Dayton for several days. When they arrived there, they found a letter from Lorraine Whittier containing specific questions she wanted answered via a reading.

Her letter was dated January 18, 1925—the day *after* Cayce had given the reading! And yet the reading had answered every question asked in the letter.

Reading From Physical Surroundings

The fact that Edgar Cayce, in trance, could attune his unconscious mind with that of another, and with such exceptional results, is remarkable enough. But consider this: on a number of occasions, when the subject of his reading was away from the location specified in the reading suggestion, Cayce went right ahead and gave his reading anyway—based on impressions from the physical surroundings normally associated with the person!

Such a case is that of Helen Barbour, who was dying of breast and lung cancer. Her friend, Frances Marks, after obtaining permission from Helen's sister to do so, requested a Cayce reading for her. She gave no information about Helen except her home address and the fact that Helen did not know the serious nature of her illness—which, of course, she did not name. When told that the reading would take place at 3:45 P.M. on February 8, 1934, Frances informed the Cayce office that at that time Helen would be away from her apartment, and gave them the two possible locations at which she might then be found.

Accordingly, when the reading suggestion was given to Edgar Cayce, it included Helen's home address, and indicated that at present she would be found either at Radio City or the Medical Center in New York City.

Cayce began speaking. "Yes, we have rather the impressions from the home surroundings, as we have transient conditions as respecting the locating of the body-individual." [Frances Marks explained, afterwards, that Helen had indeed been in transit at that moment.]

The reading proved accurate in every detail, beginning with the first statement. "There are those conditions existent wherein there is tissue in lung, in breast, involved; from conditions where they in their very activity are *creative* from that they produce in the system, or are of the malignant nature—thus not only sapping the life force but filling the blood supply through the character of the condition or the nature of the bacilli so involved throughout the system."

Included in this reading were many provable statements of fact. At times, Helen suffered excruciating pain. Only hypnotics or narcotics were being administered (which, said Cayce, "is to gradually allow the body to lose its resistance or ability for resuscitation"). Also, Cayce indicated, the treatments he outlined in such complete detail "could, and should, be applied by the nurse in charge." Helen was under twenty-four-hour nursing care, and Cayce seemed to know this.

We wish we could report that Cayce's treatments were followed, and that Helen got well, or at least was spared some needless suffering before her death. Unfortunately, such was not the case. As so often happened, her physician refused to cooperate in any way, and continued to give her the only thing medical science had to offer in 1934 for a person with terminal cancer: pain-relieving drugs.

A similar type of reading—that is, one given from the physical surroundings, rather than the body—had taken place a few months before.

It was for a man who told Cayce's office that at the time of the reading, between three and four o'clock in the afternoon of December 5, 1933, he would be on board a dredge in a shipyard in Jacksonville, Florida. If not in the shipyard, he'd be somewhere on the St. John's River near Jacksonville.

As it happened, the man forgot about his appointment, and at the time of the reading was busy in a conference some twenty miles away.

This didn't seem to disturb the reading. Cayce began it by saying, "We have the body associations with the dredge, but we don't find them together." He then proceeded to diagnose the man's back trouble. "The segments in the eighth, ninth and tenth dorsals show a tendency for settling close together, as do the activities of the muscles and the tendons about the sacral and coccyx region.

"These subluxations are not as lesions, as yet, but are rather of the nature that produces, through these areas at times, a dull aching across the hips, through the right side, low down in the caecum area. At other times a heaviness and pain through the upper portion of the body, under the shoulder blades, and a tendency for the mental body to be easily aggravated—or nothing fits just exactly right—making for a lesion in the hypogastric and pneumogastric area, or third and fourth cervicals.

"What areas, then need adjustment? In the eighth, ninth and tenth dorsals. Relaxations in the lumbar or sacral and coccyx areas."

This man, of course, had not told Cayce anything concerning his condition prior to the reading. He was amazed by the accuracy with which Cayce had described his symptoms.

He took the reading to an osteopath in Jacksonville. As he reported the experience later, "I went right down to her office and said, 'I'd like you to give me an examination. But before you do, I have a letter here I'd like you to read. I want you to read this with an open mind, no prejudice—just pick it up and read it. Don't allow yourself to be influenced by what you read. Then check my body and see how close this comes to what you find according to your science of osteopathy.'

"So she read it and said, 'Well, I've never seen anything like this before.' I then lay on the table and she went down my spine and checked each vertebra. Finally she said, 'It is one hundred percent correct. I find his description is exactly the condition existent.'

"In other words, she found the tautness particularly in the eighth, ninth, and tenth dorsals; it was very pronounced, so that there was no guesswork. Dr. W was astounded when she realized that Edgar Cayce had given that diagnosis from Virginia Beach with me in Jacksonville—and twenty miles away from where I was supposed to be keeping the appointment for him to examine my body. She was actually knocked out; she'd never heard of anything like that."

Osteopathic treatments completely cleared up the trouble.

The man stated, "From that experience I am convinced that we do leave a part of ourselves in places we occupy, say over a period of months, or days.

"There was nothing in that room outwardly indicative of me. My clothes were in a steel locker on the side. There was nothing of me there except the bed I slept on, and, as a matter of fact, the bed had been changed that day. Yet the subconscious picked it up and could tell where the trouble was in the body that occupied that room, even though I had been gone from it since six o'clock that morning. Edgar Cayce gave the reading at three-thirty in the afternoon."

A third case which comes to mind is one that occurred in September, 1929. A woman in New York City had requested a reading, and the time had been set for it.

The readings were delayed that day, however, and by the time Cayce got to it the woman had left her home. He gave it anyway, beginning with, "Now, we do not find the body—but those impressions and *surroundings* of same we find here. . . ."

There is nothing in the reading to indicate that it was not as accurate as it would have been if the woman had been in her home. However, her physical problems were attributed to nervousness and mental attitudes rather than to any organic disturbance.

Perhaps the woman was insulted by this, or somewhat disappointed by the diagnosis. At any rate, she wrote to Cayce in protest. "I fail to see where you could give a reading of my 'surroundings' and expect me to follow suggestions. Therefore, I think I am entitled to another reading . . ."

That Cayce, in Virginia Beach, could put himself to sleep and read her unconscious mind—that she could accept, just as if everyone could do the same thing every day. That he could diagnose her ailments and suggest treatment for them while in this state—that, also, she could accept. But that he could do all this while she was absent from her usual surroundings? Ridiculous!

Human nature—how very wonderful it is!

How Accurate Were the Physical Readings?

In illustrating the clairvoyance of Edgar Cayce as shown in the physical readings, it may appear that we have chosen only those cases in which there was some degree of success, if not *total* success. This has not been deliberate.

However, we necessarily chose those cases in which there was some later contact with the patient, or with the patient's doctor, for these not only bear out the accuracy of the readings, but also provide the most interesting study. There were many readings given for people who were never heard from again. In such cases, it is impossible to determine the accuracy of the readings concerning diagnosis; and it is equally impossible to determine whether or not the treatments were followed and, if they were, whether or not they were helpful.

Of course there were failures. There were times, as we have indicated earlier, when Cayce would put himself into trance, and receive the suggestion from the conductor of the reading, and then lie mute, unable to furnish any information at all. (In most cases, as we've said, later readings would be obtained.) No doubt there were some occasions on which the information received by Cayce didn't apply to the patient—or at least didn't appear to apply to the patient.

As an example of this latter contingency, we might mention one man who was given a reading which indicated that he showed the beginnings of a disturbing and extremely serious blood disorder.

"Poppycock!" he exclaimed. "I just had a thorough checkup, and there's nothing wrong with my blood." He demanded, and received, return of the small fee he'd paid for the reading.

A couple of years later, in the course of checking accuracy of the readings through follow-up letters to people who had been given them, the Cayce office contacted this man's home by mail.

The reply came from the man's wife. "I must answer your questionnaire for my husband. You see, he died six months ago—of leukemia."

The remarkable accuracy of the Edgar Cayce readings, at least those given in connection with physical problems, was confirmed by a survey conducted some years ago by Sherwood Eddy for use in his book, *You Will Survive After Death.*[1]

Mr. Eddy contacted a number of physicians who had treated patients according to the readings. In experience, they ranged all the way from one who had treated five Cayce patients to one who handled well over a hundred.

Concerning accuracy of diagnosis, estimates were all between 80 and 100 percent correct. Averaged out, this figure comes to a surprising 91 percent.

Concerning treatment, responses again indicated a range of from 80 to 100 percent showing good results. But nearly every physician reported that, where recommended treatments were followed faithfully, there was improvement in *all* cases, and astounding improvement in some. The only failure, according to one respondent, was in the area of cancer.

Considering the fact that a great many people came to Cayce as a last resort, after orthodox medicine had nothing more to offer them, it is hard to believe that the consensus showed nearly 100 percent improvement, if not complete cure!

And Tomorrow We May Discover . . .

There are indications throughout the physical readings that in many ways Cayce was well ahead of his time.

Certainly in the area of psychosomatic medicine Cayce was a ground-breaker. We couldn't begin to cite the number of cases in which proper mental attitudes were stressed, for they were an integral part of the Cayce philosophy, "Mind is the Builder." To Cayce, emotions and mental distress were as much a part of physical illness as any other factor. Just as poor mental attitudes could cause ill health, positive and healthy attitudes could result in good—or at least better—health.

"For what we think and what we eat—combined together—make what we are, physically and mentally," said Cayce in a reading given in 1934.

For an eleven-year-old girl in 1943, he said, "But this treatment should be done systematically, expectantly, not doubting! For what ye ask in His name, believing, and thyself living, ye have already."

[1] Published 1950 by Holt, Rinehart & Winston

For a patient suffering from cancer, Cayce once said, "Keep a constructive attitude ever in the prayerful manner." For another cancer patient he said, "The mental attitude has as much to do with the physical reactions as illness in the body."

Anger, said Cayce, "is certainly poison to the system. This should be a warning for every human."

"To be sure," he said in a reading for a young man, "attitudes oft influence the physical conditions of the body. No one can hate his neighbor and not have stomach or liver trouble. No one can be jealous and allow the anger of same and not have upset digestion or heart disorder. Neither of these disorders is present here, and yet those attitudes have much to do with the accumulations which have become gradually . . . tendencies towards neuritic-arthritic reactions. . . . "

We do not mean to imply that Edgar Cayce alone was concerned with the relationship between emotions and physical disorders, or that the concept of psychosomatic illness is new. It is not. But it has been only within the last few decades that medicine has begun to look at the *whole* person, just as Edgar Cayce did in his readings, rather than concern itself merely with one or more malfunctioning organs. This is a great advance, but it also brings a galaxy of complications to the business of determining the cause of any particular disease.

For example: as if the matter of solving the terrible problem of cancer in humans were not difficult enough, there is now evidence that emotions may also play a part in causing it.

This was brought out at a three-day conference sponsored by the New York Academy of Sciences held in New York in May, 1968. One report concerned a study of several hundred cancer patients conducted by a University of Rochester medical team, which strongly suggests that inner feelings of hopelessness and helplessness, caused by the death or separation of a loved one, seem somehow linked to the incidence of cancer.

In addition to this evidence, a New York psychologist conducted in-depth interviews among a group of 500 cancer patients and a group of 500 individuals with no known physical illness. According to this psychologist, the cancer patients' lives were characterized by early loss which brought pain and feelings of desertion, loneliness and even feelings of guilt and self-condemnation.

The conference chairman, Dr. Clauss Bahnson, professor of psychiatry at Jefferson Medical College in Philadelphia, reported that his studies have shown that cancer is most likely to occur in people who are unable to "discharge" their emotions following the loss of a loved one. These unexpressed emotions, said Dr. Bahnson, seem to cause changes in the body's central nervous system which can lower resistance to disease. There was general agreement among many attending the conference that cancer seems to occur most often in those whose immune defenses are down.

Psychosomatic illness, however, was only one area in which the Cayce readings seem extremely advanced for their time.

Polio, now that we have vaccines to prevent it, is on its way out. But during the years the Cayce readings were given, it was a dreaded disease that took a tremendous toll in terms of bodily health, or life itself.

Here, in part, is what Edgar Cayce had to say about polio in a reading given in August, 1936. "From the very nature of the condition, the indications are as a whole that it, the inflammation produced, is of the emunctory and lymph circulation. Hence it is infectious as well as being able to be carried by persons, or it is a carrier disease, also.

"And it arises in the individual from the conditions that exist from what may be termed body infection or bodily-infectious conditions.

"When conditions are at a balance in a body where there is that effluvium thrown off through the circulation and the activity of the superficial circulation, these [skin areas] become irritated mostly by lack of perfect cleanliness. The infectious forces entering are also enabled to do so by the depleting in those particles or effluvia of the blood itself. Which [means that they] attack, then, the mucous membranes of throat, eyes, mouth and nasal passages, but may also be absorbed by the emunctory centers from the groin, under the arm, the knees, the elbow.

"These are the sources, then, these are the manners, then, of the infection, of the infected condition that may arise, whether from contact or from the air.

"As we find, then, this is of a glandular inception, or of a type as indicated where there may be many in a household [exposed to the germ] and only a few affected. [This indicates] that the glands of some are more active than the glands of others."

As a preventive against polio, Cayce's recommendation was the use of a form of iodine developed through independent research aided by study of the Cayce readings. It was not to be taken internally while any other drug was being taken.

As a polio preventive, this iodine preparation was to be used in sponge baths, "for the elders, for the nurse, or for those about [the polio patient] . . . especially around the arms, the groin and such portions of the body. [Use] a spray of a similar 50 percent solution of commercial strength for throat, nasal passages and the like. And the taking of same internally by those that apparently have been exposed to the conditions—one to two minims morning and evening, in periods, and then a rest period, and then take it again . . ."

In 1962, a news report told of a study which seemed to indicate some antipolio properties in the conch, a large sea snail eaten extensively by people in the Bahamas.

According to this report, there had been only fifteen cases of polio in the Bahamas during the preceding ten years. Had the incidence corresponded with the rate of incidence in the United States during that same time, there would have been 177 cases there.

On the island of Bimini, the children begin eating the conch—raw, in salads, fried, in stews, etc.—from the time they stop nursing. On Nassau, the conches are eaten only occasionally. It was on Nassau that most of the fifteen cases of polio occurred.

The report contained the additional information that recent research had indicated certain antipolio qualities in the juice of abalone. Abalone, as well as conches, are of course rich in iodine. Although this is not proof of the accuracy of Cayce's pronouncements on the subject of polio, for there may be other factors involved of which we have no knowledge, we believe it merits further study.

Then there's the case of an eighteen-year-old boy suffering from leukemia, who was given a series of Cayce readings in 1941.

Among the remarks on diet, which according to the readings was of paramount importance in treating this patient, Cayce made an exceptionally interesting statement. "Include as much orange juice as may be easily assimilated by the body; preferably the Florida grown and tree-ripened fruit. This supplies the elements needed."

In an article in *Saturday Review* of June 1, 1968,[1] there is a statement by the author, Solomon Garb, M.D., concerning evidence that a relative shortage of ascorbic acid (Vitamin C) in the bodies of leukemia patients may be the cause of some of the more distressing symptoms of the disease. According to Dr. Garb, recent research indicates that leukemic cells may take up all the available ascorbic acid in the body, leaving so little of it in the plasma and tissues that the patient develops the symptoms of scurvy. Apparently normal doses of ascorbic acid are not enough; Dr. Garb suggests that experimental treatment with massive doses of ascorbic acid might well relieve some of the most distressing symptoms of leukemia. He thinks it might even prolong the victim's life.

Oranges, of course, are rich in Vitamin C.

And then there's the matter of coffee. This was often recommended in the readings to be taken not simply as a drink, but as food.

Said one reading, "For the food value and the proper strengthening, coffee should be taken without either cream or sugar." Said another, "Coffee taken properly is a food; that is, without cream or milk."

In *Rx Health* magazine for February, 1964, there was reported that, as a result of biological analyses, coffee has been shown to contain appreciable amounts of the B vitamin, niacin, as well as small amounts of other B vitamins. It contains, as well, the minerals sodium, calcium, iron and fluorine. Demitasse coffee was said to contain from 45. to 46.5 mg. of niacin per 100 grams of coffee. Further, four cups of dark roast coffee were found to supply from 9.6 to 13.4 mg. of niacin, or enough to provide the minimum daily requirement.

Space does not permit our making more than a rather casual reference to such items, and we have had to limit ourselves to a small sampling of the kinds of information given years ago in the Cayce readings that are being borne out by modern scientific research. In the areas of diet, exercise, and healing techniques much has occurred in recent years to indicate that Cayce's source of information— although presented in an everyday, commonsense manner—was actually highly sophisticated and advanced.

Only now, so many years after the death of Edgar Cayce, do we seem to be on the verge of realizing the potential worth of the material contained in the physical readings. An item in the publication, *A.R.E. News* for September, 1968, indicates that the research program among physicians associated with the Medical and Osteopathic Research Divisions of the Edgar Cayce Foundation is well under way.

States this report, "Work at a clinical research level on epilepsy, multiple sclerosis, schizophrenia, deafness, baldness and a number of other diseases and syndromes has begun to show results which should be interesting and informative. The number of cooperating physicians continues to grow apace."

[1] "Neglected Approaches to Cancer," SR June 1, 1968

CHAPTER 10

TELEPATHY AND/OR CLAIRVOYANCE
AS SHOWN IN THE LIFE READINGS

WE HAVE JUST examined, in some detail, a number of physical readings given for individuals by Edgar Cayce. We have illustrated that they were helpful, when there was cooperation on the part of patient and physician, and we have shown that they were surprisingly accurate. We do not have to *assume* they were accurate; in many cases what the readings had to say about physical conditions was borne out later by X-rays, blood tests, or other medically acceptable means. In other words, they were *provable*.

Now we move into an area where there can be little proof of accuracy. As we consider the second major type of reading given for individuals, that called the life reading, we must do so in the knowledge that there is no way to substantiate much of what Cayce had to say.

That he was able to describe accurately the personal characteristics of the subject of his reading is, at least to some extent, provable. The subject himself, or someone who knew him, might testify that Cayce had certainly described the person's attitudes, his talents, or his physical characteristics, extremely well. But there is the chance—at least in some cases—that this was a telepathic communication and nothing more.

We could suggest that, although Cayce's physical readings were astounding enough in their accuracy to shake even the most ardent skeptic, when he began to talk of the past lives of an individual and how these affected his present life, he was way out in left field. But would this be a reasonable assumption? Would it make sense to say that Cayce, in one regard, was amazingly clairvoyant, and in another regard was talking out of his psychic hat?

Would it be reasonable to assume that this humble and uncomplicated man, this Sunday school teacher, who had no interest in or knowledge of other than the most orthodox Christian beliefs, *wanted* to receive information about ancient religions, about reincarnation, and thereby "sell" such ideas to a doubting society? Hardly. For some time after the subject came up in his readings, he tried to deny its validity.

About all we can do, at this stage, is to offer some examples of life readings, and ask that you read them with an open mind. If you are skeptical about such matters, you may well come away from them just as skeptical as ever. If you are undecided about your feelings on the subject of reincarnation, you may still be undecided after you have read some of what Cayce had to say. If you happen to believe in the possibility of reincarnation, you may find some fuel to feed your belief. In any event, we think you'll find these readings highly interesting.

To understand and appreciate Cayce's clairvoyance as it was demonstrated in the life readings, it is necessary to have some knowledge of the basic philosophy behind them. A full treatment of this could well fill its own book, so we will satisfy ourselves, here, with a brief explanation.

Perhaps we should begin with a restatement of the suggestion used to obtain the life readings, which was supplied by Cayce while in trance in 1925, just after reincarnation had been introduced as a subject of the readings:

"You will have before you the body (give name and place of the individual at birth, the name at birth as given) and you will give the relation of this entity and the universe, and the universal forces, giving the conditions that are as personalities latent, and exhibited, in the present life. Also the former appearances in the earth's plane, giving time, place, name and that in that life which built or retarded the development for the entity, giving the abilities of the present entity and that to which it may attain, and how."

This suggestion, said Cayce, would make it possible to know the effect "not only of the present environment, as it has been, as it may be, but the effect of the past experiences and through what sphere these were obtained."

According to Cayce's information, as shown in the readings, God created, of Himself, souls. As he stated in one reading, "The soul is that which the Maker gave to every entity or individual in the beginning. It is seeking the home or place of the Maker."

In another reading, he said, "The soul is an individuality that may grow to be one with, or separate from the Whole."

And in another, "What, then, is a soul? What does it look like? What is its plane of experience or activity? How may ye find one?

"It may not be separated in the material world from its own place of abode in the physical body. The soul looks through the eyes of the body; it feels with the emotions; it develops awareness through the faculties in every sense—and thus adds to its body, just as food has produced a growing physical body."

A soul, according to Cayce, spends many lifetimes on earth, separated by other periods in which it resides in the spirit world, preparing itself for its next return to earth. The periods between "lifetimes" are spent in developing itself, just as it is designed to do when in earthly form, trying to reach the perfection that will make it someday worthy of returning to God.

Each earthly appearance, say the readings, has its gains and its losses. Gains, in terms of spiritual development, advance the soul toward its sought-after perfection. Losses, through succumbing to sins of the flesh, result in debts that must be paid in future earthly appearances. This is the law of karma, or the law of retribution, which Cayce clearly explained in a reading given in 1933.

"Karma is a reaction which may be compared to the reaction within the body when a piece of food is taken into the system.

"The food is translated into a part of the body itself, penetrating to every cell, and influencing the health of the body and mind. Thus it is with a soul when it enters a body for an experience in the earth. The person's thoughts are the food upon which the soul feeds, along with the actions which result from these thoughts.

"These thoughts and actions in turn have been generated by thoughts and actions behind them, and so on back to the birth of the soul.

"When a soul enters a new body, in a new environment, a door is opened leading to an opportunity for building the soul's destiny. Everything which has been previously built, both good and bad, is contained in that opportunity.

"There is always a way of redemption, but there is no way to dodge responsibilities which the soul has, itself, undertaken. Thus a life is a way of developing, a preparation for the cleansing of the soul, though it may be a hard path at times for the physical consciousness and the physical body.

"Changes come, and some people say luck has intervened. But it is not luck. It is the result of what the soul has done about its opportunities for redemption."

According to the readings, when God created souls, He gave them free will. Thus it is up to each soul, working its way through many appearances in the earth, to develop toward its original objective: to be a fit companion to God. The readings suggest that each soul chooses its time and place to be "born" into a new life on earth, selecting the environment and the company of other souls with which it may best work out its own destiny.

They also suggest that souls tend to incarnate in a kind of group pattern. This accounts for the fact that so many people who had Cayce readings were found to have had previous incarnations with others for whom readings were given. Many of them, particularly those who worked closely with Cayce in the present life, had been associated with him in some way in past incarnations. The majority of people who received readings were found to have had incarnations in one of two general patterns: Atlantis, Egypt, Rome, the Crusades period, and the early colonial American period; or Atlantis, Egypt, Rome, France in the time of Louis XIV, XV or XVI, and the time of the American Civil War. (These, however, were "highlight" incarnations given by Cayce as being most pertinent to the present life; there may have been others which did not affect the present incarnation particularly.)

Because, as we have mentioned, each soul writes its own history upon the akashic records, and retains the memory of all its experiences, it was possible for Cayce, as stated in the readings, to "tune in" and read the history for the person seeking information via Cayce's psychic abilities.

Pamela Winters: A Study in Character

One of the clearest examples of Cayce's ability to describe the personal characteristics and talents of another is seen in the case of Pamela Winters.

At the time of the reading, Pamela was fourteen years old. Thus it is possible that much of the information given in the reading was received telepathically by Cayce, for by that age personal traits are fairly well developed in the individual. Other parts of the reading may not be so easily explained, as we shall see.

We will offer the reading in its entirety, just as it was given on July 22, 1944. However, we will interject into the reading at appropriate points some portions of an A.R.E. questionnaire answered by Pamela's mother five years later, concerning her opinion of Cayce's accuracy.

Reading

"Yes, we have the entity here, Pamela Winters. Here we find very unusual abilities and also some very unusual warnings to be given for such a lovely person. [Cayce had never seen her.]

"In the interpretation of the records, these would be first directed to [the parents] who [are responsible for] giving the opportunity for the entity [to develop] its abilities, especially in that field of art which would be designated as place cards, Christmas pictures, season's greetings and that particular nature. These should be the opportunities given the entity. This necessarily would include music, but not music as a means of doing other than attuning or giving expression.

"For the entity of its inner self is very psychic. Do not submerge, but rather encourage all such."

Questionnaire

Pamela's mother indicated that Pamela had no particular interest in art or sketching, "but decided emphasis on self-adornment. She is artistic and luxurious in taste; loves elegance." As to any demonstration of psychic ability or particular interest in music, her mother answered with a question mark.

Reading

"There will be these as warnings, these for those responsible for the entity: a tendency for the body to overeat or to be overindulgent in appetites. Be warned for self, as well as associates of those who take wine or strong drink, for this may easily become a stumbling block for the entity.

"In giving the interpretation of the records for the entity, these opportunities, these privileges and these warnings should be directed more to [the parents]."

Questionnaire

Mrs. Winters indicated that Pamela had always been inclined to overeat. However, concerning a tendency to be attracted to those who overindulge in liquor, she said that Pamela had married a young man from a family of heavy drinkers, although he seemed to be quite level-headed about the problem. Pamela, said her mother, had always had a strong aversion to liquor.

Reading

"As to the entity, we find Venus, Jupiter, Mars, Saturn, all of these are parts of the entity's consciousness. Thus a very strong-minded individual, but one given to light things; and yet one very capable when talking to individuals, rather than groups or numbers of people.

"Thus those warnings should be: make the self, then embrace opportunities with groups and others. Do apply self in the direction especially of art and music. For these will offer the channels, especially as has been indicated, through which not only the material success may be gained but the interpretation of the physical, the spiritual, the psychic. Don't be afraid to acknowledge that ye see fairies as ye study, for you will nurture these experiences. Don't be afraid to say that you see the gnomes which would hinder people at times. These may be a part of the background for many of the cards, for many of the various sketches which you would make."

Questionnaire

Concerning a tendency to be with individuals, rather than groups, Mrs. Winters indicated that Pamela ". . . prefers one or two people at a time. She's quite critical of people; too discriminating. She is not outward-going!" Pamela, said her mother, "is very strong-minded, but still very much attracted to light topics of conversation and interest."

Reading

"As to the appearances in the earth, these have been quite varied.

"Before this we find the entity was in the land during that period when there were those reconstructions following the period called the American Revolution. Here we find the entity interested in building a home with the beautiful grounds about same.

"In the name then Lila Chapman, the entity gained through the period, for the home to the entity and its family and its children was that which took the greater portion of its time, save the study of the Word which was given place in that home. And yet there came from same those who took too much of the cup, as cheers. This brought disturbances, sorrows. Don't let it occur again. There will be the tendencies for attraction, not only for self, but for those about you. For that ye hate has come upon thee. Don't hate anything in the present."

Questionnaire

Mrs. Winters stated that Pamela had never shown much interest in church or the Bible. However, since childhood she had shown great concern for the care of orphans. Regarding a tendency to want a fine home and grounds, however, "Pamela's main interest, particularly since her marriage, has been in beautifying her home. She has a driving ambition to own, someday, a really elegant place."

Reading

"Before that, we find the entity was in the lands to which the Apostles went when they were driven, because of persecutions, to the Holy Land, and those parts of what is Asia Minor or the old portions and to Persia; and we find the entity, not as a 'hanger-on' but as one who aided the Disciples, who followed through in these directions with John in one portion of the land, and then with the descriptions of Bartholomew. The entity was closely associated with these in singing psalms and in the alms and good deeds for those attracted to same for the material as well as spiritual portion of their lives. In the experience the entity was then known as Ishneth.

"Before that, we find the entity was in 'the city in the hills and plains' and the entity was among those of the natives attracted by, attracted to, the peoples who came from the Grecian land, but not for any good purpose. Some succeeded in undermining peoples. Most did not, but became believers themselves. The entity was among those attracted for their beauty, for their grace and most of all for their cleanliness. For cleanliness is next to Godliness. For he who is pure as an individual should be pure in body, as clean in body also.

"In the experience the entity learned much of the mystical, not any of the

Persian, but those activities in 'the city in the hills,' which aided individuals in the artistic phases of Grecian culture and lore. Thus the interest in the body beautiful, the interest in nature and nature's dwellers in air, as well as from flowers, roses, clouds, trees, water, sounds and all of these which come from nature itself. The name then was Pleghen."

Questionnaire

Now we come to a most striking parallel between Pamela as seen by Cayce in his reading and Pamela as seen by her mother. Said Mrs. Winters, "Pamela is decidedly a clean person, even from babyhood. She never even looks slightly soiled. If a bug came upon her clothes or bedcovers, she had to immediately change them. She always smells delicious.

"In a romantic and sensual way, she appreciates beauty. However, as of this stage in her life, she has shown no particular interest in Grecian culture and lore, or in the mystical."

Reading

"Before that, we find the entity was in the Egyptian land when there were those who were a portion of that development for Ra Ta [Edgar Cayce was Ra Ta, a priest in Egypt, in an early incarnation] in bringing perfected children into the earth. The entity was among those who were of that individual's activity and yet brought into the service in the Temple of Sacrifice and the Temple Beautiful the arts which first were expressed in colored flowers upon the linen of the day, and those which made for beauty among the peoples in the homes, as a means for instruction in urging the emotional forces of body, and life-building. The name then was Itcar."

Questionnaire

Mrs. Winters was asked the question, "Is Pamela particularly susceptible or responsive to the opposite sex; or does she have decided views on relationships in home and marriage?"

She replied, "Pamela has decided views on this. She's quite opinioned, and was critical of most boys who were attracted to her because of her good looks. She is repulsed by drinking, petting, dirty jokes, even smoking. She decided at fifteen that she would marry the boy she just married last June, when she was eighteen."

Concerning an interest in flowered linens, and interior decorating, Pamela's mother replied, "She has a great appreciation of flowers and soft materials such as angora sweaters and silk underwear. She loves perfumes. She enjoys making her home as beautiful as possible.

Reading

Among the questions asked of Cayce at the end of the main portion of the reading were some concerning relationships between Pamela and her present family in previous incarnations, and the influence of this on their present lives together.

Cayce indicated that Pamela had been associated with both parents, and that their readings should be compared to Pamela's. "Parallel with the application of each or the activities in varied experiences. These ye will draw the better in the Egyptian experience."

Concerning Pamela's brother, the two had been associated in two previous incarnations: in Egypt and Persia.

However, concerning Pamela's sister, Cayce said, "You won't get along so well . . . though you love her. You were not associated."

Questionnaire

Mrs. Winters indicated that Pamela and her brother had always been congenial, though their interests were quite different. When asked if Pamela and her sister didn't get along, she replied, "They don't get along at all. Pamela can't stand her sister; the two are direct opposites."

Comments

Cayce seems to have described Pamela quite well, considering her mother's response to the questionnaire. We do not have recent reports, and can only conjecture about the possible development of such matters as an interest in the mystical, which Cayce indicated would be strong influences in this life.

It is important to remember that Cayce's readings were in no way fortune telling, or predictions of what would happen. Their purpose was to guide the individual in making the most of his life, in light of past experiences as well as present surroundings and urges. The person's own free will, and how it was applied, would determine the worth of his lifetime.

If there is one strong point that comes out of Pamela Winters' reading, it is the great influence of past lives in making the kind of person she was at the time of the reading, or is today.

Such possibilities add all sorts of complexities to our struggle to understand human nature. No wonder a psychiatrist friend of mine, who is dead-set against the idea of reincarnation, said to me recently, "Don't bug me with all this stuff about past lives. Don't you think I have enough to keep me busy, just trying to figure out all the crazy things people do from the time of their birth? If I ever have to start going back into past lives to figure out a human personality, I'll close up shop and take up basket weaving!"

And Always, the Music

Admittedly, mental telepathy might well account for Cayce's accuracy in describing Pamela Winters. She was, after all, fourteen years old at the time of her reading.

But we wonder: could telepathy alone explain such accuracy in the case of Jay Clement? His reading was given in August, 1944, when Jay was ten weeks old.

Cayce began the reading with the type of advice he frequently offered parents of young subjects. "In giving the interpretations of the records as we find them here, there is much to be chosen from. Yet, as to the developing personality of this entity, much will depend upon the guiding of same through the formative experiences in this particular sojourn."

According to the reading, Jay was an unusual entity who had once lived on the lost continent of Atlantis. In his present life, said Cayce, Jay was "one gifted, as will be indicated in the unfolding of the abilities of the body in that called the higher arts, especially of the use of the voice. All of its abilities as a composer, as a singer, should be those things to which those responsible in the present should direct this entity. For this entity was among those who first began to attempt to make music, especially American music."

The reading explained that in the incarnation preceding this one, Jay had been a musician. "These activities should be studied, not merely for meeting the problems as to the character of voice, of music, but to give the entity the advantage especially of piano and stringed instruments of every nature. For the voice will be noteworthy and such as to make a great contribution to true American music." Since he was a highly developed soul, having been once an Atlantean, Jay's parents were warned not to attempt to evade his questions, or to attempt to deceive him, "or you may make a singer on the street, and not a good one at that!"

Said Cayce, "There will be found, as with every true musician or every true artist, one with a great deal of imagination. Do not stop or confuse the entity in the imagination. Not so much as ever discouraging, but do not encourage to that point that it becomes solely imagination for the exaltation of its own ego. The entity will be found to be one quite sensitive, or a psychic of no mean ability." [There are reports from the parents indicating a number of childhood psychic experiences had by this boy.]

The reading stated that, prior to the appearance as the musician, Jay had been "in that land now known as the Holy Land, during the days when the Master walked in the earth, and during those periods when there was the establishing of churches or groups for the propagation and dissemination of the tenets and truths which were parts of the activity during those periods. The entity, young in years, was among the children in those groups at the feeding of the five thousand. Hence you will always find the entity ready to eat when it is time to eat, and he will expect it to be there, no matter where it comes from!" ["How very true!" reported Jay's parents some years later.]

"This is innate, for—created from that which was a friend's little lunch for the multitudes—why shouldn't a divine Father supply those worthy, and unworthy as well?"

During that appearance on earth, said Cayce, the entity had become a singer in the various churches throughout the land. "For the entity journeyed with Luke and Paul, Paul and Silas, Paul and Barnabas, and thus came in contact with those in many portions of the land; as a psalmsinger of real help, then, to all of the churches.

"Hence psychic experiences, the abilities to speak, the desire to go to Sunday school (and you had better go with him, not send him!) will bring activities in the experience of the entity."

There had been, said the reading, an even earlier appearance in the Holy Land. Again, he had been a psalmist, and had "led in the praises of all the leaders and those who held close to a worship of the holy influences in man's activities.

"In the present the entity will find, then, that groups, crowds, throngs, will be those things which will tend to direct, to aid or deter from the fulfilling, and yet to have the feel of the brother man; for freedom *is* America."

Prior to that appearance, the entity had been in Egypt, "among those who were trained in the Temple Beautiful, as a teacher or lecturer for those of the land of Saad, as well as the Gobi land. Thus we will find in the present the entity will be particularly interested in things oriental, especially Chinese, or the Gobi or parts of the East Indian land."

In the Egyptian experience, he had served "in the capacity of an emissary, as would be termed today, or a representative in other lands. Hence the present interest, as should and will be, in things national and international."

Before the Egyptian experience, said Cayce, the entity had been "in the Atlantean land when there were those disturbances which arose before the second breaking up of the land. This brought a period of trial for the entity. . . . The entity was a prince in the land. . . ."

Bear in mind that Edgar Cayce obtained this information, by his own description as given in the readings, through attuning his unconscious mind with that of another; in this case, that of a ten-weeks-old baby boy!

When the child was four years old, his mother reported that already there were strong indications of an interest in music.

In 1956, when Jay was eleven years old, his mother again wrote to A.R.E. to report his progress. "He has composed about five songs, one of which I feel is very good. He doesn't do so well in school, probably because he daydreams so much. His teacher told me there are times when he will look right at her and she knows he isn't hearing a word she is saying, that he is somewhere away off.

"One day he was working on his arithmetic and stopped in the middle of it. I asked him, 'Aren't you going to finish your lesson before you stop?' He answered that he was hearing music and wanted to go right to the piano and see if he could play it. His difficulty was mostly, so far, in writing it down. He wants to get a harp. He doesn't like violin music. He had an accordion at one time, but does most of his practicing on the piano. He says, 'Sometimes music comes to my mind and I have to stop whatever I'm doing and go to the piano and play.' "

In 1964, just after Jay's twentieth birthday, his aunt reported, "He's now in his second year at the music college. He is a very fine boy, tall and handsome, quiet and home-loving.

"All through high school he had his own band. One summer they played professionally, carrying their instruments around the countryside in a trailer. Jay played the organ, and was manager of the band. Much of their music is of the rock-and-roll type, which is so popular now.

"This past summer, Jay has been working with his father in the construction business, in order to earn money to help with his college expenses. He definitely shows all the signs of being headed for a musical career. He has a splendid speaking and singing voice.

"He was brought up in the Baptist Sunday school, as his parents were staunch members. He always participated and did not object, as some children do, to attending regularly.

"I do not know about his interest in things oriental, especially Chinese. Of course this might develop later, as he is still quite young. He has a wonderful taste in clothes and dresses elegantly.

"Also, I have not heard of any special interest in things national or international, as the reading mentioned, but I do know that he is a very tolerant and broad-minded individual, and a very gifted one."

That Jay has developed along the lines of his reading, both as a musician and as a human being, is probably due to many things. Not the least of these is the environment into which the reading was given.

Jay's parents had both received life readings, and in another reading had been advised by Cayce to marry. Mrs. Clement indicated their respect for this opportunity by reporting at one time, "My husband is quite an individual and a remarkable person in many ways, and we have had a great deal of happiness in being together. We are so thankful we had our readings to guide us."

It is not surprising, then, that they eagerly sought a reading for their first-born, and followed it with considerable dedication. Certainly it is evident that they encouraged Jay's early interest in music by making training in this field available to him.

But this still does not explain how Cayce knew, in giving a reading for Jay as an infant, that he would, and should, be so strongly inclined toward a career in music. And this is not a matter of training only, for Jay obviously has a natural talent for which all the training in the world cannot compensate.

It also does not explain how Cayce knew about the tendency to daydream—a manifestation of the imagination spoken of in the reading, perhaps?—or the evident love for church, and for his fellow man, which have been shown in reports concerning Jay's development. All this, said Cayce, came of earlier appearances on the earth.

It is difficult to review such a reading, and note how accurate it seems to have been in so many respects, without admitting the possibility that reincarnation is a fact, not a theory.

Sober-Sided Charlie

Charlie Roberts' parents had heard of Edgar Cayce, but saw no particular advantage in obtaining a life reading for their six-year-old son. His aunt, however, requested one for him, and it was given in May, 1944.

Again we have a reading which began with Cayce's advice to the parents. "In giving an interpretation of the records here, much rests with the parents as to how completely the entity may fit itself for its abilities and urges latent and manifested in this experience. These as characteristics will be seen with the entity.

"One always wanting to fix something, no matter what.

"The entity is always inclined to want to make something which would be an improvement.

"Thus, we will find the entity a scientific genius if the opportunities for self-expression are given full opportunity in this experience.

"Those things which would pertain to the study of mind, as well as that which would be applied in making improvements upon things, either electrically-driven or as to improvements or corrections in collecting of data, collecting of interesting experiences of or with individuals.

"There is the bringing to the entity of a tendency to be rather too much inclined to be sober and sarcastic. And this may not turn out so well unless there is given the entity such opportunities to improve the mind, or to study law as pertaining to conditions or things; not so much as having to do with material happenings as with the arbitrary expression from spiritual attributes of individuals."

In the incarnation just prior to this one, he had been "among those who improved the city or the activities in the place of the entity's [birth]. . . . In the experience the entity gained by aiding in the preparation of things pertaining to mechanical appliances which would be labor-saving to man."

In the earliest incarnation given in the reading, "the entity was in the land now known as the Holy Land when the peoples journeyed from Egypt to the Holy Land. The entity was among those who aided some of the sons or children of Dan to prepare the mechanical things for the carrying of the tables, the altar, candlesticks, and those things which were to be used by other individuals.

"In the experience the entity gained the more, and with the application of self came knowledge and power within self to control influences about the entity."

In the question-and-answer section of the reading, Cayce made the statement, "As has been indicated, the parents should make themselves responsible for the administering to the needs of the entity that which will enable him to become a scientist."

Answering an A.R.E. questionnaire in 1949 concerning Charlie Roberts' reading, the aunt replied: "Although the grandmother and parents have read this reading, they aren't interested. He is being given church training; also music." Charlie, she said, had never seen his reading.

Another questionnaire was answered by the aunt in May, 1952, when Charlie was nearly fifteen years old. Portions of her reply which seem to bear out Cayce's analysis of Charlie's nature are as follows:

"He is a very quiet boy, really too sober-minded. He can fix things, make improvements; but I have not noticed that he goes out of his way to do so. His father and mother are quite active in the Methodist Church, and they take him along with them.

"Charlie told me of an incident regarding some work, where two or three boys had to take turns. His turn came last and was difficult, so he figured out an easy way. The other boys 'jumped' him for not telling them how to go about it the easy way, and he replied, 'I never thought of it until it was my turn.'

"Another incident comes to mind. When he was six years old, he set a rabbit trap, and put a carrot inside for bait. Nothing happened. Later, when his mother inspected the trap, she saw an onion and a carrot, and she asked him about it. He said, 'Well, the rabbit could *smell* the onion, and when he saw the carrot he would investigate; then I would have him.'

"He does not like hard work, and never seems to move until a problem is presented, and then the short-cut solution comes to him. He reads constantly, and seems to be looking for explanations and answers. I have very little opportunity to guide him, since his mother opposes anything that is not orthodox. His father doesn't care much one way or the other whether I talk with him along the lines of his reading. I do think his mother is loosening up some, and as time goes on, I hope to have a chance to direct him according to his life reading.

"I have not yet noticed whether he has inclinations toward 'electrically-driven things or collecting data of interesting experiences of or with individuals,' as was indicated in his reading. At this time, he is interested in astronomy.

"I never heard him make sarcastic remarks, but I have felt it in his attitude. He is such a quiet boy. However, during the little contact I have had with him, I've noticed that he must be pushed constantly to keep going. He seems to stand aside and watch others, questioning why they are doing things in a particular way. You can only force him so far; he just won't be driven."

We do not have recent reports concerning Charlie's progress since 1952. We would hope that what seems to be a natural inventiveness and an active imagination have been encouraged to develop in the way Cayce indicated, so that he will be able to realize his full potential in this life.

"For Weal—Or Woe

Loretta Monroe was fifteen days old at the time of her reading. It is a remarkable study in personal characteristics and personal prophecy.

The reading is too long to be used in its entirety here. We will give highlights only, and from time to time will interject various reports based on comments made by those who know her. Loretta is now twenty-nine years old, married, and the mother of three children.

Reading

"Yes, we have the records of that entity now called Loretta Monroe.

"In giving the interpretations of the records as we find them here, these are chosen with the desire to be a helpful experience for the entity, as well as a helpful influence in the experience of those who will have the guiding of the formative years of the entity in this present earth plane.

"For, without the proper directions—from the experience in the sojourns (and these being many)—the emotions may influence the entity to such an extent as to become a woe in this present sojourn.

"These, then, are chosen with that purpose of making those who have the care of the entity *aware* of those inclinations, those emotions which will become manifested, especially in the formative years.

"In the composite of the latent or astrological urges, and the material sojourns, we find these as influences that will be manifest.

"One that has a temper of its own. While not stubborn—for it can be easily reasoned with—it must have a *positive* answer for every question, and not, 'Don't—because I say so!'

"One that will be beautiful in body, in figure, in the material sense. Do not allow this to become a vain experience for the entity, but keep the mind and body busy in the developing years in constructive ways and thinking.

"And let the life of each about the entity be particularly consistent with the advice that is given."

Reports

Said the mother, in a report given when Loretta was in her early teens, "She's always been just one step short of stubborn. Sometimes, when I was busy with the other children, I'd nearly be driven out of my mind with her need to know *why* something was so. She'd just stand there and stamp her little foot until I stopped what I was doing and explained. It wasn't a matter of demanding attention, per se, but simply that it was extremely important for her to have the whole answer, right now!"

Loretta Monroe is strikingly beautiful. It is quite interesting that Edgar Cayce would know this when Loretta was only fifteen days old.

The urgent warnings not to spoil the child seem directed toward the entire family. Loretta was the first grandchild, and there were many doting aunts, uncles and cousins around who would have been all too willing to spoil her beyond redemption. Cayce's heavy emphasis on this point seems to indicate that in some way he was aware of this special danger.

Reading

"From the astrological aspects, we will find that blue in the clothing, and especially in stones of every nature, should be part of the apparel for the entity; for it will bring not only the vibrations of healing for the entity but a pleasant and a beautiful reaction to the mental efficiencies of the body.

"As to astrological sojourns, we find Venus, Mercury, Uranus, Saturn and Mars as the ruling factors.

"Hence the body-beautiful will ever be as an influence either for weal or woe, as has been indicated, dependent upon that direction given in its formative years.

"From the Mercurian influence we will find that the entity will be quick at all forms of mental grasping in the spiritual or mental or any form of mental exercise, whether it be in economics or in mathematics or any other form.

"Hence those injunctions as to *consistency* in speech and activity of those about the entity in its formative periods."

Reports

Loretta Monroe has always been spritually aware, and even as a small child gave much evidence that she felt the presence of a living God. Once, when she was about four years old, her mother looked out the window to see Loretta, playing beneath a large tree in the yard, suddenly stop and kneel in prayer. Afterwards, when asked about this, she said, "I was asking God to send me a baby brother." Eight months later, her brother was born.

She was a bright, quick student, and scored extremely high in her intelligence tests. She had some poetry published in a scholastic magazine at the age of eight.

Reading

"In the Uranian influence we will find the extremes, as to moods that may arise, rather than its activity in the varied fields or spheres of meanings to the entity.

"And, as indicated, there needs to be cultivated the spiritual aptitudes; not by rote or writ, but by reasoning as to the influences wrought within the experience of the entity.

"In Saturn we find changes, that may be very much according to the aptitudes from the Uranian forces. For, much of *material* benefits will be a part of the entity's experience. Let this not spoil the entity in its formative years, in disregarding values of every nature in its experience.

"Most everyone who meets or is acquainted with the entity, because of these very influences, will wield an influence; and will *want* to give - give - give - give to the entity.

"Thus, none need ever fear as to the material benefits for the entity; but there will need to be the directing as to the evaluations of such in its experience, in its formative years.

"There will be great attractions for the entity to the opposite sex. Hence there would be the warning that there be not an early marriage for the entity, for this would bring the Saturn as well as the Uranian influences in those activities through the Venus forces—which will occur in the experience through its seventeenth to eighteenth year of experience in this sojourn."

Reports

Note again the heavy emphasis on the need for guarding against spoiling the child. Her mother has reported that this was always a problem, within such a large, loving family.

One of the most striking statements in this portion of the reading has to do with the danger of an early marriage, during the entity's seventeenth to eighteenth year. At the age of seventeen, Loretta eloped with a boy from her home town. The marriage was annulled soon afterwards.

She married again a few years later, to a fine young man who has worked a small business into quite a large one. His attitude certainly matches the part of the reading that indicated that everyone would want to give - give - give to Loretta; he works extremely long, hard hours to provide her with every possible comfort.

Reading

In discussing her previous incarnations, Cayce stated that the one just prior to the present was a well-known temperance leader who also did much work for underprivileged children. From this experience, said Cayce, "even in its early years there will be the desire to take sides with all of the little colored children, as well as all the little poor children about the entity; not caring for others."

Earlier incarnations had been in France, where she had been martyred; in the Holy Land, "during those periods when the Master walked the earth"; in Persia as a nurse; in Egypt, in the Temple Beautiful. In this experience, said Cayce, "The entity brought much of that which aided womankind, all of her sex, in greater activity; as did the entity in the sojourn just before the present bring to her fellows an aid towards freedom of speech, as well as the privilege of owning, holding possessions in the own name.

"As to the abilities of the entity, then:

"Much, as indicated, depends upon the manner in which the early periods of its experience are directed.

"If guided aright, the abilities will manifest to constructive forces. If left, it will depend upon circumstance.

"Make them rather in accordance, then, with grace and mercy—through love, through kindness, through patience—that there may be the full manifestation again of that which may bring freedom to many."

Reports

Loretta's parents, and others who know her, have reported that everything in this reading seems to apply directly to her; that it is remarkably accurate. She has a strong, quick mind, a beautiful body, and a deep concern for the welfare of others—particularly those less fortunate than she.

Her readings indicated that the major accomplishments of her life, if properly directed, will take place during the middle and later years. She is still young, and much remains to be seen as to how well she lives up to her potential.

"She Should Be Called Lilith Ann"

Thus Edgar Cayce began his reading for a two-day-old baby girl in April, 1933. Since her parents did not follow this advice, we will use the name for the purposes of this report.

Cayce explained why he had so named her. "In entering, we shall see that this name has been and is indicated in the entity's development—and the entity's appearance in the earth's plane in the present. For *many* shall be those influenced by the activities of the entity's sojourn through this experience."

Describing her personality as it would develop, he said "One, then, that will be found to be innately tending, and developing, toward headstrongness; great mental abilities. She will be able—and will have those tendencies when speaking—to argue anything down in another individual; a tendency for the obtaining and retaining of all that comes in the experience of the entity.

"Not that selfishness will prevail, but this must of necessity be one of those things that the training and environ must be warned concerning, that this does not become a fault for this entity, Lilith Ann . . ."

In her most recent incarnation before the present, said Cayce, Lilith Ann had lived in Plymouth. Her name then had been Ann Lilith Bewton. She had been beautiful, with an excellent mind, and had given "self in the services of those peoples, especially in leading the singing and the music in the spiritual service in that day." She had suffered in body "for the tenets held." This, according to Cayce, would "make in the present experience for those periods when, with a scolding or rebuke, the body will turn within itself but not forget its aim or purpose—and, unless watched, will 'do it anyway!'

"After the fifteenth to sixteenth year in the present experience, from the sojourn in Plymouth, there will be those tendencies towards the abilities to direct and lead; for the entity will ever be rather inclined to lead than be led—either by her own sex or others! For she'll make many men step around!"

In an incarnation previous to the one in Plymouth, she had been "in that land known as the Roman, when those peoples were being persecuted for their beliefs in the spiritual lessons that were being given during those periods."

She had been in the court of the rulers and, said Cayce, often had been rebuked by her associates, for she had courted favor and tried to combat the decadence of the court. "Yet," he said, "throughout the experience the entity kept self above those even of its surroundings, and never submitted of self to those indulgences as did many of the associates through the period."

Thus she had gained in that experience with regard to the development of soul. She had lost, somewhat, in that her release from an arranged and disagreeable marriage was achieved through suicide.

"In the present, then, there may be seen in the developing years those periods of sullenness; yet of cheerfulness to carry one's own point." It would be this ability, especially through the latter portion of her present life, which would "bring succor, aid, comfort and cheer to the experience of many."

Prior to the Roman incarnation, she had been in India, had suffered in body, and had been healed. She had dedicated the balance of her life to helping others. (This is interesting in light of what happened to Lilith Ann in her present life, which we will discuss later.) Her name, then, had been Lillila. (This similarity of names throughout various incarnations appears often in the Cayce readings. We cannot account for it.)

She had been in Egypt before that, in the Temple Beautiful. Her activities there had been in connection with music and dancing, and these interests, said Cayce, would be shown to be very strong in her present life.

Before that, she had been "in that period known as the Atlantean, among the sojourners from Atlantis who came to what is now known as Yucatan—and was in the temple worship there." Her name in that incarnation was, again, similar to many of her other ones: it was Lilithe.

From her activities in that experience, said Cayce, would come a strong tendency—and a desirable one—to become a vocational counselor or a teacher in the present life.

There were some interesting cautions in the reading concerning health and bodily safety.

"The greater precautions for the health, the welfare of the entity, and warnings, will come during—or should be given for—those periods in October and November of the first four years of sojourn in this experience. And especially for those things that interfere with the sensory system, in the throat and ears. In those periods, then, there should be precautions as to disease that would disturb these portions of the system particularly."

It could, of course, be mere coincidence that just after her fifth birthday, Lilith Ann had her tonsils and adenoids removed.

"And there should be precautions also in the fifth and seventh years, in December and January, as to fire. For, in those periods will the entity be passing through the fiery sign for the entity."

We have no record of any incident concerning fire during this period—or any other, for that matter.

"As to the next influence, or those periods when there come those changes in the physical and developing periods, or in the fourteenth to the fifteenth year . . . will be those periods when there may be seen the greater influence upon the entity from astrological viewpoint—in Uranus. Hence the period of the greater anxiety by or from those upon whom the training of this entity depends."

Again, it could be mere coincidence that, at the age of fourteen, a tremendous change entered the life of Lilith Ann. She contracted polio at that age, and has spent all the years since her recovery in a wheelchair.

Reports from her grandmother indicate a rather remarkable progress, despite the restrictions imposed by Lilith Ann's paralysis. (We should add that there seems to have been no particular emphasis placed on the importance of the reading in guiding her development. Her grandmother had requested it, and the parents seem to have had little interset in it.)

In October, 1947, the grandmother wrote to A.R.E., stating, "Lilith Ann is progressing from her attack of polio last April, but it is very slow. . . ."

In December of the same year, she wrote, "Lilith Ann has not recovered from the polio yet. She hopes to get to Georgia, to Roosevelt's place, in a short time. . . .

Lilith Ann's aunt wrote to A.R.E. in July, 1951. "Perhaps it would interest you to know that she is intending to teach disabled people handicrafts after she leaves school, where she is majoring in art. She is in a wheelchair. If I remember rightly, it said in her reading that she might go in for vocational guidance or teaching, and I think her work will be very similar to that. . . ."

There are several additional reports on file, all from the grandmother. In December, 1951, she wrote, "Lilith Ann carries herself with great courage and is studying hard in junior college. . . ."

In July, 1952, she reported, "Lilith Ann graduated from junior college and is full of courage. She was on the honor roll, and expects to go on to regular college, if they can make arrangements. . . ."

In March, 1955, she wrote, "Lilith Ann graduated from college with high honors and is teaching incapacitated children. . . ."

In January, 1957, the grandmother reported that, although still confined to a wheelchair, Lilith Ann had been married the previous June. "He must be a nice man, for he carried her into church. . . ."

In March, 1957, a letter from the grandmother indicated that, although still in a wheelchair, Lilith Ann was expecting a baby in April.

And she reported in April, 1958, "Lilith Ann expects her second baby shortly. Polio is a strange sickness. It affects the nerves of the limbs, but the organs are healthy. Of course, the baby will have a Caesarean birth . . ."

There seems to be no doubt that, in spite of physical hardships, Lilith Ann is fulfilling the promise indicated in her life reading. In two previous incarnations, according to her reading, she had "suffered in body," but had overcome her suffering and devoted her life to helping others. She has done the same in her present life. Certainly we cannot doubt that she possesses high mental abilities, and has put them to good and unselfish purposes.

In considering the reading, and noting its accuracy as shown in the development of Lilith Ann, it seems almost incredible that it was given when she was only two days old.

The Important Formative Years

Robert Allison's life reading was given when he was nine months old. We will print it in its entirety, inserting, at appropriate points, various reports we have concerning him.

Reading

"Yes, we have the records here of that entity now known as Robert Allison.

"Here we have rather an exceptional entity—because of preparations in the minds and hearts of the parents, especially of that entity carrying and caring for this entity through those periods of gestation.

"An exceptional musician, especially piano. If the opportunity is given here, we may have to the musical world of America what Sir Joshua Reynolds [the portrait painter] was in his field—for it is the same entity."

Reports

Robert's mother has reported that only a few weeks after conceiving him, she went into a church and prayed that her child would love music, especially the piano. There are no musicians in the family. This prayer was held throughout her pregnancy, and may account for Cayce's statement in the second paragraph of the reading.

Reading

"In giving the interpretations of the records as we find them here, we choose these with the desire especially that these may prove helpful to those responsible for the entity during the formative years of its experience in this particular sojourn.

"As we find, these are the urges:

"One who will be subtle in its manner of approach to its own individual problems, thinking long and deep, and usually having its own way. Then, unless there is some thought or care taken in meeting these, we will find that the entity may become inclined toward being overheadstrong; yet we will find a gentleness, a seriousness, though periods when there will be tendencies towards recklessness.

"These are the warnings, then, that should be considered in meeting these. Knowing what to look for as the mind unfolds for the entity, we will be capable of meeting these and of directing the entity.

"Do give the opportunity for music. Let the entity listen to and be guided by, not that character of music that is of the passing fancy but that which builds harmony, that which builds the bridge between the sublime and the finite—or from the infinite to the finite mind. Cultivate these more often in the body-mind as it unfolds. Thus we will find less and less of the tendency for headstrongness.

"But there will be periods of temper. We find that this can be controlled, for as indicated, this is an unusual entity in those fields of activity suggested."

Reports

"True," said the mother when questioned about Robert's personal characteristics several years after the reading was given. "In every respect, Cayce was 100 percent correct. My boy is a mixture of seriousness, stubbornness, high temper and at the same time a great deal of gentleness. It is a strong mixture that has puzzled and confused me at times."

Reading

"Astrologically, we find urges from Venus, Mercury, Mars, Jupiter and Uranus.

These are tempered ever by the unusual or the extremes that will be found in activities.

"From Venus we find urges related to the beautiful; inclined towards spiritual or sacred music. These backgrounds will be an excellent basis for the entity's development and unfoldment.

"As soon as it is practical for the entity to sit close to a musical instrument, especially a piano, begin to practice on same. Let it be a part of the entity's experience for the next eighteen years to practice some time during each day.

"Thus there will be brought the realms of the infinite through and to those who seek to know much of the spiritual in the experiences in the earth."

Reports

Here we have a case of a reading's being a mixed blessing. The mother, although grateful for the opportunity to understand her boy's moods and talents as shown in the reading, has been in some ways haunted by it.

She set up a schedule of piano lessons beginning at the age of seven, and Robert was excited and pleased about this. But they lived in a small town, where few if any of the boys his age studied music. Upon learning about Robert's lessons, his friends teased him, and he stubbornly refused to go ahead with them. From time to time throughout his childhood, his mother attempted to coax him to the piano. Although she would see him hanging around it, fiddling with the keys when he wasn't aware anyone was watching, he'd turn away from it as soon as the subject of lessons was broached.

He did play drums in his school band. But when he was told that, in order to continue, he would have to learn to read music, he adamantly refused.

By this time, he was aware that a Cayce reading had been given for him. His mother, afraid of overemphasizing the importance of the reading to Robert's development, tried to let him gradually drift toward music as a natural expression.

Reading

"Before this [incarnation], as indicated, the entity was an artist. Thus the harmony, the desire ever in that experience to be the musician—as it was in part during that sojourn; giving the greater expression, of course, in composition. This will be a portion of the expression in the present—the composition of sacred music and classic music. For the entity may write that which will mean from this period on as much as that by Sir Joshua Reynolds in regard to the Holy Family.

"Before that, the entity was in the Holy Land when there were those activities in which there were the gatherings of those who sought to carry on the activities of the Master.

"The entity was among those who added music to the service that brought the oneness of mind, not only in song but in the music of the instrument. For then the stringed instruments were used, but the piano—which should be used in the present—is by nature a stringed instrument.

"The entity then added to that hope, that faith, that understanding, by keeping that touch which would span the varied realms of thought.

"The name then was Sylvesta.

"Before that, the entity was in the Egyptian land during those periods when there were the preparations for greater service of individuals in specific activities.

"The entity then especially through the Temple Beautiful brought to others its activities in music—in the two, three, four, five-stringed instruments.

"The name then was Celeresbestuen."

Reports

Despite his many protestations, Robert seems to love music. Two years ago, he bought a guitar. He plucks at it often, but refuses to learn to play it properly. He enjoys listening to music of all types, particularly that played on the piano and the sitar, and has a large record collection.

He has composed songs. A few years ago, a friend wanted to publish one of them, but Robert refused permission for this.

He has just finished serving two years in the Marine Corps. Said a fellow Marine, "He sings beautifully. In the barracks, he sang us to sleep every night."

It should be noted that he did not particularly like military life. However, the serious side of his nature prevailed; he made up his mind that, if he had to spend his time in this manner, he'd make a good job of it. He finished boot camp second in his class, topped only by a young man who spent his childhood in military schools.

Stubbornness and high temper seem to prevail in his nature, just as Cayce indicated would happen if he were not allowed the tempering influence of performing music.

Reading

"As to the abilities of the entity in the present:

"Much will depend upon the formative years, as to what will be the outcome, by the manner in which the trainings begin.

"Do give the entity the opportunity for activities in the direction indicated, for it will mean much to many peoples.

"And keep the entity close in that realm of spiritual understanding."

In the question-and-answer portion of the reading, Cayce was asked, "What, specifically, are the problems he should work out for himself during this particular sojourn on earth?"

Cayce replied, "As just indicated: its stubbornness in having its own way!"

He ended the reading with the statement that has come to haunt this boy's mother for years, for she has not been able to break through the streak of resistance to see it accomplished in her son. "Do have some period each day from now on—from now—for eighteen years—to practice the music!"

Reports

Robert, with military service behind him, has entered college and is studying architectural engineering. This seems to be another of his strong talents. A family friend, reporting to A.R.E. several years ago, stated, "Robert is extremely talented along the lines of mechanical drawing; he can sit down and sketch off anything. Guess that's the trait he inherited from his great grandfather, who was a contractor." (Or is it, we can't help but wonder, a talent brought forward from his former incarnation as an artist?)

That Robert is headstrong there can be no doubt; that he is stubborn almost to a fault cannot be denied. But this is only one side of his nature.

On the positive side, he has a quick, retentive mind, a thirst for knowledge, a charming personality, and an extremely handsome and healthy body. There is no question that he has musical talent, and that one day it may be put to use. It will happen when Robert loses the mistaken impression that his reading, and his mother, were trying to *force* him to be a musician and composer, and when he realizes that he is doing it entirely on his own, simply because he wants to.

CHAPTER 11

MISSING PERSONS

THE LOCATING OF missing persons certainly could not be considered Edgar Cayce's long suit. However, he did have some successes, along with a number of misses or near-misses.

The reasons behind this are not altogether clear. There is some indication that Cayce did not feel his psychic abilities should be used for such purposes; that he felt the emphasis of his work should be concentrated in the area of physical problems, or in offering mental and spiritual guidance. He demonstrated this once, when turning down a request from a doctor to locate a friend's missing husband. Cayce's refusal was polite but firm. "We have been advised through the information not to have anything to do with such cases. I am sorry, but I cannot help you."

Often, when he did accede to such requests, he suffered emotionally and physically as a result. Once he was asked to locate a young boy who apparently had been kidnapped from his New York City home early in April, 1938. The reading offered not so much a solution to the case as a question: should Cayce's abilities be used in this way?

As a partial answer to this question, Cayce added, "This is not a condition that is out of the ordinary, but the work of a pervert. Hence it becomes all the more a question as to what the decisions are to be in same; all the more questionable to undertake [such a search.]" Following this reading, Cayce was visibly upset and nervous.

His information concerning the boy seems to have been correct, as far as it went. The child's body was found several weeks later, floating in Long Island waters. There were indications that he had suffered a long and cruel captivity, and there were fragments of heavy baling wire wrapped about one arm.

Possibly Cayce's reluctance in this case was caused, at least in part, by the fact that in 1932 he had unsuccessfully tried to locate the Lindbergh baby. At the request of a friend of the Lindbergh family, a series of readings had been given in which seemingly accurate information was furnished. However, what the readings said did not match up with facts brought out at the trial of Bruno Richard Hauptmann. Hauptmann alone was convicted of the crime, whereas the readings indicated that he had not been working alone. We hasten to add that there were enough discrepancies between the readings and the information brought out at the trial to preclude the need for any serious inquiry into the matter.

It should be noted that the Lindberghs, themselves, did not request the readings. There have been many statements in the readings to the effect that such requests were most likely to meet with successful answers if there was a close relationship between the person sought and the person seeking.

There was a case in 1939 in which Cayce did try to locate a missing sixteen-year-old boy. The boy had disappeared from his home in an eastern city on July 8 of that year. The reading was given on November 25, 1939. Cayce said, "Yes, we have the circumstances and those conditions and anxieties that are manifested here with the mother. These are not altogether pleasant surroundings or pleasant conditions. . . . In the coming months, or in August [1940] there will be full knowledge and the return of the body to the mother. . . ." (It should be noted that Cayce's use of the word "body" was usual in referring to an individual, and in no way should be considered synonymous with "corpse.")

A family friend located the boy in Los Angeles in July, 1940. The parents, who had initiated the request for the reading, went there and brought their son home. However, they would supply no information whatsoever concerning the details of the case.

The Strange Disappearance of Mark Claypool

Cayce, in trying to locate missing persons, often appears to have been affected by a peculiar sort of block that interfered with the normal performance of his psychic work. No one case better illustrates this than that of Mark Claypool.

Mark was ten years old, severely retarded and a victim of epilepsy. Between July 31, 1929, and January 11, 1932, Cayce gave thirty-four successful readings for this boy, the last of which furnished a thorough medical picture of the boy's condition, as well as a full progress report on the results of the Cayce-prescribed treatments to date. It advised Mark's admittance to a special school, named in the reading as being best suited to his needs.

Then, around noon on July 12, 1932, Mark's mother telephoned Edgar Cayce's office to request an emergency reading for the purpose of locating her son. He had disappeared just after lunch two days before, while hiking with a number of classmates in the woods at the foot of a mountain. For some reason, the school had waited until just a few minutes before to notify her of Mark's disappearance.

Mrs. Cayce, conducting the reading, began by stating the circumstances as far as they were known. Then she said, "Please trace the movements of this body from Sunday afternoon, July 10, 1932, until the present time, and tell us where he is now and give directions how best to reach him. You will answer questions as they are asked."

Cayce replied, "We do not find him among those on the hike."

"Do you find him at this school or camp during, or earlier, in the day?"

"Do not find him at this camp or school. Find him at lunch, with others."

"Please trace him from the time you locate him. Was Mark at lunch at the camp or school at lunch time?"

"We do not locate him after lunch, here on the grounds, or about the buildings or the camp here."

"Where did he go? Please trace the body from the time you locate him at lunch."

"We do not find him here."

Steadily, Mrs. Cayce continued the inquisition. "Do you find him at this school any time during—"

Cayce interrupted. "At lunch."

"He was there at lunch?"

"He was there at lunch."

"Please follow the body from lunch, tell us where he went."

"We do not find the body."

"What happened to the body?"

"We do not find the body."

"Please tell us how we may get information regarding this body through this channel."

"We do not find the body."

"Did Mark leave with the others on the hike to stay overnight about one mile from the school?"

"We find the body at lunch. We do not find him later."

Mrs. Cayce was not yet willing to give up. "Please trace the body's movements from lunch time."

"We do not find the body."

"Where were the movements of the body after he ate lunch?"

"We do not find the body."

"Can you give us any information about Mark Claypool?"

"We do not find the body."

Mrs. Cayce continued rephrasing the questions. Each time, Cayce answered, "We do not find the body." She attempted to lead Cayce into an answer by supplying the material given at the beginning of the reading, the name and address of the school, the conditions leading up to the disappearance. No matter. Cayce would only answer, "We do not find the body."

Finally she asked, "Can't you trace Mark from the lunch table?"

"Cut off there. We cannot."

"What is meant by 'cut off there'?"

"Can't see him!"

"Can you tell us if anything happened to the body which caused death?"

"We do not find the body."

"Will you please explain to us what prevents you from tracing the body?"

"Something interferes. We do not know."

"In attempting at another time to obtain information regarding Mark Claypool, will you please tell us the best suggestion to give to the body, Edgar Cayce, in order to get information regarding Mark Claypool that we may aid his parents in locating him?"

Normally, Edgar Cayce would have supplied such a suggestion without hesitation. This time, however, he simply said, "We do not find the body."

Obviously, it was hopeless. Mrs. Cayce gave the suggestion for Edgar Cayce to wake up.

Cayce, of course, was terribly disappointed, and planned another attempt at a reading that evening.

Fortunately, it proved unnecessary. About eight o'clock that night the mother called to say that Mark had just been found—on the other side of the mountain, without a stitch of clothing on, all scratched up, dazed and famished. His mental retardation prevented him from telling anything about what had happened to him. He was placed in the hospital, treated for the poison ivy rash that soon developed all over his body, and recovered completely from the effects of his two days in the woods.

It is interesting that a number of additional readings were given for Mark Claypool throughout the next several years, all dealing with his physical condition, and there was never a time when Cayce was unable to get all of the information requested!

The Call That Was Heard

Frank Johnson had once been a wealthy man. The stock market crash in 1929 had taken nearly everything, however, and instead of adapting to his new circumstances, Frank began to misappropriate funds from his firm. By April, 1934, he was in so deep that he simply gave up and dropped out of sight. A note mailed from a city several hundred miles from his home notified the family of what he had done, and indicated that he intended to commit suicide.

His daughter contacted Cayce's office immediately and requested help. There followed a remarkable series of readings in which Cayce several times indicated that he knew Frank's whereabouts, but refused to let the family know where to contact him!

Cayce's concern, it seems, was not only for Frank's safety; there was also the attitude of his family to consider. Should Frank Johnson return home, the story of his embezzlement would most surely become public knowledge. Would the family be able to survive the embarrassment this would cause and continue to love and respect him?

Cayce's readings indicate a three-way purpose: to reach out and guide Frank Johnson's steps toward home; to reassure the family that he was alive; and to prepare them for Johnson's return. They form a day-to-day drama, and we will give the highlights as they developed.

The first reading was given on April 19, 1934. It began with a statement of the circumstances, as far as they were known, as well as one possible address where Frank might be located. Cayce was asked "to give the family all the necessary instructions and advice as to how they can get to him, if possible, and just what they should do."

Cayce said, "Yes, we have those conditions that confront those of the household, the Johnson family."

The message in this reading was for the family. The overriding theme was, "Would we be forgiven, we must forgive." When asked if Frank Johnson was still alive, Cayce replied, "This should be sought, just now."

A reading given the following day echoed the "forgiveness" theme, and furnished a prayer to be used by the family. Cayce was asked if the family was doing all that it could do, and should do, at that time. He replied, "Doing well. Keep the faith. Pray the prayer, and mean it, and live it, as is given."

He answered a question concerning whether Frank Johnson had assumed a different name, "No. Is he alive, or has he passed on? Let that tell thee that would come to pass, but in His name. *His* desire prevents that which might be given in yes or no; for, he *lives*—ever."

Later that same day, another reading was given in which Cayce indicated that Frank Johnson was "still in the living—still among those that may be reasoned with, in the realm of material understanding." Otherwise, all the information given was of a spiritual nature, directed to the family—although some of it was directed to Frank Johnson.

A few more readings followed, similar to this one. Then, on April 23, Cayce was given this suggestion for a reading: "In appreciation of the help that has been given the soul of Frank Johnson through this channel, we ask that it be continued. And whatever information we or the Johnson family should have, you will give it."

For five minutes Cayce spoke in an undertone so low that nothing could be understood, with the exception of one word uttered toward the end: Philadelphia.

Then, as if speaking directly to Frank Johnson, Cayce said, "The conditions are clearing in thine own consciousness. Then, act on the impulses that prompt thee to make a more determined effort in trusting in *His* promises that what is asked in His name, *believing,* that ye may have, that the Father may be glorified in Him and He in thee." The balance of the reading also seemed directed to Frank Johnson, and was along the same lines.

On April 24, at the end of a reading which had been devoted to spiritual guidance for Frank Johnson in finding his way back to mental health, Cayce said in an undertone, just before waking, "His cough is bad."

The reading suggestion on April 25 indicates that the family had decided to trust in Cayce's ability to follow Johnson's progress and not make a concerted effort to find him. It stated, "In appreciation of the help that has been given the soul of Frank Johnson through this channel, we ask that it be continued and urge him to have faith in his desire for his home. If this condition has reached the point that the entity is not responsible for his physical actions, you will tell us if information may be given those of his family assuming the responsibility as to how to locate him at once."

Cayce stated, "To be sure, further along the way has the body gone physically." The balance of the reading indicated that there was no need for the family to try to locate Johnson at this time.

The reading given the next day was quite dramatic. Cayce opened with the statement, "We don't contact the body!"

Then he began to speak with unusual urgency. "He will come! He will come! He will come! He will come! He will come! He WILL come!

"Let not those things hinder thee! Come! These all may be met in a much more satisfactory manner than has been felt!

"You have seen the way out! COME! Come! You WILL come! You will let those know, and keep that promise to self that you will let them know! Let them know!"

After a long pause, Cayce added, "We do not get the location of the body. It *is* alive—the body.

"He WILL come! He WILL come!"

He paused again, and then said, "We are through."

Afterwards, Cayce said that during the reading he had seen woods and water, and that the night before, he had dreamed that Frank Johnson had returned to his home.

Two days later, Cayce began his reading by saying, "We are pressed too tight! We will release through here." He went through a breathing exercise, and then made a surprising statement.

"Yes. As we find, there has been a communication pencilled by Frank Johnson to the family. This should be received very soon—present day or Monday." [The note was received by the family the following day. It indicated that Frank Johnson was alive, but furnished no information concerning his whereabouts or whether or not he intended to return home.]

On April 29, Cayce was asked to "give that which will be of the most help at this time to all concerned, in a material, mental and spiritual way."

He said, "Yes. Yes. We see—we see—oh, where is it? We see the body!" He then gave some spiritual advice.

Later in the same reading he said, "About the body is—what? What is this? What IS this? What IS this? *Where* is it?"

Again there was spiritual advice. Then Cayce said, "*Where* is this? Where is this? What is this about the body that hinders so? That surrounds in such a maze that keeps aid from coming?

"When thou hast chosen those things that block the way for the greatness of the spirit of light to enter, thou makest the way hard even for those that would do thee good. Thou shuttest them out of thine companionship. Thou cuttest them off from being that help and aid that makes for the light that would guide thee.

"This backs away!

"Rise! Make known unto the Lord what thou wouldst do. The mind will clear in Him . . .

"Where is this? *Where?* . . . Still in body!"

A number of readings followed this one, all of which were devoted to aiding the mental health of Frank Johnson. In one of them, on May 3, Cayce said, "Lot of water about the body this morning!" In another, on May 10, he said, "Very much in the open now, and much better is the environ and surrounding." (Following this reading, although all the material in it was of a spiritual nature and not out of the ordinary—for a Cayce reading, that is—Cayce had a strange experience. When he awoke from the reading, he said he felt marvelous, and remarked that he had been having such a good time, he didn't want to come back. Mrs. Cayce, he said, had interrupted him by waking him up; and he couldn't remember what it was he had been doing.)

In a reading on May 11, Cayce again spoke as if directly to Frank Johnson, "More and more do you find the desire in self to make self and self's own activities known to those that long and earnestly seek to know that thou hast chosen in thine weakness and in thine strength in Him to do. . . ."

On the next day, Cayce remarked, "Everything much lighter about the body, about the activities of the soul in the present." It seems, then, that Frank Johnson was indeed breaking through the emotional problems that had so beset him!

Cayce opened the next reading, on May 14, with the statement, "Quite a lot of green about the body; more spirituality coming into the understanding of the self, as to those things that disturb and have disturbed the body in the days just passed . . ." (Green, as you will recall from the chapter on auras, is the healing color. From Cayce's statement we may gather that he was referring to improvement in Johnson's mental state, rather than to his physical surroundings.)

And at the end of the following reading, on May 16, Cayce listened to the suggestion to awaken, except that he did not wait for the final statement, "You will wake up." Instead, he said, "Jesus of Nazareth passeth by. Let Him fill thine heart with the hopes of those promises that are indeed thine, wilt thou but apply. Trust ye in the Lord."

When he was awake, Cayce said that he had seen "the Master walking down a road toward us—*all* of us, expectant, waiting for Him to come—and He was smiling."

A few more readings followed in which Cayce again seemed to be urging Frank Johnson to return home. Then, on May 21, he began a reading by saying, "Yes. The physical body lives. It is among things green, and yet it is the city of those that are called dead." He included in this reading a prayer similar to The Lord's Prayer, but not word-for-word as it is normally used. At the end of the reading, when he was being given the suggestion to awaken, Cayce coughed. He awoke much more slowly than usual, and seemed in a daze for several minutes after apparently waking up.

Still more readings were given in which spiritual advice was offered to Frank Johnson. Then, on June 9, Cayce had just completed giving a physical reading for another individual, and seemed anxious to give one for Frank Johnson. Mrs. Cayce gave him the suggestion for such a reading. At the end of it, he stated, "Much grain about the body—in fields."

The same thing happened a couple of days later, at the end of another physical reading for an individual. Cayce began his reading for Frank Johnson by saying, "More hopeful. More better conditions. Keep the way, for the law of the Lord *is* perfect—converting the soul."

A few days after that, Frank Johnson returned home to a welcoming family. He verified many of the statements in the readings concerning his state of mind at certain times, as well as his surroundings as "seen" by Cayce. For example, he felt that Cayce's description, "The body . . . is among things green, and yet it is the city of those that are called dead," referred to the fact that at the time of the reading he had been walking through a cemetery.

When questioned about whether or not he had been conscious of Cayce's telepathic messages to him, urging him to return home, he said that he had not been aware of them as such, although he had felt something "pulling" on him, influencing him in a way he couldn't quite understand.

He managed to make full restitution of the funds he had stolen, and thereafter lived a full and useful life.

Cayce's "Search" for Amelia Earhart

We can make no claims concerning the accuracy of two readings given in 1937 in connection with the disappearance of Amelia Earhart and her navigator, Fred Noonan, during the last leg of their around-the-world flight. No positive statement has ever been made concerning what really happened to them. However, the readings are interesting, and we thought you might like to share some of the highlights.

The first was given on July 5 in answer to a request by a close friend of Amelia.

The reading suggestion was, "You will have before you the request from . . . for information regarding locating Amelia Earhart who, according to radio reports on July 2, 1937, was approximately one hundred miles from Howland Island in the South Pacific Ocean, in her plane. You will locate the plane as of this time and then trace it to its present position, giving specific directions for locating this plane now. You will answer questions regarding this."

Cayce said, "Yes, we have the request, and the anxiety that is manifested in the minds of many at this time. . . .

"As we find, while the conditions are rather serious, by the early morning hours (for it is night there now) there should be the locating from those that are searching in the area.

"This as we find lies in that position opposite from the ordinary for those who lose their way; to the north and to the west of Howland Island, upon the reef that extends from this western portion of the island—about, or in the proximity of less than a hundred miles from the main body of Howland Island; and from Howland Island in that of a westerly, northwesterly, direction."

"What is the present condition of Amelia Earhart and her companion?" he was asked.

"Amelia Earhart in the present is much better, standing the conditions much better than the companion; for the companion has been panicky, and with two these become conditions very much to be reckoned with.

"Not injured bodily so much as from exposure, and the mental condition."

"What happened to the plane? What is the condition of the plane?"

"It is broken up somewhat, but this as we find is more from the attempt in the landing when gas was gone than from anything else; though, to be sure, the winds and the inability to stabilize same has made all very out of order. Not able to proceed even with gas."

Cayce was asked for suggestions in connection with locating Amelia and her companion.

"Serious," he said. "Yet [there are] prospects of locating in this area in the early morning. But it will necessitate light, for there is no way of light for them except flashes—and this is soon giving way."

"Do they have food and water?"

"Mighty little of either.

"Conditions, to be sure, are gradually growing worse all the time. But there should be the rescue with that set in motion, in the early morning of tomorrow—

six—which is already beginning, but not fully complete as yet, and more activity is being shown in the right direction now."

At the end of the reading, Cayce remarked that he had seen "myriads of wire netting; some diamond-shaped and others square." This may have been a highly significant statement, as we shall see.

A second reading was given on August 1,1937, at the request of Amelia's husband, George P. Putnam, through A.R.E. contact of the friend who had requested the first one.

Cayce stated, "As we find, the twenty-first [of July] saw the experience of change in the experience of Amelia Earhart.

"Then, little helpful information may be given, save that: alone she perished.

"Then, this between eighty-nine and ninety miles northwest from her intended destination, or Howland Island.

"Storm—and heat.

"We are through."

Planes had searched the area until July 18. According to Cayce, Amelia had lived three days longer.

Throughout the years since Amelia Earhart and Fred Noonan disappeared, there has been much speculation concerning what might have happened to them. Many stories reporting knowledge of their fate have come to light, but none has survived serious investigation.

None, that is, until a Japanese-born woman living in San Mateo, California, reported to the San Mateo *Times* that she had seen two American flyers, a man and a woman, taken by guards on Saipan Island in the Marianas in 1937. This woman, whose name is Josephine Blanco Akiyama, gave accurate descriptions of Amelia and Fred, and furnished a good deal of evidence to support the truth of her story.

Her disclosure was made in May, 1960. It was not the first time she had told her story, but it was the first time it was to be acted upon.

What she had to say did not constitute proof of what had happened to the two flyers, but it was enough to prod a San Francisco radio newsman, Fred Goerner, into beginning an investigation. A joint venture involving Goerner, the Columbia Broadcasting System, the Scripps League of Newspapers, the San Mateo *Times*, and the Associated Press, this intensive investigation spanned the years from 1960 through 1966, and has been fully reported by Goerner in his book, *The Search for Amelia Earhart*, published by Doubleday in 1966.

The conclusions reached at the end of this investigation bear some resemblance to the information contained in the Cayce readings. Neither the investigation, nor the readings, give the final answer to what happened to the two flyers, for as Goerner himself says in summarizing the conclusion, "This is what *probably* happened, based on what we found."

In Goerner's version, Amelia and Fred did not fly directly from Lae, New Guinea toward Howland Island as had been announced in the original flight plan. Instead, they headed north to Truk in the Central Carolines, on an unofficial mission for the United States—that of checking Japanese airfields and fleet-servicing facilities in the Truk complex.

Goerner, an experienced pilot himself, suggests that their Electra, powered by Wasp Senior engines, was capable of speeds ranging from 200 to 220 miles per hour, rather than the 150 miles per hour which had been their top speed during the entire flight. He thinks the higher speed capability may have been deliberately concealed. Thus they would be able to detour over Truk and make good enough time that such a detour wouldn't "show" on the flight records.

When they encountered terrible weather conditions, in the form of strange wind currents—now perfectly calm, now turbulent—they knew they were in trouble. Because Amelia didn't want to be "caught" off to the Northwest of Howland, where she had no business being according to the flight plan, she kept her radio transmissions brief. Clouds obscured the sea for long periods of time, and navigation soon became confused.

Finally, with the gas nearly gone, Amelia, thinking they had overshot Howland, turned the plane around; thus they were actually heading away from their destination. She brought the plane down on a small island which was part of a larger atoll. It seems most probable, says Goerner, that the plane crash-landed in a lagoon at Mili Atoll in the southeastern Marshalls, which was territory mandated to Japan.

According to Goerner's summary of what probably happened, Amelia was not hurt, but Noonan struck his head against some metal in the cabin. His head was cut and he was knocked unconscious. Amelia bound his wounds, and when Noonan regained consciousness, Amelia left the plane to scout the area. Wading ashore, she encountered a number of natives, and managed through sign language to get them to understand that they were to carry Noonan ashore. This accomplished, Amelia then proceeded to send S.O.S. messages from the damaged plane.

Then, said Goerner's summary, on or about July 13, 1937, a Japanese fishing boat picked up Amelia and Fred and carried them either to the Japanese seaplane tender *Kamoi,* or the survey ship *Koshu.* They were taken to Jaluit, then to Kwajalein, and finally to Saipan, Japan's military headquarters in the Pacific. There they were interrogated—cruelly, it is suggested—and there they died; Amelia from dysentery, Noonan beheaded.

On the surface, it may seem that Cayce's readings bore little resemblance to what Goerner has reported in his book as having probably happened.

And yet there are similarities.

The location given in the readings does not seem to jibe. In the first place, there *is* no island 90 to 100 miles northwest of Howland. However, that's where Amelia thought she was when she brought the plane down, and it's possible that Cayce telepathically picked up her conscious thought in this regard; or possibly he accepted the reading suggestion as fact. His statement that they were "in that position opposite from the ordinary for those who lose their way" seems telling, in view of the Goerner statement that they had deliberately gone off course to fly over Truk.

Cayce mentioned high winds and storm. This may well have been a reference to the conditions which had caused them to bring the plane down. He also mentioned lack of gas, which according to the Goerner report was certainly true. Both Cayce and Goerner suggest that the plane was "landed," as opposed to an uncontrolled crash.

In his second reading, Cayce indicated that Amelia had died on the twenty-first of July. This would seem a reasonable date when compared to the Goerner report of their being picked up on July 13 and taken to Saipan for interrogation. Oddly,

Cayce, in the second reading, did not mention Noonan's fate—although this might be because Noonan's name was not furnished in the reading suggestion. Cayce also did not give the cause of death in Amelia's case, although his first reading had mentioned "exposure" as contributing to the poor conditions.

The most striking statement, in light of the Goerner report, is the statement at the end of Cayce's first reading, when he indicated that he had seen "myriads of wire netting—some diamond-shaped and others square." This could well refer to the capture and interrogation by the Japanese indicated in Goerner's report. Given on July 5, it could have been a prophetic vision, either symbolic or clairvoyant, concerning their eventual capture. Or perhaps they were captured sooner than July 13, the date fixed by Goerner.

The investigation in which Fred Goerner was involved was a painstaking one, with no arbitrary jumping to conclusions. He told me on the telephone a few weeks ago that it is continuing. So perhaps one day we will have *all* the answers to this thirty-two-year-old mystery.

CHAPTER 12

HISTORICAL DATA AS SHOWN IN THE EDGAR CAYCE READINGS

THERE IS A wealth of historical data in the Cayce readings. Most often it came as a result of life readings for individuals, wherein historical details concerning previous incarnations reflected the larger history of the entity's time.

Fortunately, on a great many occasions such statements were brought back to the sleeping Cayce for further explanation. Sometimes what he had to say disagreed with accepted knowledge, while at other times his words added to what was already known. In a striking number of cases the data given by Cayce made little sense at the time, only to be proved true in later years by archaeological discoveries or other supporting evidence.

In an earlier chapter, we discussed the case of the reincarnated Salome. Cayce, reading for this woman, indicated that as Salome, she had been present at Jesus' raising of Lazarus from the dead. Years passed before this information, which was at variance with that given in the Gospels, was confirmed through the discovery of ancient written documents.

The range of history found in the readings is astounding. We cannot begin to cover it all within the confines of this chapter, but we can indicate the scope of the material by providing a few examples drawn from readings given by Cayce for various individuals.

In a reading for a four-year-old boy, Cayce said, "Before this, we find the entity was in that land now known as the Arabian . . . then in the name Xertelpes . . ." (Other portions of the reading make it clear that "Arabian," here, meant Persia—which is now Iran.)

"And the entity was among those that became the first of the crop of judges in the city. . . ."

"There still may be found those remains of the entity near where Uhjltd [Cayce, in a previous incarnation] was entombed, in the cave outside of the city that had recently been builded and termed, or called, Shushtar; this to the south and west of that city, in the cave there."

For a forty-two-year-old woman, Cayce said, "Before that we find the entity was in the Chaldean land during those periods when there were the preparations for the peoples called the Jewish or Hebraic to return to their own land, for their establishing again of the activities in their home land.

"The entity may be said to have been the counsellor then to the king, Xerxes.

"The entity then was of the Chaldeans. And there may be found . . . in those excavations—look for same—that rod ye once used in thy divining of the individual purposes during that experience. This will be among those things that will soon be uncovered. It is of ebony and of gold."

For a forty-three-year-old woman, Cayce said, "Before this the entity was in the earth when there were those journeyings from the east to the west—GOLD! In '49 did the entity, with its associates and companions, journey to the western lands.

"Hardships were experienced on the way, yet the entity was among those that did attain, and saw, experienced, was associated in those acts with those that were comparable in their relationships to such conditions: rowdy, drink, spending.

"The name was Etta Tetlow. Records of these may be found in some of the questioned places in portions of California, even in the present."

For a twenty-year-old man, Cayce said, "Before this the entity was in the Norse land, and among those who were the daring, as the sailors; and the entity was Eric, as called through that experience; journeying to or settling in the land of its present nativity [America]."

Cayce was asked, "In the Norse land experiences, how often and in what years did he cross the ocean?"

He replied, "In 1552, 1509 and 1502." (Note that here, as always, Cayce went backwards in giving the dates. This seems to be another indication of his consulting the "record book" mentioned in an earlier chapter—a sort of mental leafing back through its pages.)

In discussing these journeys, he added, "In this country there were the settlements in the northwestern lands; portions even of Montana were reached by the entity—because the entrance then was through the St. Lawrence, through the Lakes."

Asked for proofs that might be found to substantiate this, he replied, "They have just been uncovered by a recent expedition there in Wisconsin . . . Among the knives and stones that were found, one of those was Eric's!"

Even from this small sampling, it is evident that Cayce's sense of geography and history was remarkable. There is also a compelling argument for the accuracy of such statements, it seems to me, in the fact that names furnished for various entities throughout the Cayce files are somehow "right" for the time and place. The name Xertelpes, for instance, given for the young boy mentioned above, fits perfectly in its place in the history of Iran. As was his custom, Cayce paused after reciting the name and carefully spelled it for the benefit of the stenographer recording the reading. (Once again we must remind the reader that Cayce had an extremely limited formal education, and read little outside the Bible during his lifetime.)

There is one more striking quality apparent in the readings. It is possible to go to the Cayce files and pull out any number of readings in which similar incarnations for different individuals are mentioned. Regardless of the number of years that passed between the readings, the facts will be found to coincide, to weave themselves into an intricate whole, with no real contradictions!

The Royal Family

To illustrate this last point, let's examine some readings given by Cayce for several members of the same family.

There are a couple of exceptional circumstances concerning these readings. First, they indicated that some of the entities had been famous during earlier incarnations, whereas the vast majority of Cayce readings were for people whose previous names were not well known. Second, three of these entitites were related to each other exactly as before; that is, father, mother and son in one incarnation were again father, mother and son—a rarity among the Cayce readings.

The father, whom we'll call Roger Morrison, received his reading on August 6, 1926. Cayce stated that in his previous incarnation, he had been in France, and had been "the entity known as [King] Louis XVI."

Roger's wife, Sarah, had received her reading about a year earlier, on July 15, 1925. Of her earlier incarnation, Cayce said, "We find in that of the Queen who was beheaded, in that of Marie Theresa, or Marie Antoinette, as known in the historic forces. . . ."

In a reading for their son, Charles, on July 23, 1925, Cayce said, "In the appearance before this, we find in that of the entity who was the one to become the King in France, when the father and mother were at that time beheaded. The entity then only gained in the knowledge of the earth's forces through the things which the entity suffered, for the life at that time was only half a score years plus five."

Sarah Morrison seems to have retained, unconsciously, many "reminders" of the French incarnation. According to notes made in the files by members of the A.R.E. staff who knew her well, we find that Sarah was a woman of "regal bearing. She *is* sort of a 'queen' of a large family, and has the last word on any decision of importance." She was quite tall, and very beautiful.

Another interesting report on her states, "When traveling by train, she would never go from one car to another, for she said she could not bear the sound of the rumbling wheels. Could this be a throwback to the ride over cobblestones to her death?"

Sarah had a great love for beautiful and luxurious things. She was an accomplished painter, and collected fine furniture, old silver and linens. "When she died," says another note in the file, "she left trunks of elaborately embroidered linens. All her life, since a very young girl, she never sat even for a few minutes without picking up her embroidery." (This could well be an influence brought forward not only from the French, but from a much earlier incarnation in Egypt, of which Cayce said, "The entity then giving much to the people, and the desire to preserve relics, old and new, the desire to preserve the best for the worship of every nature. . . . The urges show also in the artistic abilities, and the ability to design of every character, anew, as it were, from others, for much of the Temple decorations in that day were of the mind of this entity. . . ."

To continue the chronicle of this family, let's look now at a reading given on July 1, 1930 for Barbara Withers, who was to marry Charles Morrison six years later. They had known each other for several years, and were dating at the time the reading was given. (On the day they met, Barbara came home from school and exclaimed to her mother, "He's the most wonderful boy! I love him. I know that sounds silly — but I feel as though I've known him for a long, long time.")

Concerning Barbara, Cayce said, "In the appearance before this we find during that period when there were troublesome times in the land known as France. The entity then the one to whom the young King [the Dauphin] was given in charge, and was the keeper of same—even until the time of the passing from the body. The entity lost and gained through that influence. During the first portion of this period the entity lost, for oft were the stripes laid on the body [of the Dauphin] by the entity. Then in the latter period were there the sorrows as were known from the conditions as surrounded that brought for the entity much of an under- standing of the better relationships between those of high estate and those that were of the keeper, or the servant, in such periods."

So we find that in her French incarnation, Barbara had been in charge of the young man who would have been King Louis XVII, had the Revolution not intervened. Generally, the assumption has been that her position was that of nursemaid. However, in this reading Cayce departed from his usual practice and did not furnish her name for that incarnation. Since the sex of the entity was rarely designated in the readings, an interesting point is raised.

There has always been some question concerning the fate of the young Dauphin following the execution of his parents. Rumors have persisted, but have never been substantiated, that he escaped the country. However, the records of the French government indicate that he was placed in the care of a cobbler named Simon, suffered neglect, and died at the age of ten. Considering the complete confusion existing in France in the years of the Revolution, it is possible that the records are incorrect. It is equally possible, of course, that Cayce erred in stating that the Dauphin died at the age of fifteen.

Noting Cayce's harsh statements in Barbara's reading concerning the person caring for the Dauphin, we wonder if possibly she was the person the French records show as "Simon." Cayce's remarks to the effect that the Dauphin was often whipped, and suffered much, would make this seem plausible. His statement that she had been with the Dauphin until the time of his death does raise this perplexing question: was Barbara a man in that incarnation—a man named Simon? Or was she, as has been assumed, a nursemaid—possibly one who was in the French court, later took the boy to Simon, and stayed on, thus sharing in the care (and neglect) of the child until his death? Spanking a child occasionally—or even often—would not seem to be sufficient basis for Cayce's claiming that the entity (now Barbara) had suffered soul retrogression which was somewhat cancelled out by an understanding, later in her life, "of the better relationships between those of high estate and those that were . . . the servant in such periods."

Barbara's sister received a life reading, in December, 1930. Said Cayce, "In the one before this we find during that period when there were rebellions or oppressions in the land known as the French. The entity was among those peoples who were in touch with those in authority as rulers, for the entity [was] one of the offspring [of those] to whom these peoples went upon their attempt to escape from the land. . . ."

Taken by itself, this statement doesn't particularly advance our knowledge of French history. It undoubtedly refers to the known fact that, on the night of June 20, 1791, the King and Queen and their family, disguised as ordinary travelers, went by coach toward Malmédy on the eastern border of France. They were detected at Varennes, and were forced to return to Paris.

This episode in history was elaborated on in a Cayce reading given in October, 1939, for Charles and Barbara Morrison's daughter. "Before that we find the entity was in the French land; being a child, or a young lady thirteen to fourteen years of age in the experience, when the entity's present father and its present mother (an attendant to the present father) were, with the King and the Queen, turned back."

(This statement, of course, shoots a few holes in our speculations about the possibility that Barbara, in her French incarnation, had been a cobbler named Simon to whom the Dauphin was given in charge. It does not rule out the possibility that she later went with the Dauphin to Simon—or, indeed, that there *was* no Simon, after all; that the French records were wrong. We could have eliminated all mention of such speculations on our part, but instead we have included them to show the kind of things many people went through upon receiving their readings and, trying to match up what Cayce had to say with what has been recorded in history, found mystifying discrepancies.)

To continue the reading for Barbara's daughter, we find that Cayce said, "The entity was then in the household of the tavern where that turning back took place—in the name then Arabela.

"In the experience the entity suffered through its feelings for those who were to the entity so royal, so above others; and, because of their gentleness, their kindness, their feelings, the entity has sought expression in such environs in the present. . . ." (There was an unusually strong tie between this child and her grandmother, the "former" Marie Antoinette. Her grandfather died before the child was born.)

The Morrisons also had a son. His life reading, interestingly enough, shows no French incarnation—although he had been associated with some members of his family in an early appearance in Egypt.

When these readings are put together, it is easy to see that Cayce has furnished a good portion of French history. Presented over a span of some *fourteen years,* he has given facts concerning each individual which, combined with facts given to other members of the family, form a complete story. There are no deviations from accepted facts concerning the French royal family, with the exception noted above concerning the fate of the Dauphin. (Later readings were given for the purpose of expanding this information, and although much was added, nothing was altered.)

All these statements were made spontaneously during the course of the readings. None came as a result of direct questioning or prompting of any kind.

The Essenes and the Dead Sea Scrolls

There are a number of Cayce readings on file in which an individual was said to have been connected, in a former incarnation, with an Essene community. These readings gave much information concerning such communities which at that time could not be confirmed.

This was because, at the time of the readings, hardly anything was known of the Essenes. What little was known came principally from the writings of three men, all of whom lived during the first century after the birth of Christ: the Jewish historian, Josephus; the philosopher, Philo; and the Roman historian, Pliny the Elder.

What made things even more confusing was that often what Cayce said about the entity's experience during that time did not match up completely with what was known about the Essenes, or, for that matter, what we know about them today.

Present knowledge—admittedly still scanty—has it that the Essenes were a Jewish religious group which flourished in the two centuries before and after the period of Christ's appearance on the earth. They were a communal society, extremely pious, who emphasized the virtue of physical and spiritual purity. They refused to take oaths or engage in animal sacrifices as did the Sadducees and the Pharisees. Their major endeavors centered around agriculture and hand-icrafts, for they felt these two occupations were the least sinful. They abhorred commerce, believing that it led to the covetousness and to the making of the weapons of war. Until recent years, when skeletons of women were found in the graveyards of some Essene communities, it was believed that they were inhabited only by men. (This, incidentally, confirmed statements made years earlier by Cayce.)

The Essenes were thought by some to be celibate, but their numbers did not die out because of the practice of taking in young boys and bringing them up as novices, as well as accepting adult males who rejected life outside the communities. Enrichment of the soul was the main emphasis of their religion. It has been widely speculated—although not yet proved—that John the Baptist was an Essene.

The Essenes were highly respected, and became famous for their mysticism and esoteric knowledge—the nature of which is little known, since the Essene communities were essentially secret societies.

There has been much controversy, through the years, concerning whether or not Jesus Christ was associated with the Essenes. Although there is no consequential evidence to support either side of the debate, the consensus seems to be that Jesus was not connected with them, but that some of his disciples may have come out of such communities—particularly those who were formerly disciples of John the Baptist.

The Cayce readings, however, indicate otherwise. Bearing in mind that there can be no proof, as yet, of the accuracy of what he had to say on the subject, here is a brief rundown of the life of Jesus as it is shown in the Cayce files.

First we should mention that Cayce, in his many discussions of the Essenes through the readings, said that in Palestine their principal center was at Mount Carmel, near the shores of the Mediterranean Sea. (Practically no archaeological surveys have been done in this area, as yet; it is interesting to speculate on what might be uncovered in future years.)

Here is what Cayce had to say in one reading. "In the days when more and more leaders of the people had been trained in the temple at Mount Carmel, the original place where the school of the prophets was established during Elijah's time, there were those leaders called Essenes—students of what ye would call astronomy, astrology, phrenology, numbers and numerology, and that study of the return of individuals—or reincarnation.

"There were reasons why these proclaimed that certain periods formed a cycle— reasons which grew out of the studies of Aristotle, Enos, Mathias, Judy and others who supervised the school, as ye would term it in the present.

"These individuals had been persecuted by leaders of the people, and this caused the saying of which ye have an interpretation, as given by the Sadducees, 'There is no resurrection' or 'There is no reincarnation'—which is what the word meant in those days. . . ."

"Hence there was continued preparation and dedication of those who might be channels through whom the chosen vessel could enter—through choice—into materiality. Those in charge at that time were Mathias, Enos and Judy. Thus in Carmel where there were the priests of this faith . . . twelve maidens were chosen who were dedicated to this purpose, this office, this service. Among them was Mary, the beloved, the chosen one; and she, as had been foretold, was chosen as the channel. Thus she was separated and kept in closer associations with and in the care of this office.

"That was the beginning, that was the foundation of what ye term the Church."

According to the readings, then, it was the Essenes who chose Mary to be the Virgin Mother. She had been chosen at the age of four, and had been placed in the custody of the temple priests at Carmel. There she had begun a long and arduous training period which included mental and physical exercises, special foods and diet, learning the wisdom and necessity of chastity, purity, love, patience and endurance. She was twelve before she was told the purpose of her training.

The readings indicate that Joseph, also selected by the Essenes, objected at first to the union with Mary. He was, after all, thirty-six years old, whereas Mary was only sixteen. He was concerned about what people would say, not only because of the difference in their ages, but because of the very nature of a virgin birth. However, through a dream and a vision he became convinced that it was Divine Will, and he consented.

The marriage ceremony, said Cayce, was performed at Carmel in the temple of the Essenes, after which Joseph returned to his home in Nazareth and Mary retired to the hill country of Judea to await the birth of Jesus.

Near the end of her pregnancy, Mary joined Joseph at Nazareth and they began the journey to Bethany—some seventy miles away—to register for taxation as required by law.

It was about this time that the wise men, who were initiates in the Mysteries, perceived the signs of the coming of Jesus, and came from Egypt, India and the Gobi, to serve as emissaries of the religious leaders in those countries. They bore their gifts of gold, frankincense and myrrh, representing, according to Cayce, the healing force—or body, mind and soul.

Then, at midnight on January 6 of the present Gregorian calendar, Jesus was born in the stable of a hillside inn in Bethlehem. The innkeeper's daughter acted as midwife.

One reading elaborated on this journey to Bethany. "Each individual was required by Roman law to be present in the city of his birth for this polling. Both Joseph and Mary were members of the sect called Essenes; and thus they were to be polled and questioned not only by those in political, but also in religious authority in the City. . . .

"For remember, many of those present [at the inn] were also of that questioned group, the Essenes. They had heard of the girl, that lovely wife of Joseph, who had been chosen by the angel on the stair; they had heard of what had taken place in the hills where Elizabeth had gone, when she [Elizabeth] had been visited by this girl, her cousin . . ."

According to the readings, Mary had spent the required period of purification following the birth of Jesus. Then the Infant had been taken to the temple to be blessed by Anna, Mary's mother, and by the high priest. The family then returned to Nazareth. Herod's edict, ordering the death of the Jews, had forced them to flee to Egypt; they remained there for five years. A handmaid called Josie, and at other times called Sophie, stayed with Mary for many years, helping with the care of the young Jesus, as well as with the other children who came later. She also cared for Joseph in his last days. Josie was an Essene; thus the readings indicate a continuing influence of the Essenes upon the life of Jesus.

After the five-year stay in Egypt, the family went to Judea, then to Capernaum, and then settled once again in Nazareth. At the age of ten, Jesus was presented in the temple. There was much counseling and discussion among the rabbis, leading to Jesus' going to Egypt to begin His schooling in the secret doctrines of the law. The readings do not specify whether or not these rabbis were Essenes; however, they do indicate that Jesus had some teaching by the Essenes.

"The return was made to Capernaum, not Nazareth, and not just because of political reasons following the death of Herod. But a division of the kingdom had been made after the death of Herod. And the return [to Capernaum] was so that there might be the ministry or teaching that was to be a part of the Brotherhood, supervised in that period by Judy, as one of the leaders of the Essenes in that particular period."

According to the readings, Jesus spent only a short time in Egypt in connection with His training. He was then sent to India, and then "into what is now Persia."

Jesus spent one year in Egypt, India and Persia. He was called home upon the death of Joseph, and then returned to Egypt for more schooling. The readings indicate that during part of this time He was with John the Messenger. Between the ages of thirteen and sixteen, He was in India and studied under Kshijiar. In Persia He studied under Junner; in Egypt, under Zar.

Then, "after the return to Jerusalem there were the periods of education in Syria, India and the completion of the studies in Egypt; and the passing of the tests there by those who were of the Essene group, as they entered into the service; as did the Master, and John before him."

Once His schooling was completed, Jesus went to Capernaum, Cana and the land of Judea. Here the readings coincide with what has been written in the Gospels concerning Jesus' ministry. He taught the lessons of Isaiah, Jeremiah and the lesser prophets, in the synagogues.

Jesus, as portrayed in the readings, was not of the sad countenance and frail body generally depicted by others. Indeed, said Cayce, He smiled often, and sometimes spoke lightly. He excelled in playing the harp.

He attended the wedding of His sister Ruth, who married a Roman tax supervisor.

There are a great many readings given for individuals which support the story of Jesus and fill in many gaps in present knowledge of the Essenes.

A summary of this information might contain the following: there were many Essene communities, widely scattered throughout the Middle East area, from Egypt to India. In Palestine, their center was not on the Dead Sea, but at Mount Carmel, some seventy miles to the north.

Although Jesus, according to the readings, was raised and educated by Essenes, He seems to have differed with them in some aspects of their beliefs. Indeed, some of His admonishments seem to have been directed toward them.

The readings indicate that the Essene community on the Dead Sea was evidently dispersed around 70 A.D., when large numbers of Roman soldiers drove them from their site.

With the discovery of the Dead Sea Scrolls of Khirbet Qumran in 1947, and the extensive excavations of the various caves in the area since that time, we now seem to be on the way to finding out whether Cayce's readings were completely accurate, partly accurate, or absolutely wrong. So far, there seems to have been no discovery that disproves what he had to say. Some discoveries have confirmed material given in the readings.

Restoring the Scrolls—tens of thousands of bits of papyrus, copper and leather, in a dreadful state of decay—is a monumental task, and it has been estimated that it may take at least fifty years to decipher and translate those already recovered. Even as this is accomplished, there will surely be growing debates concerning their content and their meaning to Christianity.

One piece of Essene literature recently deciphered indicates that the communion meal of that day, almost identical to that used today, was a liturgical anticipation of the Messianic banquet. It details the offering of the bread, and then the wine, to the congregation of the community. It ends with the statement, "And they shall follow this prescription whenever [the meal is ar]ranged, when as many as ten meet together."

The Last Supper Described by Edgar Cayce

The foregoing was not presented as a means of trying to establish proof of the accuracy of Cayce's readings concerning Jesus. Such an attempt would be, at the least, extremely premature. But because of information coming to light as a result of the discovery of the Dead Sea Scrolls, we thought you would find Cayce's words interesting. The same might be said for the following reading.

It was given at the end of a physical reading for a woman on June 14, 1932. Cayce, after being given the suggestion to awaken three times, refused to do so. Instead, he began to recite this story of the Last Supper:

"Here, with the Master. See what they have for supper . . . boiled fish, rice with leeks, wine, and loaf. One of the pitchers in which it is served is broken. The handle is broken as is the lip to same.

"The whole robe of the Master is not white, but pearl gray—all combined into one—the gift of Nicodemus to the Lord.

"The better looking of the twelve, of course, was Judas. The younger was John: oval face, dark hair, smooth face, the only one with the short hair. Peter, the rough and ready, always that of very short beard, rough, and not altogether clean. Andrew's is just the opposite: very sparse, but inclined to be long more on the side and under the chin—long on the upper lip. His robe was always near gray or black, while his clouts or breeches were striped; while those of Philip and Bartholomew were red and brown.

"The Master's hair is 'most red, inclined to be curly in portions, yet not feminine or weak. Strong, with heavy piercing eyes that are blue or steel-gray.

"His weight would be at least a hundred and seventy pounds. Long, tapering fingers, nails well kept. Long nail, though, on the left little finger.

"Merry—even in the hour of trial. Joke—even in the moment of betrayal.

"The sack is empty. Judas departs.

"The last is given of the wine and loaf, with which He gives the emblems that should be so dear to every follower of Him. Lays aside His robe, which is all of one piece. Girds the towel about His waist, which is dressed with linen that is blue and white. Rolls back the folds, kneels first before John, James, then to Peter—who refuses.

"Then the dissertation as to 'He that would be the greatest would be servant of all.'

"The basin taken is without handle, and is made of wood. The water is from the gherkins, that are in the wide-mouth shibboleths that stand in the house of John's father, Zebedee.

"And now comes, 'It is finished.'

"They sing the ninety-first Psalm: 'He that dwelleth in the secret place of the Most High shall abide under the shadow of the Almighty. I will say of the Lord, He is my refuge and my fortress; my God, in Him will I trust.'

"He is the musician as well, for He uses the harp.

"They leave for the garden."

Here again, as in the case of the Essenes, and Jesus' connection with them, we find that Cayce has provided a most interesting situation. He has interwoven accepted versions of Biblical history and material supplied from his own source of information, presumably the akashic records.

His version of the Last Supper is unique, so far as we can determine. It agrees in some respects with the accounts given in the four Gospels—which, themselves, do not completely agree—and seems to be an attempt to fill out the story for us, to expand our knowledge of this important and moving event.

It would be difficult, if not impossible, to believe that such a narration amounted to nothing more than a fanciful journey through the unconscious mind of Edgar Cayce.

Who Built Stonehenge—And When?

The famous ruined monument—now no more than a complex arrangement of ditches, pits and stone columns on England's Salisbury plain—continues to be a mystery.

My 200-year-old Encyclopaedia Britannica indicates that around 1768 Stonehenge consisted of "the remains of four ranks of rough stones, ranged one within another, some of them, especially in the outermost and third rank, twenty feet high, and seven broad; sustaining others laid across their heads and fastened by mortises, so that the whole must have anciently hung together. . . ."

In those days, people were pretty well convinced that it was a British temple. However, said the encyclopaedia, the English architect Inigo Jones had "given a fine scheme of the work, and strives hard to persuade the world that it was Roman."

In 1797, amateur archaeological expeditions caused some of the enormous stones to topple to the ground.

Then, in 1950, the theory that the monument had been built by Druids was finally laid to rest. Interest, which had flagged over the centuries, was revived.

In 1952, Professor W. F. Libby of the University of Chicago estimated that Stonehenge had been constructed about 3,800 years before, or around 1850 B.C.

In 1958, Richard J. C. Atkinson reported his view that the monuments were not of British design or construction, but the work of "an itinerant architect from one of the two great Mediterranean civilizations—the Minoan in Crete or the Mycenean in Greece." Mr. Atkinson, together with Professor Stuart Piggott, had been put in charge of a British-financed project to raise the six 45-ton stones which had fallen in 1797.

In 1959, the British Museum announced that radiocarbon dating of bits of deer antler found at Stonehenge proved that the monuments had been built around 3,670 years before. In other words, they supported the estimate of Professor Libby.

In 1964, Dr. Gerald Hawkins of the Smithsonian Astrophysical Observatory reported on experiments he had made which indicated that Stonehenge may have been a huge astronomical calendar. He calculated the directions of the lines joining the various stones and holes of the compound, gathered data relative to the movements and positions of the heavenly bodies at the time Stonehenge was built (1500 B.C., according to his estimate) and fed this data into a computer. The results showed twenty-four close correlations with solar and lunar directions. Dr. Hawkins, said the report, is convinced that Stonehenge was built as a device for predicting seasons and for signalling the approach of eclipses. This, he said, indicated a remarkably advanced solar-lunar lore, in some ways superior to that of the Egyptians and Mesopotamians of the period.

The mystery would seem to be still quite a mystery.

So let's turn to what Edgar Cayce had to say about Stonehenge in several readings given in which the subject came up.

In one, he was asked outright to tell who built Stonehenge, and for what purpose.

He answered, "In the Holy Land when there were those dredgings up in the period when the land was being sacked by the Chaldeans and Persians . . . among those groups who escaped in ships and settled in portions of the English land near what is now Salisbury, and there builded those altars that were to represent the dedication of individuals to the service of a living God."

In other words, Stonehenge was built around 1800 B.C. by Jews escaping the Chaldeans and Persians. This date would seem to agree with the estimates of Professor Libby and the British Museum.

Another time, Cayce said, "Before that the entity was in England . . . and there should be many of those lands, especially in the areas where altars were once set up by the peoples from the Holy Land, that should be of interest as well as bring to the mind of the consciousness of the entity the happenings of that period. . . ."

And in another reading, "in the land of the present nativity [England] during those periods when there was the expanding of the activities of the groups that had settled there from the Holy Land . . . A home builder, in the name of Ersa Kent. . . ."

Still another reading stated, "Before this the entity was in England when the people from the Holy Land were coming in. The entity was with a group which had been part of the temple watch in Jerusalem, which had established the outer courts of the temple for individual service and activity. The entity helped set up altars which long since have been torn away, though evidence yet remains of stones set up in the form of a court, with an inner court for those who sought to learn of the Lord." Thus, in this reading, Edgar Cayce described not only the earlier temple, but the ruins as they appear today!

In another reading he said, ". . . before that we find the entity was in the English land in the early settlings of the children of Israel who were foregathered with the daughters of Hezekiah in what is now Somerland, Somerhill, or Somerset. There the entity saw group organization for the preservation of tenets and truths of the Living God. . . ."

And finally, this: "Before that the entity was in the English land during those periods when there was the breaking up of the tribes of Israel. The entity was a granddaughter of Hezekiah the King, and among those who set sail to escape when the activities brought the rest of the people into servitude in the Persian land. Then the entity was among those who landed and set up the seat of customs as indicated in the altars built near what is now Salisbury, England."

These readings, were for different individuals, given over a considerable span of years. And yet the information in each of them seems to parallel all the others. Although this, in itself, cannot prove the accuracy of the readings, it certainly makes a thought-provoking statement.

PRECOGNITION AND PROPHECY

EDGAR CAYCE CERTAINLY did not consider himself a prophet. And yet he uttered, over a period of some forty-three years, an almost incredible number of prophetic statements—a great many of which have already come true.

In scope, these statements seem limitless. They range all the way from a simple one, made at the end of a physical reading for a woman suffering from a severe cold, "Then—be well by Wednesday!" to a complex and frightening one indicating that great earth changes would begin to take place during the period 1958 to 1998. The woman with the cold *was* completely well by Wednesday. And a lot of the earth changes prophesied by Edgar Cayce *have begun*.

There are enough Cayce prophecies on file to fill a book. Fortunately, they do fill one: a book in this series, entitled, *Edgar Cayce on Prophecy*. Since its author, Mary Ellen Carter, has done a fine job of pulling this material together and putting it into focus, we will not attempt to cover the subject in any depth within this chapter. Instead, we will try to indicate the scope of the material by citing a few examples from the Cayce readings.

Prophecy: Concerning the Individual

Edgar Cayce, in 1934, was asked if it is possible, by psychic means, to absolutely prophesy specific events in the future of an individual.

He answered, "Such things should rather be builded from within. And if the soul merits such [success], through that it metes to its fellow man, it will bring such into the experience of the body. But to say that it *will* happen—it can't be done! For the Father, Himself, has given each soul that portion of Himself. What the soul *does* about his knowledge, about his abilities or opportunities, depends upon the *will* of the soul.

"Hence, as to whether this is to come to pass or may not come to pass—it may, my brother, to *any* soul. What wilt thou do about the opportunities that have been and are being presented to thee?"

So we see that Cayce's words concerning the future of an individual were never to be considered fortune telling. Rather, and this is particularly evident in the life readings, Cayce told of personal characteristics and talents as he "read" them from the person's unconscious mind. It was then up to the individual to do something about his talents, to make the most of the opportunities that came his way. If the reading indicated a need for caution in certain areas, then it was up to the individual to exercise such caution. Nevertheless, a great many statements Cayce made in the life readings seemed prophetic—and were proven by the passage of time. This is because the individual followed his reading, or his natural bent, or both.

In the physical readings, a statement such as, "Then—be well by Wednesday!" meant simply, "This is the best treatment for this particular body. Follow it faithfully, with the correct mental attitude, and you will be well." If the patient obeyed instructions, the "prophecy" generally came true.

We have seen many examples of such statements contained in readings covered in earlier chapters; indeed, some degree of prophecy is to be found in the majority of life and physical readings. But we did not specifically point to certain portions of the readings and exclaim, "Prophecy!" We will do so now, with a couple of interesting readings from the Cayce files.

John Marshall's reading was given when he was only eight months old, and yet we find that Cayce was most explicit—and prophetic—in suggesting his career potentials. "We find those influences will be in the direction of mathematical calculations," he said. "Especially as pertaining to electrical energy." The parents were directed to give the boy every opportunity to develop interest in mathematics and electricity. "Then we would find the wonderful mental development of the entity in the present earth's plane. . . .

"In the urge as will be found in the present entity: that of the ability to correlate data in a manner that will be at fingertips, as it were, in memory and mathematical form. . . .

"Then, that to which the entity may attain in the present earth's plane, and how: with the correct guiding through the moulding age, the entity will take on those urges of the electrical forces and application of same in a mathematical manner beyond that as has been undertaken heretofore . . ."

At the age of fourteen, John Marshall announced to his mother that he intended to become an airplane designer. He took a part-time job in an electric shop.

When he was nineteen, John's mother wrote to A.R.E. to say that he was working with the Air Transport Command as an aviation mechanic. He was also attending night school.

When John was twenty-nine, his mother reported that he had gone into partnership in an electrical construction business. "He likes it very much, and is doing well," she said.

Three years later, she indicated that John's abilities were still being cultivated, even at the age of thirty-two. "He goes to college two nights a week, still taking physics. He has to study other evenings and also puts in some overtime. He is now a Production Engineer. I believe he will be married soon. . . ."

It is evident from the correspondence that John Marshall's road was not paved with gold, and he pretty much had to make his own opportunities. He had to work hard to reach the potential indicated in the Cayce reading, but he accomplished it with singleminded determination. He is married now, with children, and has become highly successful in his field as well as in his family and social life.

In contrast, consider the case of Peter Matson, who was given a life reading in 1944. He was twelve years old. Cayce had many warnings concerning his future. "In giving the interpretations of the records here of this entity, it would be very easy to interpret same either in a very optimistic or a very pessimistic vein. For there are great possibilities and great obstacles. But know, in either case, the real lesson is within self. For here is the opportunity for an entity (while comparisons are odious, these would be good comparisons) to be either a Beethoven or a Whittier or a Jesse James or some such entity! For the entity is inclined to think more highly of himself than he ought to think, as would be indicated. That's what these three individuals did, in themselves. As to the application made of it, depends upon the individual self."

Cayce indicated that Peter had a strong latent ability to become a musician, a poet or a writer, "which few would ever excel. Or there may be the desire to have its own way to such an extent that the entity will be in the position to disregard others altogether in every form, just so self has its own way."

Depending upon how well the boy might be brought under control, without breaking his spirit, Cayce said, "we will not only give to the world a real individual with genius, but make for individual soul development. Otherwise, we will give to the world one of genius in making trouble for somebody."

Peter's parents tried very hard to follow the reading. They sent him to a strict boarding school, and sought professional help for their son in an attempt to understand and guide his difficult personality.

At the age of sixteen, however, Peter became emotionally unbalanced. Three years later, he shot his father and his grandmother. He was confined to a mental hospital for several years.

In 1956, when Peter was twenty-four, his mother reported to A.R.E. that, although Peter was still in an institution, she was optimistic about his future. "With only one setback, he has steadily improved and we have great hopes that he will ultimately recover. . . ."

We certainly would not want to imply that anyone could have done anything to prevent the tragedy in Peter's life. His parents spared no effort or expense in getting the best professional help available for this young man both before and after his emotional problems erupted in violence.

Rather, we offer the case to illustrate how well Cayce foretold, through explaining the natural inclinations of twelve-year-old Peter Matson, the difficulties that lay ahead.

Prophecy: Concerning the Human Body

Philip Andrews was suffering from a serious form of arthritis which affected his back and legs. In one of a series of readings given for this condition, Cayce was asked if the prescribed treatments would check the atrophying of the muscles in Philip's right leg and thigh.

"They will check the atrophying of the muscles in the limbs," he stated.

"Can the leg be brought back to normal?"

"Try it!" Cayce said. "It's worth trying! It will, if there are the applications in the manners indicated."

This statement was made on September 12, 1937. Exactly one month later,

Philip wrote to Edgar Cayce, "First of all, there was immediate relief as a result of the treatment outlined in my last reading. The leg, which was rapidly atrophying, has put on flesh, and Dr. D. is amazed at it. . . ."

This is not an unusual case at all. The A.R.E. files are full of such prophetic statements which came true *because of the application made by the individual—* the one ingredient stressed in the Cayce readings as being essential to success.

In the physical readings, both those for individuals and those covering a specific malady for which a special reading was given (such as the common cold) we find much prophecy—although often it is so subtle that it might easily be missed, had it not been repeated so often.

For example, Edgar Cayce prescribed the use of gold, in various forms, for use in many different illnesses.

The sands at Virginia Beach, he said, contained much chloride of gold, and arthritis patients, particularly, were directed to lie on the beach with affected portions of the body covered by the sand in order to let the sun "bake" it in. (My grandfather was one of these, and it helped him immeasurably.)

Chloride of gold, said Cayce in a reading given many years ago, would be particularly useful in "any condition wherein there is any form of the condition bordering on rheumatics, or of the necessity of rejuvenating any organ of the system showing the delinquency in action, see?"

In the same reading, he stated, "Many of the conditions as are existent in alcoholic stimulants, as have been applied to the system, that has destroyed the tissue in central portion of the body, destroyed tissue in the recreative forces in the generative system, destroyed tissue in other portions of the system, even unto the brain itself, give these (the various ails of the body); gold or silver, or both, would add and rebuild—rejuvenate, as it were, in the system. Give these, for they are good."

Among many conditions for which chloride of gold was specified by Cayce in his readings were the physical problems associated with alcoholism, arthritis, assimilations, asthenia, blindness, bursitis, cancer, circulatory disturbances, diverticulitis, eliminations, glands, insanity, menopause, multiple sclerosis, and so on. In some cases it was to be administered orally. In others, it was to be given through use of a so-called "wet cell appliance," a vibratory device developed out of the Cayce readings which, in effect, electrically transmitted certain substances into the body—or, as suggested in at least one reading, enabled inactive elements in the body, such as gold, to become stimulated into action.

The main factor in the specification of gold in the readings seems to be that gold has a rejuvenating power for the body. Its use, as shown in many readings, goes back over a period of many years.

Four years ago, we began to get reports of the use of gold by "orthodox" medicine. A report in *Science News Letter* of October 3, 1964, carried the information that electrically charged gold leaves, *used for the first time on humans and animals* [author's italics] in a Washington, D.C., hospital, had been found to prevent troublesome adhesions and to patch blood vessels!

According to this report, fractures had been successfully treated in that way. "And," said the article, "in some cases it can replace silk sutures as well as form a protective layer over surgical suture lines." (Silk sutures can cause an adverse tissue reaction, whereas gold leaf has been proved not to do so.)

This success led to a review of medical literature, which disclosed the fact that gold salts had been used in the treatment of disease, especially arthritis; gold leaves—not electrically charged, however—had been applied to the pustules of smallpox to prevent scarring; gold foil had been used for the healing and closing of perforations of the eardrum; and gold plate had been used to cover a defect in the cranium.

In the Washington, D.C., *Sunday Star,* dateline September 5, 1965, there was this statement: "Doctors here are fashioning the fanciest bandages ever—out of gold leaf.

" 'Nobody knows why,' one said. 'But damn it, it works!'

"It seems to relieve pain and stop the oozing from severe burns and skin ulcers and sores. Best of all, it apparently speeds the wounds' healing.

"Deep wounds as big around as a hand seem to start healing in a couple of days in some cases, the doctors say.

"Patients who might ordinarily be expected to heal only after weeks or months in a hospital are sometimes able to continue work while letting the gold do its work."

The newspaper account continued with a description of a surgical technique developed by Doctors John P. Gallagher and Charles F. Geschickter which had been perfected through use on experimental animals. Dr. Gallagher had later used the technique on a nine-year-old boy with severe head injuries, and thereby saved his life.

The technique had been reported in the *Journal* of the American Medical Association and, said the news report, was now being used by a number of physicians and surgeons.

The *Sunday Star* report continued with news of work being done at the Hebrew Home for the Aged in Washington, D.C. in which thin sheets of gold had been applied to big, open wounds and sores with spectacular results. It mentioned the experiences of Dr. Naomi M. Kanof, a dermatologist, who had been getting good results with the application of gold leaf to "long-standing, deep and open skin ulcers resulting from injuries, diabetic and varicose conditions, and from the deterioration known by the mild name of 'bedsores.' "

Also, said the report, Dr. Linwood L. Rayford, Jr., of Washington, D.C., had "transferred the gold leaf technique into the treatment of large, painful second degree burns. In the severest case, the burns covered 25 percent of the patient's body.

"The gold, Rayford said, cuts the severe pain and dries the wound—from which burn patients may lose important body fluids."

The news report quoted Dr. Rayford as saying, "I have the impression that it also quickens the healing."

It is difficult to look at Cayce readings dealing with the use of gold, and then at subsequent reports of the advances of "modern" medicine, and affix a tag which reads "prophecy." Maybe this is because we generally think of prophecy as being manifested in an individual who says, "I predict . . ." or "I see in the future . . ." This is not what Edgar Cyce did at all. He merely used techniques and substances that "orthodox" medicine did not come to use until a number of years after Cayce specified them in his readings. Thus his *work*, and not simply his *words*, could be said to have been prophetic.

There is a wealth of such evidence in the files, and there is hardly an area, within the broad concept of bodily health, that is not touched on in some way.

The dietary advice, alone, as given in the Cayce readings, was at least a generation ahead of its time. We referred to this in an earlier chapter in discussing the orange juice specified in massive doses for a young boy with leukemia; in Cayce's words concerning the food value to be found in coffee; and in other such instances.

Concerning coffee, by the way, Cayce said that not only was it a food when taken *without* cream or milk, but that *with* cream or milk it might well harm the digestion. This kind of statement was repeated, again and again, in many readings for individuals. It seemed curiously eccentric advice.

However, in the Sunday Magazine Section of the *Philadelphia Inquirer* dated March 9, 1958, we find this item: "If you suffer dyspeptic distress after drinking coffee, it may be caused by the cream. Doctors at the University of Turku, Finland, have concluded that upset stomach results more from coffee with cream than from black coffee alone."

Cayce often urged against the indiscriminate use of vitamin supplements, maintaining that vitamins were properly to be obtained from an adequate, nutritious diet. Whenever he specified vitamin pills or tonics, he indicated that they were to be taken for a stated period, then left off in order to prevent the body's becoming dependent upon them. Otherwise, he said, the system would cease to assimilate and manufacture vitamins from even the most adequate diet. "It is much better for these vitamins to be produced in the body," he explained, "from the normal development, than supplied mechanically, for nature is much better, still, than science!"

Many years later, in February, 1961, the American Medical Association issued a warning: don't munch too many vitamin pills! The *Journal* of the A.M.A., reporting a widespread belief that people must consume multi-vitamin pills to keep healthy, stated, "On the contrary, only in a deficiency state or in an anticipated deficiency state are vitamin supplements necessary." An overdose of vitamins, added the *Journal,* can cause loss of appetite, irritability, skin eruptions, liver enlargement, and gastro-intestinal symptoms.

Cayce once stated, concerning the acid-alkaline balance in the human body, "Overalkalinity is much more harmful than a little tendency for acidity."

In a report in the *National Health Federation Bulletin* of December, 1962, Dr. George A. Wilson stated that, as a result of tests he had made on hundreds of patients of the renowned Spears Chiropractic Hospital in Denver, Colorado, over a fourteen-year period, and backed up by his forty-five years of experience, he was convinced that most sick people are too alkaline, rather than too acid, as has generally been thought. This was found to be especially true of people with chronic illnesses, he said.

And consider: almost twenty-five years ago, Edgar Cayce said this about human blood: "There is no condition existent in a body, the reflection of which may not be traced in the blood supply. Not only does the blood stream carry the rebuilding forces to the body; it takes the used forces and eliminates them through their proper channels in the various portions of the system. We find red blood, white blood and lymph, all carried in the veins. These are only separated by the very small portions that act as builders, strainers, destroyers, or resuscitating portions of the system. For there is always seen in the blood stream the reflection or the evidence of that condition being enacted in the physical body. *The day may yet arrive when one may take a drop of blood and diagnose the condition of any physical body."* [Author's italics.]

On March 20, 1958, a story was carried in the Norfolk (Virginia) *Virginian-Pilot* concerning research being conducted by Dr. Winston Price at Johns Hopkins Hospital on medical diagnosis, involving analysis of particles in the blood steam. Said the report, "His discovery could mean that a medical laboratory can tell what ails you—cancer, tuberculosis, ulcers, or even mental disorders—*simply by examination of a drop of your blood."* [Author's italics.]

On February 16, 1960, the Washington (D.C.) *Daily News* ran a short feature describing a method of analyzing a single drop of blood or a tiny bit of tissue to identify the enzymes present.

By means of a so-called "zymograph," said the paper, its developers—Doctors R. L. Hunter and C. L. Markest, working at the University of Michigan with financial support of the American Cancer Society, hoped that it would be "possible, by observing and analyzing the enzymes in the blood, to trace the changes which take place in the process of growth from the embryonic state to old age."

By studying the chemical changes that accompany various diseases, then, the doctors felt it might in time be possible to diagnose some diseases, possibly even cancer, before clinical symptoms have appeared.

Business Week, on November 21, 1964, covered this same subject. The magazine reported that Dr. John B. Henry, Professor of Pathology at the Medical Center of New York, Syracuse, speaking before a meeting of the American College of Clinical Pathologists in New York, had discussed the role of enzymes in diagnosing disease.

The article stated that it had been known for some time that the quantity of enzymes in the blood and other body fluids could be used to measure cell death or damage. For example, cancer sometimes produces high enzyme levels, whereas lower enzyme levels might indicate some other type of disease.

Dr. Henry's ultimate hope, said this story, was that some day a series of laboratory tests—a single enzyme "profile"—might be developed as a kind of chart for use in conjunction with blood tests to determine, within a matter of hours, the presence of any of a number of possible diseases.

About a year and a half earlier, *Business Week* (March 9, 1963) had also reported a new diagnostic test to detect Wilson's disease, a rare malady that strikes people of all ages and is often diagnosed as mental or emotional illness.

The test was developed by the Albert Einstein College of Medicine in New York. Doctors there were reported as saying that, if detected early enough, Wilson's disease should be treatable with drugs, diet and psychotherapy.

The test, said the report, now made it possible to detect the presence of the disease before the appearance of any clinical signs. *All that is needed for the test is one drop of blood from the patient.*

These, of course, are only a few examples out of the Cayce files to illustrate the kind of prophetic material that may be found there. Considering this, we wonder if it isn't just a matter of time before the "orthodox" medical world catches up with the "Cayce" medical world and supplies the scientific facts behind a great many more of his statements.

For starters, in the dietary department, how about these?

Cayce frequently insisted that certain foods should not be combined at the same meal (e.g. citrus fruits or juices with wheat cereals.) Why?

Cayce specified that fruits and vegetables are more easily assimilated into the body when combined with gelatin. Why?

Cayce made the flat-out statement, many years ago, that within the blueberry there is "a property which someone, someday, will use in its proper place!" What is this property?

Prophecy: Is It Rooted in History?

Suppose, for the moment, that you are living in the year 1934. You are sitting in a rather small room, watching a man lying on a couch and talking in his "sleep," while a stenographer jots down his words. Suppose this sleeping man has just told you that you once lived, more than 29,000 years ago, in a society which in many ways was more advanced than the one you're living in today. Incredibly, this sleeping man has just said that you were "in the Atlantean land at the time of development of electrical forces that dealt with transportation of craft from place to place, photographing at a distance, reading inscriptions through walls even at a distance, overcoming gravity itself, preparation of the crystal, the terrible mighty crystal. Much of this brought destruction."

Would you believe this sleeping man? Probably not. You might even think he had taken leave of his senses—unconscious or otherwise.

You might think this, unless you later compared what Edgar Cayce had said about *your* experiences on the legendary continent of Atlantis with what he had said about the experiences of others, and found that, regardless of the number of years separating the readings, all the experiences meshed together to make a cohesive and fascinating whole, a compelling argument for the *reality* of Atlantis! Then you would be left to wonder. . . .

Hugh Lynn Cayce, in the Preface to another book in this series, *Edgar Cayce on Atlantis,* written by Edgar Evans Cayce, discussed this perplexing subject. "My brother, the author, and I know that Edgar Cayce did not read Plato's material on Atlantis, or books on Atlantis, and that he, so far as we know, had absolutely no knowledge of this subject. If his unconscious fabricated this material or wove it together from existing legends and writings, we believe that it is the most amazing example of telepathic-clairvoyant scanning of existing legends and stories in print or of the minds of persons dealing with the Atlantis theory. As my brother and I have said from time to time, life would be simpler if Edgar Cayce had never mentioned Atlantis."

However, Edgar Cayce did mention Atlantis. Of the 2,500 life readings on file at A.R.E., at least 30 percent contain references to previous incarnations on this lost continent.

Unfortunately, few dates concerning Atlantis appear in the readings. This is because few were requested, and few were volunteered by the sleeping Cayce. However, enough were given that it has been possible to pull together a chronologically consistent picture of this ancient land and its people.

He described the location of the lost Atlantis as lying "between the Gulf of Mexico on one side and the Mediterranean on the other. Evidences of Atlantean civilization," he said, "may be found in the Pyrenees and Morocco and in British Honduras, Yucatan and parts of the Americas—especially near Bimini and in the Gulf Stream, in this vicinity."

Roughly, the three distinct periods in the history of Atlantis described by Cayce break down into three eras marked by destruction of part of the land: around 50,000 B.C., around 28,000 B.C., and the final, complete sinking under the sea between the years 10,500 and 10,000 B.C. This latter period was one of gradual disappearance over some 7,500 years until, finally, Atlantis was no more.

The man inhabiting Atlantis, said Cayce, was of the red race. Asked in November, 1932, to elaborate on the origin of the five races, Cayce stated that they had come into existence simultaneously. Where? "As we find—those in the Gobi the yellow, the white in the Carpathians, the red in the Atlantean and in the American, the brown in the Andean, the black in the plain and the Sudan or in the African."

Many readings on file discuss incarnations in Atlantis prior to 50,000 B.C. It was a time of friction between two groups: those who represented good (Cayce called them the "children of the Law of One ") and those who were evil (called "the Sons of Belial"). Their warring led eventually to destruction of a portion of the continent.

Concerning this awful time, Cayce once said, "There were those who questioned the expedience of acquainting the workers with applications of material and spiritual laws—saw divine and spiritual laws become destructive. For when the facets were prepared for the motivative forces from the rays of the sun to be effective upon those ships and electrical forces, when these were turned upon the elements of the earth, the first upheavals occurred."

In another reading, he said, ". . . in the Atlantean land during the period of the first destruction or separation of land . . . [the entity] aided in the preparation of explosives or those things that set in motion the fires of the inner portion of the earth."

Is it possible that there was a civilization prior to 50,000 B.C. so advanced that solar rays were controlled and directed at one's enemies with a force powerful enough to trigger volcanic eruptions? Is it *possible?*

Another living in that same time, Cayce stated, was "in the Atlantean land just preceding the first breaking up of the land, when there was the use of those influences *that are again being discovered* [Author's italics]—that may be used for benefits in communications, transportation, etc., or turned into destructive forces." This reading was given in May, 1941. On December 2, 1942, the first sustained controlled production of atomic energy was accomplished.

This was not an isolated case. There were many others, given over a number of years, that supplied the same general information—with variations, but never at variance with each other.

Here's an excerpt from another reading, in 1933: "In Atlantis the entity attended the meeting of many representatives of many countries to devise ways of dealing with the great animals overruning the earth. Means were devised to change environs suitable for beasts. This was administered by sending out death rays or super cosmic rays from various central plants. *These rays will be discovered within the next twenty-five years.*" [Author's italics.] Cayce, answering a question concerning the date of this meeting, said that the year was 50,772 B.C.

Adding twenty-five years to the date of this 1933 reading would place the time of discovery of such rays at 1958. In 1955, the antiproton was discovered. Out of this came the discovery, in 1957, of the antineutron. Thus we had, by 1958, the theoretical possibility, through the combination—in principal—of antiprotons and antineutrons which would form "antimatter." Should antimatter come into contact with ordinary matter, all its mass would be converted into energy, rather than the fraction of it as in the case of nuclear fission and fusion reactions.

Another scientific advance in 1958 seems to be in line with the prophecy in this reading; the development of a workable maser—short for "microwave amplification by stimulated emission of radiation." Amplification is accomplished as a result of storing up energy in a small insulating crystal of special magnetic properties. An incident signal triggers off the release of energy, and the crystal passes on more energy than it has taken in.

Since that time, the maser has been considerably developed. The same is true of the laser—which stands for "light amplification by stimulated emission of radiation"; in other words, an optical maser. It, too, was developed in 1958.

There are a number of Cayce readings which refer to the use of crystals that sound suspiciously like a type of maser or laser. These mentions were most often found in connection with incarnations in Atlantis during the second period, ending with the destruction in 28,000 B.C., and the third period, ending with the final destruction in 10,000 B.C.

Concerning what life in Atlantis was like around the year 28,000 B.C., Cayce had this to say in a reading for an individual: "In the Atlantean land before the second destruction, when there was the dividing of the islands, the entity was among those that interpreted the messages received through the crystal and the fires that were to be the eternal fires of nature. New devlopments in air and water travel are no surprise to the entity, as these were beginning development at that period."

Another individual, he said, had been "in Atlantis when there were those activities which later brought about the second upheaval in the land. The entity was what would be in the present the electrical engineer, [and] applied those forces or influences for aircraft, ships and what you would today call radio in a form for constructive or destructive purposes."

Still another individual, Cayce said, "was associated with those who dealt with mechanical appliances and their application, during the experience. And as we find, it was a period when there was much that has not even been thought of yet, in the present experience."

In 1933, Cayce gave a long description of technological developments in Atlantis, together with elaborate instructions for construction of the building which housed the "firestone," or crystal, mentioned earlier. According to the reading, it was this crystal which, through "unintentionally being set too high," had caused the second destruction in Atlantis and had broken up the land into islands which eventually led to the final sinking.

Said Cayce of this crystal, "The records as to ways of constructing same are in three places in the earth, as it stands today: in the sunken portion of Atlantis, or Poseidia, where a portion of the temples may yet be discovered under the slime of ages of sea water—near what is known as Bimini, off the coast of Florida. And, secondly, in the temple records that were in Egypt, where the entity acted later in cooperation with others towards preserving the records that came from the land where these had been kept. Also, thirdly, the records that were carried to what is now Yucatan, in America, where these stones (which they know so little about) are now—during the last few months—being uncovered.

"In Yucatan there is the emblem of same. Let's clarify this, for it may be more easily found. For they will be brought to this America, these United States. A portion is to be carried, as we find, to the Pennsylvania State Museum. A portion is to be carried to the Washington preservations of such findings; or to Chicago."

Cayce was unquestionably correct in saying that too little was known of these stones—drawings or carvings of which, possibly from some temple, he said were being uncovered at the time of his 1933 reading. At any rate, if they were discovered they have yet to be identified and announced by any archaeologist or museum.

The third and final destruction of Atlantis, of what remained of the islands, took place during the period between 10,500 and 10,000 B.C. Edgar Evans Cayce has speculated that this may be the portion alluded to by Plato. Approximately 50 percent of the life readings which mention Atlantis incarnations are concerned with this era, and with the parallel activities in pre-history Egypt.

The readings indicate that many of the people who fled the sinking Atlantis islands went to Egypt; others to the Pyrenees, or to Europe, Africa, and even to the Americas.

Perhaps it is in Egypt that the full story of Atlantis may someday be uncovered. For, said Cayce, copies of all the important documents and records dealing with the history of the lost continent and its civilization were taken to Egypt by fleeing Atlanteans, and were eventually placed in the Hall of Records, a small tomb or pyramid which lies between the right paw of the Sphinx and the Nile River. This enclosure also contains the bodies of many of the Atlanteans who brought these materials to Egypt, said Cayce, as well as a number of artifacts which will verify the former existence of Atlantis. There will be found, when the Hall of Records is uncovered, musical instruments, "the hangings, the accoutrements for the altar in the temple of the day," plaques and life seals, surgical instruments and medical compounds, gold and precious stones, linens. All that remains is for us to *find* the Hall of Records!

Of course, we may not have to wait much longer for some sign of the former existence of this strange continent. On June 28, 1940, the sleeping Cayce made this startling statement. "Poseidia will be among the first portions of Atlantis to rise again. Expect it in '68 and '69—not so far away!" The second of the three sacred temples, holding the secrets of Atlantis, was said to be there.

Or we may find the answer to some of the mysteries surrounding Atlantis in Yucatan. There, said Cayce in a reading in 1933, will be found the Temple of

Iltar, the third of the spots in which the Atlantis records were placed. (The readings state that the people who migrated there from Atlantis came not only by ship, but by air!) Cayce once discussed the fate of Iltar's people. "Those in Yucatan, those in the adjoining lands as begun by Iltar, gradually lost in their activities (through generations) and came to be that people termed, in other portions of America, the Mound Builders."

According to Cayce, there are many secrets still to be disclosed within The Great Pyramid of Gizeh, the oldest pyramid in Egypt and the one closest to the Nile. It is generally assumed to have been built around 2885 B.C. Cayce, however, stated that it was built in the one hundred years between 10,490 to 10,390 B.C., and that the Sphinx was constructed around the same time.

We find some clues to their construction in a portion of a reading for an individual who, according to Cayce, had helped to build the Sphinx. "As the monuments were being rebuilt in the plains of that now called the Pyramid of Gizeh," he said, "this entity builded, laid, the foundations. That is, supervised same, figured out the geometrical position of same as [in] relation to those buildings as were put up of that connecting the Sphinx, and the data concerning same may be found in the vaults in the base of the Sphinx. The entity was with that dynasty . . . when these buildings [were] begun. This laid out, base of Sphinx, in channels, and in the corner facing the Gizeh may be found that of the wording of how this was founded, giving the history . . ."

Information concerning the Sphinx, said Cayce, would be found "in the base of the left forearm, or leg, of the prostrate beast, in the base of foundation. Not in the underground channel—as was opened by the ruler many years, many centuries, later—but in the real base, or that as would be termed in the present parlance as the cornerstone. . . ."

Within the Pyramid of Gizeh, he said, would be found all the information dealing with the period in which great advances were made in pre-history Egypt, following the migration from Atlantis of a people more advanced than those in Egypt in that era. But that's not all. The information in Gizeh concerns not only pre-history Egypt; it covers *the entire history of mankind from that time until the year 1998*—which is, said Cayce, "that period when there is to be the change in the earth's position, and the return of the Great Initiate to that and other lands, for the fulfillment of those prophecies depicted there.

"All changes that occurred in the religious thought in the world are shown there: in the variations in which the passage through same is reached, from the base to the top—or to the open tomb and the top. These [changes] are signified both by the layer and the color and the direction of the turn."

Cayce, in his readings, often referred to The Great Pyramid as the "Pyramid of Understanding." Built as a hall of initiation—through the process of levitation, "by those universal laws and forces of nature which cause iron to float," Cayce explained—it served as the "House Initiate" for those dedicating themselves to special services in the secrets of the mystery religion of Egypt. Here the masters performed their vows, consecrating themselves to holy service. It had a much higher purpose, then, than that of a burial place.

Within the Great Pyramid, say the readings, is a record in stone of the history and development of man from the time of Araaraat (the King) and Ra (the High

Priest: Cayce in an earlier incarnation, during which he was also known as Ra Ta) to the end of the present earth cycle, or 1998. Its records are written in the language of mathematics, geometry and astronomy, as well as in the kinds of stone used, with their symbology. At the end of the cycle, there is to be another change in the earth's position (generally taken to mean a shifting of the poles) and the return of the Great Initiate for the culmination of the prophecies. All changes that have come and are to come, said Cayce, are shown there in the passages from the base to the top. Changes are signified by the layer of stone, the color of it, and the direction in which the turns are made. Thus the real message of the Great Pyramid, according to Cayce, is in code; there are no undiscovered rooms, as such, there.

The smaller pyramid, the Hall of Records still covered by sand, does contain a sealed room. The readings describe it as a vault sealed with heavy metal, and state that, among other things, it contains the prophecy for the period from 1958 to 1998!

Prophecy: What Lies Ahead?

In the first chapter of this book, we mentioned some of the Cayce prophecies that have been proved by the passage of time. These have been covered completely in other books, together with prophecies for the future years: notably, in Jess Stearn's *Edgar Cayce—The Sleeping Prophet,* and Mary Ellen Carter's *Edgar Cayce on Prophecy.*

Naturally enough, it is the Cayce prophecies concerning earth changes which have garnered the most public attention, particularly those predicted for the period 1958 to 1998. They are literally earth-shaking, and should they come true would affect great numbers of people.

I think it is right that these should be noticed, because I feel there was some purpose, probably a great one, in Cayce's giving them to us.

But I will not list them here. Space does not permit my discussing them adequately, and anything short of that, I think, would be irresponsible. Instead, I would suggest that the reader get the full information from the above-listed books, as well as from a booklet published by A.R.E. entitled "Earth Changes."

I do, however, have one point—a personal one—to make. The Cayce prophecy concerning the future destruction of Los Angeles, San Francisco and New York City has caused me much anxiety, for I happen to live just a few miles south of San Francisco. Common sense tells me that, living as I do on the very edge of one of America's most active faults, the San Andreas, my chances of being caught up in the massive destruction—predicted by Cayce to occur within the years 1958 to 1998—are quite good. Geologists tell us that, as far as severe earthquakes are concerned, our area is overdue for at least one—and that it can occur ten minutes or ten years from now. And yet building heights continue to rise, and power plants and communications centers and schools and public buildings continue to be built *directly along the line of the fault!* I need no psychic to tell me that I am living on top of a time bomb.

But I must admit that my first reaction, upon hearing about Cayce's prophecy, was to consider the possibility of moving away. I thought about it quite a lot.

And then it occurred to me that it was not the threat of sudden death that disturbed me—it was the idea that my home and everything in it might be destroyed, and that I'd have to start all over again, building from the ruins.

This is an unpleasant admission, even to oneself, for it reflects the one human failing above all others that Edgar Cayce in his readings was trying to get across to us: our tendency to let the material side of life govern the spiritual. In one reading, he put it this way: "These experiences then, that have shattered hopes, that have brought disappointment, that have produced periods when there seemed little or nothing left in material life—if they are used as stepping stones and not as those things that bring resentment, accusation of others, discontent, we will find they will become helpful experiences that may guide one into a haven that is quiet and peaceful."

CHAPTER 14

DREAMS

OF THE MORE than 14,000 psychic readings in the Cayce files, approximately 1,000 deal in some way with the most personal activity of the human mind: the process of dreaming.

Some of these readings were given in order to advance our general knowledge of what happens when we surrender ourselves to sleep. Some were given for the purpose of interpreting the dreams of others. And some were devoted to interpretation of Edgar Cayce's own dreams.

It was in October, 1923, that Cayce first described the subject. "As in dream, those forces of the subconscious when taken as correlated with those [dream] forms that relate to the various phases of the individual, give to that individual a better understanding of self, when correctly interpreted, or when correctly answered.

"Forget not that it has been said correctly that the Creator, the gods and the God of the Universe, speak to man through his individual self. Man approaches the more intimate conditions of that field of the inner self when the conscious [self] is at rest in sleep or slumber, at which time more of the inner forces are taken into consideration and studied by the individual, and not someone else. It is each individual's job, if he will study to show himself approved (by God, his Maker) to understand his individual condition, his individual position in relation to others, his individual manifestation, through his individual receiving of messages from the higher forces themselves (thus, through dreams).

"In this age—at present 1923—there is not sufficient credence given dreams; for the best development of the human family is to give the greater increase in knowledge of the subconscious soul or spirit world."

Perhaps we should restate, here, the human mind as it was described in the readings. The conscious mind, said Cayce, is that which has to do with the activities of the physical body. The subconscious mind is that of the soul; and the readings emphasize that the more authority given to the unconscious, the more creative and useful work it is able to do. The superconscious mind, that term which infuriates so many literal-minded men of science, is the mind of the spirit—that part of us which is attuned to the forces of God.

Immediately after the series of "sleep" readings given by Cayce in 1923, a number of people closely associated with his work began to record their dreams and bring them to him for interpretation through his psychic source. This led to a most interesting discovery: it is possible, through concentration and practice, to greatly increase our awareness of dreams, as well as our ability to remember them long enough to get them recorded. The dreams, and their interpretations, were closely studied, and a good deal of information came out of this informal "Cayce sleep laboratory."

In 1932, Cayce was asked in a reading to "outline clearly and comprehensively the material which should be presented to the general public in explaining just what occurs in the conscious, subconscious, and spiritual forces of an entity while in the state known as sleep."

He answered, "Yes. While a great deal has been written and spoken regarding the experiences of individuals in that state called sleep, only recently has there been the attempt to control it or form any definite idea of what produces conditions in the unconscious, subconscious, subliminal or subnormal mind. These attempts have been to produce—or to determine that which produces—the kinds of dreams experienced by an individual entity.

"For some minds such experiments may determine questions respecting the claim of some psychiatrist or psychoanalyst. Such experiments may refute or determine the value of such claims in the study of certain kinds of mental disturbances in individuals. Yet little of this can be called a true analysis of what really happens to the body—either physical, mental, subconsciuos or spiritual—when it loses itself in such repose.

"There are certain definite conditions, to be sure, which take place respecting the physical, the conscious, and the subconscious, as well as the spiritual forces of the body."

That reading, of course, was in the early 'thirties, long before the discoveries about sleep and dreaming that have come—only within the past decade—as a result of sleep laboratories utilizing the most sophisticated electronic equipment available.

The experiments mentioned by Cayce might well have referred to those being conducted, around the time of the reading, by the foremost pioneer in sleep research, Dr. Nathaniel Kleitman, a professor of physiology at the University of Chicago. An interesting point of conjecture is that at that time Kleitman was only at the threshold of his work, for he was approaching it from a physiological standpoint alone, studying the physical processes of sleep. Another twenty years were to pass before Kleitman would recognize the physical processes of *dreaming*, when he noticed that the eyes of all individuals continue to flutter beneath their lids after all signs of consciousness have passed. It was from this base that the modern sleep laboratory was built. And from this laboratory has come solid proof that *everyone* dreams.

On a typical night of sleeping, a person has four or five dreams—the first beginning about 90 minutes after sleep has come. Of these, the first dreams are short; later ones are more extended. The fluttering of the eyes, called "rapid eye movements," correspond to periods of dreaming. While outwardly the body may seem completely calm, the process of dreaming brings inner tumult for the physical body, involving changes in heartbeat, breathing, secretion of hormones and gastric juices, and so forth. The brain undergoes measurable changes, and at times seems even more active than in some states of wakefulness (such as while listening to the radio.) Brain temperature increases slightly, and the rate of metabolism in the brain seems to indicate that tremendous amounts of energy are being expended while dreaming.

These, of course, are the physiological signs of dreaming. They are extremely important, for out of the laboratory may come scientific establishment of what Cayce discussed in his readings many years ago: the significance of dreams, and their involvement with the *sixth sense!*

Cayce stated it this way, in excerpts from a series of sleep readings given in 1932:

"First, we would say, sleep is a shadow of the intermission in the earth's experiences—that state called death. For physical consciousness becomes unaware of existent conditions in sleep, save as attributes of the physical partake of attributes of the imaginative, or the subconscious and unconscious forces of the same body. That is, in a normal sleep (from the physical standpoint we are reasoning now) the senses are on guard, so to speak, so that the auditory forces are the ones which are more sensitive . . .

"So, then, we find that there are what is ordinarily known as four other senses, acting independently but coordinating in awareness, for the physical body to be conscious. These four, in the state of sleep or repose, or rest, or exhaustion (and when induced by any influence from the outside) have become unaware of that which is taking place about the individual so resting. . . ."

With the "relaxation" of the four senses of taste, touch, sight and smell, say the readings, comes a division of the sense of hearing. This one sense, during sleep, functions in place of the five conscious senses, and does something more: it creates a sixth sense which is capable of a whole new activity.

This activity was described by Cayce in another reading. "There is an active force within each individual which functions in the manner of a sense when the body-physical is in sleep, repose or rest. We would outline what are the functions of this thing we have chosen to call a sixth sense.

"This sixth sense activity is the activating force or power of the other self. What other self? That which has been built by the entity or body, or soul, throughout all its experiences as a whole, in the material and cosmic world, see? It may be termed a faculty of the soul-body itself."

Cayce elaborated on this. "Sleep is that period of time when the soul takes stock of what it has acted upon from one rest period to another; drawing comparisons—as it were—which comprise life itself, in its essence.

"In sleep all things become possible. One finds himself flying through space, or being pursued . . . by those very components which make for comparisons with what has been built by the very soul of the body itself."

Among those who brought their dreams to the sleeping Cayce for interpretation were some who seemed to have a good deal of psychic awareness, possibly even a talent for prophecy as it came to them through their dreaming.

One often-reported case is that of a young woman who dreamed, soon after her marriage, of the birth of a weakminded baby. Cayce's interpretation of the dream indicated that it might well be a warning of things to come. The child who was born two years later seemed perfectly healthy and normal. However, at the age of twenty-five he was committed to a mental institution.

Had this been an isolated instance in the life of this young woman, we might toss it off as coincidence, or even as the result of marital difficulties, divorce and all manner of unpleasant occurrences in her family life, for certainly her son must have been affected by these things. However, she had a total of eighty-five dreams interpreted by Edgar Cayce between the years 1925 and 1930, and a number of them seem to indicate some telepathic, even precognitive ability.

In December, 1926, for example, she mentioned one dream in which her friend, Emmie, had committed suicide. Cayce's interpretation of this was, "This shows to the entity, through this correlation of mental forces of the body-mind itself and those of the body-mind of Emmie, that such conditions had passed through this mind—or had contemplated such conditions, see? They have passed."

The dreamer had not been in touch with Emmie for several years. She wrote to her and learned that Emmie had, indeed, contemplated suicide around the time of the dream, but had since managed to get into a better frame of mind.

Cayce was asked to explain how the information about Emmie had come through the dream. He first gave an outline of the various types of dreams: nightmares, resulting from physical discomforts; symbolic dreams; problem solving; and psychic dreams. The dream about Emmie, said Cayce, had been a psychic one. He explained, "Others there are, a correlation between mentalities or subconscious entities, wherein there has been attained, physically or mentally, a correlation of individual ideas or mental expressions, that bring from one subconscious to another those of actual existent conditions, either direct or indirect, to be acted upon or that are ever present, see?

"Hence we find visions of the past, visions of the present, visions of the future. For the subconscious there is no past or future—all is present. This would be well to remember in much of the information as may be given through such forces as these."

In the A.R.E booklet, "Dreams: The Language of the Unconscious," there is an article by Tom C. Clark dealing with his study of the readings in which ninety-one of Edgar Cayce's own dreams were interpreted, between January, 1925, and February, 1940. There were many curious circumstances involved in these readings.

First, there was the matter of eleven dreams experienced by Edgar Cayce while he was in the self-induced sleep necessary to give a reading for someone else! It is almost impossible to accept the complexity of a situation in which Edgar Cayce, at his home in Virginia Beach and reading for someone, say, in New York City, might suddenly become aware of the fact that he was not only getting the information requested for the reading, but was dreaming his own dream as well! Even more puzzling, he would remember the dream afterwards, but as usual would have no recollection whatsoever about the subject of the reading.

That even so talented a psychic as Edgar Cayce might have trouble living up to the messages received in his readings is difficult to imagine. And yet, after examining Cayce's early readings in which he interpreted his own dreams, Mr.

Clark had this to say. "In the early dreams between 1925 and 1930, Cayce is revealed as struggling and fighting with himself. He had a premonition that what came through him was of divine nature and his dreams revealed to him that he was anything but a divine individual. He struggled desperately with himself to live by and bring into his conscious life a few divine principles. At one time his psychic source, when asked to interpret a dream, refused the information because, it said, in the past, in connection with similar dreams which had been interpreted, Edgar Cayce had ignored the lesson and done nothing in his life to make correction or adjustment. Even his psychic informant, then, turned against him with impatience and criticism. In certain respects—and unfortunately they were important—he was a weak man, even as most of us in these respects are weak.

"After 1932, the content of the dreams started to alter. Fewer dreams were submitted to the psychic source for interpretation and there was evident a definite change in Edgar Cayce's spiritual development. The conflicts and doubts were pretty well resolved and he had a clearer intuitive comprehension of the meaning, importance, and validity of the information which came through him."

This would seem to provide a striking example of the way an individual, any individual, may profit from an understanding of what his dreams may mean.

Lacking an Edgar Cayce to interpret our dreams, however, what chance do we have of learning to understand them? Well, our first step must be to become aware of them.

Experiments conducted several years ago by A.R.E., working with a group of volunteers, showed that this is more easily accomplished than one might think. People who reported, the first week, that they had not dreamed at all were reporting, by the third week, not only types of dreams brought on by physical conditions and surroundings, but even those in which some psychic source seemed evident.

In discussing this with Hugh Lynn Cayce some months ago, I mentioned my own problem—a not unusual one. I explained that I have many dreams during the night, but generally cannot hold on to them, during the process of waking up (a slow and painful ordeal for me) long enough for my conscious mind to grab on to them.

He suggested that I do as his volunteers had done: place a pad and pencil on the night stand, and form the habit of jotting down my dreams even before coming completely awake. Then I explained that my mind wakes up before my body does, so that by the time I could get my writing arm in action, the dream would be gone. He made a simple and logical suggestion: that I place a tape recorder beside the bed.

Feeling slightly foolish at first, I did just that. My early attempt gave me little more than gibberish, but by the end of ten days I found myself doing a fairly efficient job of it. Now I've progressed a step further; generally, I simply transfer the dream directly to my conscious mind and find that, by just thinking out the dream in this way, I can retain it. I've been amazed by the number of prophetic dreams I've experienced in the past several months—some purely personal, and many on a national or international scale. I've also solved some real problems by saying, before going to sleep, that they will be worked out during the night while I'm "resting."

Which brings up the other major suggestion given to me by Hugh Lynn Cayce. That is, several times before dropping off to sleep, I say to myself, "I will recall what I dream." No doubt this mechanism is as simple as it seems; that it's merely a matter of making the conscious mind aware of the importance of the dream, and thus receptive to it.

But once awareness, and memory, of a dream are achieved, what does the dream mean? This is where things get a bit more complicated—though not impossible.

Many dreams can be easily explained by physical conditions (the body or the surroundings); or by events going on in the person's life which are continued on into the dream world. Probably the majority of dreams fall into this category.

Others are clothed in symbolism, and in order to understand them we must understand the symbols. But not all symbols are the same for all people—although once established for the individual, they generally remain constant.

The following list, then, is not meant to apply to each individual, but merely to supply the sort of pattern that symbols will be found to make. These are the symbols that have been taken from the Cayce readings as being most universal in nature:

> *Water*—Source of life, spirit, unconscious
> *Boat*—Voyage of life
> *Explosion*—Turmoils
> *Fire*—Wrath, cleansing, destroying
> *A Person*—Represents what the dreamer feels toward that person
> *Clothing*—The way one appears to others
> *Animals*—Represent some phase of self, according to what one feels about the animal seen. In this area especially the universal, historical and racial quality of meaning must be considered. For example, the bull, sexless human figure, lion and eagle may for many persons symbolize the four lower vital centers of the body; the sex glands, cells of Leydig, adrenals, and thymus, in that order. The snake is both a wisdom symbol and a sex symbol, associated with the kundalini. When raised to the higher centers in the head it becomes the wisdom symbol.
> *Fish*—Christ, Christian, spiritual food
> *Dead Leaves*—Body drosses
> *Mud, Mire, Tangled Weeds*—That which needs cleansing
> *Naked*—Open to criticism, exposed

This list is intended to serve only as a starting point. The person who records his dreams for a few weeks will see a general pattern emerging. Certain symbols will be seen to recur in such a way that their meaning will soon become clear—at which time the individual's own list of symbols can be compiled.

Whether or not a dreamer goes so far as to develop a list of symbols, however, he'll find it interesting to begin to "listen" to what his unconscious mind, speaking the language of dreams, has to say to him.

For, through dreaming, we have the most natural, and certainly the safest, bridge to a part of the mind that is hidden from a waking world. It can tell us a good deal about our emotions, our physical health, our talents, our failings, and even—with practice in understanding its messages—a great deal about the psychic and spiritual sides of our being.

CHAPTER 15

CONCLUSION

I GREW UP at Virginia Beach, during the years in which Cayce lived and worked there. I thought I knew him. But I have only truly come to know him through study of his psychic readings.

The modest, humble man who was my friend and neighbor was only part of the story; just as this book is only part of the story. But I was a child when I knew him, and was still a child when he died. Although I knew that he did strange, wonderful things when he "went to sleep" it was not this part of Edgar Cayce that I knew. The man I knew grew the largest, juiciest strawberries I had ever seen, and certainly the sweetest I had ever tasted. The man I knew was a quiet man, and I was surprised to learn, only a few years ago, that he had a terrible temper at times that bothered him more than it bothered anybody else, for I never saw a sign of temper in him. The man I knew was towering-tall, laughed often, and had an ability to communicate with children that is given to few men.

I was too young to understand the depth of the man, or the depth of the matters of which he spoke while asleep. I knew that through his readings he was able to bring health back to ailing bodies, for I had seen such "miracles" performed for members of my own family. I was wise enough to know that he did not tell fortunes; but not wise enough to know that the life reading that would have been given for me, had I accepted it when it was offered, would have helped me find my real work in life much earlier than the age of thirty-six, and possibly to avoid some of the more serious mistakes of my life—or at least to understand why I made them!

Since I didn't have my own life reading, then, I've had to find my own benefits in the readings through studying those given for others. The benefits have been many, and the pleasures too numerous to mention.

Serious study of the readings has brought me—through its complete involvement with matters concerning the human body, the human mind, and the human spirit—to a new awareness of man's real purpose in the earth. Concentration on the vast scope, the universal nature of the Cayce readings, dealing as they do with past, present and future, has broadened my respect for this most talented of all psychics.

It seems to me, as I look back over the great number of readings I studied for the purpose of this effort—far too many of which were excluded for one reason alone; a lack of space—that there is enough material here to keep thousands of researchers busy for at least another century. Where there is so much still to be learned about the workings of the human body and the human mind, I cannot help believing that many of the ultimate answers may well be found within the readings. As has been said, some research is now being conducted along these lines—but surely there is much more that could be done, *should* be done.

That some of the methods of treatment seem clumsy by today's standards should not deter doctors of medicine, and doctors of psychology, from examining what Cayce had to say. As long as there are the tragedies of multiple sclerosis, arthritis, cancer, schizophrenia, drug addiction and other ills plaguing mankind, does orthodox medicine have a right to close the door on the possibility that Cayce was giving the true answers to these problems? Does the psychiatrist have a right to refuse to consider that man may have lived before, and that the reason he acts the way he does may be at least partially due to past experiences of other lifetimes?

As a child, I often heard the phrase used in connection with Cayce's work, "first for the few; then for the masses." This phrase had come directly from the readings, to indicate that Cayce's readings would apply, first, to the individual; would then be studied in small groups; and finally would be explained to the general public. I understood this, or thought I did.

At the same time, I wondered why so many people thought of Mr. Cayce as a strange man who did strange things, and why so many people said they did not believe in the things they'd heard about him. I heard stories about people who came—sometimes several at a time—to show him up as a fake, a charlatan. I knew that these people always went away saying things like, "I don't know what it is he does; but it certainly seems to work."

Now, from the vantage point of my middle years, I think I understand it all a bit better. I am still dismayed that so many people of science will slam the door on any investigation into psychic phenomena in general, or Edgar Cayce's work in particular, for it seems to me that we accept all sorts of things as possible, even if we can't explain them fully. Electricity, for one. The miracle of conception and birth, for another. These things have no business working, but they do. The Cayce readings worked, too, even if we don't know quite how, and why, they did.

I used to wonder why Cayce was a man of *this* particular century, rather than the next, which might be somewhat more willing to accept and *use* the information he had to offer. But I look at man today, with all his faults; and then I look at man's ideal, as shown in the readings, and it seems to me that if there was ever needed an understanding of man's purpose in the earth, and a reiteration of the spiritual values that must guide his steps as he strives to make sure that there *will* be a next century, then this, most certainly, is the time!

For the focus in the readings is on the individual. It is for the individual, by understanding himself and his fellow man, to find his own reason for existing, to shape his own destiny—with the help of a living God.

At a time when we are being more and more computerized, more and more made a part of a don't-staple-or-mutilate-this-card society, it is good to be reminded that we are, after all, individuals. And that what we do as individuals—as individual souls—goes to make up the story of mankind. We can change the world, or we can destroy it.